Perspectives on
Behavior in
Organizations

Perspectives on Behavior in Organizations

Edited by
J. Richard Hackman
Yale University

Edward E. Lawler III
University of Michigan and
Battelle Memorial Institute

Lyman W. Porter
University of California, Irvine

McGraw-Hill Book Company

New York St. Louis San Francisco Auckland Bogotá Düsseldorf
Johannesburg London Madrid Mexico Montreal New Delhi
Panama Paris São Paulo Singapore Sydney Tokyo Toronto

Perspectives on
Behavior in
Organizations

Each of the following articles is copyrighted by, and used with the permission of, the
author or authors noted:

"Motivation: A Diagnostic Approach" (pages 26–38), by David A. Nadler and
   Edward E. Lawler III
"A Diagnostic Model for Organizational Behavior" (pages 85–98), by David A.
   Nadler and Michael Tushman
"Organizational Entry: The Individual Viewpoint" (pages 126–135), by John P.
   Wanous
"Making Effective Use of Control Systems" (pages 215–224), by Cortlandt Cammann
   and David A. Nadler
"An Intergroup Perspective on Individual Behavior" (pages 359–372), by Ken K.
   Smith
"Leaders and Leadership: Of Substance and Shadow" (pages 375–386), by Morgan
   W. McCall, Jr.

1 2 3 4 5 6 7 8 9 0 D O D O 7 8 3 2 1 0 9 8 7

This book was set in Times Roman by Black Dot, Inc.
The editors were Richard R. Wright and Susan Gamer;
the cover was designed by Jo Jones;
the production supervisor was Charles Hess.
The drawings were done by Scalor Publications, Inc.
R. R. Donnelley & Sons Company was printer and binder.

Library of Congress Cataloging in Publication Data
Main entry under title:

Perspectives on behavior in organizations.

   1.   Organizational behavior—Addresses, essays, lectures.   I.   Hackman, J.
Richard.   II.   Lawler, Edward E.   III.   Porter, Lyman W.
HD58.7.P47   658.4′008   76-39843
ISBN 0-07-025413-3

Contents

PART FIVE   IMPROVING ORGANIZATIONAL EFFECTIVENESS

Preface

Knowledge about behavior in organizations has been expanding at a rapid rate. This book provides some perspectives on that knowledge, with special emphasis on factors that affect the lives of those who work in organizations. Each of the articles included here describes some important aspect of behavior in organizations, analyzes why things happen the way they do, or provides some guidelines for managing and changing organizations.

The book does *not* include articles that report the details of specific research projects, nor does it delve into the complexities of organizational research methodology. Instead, our attempt has been to provide a general and informative overview of current thinking about behavior in organizations, including ideas about how organizations can be changed for the better.

The book is primarily intended for students—particularly those enrolled in junior-senior and beginning graduate-level courses in organizational behavior, organizational psychology, and management. We also believe that the book can be informative for the practicing manager. No extensive background in the behavioral sciences is assumed.

The organization of the book parallels that of our text (L. W. Porter, E. E. Lawler, and J. R. Hackman, *Behavior in organizations*, McGraw-Hill, 1975), and we hope that this book will prove useful in supplementing and updating the material presented in that text. In selecting materials for this book, however, we had in mind students in a wide variety of courses on organizations—not just those in which our own text is used. We hope these students also find the perspectives presented here helpful in rounding out their understanding of organizational behavior.

The book is organized into five major parts. Part One considers the nature of individuals and of organizations, as a point of departure for addressing the interaction between individual and organization that forms the heart of organizational behavior. Then, in Part Two, we discuss the development of relationships between individuals and organizations—how each party chooses the other, adapts to the other, and develops continuing relationships. Part Three examines the impact of structural factors on behavior in organizations, including both the structure of the organization itself and the design of the work that members of organizations do. In Part Four we turn to ways that organizational practices and social processes affect the attitudes and behavior of employees. In this section special attention is given to the dynamics of interacting work groups and to leadership in organizational settings. Finally, in Part Five, a number of articles address the assumptions and strategies involved in various approaches to organizational change and development.

We are indebted to many people for their help in completing this book. About one-quarter of the book is made up of articles written especially for inclusion here; our special thanks go to our colleagues who wrote those articles, and to others who gave us permission to reprint articles they had published elsewhere. Finally, we wish to acknowledge the faithful and expert work of Carol Truxal in gathering materials for inclusion and preparing them for the publisher.

J. Richard Hackman

Edward E. Lawler III

Lyman W. Porter

Part One

Individuals and Organizations

Chapter 1

The Nature of Individuals

Basic to the understanding and prediction of human behavior in organizations is knowledge of the nature of individuals and how they deal with the work environments they face. A vast amount of knowledge exists about how the characteristics of individuals affect their behavior. Anyone who is familiar with the study of human behavior will recognize that, in this section, we have not included a great deal of this work. By necessity, we have limited ourselves to a consideration of a few key areas of research. In choosing these areas we kept in mind that we were trying to help the reader understand behavior in *organizations*. Behavioral scientists have pointed out repeatedly that behavior in organizations is a function of two factors: ability and motivation. These two factors frequently are stressed by psychologists when they try to determine the causes of poor individual performance.

The emphasis on ability follows naturally from the basic nature of organizations and how they function. Most jobs demand that individuals perform in a certain manner. In some cases (e.g., many assembly-line jobs), most people can easily perform at the level required by the job. In many other cases, however, the job requires a high level of physical or intellectual ability (e.g., being a company president or playing professional tennis). Because there are jobs in most organizations that not everyone can perform, the measurement of—and understanding of—human ability is important in all work organizations. The first two readings in this chapter deal with the issue of human abilities. The first, by Dunnette, presents an overview of the type of work that psychologists have done on this topic and shows how this work is relevant to understanding behavior in organizations.

3

The article describes some of the measures that have been developed by psychologists and shows how these measures can be used. In short, it is a review of the fundamentals of human-ability measurement and conceptualization.

The second article, by Wallace, is a different kind of article. It attempts to take a difficult area, *personality*, and discuss it from a unique perspective. Wallace emphasizes that personality is influenced by an abilities dimension as well as by a motivational or "can do" dimension. Most other writers in this area have tended to ignore the abilities dimension while stressing the motivational side of personality. Wallace's perspective seems particularly relevant for organizations because recent research has suggested that if people are to change their interpersonal behavior they need to *learn* how to behave in new ways. The article also provides a natural link to the final two articles in this chapter, since it stresses the importance of motivation.

It is not surprising that a great deal of research on organizations has focused on the issue of motivation. It is obvious to even the casual observer of organizations that many people do not perform their jobs to the best of their abilities. Why don't they? At this point there is no answer that is universally accepted. We have chosen to deal with the question of motivation by emphasizing one particular approach to the topic, one that is probably most widely accepted by people concerned with behavior in organizations. This approach is described in the article by Nadler and Lawler. It has the advantage of being a useful tool for understanding why individuals may not be performing as well as they might, and it is based upon a well-accepted body of research. When this approach is combined with that taken by Lawler in our last reading, the reader should possess a good understanding of why people perform their jobs as they do, and why they join and remain members of organizations.

Reading 1

Measuring Differences between People

Marvin D. Dunnette

THE RECOGNITION OF HUMAN DIFFERENCES

For centuries, philosophers speculated about the nature of man. Kant argued against a science of psychology because he believed that human feelings, sensations, images, and thoughts could never be accessible to observation and measurement. But this does not rule out the observation of human *behavior* and of the external conditions or stimuli under which the behavior occurs. The early Greeks were strongly aware of human differences in the ability to learn. Socrates developed and refined tests of how much his students learned, and he used the tests to assess and to enrich their learning. The Greeks also graded boys on an elaborate series of physical tests to keep tab on them as they matured and acquired the skills of manhood. Plato clearly recognized the differing abilities of men and saw the need for accurate assignment of individuals to the particular occupations (soldier, statesman, teacher, etc.) for which they were best suited so that they would make maximum contributions to society.

Measurement of Human Differences

However, true measurement of individual differences (that is, the assignment of quantitative values to observable differences in human behavior) had to await someone with a desire to understand differences between people and who had the wherewithal for developing mathematical methods for measuring such differences. Both the desire and the means were provided by the genius of Sir Francis Galton,

who founded the study of individual differences. In his book *Hereditary Genres*, published in 1869, he presented the elements of a system for classifying men according to their eminence (abilities). He stated that true eminence was extremely rare, characterizing only one person out of every 4,000, that *all* human abilities were distributed according to the normal probability curve, and that persons could therefore be classified according to the known frequencies of the normal distribution.

Galton's first efforts (illustrated in Figure 1-1) simply ordered people in a number of broad categories. However, he also recognized the desirability of expressing each person's relative standing in the form of a single score or index, and, to do this, he invented the standard score.

THE DEVELOPMENT OF PSYCHOLOGICAL MEASURES

Galton's concern with eminence and the relative contributions made by men to society led him and others to seek ways of measuring human differences in learning ability. At first, it was expected that learning ability should be reflected in such things as sensory sensitivity, quickness of response, and various physical proficiencies. As a consequence, the "mental tests" of the late 1800s consisted of reaction times and measures of tactual sensitivity, keenness of vision and hearing, strength of grip, tapping speed, and the like. However, differences on these measures showed no relation to differences in the ability to learn as reflected by school grades or teachers' ratings of pupil performance.

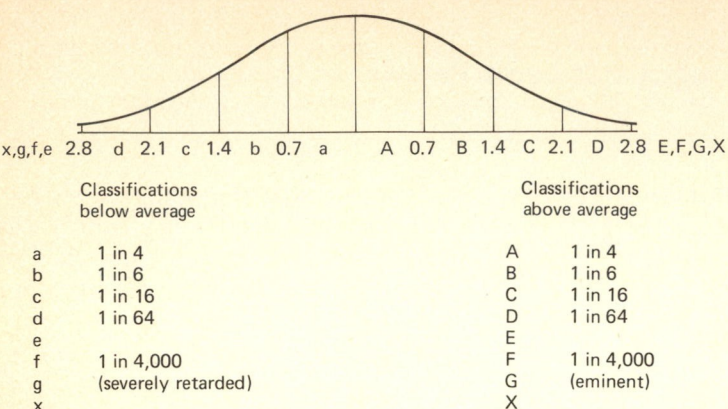

Figure 1-1 Galton's classification of persons according to their abilities and the proportion of persons in each class.

Toward Complex Processes

In 1895, the French psychologist Alfred Binet published an article severely criticizing the practices of sensory and motor testing. With his colleague Henri, Binet argued that more complex mental processes should be studied; he emphasized the importance of studying and *measuring* the higher faculties such as memory, imagery, imagination, attention, and comprehension—an argument that probably would have been "laughed out of court" had it not been for the groundwork laid by Galton's earlier emphasis on the meaningfulness and importance of measuring individual differences and the classification of persons "according to their natural abilities."

During the next decade, Binet tried a number of short tasks designed to tap the complex mental processes of school children. He reasoned that as children grow they are exposed to similar things, and they have opportunities to learn and to develop skills in dealing with the world they live in. He thought mental ability might be estimated by simply observing how a child copes with tasks similar to the ones he has faced in his day-to-day activities. Binet asked youngsters to identify familiar objects, name the months in order, name coins, arrange scrambled words into meaning-

ful sentences, and define abstract words. These tasks obviously were far more complex and closer to the kind of functioning demanded in the real world than the reaction-time, sensory, and motor tests being espoused by most of the laboratory psychologists of the time.

Binet was an *empiricist* who did not completely trust his own judgment for choosing test items. He demanded that children's responses to each of his test tasks be compared with other aspects of their behavior. He reasoned that, to be useful, a test item should yield different responses from children identified by their teachers as quick learners and those identified as slow learners. Thus, Binet was probably the first psychologist to use methods of *item analysis* to decide whether responses to any given item were or were not related to important behaviors outside the test. As we shall see, this *empirical* approach to test development has much to recommend it and is, in fact, the method used by the authors of nearly all our more widely used and most effective psychological tests today.

In Binet's approach, children of the same age were rated by their teacher as "quick" and "slow" learners, and these ratings were compared with the children's performance on sev-

Table 1-1

	Percentage of children performing task correctly		Difference
	Quick learners (N = 10)	Slow learners (N = 10)	(Quick − Slow)
Task 1: Count to five without error.	60%	20%	+40%
Task 2: Follow a lighted match with the eyes.	90	100	−10
Task 3: Use the word *home* correctly in a sentence.	80	60	+20
Task 4: Define the meaning of the word *sorry*.	20	0	+20
Task 5: Point to objects of different colors, red, yellow, and blue.	70	20	+50

eral simple tasks. (See hypothetical data in Table 1-1.)

Tasks 1 and 5 discriminate sharply between quick and slow learners. Many more quick learners perform the two tasks correctly. Tasks 1 and 5 can be said, therefore, to be good indicators of whatever behaviors are involved in this particular teacher's rating of learning ability; tasks 2, 3, and 4 are poor indicators. Tasks 1 and 5 are worthy of further study as possible measures of learning ability or "intelligence." However, knowledge about these tasks would need to be extended in a number of ways. Since the numbers of children used for this comparison were so small, it would be well to repeat the study on other children to see whether the same two tasks prove to be best. This would provide other sets of teacher observations against which to compare the results. Moreover, it would be well to obtain information on other kinds of estimates of learning ability. Another that Binet used was a simple age comparison; he assumed that older children, because of their greater exposure to learning situations and because of their greater growth, should develop more ability to learn than younger children.

The Empirical Method of Test Development

We have gone into detail in describing Binet's approach because it so aptly illustrates the crucial steps in the empirical development of psychological measures.

First, people are observed to differ in a particular behavior—a behavior sufficiently important to society that it seems worthwhile to seek to understand it better. For Binet, the important behavior was *learning ability*.

Second, behavioral observations are made of a number of individuals; they are rated, labeled, or categorized according to the amount they show of the behavior being studied. For Binet, teacher's ratings, school attainment, and age comparisons served this purpose.

Third, a series of standardized tasks, questions, statements, or other stimuli are prepared which seem to be related to the behavior being studied. As we have seen, Binet rejected sensory and motor testing in favor of developing more complex tasks that seemed more accurate indicators of learning ability.

Fourth, the stimuli are presented to the individuals whose behavior has been observed; their responses are studied (item analysis) to discover which stimuli elicit behavior related to the behavior being studied. Most psychological measures *do not* measure the relevant behavior directly. As Chauncey and Dobbin (1963) have pointed out, this method of empirically studying the responses to test items is very much like the methods used by physicists to detect the forces released by the atom. The cloud chamber does not measure the atom or its components directly, but the tracks of ionizing particles do permit deductions about the nature of the atom and the forces holding it together. In the same way, responses shown to be related to observations of the behavior we label *learning ability* enable the psychologist to deduce things about learning ability. Binet's greatest contribution was his application of empirical methods to the measurement of an important area of human behavior.

MEASURING INTELLIGENCE

In 1905, the first Binet Test, consisting of thirty tasks ranging from very simple to rather difficult, was published and began to be used in the Paris schools. He called his series of tasks a *metrical scale of intelligence*, and with this contribution Binet set off an immediate worldwide response.

It was soon apparent to other investigators that the Binet Test yielded accurate estimates of children's mental status and good predictions of school accomplishment. In this country, Lewis Terman of Stanford University translated, revised, and greatly extended the Binet Test. In 1916, his Stanford-Binet Test was published; it consisted of ninety tasks arranged in order of increasing difficulty. Terman chose to express scores on the test as an Intelligence Quotient (IQ),[1] the ratio (multi-

plied by 100) between an individual's "mental age" (calculated from the tasks he successfully completed) and his chronological age. With this test, the measurement of individual differences came of age; an important aspect of human variation had been studied and a measure successfully developed. This development was met with a widespread response of research activity directed toward learning more about this new test and the nature of the underlying construct (intelligence) it was designed to measure.

The General Factor, Factor Analysis, and Multiple Factors

Charles Spearman (1927), an English statistician and contemporary of Binet's, held that humans possessed an underlying *general intelligence* or *g* factor accompanied by a myriad of *specific* abilities called *s* factors. He argued that a high correlation between grades in French and grades in the study of the classics was evidence of the common action of the underlying ability, *g*, but that the correlation was less than perfect because of the singular actions of abilities specific to the study of French and to the study of the classics.

The correlational procedures Spearman used to support his theoretical statements about intelligence marked the beginning of *factor analysis*. . . . Factor analysis is a method for summarizing the correlations among a large number of measures in terms of a smaller number of clusters or factors. It is presumed that the factors constitute relatively more basic or fundamental dimensions underlying the many different measures on which the correlation matrix is based.

Subsequent factor analysts, notably L. L. Thurstone and J. P. Guilford, have argued that

---

[1]The choice of IQ as a method of expressing scores was unfortunate, for it implied that "intelligence" was a global, all-encompassing, and unchanging human quality. The IQ came to be widely misinterpreted and misused.

Finally, in 1960, it was decided to express scores on the third edition of the Stanford-Binet Test in terms of standard score units with a mean of 100 and a standard deviation of 16.

several factors are necessary to account for the range of observable differences among people. Intelligence appears to be many faceted, made up of a number of broad groupings of relatively independent aptitudes. For example, Thurstone concluded that the major cognitive abilities of man could be grouped into seven categories:

Verbal comprehension: to understand the meaning of words and their relations to each other; to comprehend readily and accurately what is read; measured by test items such as:

Which one of the following words means most nearly the same as *effusive*?

1. evasive
2. affluent
3. gushing
4. realistic.
5. lethargic

Word fluency: to be fluent in naming or making words, such as making smaller words from the letters in a large one or playing anagrams; measured by test items such as:

Using the letters in the word *Minneapolis*, write as many four letter words as you can in the next two minutes.

_____
_____

_____

Number aptitude: to be speedy and accurate in making simple arithmetic calculations; measured by test items such as:

Carry out the following calculations:

346	8732	$422 \times 32 =$ _____
+ 722	− 4843	$3630 \div 5 =$ _____

Inductive reasoning: to be able to discover a rule or principle and apply it to the solution of a problem, such as determining what is to come next in a series of numbers or words; measured by test items such as:

What number should come next in the sequence of the following five numbers?

1 5 2 4 3

1. 7
2. 1
3. 2
4. 4
5. 3

Memory: to have a good rote memory for paired words, lists of numbers, etc.; measured by test items such as:

The examinee may be given a list of letters paired with symbols such as:

A *	E ?
B ,	F ;
C ☆	G :
D !	H .

He is given a brief period to memorize the pairs. Then he is told to turn the page and write the appropriate symbols after each of the letters appearing there.

Spatial aptitude: to perceive fixed geometric relations among figures accurately and to be able to visualize their manipulation in space; measured by test items such as:

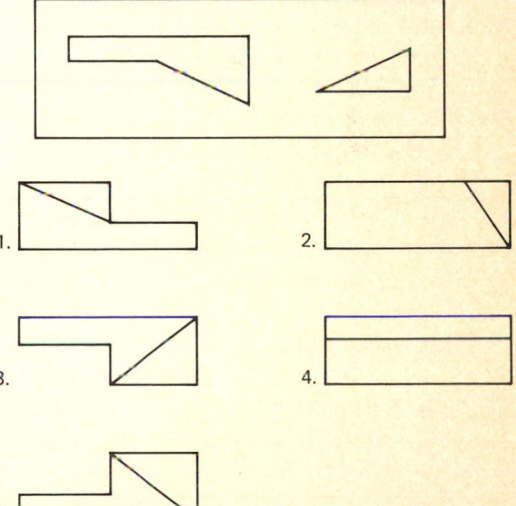

Which figure would result if the two pieces in the picture above were put together?

Perceptual speed: to perceive visual details

quickly and accurately; measured by test items such as:

Make a check mark in front of each pair below in which the numbers are identical.

1. 367773_____367713
2. 471352_____471352
3. 581688_____581688
4. 324579_____334579
5. 875989_____876898

Empiricism and Factor Analysis

At this point, it is well to note some of the differences between Binet's approach to measuring intelligence and the factor-analytic approach. First, even though Binet did believe that human cognitive ability (intelligence) consisted of a number of faculties such as imagination, memory, attention, and comprehension, he made no pretense of separately identifying and measuring each one. Instead, he found it more useful to define intelligence as the sum total of a student's proficiency on all the problems or test items. This approach differs from that of factor analysis because factor analysis seeks to classify human abilities according to the patterns of their similarities and differences as expressed by correlation coefficients.

Second, as we have seen, Binet's justification for the selection of test items was an empirical relationship between success on an item and some observation of nontest behavior such as teachers' ratings or other estimates of school success or intellectual growth. In contrast, factor analysis is directed toward sampling and classifying adequately a large domain of *tested* abilities. The names or labels given to factors (such as Inductive Reasoning, Number Ability, or Word Fluency) are based on the investigator's knowledge of or presumptions about the content of the tests making up a factor rather than on any effort to classify observed behavior outside the test. This characteristic of the factor-analytic approach is one reason why efforts to show relationships between scores on factorially developed tests and nontest behavior are often disappointing. Job behavior and behavioral observations of persons on jobs appear to be very complex factorially. We should not be surprised, therefore, to learn that any one factor of tested ability may be only a limited sampling and, therefore, a rather poor indicator of the complex behaviors demanded in most job situations. Because of this, it is often necessary to combine several of the factored tests of ability, and in many instances it is more efficient to use Binet's empirical approach.

Nevertheless, the classification of human tested abilities is important theoretically, and such a taxonomy may also take on added practical significance when more clearly defined and more complete classifications of nontest and job behaviors become available. Because of this, the work of factor analysts has continued unabated. By analyzing human tested abilities more and more thoroughly (for example, by factor analyzing sets of tests *within* each of the broad groupings defined by Thurstone), nearly 60 additional factors have been found.

The Three Faces of Intellect

In 1956 Guilford (1956, 1959) summarized his own and others' factor-analytic results, systematizing for the first time the many factors observed. He viewed mental organization as lying along three dimensions. Along one dimension are the *operations* (the things a person can do); along a second are the *contents* (the kinds of material or content on which the operations may be performed); and along the third dimension are the *products* (the outcomes or results of the operations being performed on one or more of the contents). The classifications within each of the three areas are as follows:

Operations

1 Cognition—becoming aware of the existence of something.

2 Memory—remembering what was once known.

3 Convergent Thinking—organizing content in such a way as to produce a single correct solution to a problem.

4 Divergent Thinking—utilizing content to produce a wide range or variety of possible solutions to a problem.

5 Evaluation—making judgments or decisions.

Contents

1 Semantic—contents involving language.

2 Symbolic—contents involving numerical ideas and concepts.

3 Figural—contents involving various configurations, patterns, or shapes.

4 Behavioral—contents involving the way persons behave toward one another.

Products

1 Units—bits of information.

2 Classes—groupings of units.

3 Relations—similarities, differences, and contingencies among classes.

4 Systems—groupings of relations.

5 Transformations—concepts of how things change.

6 Implications—projections of concepts to deduce events that have not yet been observed.

According to Helmstadter (1964), a person performing successfully all the operations containing semantic content would be said to have high verbal ability; a person performing all operations containing symbolic content would have high mathematical ability; one performing effectively the operations with figural content would have high spatial or artistic ability; and a person who could recognize, remember, solve, and evaluate contents involving interpersonal behavior would be said to possess high social ability.

Obviously, Guilford's suggested taxonomy of human abilities is a far cry from the intentions of Binet when he set out rather simply to develop indicators of school learning ability. Even so, it is interesting that Binet's early tests and certainly the 1960 revision of the Stanford-Binet Test include items sampling many of the factors suggested by Guilford's classification. The most notable lack, perhaps, is in the Operations area of Divergent Thinking. School performance, teachers' ratings, learning ability, etc., have typically emphasized convergent thinking—that is, finding a single correct answer to problems. It is no surprise that Binet "missed" this important aspect of human ability; he based his selection of items on ratings of nontest behaviors that failed to emphasize divergent thinking abilities. Only recently have psychologists and educators come to recognize the potential importance of the divergent thinking abilities in jobs placing a premium on creativeness and originality. The rationally derived tests of divergent thinking may fill the gap caused by Binet's early dependence on behavioral observations that were incomplete estimates of the ability to cope successfully with problems. Raw empiricism may succeed in developing good indicators of nontest behaviors, but it may miss important aspects of human variation if the criterion observations of the nontest behaviors are deficient or limited in some way. Ideally, both methods should be employed as we seek to measure individual differences and to understand human behavior more fully. The history of the development of our present knowledge of what constitutes human intelligence and the specification of the wide variety of human abilities is a clear illustration of the interactive and additive contributions of the two methods.

MEASURING OTHER HUMAN DIFFERENCES

Motor Skills

So far, we have traced and discussed the development of measures of human cognitive abilities—those abilities crucial in developing an awareness and understanding of the elements of our environment. We have said nothing about the physical manipulation of objects in the environment. This involves the specification and measurement of *motor skills*, many of which have obvious relevance to the world of work. For example, the job of secretary involves not only a wide range of cognitive abilities such as verbal comprehension, perceptual speed, memory, and reasoning, but also, possibly, whatever motor skills may be necessary to handle a typewriter adequately. Scores of other jobs could be named (for example, bricklayer, auto mechanic, and watch repairman) that require relatively greater amounts of motor proficiency. Thus, the measurement of motor abilities is also important if an effective job of personnel selection and placement is to be done.

The major conclusion from a wealth of research on motor skills is that these abilities are highly specific. Tests designed to measure skills such as finger dexterity, steadiness, speed of response, and eye-hand coordination show only low intercorrelations. Summarizing over a decade of factor-analytic results with motor skills tests, Fleishman (1962) concluded that there are eleven fairly independent groupings of motor skills. These are:

1   *Control precision*, involving tasks requiring finely controlled muscular adjustments, such as moving a lever to a precise setting.

2   *Multilimb coordination*, involving the ability to coordinate the movements of a number of limbs simultaneously, such as packing a box with both hands.

3   *Response orientation*, involving the ability to make correct and accurate movements in relation to a stimulus under highly speeded conditions, such as reaching out and flicking a switch when a warning horn sounds.

4   *Reaction time*, involving the speed of a person's response when a stimulus appears, such as pressing a key in response to a bell.

5   *Speed of arm movement*, involving the speed of gross arm movements where accuracy is not required, such as gathering trash or debris and throwing it into a large pile.

6   *Rate control*, involving the ability to make continuous motor adjustments relative to a moving target changing in speed and direction, such as holding a rod on a moving rotor.

7   *Manual dexterity*, involving skillful arm and hand movements, in handling rather large objects under speeded conditions, such as placing blocks rapidly into a form board.

8   *Finger dexterity*, involving skillful manipulations of small objects (such as nuts and bolts) with the fingers.

9   *Arm-hand steadiness*, involving the ability to make precise arm-hand positioning movements that do not require strength or speed, such as threading a needle.

10   *Wrist-finger speed*, involving rapid tapping movements with the wrist and fingers, such as transmitting a continuous signal with a telegraphic key.

11   *Aiming*, involving an extremely narrow ability defined by a test in which the examinee places dots in circles as rapidly as possible.

Unfortunately, not much research has been done on the relative importance of each of these basic motor skills in successfully performing various industrial tasks. However, tests are available to measure each of the above abilities, either singly or in combination.

Typical Behavior Measures

Cronbach (1960) has chosen the term *maximum performance* measures to denote tests of cognitive and motor abilities. Such tests are designed primarily to determine how much a person can do or how well he can perform on any given test. In contrast, a number of tests have been developed with no distinction between so-called right and wrong answers. Cronbach calls these tests *typical behavior* measures. These are the tests of attitudes, interests, personality, and the like; their prime purpose is to yield descriptions of an individual's typical behavior as he pursues his daily activities. There are no right or wrong answers except as they are descriptive of individual behavioral tendencies; instead of just one scoring key, such inventories tend to have several—each representing a mode or pattern of observed behavior relevant for describing differences between people. Information of this kind has obvious potential importance for making selection decisions because it indicates the pattern of behavior to be expected from a person after he has been placed on a job.

As a means of describing the kinds of typical behavior tests available, we can consider the methods used for developing such tests and some of the results obtained. The three major methods are *armchair theoretic*, *factor analytic*, and *empirical*.

The Armchair Theorist Based on his pet theory of human behavior, a test developer might simply sit at his desk (or in his armchair) and devise a set of stimulus materials (such as verbal statements, ambiguous pictures, inkblots) to be used in eliciting responses from persons. He would then administer the test materials to a group of persons and decide, on the basis of his theory, what their responses might mean in terms of each person's major behavior tendencies. The final step would be to confirm or disconfirm the behavioral inferences by observing and measuring the actual subsequent behavior of the persons tested. However, this last step is very rarely undertaken by users of this method. Instead, evaluation of such tests usually occurs from the same place they were created—the armchair.

It should be obvious that the armchair ap-proach has little to recommend it for developing tests useful in selection and placement programs. Most existing behavioral theories have at best doubtful validity, and it is unlikely that any test developer is so omniscient that he can accurately intuit what a person's responses to a set of stimuli may mean in terms of later observed behavior. Unfortunately, however, many tests and methods of this kind are still being used in industrial selection programs. Some examples of such methods are handwriting analysis, the Rorschach Test, and the Thematic Apperception Test.

The Factor Analyst The factor-analytic ap-proach should already be fairly familiar from our discussion of developing and defining cognitive and motor skill measures. Its use in developing typical behavior tests usually begins with a lengthy listing of terms (for example, all possible adjectives) or statements commonly used to describe human behavior. Observers then use the terms in rating or describing the actual behavior shown by persons who are well known to them. For example, sorority or fraternity members might describe each other, or clinical psychologists might describe their patients. The descriptions can then be correlated and factor analyzed to yield the basic dimensions (taxonomy) of typically observed human behaviors. This approach has been used in many studies and as a basis for developing many inventories. Eight such studies have been summarized by Tupes and Christal (1961). The persons rated in the various studies ranged from airmen with only high school education to male and female college students and first-year graduate students. The observers carrying out the ratings ranged from psychologically unsophisticated persons (for example, the airmen) to clinical psychologists and psychiatrists with years of experience in observing human behavior. In spite of these wide differences among subjects and raters, the same five factors of typical behavior emerged from all studies.

1 *Surgency*—the tendency to be assertive, talkative, out-going, and cheerful as opposed to being meek, mild, and reserved.
2 *Agreeableness*—the tendency to be good-natured, cooperative, emotionally mature, and attentive to people.
3 *Dependability*—the tendency to be orderly, responsible, conscientious, and persevering.
4 *Emotional stability*—the tendency to be poised, calm and self-sufficient.
5 *Culture*—the tendency to be imaginative, cultured, socially polished, and independently minded.

The factor-analytic approach has a good deal to recommend it because it starts with observable behavioral tendencies and seeks to identify the minimum number of dimensions necessary for usefully describing the behavior shown by people in normal day-to-day intercourse. As suggested by the Tupes and Christal summary, factor-analytic studies have yielded a stable and useful classification of different modes of human interpersonal behavior. Tests designed to measure these behavioral tendencies are available and warrant inclusion in experimental selection and placement test batteries.

The Empiricist   The empiric approach follows much the same pattern of test development used by Binet and outlined in the early pages of this chapter. Whereas Binet was seeking a measure indicative of learning ability, the method has been employed to identify other patterns of behavior. The method has been used with notable success to identify the characteristic patterns of likes and dislikes of persons who have entered and persisted in a variety of professions (physician, lawyer, engineer, personnel director, etc.) and skilled trades (electrician, plumber, carpenter, etc.).

In these instances, the behavior chosen for study has been occupational choice and occupational persistence, and the groups against which the statements of various kinds of likes and dislikes have been compared (item analyzed) are classified simply on the basis of occupational belonging. Two of the most widely used and successful measures of vocational interest were developed in this way— the *Strong Vocational Interest Blank* (SVIB) and the *Minnesota Vocational Interest Inventory* (MVII).

Other patterns of behavior, less easily defined and specified, have been used as a basis for test development. For example, the first scales of the widely used *Minnesota Multiphasic Personality Inventory* (MMPI) were chosen by comparing responses of groups of persons with different psychiatric disturbances (paranoia, schizophrenia, severe depression, etc.) with those given by emotionally undisturbed ("well") persons. Thus, the MMPI has come to play an important role in psychiatric diagnosis.

A similar test is the *California Psychological Inventory* (CPI). In this test the responses have been validated against "normal" patterns of observed behavior (such as dominance, sociability, social maturity, achievement motivation, etc.). Here, the behavioral criterion consisted of ratings of observed behavioral patterns occurring in everyday life. Item responses differentiating persons with different rated behaviors were chosen and scored to form the various scales; thus, the typical behaviors measured by the CPI are potentially more relevant to the world of work than the psychiatrically relevant behaviors tapped by the MMPI.

Since the empirical method is so strongly behaviorally based, it is the most desirable method for developing typical behavior tests. Consider, for example, the relative degree of confidence that may be attached to behavioral inferences based respectively on armchair and on empirically developed tests. Experience shows the chances to be extremely slight that inferences derived from armchair inventories will prove valid. This is because so many *untested* assumptions necessarily lie between the enunciation of a behavior theory and the ultimate observation of behavior in the real world. Even if the major elements of a behavior theory undergirding a test were essentially correct (and this, unfortunately, is extremely unlikely for most of psychology's present "theories"), there would be no assurance that the stimuli (test items) chosen intuitively or the theorists' inferences about the behavioral meaning of an examinee's responses would have any semblance of reality or fact.

In contrast, the empirical method places no such burden on the shoulders of the test author. He simply accumulates experimental evidence that certain test item responses are or are not associated with certain defined patterns of behavior in the real world, and he chooses for his test those responses that are empirically related to the particular pattern of behavior he is interested in. There probably is no more clear example of the failure of the armchair method than of the failure of early sensory tests to reflect the real world of human behavior. Binet was successful because he broke with current theorizing and proceeded to select his test stimuli on empirical rather than on theoretical grounds.

Possible Problems with Empiricism It is imperative in the development of any test or specialized scoring key to determine the relative stability of the association between item responses and behavior patterns. It is possible, particularly if only a few persons have been used as experimental subjects, that apparent response differences may be the result of only random or chance fluctuations. The best way to check stability of any scoring key is *cross-validation....* (A similar approach—the one used by Binet—is simply to carry out item analyses on several different groups and to select for the final test or scale only those items and responses showing consistent differences between persons with different observed behaviors—for example, high- versus low-rated learning ability.) The necessity for cross-validation is obvious; it is a safeguard for assuring that empirical results are based on real and not on chance differences. Even so, some tests on the market have *not* been properly cross-validated against the behavioral descriptions they are designed to measure. No confidence can be placed in a typical behavior test that has not been properly cross-validated.

A second problem with empirically developed tests grows out of the very strengths such tests possess. Such a test identifies certain specific behaviors used as the basis for item validation and selection, but little additional meaning can be attached initially to scores on the test. The lack of any cohesive theory during test development and the dependence of item selection on a rather narrowly specified behavior may result in interpretive sterility for scores. A critic of such a test might, for example, say, "Yes. I know that a high score means that a person has likes and dislikes similar to those of lawyers, but what does this *really* mean in terms of the behavior I might expect from such a person?" Such a critic is really asking for further definition of relationships between scores on the test and other observed behaviors. The initial empirical development of a test does not usually provide such additional information. Ordinarily, the test author should assume responsibility, along with other interested researchers, for seeking out and publicizing lawful relations between his measure and additional behavior observations and measures. The process is never ending, and a variety of research methods may be used.

Consider some of the research with the *Strong Vocational Interest Blank*. The first scales showed substantial differences between the likes and dislikes of persons in different occupations, but many questions about the scales remained unanswered. How stable over time were different patterns of response on the SVIB? Which, if any, patterns of occupational interests tended to be relatively more and less similar to one another? Given early in persons' educational or work careers, did occupational interest scales on the SVIB predict tendencies to enter and remain in an occupation or were they useful only for identifying the occupation that a person had already entered? Over many years of research, Strong (1943, 1955) and others have managed to answer these questions. It is known now that after age 18 or 19, measured interests *are* highly stable individual qualities. It is also known that on the average, male college students scoring high on a specific occupational scale of the SVIB are about four times as likely to be in that occupation nearly twenty years later than college men scoring low on the same scale. Moreover, men most satisfied with their chosen professions at ages 40–45 tend to be those whose measured interests in college were most compatible with their actual career choices. Factor analyses have also aided in understanding the way in which measured vocational likes and dislikes group together—that is, the basic dimensions of vocational interests. Summarizing the results of many such studies, Super and Crites (1962) suggest the following major factors of vocational interest:

Scientific activities
Social welfare activities (a helpful interest in people)
Literary, linguistic, and verbal activities (for example, journalism and law)
Materials manipulation (such as carpentry)
Systems interests (clerical and business detail jobs)
Persuasive personal contact activities (a manipulative interest in people)

Aesthetic expression
Aesthetic appreciation

These lines of evidence add greatly to what we know about scores on the SVIB. Similar research has been done on many other existing typical behavior inventories, such as the CPI and MMPI. The important point is, that the empirical method of item selection, *crucial* as it is as a first step in test development, still needs to be supplemented by further empirical studies designed to round out the meaning and interpretive significance of scores on the test.

Biographical Information   One of the most promising reasons for developing typical behavior inventories is that one of the best predictors of future behavior is past behavior. Nearly all programs of personnel selection seek to tap elements of past behavior by interviewing, checking references, analyzing application blanks and personal data sheets, reviewing scholastic records, and the like. Unfortunately, it is difficult to know exactly how past behaviors relate to specific future behaviors that may be of interest. The methods mentioned above are usually poorly standardized. The nature and extent of the information attained differ from applicant to applicant; predictions must be based on varying knowledge with the usual result that they can be little more than vague impressions, subjective hunches, and intuitive feelings.

The most commonly used method in selection, the personal interview, is notoriously bad in this regard. It is handled differently by each interviewer, who in turn probably uses different methods with each applicant. At its worst, the personal interview may bog down into merely "passing the time of day," with little time devoted to learning about an applicant's typical past behavior patterns. Under the best conditions, a highly skilled interviewer may be able to gather a wide range of fairly accurate information from the past, but even then it is difficult to interpret the meaning of this data for predicting future behavior; and again reliance must be placed on intuitive hunches and guesses. Some interviewers' hunches turn out to be much better than those of others, but it is difficult to know ahead of time who the better and more accurate interviewers are.

In spite of all this, no one would suggest dispensing with the interview in personnel selection; it is the only way of seeing what the applicant looks like, of getting a feeling for how his personality "clicks" with yours, and of getting acquainted with him as a person. Moreover, it is still the best way for "selling" the company to a promising applicant and of creating in him a good impression of how he was dealt with during the selection process. Thus, as a public relations device, the interview is crucial; as a means of predicting expected future job behavior, it often is not much good.

The best way to capitalize on past behavior for predicting future behavior is to use the empirical method with a standardized biographical inventory to learn what job behaviors may be predicted from various elements of past behavior. In effect, elements of a person's past behavior—marital history, jobs held, activities in high school and college, amount of education, hobbies, past successes and failures, etc.—are treated as separate items to be compared against defined job behavior categories in much the same way that Binet compared performance on test items with learning ability ratings. In this way, items of a biographical inventory may be scored to yield predictions of typical behavior in the future. The resulting typical behavior inventory does not suffer from many of the usual difficulties encountered by personality and interest tests. For example, (1) the inventory is empirically developed; (2) it is linked directly to job behavior, thereby forcing a more careful study of job behavior than has been done for most typical behavior invento-

ries; and, best of all, (3) it is much less likely to be "faked" because it includes information of actual past behavior which can, if necessary, be checked by independent means.

Since biographical inventories first came into wide use about twenty years ago, they have been used in a wide variety of studies and in many selection programs. Very often, a carefully developed typical behavior inventory based on biographical information has proved to be the single best predictor of future job behavior. Thus, biographical information constitutes one of the most fruitful sources of predictive data, to be considered along with measures of cognitive abilities, motor skills, and personality and interest measures.

REFERENCES

Chauncey, H., and Dobbin, J. E. *Testing: Its place in education today.* New York: Harper & Row, 1963.

Cronbach, L. J. *Essentials of psychological testing.* New York: Harper & Row, 1960. 2nd Ed.

Fleishman, E. A. The description and prediction of perceptual-motor skill learning. In Glaser, R. (Ed.), *Training research and education.* Pittsburgh: Univ. of Pittsburgh Press, 1962.

Guilford, J. P. The structure of intellect. *Psychol. Bull.*, 1956, *53*, 267–293.

Guilford, J. P. Three faces of intellect. *Amer. Psychologist*, 1959, *14*, 469–479.

Helmstadter, G. C. *Principles of psychological measurement.* New York: Appleton-Century-Crofts, 1964.

Spearman, C. *The abilities of man.* London: Macmillan, Ltd., 1927.

Strong, E. K., Jr. *Vocational interests of men and women.* Stanford: Stanford Univ. Press, 1943.

Strong, E. K., Jr. *Vocational interests 18 years after college.* Minneapolis: Univ. of Minn. Press, 1955.

Super, D. C., and Crites, J. O. *Appraising vocational fitness.* New York: Harper & Row, 1962.

Tupes, E. C., and Christal, R. E. *Recurrent personality factors based on trait ratings.* Technical Report ASD-TR-61-97. Personnel Laboratory, United States Air Force, Lackland Air Force Base, 1961.

Reading 2

An Abilities Conception of Personality: Some Implications for Personality Measurement

John Wallace

Anybody who has taught an introductory course in personality theory knows from past experience that the first thing one must do is clarify certain misconceptions that students hold. Among these multifarious naivetés which instructors anticipate, none is construed as more deserving of rapid extinction than the concept of personality as social skill. In one way or another, our ingenuous students must be led to eschew efficiency-evaluative conceptions of personality, i.e., personalities are "good" or "bad," and come to embrace what must certainly appear to them a bewildering phantasmagoria of putative underlying mediating structures and mechanisms. In exchange for a concept of personality which emphasizes the *efficiency* with which a person can elicit positive statements and actions from others, the student is invited to consider alternative constructs such as needs, traits, drives, cathexes, and a host of energy transformations apparently involving as many structures and mechanisms of change as there are theorists. Occasionally the instructor may encounter a student whose "misconceptions" about personality show considerable resistance to extinction. And perhaps this is as it should be. It may very well be the case that a social-skills conception is not so much wrong as it is narrow and incomplete.

Psychologists much like other scientists have shown a strong penchant for categorization. While cognizant of the arbitrary boundaries which, as a matter of convenience, separate one behavioral domain from another, we frequently *act* as if our categories were indeed mutually exclusive and nonoverlapping. Perhaps our preference for neat and unambiguous categories led to the rather humorous subtractive definition of personality as that which remains after intelligence, aptitudes, interests, and attitudes have been removed. The fact that the extant literature in personality research abounds with an enormous number of studies concerning needs or traits, while the first study which would follow logically from an explicit "abilities" conception of personality remains to be accomplished, certainly attests to the fact that most psychologists have tended to regard the domains of personality and ability as separate. This unfortunate separation has resulted in a necessary confounding of two important response properties in personality research, i.e., *response predisposition and response capability*. The present paper comprises an attempt to explore the consequences of conceiving personality as sets of abilities—abilities which, with regard to acquisition, maintenance, and modification, share much in common with other abilities.

RESPONSE PREDISPOSITION VERSUS RESPONSE CAPABILITY

The manner in which we choose to construe personality will obviously affect our research efforts. Construing personality as *essence* leads one to embrace somewhat different sets of theoretical constructs and research operations from those that would result from a construction of personality as response capability. And this is as it should be since the implications for personality measurement, de-

American Psychologist, 1966, **21**, 132–138. Copyright 1966 by the American Psychological Association. Reprinted by permission.

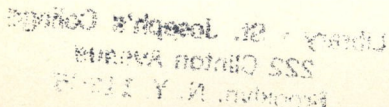

scription, and modification are of necessity quite different when we choose to search for *man as he really is* rather than *that of which he is capable*.

The bulk of research in personality has stemmed from essence concepts of personality and has focused upon such concepts as needs which, while accorded hypothetical status, stand in some relationship to underlying physiological processes (Murray, 1938) or traits which presumably possess a reality independent of the construct systems of observers (Allport, 1937). Both needs and traits possess the capacity to initiate and guide behavior, i.e., predispose the individual to respond in certain ways. While many who align themselves with trait or need concepts might reject the extreme critical realism as typified by the thought of Allport and might correspondingly embrace a position of nominalism to some degree or another, the fact remains that it would prove difficult to distinguish such positions from research operations alone. Essence concepts of personality have channelized research activities in directions that appear to have become "functionally autonomous."

In order to clarify the distinction made between response predisposition and response capability, let us consider a concrete example. Imagine a situation in which a child is observed striking another child repeatedly and in a forceful and excited fashion. A need theorist might infer the existence of an underlying construct, need for aggression. The trait theorist would probably demand more information and, depending upon the frequency of the behavior, the similarities among struck children, and the number of objectively diverse situations in which striking takes place, might infer the existence of a secondary, central, or cardinal trait of aggressiveness. In both cases, it is assumed that the individual is predisposed to respond aggressively. Curiously enough, neither trait nor need theory takes into account the simple but important matter of whether or not the child is capable of responding in a different way. Equally important but perhaps trivial at first blush is the fact that the child in question is indeed *capable* of an aggressive response in the first place, i.e., he is capable of assuming an aggressive role. Rather than inferences about predisposition in terms of operative needs or traits one can with equal justification assert that given individuals are simply either capable or incapable of certain responses in certain stimulus situations.

Is it possible that accurate knowledge of the breadth and diversity of *extant behavioral repertoires* in conjunction with detailed *knowledge of specific stimulus situations* would render motivational inferences superfluous? In conceiving of situations in which social needs or traits are presumed operative, it seems difficult to think of any in which capability statements appear less justified than predisposition statements. For example, consider the individual who may be described as gregarious or high in need for affiliation. Rather than describe such an individual as possessed of a strong need to "draw near and enjoyably co-operate or reciprocate with an allied other [Murray, 1938, p. 154]," could we not describe him equally well in terms of his utter inability to withstand social isolation or [say] that he is quite incapable of independent effort? Turning to essence conceptions in terms of traits, might we not describe a "shy" person as one who is incapable of making assertive responses in certain situations? Or to take an example from psychopathology, a world of difference exists between the statements, "Patient A *is* schizophrenic" and "Patient A is *capable* of schizophrenic behavior." The first of the statements, an essence concept, is somewhat incongruous with the observation that hospitalized psychotics infrequently show overt psychotic symptoms (Lindsley, 1962). Capability statements, on the other hand, do not imply "continuous pathology" and are not rendered problematic by the intermittent expression of pathological behavior.

Essence conceptions of personality typically involve hierarchical arrangements of personality structure. Thus, for example, needs are thought to vary with regard to intensity or strength. And traits are described as secondary, central, or cardinal. Perhaps the most extreme example of hierarchical organization is found in Freud's bifurcation of mental life into conscious and unconscious. The problems posed by hierarchical conceptions of the organization of personality structure are still unresolved. For example, the assumption that needs are hierarchically arranged in order of increasing strength renders *frequency* of response to projective stimuli a plausible measure of need strength. But, frequency will prove to be a useful measure of response strength and hence of response predisposition if and only if our assumption concerning the organization of needs is reasonable. It is not unreasonable to suppose that "needs" can be organized in other than hierarchical arrangements. For example, consider the extreme case of an individual who possesses relative balance among his operative needs. Of what significance is a given "need-related" response when it is but one of numerous possible need-related responses all of which are equivalent in strength and, hence, in probability of occurrence. Clearly, in such a case, one is in considerable danger of confusing response capability with response predisposition. Moreover, if one assumes a need organization other than a hierarchical one, how can one predict what particular need-related response will occur in response to a projective stimulus? And even more important, how can one ever hope to establish extratest correlates of such responses? As the organization of needs approaches balance within the individual, his responses to projective instruments should more clearly indicate his *capabilities* rather than his predispositions.

In order to allay the reader's fears that the preceding amounts to nothing more than a play upon words, let us now turn to some of the implications of an abilities conception for personality measurement.

IMPLICATIONS FOR PERSONALITY MEASUREMENT

In the measurement of abilities, attempts are made to elicit indices of *maximal* performance under *optimal* conditions of measurement. The phrase optimal conditions of measurement refers to the selection, development, and maintenance of both extratest and test stimuli in a manner considered most favorable for demonstration of the ability in question. Considerable care is exercised in the selection of items such that ambiguity is at a minimum and difficulty levels are known. Moreover, in abilities testing, ambiguity in *the purpose of testing* is generally quite low, i.e., the subject is frequently informed of the nature of the instrument, the possible range of inferences which are permissible from the resulting data, and the type of decisions which may take place either by the subject himself or by some external agent as a consequence of performance in the testing situation. Finally, response uncertainty is reduced since the subject is informed that convergent solutions exist, i.e., there is one and only one correct response to a given item rather than a range of responses.

In order to clarify differences, consider the most extreme example of predisposition measurement, i.e., projective techniques. In contrast to abilities measurement, projective techniques as originally conceived were thought to constitute rather pure measures of response predisposition. While great effort is expended in the construction of abilities measures to avoid ambiguity, the classical view of projective measurement which stemmed from well-known psychoanalytic notions of projection would imply the more ambiguity the better. Deliberate attempts were made to achieve stimuli highly unstructured as well as ambiguous. It was thought that when the subject was presented with stimuli whose components permitted multiple organizations and upon which numerous interpretations could be placed, his responses would reflect central tendencies, i.e., projections. Moreover, since maximum structure in the testing situation itself might obscure response predispositions, efforts were made to disguise the real purpose of testing, i.e., subjects were provided with vague instructional sets such as "tests of imagination," etc. Given the rather novel nature of tasks such as the Rorschach or the Thematic Apperception Test (TAT) as well as the rather wide publicity of projective techniques through educational and mass media channels, few subjects could be expected to accept these explanations of the nature of the task by the examiner. In contrast to abilities measurement, ambiguity in the purpose of testing when projective techniques are employed is quite high.

The subject is free to interpret (and usually does so) the nature of the test as he chooses. In addition, subjects are typically quite uncertain as to the range of inferences which are permissible from the resulting data as well as the type of decisions that might result as function of their performance in the testing situation. Response uncertainty is at a maximum since the subject is typically informed that convergent solutions do not exist, i.e., there are no right or wrong answers.

Obviously, then, predisposition conceptions of personality *can* lead to operations which are clearly at odds with those demanded by an abilities conception. In short, the projective-techniques setting in which highly ambiguous materials are employed comprises the most inefficient and nonoptimal of all possible situations one could imagine for the demonstration by subjects of their *capabilities*. It would follow from an abilities conception that the usefulness of any measuring instrument would *decrease* as ambiguity in the measuring instrument is *increased*. Curiously enough, although some lack of agreement is apparent, this is precisely what research on the matter of ambiguity in the TAT seems to show. Two researches by Kagan (1956, 1959) provide clear support for the notion that the usefulness of TAT-like responses varies as a function of level of stimulus ambiguity. In the first, Kagan (1956) found that fantasy productions to highly structured hostile pictures differentiated aggressive boys from nonaggressive boys while responses to ambiguous pictures did not. In the second study, Kagan (1959) examined the stability of content scores over time. Two content measures, need for achievement and need for aggression, were the only fantasy motives showing stability. Both of these measures were derived from stimulus cards highly structured for these needs.

Several researches (Leiman, 1961; Leiman & Epstein, 1961; Strizver, 1961) seem to indicate quite clearly that subjects respond to highly structured stimuli quite in line with a "capability" conception. Leiman and Epstein (1961) obtained self-report measures on their subjects for guilt associated with sexuality. The subjects were divided into low- and high-guilt groups. On pictures highly structured for sexual themes, those who reported themselves high on guilt over sexual matters projected less sexual imagery than those who had reported low guilt. Leiman (1961), in a separate study, found that subjects with conflict over sexual expression responded with less magnitude to high-relevance pictures than subjects with minimal or no conflict. In an experiment which involved induced sexual drive and experimental manipulation of inhibition, Strizver (1961) found that pictures of high relevance coupled with low inhibition yielded considerable sexual imagery. These studies involving highly structured pictures and socially "ques-

tionable" behaviors, i.e., hostility and sexuality, seem to suggest that subjects who appear
capable of responding to the "stimulus pull"
of highly structured cards do so while subjects
who appear incapable for whatever reason,
e.g., guilt, inhibition, do not. Murstein (1963),
after reviewing the literature on ambiguity
levels and the TAT, reaches a conclusion
which is in partial agreement when he asserts
that "low and medium-structure cards are
most sensitive to the direct expression of
drive, *while the highly structured cards* are
most diagnostic through the avoidance of
stimulus pull [p. 193]."

Considering the fact that projective techniques were once thought (and apparently still
are by some) to constitute a "royal road to the
unconscious," it seems of great interest to
note that such responses become more predictable when *self-reported* guilt over expression of the drive in question is considered. It
would appear that some relationship exists
between the *ability* to assume roles in a stimulus situation which contains discriminable
cues relevant to such roles (the TAT testing
situation) and the ability to assume such roles
in a second stimulus environment (a self-
report testing situation). One may readily rephrase this relationship in terms of a broad
general question as follows: What is the relationship between the ability to make certain
verbal responses in a make-believe setting and
the ability to respond in a similar fashion in
overt behavior? In seeking an answer to this
question, the ambiguity factor is crucial. In
contrast to the classical view of projective
techniques, which would imply the more ambiguity the better, an abilities conception
would hold that, as ambiguity is reduced
through the addition of discriminable cues
highly relevant to the examiner's purpose in
testing, optimal conditions for the demonstration of maximal performance are achieved.
Following this line of reasoning, one might
achieve maximum clarity in projective-
technique settings by simply directly request-

ing responses which correspond to the examiner's purposes in testing.

Murstein (1963) has indicated that a "test
the limits" procedure employed by R. S. Laza-
rus with the TAT has yielded tentative
findings of interest. Some observations from a
study by the author and Michael Conant currently in progress appear most intriguing. Fraternity boys were presented with two cards
from the TAT, Card 7BM and Card 6GF. Card
7BM has been shown to have moderate pull
for hostile thema (Murstein, 1963) while Card
6GF seemed to be one which would have at
least moderate pull for sexuality. Responses
were first gathered under the typical McClel-
land "predisposition" instructions. After the
subjects had written a story to each of the
cards, the stimuli were immediately reshown
and the subjects were asked to write the
"sexiest story" of which they were capable to
one and the "most hostile" story of which
they were capable to the other. The stories which follow were obtained from two
different subjects under the instructions to
write the "sexiest" story of which they were
capable.

Story 1. Martin leaned over her shoulder and
while appearing to look at her face, he was
actually viewing the bulge at her chest. He was
suddenly overcome with desire wanting to grab
them, rip open her dress, put his mouth all over
them, suck them, bite them—and lower, yes
lower. His hands wanted to roam, to enter secret
places, to weave through pubic hairs. But his
mouth and tongue too were moist with the desire
to lick.

Suddenly he seizing, and she let out a moan
deep in the throat—half passionate, half-
terrified.

But she let him anyway, she wanted it.

She quickly unbuttoned and his hands
wormed into the opening.

He pulled her to him, waiting and trying to
touch all over as her dress fell.

"Do you want me to touch you too?" she
pleaded.

Yes, yes!
Here?
Yes!
And here?
Yes, yes!
His hands roamed wildly, seeking hard breasts and dark crevices.
Soon he laid her on the bed and began.

Story 2. The young woman has been living with another man for several weeks. Now she is pregnant and has come to her father for help. The old man is at first shocked since he thought his daughter was away at school. But he advises his daughter not to marry her lover if he does not really love her as she says. He is not a prudish man and understands that these can happen. He sees nothing wrong in keeping the child when it is born even though the mother is unmarried.

Eventually the girl meets a man who loves her for herself and is willing to accept the child. The woman is fully capable of offering sexual fulfillment to this man even though she suffers from a guilt feeling from the previous affair. It is unfortunate that society should force such a guilty complex upon her. She should feel free to give a man sexual fulfillment without marriage if she wants to. She does get married to this man, in this case, but only after she has lived with him long enough to know that she has a good deal more to offer him than sex.

While our research is still in its developmental stages, one cannot help but be impressed with the rather striking differences among subjects with regard to their ability to comply with the instructions. Equally intriguing are the marked differences in what subjects construe as constituting a "sexy" story. Lacking knowledge of the specific instructional set employed, one would hardly conclude that each of these subjects was in fact writing the "sexiest" story of which he was capable. The author of Story 1 appears quite capable of complying with the instructions. His account of the sexual act is liberally sprinkled with a variety of erotic acts. His characters behave with nearly total abandon and the conse-

quences of engaging in sexual behavior for both male and female appear wildly pleasurable. On the other hand, the author of Story 2 omits description of the sexual act itself and concentrates upon unhappy consequences of sexual intercourse, e.g., an illegitimate pregnancy, guilt feelings, etc. Story 2 ends with a strong denial of the importance of sexual relations at all in male-female relationships. While it is obvious that striking differences in story content are obtained by "capability" instructions, it is, of course, necessary to show that such differences are useful in predicting extratest behavior.

In the preceding material, the implications of a response-capability conception of personality for projective measurement has been treated in some detail. It seems reasonable to draw implications for other methods of measurement as well. In fact, one may draw reasonable conclusions as to what methods of measurement may prove of value in personality assessment. The use of role playing in well-defined stimulus situations will most likely be of considerable value as an assessment method. By varying systematically given attributes of the stimulus situations under which roles are assumed, it may prove quite feasible to specify the conditions under which the individual becomes capable of performing given responses. It would appear most reasonable to assume that the closer the approximation of the role-playing situation to the predictive situation, the greater should be the accuracy of the predictions. If an individual can demonstrate response capability under a given set of conditions, he ought to be able to demonstrate the same capability under other highly similar conditions.

RESPONSE DEFICITS OR RESPONSE INHIBITION

Those interested in the assessment of personality in research as well as clinical settings have overlooked an assessment question of considerable importance. Emphasis upon psychodynamics and matters such as "unconscious conflict" dictate a search for internal states which presumably mediate and guide overt behavior. Psychoanalytic theorizing of the classical vintage assumes that powerful but unconscious controlling forces over overt behavior must be made conscious before overt behavior can be changed. Learning-theory conflict models emphasize the importance of lowering the avoidance gradient before approach responses can be made. Both positions are in a sense "subtractive." The classical analytical model emphasizes the importance of libidinal discharge, i.e., catharsis. And the learning-theory conflict model indicates the importance of the unlearning of inhibitory tendencies, i.e., extinction of underlying conditioned emotional responses such as "anxiety." Neither position considers the important question of whether or not the alternative responses which are to be performed or the components of these responses are a part of the individual's repertoire of responses in the first place. It is an altogether erroneous assumption to assume that nonperformance of appropriate (as defined by an observer) responses *always* reflects the operation of response inhibition, avoidance, anxiety, or some other internal state. Certainly, it is difficult to see how an individual can perform given responses if he has never learned them, i.e., they are not a part of his response repertoire. A meaningful assessment problem then revolves around the question of the maintaining factors in behavior. It is most conceivable that some behaviors of the individual reflect *inadequate learning*, i.e., response deficits, while others may reflect *overlearning*, i.e., extraordinary conditioned emotional responses. In personality assessment, then, one must bear in mind that response incapability may be attributable to *either* a learning deficit or response inhibition.

RESPONSE CAPABILITY AND PSYCHOPATHOLOGY

An emphasis upon response capability would do much to bring order to one of the most confused areas of psychology, that of psychopathology. The difficulties posed by psychiatric nosology are well known. While many have criticized traditional classificatory schema, a satisfactory and *useful* diagnostic nomenclature has not appeared. The reliability (diagnostic agreement among those who use a given nomenclature) of such systems remains less than adequate. And the validity (demonstrated intraclassification and extraclassification correlates) leaves much to be desired. While some may feel that it is premature to abandon the search for an adequate classificatory system (e.g., Zigler & Phillips, 1961), it may very well be the case that our traditional approaches to psychiatric diagnosis are inherently wrong. The search for "disease entities" is, in actuality, a search for essences. Disease entity conceptions, regardless of the way the "symptomatic pie" is cut, have, without exception, ignored the conditions under which behavior occurs. Thus, for example, while hundreds of studies have been conducted upon the various attributes of persons classified as schizophrenic, few have concerned themselves with the conditions under which such behavior becomes apparent. Considering the fact that Lindsley's (1962) study of hospitalized patients indicated that such patients rather infrequently display overt psychotic behavior, a logical first step might be a careful analysis of given stimulus conditions in the hospital milieu under which the patient becomes capable of hallucinatory behavior, assaultive behavior, etc. Our assumption that schizophrenia is an entity, disease, or disorder has precluded sensitive analysis of situational determinants of the behavior of persons so diagnosed. Szasz's (1957) plea for a situational analysis of psychiatric operations is certainly a step in the right direction.

While clinicians who have embraced psychodynamic models of psychopathology have eschewed traditional nosological efforts in favor of description of underlying dynamics, it would appear that such efforts have simply directed the search for essences to a different level of functioning. The Freudian emphasis upon unconscious determinants of behavior and underlying structure typifies such efforts. It would certainly appear to make a world of difference, both to the patient and his therapist, to construe the patient as capable of homicidal behavior rather than, "underneath it all," a homicidal person. The former would lead to an examination of the conditions under which such behavior might occur. The latter might very well suggest little beyond immediate confinement!

In conclusion, many of the problems in personality assessment with which we are currently faced seem attributable, in large part, to the marked influence of "essence" conceptions of personality which have captured the imaginations of those interested in personality over the past 60-odd years. Conceiving personality in terms of response capability would appear to have meaningful and tangible implications for personality assessment. Certainly, a response-capability conception would do much toward providing the means by which the persistent epistemological quandary inherent in essence conceptions could be resolved. When faced with the inevitably incompatible evidence, how does one decide as to the *level* at which, or the *particular* stimulus situation in which, the "real" person (whatever that may mean) can be found?

In short, whether we choose to search for man "as he really is" or that "of which he is capable" is of utmost importance. Construing personality as response capability reemphasizes the importance of the stimulus conditions under which behavior occurs—something which, in my opinion, has been neglected by those interested in personality description, measurement, and development.

REFERENCES

Allport, G. W. *Personality: A psychological interpretation.* New York: Holt, 1937.

Kagan, J. The measurement of overt aggression from fantasy. *Journal of Abnormal and Social Psychology*, 1956, **52**, 390–393.

Kagan, J. The stability of TAT fantasy and stimulus ambiguity. *Journal of Consulting Psychology*, 1959, **23**, 226–271.

Leiman, A. H. Relationship of TAT sexual responses to sexual drive, sexual guilt, and sexual conflict. Unpublished doctoral dissertation. University of Massachusetts, 1961.

Leiman, A. H., & Epstein, A. Thematic sexual responses to sexual drive and guilt. *Journal of Abnormal and Social Psychology*, 1961, **63**, 169–175.

Lindsley, O. L. Characteristics of the behavior of chronic psychotics as revealed by free-operant conditioning methods. In T. R. Sarbin (Ed.), *Studies in behavior pathology.* New York: Holt, Rinehart & Winston, 1962.

Murray, H. A. *Explorations in personality.* New York: Oxford Univer. Press, 1938.

Murstein, B. I. *Theory and research in projective techniques.* New York: Wiley, 1963.

Strizver, G. L. Thematic sexual and guilt responses as related to stimulus-relevance and experimentally induced drive and inhibition. Unpublished doctoral dissertation, University of Massachusetts, 1961.

Szasz, T. S. The problem of psychiatric nosology: A contribution to a situational analysis of psychiatric operations. *American Journal of Psychiatry*, 1957, **114**, 405–413.

Zigler, E., & Phillips, L. Psychiatric diagnosis: A critique. *Journal of Abnormal and Social Psychology*, 1961, **63**, 607–618.

Reading 3

Motivation: A Diagnostic Approach

David A. Nadler
Edward E. Lawler III

- What makes some people work hard while others do as little as possible?
- How can I, as a manager, influence the performance of people who work for me?
- Why do people turn over, show up late to work, and miss work entirely?

These important questions about employees' behavior can only be answered by managers who have a grasp of what motivates people. Specifically, a good understanding of motivation can serve as a valuable tool for *understanding* the causes of behavior in organizations, for *predicting* the effects of any managerial action, and for *directing* behavior so that organizational and individual goals can be achieved.

EXISTING APPROACHES

During the past twenty years, managers have been bombarded with a number of different approaches to motivation. The terms associated with these approaches are well known—"human relations," "scientific management," "job enrichment," "need hierarchy," "self-actualization," etc. Each of these approaches has something to offer. On the other hand, each of these different approaches also has its problems in both theory and practice. Running through almost all of the approaches with which managers are familiar are a series of implicit but clearly erroneous assumptions.

Assumption 1: All Employees Are Alike
Different theories present different ways of looking at people, but each of them assumes that all employees are basically similar in their makeup: Employees all want economic gains,

or all want a pleasant climate, or all aspire to be self-actualizing, etc.

Assumption 2: All Situations Are Alike
Most theories assume that all managerial situations are alike, and that the managerial course of action for motivation (for example, participation, job enlargement, etc.) is applicable in all situations.

Assumption 3: One Best Way Out of the other two assumptions there emerges a basic principle that there is "one best way" to motivate employees.

When these "one best way" approaches are tried in the "correct" situation they will work. However, all of them are bound to fail in some situations. They are therefore not adequate managerial tools.

A NEW APPROACH

During the past ten years, a great deal of research has been done on a new approach to looking at motivation. This approach, frequently called "expectancy theory," still needs further testing, refining, and extending. However, enough is known that many behavioral scientists have concluded that it represents the most comprehensive, valid, and useful approach to understanding motivation. Further, it is apparent that it is a very useful tool for understanding motivation in organizations.

The theory is based on a number of specific assumptions about the causes of behavior in organizations.

Assumption 1: Behavior Is Determined by a Combination of Forces in the Individual and Forces in the Environment Neither the individual nor the environment alone determines behavior. Individuals come into organizations with certain "psychological baggage." They have past experiences and a developmental history which has given them unique sets of needs, ways of looking at the world, and expectations about how organizations will treat them. These all influence how individuals respond to their work environment. The work environment provides structures (such as a pay system or a supervisor) which influence the behavior of people. Different environments tend to produce different behavior in similar people just as dissimilar people tend to behave differently in similar environments.

Assumption 2: People Make Decisions about Their Own Behavior in Organizations While there are many constraints on the behavior of individuals in organizations, most of the behavior that is observed is the result of individuals' conscious decisions. These decisions usually fall into two categories. First, individuals make decisions about *membership behavior*—coming to work, staying at work, and in other ways being a member of the organization. Second, individuals make decisions about the amount of *effort* they will direct *towards performing their jobs*. This includes decisions about how hard to work, how much to produce, at what quality, etc.

Assumption 3: Different People Have Different Types of Needs, Desires and Goals Individuals differ on what kinds of outcomes (or rewards) they desire. These differences are not random; they can be examined systematically by an understanding of the differences in the strength of individuals' needs.

Assumption 4: People Make Decisions among Alternative Plans of Behavior Based on Their Perceptions (Expectancies) of the Degree to Which a Given Behavior will Lead to Desired Outcomes In simple terms, people tend to do those things which they see as leading to outcomes (which can also be called "rewards") they desire and avoid doing those things they see as leading to outcomes that are not desired.

In general, the approach used here views people as having their own needs and mental maps of what the world is like. They use these maps to make decisions about how they will behave, behaving in those ways which their mental maps indicate will lead to outcomes that will satisfy their needs. Therefore, they are inherently neither motivated nor unmotivated; motivation depends on the situation they are in, and how it fits their needs.

THE THEORY

Based on these general assumptions, expectancy theory states a number of propositions about the process by which people make decisions about their own behavior in organizational settings. While the theory is complex at first view, it is in fact made of a series of fairly straightforward observations about behavior. (The theory is presented in more technical terms in Appendix A.) Three concepts serve as the key building blocks of the theory:

Performance-Outcome Expectancy Every behavior has associated with it, in an individual's mind, certain outcomes (rewards or punishments). In other words, the individual believes or expects that if he or she behaves in a certain way, he or she will get certain things.

Examples of expectancies can easily be described. An individual may have an expectancy that if he produces ten units he will receive his normal hourly rate while if he produces fifteen units he will receive his hourly pay rate plus a bonus. Similarly an individual may believe that certain levels of performance will lead to approval or disapproval from members of her work group or from her supervisor. Each performance can be seen as leading to a number of different kinds of outcomes and outcomes can differ in their types.

Valence Each outcome has a "valence" (value, worth, attractiveness) to a specific individual. Outcomes have different valences for different individuals. This comes about because valences result from individual needs and perceptions, which differ because they in turn reflect other factors in the individual's life.

For example, some individuals may value an opportunity for promotion or advancement because of their needs for achievement or power, while others may not want to be promoted and leave their current work group because of needs for affiliation with others. Similarly, a fringe benefit such as a pension plan may have great valence for an older worker but little valence for a young employee on his first job.

Effort-Performance Expectancy Each behavior also has associated with it in the individual's mind a certain expectancy or probability of success. This expectancy represents the individual's perception of how hard it will be to achieve such behavior and the probability of his or her successful achievement of that behavior.

For example, you may have a strong expectancy that if you put forth the effort, you can produce ten units an hour, but that you have

only a fifty-fifty chance of producing fifteen units an hour if you try.

Putting these concepts together, it is possible to make a basic statement about motivation. In general, the motivation to attempt to behave in a certain way is greatest when:

a The individual believes that the behavior will lead to outcomes (performance-outcome expectancy)
b The individual believes that these outcomes have positive value for him or her (valence)
c The individual believes that he or she is able to perform at the desired level (effort-performance expectancy)

Given a number of alternative levels of behavior (ten, fifteen, and twenty units of production per hour, for example) the individual will choose that level of performance which has the greatest motivational force associated with it, as indicated by the expectancies, outcomes, and valences.

In other words, when faced with choices about behavior, the individual goes through a process of considering questions such as, "Can I perform at that level if I try?" "If I perform at that level, what will happen?" "How do I feel about those things that will happen?" The individual then decides to behave in that way which seems to have the best chance of producing positive, desired outcomes.

A General Model

On the basis of these concepts, it is possible to construct a general model of behavior in organizational settings (see Figure 3-1). Working from left to right in the model, motivation is seen as the force on the individual to expend effort. Motivation leads to an observed level of effort by the individual. Effort, alone, however, is not enough. Performance results from a combination of the effort that an individual

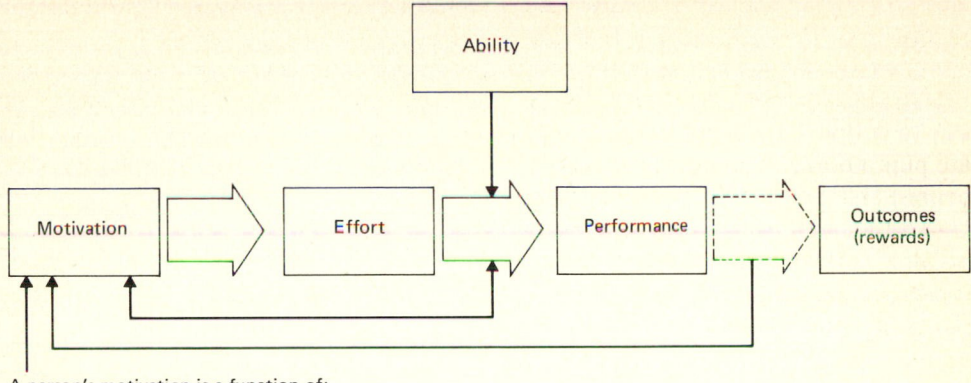

A person's motivation is a function of:

    a. Effort-to-performance expectancies
    b. Performance-to-outcome expectancies
    c. Perceived valence of outcomes

Figure 3-1   The basic motivation-behavior sequence.

puts forth *and* the level of ability which he or she has (reflecting skills, training, information, etc.) Effort thus combines with ability to produce a given level of performance. As a result of performance, the individual attains certain outcomes. The model indicates this relationship in a dotted line, reflecting the fact that sometimes people perform but do not get desired outcomes. As this process of performance-reward occurs, time after time, the actual events serve to provide information which influences the individual's perceptions (particularly expectancies) and thus influences motivation in the future.

Outcomes, or rewards, fall into two major categories. First, the individual obtains outcomes from the environment. When an individual performs at a given level he or she can receive positive or negative outcomes from supervisors, coworkers, the organization's rewards systems, or other sources. These environmental rewards are thus one source of outcomes for the individual. A second source of outcomes is the individual. These include outcomes which occur purely from the performance of the task itself (feelings of

accomplishment, personal worth, achievement, etc.). In a sense, the individual gives these rewards to himself or herself. The environment cannot give them or take them away directly; it can only make them possible.

Supporting Evidence

Over fifty studies have been done to test the validity of the expectancy-theory approach to predicting employee behavior.[1] Almost without exception, the studies have confirmed the predictions of the theory. As the theory predicts, the best performers in organizations tend to see a strong relationship between performing their jobs well and receiving rewards they value. In addition they have clear performance goals and feel they can perform well. Similarly, studies using the expectancy theory to predict how people choose jobs also

[1]For reviews of the expectancy theory research see Mitchell, T. R. Expectancy models of job satisfaction, occupational preference and effort: A theoretical methodological, and empirical appraisal. *Psychological Bulletin,* 1974, **81**, 1053–1077. For a more general discussion of expectancy theory and other approaches to motivation see Lawler, E. E. *Motivation in work organizations,* Belmont Calif.: Brooks/Cole, 1973.

show that individuals tend to interview for and actually take those jobs which they feel will provide the rewards they value. One study, for example, was able to correctly predict for 80 percent of the people studied which of several jobs they would take.[2] Finally, the theory correctly predicts that beliefs about the outcomes associated with performance (expectancies) will be better predictors of performance than will feelings of job satisfaction since expectancies are the critical causes of performance and satisfaction is not.

Questions about the Model

Although the results so far have been encouraging, they also indicate some problems with the model. These problems do not critically affect the managerial implications of the model, but they should be noted. The model is based on the assumption that individuals make very rational decisions after a thorough exploration of all the available alternatives and on weighing the possible outcomes of all these alternatives. When we talk to or observe individuals, however, we find that their decision processes are frequently less thorough. People often stop considering alternative behavior plans when they find one that is at least moderately satisfying, even though more rewarding plans remain to be examined.

People are also limited in the amount of information they can handle at one time, and therefore the model may indicate a process that is much more complex than the one that actually takes place. On the other hand, the model does provide enough information and is consistent enough with reality to present some clear implications for managers who are concerned with the question of how to motivate the people who work for them.

[2]Lawler, E. E., Kuleck, W. J., Rhode, J. G., & Sorenson, J. E. Job choice and post-decision dissonance. *Organizational Behavior and Human Performance*, 1975, 13, 133–145.

Implications for Managers

The first set of implications is directed toward the individual manager who has a group of people working for him or her and is concerned with how to motivate good performance. Since behavior is a result of forces both in the person and in the environment, you as manager need to look at and diagnose both the person and the environment. Specifically, you need to do the following:

Figure out what outcomes each employee values As a first step, it is important to determine what kinds of outcomes or rewards have valence for your employees. For each employee you need to determine "what turns him or her on." There are various ways of finding this out, including (a) finding out employees' desires through some structured method of data collection, such as a questionnaire, (b) observing the employees' reactions to different situations or rewards, or (c) the fairly simple act of asking them what kinds of rewards they want, what kind of career goals they have, or "what's in it for them." It is important to stress here that it is very difficult to change what people want, but fairly easy to find out what they want. Thus, the skillful manager emphasizes diagnosis of needs, not changing the individuals themselves.

Determine what kinds of behavior you desire Managers frequently talk about "good performance" without really defining what good performance is. An important step in motivating is for you yourself to figure out what kinds of performances are required and what are adequate measures or indicators of performance (quantity, quality, etc.). There is also a need to be able to define those performances in fairly specific terms so that observable and measurable behavior can be defined and subordinates can understand what is desired of them (e.g., produce ten products of a certain quality standard—rather than only produce at a high rate).

Make sure desired levels of performance are reachable The model states that motivation is determined not only by the performance-to-outcome expectancy, but also by the effort-to-performance expectancy. The implication of this is that the levels of performance which are set as the points at which individuals receive desired outcomes must be reachable or attainable by these individuals. If the employees feel that the level of performance required to get a reward is higher than they can reasonably achieve, then their motivation to perform well will be relatively low.

Link desired outcomes to desired performances The next step is to directly, clearly, and explicitly link those outcomes desired by employees to the specific performances desired by you. If your employee values external rewards, then the emphasis should be on the rewards systems concerned with promotion, pay, and approval. While the linking of these rewards can be initiated through your making statements to your employees, it is extremely important that employees see a clear example of the reward process working in a fairly short period of time if the motivating "expectancies" are to be created in the employees' minds. The linking must be done by some concrete public acts, in addition to statements of intent.

If your employee values internal rewards (e.g., achievement), then you should concentrate on changing the nature of the person's job, for he or she is likely to respond well to such things as increased autonomy, feedback, and challenge, because these things will lead to a situation where good job performance is inherently rewarding. The best way to check on the adequacy of the internal and external reward system is to ask people what their perceptions of the situation are. Remember it is the perceptions of people that determine their motivation, not reality. It doesn't matter for example whether you feel a subordinate's

pay is related to his or her motivation. Motivation will be present only if the subordinate sees the relationship. Many managers are misled about the behavior of their subordinates because they rely on their own perceptions of the situation and forget to find out what their subordinates feel. There is only one way to do this: ask. Questionnaires can be used here, as can personal interviews. (See Appendix B for a short version of a motivation questionnaire.)

Analyze the total situation for conflicting expectancies Having set up positive expectancies for employees, you then need to look at the entire situation to see if other factors (informal work groups, other managers, the organization's reward systems) have set up conflicting expectancies in the minds of the employees. Motivation will only be high when people see a number of rewards associated with good performance and few negative outcomes. Again, you can often gather this kind of information by asking your subordinates. If there are major conflicts, you need to make adjustments, either in your own performance and reward structure, or in the other sources of rewards or punishments in the environment.

Make sure changes in outcomes are large enough In examining the motivational system, it is important to make sure that changes in outcomes or rewards are large enough to motivate significant behavior. Trivial rewards will result in trivial amounts of effort and thus trivial improvements in performance. Rewards must be large enough to motivate individuals to put forth the effort required to bring about significant changes in performance.

Check the system for its equity The model is based on the idea that individuals are different and therefore different rewards will need to be used to motivate different individuals.

On the other hand, for a motivational system to work it must be a fair one—one that has equity (not equality). Good performers should see that they get more desired rewards than do poor performers, and others in the system should see that also. Equity should not be confused with a system of equality where all are rewarded equally, with no regard to their performance. A system of equality is guaranteed to produce low motivation.

Implications for Organizations

Expectancy theory has some clear messages for those who run large organizations. It suggests how organizational structures can be designed so that they increase rather than decrease levels of motivation of organization members. While there are many different implications, a few of the major ones are as follows:

Implication 1: The design of pay and reward systems Organizations usually get what they reward, not what they want. This can be seen in many situations, and pay systems are a good example.[3] Frequently, organizations reward people for membership (through pay tied to seniority, for example) rather than for performance. Little wonder that what the organization gets is behavior oriented towards "safe," secure employment rather than effort directed at performing well. In addition, even where organizations do pay for performance as a motivational device, they frequently negate the motivational value of the system by keeping pay secret, therefore preventing people from observing the pay-to-performance relationship that would serve to create positive, clear, and strong performance-to-reward expectancies. The implication is that organizations should put more effort into rewarding people (through pay, promotion, better job opportunities, etc.) for the performances which are desired, and that to keep these rewards secret is clearly self-defeating. In addition, it underscores the importance of the frequently ignored performance evaluation or appraisal process and the need to evaluate people based on how they perform clearly defined specific behaviors, rather than on how they score on ratings of general traits such as "honesty," "cleanliness," and other, similar terms which frequently appear as part of the performance appraisal form.

Implication 2: The design of tasks, jobs, and roles One source of desired outcomes is the work itself. The expectancy-theory model supports much of the job enrichment literature, in saying that by designing jobs which enable people to get their needs fulfilled, organizations can bring about higher levels of motivation.[4] The major difference between the traditional approaches to job enlargement or enrichment and the expectancy-theory approach is the recognition by the expectancy theory that different people have different needs and, therefore, some people may not want enlarged or enriched jobs. Thus, while the design of tasks that have more autonomy, variety, feedback, meaningfulness, etc., will lead to higher motivation in some, the organization needs to build in the opportunity for individuals to make choices about the kind of work they will do so that not everyone is forced to experience job enrichment.

Implication 3: The importance of group structures Groups, both formal and informal, are powerful and potent sources of desired outcomes for individuals. Groups can provide or withhold acceptance, approval, affection, skill training, needed information, assistance, etc. They are a powerful force in the total motivational environment of individuals. Several im-

---

[3]For a detailed discussion of the implications of expectancy theory for pay and reward systems, see Lawler, E. E. *Pay and organizational effectiveness: A psychological view.* New York: McGraw-Hill, 1971.

[4]A good discussion of job design with an expectancy theory perspective is in Hackman, J. R., Oldham, G. R., Janson, R., & Purdy, K. A new strategy for job enrichment. *California Management Review*, Summer, 1975, p. 57.

plications emerge from the importance of groups. First, organizations should consider the structuring of at least a portion of rewards around group performance rather than individual performance. This is particularly important where group members have to cooperate with each other to produce a group product or service, and where the individual's contribution is often hard to determine. Second, the organization needs to train managers to be aware of how groups can influence individual behavior and to be sensitive to the kinds of expectancies which informal groups set up and their conflict or consistency with the expectancies that the organization attempts to create.

Implication 4: The supervisor's role   The immediate supervisor has an important role in creating, monitoring, and maintaining the expectancies and reward structures which will lead to good performance. The supervisor's role in the motivation process becomes one of defining clear goals, setting clear reward expectancies, and providing the right rewards for different people (which could include both organizational rewards and personal rewards such as recognition, approval, or support from the supervisor). Thus, organizations need to provide supervisors with an awareness of the nature of motivation as well as the tools (control over organizational rewards, skill in administering those rewards) to create positive motivation.

Implication 5: Measuring motivation   If things like expectancies, the nature of the job, supervisor-controlled outcomes, satisfaction, etc., are important in understanding how well people are being motivated, then organizations need to monitor employee perceptions along these lines. One relatively cheap and reliable method of doing this is through standardized employee questionnaires. A number of organizations already use such techniques, surveying employees' perceptions and attitudes at regular intervals (ranging from once a month to once every year-and-a-half) using either standardized surveys or surveys developed specifically for the organization. Such information is useful both to the individual manager and to top management in assessing the state of human resources and the effectiveness of the organization's motivational systems.[5] (Again, see Appendix B for excerpts from a standardized survey.)

Implication 6: Individualizing organizations   Expectancy theory leads to a final general implication about a possible future direction for the design of organizations. Because different people have different needs and therefore have different valences, effective motivation must come through the recognition that not all employees are alike and that organizations need to be flexible in order to accommodate individual differences. This implies the "building in" of choice for employees in many areas, such as reward systems, fringe benefits, job assignments, etc., where employees previously have had little say. A successful example of the building in of such choice can be seen in the experiments at TRW and the Educational Testing Service with "cafeteria fringe-benefits plans" which allow employees to choose the fringe benefits they want, rather than taking the expensive and often unwanted benefits which the company frequently provides to everyone.[6]

SUMMARY

Expectancy theory provides a more complex model of man for managers to work with. At the same time, it is a model which holds promise for the more effective motivation of

[5]The use of questionnaires for understanding and changing organizational behavior is discussed in Nadler, D. A. *Feedback and organizational development: Using data-based methods.* Reading, Mass.: Addison-Wesley, 1977.

[6]The whole issue of individualizing organizations is examined in Lawler, E. E. The individualized organization: Problems and promise. *California Management Review*, 1974, **17**(2), 31–39.

individuals and the more effective design of organizational systems. It implies, however, the need for more exacting and thorough diagnosis by the manager to determine (a) the relevant forces in the individual, and (b) the relevant forces in the environment, both of which combine to motivate different kinds of behavior. Following diagnosis, the model implies a need to act—to develop a system of pay, promotion, job assignments, group structures, supervision, etc.—to bring about effective motivation by providing different outcomes for different individuals.

Performance of individuals is a critical issue in making organizations work effectively. If a manager is to influence work behavior and performance, he or she must have an understanding of motivation and the factors which influence an individual's motivation to come to work, to work hard, and to work well. While simple models offer easy answers, it is the more complex models which seem to offer more promise. Managers can use models (like expectancy theory) to understand the nature of behavior and build more effective organizations.

APPENDIX A: The Expectancy Theory Model in More Technical Terms

A person's motivation to exert effort towards a specific level of performance is based on his or her perceptions of associations between actions and outcomes. The critical perceptions which contribute to motivation are graphically presented in Figure 3-2. These perceptions can be defined as follows:

a The effort-to-performance expectancy ($E \rightarrow P$): This refers to the person's subjective proba-

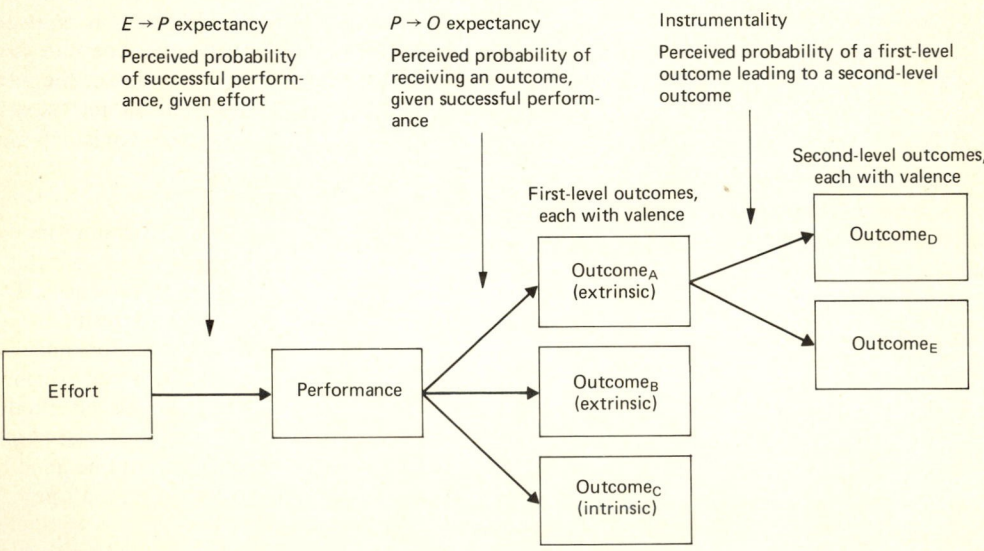

Motivation is expressed as follows: $M = [E \rightarrow P] \times \Sigma [(P \rightarrow O)(V)]$

Figure 3-2 Major terms in expectancy theory.

bility about the likelihood that he or she can perform at a given level, or that effort on his or her part will lead to successful performance. This term can be thought of as varying from 0 to 1. In general, the less likely a person feels that he or she can perform at a given level, the less likely he or she will be to try to perform at that level. A person's $E \rightarrow P$ probabilities are also strongly influenced by each situation and by previous experience in that and similar situations.

b The performance-to-outcomes expectancy ($P \rightarrow O$) and valence (V): This refers to a combination of a number of beliefs about what the outcomes of successful performance will be and the value or attractiveness of these outcomes to the individual. Valence is considered to vary from +1 (very desirable) to −1 (very undesirable) and the performance-to-outcomes probabilities vary from +1 (performance sure to lead to outcome) to 0 (performance not related to outcome). In general, the more likely a person feels that performance will lead to valent outcomes, the more likely he or she will be to try to perform at the required level.

c Instrumentality: As Figure 3-2 indicates, a single level of performance can be associated with a number of different outcomes, each having a certain degree of valence. Some outcomes are valent because they have direct value or attractiveness. Some outcomes, however, have valence because they are seen as leading to (or being "instrumental" for) the attainment of other "second level" outcomes which have direct value or attractiveness.

d Intrinsic and extrinsic outcomes: Some outcomes are seen as occurring directly as a result of performing the task itself and are outcomes which the individual thus gives to himself (i.e., feelings of accomplishment, creativity, etc.). These are called "intrinsic" outcomes. Other outcomes that are associated with performance are provided or mediated by external factors (the organization, the supervisor, the work group, etc.). These outcomes are called "extrinsic" outcomes.

Along with the graphic representation of these terms presented in Figure 3-2, there is a simplified formula for combining these perceptions to arrive at a term expressing the relative level of motivation to exert effort towards performance at a given level. The formula expresses these relationships:

a The person's motivation to perform is determined by the $P \rightarrow O$ expectancy multiplied by the valence (V) of the outcome. The valence of the first order outcome subsumes the instrumentalities and valences of second order outcomes. The relationship is multiplicative since there is no motivation to perform if either of the terms is zero.

b Since a level of performance has multiple outcomes associated with it, the products of all probability-times-valence combinations are added together for all the outcomes that are seen as related to the specific performance.

c This term (the summed $P \rightarrow O$ expectancies times valences) is then multiplied by the $E \rightarrow P$ expectancy. Again the multiplicative relationship indicates that if either term is zero, motivation is zero.

d In summary, the strength of a person's motivation to perform effectively is influenced by (1) the person's belief that effort can be converted into performance, and (2) the net attractiveness of the events that are perceived to stem from good performance.

So far, all the terms have referred to the individual's perceptions which result in motivation and thus an intention to behave in a certain way. Figure 3-3 is a simplified representation of the total model, showing how these intentions get translated into actual behavior.[7] The model envisions the following sequence of events:

a First, the strength of a person's motivation to perform correctly is most directly reflected in his or her effort—how hard he or she works. This effort expenditure may or may not result in good performance, since at least two factors must be right if effort is to be converted into performance. First, the person must possess the necessary abilities in order to perform the job well. Unless both ability and effort are high, there cannot be good performance. A second factor is the person's perception of

[7]For a more detailed statement of the model see Lawler, E. E. Job attitudes and employee motivation: Theory, research and practice. *Personnel Psychology,* 1970, 23, 223–237.

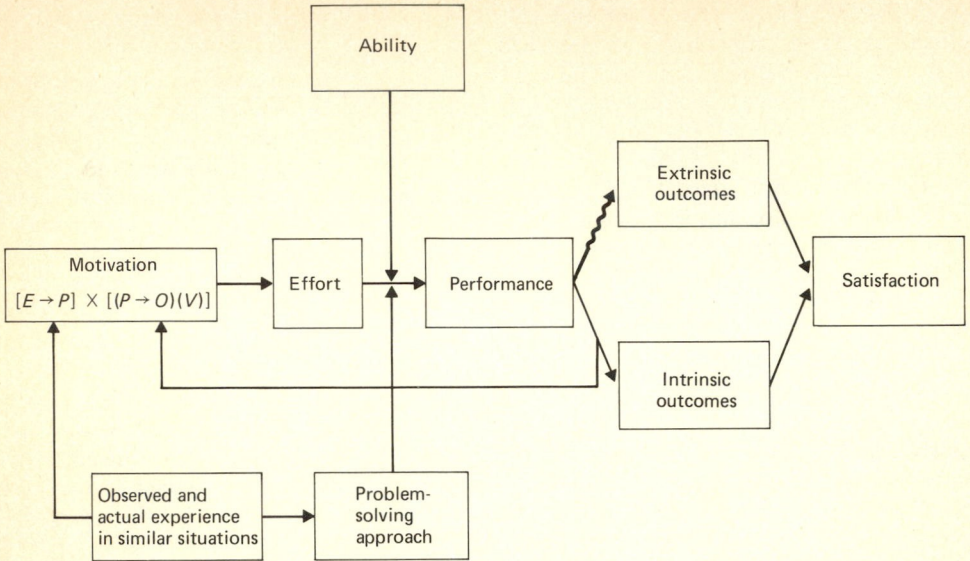

Figure 3-3 Simplified expectancy-theory model of behavior.

how his or her effort can best be converted into performance. It is assumed that this perception is learned by the individual on the basis of previous experience in similar situations. This "how to do it" perception can obviously vary widely in accuracy, and—where erroneous perceptions exist—performance is low even though effort or motivation may be high.

b Second, when performance occurs, certain amounts of outcomes are obtained by the individual. Intrinsic outcomes, not being mediated by outside forces, tend to occur regularly as a result of performance, while extrinsic outcomes may or may not accrue to the individual (indicated by the wavy line in the model).

c Third, as a result of the obtaining of outcomes and the perceptions of the relative value of the outcomes obtained, the individual has a positive or negative affective response (a level of satisfaction or dissatisfaction).

d Fourth, the model indicates that events which occur influence future behavior by altering the $E \rightarrow P$, $P \rightarrow O$, and V perceptions. This process is represented by the feedback loops running from actual behavior back to motivation.

APPENDIX B: Measuring Motivation Using Expectancy Theory

Expectancy theory suggests that it is useful to measure the attitudes individuals have in order to diagnose motivational problems. Such measurement helps the manager to understand why employees are motivated or not, what the strength of motivation is in different parts of the organization, and how effective different rewards are for motivating performance. A short version of a questionnaire used to measure motivation in organizations is included here.[8] Basically, three different questions need to be asked (see Tables 3-1, 3-2, and 3-3).

[8]For a complete version of the questionnaire and supporting documentation see Nadler, D. A., Cammann, C., Jenkins, G. D., & Lawler, E. E. (Eds.) *The Michigan organizational assessment package* (Progress Report II). Ann Arbor: Survey Research Center, 1975.

Table 3-1 *Question 1:* Here are some things that could happen to people if they do their jobs *especially well.* How likely is it that each of these things would happen if you performed your job *especially well?*

		Not at all likely		Somewhat likely		Quite likely		Extremely likely
a	You will get a bonus or pay increase	(1)	(2)	(3)	(4)	(5)	(6)	(7)
b	You will feel better about yourself as a person	(1)	(2)	(3)	(4)	(5)	(6)	(7)
c	You will have an opportunity to develop your skills and abilities	(1)	(2)	(3)	(4)	(5)	(6)	(7)
d	You will have better job security	(1)	(2)	(3)	(4)	(5)	(6)	(7)
e	You will be given chances to learn new things	(1)	(2)	(3)	(4)	(5)	(6)	(7)
f	You will be promoted or get a better job	(1)	(2)	(3)	(4)	(5)	(6)	(7)
g	You will get a feeling that you've accomplished something worthwhile	(1)	(2)	(3)	(4)	(5)	(6)	(7)
h	You will have more freedom on your job.	(1)	(2)	(3)	(4)	(5)	(6)	(7)
i	You will be respected by the people you work with . .	(1)	(2)	(3)	(4)	(5)	(6)	(7)
j	Your supervisor will praise you	(1)	(2)	(3)	(4)	(5)	(6)	(7)
k	The people you work with will be friendly with you. . .	(1)	(2)	(3)	(4)	(5)	(6)	(7)

Table 3-2 *Question 2:* Different people want different things from their work. Here is a list of things a person could have on his or her job. How *important* is each of the following to you?

How Important Is . . . ?

		Moderately important or less		Quite important		Extremely important		
a	The amount of pay you get	(1)	(2)	(3)	(4)	(5)	(6)	(7)
b	The chances you have to do something that makes you feel good about yourself as a person	(1)	(2)	(3)	(4)	(5)	(6)	(7)
c	The opportunity to develop your skills and abilities . .	(1)	(2)	(3)	(4)	(5)	(6)	(7)
d	The amount of job security you have	(1)	(2)	(3)	(4)	(5)	(6)	(7)

How Important Is . . . ?

e	The chances you have to learn new things	(1)	(2)	(3)	(4)	(5)	(6)	(7)
f	Your chances for getting a promotion or getting a better job	(1)	(2)	(3)	(4)	(5)	(6)	(7)
g	The chances you have to accomplish something worthwhile.	(1)	(2)	(3)	(4)	(5)	(6)	(7)
h	The amount of freedom you have on your job.	(1)	(2)	(3)	(4)	(5)	(6)	(7)

How Important Is . . . ?

i	The respect you receive from the people you work with	(1)	(2)	(3)	(4)	(5)	(6)	(7)
j	The praise you get from your supervisor.	(1)	(2)	(3)	(4)	(5)	(6)	(7)
k	The friendliness of the people you work with	(1)	(2)	(3)	(4)	(5)	(6)	(7)

Table 3-3 *Question 3:* Below you will see a number of pairs of factors that look like this:

Warm weather→sweating   (1) (2) (3) (4) (5) (6) (7)

You are to indicate by checking the appropriate number to the right of each pair how often it is true for **you** personally that the first factor leads to the second on **your job**. Remember, for each pair, indicate how often it is true by checking the box under the response which seems most accurate.

		Never		Sometimes		Often		Almost always
a	Working hard → high productivity	(1)	(2)	(3)	(4)	(5)	(6)	(7)
b	Workind hard → doing my job well	(1)	(2)	(3)	(4)	(5)	(6)	(7)
c	Working hard → good job performance	(1)	(2)	(3)	(4)	(5)	(6)	(7)

Using the Questionnaire Results

The results from this questionnaire can be used to calculate a *work-motivation score*. A score can be calculated for each individual and scores can be combined for groups of individuals. The procedure for obtaining a work-motivation score is as follows:

   a   For each of the possible positive outcomes listed in questions 1 and 2, multiply the score for the outcome on question 1 ($P→O$ expectancies) by the corresponding score on question 2 (valences of outcomes). Thus, score 1a would be multiplied by score 2a, score 1b by score 2b, etc.

   b   All of the 1 times 2 products should be added together to get a total of all expectancies times valences _____.

   c   The total should be divided by the number of pairs (in this case, eleven) to get an average expectancy-times-valence score _____.

   d   The scores from question 3 ($E→P$ expectancies) should be added together and then divided by three to get an average effort-to-performance expectancy score _____.

   e   Multiply the score obtained in step c (the average expectancy times valence) by the score obtained in step d (the average $E→P$ expectancy score) to obtain a total work-motivation score

Additional Comments on the Work-Motivation Score

A number of important points should be kept in mind when using the questionnaire to get a work-motivation score. First, the questions presented here are just a short version of a larger and more comprehensive questionnaire. For more detail, the articles and publications referred to here and in the text should be consulted. Second, this is a general questionnaire. Since it is hard to anticipate in a general questionnaire what may be valent outcomes in each situation, the individual manager may want to add additional outcomes to questions 1 and 2. Third, it is important to remember that questionnaire results can be influenced by the feelings people have when they fill out the questionnaire. The use of the questionnaire as outlined above assumes a certain level of trust between manager and subordinates. People filling out questionnaires need to know what is going to be done with their answers and usually need to be assured of the confidentiality of their responses. Finally, the research indicates that, in many cases, the score obtained by simply averaging all the responses to question 1 (the $P→O$ expectancies) will be as useful as the fully calculated work-motivation score. In each situation, the manager should experiment and find out whether the additional information in questions 2 and 3 aid in motivational diagnosis.

Reading 4

Satisfaction and Behavior

Edward E. Lawler III

Compared to what is known about motivation, relatively little is known about the determinants and consequences of satisfaction. Most of the psychological research on motivation simply has not been concerned with the kinds of affective reactions that people experience in association with or as a result of motivated behavior. No well-developed theories of satisfaction have appeared and little theoretically based research has been done on satisfaction. The influence of behaviorism on the field of psychology had a great deal to do with this lag in research. While psychology was under the influence of behaviorism, psychologists avoided doing research that depended on introspective self-reports. Behaviorists strongly felt that if psychology were to develop as a science, it had to study observable behavior. Since satisfaction is an internal subjective state that is best reported by the people experiencing it, satisfaction was not seen as a proper subject for study. Psychologists thought they should concentrate on those aspects of motivation that are observable (for example, performance, hours of deprivation, strength of response, and so on).

Most of the research on the study of satisfaction has been done by psychologists interested in work organizations. This research dates back to the 1930s. Since that time, the term "job satisfaction" has been used to refer to affective attitudes or orientations on the part of individuals toward jobs. Hoppock published a famous monograph on job satisfaction in 1935, and in 1939 the results of the well-known Western Electric studies were published. The Western Electric studies (Roethlisberger & Dickson, 1939) emphasized the importance of studying the attitudes, feelings, and perceptions employees have about their jobs. Through interviews with over 20,000 workers, these studies graphically made the point that employees have strong affective reactions to what happens to them at work. The Western Electric studies also suggested that affective reactions cause certain kinds of behavior, such as strikes, absenteeism, and turnover. Although the studies failed to show any clear-cut relationship between satisfaction and job performance, the studies did succeed in stimulating a tremendous amount of research on job satisfaction. During the last 30 years, thousands of studies have been done on job satisfaction. Usually these studies have not been theoretically oriented; instead, researchers have simply looked at the relationship between job satisfaction and factors such as age, education, job level, absenteeism rate, productivity, and so on. Originally, much of the research seemed to be stimulated by a desire to show that job satisfaction is important because it influences productivity. Underlying the earlier articles on job satisfaction was a strong conviction that "happy workers are productive workers." Recently, however, this theme has been disappearing, and many organizational psychologists seem to be studying job satisfaction simply because they are interested in finding its causes. This approach to studying job satisfaction is congruent with the increased prominence of humanistic psychology, which emphasizes human affective experience.

The recent interest in job satisfaction also ties in directly with the rising concern in many countries about the quality of life. There is an

Excerpt from chap. 4 of E. E. Lawler III, *Motivation in work organizations*. Monterey, Calif.: Brooks/Cole, 1973.

increasing acceptance of the view that material possessions and economic growth do not necessarily produce a high quality of life. Recognition is now being given to the importance of the kinds of affective reactions that people experience and to the fact that these are not always tied to economic or material accomplishments. Through the Department of Labor and the Department of Health, Education, and Welfare, the United States government has recently become active in trying to improve the affective quality of work life. Job satisfaction is one measure of the quality of life in organizations and is worth understanding and increasing even if it doesn't relate to performance. This reason for studying satisfaction is likely to be an increasingly prominent one as we begin to worry more about the effects working in organizations has on people and as our humanitarian concern for the kind of psychological experiences people have during their lives increases. What happens to people during the work day has profound effects both on the individual employee's life and on the society as a whole, and thus these events cannot be ignored if the quality of life in a society is to be high. As John Gardner has said:

> Of all the ways in which society serves the individual, few are more meaningful than to provide him with a decent job. . . . It isn't going to be a decent society for any of us until it is for all of us. If our sense of responsibility fails us, our sheer self-interest should come to the rescue [1968, p. 25].

As it turns out, satisfaction is related to absenteeism and turnover, both of which are very costly to organizations. Thus, there is a very "practical" economic reason for organizations to be concerned with job satisfaction, since it can influence organizational effectiveness. However, before any practical use can be made of the finding that job dissatisfaction causes absenteeism and turnover, we must understand what factors cause and influence

job satisfaction. Organizations can influence job satisfaction and prevent absenteeism and turnover only if the organizations can pinpoint the factors causing and influencing these affective responses.

Despite the many studies, critics have legitimately complained that our understanding of the causes of job satisfaction has not substantially increased during the last 30 years (for example, see Locke, 1968, 1969) for two main reasons. The research on job satisfaction has typically been atheoretical and has not tested for causal relationships. Since the research has not been guided by theory, a vast array of unorganized, virtually uninterpretable facts have been unearthed. For example, a number of studies have found a positive relationship between productivity and job satisfaction, while other studies have found no evidence of this relationship. Undoubtedly, this disparity can be explained, but the explanation would have to be based on a theory of satisfaction, and at present no such theory exists. One thing the research on job satisfaction has done is to demonstrate the saying that "theory without data is fantasy; but data without theory is chaos!"

Due to the lack of a theory stating causal relationships, the research on job satisfaction has consistently looked simply for relationships among variables. A great deal is known about what factors are related to satisfaction, but very little is known about the causal basis for the relationships. This is a serious problem when one attempts to base change efforts on the research. This problem also increases the difficulty of developing and testing theories of satisfaction. Perhaps the best example of the resulting dilemma concerns the relationship between satisfaction and performance. If satisfaction causes performance, then organizations should try to see that their employees are satisfied; however, if performance causes satisfaction, then high satisfaction is not necessarily a goal but rather a by-product of an effective organization.

A MODEL OF FACET SATISFACTION

Figure 4-1 presents a model of the determinants of facet satisfaction. The model is intended to be applicable to understanding what determines a person's satisfaction with any facet of the job. The model assumes that the same psychological processes operate to determine satisfaction with job factors ranging from pay to supervision and satisfaction with the work itself. The model in Figure 4-1 is a discrepancy model in the sense that it shows satisfaction as the difference between a, what a person feels he should receive, and b, what he perceives that he actually receives. The model indicates that when the person's perception of what his outcome level is and his perception of what his outcome level should be are in agreement, the person will be satisfied. When a person perceives his outcome level as falling below what he feels it should be, he will be dissatisfied. However, when a person's perceived outcome level exceeds what he feels it should be, he will have feelings of guilt and inequity and perhaps some discomfort (Adams, 1965). Thus, for any job factor, the assumption is that satisfaction with the factor will be determined by the difference between how much of the factor there is and how much of the factor the person feels there should be.

Present outcome level is shown to be the key influence on a person's perception of what rewards he receives, but his perception is also shown to be influenced by his perception of what his "referent others" receive. The higher the outcome levels of his referent others, the lower his outcome level will appear. Thus, a person's psychological view of how much of a factor he receives is said to be influenced by more than just the objective amount of the factor. Because of this psychological influence, the same amount of reward often can be seen quite differently by two people; to one person it can be a large amount, while to another person it can be a small amount.

The model in Figure 4-1 also shows that a person's perception of what his reward level should be is influenced by a number of factors. Perhaps the most important influence is perceived job inputs. These inputs include all of the skills, abilities, and training a person

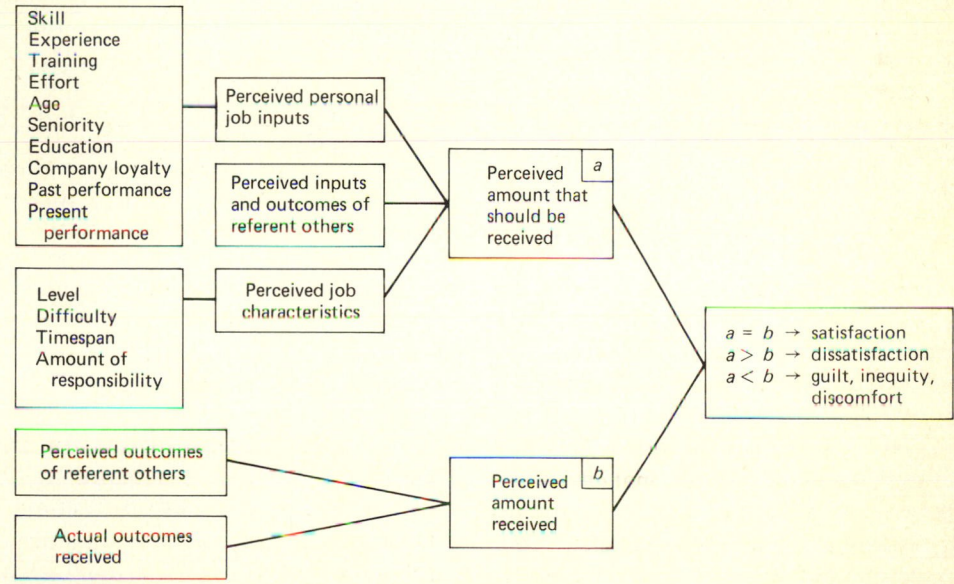

Figure 4-1 Model of the determinants of satisfaction.

brings to the job as well as the behavior he exhibits on the job. The greater he perceives his inputs to be, the higher will be his perception of what his outcomes should be. Because of this relationship, people with high job inputs must receive more rewards than people with low job inputs or they will be dissatisfied. The model also shows that a person's perception of what his outcomes should be is influenced by his perception of the job demands. The greater the demands made by the job, the more he will perceive he should receive. Job demands include such things as job difficulty, responsibilities, and organization level. If outcomes do not rise along with these factors, the clear prediction of the model is that the people who perceive they have the more difficult, higher level jobs will be the most dissatisfied.

The model shows that a person's perception of what his outcomes should be is influenced by what the person perceives his comparison-other's inputs and outcomes to be. This aspect of the model is taken directly from equity theory and is included to stress the fact that people look at the inputs and outcomes of others in order to determine what their own outcome level should be. If a person's comparison-other's inputs are the same as the person's inputs but the other's outcomes are much higher, the person will feel that he should be receiving more outcomes and will be dissatisfied as a result.

The model allows for the possibility that people will feel that their outcomes exceed what they should be. The feelings produced by this condition are quite different from those produced by under-reward. Because of this difference, it does not make sense to refer to a person who feels over-rewarded as being dissatisfied. There is considerable evidence that very few people feel over-rewarded, and this fact can be explained by the model. Even when people are highly rewarded, the social-comparison aspect of satisfaction means that people can avoid feeling over-rewarded by

looking around and finding someone to compare with who is doing equally well. Also, a person tends to value his own inputs much higher than they are valued by others (Lawler, 1967). Because of this discrepancy, a person's perception of what his outcomes should be is often not shared by those administering his rewards, and is often above what he actually receives. Finally, the person can easily increase his perception of his inputs and thereby justify a high reward level.

As a way of summarizing some of the implications of the model, let us briefly make some statements about who should be dissatisfied if the model is correct. Other things being equal:

1 People with high perceived inputs will be more dissatisfied with a given facet than people with low perceived inputs.
2 People who perceive their job to be demanding will be more dissatisfied with a given facet than people who perceive their jobs as undemanding.
3 People who perceive similar others as having a more favorable input-outcome balance will be more dissatisfied with a given facet than people who perceive their own balance as similar to or better than that of others.
4 People who receive a low outcome level will be more dissatisfied than those who receive a high outcome level.
5 The more outcomes a person perceives his comparison-other receives, the more dissatisfied he will be with his own outcomes. This should be particularly true when the comparison-other is seen to hold a job that demands the same or fewer inputs.

OVERALL JOB SATISFACTION

Most theories of job satisfaction argue that overall job satisfaction is determined by some combination of all facet-satisfaction feelings. This could be expressed in terms of the facet-satisfaction model in Figure 4-1 as a simple sum of, or average of, all $a - b$ discrepancies. Thus, overall job satisfaction is determined by the difference between all the things a person feels he should receive from his job and all the things he actually does receive.

A strong theoretical argument can be made for weighting the facet-satisfaction scores according to their importance. Some factors do make larger contributions to overall satisfaction than others. Pay satisfaction, satisfaction with the work itself, and satisfaction with supervision seem to have particularly strong influences on overall satisfaction for most people. Also, employees tend to rate these factors as important. Thus, there is a connection between how important employees say job factors are and how much job factors influence overall job satisfaction (Vroom, 1964). Conceptually, therefore, it seems worthwhile to think of the various job-facet-satisfaction scores as influencing total satisfaction in terms of their importance. One way to express this relationship is by defining overall job satisfaction as being equal to Σ (facet satisfaction $\times$ facet importance). However, as stressed earlier, actually measuring importance and multiplying it by measured facet satisfaction often isn't necessary because the satisfaction scores themselves seem to take importance into account. (The most important items tend to be scored as either very satisfactory or very dissatisfactory; thus, these items have the most influence on any sum score.) Still, on a conceptual level, it is important to remember that facet-satisfaction scores do differentially contribute to the feeling of overall job satisfaction.

A number of studies have attempted to determine how many workers are actually satisfied with their jobs. Our model does not lead to any predictions in this area. The model simply gives the conditions that lead to people experiencing feelings of satisfaction or dissatisfaction. Not surprisingly, the studies that have been done do not agree on the percent-

age of dissatisfied workers. Some suggest figures as low as 13 percent, others give figures as high as 80 percent. The range generally reported is from 13 to 25 percent dissatisfied. Herzberg et al. (1957) summarized the findings of research studies conducted from 1946 through 1953. The figures in their report showed a yearly increase in the median percentage of job-satisfied persons (see Table 4-1). Figure 4-2 presents satisfaction-trend data for 1948 through 1971. These data also show an overall increase in the number of satisfied workers, which is interesting because of recent speculation that satisfaction is decreasing. However, due to many measurement problems, it is impossible to conclude that a real decline in number of dissatisfied workers has taken place.

The difficulty in obtaining meaningful conclusions from the data stems from the fact that different questions yield very different results. For example, a number of studies, instead of directly asking workers "How satisfied are you?," have asked "If you had it to do over again, would you pick the same job?" The latter question produces much higher dissatis-

Table 4-1 Median Percentage of Job-dissatisfied Persons Reported from 1946–1953
(From Herzberg et al., *Job Attitudes: Review of Research and Opinion.* Copyright 1957 by the Psychological Service of Pittsburgh. Reprinted by permission.)

Year	Median percentage of job dissatisfied
1953	13
1952	15
1951	18
1949	19
1940	19
1946–1947	21

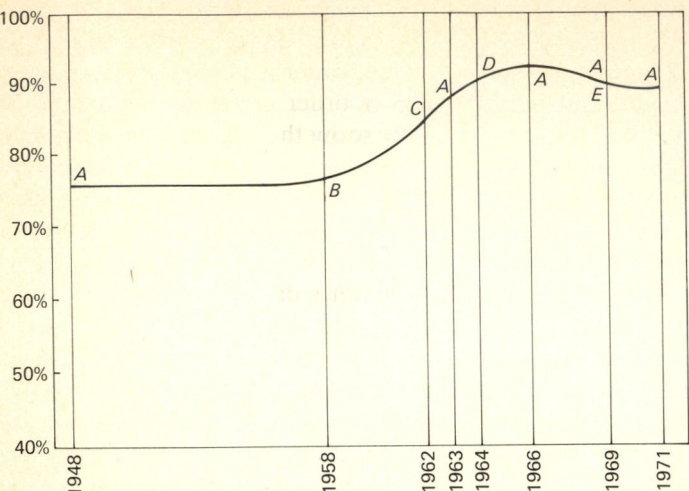

Figure 4-2 Percentage of "satisfied" workers, 1948–1971. *(From Quinn, Staines, & McCullough, 1973.) Note*: "Don't know" and "uncertain" have been excluded from the base of the percentages. *Sources*: A = Gallup, or Gallup as reported by Roper; B = Survey Research Center (Michigan); C = NORC; D = Survey Research Center (Berkeley); E = 1969–1970 Survey of Working Conditions.

faction scores than does the simple "how satisfied are you" question. One literature review showed that 54 percent of the workers tended to say that they were sufficiently dissatisfied with their jobs that they would not choose them again. On the other hand, the straight satisfaction question shows between 13 and 25 percent dissatisfied. However, even this figure is subject to wide variation depending on how the question is asked. When the question is asked in the simple form, "Are you satisfied, yes or no?," the number of satisfied responses is large. When the question is changed so that the employees can respond yes, no, or undecided—or satisfied, dissatisfied, or neutral—the number of satisfied responses drops.

Because of these methodological complexities, it is difficult to draw conclusions about the number of workers who are or are not satisfied with their jobs or with some facet of their jobs. This drawback does not mean, however, that meaningful research on satisfaction is impossible. On the contrary, interesting and important research has been and can be done on the determinants of job satisfaction. For example, the relationship between personal-input factors—such as education level, sex, and age and seniority—and job or facet satisfaction can be ascertained by simply comparing those people who report they are satisfied with those people who report they are dissatisfied and checking the results to see if the two groups differ in any systematic manner. The number of people reporting satisfaction is not crucial for this purpose. What is important is that we distinguish those people who tend to be more satisfied from those people who tend to be less satisfied. This distinction can be made with many of the better-known satisfaction-measuring instruments, such as the Job Description Index (Smith, Kendall, & Hulin, 1969) and Porter's (1961) need-satisfaction instrument.

A number of studies have tried to determine the amount of employee dissatisfaction that is associated with different job facets. Although these studies have yielded interesting results, some serious methodological problems are involved in this work. As with overall job satisfaction, factors such as type of measurement scale used and manner of wording questions seriously affect the number of people who express dissatisfaction with a given facet. For example, a question about pay satisfaction can be asked in a way that will cause few people to express dissatisfaction, while a question about security satisfaction can be asked in a way that will cause many people to express dissatisfaction. In this situation, comparing the number of people expressing security satisfaction with the number of people expressing pay dissatisfaction might produce very misleading conclusions. This problem is always present no matter how carefully the various items are worded because it is impossible to balance the items so they are comparable for all factors.

Despite methodological problems, the data on relative satisfaction levels with different job factors are interesting. These data show that the factors mentioned earlier as being most important—that is, pay, promotion, security, leadership, and the work itself—appear in these studies as the major sources of dissatisfaction. Porter (1961) designed items using Maslow's needs as a measure of satisfaction. With these items, he collected data from various managers. The results of his study (see Table 4-2) show that more managers express higher order need dissatisfaction than express lower order need dissatisfaction. The results also show that a large number of managers are dissatisfied with their pay and with the communications in their organizations and that middle level managers tend to be better satisfied in all areas than lower level managers.

Porter's data also show that managers consider the areas of dissatisfaction to be the most important areas. It is not completely clear whether the dissatisfaction causes the importance or the importance causes the dissatisfaction. The research reviewed earlier suggests that the primary causal direction is from dissatisfaction to importance, although there undoubtedly is a two-way-influence process operating. The important thing to remember is that employees do report varying levels of satisfaction with different job factors, and the factors that have come out high on dissatisfaction have also been rated high on importance and have the strongest influence on overall job satisfaction.

A study by Grove and Kerr (1951) illustrates how strongly organizational conditions can affect factor satisfaction. Grove and Kerr measured employee satisfaction in two plants where normal work conditions prevailed and

Table 4-2 Differences between Management Levels in Percentage of Subjects Indicating Need-Fulfillment Deficiencies (Adapted from Porter, 1961)

Questionnaire items	% Bottom management (N = 64)	% Middle management (N = 75)	% Difference
Security needs	42.2	26.7	15.5
Social needs	35.2	32.0	3.2
Esteem needs	55.2	35.6	19.6
Autonomy needs	60.2	47.7	12.5
Self-actualization needs	59.9	53.3	6.6
Pay	79.7	80.0	−0.3
Communications	78.1	61.3	16.8

found that 88 percent of the workers were satisfied with their job security, which indicated that security was one of the least dissatisfying job factors for employees in these two plants. In another plant where layoffs had occurred, only 17 percent of the workers said they were satisfied with the job security, and job security was one of the most dissatisfying job factors for this plant's employees.

The research on the determinants of satisfaction has looked primarily at two relationships: (1) the relationship between satisfaction and the characteristics of the job, and (2) the relationship between satisfaction and the characteristics of the person. Not surprisingly, the research shows that satisfaction is a function of both the person and the environment. These results are consistent with our approach to thinking about satisfaction, since our model (shown in Figure 4-1) indicates that personal factors influence what people feel they should receive and that job conditions influence both what people perceive they actually receive and what people perceive they should receive.

The evidence on the effects of personal-input factors on satisfaction is voluminous and will be only briefly reviewed. The research clearly shows that personal factors do affect job satisfaction, basically because they influence perceptions of what outcomes should be. As predicted by the satisfaction model in Figure 4-1, the higher a person's perceived personal inputs—that is, the greater his education, skill, and performance—the more he feels he should receive. Thus, unless the high-input person receives more outcomes, he will be dissatisfied with his job and the rewards his job offers. Such straightforward relationships between inputs and satisfaction appear to exist for all personal-input factors except age and seniority. Evidence from the study of age and seniority suggests a curvilinear relationship (that is, high satisfaction among young and old workers, low satisfaction among middle-age workers) or even a

relationship of increasing satisfaction with old age and tenure. The tendency of satisfaction to be high among older, long-term employees seems to be produced by the effects of selective turnover and the development of realistic expectations about what the job has to offer.

CONSEQUENCES OF DISSATISFACTION

Originally, much of the interest in job satisfaction stemmed from the belief that job satisfaction influenced job performance. Specifically, psychologists thought that high job satisfaction led to high job performance. This view has now been discredited, and most psychologists feel that satisfaction influences absenteeism and turnover but not job performance. However, before looking at the relationship among satisfaction, absenteeism, and turnover, let's review the work on satisfaction and performance.

Job Performance

In the 1950s, two major literature reviews showed that in most studies only a slight relationship had been found between satisfaction and performance. A later review by Vroom (1964) also showed that studies had not found a strong relationship between satisfaction and performance; in fact, most studies had found a very low positive relationship between the two. In other words, better performers did seem to be slightly more satisfied than poor performers. A considerable amount of recent work suggests that the slight existing relationship is probably due to better performance indirectly causing satisfaction rather than the reverse. Lawler and Porter (1967) explained this "performance causes satisfaction" viewpoint as follows:

> If we assume that rewards cause satisfaction, and that in some cases performance produces rewards, then it is possible that the relationship found between satisfaction and performance

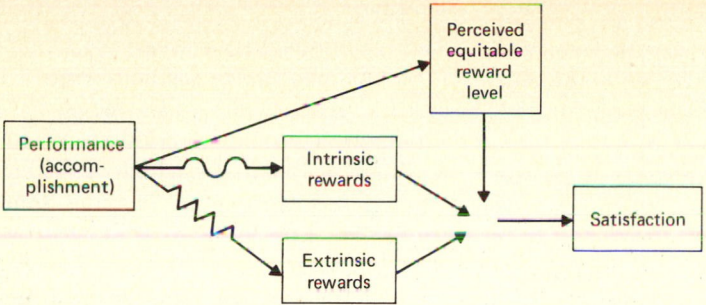

Figure 4-3 Model of the relationship of performance to satisfaction. (*From Lawler, E. E., and Porter, L. W. The effect of performance on job satisfaction.* Industrial Relations, *1967*, **7**, *20–28. Reprinted by permission of the publisher,* Industrial Relations.)

comes about through the action of a third variable—rewards. Briefly stated, good performance may lead to rewards, which in turn lead to satisfaction; this formulation then would say that satisfaction rather than causing performance, as was previously assumed, is caused by it.

[Figure 4-3] shows that performance leads to rewards, and it distinguishes between two kinds of rewards and their connection to performance. A wavy line between performance and extrinsic rewards indicates that such rewards are likely to be imperfectly related to performance. By extrinsic rewards is meant such organizationally controlled rewards as pay, promotion, status, and security—rewards that are often referred to as satisfying mainly lower-level needs. The connection is relatively weak because of the difficulty of tying extrinsic rewards directly to performance. Even though an organization may have a policy of rewarding merit, performance is difficult to measure, and in dispensing rewards like pay, many other factors are frequently taken into consideration.

Quite the opposite is likely to be true for intrinsic rewards, however, since they are given to the individual by himself for good performance. Intrinsic or internally mediated rewards are subject to fewer disturbing influences and thus are likely to be more directly related to good performance. This connection is indicated in the model by a semi-wavy line. Probably the best example of an intrinsic reward is the feeling of having accomplished something worthwhile. For

that matter any of the rewards that satisfy self-actualization needs or higher order growth needs are good examples of intrinsic rewards [p. 23–24].[1]

Figure 4-3 shows that intrinsic and extrinsic rewards are not directly related to job satisfaction, since the relationship is moderated by perceived equitable rewards (what people think they should receive). The model in Figure 4-3 is similar to the model in Figure 4-1, since both models show that satisfaction is a function of the amount of rewards a person receives and the amount of rewards he feels he should receive.

Because of the imperfect relationship between performance and rewards and the important effect of perceived equitable rewards, a low but positive relationship should exist between job satisfaction and job performance in most situations. However, in certain situations, a strong positive relationship may exist; while in other situations, a negative relationship may exist. A negative relationship would be expected where rewards are unrelated to performance or negatively related to performance.

[1]Lawler, E. E., and Porter, L. W. The effect of performance on job satisfaction, *Industrial Relations*, 1967, 7, 20–28. Reprinted by permission of the publisher, Industrial Relations.

To have the same level of satisfaction for good performers and poor performers, the good performers must receive more rewards than the poor performers. The reason for this, as stressed earlier, is that performance level influences the amount of rewards a person feels he should receive. Thus, when rewards are not based on performance—when poor performers receive equal rewards or a larger amount of rewards than good performers—the best performers will be the least satisfied, and a negative satisfaction-performance relationship will exist. If, on the other hand, the better performers are given significantly more rewards, a positive satisfaction-performance relationship should exist. If it is assumed that most organizations are partially successful in relating rewards to performance, it follows that most studies should find a low but positive relationship between satisfaction and performance. Lawler and Porter's (1967) study was among those that found this relationship; their study also found that, as predicted, intrinsic-need satisfaction was more closely related to performance than was extrinsic-need satisfaction.

In retrospect, it is hard to understand why the belief that high satisfaction causes high performance was so widely accepted. There is nothing in the literature on motivation that suggests this causal relationship. In fact, such a relationship is opposite to the concepts developed by both drive theory and expectancy theory. If anything, these two theories would seem to predict that high satisfaction might reduce motivation because of a consequent reduction in the importance of various rewards that may have provided motivational force. Clearly, a more logical view is that performance is determined by people's efforts to obtain the goals and outcomes they desire, and satisfaction is determined by the outcomes people actually obtain. Yet, for some reason, many people believed—and some people still do believe—that the "satisfaction causes performance" view is best.

Turnover

The relationship between satisfaction and turnover has been studied often. In most studies, researchers have measured the job satisfaction among a number of employees and then waited to see which of the employees studied left during an ensuing time period (typically, a year). The satisfaction scores of the employees who left have then been compared with the remaining employees' scores. Although relationships between satisfaction scores and turnover have not always been very strong, the studies in this area have consistently shown that dissatisfied workers are more likely than satisfied workers to terminate employment; thus, satisfaction scores can predict turnover.

A study by Ross and Zander (1957) is a good example of the kind of research that has been done. Ross and Zander measured the job satisfaction of 2680 female workers in a large company. Four months later, these researchers found that 169 of these employees had resigned; those who left were significantly more dissatisfied with the amount of recognition they received on their jobs, with the amount of achievement they experienced, and with the amount of autonomy they had.

Probably the major reason that turnover and satisfaction are not more strongly related is that turnover is very much influenced by the availability of other positions. Even if a person is very dissatisfied with his job, he is not likely to leave unless more attractive alternatives are available. This observation would suggest that in times of economic prosperity, turnover should be high, and a strong relationship should exist between turnover and satisfaction; but in times of economic hardship, turnover should be low, and little relationship should exist between turnover and satisfaction. There is research evidence to support the argument that voluntary turnover is much lower in periods of economic hardship. However, no study has compared the relationship between satisfaction and turnover under different economic conditions to see if it is stronger under full employment.

Absenteeism

Like turnover, absenteeism has been found to be related to job satisfaction. If anything, the relationship between satisfaction and absenteeism seems to be stronger than the relationship between satisfaction and turnover. However, even in the case of absenteeism, the relationship is far from being isomorphic. Absenteeism is caused by a number of factors other than a person's voluntarily deciding not to come to work; illness, accidents, and so on can prevent someone who wants to come to work from actually coming to work. We would expect satisfaction to affect only voluntary absences; thus, satisfaction can never be strongly related to a measure of overall absence rate. Those studies that have separated voluntary absences from overall absences have, in fact, found that voluntary absence rates are much more closely related to satisfaction than are overall absence rates (Vroom, 1964). Of course, this outcome would be expected if satisfaction does influence people's willingness to come to work.

Organization Effectiveness

The research evidence clearly shows that employees' decisions about whether they will go to work on any given day and whether they will quit are affected by their feelings of job satisfaction. All the literature reviews on the subject have reached this conclusion. The fact that present satisfaction influences future absenteeism and turnover clearly indicates that the causal direction is from satisfaction to behavior. This conclusion is in marked contrast to our conclusion with respect to performance—that is, behavior causes satisfaction.

The research evidence on the determinants of satisfaction suggests that satisfaction is very much influenced by the actual rewards a person receives; of course, the organization has a considerable amount of control over these rewards. The research also shows that, although not all people will react to the same reward level in the same manner, reactions are predictable if something is known about how people perceive their inputs. The implication is that organizations can influence employees' satisfaction levels. Since it is possible to know how employees will react to different outcome levels, organizations can allocate outcomes in ways that will either cause job satisfaction or job dissatisfaction.

Absenteeism and turnover have a very direct influence on organizational effectiveness. Absenteeism is very costly because it interrupts scheduling, creates a need for overstaffing, increases fringe-benefit costs, and so on. Turnover is expensive because of the many costs incurred in recruiting and training replacement employees. For lower-level jobs, the cost of turnover is estimated at $2000 a person; at the managerial level, the cost is at least five to ten times the monthly salary of the job involved. Because satisfaction is manageable and influences absenteeism and turnover, organizations can control absenteeism and turnover. Generally, by keeping satisfaction high and, specifically, by seeing that the best employees are the most satisfied, organizations can retain those employees they need the most. In effect, organizations can manage turnover so that, if it occurs, it will occur among employees the organization can most afford to lose. However, keeping the better performers more satisfied is not easy, since they must be rewarded very well.

REFERENCES

Adam, J. S. Injustice in social exchange. In L. Berkowitz (Ed.), *Advances in experimental social psychology*, Vol. 2. New York, Academic Press, 1965.

Gardner, J. W. *No easy victories.* New York, Harper & Row, 1968.

Grove, E. A., & Kerr, W. A. Specific evidence on

origin of halo effect in measurement of employee morale. *Journal of Social Psychology*, 1951, **34**, 165–170.

Herzberg, F., Mausner, B., Peterson, R. O., & Capwell, D. I. *Job attitudes: Review of research and opinion.* Pittsburgh, Psychological Service of Pittsburgh, 1957.

Lawler, E. E. The multitrait multirater approach to measuring managerial job performance. *Journal of Applied Psychology*, 1967, **51**, 369–381.

Lawler, E. E., & Porter, L. W. The effect of performance on job satisfaction. *Industrial Relations*, 1967, **7**, 20–28.

Locke, E. A. What is job satisfaction? Paper presented at the APA Convention, San Francisco, September 1968.

Locke, E. A. What is job satisfaction? *Organizational Behavior and Human Performance*, 1969, **4**, 309–336.

Porter, L. W. A study of perceived need satisfactions in bottom and middle management jobs. *Journal of Applied Psychology*, 1961, **45**, 1–10.

Quinn, R. P., Staines, G., & McCullough, M. Job satisfaction in the 1970's. Recent history and a look to the future. *Manpower Monograph*, 1973.

Roethlisberger, F. I., & Dickson, W. I. *Management and the worker.* Cambridge, Mass., Harvard University Press, 1939.

Ross, I. E., & Zander, A. F. Need satisfaction and employee turnover. *Personnel Psychology*, 1957, **10**, 327–338.

Smith, P., Kendall, I., & Hulin, C. *The measurement of satisfaction in work and retirement.* Chicago, Rand McNally & Company, 1969.

Vroom, V. H. *Work and motivation.* New York, John Wiley & Sons, 1964.

Chapter 2

The Nature of Organizations

Any attempt to understand behavior in organizations cannot be complete unless one takes into account the nature of organizations as well as the nature of people. Over the past several decades, both practitioners and scholars have spent considerable effort in defining organizations and in analyzing their nature and structure. From these endeavors have emerged some identifiable approaches and some broad conclusions. However, as one reads through the selections in this chapter, it will be apparent that unanimity of opinion is lacking. Rather, what can be observed is that there are a variety of useful ways of looking at and thinking about organizations; and, perhaps most important, each of these ways has both advantages and limitations. It will be one of the tasks of the reader to decide what is most important and useful among the various viewpoints and approaches described.

The first article, by Scott, traces the development of "organization theory." It describes and analyzes three different theories: "classical," "neoclassical," and "modern." These are labels supplied by Scott, but they are ones that are frequently used by scholars when talking about theories of organizations. While Scott does not explicitly adopt a historical or chronological framework for presenting the three theories, it will be useful for the reader to keep in mind that they do follow in a more or less sequential order with respect to time. That is, the so-called classical theory of organizations emerged first, and thus for a time in the early part of this century was the only theory available. Later on, as some deficiencies in this viewpoint became fairly obvious, the "neoclassical" school emerged as a refinement of the classical approach. Most recently, of course, what Scott and others have termed "modern organization theory" has come on the scene, with its heavier empirical basis and its emphasis on a system-type perspective. What is important to note is that supporters of the neoclassical theory had the benefit of the work of the classical theorists before them, and the modern organization theorists could take into account the ideas of both of the preceding groups. Put another way, present-day theories have built upon, and have utilized, the accumulated wisdom of the past.

The second paper, by Pugh, is an intensive look at modern organization theory, especially in terms of its multidisciplinary nature. Pugh suggests that a number of disciplines have made important contributions to the development of organization theory, and will continue to do so. In this article, six different approaches to organizations are described: management, structural, group, individual, technological, and economic. In each instance, the author evaluates both the contributions *and* the limitations of the particular approach. For example, the structural theorists, according to Pugh, have helped us focus on the "regularities" in continuing activities such as task allocations, exercise of authority, and coordination of functions. At the same time, though, the structuralists have tended to give very little weight to the psychology of behavior in organizations and to the effects that individuals can have on organizations (in addition to the obvious effects organizations can have on individuals). Pugh concludes his review of the major approaches to modern organization the-

ory by emphasizing that if such theory is to develop and provide increasing understanding of organizations it must ignore what he calls "artificial disciplinary boundaries." It must become, in effect, a true interdisciplinary field of science.

The final selection in this chapter, by Nadler and Tushman, shifts from broad theories of organizations to a proposed diagnostic model for understanding behavior in organizations. As this article is read, it will be important to recognize that the authors are particularly interested in the utility of this model from the *manager's* point of view. The model described in the article rests on a set of basic assumptions: (1) that organizations are dynamic, (2) that behavior in organizations exists at multiple levels (individual, group, and organizational), (3) that behavior in organizations occurs not in a vacuum but surrounded by a variety of technologies, and (4) that organizations have the characteristics of *open* social systems. In fact, the model makes explicit use of a "systems theory" perspective, in that it concentrates on analyzing inputs, transformation processes, and outputs. The authors stress a "problem-solving" orientation for managers to use in diagnosing organizations and the behavior of people in them, especially with respect to the necessity for continual evaluation of actions and their consequences. It will be interesting for the reader to assess this model and approach in the light of the various theories of organizations that are discussed in the first two readings in the chapter.

Reading 5

Organization Theory: An Overview and an Appraisal

William G. Scott

Man is intent on drawing himself into a web of collectivized patterns. "Modern man has learned to accommodate himself to a world increasingly organized. The trend toward ever more explicit and consciously drawn relationships is profound and sweeping; it is marked by depth no less than by extension."[1] This comment by Seidenberg nicely summarizes the pervasive influence of organization in many forms of human activity.

Some of the reasons for intense organizational activity are found in the fundamental transitions which revolutionized our society, changing it from a rural culture, to a culture based on technology, industry, and the city. From these changes, a way of life emerged characterized by the *proximity* and *dependency* of people on each other. Proximity and dependency, as conditions of social life, harbor the threats of human conflict, capricious antisocial behavior, instability of human relationships, and uncertainty about the nature of the social structure with its concomitant roles.

Of course, these threats to social integrity are present to some degree in all societies, ranging from the primitive to the modern. But, these threats become dangerous when the harmonious functioning of a society rests on the maintenance of a highly intricate, delicately balanced form of human collaboration. The civilization we have created depends on the preservation of a precarious balance. Hence, disrupting forces impinging on this shaky form of collaboration must be eliminated or minimized.

Traditionally, organization is viewed as a vehicle for accomplishing goals and objectives. While this approach is useful, it tends to obscure the inner workings and internal purposes of organization itself. Another fruitful way of treating organization is as a mechanism having the ultimate purpose of offsetting those forces which undermine human collaboration. In this sense, organization tends to minimize conflict, and to lessen the significance of individual behavior which deviates from values that the organization has established as worthwhile. Further, organization increases stability in human relationships by reducing uncertainty regarding the nature of the system's structure and the human roles which are inherent to it. Corollary to this point, organization enhances the predictability of human action, because it limits the number of behavioral alternatives available to an individual. As Presthus points out:

> Organization is defined as a system of structural interpersonal relations . . . individuals are differentiated in terms of authority, status, and role with the result that personal interaction is prescribed. . . . Anticipated reactions tend to occur, while ambiguity and spontaneity are decreased.[2]

In addition to all of this, organization has built-in safeguards. Besides prescribing acceptable forms of behavior for those who elect to submit to it, organization is also able to counterbalance the influence of human ac-

[1] Roderick Seidenburg, *Post Historic Man* (Boston: Beacon Press, 1951), p. 1.

[2] Robert V. Presthus, "Toward a Theory of Organizational Behavior," *Administrative Science Quarterly*, June, 1958, p. 50.

Excerpt from *Journal of the Academy of Management*, 1961, **4**, 7–26.

tion which transcends its established patterns.[3]

Few segments of society have engaged in organizing more intensively than business.[4] The reason is clear. Business depends on what organization offers. Business needs a system of relationships among functions; it needs stability, continuity, and predictability in its internal activities and external contacts. Business also appears to need harmonious relationships among the people and processes which make it up. Put another way, a business organization has to be free, relatively, from destructive tendencies which may be caused by divergent interests.

As a foundation for meeting these needs rests administrative science. A major element of this science is organization theory, which provides the grounds for management activities in a number of significant areas of business endeavor. Organization theory, however, is not a homogeneous science based on generally accepted principles. Various theories of organization have been, and are being evolved. For example, something called "modern organization theory" has recently emerged, raising the wrath of some traditionalists, but also capturing the imagination of a rather elite *avant-garde*.

The thesis of this paper is that modern organization theory, when stripped of its irrelevancies, redundancies, and "speech de-

fects," is a logical and vital evolution in management thought. In order for this thesis to be supported, the reader must endure a review and appraisal of more traditional forms of organization theory which may seem elementary to him.

In any event, three theories of organization are having considerable influence on management thought and practice. They are arbitrarily labeled in this paper as the classical, the neoclassical, and the modern. Each of these is fairly distinct; but they are not unrelated. Also, these theories are on-going, being actively supported by several schools of management thought.

THE CLASSICAL DOCTRINE

For lack of a better method of identification, it will be said that the classical doctrine deals almost exclusively with the *anatomy of formal organization*. This doctrine can be traced back to Frederick W. Taylor's interest in functional foremanship and planning staffs. But most students of management thought would agree that in the United States, the first systematic approach to organization, and the first comprehensive attempt to find organizational universals, is dated 1931 when Mooney and Reiley published *Onward Industry*.[5] Subsequently, numerous books, following the classical vein, have appeared. Two of the more recent are Brech's, *Organization*[6] and Allen's, *Management and Organization*.[7]

Classical organization theory is built around four key pillars. They are the division of labor, the scalar and functional processes,

---

[3]Regulation and predictability of human behavior are matters of degree varying with different organizations on something of a continuum. At one extreme are bureaucratic type organizations with tight bonds of regulation. At the other extreme are voluntary associations, and informal organizations with relatively loose bonds of regulation.

This point has an interesting sidelight. A bureaucracy with tight controls and a high degree of predictability of human action appears to be unable to distinguish between destructive and creative deviations from established values. Thus the only thing which is safeguarded is the *status quo*.

[4]The monolithic institutions of the military and government are other cases of organizational preoccupation.

[5]James D. Mooney and Alan C. Reiley, *Onward Industry* (New York: Harper and Brothers, 1931). Later published by James D. Mooney under the title *Principles of Organization*.

[6]E. F. L. Brech, *Organization* (London: Longmans, Green and Company, 1957).

[7]Louis A. Allen, *Management and Organization* (New York: McGraw-Hill Book Company, 1958).

structure, and span of control. Given these major elements just about all of classical organization theory can be derived.

1.   *The division of labor* is without doubt the cornerstone among the four elements.[8] From it the other elements flow as corollaries. For example, *scalar* and *functional* growth requires specialization and departmentalization of functions. Organization *structure* is naturally dependent upon the direction which specialization of activities travels in company development. Finally, *span of control* problems result from the number of specialized functions under the jurisdiction of a manager.

2.   *The scalar and functional processes* deal with the vertical and horizontal growth of the organization, respectively.[9] The scalar process refers to the growth of the chain of command, the delegation of authority and responsibility, unity of command, and the obligation to report.

The division of the organization into specialized parts and the regrouping of the parts into compatible units are matters pertaining to the functional process. This process focuses on the horizontal evolution of the line and staff in a formal organization.

3.   *Structure* is the logical relationships of functions in an organization, arranged to accomplish the objectives of the company efficiently. Structure implies system and pattern. Classical organization theory usually works with two basic structures, the line and the staff. However, such activities as committee and liaison functions fall quite readily into the purview of structural considerations. Again, structure is the vehicle for introducing logical and consistent relationships among the diverse functions which comprise the organization.[10]

4.   *The span of control* concept relates to the number of subordinates a manager can effectively supervise. Graicunas has been credited with first elaborating the point that there are numerical limitations to the subordinates one man can control.[11] In a recent statement on the subject, Brech points out, "span" refers to ". . . the number of persons, themselves carrying managerial and supervisory responsibilities, for whom the senior manager retains his over-embracing responsibility of direction and planning, co-ordination, motivation, and control."[12] Regardless of interpretation, span of control has significance, in part, for the shape of the organization which evolves through growth. Wide span yields a flat structure; short span results in a tall structure. Further, the span concept directs attention to the complexity of human and functional interrelationships in an organization.

It would not be fair to say that the classical school is unaware of the day-to-day administrative problems of the organization. Paramount among these problems are those stemming from human interactions. But the interplay of individual personality, informal groups, intraorganizational conflict, and the decision-making processes in the formal structure appears largely to be neglected by classical organization theory. Additionally, the classical theory overlooks the contributions of the behavioral sciences by failing to incorporate them in its doctrine in any systematic way. In summary, classical organiza-

[8]Usually the division of labor is treated under a topical heading of departmentation, see for example: Harold Koontz and Cyril O'Donnell, *Principles of Management* (New York: McGraw-Hill Book Company, 1959), Chapter 7.

[9]These processes are discussed at length in Ralph Currier Davis, *The Fundamentals of Top Management* (New York: Harper and Brothers, 1951), Chapter 7.

[10]For a discussion of structure see: William H. Newman, *Administrative Action* (Englewood Cliffs: Prentice-Hall, Incorporated, 1951), Chapter 16.

[11]V. A. Graicunas, "Relationships in Organization," *Papers on the Science of Administration* (New York: Columbia University, 1937).

[12]Brech, *op. cit.*, p. 78.

tion theory has relevant insights into the nature of organization, but the value of this theory is limited by its narrow concentration on the formal anatomy of organization.

NEOCLASSICAL THEORY OF ORGANIZATION

The neoclassical theory of organization embarked on the task of compensating for some of the deficiencies in classical doctrine. The neoclassical school is commonly identified with the human relations movement. Generally, the neoclassical approach takes the postulates of the classical school, regarding the pillars of organization as givens. But these postulates are regarded as modified by people, acting independently or within the context of the informal organization.

One of the main contributions of the neoclassical school is the introduction of behavioral sciences in an integrated fashion into the theory of organization. Through the use of these sciences, the human relationists demonstrate how the pillars of the classical doctrine are affected by the impact of human actions. Further, the neoclassical approach includes a systematic treatment of the informal organization, showing its influence on the formal structure.

Thus, the neoclassical approach to organization theory gives evidence of accepting classical doctrine, but superimposing on it modifications resulting from individual behavior, and the influence of the informal group. The inspiration of the neoclassical school was the Hawthorne studies.[13] Current examples of the neoclassical approach are found in human relations books like Gardner and Moore, *Human Relations in Industry*,[14] and Davis, *Human Relations in Business*.[15] To a more limited extent, work in industrial sociology also reflects a neoclassical point of view.[16]

It would be useful to look briefly at some of the contributions made to organization theory by the neoclassicists. First to be considered are modifications of the pillars of classical doctrine; second is the informal organization.

Examples of the Neoclassical Approach to the Pillars of Formal Organization Theory

1. The *division of labor* has been a long standing subject of comment in the field of human relations. Very early in the history of industrial psychology study was made of industrial fatigue and monotony caused by the specialization of the work.[17] Later, attention shifted to the isolation of the worker, and his feeling of anonymity resulting from insignificant jobs which contributed negligibly to the final product.[18]

Also, specialization influences the work of management. As an organization expands, the need concomitantly arises for managerial motivation and coordination of the activities of others. Both motivation and coordination in turn relate to executive leadership. Thus, in part, stemming from the growth of industrial specialization, the neoclassical school has developed a large body of theory relating to motivation, coordination, and leadership. Much of this theory is derived from the social sciences.

2. Two aspects of the *scalar and functional* processes which have been treated with some degree of intensity by the neoclassical school are the delegation of authority and

---

[13]See: F. J. Roethlisberger and William J. Dickson, *Management and the Worker* (Cambridge: Harvard University Press, 1939).

[14]Burleigh B. Gardner and David G. Moore, *Human Relations in Industry* (Homewood: Richard D. Irwin, 1955).

[15]Keith Davis, *Human Relations in Business* (New York: McGraw-Hill Book Company, 1957).

[16]For example see: Delbert C. Miller and William H. Form, *Industrial Sociology* (New York: Harper and Brothers, 1951).

[17]See: Hugo Munsterberg, *Psychology and Industrial Efficiency* (Boston: Houghton Mifflin Company, 1913).

[18]Probably the classic work is: Elton Mayo, *The Human Problems of an Industrial Civilization* (Cambridge: Harvard University, 1946, first printed 1933).

responsibility, and gaps in or overlapping of functional jurisdictions. The classical theory assumes something of perfection in the delegation and functionalization processes. The neoclassical school points out that human problems are caused by imperfections in the way these processes are handled.

For example, too much or insufficient delegation may render an executive incapable of action. The failure to delegate authority and responsibility equally may result in frustration for the delegatee. Overlapping of authorities often causes clashes in personality. Gaps in authority cause failures in getting jobs done, with one party blaming the other for shortcomings in performance.[19]

The neoclassical school says that the scalar and functional processes are theoretically valid, but tend to deteriorate in practice. The ways in which they break down are described, and some of the human causes are pointed out. In addition the neoclassicists make recommendations, suggesting various "human tools" which will facilitate the operation of these processes.

3. *Structure* provides endless avenues of analysis for the neoclassical theory of organization. The theme is that human behavior disrupts the best laid organizational plans, and thwarts the cleanness of the logical relationships founded in the structure. The neoclassical critique of structure centers on frictions which appear internally among people performing different functions.

Line and staff relations is a problem area, much discussed, in this respect. Many companies seem to have difficulty keeping the line and staff working together harmoniously. Both Dalton[20] and Juran[21] have engaged in

research to discover the causes of friction, and to suggest remedies.

Of course, line-staff relations represent only one of the many problems of structural frictions described by the neoclassicists. As often as not, the neoclassicists will offer prescriptions for the elimination of conflict in structure. Among the more important harmony-rendering formulae are participation, junior boards, bottom-up management, joint committees, recognition of human dignity, and "better" communication.

4. An executive's *span of control* is a function of human determinants, and the reduction of span to a precise, universally applicable ratio is silly, according to the neoclassicists. Some of the determinants of span are individual differences in managerial abilities, the type of people and functions supervised, and the extent of communication effectiveness.

Coupled with the span of control question are the human implications of the type of structure which emerges. That is, is a tall structure with a short span or a flat structure with a wide span more conducive to good human relations and high morale? The answer is situational. Short span results in tight supervision; wide span requires a good deal of delegation with looser controls. Because of individual and organizational differences, sometimes one is better than the other. There is a tendency to favor the looser form of organization, however, for the reason that tall structures breed autocratic leadership, which is often pointed out as a cause of low morale.[22]

The Neoclassical View of the Informal Organization

Nothing more than the barest mention of the informal organization is given even in the

[19]For further discussion of the human relations implications of the scalar and functional processes see: Keith Davis, *op. cit.*, pp. 60–66.

[20]Melville Dalton, "Conflicts between Staff and Line Managerial Officers," *American Sociological Review*, June, 1950, pp. 342–341.

[21]J. M. Juran, "Improving the Relationship between Staff and Line," *Personnel*, May, 1956, pp. 515–524.

[22]Gardner and Moore, *op. cit.*, pp. 237–243.

most recent classical treatises on organization theory.[23] Systematic discussion of this form of organization has been left to the neoclassicists. The informal organization refers to people in group associations at work, but these associations are not specified in the "blueprint" of the formal organization. The informal organization means natural groupings of people in the work situation.

In a general way, the informal organization appears in response to the social need—the need of people to associate with others. However, for analytical purposes, this explanation is not particularly satisfying. Research has produced the following, more specific determinants underlying the appearance of informal organizations.

1.   The *location* determinant simply states that in order to form into groups of any lasting nature, people have to have frequent face-to-face contact. Thus, the geography of physical location in a plant or office is an important factor in predicting who will be in what group.[24]

2.   *Occupation* is key factor determining the rise and composition of informal groups. There is a tendency for people performing similar jobs to group together.[25]

3.   *Interests* are another determinant for informal group formation. Even though people might be in the same location, performing similar jobs, differences of interest among them explain why several small, instead of one large, informal organizations emerge.

4.   *Special issues* often result in the formation of informal groups, but this determinant is set apart from the three previously mentioned. In this case, people who do not necessarily have similar interests, occupations, or locations may join together for a common cause. Once the issue is resolved, then the tendency is to revert to the more "natural" group forms.[26] Thus, special issues give rise to a rather impermanent informal association; groups based on the other three determinants tend to be more lasting.

When informal organizations come into being they assume certain characteristics. Since understanding these characteristics is important for management practice, they are noted below:

1.   Informal organizations act as agencies of *social control*. They generate a culture based on certain norms of conduct which, in turn, demands conformity from group members. These standards may be at odds with the values set by the formal organization. So an individual may very well find himself in a situation of conflicting demands.

2.   The form of human interrelationships in the informal organization requires *techniques of analysis* different from those used to plot the relationships of people in a formal organization. The method used for determining the structure of the informal group is called sociometric analysis. Sociometry reveals the complex structure of interpersonal relations which is based on premises fundamentally unlike the logic of the formal organization.

3.   Informal organizations have *status and communication* systems peculiar to themselves, not necessarily derived from the formal systems. For example, the grapevine is the subject of much neoclassical study.

4.   Survival of the informal organization requires stable continuing relationships among the people in them. Thus, it has been observed that the informal organization *resists*

[23]For example: Brech, *op. cit.*, pp. 27–29; and Allen, *op. cit.*, pp. 61–62.

[24]See: Leon Festinger, Stanley Schachter, and Kurt Back, *Social Pressures in Informal Groups* (New York: Harper and Brothers, 1950), pp. 153–163.

[25]For example see: W. Fred Cottrell, *The Railroader* (Palo Alto: The Stanford University Press, 1940), Chapter 3.

[26]Except in cases where the existence of an organization is necessary for the continued maintenance of employee interest. Under these conditions the previously informal association may emerge as a formal group, such as a union.

change.[27] Considerable attention is given by the neoclassicists to overcoming informal resistance to change.

5. The last aspect of analysis which appears to be central to the neoclassical view of the informal organization is the study of the *informal leader.* Discussion revolves around who the informal leader is, how he assumes this role, what characteristics are peculiar to him, and how he can help the manager accomplish his objectives in the formal organization.[28]

This brief sketch of some of the major facets of informal organization theory has neglected, so far, one important topic treated by the neoclassical school. It is the way in which the formal and informal organizations interact.

A conventional way of looking at the interaction of the two is the "live and let live" point of view. Management should recognize that the informal organization exists, nothing can destroy it, and so the executive might just as well work with it. Working with the informal organization involves not threatening its existence unnecessarily, listening to opinions expressed for the group by the leader, allowing group participation in decision-making situations, and controlling the grapevine by prompt release of accurate information.[29]

While this approach is management centered, it is not unreasonable to expect that informal group standards and norms could make themselves felt on formal organizational policy. An honestly conceived effort by managers to establish a working relationship with the informal organization could result in an association where both formal and informal views would be reciprocally modified. The danger which at all costs should be avoided is that "working with the informal organization" does not degenerate into a shallow disguise for human manipulation.

Some neoclassical writing in organization theory, especially that coming from the management-oriented segment of this school, gives the impression that the formal and informal organizations are distinct, and at times, quite irreconcilable factors in a company. The interaction which takes place between the two is something akin to the interaction between the company and a labor union, or a government agency, or another company.

The concept of the social system is another approach to the interactional climate. While this concept can be properly classified as neoclassical, it borders on the modern theories of organization. The phrase "social system" means that an organization is a complex of mutually interdependent, but variable, factors.

These factors include individuals and their attitudes and motives, jobs, the physical work setting, the formal organization, and the informal organizations. These factors, and many others, are woven into an overall pattern of interdependency. From this point of view, the formal and informal organizations lose their distinctiveness, but find real meaning, in terms of human behavior, in the operation of the system as a whole. Thus, the study of organization turns away from descriptions of its component parts, and is refocused on the system of interrelationships among the parts.

One of the major contributions of the Hawthorne studies was the integration of Pareto's idea of the social system into a meaningful method of analysis for the study of behavior in human organizations.[30] This concept is still

---

[27]Probably the classic study of resistance to change is: Lester Coch and John R. P. French, Jr., "Overcoming Resistance to Change," in Schuyler Dean Hoslett (editor). *Human Factors in Management* (New York: Harper and Brothers, 1951). pp. 242–268.

[28]For example see: Robert Saltonstall, *Human Relations in Administration* (New York: McGraw-Hill Book Company, 1959), pp. 330–331; and Keith Davis, *op. cit.,* pp. 99–101.

[29]For an example of this approach see: John T. Doutt, "Management Must Manage the Informal Group, Too," *Advanced Management*, May, 1959, pp. 26–28.

[30]See Roethlisberger and Dickson, *op. cit.,* Chapter 24.

vitally important. But unfortunately some work in the field of human relations undertaken by the neoclassicists has overlooked, or perhaps discounted, the significance of this consideration.[31]

The fundamental insight regarding the social system, developed and applied to the industrial scene by the Hawthorne researchers, did not find much extensĩon in subsequent work in the neoclassical vein. Indeed, the neoclassical school after the Hawthorne studies generally seemed content to engage in descriptive generalizations, or particularized empirical research studies which did not have much meaning outside their own context.

The neoclassical school of organization theory has been called bankrupt. Criticisms range from, "human relations is a tool for cynical puppeteering of people," to "human relations is nothing more than a trifling body of empirical and descriptive information." There is a good deal of truth in both criticisms, but another appraisal of the neoclassical school of organization theory is offered here. The neoclassical approach has provided valuable contributions to lore of organization. But, like the classical theory, the neoclassical doctrine suffers from incompleteness, a shortsighted perspective, and lack of integration among the many facets of human behavior studied by it. Modern organization theory has made a move to cover the shortcomings of the current body of theoretical knowledge.

MODERN ORGANIZATION THEORY

The distinctive qualities of modern organization theory are its conceptual-analytical base, its reliance on empirical research data and,

above all, its integrating nature. These qualities are framed in a philosophy which accepts the premise that the only meaningful way to study organization is to study it as a system. As Henderson put it, the study of a system must rely on a method of analysis, ". . . involving the simultaneous variations of mutually dependent variables."[32] Human systems, of course, contain a huge number of dependent variables which defy the most complex simultaneous equations to solve.

Nevertheless, system analysis has its own peculiar point of view which aims to study organization in the way Henderson suggests. It treats organization as a system of mutually dependent variables. As a result, modern organization theory, which accepts system analysis, shifts the conceptual level of organization study above the classical and neoclassical theories. Modern organization theory asks a range of interrelated questions which are not seriously considered by the two other theories.

Key among these questions are: (1) What are the strategic parts of the system? (2) What is the nature of their mutual dependency? (3) What are the main processes in the system which link the parts together, and facilitate their adjustment to each other? (4) What are the goals sought by systems?[33]

Modern organization theory is in no way a unified body of thought. Each writer and researcher has his special emphasis when he considers the system. Perhaps the most evident unifying thread in the study of systems is the effort to look at the organization in its totality. Representative books in this field are March and Simon, *Organizations*,[34] and

[31]A check of management human relations texts, the organization and human relations chapters of principles of management texts, and texts on conventional organization theory for management courses reveals little or no treatment of the concept of the social system.

[32]Lawrence J. Henderson, *Pareto's General Sociology* (Cambridge: Harvard University Press, 1935), p. 13.

[33]There is another question which cannot be treated in the scope of this paper. It asks, what research tools should be used for the study of the system?

[34]James G. March and Herbert A. Simon, *Organizations* (New York: John Wiley and Sons, 1958).

Haire's anthology, *Modern Organization The-ory.*[35]

Instead of attempting a review of different writers' contributions to modern organization theory, it will be more useful to discuss the various ingredients involved in system analy-sis. They are the parts, the interactions, the processes, and the goals of systems.

The Parts of the System and Their Interdependency

The first basic part of the system is the *individual,* and the personality structure he brings to the organization. Elementary to an individual's personality are motives and atti-tudes which condition the range of expectan-cies he hopes to satisfy by participating in the system.

The second part of the system is the formal arrangement of functions, usually called the *formal organization.* The formal organization is the interrelated pattern of jobs which make up the structure of a system. Certain writers, like Argyris, see a fundamental conflict result-ing from the demands made by the system, and the structure of the mature, normal per-sonality. In any event, the individual has ex-pectancies regarding the job he is to perform; and, conversely, the job makes demands on, or has expectancies relating to, the perform-ance of the individual. Considerable attention has been given by writers in modern organiza-tion theory to incongruencies resulting from the interaction of organizational and individu-al demands.[36]

The third part in the organization system is the *informal organization.* Enough has been said already about the nature of this organiza-tion. But it must be noted that an interactional

pattern exists between the individual and the informal group. This interactional arrange-ment can be conveniently discussed as the mutual modification of expectancies. The in-formal organization has demands which it makes on members in terms of anticipated forms of behavior, and the individual has expectancies of satisfaction he hopes to de-rive from association with people on the job. Both these sets of expectancies interact, re-sulting in the individual modifying his behav-ior to accord with the demands of the group, and the group, perhaps, modifying what it expects from an individual because of the impact of his personality on group norms.[37]

Much of what has been said about the various expectancy systems in an organization can also be treated using status and role concepts. Part of modern organization theory rests on research findings in social-psychology relative to reciprocal patterns of behavior stemming from role demands generated by both the formal and informal organizations, and role perceptions peculiar to the individual. Bakke's *fusion process* is largely concerned with the modification of role expectancies. The fusion process is a force, according to Bakke, which acts to weld divergent elements together for the preservation of organizational integrity.[38]

The fifth part of system analysis is the *physical setting* in which the job is performed. Although this element of the system may be implicit in what has been said already about the formal organization and its functions, it is well to separate it. In the physical surround-ings of work, interactions are present in com-plex man-machine systems. The human "engi-

---

[35]Mason Haire, (editor) *Modern Organization Theory* (New York: John Wiley and Sons, 1959).

[36]See Chris Argyris, *Personality and Organization* (New York: Harper and Brothers, 1957), esp. Chapters 2, 3, 7.

[37]For a larger treatment of this subject see: George C. Homans, *The Human Group* (New York: Harcourt, Brace and Company, 1950), Chapter 5.

[38]E. Wight Bakke, "Concept of the Social Organiza-tion," in *Modern Organization Theory,* Mason Haire, (editor) (New York: John Wiley and Sons, 1959), pp. 60–61.

neer" cannot approach the problems posed by such interrelationships in a purely technical, engineering fashion. As Haire says, these problems lie in the domain of the social theorist.[39] Attention must be centered on responses demanded from a logically ordered production function, often with the view of minimizing the error in the system. From this standpoint, work cannot be effectively organized unless the psychological, social, and physiological characteristics of people participating in the work environment are considered. Machines and processes should be designed to fit certain generally observed psychological and physiological properties of men, rather than hiring men to fit machines.

In summary, the parts of the system which appear to be of strategic importance are the individual, the formal structure, the informal organization, status and role patterns, and the physical environment of work. Again, these parts are woven into a configuration called the organizational system. The processes which link the parts are taken up next.

The Linking Processes

One can say, with a good deal of glibness, that all the parts mentioned above are interrelated. Although this observation is quite correct, it does not mean too much in terms of system theory unless some attempt is made to analyze the processes by which the interaction is achieved. Role theory is devoted to certain types of interactional processes. In addition, modern organization theorists point to three other linking activities which appear to be universal to human systems of organized behavior. These processes are communication, balance, and decision making.

1. Communication is mentioned often in

neoclassical theory, but the emphasis is on description of forms of communication activity, i.e., formal-informal, vertical-horizontal, line-staff. Communication, as a mechanism which links the segments of the system together, is overlooked by way of much considered analysis.

One aspect of modern organization theory is study of the communication network in the system. Communication is viewed as the method by which action is evoked from the parts of the system. Communication acts not only as stimuli resulting in action, but also as a control and coordination mechanism linking the decision centers in the system into a synchronized pattern. Deutsch points out that organizations are composed of parts which communicate with each other, receive messages from the outside world, and store information. Taken together, these communication functions of the parts comprise a configuration representing the total system.[40] More is to be said about communication later in the discussion of the cybernetic model.

2. The concept of *balance* as a linking process involves a series of some rather complex ideas. Balance refers to an equilibrating mechanism whereby the various parts of the system are maintained in a harmoniously structured relationship to each other.

The necessity for the balance concept logically flows from the nature of systems themselves. It is impossible to conceive of an ordered relationship among the parts of a system without also introducing the idea of a stabilizing or an adapting mechanism.

Balance appears in two varieties—quasi-automatic and innovative. Both forms of balance act to insure system integrity in face of changing conditions, either internal or external to the system. The first form of balance,

[39]Mason Haire, "Psychology and the Study of Business: Joint Behavioral Sciences," in *Social Science Research on Business: Product and Potential* (New York: Columbia University Press, 1959), pp. 53–59.

[40]Karl W. Deutsch "On Communication Models in the Social Sciences," *Public Opinion Quarterly*, 16 (1952), pp. 356–380.

quasi-automatic, refers to what some think are "homeostatic" properties of systems. That is, systems seem to exhibit built-in propensities to maintain steady states.

If human organizations are open, self-maintaining systems, then control and regulatory processes are necessary. The issue hinges on the degree to which stabilizing processes in systems, when adapting to change, are automatic. March and Simon have an interesting answer to this problem, which in part is based on the type of change and the adjustment necessary to adapt to the change. Systems have programs of action which are put into effect when a change is perceived. If the change is relatively minor, and if the change comes within the purview of established programs of action, then it might be fairly confidently predicted that the adaptation made by the system will be quasi-automatic.[41]

The role of innovative, creative balancing efforts now needs to be examined. The need for innovation arises when adaptation to a change is outside the scope of existing programs designed for the purpose of keeping the system in balance. New programs have to be evolved in order for the system to maintain internal harmony.

New programs are created by trial and error search for feasible action alternatives to cope with a given change. But innovation is subject to the limitations and possibilities inherent in the quantity and variety of information present in a system at a particular time. New combinations of alternatives for innovative purposes depend on:

a the possible range of output of the system, or the capacity of the system to supply information.

b the range of available information in the memory of the system.

c the operating rules (program) governing

the analysis and flow of information within the system.

d the ability of the system to "forget" previously learned solutions to change problems.[42] A system with too good a memory might narrow its behavioral choices to such an extent as to stifle innovation. In simpler language, old learned programs might be used to adapt to change, when newly innovated programs are necessary.[43]

Much of what has been said about communication and balance brings to mind a cybernetic model in which both these processes have vital roles. Cybernetics has to do with feedback and control in all kinds of systems. Its purpose is to maintain system stability in the face of change. Cybernetics cannot be studied without considering communication networks, information flow, and some kind of balancing process aimed at preserving the integrity of the system.

Cybernetics directs attention to key questions regarding the system. These questions are: How are communication centers connected, and how are they maintained? Corollary to this question: what is the structure of the feedback system? Next, what information is stored in the organization, and at what points? And as a corollary: how accessible is this information to decision-making centers? Third, how conscious is the organization of the operation of its own parts? That is, to what extent do the policy centers receive control information with sufficient frequency and relevancy to create a real awareness of the operation of the segments of the system? Finally, what are the learning (innovating) capabilities of the system?[44]

[41]March and Simon, *op. cit.*, pp. 139–140.

[42]Mervyn L. Cadwallader "The Cybernetic Analysis of Change in Complex Social Organization," *The American Journal of Sociology*, September, 1959, p. 156.

[43]It is conceivable for innovative behavior to be programmed into the system.

[44]These are questions adapted from Deutsch, *op. cit.*, 368–370.

Answers to the questions posed by cybernetics are crucial to understanding both the balancing and communication processes in systems.[45] Although cybernetics has been applied largely to technical-engineering problems of automation, the model of feedback, control, and regulation in all systems has a good deal of generality. Cybernetics is a fruitful area which can be used to synthesize the processes of communication and balance.

3. A wide spectrum of topics dealing with types of decisions in human systems makes up the core of analysis of another important process in organizations. Decision analysis is one of the major contributions of March and Simon in their book *Organizations*. The two major classes of decisions they discuss are decisions to produce and decisions to participate in the system.[46]

Decisions to produce are largely a result of an interaction between individual attitudes and the demands of organization. Motivation analysis becomes central to studying the nature and results of the interaction. Individual decisions to participate in the organization reflect on such issues as the relationship between organizational rewards versus the demands made by the organization. Participation decisions also focus attention on the reasons why individuals remain in or leave organizations.

March and Simon treat decisions as internal variables in an organization which depend on jobs, individual expectations and motivations, and organizational structure. Marschak[47] looks on the decision process as an independent variable upon which the survival of the

organization is based. In this case, the organization is viewed as having, inherent to its structure, the ability to maximize survival requisites through its established decision processes.

The Goals of Organization

Organization has three goals which may be either intermeshed or independent ends in themselves. They are growth, stability, and interaction. The last goal refers to organizations which exist primarily to provide a medium for association of its members with others. Interestingly enough these goals seem to apply to different forms of organization at varying levels of complexity, ranging from simple clockwork mechanisms to social systems.

These similarities in organizational purposes have been observed by a number of people, and a field of thought and research called general system theory has developed, dedicated to the task of discovering organizationed universals. The dream of general system theory is to create a science of organizational universals, or if you will, a universal science using common organizational elements found in all systems as a starting point.

Modern organization theory is on the periphery of general system theory. Both general system theory and modern organization theory studies:

1 the parts (individuals) in aggregates, and the movement of individuals into and out of the system.
2 the interaction of individuals with the environment found in the system.
3 the interactions among individuals in the system.
4 general growth and stability problems of systems.[48]

Modern organization theory and general

---

[45]Answers to these questions would require a comprehensive volume. One of the best approaches currently available is Stafford Beer, *Cybernetics and Management* (New York: John Wiley and Sons, 1959).

[46]March and Simon, *op. cit.*, Chapters 3 and 4.

[47]Jacob Marschak, "Efficient and Viable Organizational Forms" in *Modern Organization Theory*, Mason Haire, editor (New York: John Wiley and Sons, 1959), pp. 307–320.

[48]Kenneth E. Boulding, "General System Theory—The Skeleton of a Science," *Management Science*, April, 1956, pp. 200–202.

system theory are similar in that they look at organization as an integrated whole. They differ, however, in terms of their generality. General system theory is concerned with every level of system, whereas modern organizational theory focuses primarily on human organization.

The question might be asked, what can the science of administration gain by the study of system levels other than human? Before attempting an answer, note should be made of what these other levels are. Boulding presents a convenient method of classification:

1 The static structure—a level of framework, the anatomy of a system; for example, the structure of the universe.

2 The simple dynamic system—the level of clockworks, predetermined necessary motions.

3 The cybernetic system—the level of the thermostat, the system moves to maintain a given equilibrium through a process of self-regulation.

4 The open system—level of self-maintaining systems, moves toward and includes living organisms.

5 The genetic-societal system—level of cell society, characterized by a division of labor among cells.

6 Animal systems—level of mobility, evidence of goal-directed behavior.

7 Human systems—level of symbol interpretation and idea communication.

8 Social system—level of human organization.

9 Transcendental systems—level of ultimates and absolutes which exhibit systematic structure but are unknowable in essence.[49]

This approach to the study of systems by finding universals common at all levels of organization offers intriguing possibilities for administrative organization theory. A good deal of light could be thrown on social systems

if structurally analogous elements could be found in the simpler types of systems. For example, cybernetic systems have characteristics which seem to be similar to feedback, regulation, and control phenomena in human organizations. Thus, certain facets of cybernetic models could be generalized to human organization. Considerable danger, however, lies in poorly founded analogies. Superficial similarities between simpler system forms and social systems are apparent everywhere. Instinctually based ant societies, for example, do not yield particularly instructive lessons for understanding rationally conceived human organizations. Thus, care should be taken that analogies used to bridge system levels are not mere devices for literary enrichment. For analogies to have usefulness and validity, they must exhibit inherent structural similarities or implicitly identical operational principles.[50]

Modern organization theory leads, as it has been shown, almost inevitably into a discussion of general system theory. A science of organization universals has some strong advocates, particularly among biologists.[51] Organization theorists in administrative science cannot afford to overlook the contributions of general system theory. Indeed, modern organization concepts could offer a great deal to those working with general system theory. But the ideas dealt with in the general theory are exceedingly elusive.

Speaking of the concept of equilibrium as a

[49]*Ibid.*, pp. 202–205.

[50]Seidenberg, *op. cit.*, p. 136. The fruitful use of the type of analogies spoken of by Seidenberg is evident in the application of thermodynamic principles, particularly the entropy concept, to communication theory. See: Claude E. Shannon and Warren Weaver, *The Mathematical Theory of Communication*, (Urbana: The University of Illinois Press, 1949). Further, the existence of a complete analogy between the operational behavior of thermodynamic systems, electrical communication systems, and biological systems has been noted by: Y. S. Touloukian, *The Concept of Entropy in Communication, Living Organisms, and Thermodynamics*, Research Bulletin 130, Purdue Engineering Experiment Station.

[51]For example see: Ludwig von Bertalanffy, *Problem of Life* (London: Watts and Company, 1952).

unifying element in all systems, Easton says, "It (equilibrium) leaves the impression that we have a useful general theory when in fact, lacking measurability, it is a mere pretence for knowledge."[52] The inability to quantify and measure universal organization elements undermines the success of pragmatic tests to which general system theory might be put.

Modern organization theory needs tools of analysis and a conceptual framework uniquely

its own, but it must also allow for the incorporation of relevant contributions of many fields. It may be that the framework will come from the theory of general systems. New areas of research such as decision theory, information theory, and cybernetics also offer reasonable expectations of analytical and conceptual tools. Modern organization theory represents a frontier of research which has great significance for management. The potential is great, because it offers the opportunity for uniting what is valuable in classical theory with the social and natural sciences into a systematic and integrated conception of human organization.

[52]David Easton, "Limits of the Equilibrium Model in Social Research," in *Profits and Problems of Homeostatic Models in the Behavioral Sciences*, Publication 1, Chicago Behavioral Sciences, 1953, p. 39.

Reading 6

Modern Organization Theory: A Psychological and Sociological Study

D. S. Pugh

"Organization theory" is the study of the structure and functioning of organizations and the behavior of groups and individuals within them. It is an emerging interdisciplinary quasi-independent science, drawing primarily on the disciplines of sociology and psychology, but also on economics and, to a lesser extent, on production engineering. The purpose of this paper is to discuss the lines of development which compose this subdiscipline (some of which may be relatively little known to psychologists) and to present an overview of attempts to develop a unified science of man in organizations.

The importance of developing such a science cannot be overemphasized. Most people spend a considerable portion of their time in formal organizations. Preschool children, non-

working wives, and old people are the only sizable groups not necessarily so involved as members, and even they are affected as patients, clients, customers, or citizens. The bureaucratic organization, and the individual operating within it, is one of the dominant institutions of our time. Of course organizations do not exist in a vacuum, they have to respond to the pressures impinging on them from the society in which they exist. The demands of a market economy, political decisions, legal restrictions, technological requirements, etc., all affect organizational operations. But just as the O is coming back into the S-R bond in contemporary psychology, so the "O," in this case the organization, is the mediating organism between the "S" (Society) and the "R" (the Resultant achievement of

Psychological Bulletin, 1966, **66,** 235–251. Copyright 1966 by the American Psychological Association. Reprinted by permission.

goals, the higher standard of living, the longer expectation of life, etc.). Highly colored exaggerations of this situation, such as Burnham's (1941) *The Managerial Revolution* and Whyte's (1956) *The Organization Man*, only serve to underline the organization's important place in society.

There is a second reason for the importance of organization theory which is of particular interest to those psychologists who believe that the proper study of mankind is man *outside* the laboratory. Those of us who are concerned with the empirical study of man *in situ* cannot fail to be impressed with the achievements of the laboratory method in other sciences, even though we are more uncertain of its usefulness in our own. But the fact that we substitute the statistical method for the laboratory one in our experiments and use statistics to control our independent variables rather than laboratory simulation only serves to emphasize that we are working within the same basic underlying experimental "model." The study of men in organizations can offer possibilities of direct comparisons between individuals approximating to a laboratory investigation, but without its artificiality. For example, a factory can have a row of people sitting at a bench doing the same *real* job. This makes the achievement of experimental control outside the laboratory much easier. Studies of factors affecting the motivation to perform, the effects of personality on role behavior, the transmission of information along communication channels—all these can benefit from study in a real situation which has in it many of the advantages of the artificial laboratory situation, such as repeatability on large numbers, specificity of process studied, etc.

One may ask why it is considered less artificial to study men getting paid for standing on the assembly line at a motor factory screwing on car-door handles than to study men getting paid for taking part in a laboratory ergograph experiment. The answer is that it is not so much the actual laboratory task itself

that is artificial—although there are difficulties here (Rolfe & Corkindale, 1964)—as the social situation in which it is performed. The social role of mass production operator is far removed from that of laboratory subject. The enormous disparity in the duration of role occupancy is sufficient to ensure differences in sanctions and motivations, with consequent divergence in performance.

DEFINITION OF THE SUBJECT

Defining a new subject carries with it a built-in dilemma. One can either use the technical terms of the established disciplines to indicate the area of interest (this has the advantage of containing verbal stimuli which produce recognition responses in potential recruits in relevant fields, and might therefore be called a "political" definition) or one can create new terms which define exactly what is meant in terms of the new discipline (this has the obvious advantage of precision, and might thus be called a "scientific" definition). The disadvantage of the political definition is that the established terms may carry with them connotations and overtones, to overcome which may be the precise purpose of setting up the new discipline. The disadvantage of the scientific definition is that it conveys little to the uninitiated, which is a limitation in encouraging potential interest.

The definition of organization theory given above is clearly a political one. It indicates in general terms the areas of interest, using established social science terminology: structure, functioning, organization, behavior, groups, individuals. It seems to form a nice balance between sociological and psychological "clang" words and thus to interest practitioners in both fields. But it suffers from the disadvantage of a political definition in that there may be read into it the implication that the structure and functioning of organizations is the province of the sociologist, the behavior of individuals is dealt with by the psychologist, while groups are left to a peculiar man in the middle, the social psychologist. He appears to be so peculiar that one writer (Smith, 1954) has suggested that he could be divided up and a distinction made between the "sociological social psychologist" and the "psychological social psychologist."

It is precisely because this compartmentalization is unhelpful that we wish to break away from the traditional division of the ground, and have used the concept of organization theory as a way of integrating these disciplines (and some others) into a unified science of individual, group, and organizational behavior. The behavior itself at these three levels is intimately interrelated, and so, therefore, should be the study of it. It is our contention that sociologists and psychologists can jointly make contributions to all problems of organization theory.

Let us take two examples: a considerable limitation on all major sociological theories of organizational functioning is an extremely naïve treatment of human motivation combined with a neglect of individual differences which are characteristically devalued into "personal idiosyncrasies." An organization is a system of functioning human beings who are different, and if the sociologist neglects these differences he is not leaving them *out of account*, he is saying that for the processes with which he is concerned, these differences are of *no account*—that is, they are equal to zero. This is a most important psychological statement which may very well be true—or not, as the case may be—but which requires empirical investigation rather than a priori assertion. Similarly, psychological studies of leadership patterns in relation to personality and social skill training imply a very naïve view of the relationship between personality and role behavior, combined with a neglect of structural differences in organizational positions. Again the psychologist cannot say that he is not concerned with differences in organi-

zation structure since he is only discovering the best leadership style to suit the particular personality. Leadership is exercised within different organizational structures, and if he neglects these differences the psychologist is not leaving them *out of account*, he is maintaining that for the processes with which he is concerned they are of *no account*. This is a very important sociological statement, which may very well be true—or not—but which again requires empirical investigation.

It was considerations such as these which led us to conceptualize our work as the attempt to develop an interdisciplinary unified study of organization theory. It would be impossible to describe all the lines of development which affect a new study even if one were aware of them. We can only briefly and summarily give here a number of main strands which have been particularly formative. Pugh, Hickson, and Hinings (1964) summarized in greater detail the work of many of these writers. They are not given here in any order of importance, overt or implied. Indeed, we would wish explicitly to disavow the primacy of any particular approach and to maintain that an integrated unified orientation, drawing on all these approaches and interrelating them (and, most importantly, *rejecting* something of all of them), offers the best promise for future development.

MANAGEMENT THEORISTS

Managers, administrators, and government officials have always had an interest in describing their experiences with more or less insight, but the first manager whose theoretical analysis of organizational functioning has had a lasting impact was a Frenchman—Henri Fayol (1949), who was writing about 50 years ago. His "General Principles of Management" have little in the way of systematic evidence to support them, but most managers find that they square with experience. As empirical scientists, we are right to be wary of such "proverbs" as these, but not to dismiss them out of hand. They include such tenets as "authority must equal responsibility," "one man, one boss," and so on. A whole series of managers (and others) have developed these practical insights. "Specialization increases efficiency" is a favorite one. "The span of control of a manager, that is, the number reporting directly to him, should never be more than six," is another. The almost completely descriptive writings of political scientists and industrial relations experts belong here too (Dahl, 1959; Drucker, 1955; Goldstein, 1952).

From the scientific point of view, there are two main difficulties in this approach. There is first the very considerable prescriptive content. Very much more is said about how organizations should be run than about how they are run—not unnaturally since these are guides to the manager on what he ought to do. The contemporary British manager Wilfred Brown (1960) illustrated this attitude very well. He noted that wherever there is an authority system (i.e., a situation in which some people are in a position to make decisions, give orders, allocate work, etc., to others) there are also developed ways of letting those in authority know what the people underneath them think and feel about these decisions, even if in only the most rudimentary and unsystematic way. Since this will happen anyway, it is clearly bad management to allow it to happen inefficiently. Brown therefore maintained that wherever there is an executive authority system, there must be set up feedback channels of equivalent formality and complexity (which he called a "Representative System") if communication is to improve and the organization to function efficiently. Brown's own firm has a highly complex system of representative committees formally elected by all levels of employees. It will be seen that Brown represents a considerable

increase in sociological and psychological sophistication from the common sense analyses of Fayol, but the normative orientation is still very much to the fore.

The second difficulty with the management theorists, particularly the common sense ones, is that not being scientists, their statements do not usually have sufficient precision to enable crucial experiments to be undertaken to test their validity. This is their attraction for the layman, since the proverbs appear to be wise and true for all occasions. But scientific statements are precisely *not* true for *all* occasions, and it is an integral part of the process of science to look for occasions for which they are not true. A scientific hypothesis is essentially a falsifiable statement. When the statements of the management theorists are subject to the same scrutiny, and attempts made to operationalize them, it is usually found that they do not stand up to such analysis very well (Simon, 1957).

For example, consider the principle already mentioned: "specialization increases efficiency," which spelled out would presumably mean "increased specialization will lead to greater efficiency." Does this mean that *any* increase in specialization will increase efficiency? Take the case of a firm with three factories: Factory A makes washing machines, Factory B makes refrigerators, and Factory C makes vacuum cleaners—in each case complete. How do we increase efficiency by increasing specialization? Could we let Factory A make the electric motors which are required for all three products; Factory B do the machine shop work for all three; and Factory C do the assembly and finishing work for all three? Would this be an increase in specialization? As soon as the problem is stated in these concrete terms, it is clear that the proverb is no help in making the decision. It does not define what is an "increase in specialization" as distinct from a change in specialization except in terms of an increase in efficiency. Specialization is an inevitable concomitant of organization (efficient or inefficient), and the problem is not "how to specialize" but "how to specialize efficiently." The operational translation of the principle would be: Efficiency is increased by such specialization as will lead to increased efficiency!

In fact, the specialization problem is an absolutely fundamental one, having its ramifications throughout the whole of organization theory, at the organization, group, and individual levels. At the organization level, it is the "assignment" problem. Given an overall set of tasks which can be partitioned in a number of ways and a total set of resources which can be partitioned in a number of ways, what partitioning of the resources assigned to what partitioning of the tasks will yield the maximum efficiency? There are three sets of decisions here; the partitioning of the tasks, the partitioning of the resources, and the assignment; and the difficulty lies in the fact that the efficiencies are nonadditive. For example, the man-hours required for 100 jobs if 10 men each do 10 jobs may be more than or less than, but it is unlikely to be equal to, the man-hours required for 1 man to do all the 100 jobs or for 100 men to do 1 job each. Since the factors which affect efficiency range from machine set-up costs through operator skills and restriction of output to technological know-how and administrative flexibility, it is not surprising that no underlying principles for tackling this problem have emerged. The only available solution is a "brute force" one, involving testing all the possible partitions of the resources assigned to all the possible partitions of the task. This is normally an unrealistic undertaking, and although with computer techniques there are methods of reducing the magnitude of the computational task involved (Kuhn, 1955), no general propositions about optimal assignment have emerged, only methods of obtaining the best solution in a particular case.

In the face of this major unsolved problem of operations research, the management principle "specialization increases efficiency" does no more than serve to point out the existence of the problem. Management theory has great interest for the social scientist, for the problems with which it deals nearly always point to topics with which he is concerned. But it has great dangers too, for if the social scientist allows outsiders to set the topics on which he works, his contribution to the development of the discipline (which should be his main concern) is much hampered.

STRUCTURAL THEORISTS

All organizations have to make provision for continuing activities directed towards the achievement of given aims. Regularities in such activities as task allocation, the exercise of authority, and coordination of functions are developed. Such regularities constitute the organization's structure, and sociologists have studied systematic differences in structure related to variations in such factors as the objectives of the organization, its size, ownership, geographical location, and technology of manufacture, which produce the characteristic differences in structure of a bank, a hospital, a mass production factory or a local government department.

The concept of bureaucracy as described by the German sociologist Max Weber (1947) is central to this approach. In popular discussion, bureaucracy is synonymous with inefficient administration, pettifogging legalism, and red tape, and yet the bureaucratic form of organization has become the dominant one in all modern societies. Weber drew critical attention to the strengths of the bureaucratic structure of organization. He noted that characteristically in a bureaucracy, authority is exercised by means of a system of rules and procedures through the official position which an individual occupies. These positions are arranged in a hierarchy, each successive step embracing in authority all those beneath it. Rules and procedures are drawn up for every theoretically possible contingency. There is a "bureau" for the safekeeping of all written records and files—it being an important part of the rationality of the system that information is written down. Particularly important is the stress on the appointment of experts who are specialists with formal qualifications for their positions. The system thus aims to develop the most efficient methods for achieving its goals by depersonalizing the whole administrative process. Written rulebooks, standardized procedures, and formal training and qualification for appointment all act to minimize capricious differences in the treatment of the same problem, eliminate nepotism in promotion, and set and maintain high standards of efficiency in working. In modern computer jargon, a bureaucracy is an organization which is completely programmed.

The major development of this approach has been to compare the organization's structure and functioning with Weber's description of bureaucracy and to point out that he was incomplete and inadequate in his formulations of bureaucratic action. These are the classic studies of bureaucratic dysfunction of Merton (1940), Dubin (1949), and Gouldner (1955), among others. They underline that Weber gave only a description of the formal (i.e., intended) characteristics of bureaucracy and left out the unintended consequences which may have very important disrupting effects upon the organization. Crucial significance must be given to the attitudes, values, and goals of specialist subunits and individuals and the way in which these continuously modify the organization's formal structure.

Selznick (1949), for example, on the basis of a study of the Tennessee Valley Authority, showed that Weber's formal description of an efficient bureaucracy left out the dysfunctions which must occur when the top administrators in a large organization inevitably delegate some of their authority. They do so differentially, and this has several consequences. As intended, it increases the specialized competences of the various groups which now have authority over the different parts of the organization's functioning. But at the same time, it also has the unintended effect of increasing departmentalization and underlining the differences of interest between the department and the organization as a whole. Each department soon develops its own goals and values, and conflict between departments ensues with consequent greater identification of the individual with his own department and smaller identification with the organization. A man's career comes to appear to be best served by conforming to his department's ideology, rather than by optimizing his contribution to the whole organization if this involves flouting his department. This is the problem of specialization again, at the group level. Specialist competence can certainly increase efficiency, but the price has to be paid in increased division of interest. The problem is: At what point does the price become too high?

Burns and Stalker (1961) have developed a consideration of these dysfunctions into a postulated continuum of organizations in terms of their flexibility of structure. The mechanistic type of organization is adapted to relatively stable conditions. In it, the problems and tasks of management are broken down into specialisms within which each individual carries out his assigned, precisely defined task. There is a clear hierarchy of control and responsibility for overall knowledge, and coordination rests exclusively at the top. The organic type (later called "organismic," Burns, 1963) is adapted to unstable conditions when new and unfamiliar problems continually arise which cannot be broken down and distributed among the existing specialist roles. There is therefore a continual adjustment and redefinition of individual tasks; interaction and communication (information and advice rather than orders) occur across any level as required and reliance on the normal hierarchical processes is rejected in favor of going out and getting things done. A much higher degree of commitment to the success of the organization is generated, presumably at a greater cost in ulcers and coronaries.

Burns and Stalker studied the attempts of traditional, mechanistic Scottish firms to absorb electronics research and development engineers into their organizations. The almost complete failure of these attempts led them to doubt whether a mechanistic firm can consciously change into an organismic one. This is because the individual in a mechanistic organization is not only committed to the organization as a whole, he is also a member of a group or department with a stable career structure and with sectional interests in conflict with those of other groups. Thus there develop power struggles between established sections to obtain control of the new functions and resources. These divert the organization from purposive adaptation and allow out-of-date mechanistic structures to be perpetuated and "pathological" systems to develop.

The first major limitation of structural theory is that it involves what one might call "Hebb's fallacy." Hebb (1949) wished to explain psychological behavior in terms of physiological intervening variables, but his data was solely psychological. His physiology was purely speculative—reverberating neural feedback mechanisms, etc. Structural organization theorists deal with sociological phenomena and use psychological concepts as explanatory intervening variables—such concepts as "the process of sanctification of the rules of the organization" (meaning the internalization of rules by bureaucrats), "the development of esprit de corps," and "the resort to categorization" in decision-making. But the data are purely sociological; the psychology is only speculative—or perhaps it would be bet-

ter to say "common sense." Merton's (1940) famous paper criticizing Weber was entitled "Bureaucratic Structure and Personality" and it used the three concepts just mentioned, but a psychologist reading it for signs of a link between structural theory and personality theory can only have the same feelings of exasperation as a physiologist reading Hebb. There is a continual use of lower order concepts as intervening variables and yet no attempt to devise ways of operationalizing them in order to carry out direct empirical tests of their validity. The use of a concept such as "sanctification of rules" must surely imply consideration of individual differences in such sanctification. The difficulty is that sociologists consider that they know enough speculative psychology for their purposes, just as psychologists think they know enough speculative physiology for theirs. But speculative "common sense" explanations, if they are not used as a spur to direct empirical investigation, are the enemy of scientific ones.

The second major limitation of structural theory is that it has been subject to what a sociologist (Wrong, 1961) has characterized as "the oversocialized conception of man in modern sociology." It is implicit in the structural approach that conformity to social expectations is the only effective motivation. Any more complex motivations are ignored. In addition, consideration is given only to the effects of the organization's demands and the expectations of other members in their roles, on the behavior and personality of the individual. These are assumed to be all-pervading. Merton's (1940) paper, referred to above, listed a number of problems for research such as: To what extent are particular personality types selected by various bureaucracies? Does holding bureaucratic office increase ascendancy traits of personality? What are the mechanisms for obtaining emotional commitment to the correct enforcement of the rules? Typically, they are all concerned with the effects of the organization on the individual. The most that an individual can do, it appears, if he does not conform, is to leave the job.

The structural approach gives no reciprocal account of the possible effects of the individual and his personality on the organization. For those of us who want a balanced understanding of integrated individual and organizational functioning, this is too limiting. What is required is a conceptual frame of reference which admits the equal validity of the demands of both the organizational structure *and* the individual personality; which looks for the way in which the structure determines the role behavior, but also notes that many role demands are permissive rather than mandatory so that the individual's behavior within the role may legitimately vary according to his personality—and that these variations may act *to change the structure.*

GROUP THEORISTS

This approach stems from Elton Mayo (1933) and Kurt Lewin (1943), and their "discovery" of the influence of the immediate informal group on motivation and behavior. Some of the findings of those who have developed this line of approach are: the amount of work carried out by a worker is determined not by his physical capacity but by his social capacity; noneconomic rewards are most important in the motivation and satisfaction of workers, who react to their work situations as groups and not as individuals; the leader is not necessarily the person appointed to be in charge, informal leaders can develop who have more power; the effective supervisor is "employee-centered" and not "job-centered," that is, he regards his job as dealing with human beings rather than with the work; communication and participation in decision making are some of the most significant rewards which can be offered to obtain the commitment of the individual. The prewar Hawthorne and leadership

studies (Lewin, Lippit, & White, 1939; Roethlisberger & Dickson, 1939), the postwar studies of groups in the restaurant, pajama, and ball-bearing industries (Coch & French, 1948; Jaques, 1951; Whyte, 1948), and in the Army (Shils, 1950); Holmans' (1951) survey of "*The Human Group*," Cartwright and Zander's (1953) of *Group Dynamics*, Likert's (1961) *New Patterns of Management* all add up to an impressive body of data.

The first limitation of the group theorists is that they have restricted their sights to too narrow a range of variables. Most of their studies are industrial ones, yet they have had little, if anything, to say about the political, social, and industrial power relationships that form the setting for work behavior. It may well be true that in the Hawthorne interviewing program—which was completed by 1932—not one worker spontaneously mentioned a trade union (as Landsberger, 1958, has confirmed), yet that would hardly be the case today. Having discovered the informal group and its importance, investigators in this tradition seem loath to allow other institutions some importance too. Even the formal executive organization seems to be looked upon as a sort of necessary evil. Many of the structural theorists, reacting against Weber and management theory, also seem to have this implicit bias against the formal organization.

Cartwright (1953) took up another aspect of this same criticism when he accused group psychology of being "soft on power." Concepts such as leadership, authoritarianism, and influence have been well-investigated in social psychology, but not factors such as power or control. Partly as a result of Cartwright's observations, what might be thought of as the "second generation" Michigan investigators have recently begun to make good this deficiency (French, 1956; Kahn, 1964; Tannenbaum, 1962). In view of the long tradition in group theory that it is "psychological participation"—the *feeling* that one is participating in decision-making, not the actual participation itself—which matters, a study by Tannenbaum and Smith (1964) must be regarded as something of a breakthrough. They showed that in a voluntary organization with a large number of local groups, when individual perception of ability to influence decisions is held constant, there remains a significant relationship between the groups' average perception of influence and the level of loyalty and activity. Thus, members' participation was not just a function of subjective perceptions, although this factor was present. The average perceptions—which reflect the actual power exerted—must also be regarded as a causative factor. The emerging acceptance of the structured social relationship as real is an important stage in the development of group theory and is the innovation which best warrants the use of the new term "organizational psychology" (Bass, 1965; Schein, 1965). The studies of Porter and his associates (Porter & Henry, 1964; Porter & Lawler, 1964, 1965) have also contributed to this development by linking attitudes and job satisfaction firmly to positions in the formal organization structure.

The second limitation of the group theorists is theoretically more important though ideologically not so dramatic. It applies with equal force to both the structural and management theorists, but is dealt with here because it does not apply to the remaining approaches to be considered. There have been few attempts so far to relate organizational functioning and group behavior in any systematic way. This is not surprising, as a striking characteristic of all these approaches is that the analysis has been primarily processual as opposed to factorial, as Komarovsky (1957) would put it, or clinical as opposed to statistical, using Meehl's (1954) terms. These writers have discussed the administrative process or the processes of group interaction, and their work has led to the development of management control systems and techniques in human relations. There

has been almost no systematic statistical exploration of the causal connection between contextual factors and certain administrative systems rather than others, or certain group and individual behavior rather than others. The method of dealing with the problems has been the adumbration of broad generalizations based either on the experience and insights of the writer, or on the intensive one-case study of the empirical researcher. Because the problems have been conceived entirely in processual-clinical terms, the fact that the one-case study is of a particular work group, in a particular factory, in a particular firm, in a particular industry, in a particular country, or at a particular time has not prevented the development of generalizations that claim to apply to all individuals and all groups in all organizations and in all contexts. The inadequacies of this non-comparative approach are apparent. It may postulate that the designation of the correct mode of functional specialization is a vital part of the task of administration, but, as we have seen, it will give no systematic leads as to why a particular form of specialization exists in a particular organization. It may discover that some supervisory practices lead to a decrease in conflict, but it will not explain why particular industries (e.g., the chemical industry), which certainly do not have a monopoly of these practices, nevertheless have consistently less conflict than others (Kerr & Fisher, 1957).

The concept that the processual-clinical and the factorial-statistical approaches to analysis are in conflict has rightly been labelled by Komarovsky (1957) as a "pseudo-issue" in social science. Both approaches are vital. But processual analysis must take place in relation to the contextual framework provided by factorial analysis, not in neglect of it. The present study of work organization and behavior can no longer be content with a priori postulations or a continuing succession of one-case studies.

INDIVIDUAL THEORISTS

The investigation of psychological factors affecting a worker's performance on the job has a long tradition stemming from the Health of Munition Workers Report and the Industrial Fatigue Research Board during World War I. Since then, a considerable series of studies has developed designed to achieve the task of the applied psychologist, which is as Rodger (1950) put it "to fit the man to the job, and to fit the job to the man."

In many ways, this approach, concerned as it is with such concrete problems as counselling, selection, training, human engineering, conditions of work, and methods of payment, is the one where the psychologist can demonstrate that he has made a real contribution. Using his complementary twin objectives of, in Heron's (1954) neat formulation, "job satisfaction" and "job satisfactoriness," he has been able to concentrate his efforts on the mechanics of the work situation to the exclusion of wider factors such as group dynamics, social norms and values, and institutional conflict. But the growing body of data which indicates that satisfaction and productivity are not necessarily complementary (Brayfield & Crockett, 1955; Kahn, 1960) and that job satisfaction itself is by no means a unitary concept (Hertzberg, Mausner, & Snyderman, 1959) suggests that this approach too, as that of the group theorists, is embarking on a new stage of development.

The great contribution of the individual theorists has been in terms of methods. The management approach and the structural approach have relied on "intensive" rather than "systematic" methods of data collecting. The group approach has used Likert-type questionnaires. But if we wish to seek any more sophisticated or potent techniques, then we must go to the individual theorists. If we wish to have tests of demonstrated reliability, or attitude questionnaires which have more than face validity; if we wish to use activity sampling or the critical incident technique—for all of these we must go to the individual theorists. Their overwhelming limitation is that almost without exception, they have defined their work in terms of management problems not psychological ones, and this has turned them from scientists into applied scientists or technologists. (This is also true to a considerable, but much less, extent of the group theorists.) It is no criticism to be an applied scientist if there is some science to apply. But applied psychology is a contradiction in terms because there is yet no coherent body of acceptable theory and data which can be drawn upon and applied once we get beyond the level of learning of perceptual and motor skills in ergonomics. There are some empirical techniques (e.g., intelligence testing, selection procedures), but no corpus of theory.

The choice of management problems for study rather than scientific ones imposes a considerable limitation. The whole of the work on industrial selection, for example, has contributed little more to the understanding of human behavior than a series of (usually modest) validity coefficients. This does not detract from the individual theorists' achievement in being the only ones who have tackled the problem of validity of data at all. But their concentration on the factorial-statistical approach to the almost complete exclusion of processual-clinical studies has buttressed the theoretical aridity of their formulation, although Fleishman's (1953) study of the International Harvester Company's supervisory training scheme is a notable exception. Such other processual studies of the effects of selection and training have drawn on the group and structural approaches (Sykes, 1962; Wilson, 1959).

The one example there has been of the wholesale application of a body of psychological theory—that of psychoanalysis—has not been very encouraging. Consideration is given only to the effects of the individual's personality structure and mechanisms on his behavior. These are assumed to be all-pervading and no systematic account is given of the effects of the organization and his role in it. Since the development of psychoanalysis relies so much on clinical insights obtained when the people concerned are not in their normal roles (i.e., they are patients, clients, interviewees; not managers, teachers, clerks), it is the subjective aspects of reality which receive major emphasis. Reality is out there, pressing, often hostile, but basically unstructured, so that it is an individual's personality dynamics which cause him to carve out for himself his role in life. A man's projection of his relationship to his father assumes more importance than the actual behavior of his boss (Cohen & Cohen, 1954; Holt & Salverson, 1960).

There has been one recent study in Britain, by Rogers (1963), in this tradition. He studied firms in the domestic appliance market and related their success to a psychoanalytic discussion of the motivation of their sales executives. He maintained that the successful executives had more dominant mothers and thus were able to identify better with the housewife to whom they were trying to sell their products. Unfortunately, his thesis was maintained by reference to a small number of case studies of individuals, which are notoriously unreliable. We are nowhere near the stage where we can apply established theories. A discussion of the motivation to undertake a sales rather than manufacturing career which goes into great detail about the subject's identification with his mother but says nothing about his mechanical intelligence or level of technical ability leaves much to be desired. A much wider range of psychological variables than Rogers took account of must be considered. As was suggested at the beginning of this paper, the study of the individual in the organization is just as much a theoretical adventure and has potentially just as much to con-

tribute to the development of psychology as any other part of the discipline. But this will only happen if the individual theorists widen their sights and choose the problems that they wish to study in terms of the development of the discipline.

There has already been one monumental effort in this direction—March and Simon's (1958) book, *Organizations*. The title may be a bit misleading for those who do not think of organization theory as a unified discipline, since March and Simon are very much in the individual theorist's approach. They viewed an organization as a system of decision-making individuals, and they were concerned with discovering the factors which affect the individual in making his decisions. They were insistent that it is the individual organism which mediates decision making and behavior (in contrast to the group theorists), and their variables were put in subjective terms: "the perceived consequence of evoked alternatives," "the expected value of reward," "the visibility of the organization." These are the "plans" of Miller, Galanter, and Pribram (1960); the "personal constructs" of Kelly (1955): and the March and Simon book is just as important to the present development of theoretical psychology as those two.

TECHNOLOGY THEORISTS

The techniques involved in achieving the goals of an organization, and, in industry, particularly the technology of manufacture, have generally been regarded as an important factor in organizational functioning. But there are some theorists who give it considerably greater emphasis than this, regarding it as the preemptive determinant of structure, functioning, and behavior. This approach is very much more heterogeneous than the others that have been considered, since its protagonists range from production engineers to political scientists and there are few signs that the members are aware of each others' work. Each of them has many affinities with one or other of the previous approaches, but they can be usefully classified together because their general impact on organization theory has been to underline the causal importance of technology.

At the societal level, it is the process of industrialization. This is considered by some political scientists and economic sociologists (Hoselitz, 1952) to be *the* major contemporary phenomenon. The modern world is divided into countries which are industrial and those in the process of becoming so: everything else is overshadowed by this distinction. The Soviet revolution was an instrument for industrializing Russia in one generation instead of five, and revolution is presumably serving the same purpose in China today. But when industrialization has been achieved, Communist industrial man, as he serves and is served by the same technology of manufacture, is no different from his Western capitalist counterpart.

This is an extremely global theory which is the subject of considerable dispute (Halmos, 1964). Such psychological evidence as there is (c.g., Harbison & Myers, 1960) suggests that it is a considerable over-simplification. Organizational functioning appears to be as much a product of cultural tradition as of technological level. Attitudes of managers in a highly industrialized Catholic country such as France appear to have more in common with those in a relatively poorly industrialized Catholic country like Spain than with their counterparts in the equally industrialized, but Protestant, Sweden (Haire, Ghiselli, & Porter, 1963).

At the other extreme of the individual and physiological levels, there is the whole of the tradition which has developed from the work of F. W. Taylor: time-study, work-study, industrial engineering, and ergonomics. Taylor was a production engineer who functioned in the early years of the century when mass production techniques with their consequent

need for the specification and control of the process and the product were just coming to the fore. The technology also required specification and control of the human operator as well as the machine, and Taylor (1911) devised methods to achieve this. His ideas led to bitter controversy at the time over the alleged inhumanity of his system which was said to reduce men to the level of machines, and his activities and those of his successors have remained a subject for argument. His importance for organization theory, as distinct from management techniques, is that from him has flowed the demonstration that given the right selection and training, and a suitable incentive scheme, it certainly is possible for men's working behavior to be narrowly restricted and specialized, as determined by the demands of the machine and technology. Not completely, of course; there are strikes, there is "restriction of output," there are "fiddles" on the bonus scheme. But these are relatively minor compared with the basic determinism which allowed the mass-production revolution to happen and to bring with it the consumer society. When Taylor's latest successor, the modern ergonomist, talks about man-machine systems he can do so in the knowledge that the control of the man by the machine is merely the reciprocal of the control of the machine by the man.

This is the problem of specialization at the individual level. The continual narrowing down and deskilling of man's job—the transfer of intelligence from the shop floor, as an early advocate, Elbourne (1934), called it—has been regarded as the cause of much of the malaise in modern industry and indeed in modern society (Argyris, 1960; Friedman, 1955). The advocates of "job enlargement" (Walker & Guest, 1952) are saying that the human costs of tailoring jobs completely to the demands of the machine are too high a price to pay.

At the structural level, the work of Woodward (1958, 1965) has had the most impact. As a result of a survey of manufacturing firms, she developed a scale of the technical complexity of the production systems used, running from unit production through batch and mass to process production, and found systematic relationships between a firm's technology and its pattern of organization. This led her to criticize the management theorists very strongly. Their "principles of management" have no general validity, she maintained. Even as intuitive rules of thumb, they have relevance mainly for mass-production firms: unit production firms and process firms have quite different organization structures.

By far the most sophisticated use of the concept of technology has been at the group level in the work of Trist and his colleagues at the Tavistock Institute (Trist & Bamforth, 1951; Trist, Higgin, Murray, & Pollock, 1963). From a study of the changeover from the shortwall to the longwall method of coal mining (which may be thought of roughly as being the change from the "individual craftsman" miner to the "mass-production operator" miner), Trist developed the conception of the working group as being neither a social system (as viewed by the group theorists) nor a technical system (as viewed by the engineers) but an interdependent "socio-technical" system. From this point of view, it makes as little sense to regard social relationships at work as being determined by the technology as it does to regard the manner in which a job is performed as being determined by the social psychological characteristics of the workers. The social and technical requirements are mutually interactive.

The Tavistock work has also been the most consistent in applying the systems approach in organization theory. The organization and the group have come to be regarded in the light of the cybernetic concept of an "open system" (von Bertalanffy, 1950). The systems are regarded as having inputs (resources such as raw materials, people, information), on which they operate a conversion process to produce outputs (such as products, services). Both the inputs and the outputs must take account of the environmental opportunities and demands (Rice, 1963; Emery & Trist, 1965). The systems theory approach has great potential for organization theory, particularly with its emphasis that the organization is a self-maintaining "organism" rather than a "mechanism" which can be designed and redesigned to achieve given ends. But it is the "political" impact (using the term as defined at the beginning of this paper) which is most impressive. Any concept which can be used by mathematicians (Weiner, 1948), biologists (Ashby, 1954), physiologists (Walter, 1953), engineers (Tustin, 1953), economists (Boulding, 1956), experimental psychologists (George, 1956), social psychologists (Herbst, 1954), sociologists (Etzioni, 1960), managers (Vickers, 1957), and operational researchers (Beer, 1959), to give only one example of each, must command respect by that very fact. Saying this still allows us to keep an open mind on the wisdom of attempting to develop a general systems theory to encompass all knowledge or the usefulness of writing on the "comparative physiology of the enterprise" (Lombard, 1960).

One limitation of the technology theorists is that the concept has been systematically applied only in respect of manufacturing and extractive industry. Technology in its widest sense of techniques to achieve the purposes of the organization is clearly applicable to a much wider range. Work is beginning to extend the concept as in Thompson and Bates (1957) who compared a mine, a manufacturing plant, a hospital, and a university. But technology must be treated as one of a number of causative variables, and the main limitation of the technology theorists is their comparative devaluation of other factors. With the acceptance of multiple causation and the availability of multivariate analysis, this is a considerable lack. Even the nondeterministic approach of the Tavistock group is still highly biased in this respect. In the long run, we shall come to regard the attempt to interpret all organization functioning and behavior in relation to the technology of the means of production in the same light as we now regard the Marxist attempt to relate it all to the ownership of the means of production.

ECONOMIC THEORISTS

The traditional economic theory of the firm (Marshall, 1890) assumed that the firm was an entrepreneur operating to maximize profits in a perfectly competitive market. This "personalization" of the firm meant that problems of internal organization did not arise, and the focus was on the market viewed in terms of marginal analysis. This emphasis remained when the theory was made more complex to cover imperfect competition (Robinson, 1934) although, as Boulding (1960) has pointed out, in the imperfect situation the way in which information is obtained and processed for decision making becomes crucial. The behavior of the firm itself is now regarded as an active participator in economic decisions, rather than as a passive resultant of market forces; and this change of focus has led economists to study the problems of decision making under conditions of uncertainty.

The development of econometrics, linear programming, and game theory are formal attempts of economists to tackle this problem in mathematical terms. Their interest in organization theory also comes from its attempt to deal with psychological and sociological factors affecting decision making, and has led to the "behavioral theory of the firm" (Cyert & March, 1963), and the theory of "managerial capitalism" (Marris, 1964). The more specifically structural aspects have been discussed by Leibenstein (1960).

The interest of economists in organization theory is a very fruitful source of development. The main traffic at the moment is from social science to economics—Cyert and March, for example, may be regarded as, roughly, applied March and Simon. To an empirically oriented science like organization theory, the development of formal models derived from simulation has less impact than empirical studies of actual decisions being taken; economics has always been light on data at this level of empiricism. But this situation can be expected to change and the potential contribution of economics to organization theory is considerable. The facts that all organizations operate in an economic environment and the success or failure of many is judged on economic terms mean that the study of the context and the performance of organizations must rely primarily on economic concepts. The intriguing analysis by Goode (1960) of the phenomenon of role conflict in organizations in terms of marginal utility theory illustrates what potential there is for cross-fertilization of ideas.

CONCLUSIONS

What lessons can be drawn for organization theory from this brief survey? There are two important ones. Organization theory must be left free to find its own problems and develop its own formulations (a) unrestricted by the need to choose managerial problems for study rather than scientific ones and (b) unfettered by artificial boundaries between established disciplines.

The need to develop by choosing scientific problems for study is basic to the establishment of any discipline. Management problems always give interesting pointers and often insightly analytic concepts for hypotheses. But these have to be tested out in systematically designed investigations if we are to carry forward the scientific process of developing new theories to cover the known facts and discovering new facts to upset the known theories. Science is essentially a theoretical venture, and in the face of outside demands a scientist should never forget that he is wedded to Lewin's dictum: "There is nothing so practical as a good theory." A continual diet of management oriented problems (selection, morale, restriction of output, resistance to change, overcentralization, productivity, etc.) with their almost inevitably *ex post facto* design, at best distorts, and at worst frustrates, development.

For example, the translation of the management problem of "restriction of output" into psychological terms, as "social factors affecting motivation [Hickson, 1961]," or into sociological terms, as "the development of norms in a social system [Lupton, 1963]," is not simply an unnecessary change of jargon. It is a way of bringing to bear a whole new range of variables on a much wider topic. Lupton found in a comparative study that restrictive norms prevailed in a large factory employing mainly men, whereas no restrictions were found in a small factory employing mainly women. In an effort to tease out these and other relevant factors, he then directed a study of the production norms of a large factory employing mainly women. This is the only study known to the present author, in the whole history of the investigation of this phenomenon from the Hawthorne Bank Wiring Observation Room onwards, where the investigators did not happen to come across worker restriction of output and then try to explain it *ex post facto*, but where they chose the site and the group of subjects to be studied in the light of the need to test out their own hypotheses. This is an infinitely more efficient way of developing a valid body of knowledge, and now at least we do know that size of firm is as relevant a factor as sex of operative, since girls in this large factory developed restrictive

norms although not to the same extent as the men (Lupton & Cunnison, 1965).[1]

The need to develop by abolishing artificial boundaries between disciplines is vital. We have already seen how managers provide many useful insights which have to be operationalized and tested out by social scientists. One of the most common views held by practicing managers is that the structure of an organization is a reflection of the personality of its chief executive. The author knows of no evidence bearing on this hypothesis because it cannot be tackled in terms of the separate disciplines of psychology and sociology.

The sociologist, with his conceptual limitation against accepting that an individual can more than marginally affect an organization, tends to regard the hypothesis as naïve; while the psychologist's conceptual limitations make him regard the notion of organization structure with suspicion as being unreal since it cannot be reduced to behavior. But to anyone who has not had the benefit of a specifically sociological or specifically psychological training, it seems an eminently reasonable hypothesis and well worth further study. But this can only be done by people who are equally at home in the structural and individual traditions and who are therefore prepared to develop a balanced model of the relationship between the two. Argyris (1957) and Bennis (1959) are two writers who attempted this, but there are not many as yet. An essay of the present author's on T-group training (Pugh, 1965) may be cited as an attempt to examine a topic in organization theory from a consciously interdisciplinary point of view.

Many other examples can be given of how fruitful development depends upon an interdisciplinary approach. The work of Likert (1961) on the effectiveness of employee-

[1]T. Lupton and S. Cunnison, personal communication, 1965.

centered leadership contrasts strongly with the work of Fiedler (1960), who has evidence to show that the effective leader needs to be "psychologically distant" from his subordinates. That is, he must be able and prepared to evaluate his subordinates, rejecting some as being less efficient than others rather than playing down the differences between the best and the worst because "we are all members of a team together." Within a psychological frame of reference, there does not seem to be a way in which these contradictory findings can be reconciled. It was Daniel (1965) who noted that Fiedler's groups tended to be in fairly well-structured tasks—bomber and tank crews; open hearth steel gangs, baseball teams—whereas Likert, running a consultancy organization, tends to be called in to study organizations under conditions of change and stress. Daniel suggested that if we combine the study of leadership style with organization structure we might find that employee-centeredness is linked with success in organismic organizations (Burns, 1963), whereas psychological distance is linked with success in mechanistic ones. He thus opened out a fruitful line of, inevitably interdisciplinary, study.

The contribution of the individual theorists in terms of methods cannot be over-estimated. Role theory, which at one time was hailed as a basic interlocking explanatory concept for all the social sciences, has in fact proved to be relatively sterile as a heuristic device (Levinson, 1959). This has to a large extent been due to its holistic use. The term has been used in a blanket way and not enough attention has been given to separating expectations from behavior and legitimate from illegitimate expectations; consensus on role definition has been assumed among groups and even in society-at-large and thus not subjected to verification. In the past few years, this picture has been completely altered by the appearance of two major studies which have applied the methods of the individual theorists to this field (Gross, Mason, & McEachern, 1958; Kahn, Wolfe, Quinn, Snoek, & Rosenthal, 1964). The concepts involved have been operationally defined and not just described, the information has been collected systematically and reliably and not just impressionistically, the data have been subjected to statistical analysis and not just discussed, and so on. As a result, role theory has again become one of the growing points of social science, and, particularly in organization theory, its explanatory power at all three levels of organization, group, and individual, is beginning to be explored.

Organization theory itself is a growth point at the present time in the social sciences. In particular, the attempt to draw from all the approaches here mentioned, and interrelate them, is proving to have considerable potential. Attempts are being made to generalize and develop the study of work organization into a consideration of the interdependence of three conceptually distinct levels of analysis of behavior in organizations: (*a*) organizational structure and functioning, (*b*) group composition and interaction, and (*c*) individual personality and behavior. It thus becomes possible to study a particular level of analysis, say group composition and interaction, systematically in relation to particular organizational structures, not, as so often in the past, in neglect of them (Argyris, 1964; Kahn et al., 1964; Pugh, Hickson, Hinings, MacDonald, Turner, & Lupton, 1963).

Kahn et al. (1964) concluded their important study with the view that

knowledge can best be advanced by research which attempts to deal simultaneously with data at different levels of abstraction—individual, group, and organization. This is a difficult task, and the outcome is not uniformly satisfactory. It is, nevertheless, a core requirement for understanding human organizations. Organizations are reducible to individual human acts; yet they are lawful and in part understandable only at the level of collective behaviour. This duality of level, which is the essence of human organization as it is of social psychology, we have attempted to recognise in our theoretical model and in our research design. Our hope is that the effort and its product may contribute to the understanding of organized human behaviour. We know of no more urgent problem [pp. 397–398].

Organization theorists can only concur, grateful in the knowledge that the *Zeitgeist* is with us.

REFERENCES

Argyris, C. *Personality and organization.* New York: Harper, 1957.

Argyris, C. *Understanding organizational behaviour.* London: Tavistock, 1960.

Argyris, C. *Integrating the individual and the organization.* New York: Wiley, 1964.

Ashby, W. R. *Design for a brain.* London: Chapman & Hall, 1954.

Bass, B. M. *Organizational psychology.* Boston: Allyn & Bacon, 1965.

Beer, S. *Cybernetics and management.* London: English Universities Press, 1959.

Bennis, W. G. Leadership theory and administrative behavior: The problem of authority. *Administrative Science Quarterly*, 1959, **4**, 259–301.

Boulding, K. E. General systems theory—A skeleton of a science. *Management Science*, 1956, **2**, 197–208.

Boulding, K. E. The present position of the theory of the firm. In K. E. Boulding & W. A. Spivey, *Linear programming and the theory of the firm.* New York: Macmillan, 1960. Pp. 1–17.

Brayfield, A. H., & Crockett, W. H. Employee attitudes and employee performance. *Psychological Bulletin*, 1955, **52**, 396–424.

Brown, W. *Exploration in management.* London: Heinemann, 1960.

Burnham, J. *The managerial revolution.* New York: Day, 1941.

Burns, T. Industry in a new age. *New Society*, 1963, No. 18, 17–20.

Burns, T., & Stalker, G. M. *The management of innovation.* London: Tavistock, 1961.

Cartwright, D. Toward a social psychology of groups. Address to the Annual Meeting of the Society for the Psychological Study of Social Issues, 1953. Quoted in R. L. Kahn & E. Boulding (Eds.), *Power and conflict in organizations.* London: Tavistock, 1964.

Cartwright, D., & Zander, A. *Group dynamics.* Evanston: Row, Peterson, 1953.

Coch, L., & French, J. P. R., Jr. Overcoming resistance to change. *Human Relations*, 1948, **1**, 512–532.

Cohen, M., & Cohen, R. A. Personality as a factor in administrative decisions. *Psychiatry*, 1954, **14**, 47–53.

Cyert, R., & March, J. G. *A behavioural theory of the firm.* London: Prentice-Hall, 1963.

Dahl, R. A. Business and politics: A critical appraisal of political science. In R. A. Dahl, M. Haire, & P. F. Lazarsfeld, *Social science research on business: Product and potential.* New York: Columbia University Press, 1959. Pp. 3–44.

Daniel, W. W. How close should a manager be? *New Society*, 1965, No. 158, 6–9.

Drucker, P. F. *The practice of management.* London: Heinemann, 1955.

Dubin, R. Decision-making by management in industrial relations. *American Journal of Sociology*, 1949, **54**, 292–297.

Elbourne, E. *Fundamentals of industrial administration.* London: Macdonald & Evans, 1934.

Emery, F. E., & Trist, E. L. The causal texture of organizational environments. *Human Relations*, 1965, **18**, 21–32.

Etzioni, A. Two approaches to organizational analysis: A critique and a suggestion. *Administrative Science Quarterly*, 1960, **5**, 257–278.

Fayol, H. *General and industrial management.* London: Pitman, 1949.

Fiedler, F. E. The leader's psychological distance and group effectiveness. In D. Cartwright & A. Zander (Eds.), *Group dynamics.* (2nd ed.) Evanston: Row, Peterson, 1960. Pp. 586–606.

Fleishman, E. A. Leadership climate, human relations training, and supervisory behavior. *Personnel Psychology*, 1953, **6**, 205–222.

French, J. R. P., Jr. A formal theory of social power. *Psychological Review*, 1956, **63**, 181–194.

Friedmann, G. *Industrial society: The emergence of human problems of automation.* Glencoe: Free Press, 1955.

George, F. H. Logical networks and behavior. *Bulletin of Mathematical Biophysics*, 1956, **18**, 337–348.

Goldstein, J. *The government of British trade unions.* London: Allen & Unwin, 1952.

Goode, W. J. A theory of role strain. *American Sociological Review*, 1960, **25**, 483–496.

Gouldner, A. W. *Patterns of industrial bureaucracy.* London: Routledge & Kegan Paul, 1955.

Gross, N., Mason, W. S., & McEachern, A. W. *Explorations in role analysis.* New York: Wiley, 1958.

Haire, M., Ghiselli, E. E., & Porter, L. W. Cultural patterns in the role of the manager. *Industrial Relations*, 1963, **2**, 95–117.

Halmos, P. (Ed.) *The development of industrial societies.* (The Sociological Review Monograph No. 8) Keele: University of Keele Press, 1964.

Harbison, F., & Myers, C. *Management in the industrial world.* New York: McGraw-Hill, 1960.

Hebb, D. O. *The organization of behavior.* New York: Wiley, 1949.

Herbst, P. G. The analysis of social flow systems. *Human Relations*, 1954, **1**, 327–353.

Heron, A. Satisfaction and satisfactoriness: Complementary aspects of occupational adjustment. *Occupational Psychology*, 1954, **28**, 140–153.

Herzberg, F., Mausner, B., & Snyderman, B. *The motivation to work.* (2nd ed.) New York: Wiley, 1959.

Hickson, D. J. Motivation of work people who restrict their output. *Occupational Psychology*, 1961, **35**, 111–121.

Holt, H., & Salverson, M. E. Psychoanalytic processes in management. In C. W. Churchman & M. Verhulst (Eds.), *Management sciences: Models and techniques.* Vol. 2. Oxford: Pergamon Press, 1960. Pp. 45–66.

Holmans, G. *The human group.* London: Routledge & Kegan Paul, 1951.

Hoselitz, B. F. (Ed.) *The progress of underdeveloped areas.* Chicago: University of Chicago Press, 1952.

Jaques, E. *The changing culture of a factory.* London: Tavistock, 1951.

Kahn, R. L. Productivity and job satisfaction. *Personnel Psychology*, 1960, **13**, 275–287.

Kahn, R. L. Field studies of power in organizations. In R. L. Kahn & E. Boulding, *Power and conflict in organizations.* London: Tavistock, 1964. Pp. 52–66.

Kahn, R. L., Wolfe, D., Quinn, R., Snoek, J. D., & Rosenthal, R. A. *Organizational stress.* New York: Wiley, 1964.

Kelly, G. A. *The psychology of personal constructs.* New York: Norton, 1955.

Kerr, C., & Fisher, L. H. Plant sociology: The elite and the aborigines. In M. Komarovsky (Ed.), *Common frontiers of the social sciences.* Glencoe: Free Press, 1957. Pp. 281–309.

Komarovsky, M. (Ed.) *Common frontiers of the social sciences.* Glencoe: Free Press, 1957.

Kuhn, H. W. The Hungarian method for the assignment problem. *Naval Research Logistics Quarterly*, 1955, **1**, 83–97.

Landsberger, H. A. *Hawthorne revisited.* New York: Cornell University Press, 1958.

Leibenstein, H. *Economic theory and organizational analysis.* New York: Harper, 1960.

Levinson, D. J. Role, personality and the social structure in the organizational setting. *Journal of Abnormal and Social Psychology*, 1959, **58**, 170–181.

Lewin, K. Forces behind food habits and methods of change. *Bulletin of the National Research Council*, 1943, **108**, 35–65.

Lewin, K., Lippit, R., & White, R. K. Patterns of aggressive behavior in experimentally created "social climates." *Journal of Social Psychology*, 1939, **10**, 271–299.

Likert, R. *New patterns of management.* New York: McGraw-Hill, 1961.

Lombard, R. *La Physiologie Comparee de L'Entreprise.* Paris: Editions d'Organization, 1960.

Lupton, T. *On the shop floor.* Oxford: Pergamon Press, 1963.

March, J. G., & Simon, H. A. *Organizations.* New York: Wiley, 1958.

Marris, R. *The economic theory of "managerial" capitalism.* London: Macmillan, 1964.

Marshall, A. *Principles of economics.* London: Macmillan, 1890. (8th ed. 1920, reprinted 1947)

Mayo, E. *The human problems of industrial civilization.* New York: Macmillan, 1933.

Meehl, P. E. *Clinical versus statistical prediction.* Minneapolis: University of Minnesota Press, 1954.

Merton, R. K. Bureaucratic structure and personality. *Social Forces*, 1940, **18**, 560–568.

Miller, G. A., Galanter, E., & Pribram, K. H. *Plans and the structure of behavior.* New York: Holt, 1960.

Porter, L. W., & Henry, M. M. Job attitudes in management: Perceptions of the input of certain personality traits as a function of job level. *Journal of applied Psychology*, 1964, **48**, 31–36.

Porter, L. W., & Lawler, E. E. The effects of "tall" versus "flat" organization structures on managerial job satisfaction. *Personnel Psychology*, 1964, **17**, 135–148.

Porter, L. W., & Lawler, E. E. Properties of organization structure in relation to job attitudes and job behavior. *Psychological Bulletin*, 1965, **64**, 23–51.

Pugh, D. S. T-group training from the point of view of organization theory. In G. Whitaker (Ed.), *T-group training: Group dynamics in management education.* (A.T.M. Occasional Paper No. 2) Oxford: Blackwell, 1965. Pp. 44–50.

Pugh, D. S., Hickson, D. J., & Hinings, C. R. *Writers on organizations.* London: Hutchinson, 1964.

Pugh, D. S., Hickson, D. J. Hinings, C. R., MacDonald, K. M., Turner, C., & Lupton, T. A conceptual scheme for organizational analysis. *Administrative Science Quarterly*, 1963, **6**, 289–315.

Rice, A. K. *The enterpise and its environment.* London: Tavistock, 1963.

Robinson, J. *The economics of imperfect competition.* London: Macmillan, 1934.

Roethlisberger, F. J., & Dickson, W. J. *Management and the worker.* Massachusetts: Harvard University Press, 1939.

Rodger, A. Industrial psychology. In, *Chambers Encyclopaedia.* Vol. 7. London: Newnes, 1950. Pp. 542–548.

Rogers, K. *Managers—Personality and performance.* London: Tavistock, 1963.

Rolfe, J. M., & Corkindale, K. G. The influence of the excluded variable. *Bulletin of the British Psychological Society*, 1964, **17**, 31–38.

Schein, E. H. *Organizational psychology.* Englewood Cliffs, N. J.: Prentice-Hall, 1965.

Selznick, P. *TVA and the grass roots.* Berkeley: University of California Press, 1949.

Shils, E. A. Primary groups in the American army. In R. K. Merton & P. F. Lazarsfeld (Eds.), *Continuities in social research.* Glencoe: Free Press, 1950. Pp. 16–39.

Simon, H. A. *Administrative behavior.* (2nd ed.) New York: Macmillan, 1957.

Smith, M. B. Anthropology and psychology. In J. Gillin (Ed.), *For a science of social man.* New York: Macmillan, 1954. Pp. 19–23.

Sykes, A. J. M. The effect of a supervisory training course in changing supervisor's perceptions and expectations of the role of management. *Human Relations*, 1962, **15**, 227–243.

Tannenbaum, A. S. Control in organizations: Individual adjustment and organizational performance. *Administrative Science Quarterly*, 1962, **7**, 236–257.

Tannenbaum, A. S., & Smith, C. G. Effects of member influence in an organization: Phenomenology versus organization structure. *Journal of Abnormal and Social Psychology*, 1964, **69**, 401–410.

Taylor, F. W. *Principles of scientific management.* New York: Harper, 1911. (Reprinted: In F. W. Taylor, *Scientific management.* New York: Harper, 1947. Pp. 5–143.)

Thompson, J. D., & Bates, F. L. Technology, organization and administration. *Administrative Science Quarterly*, 1957, **2**, 325–343.

Trist, E. L., & Bamforth, D. W. Some social and psychological consequences of the longwall method of coal-getting. *Human Relations*, 1951, **4**, 3–38.

Trist, E. L., Higgin, G. W., Murray, H., & Pollock, A. B. *Organization choice.* London: Tavistock, 1963.

Tustin, A. *The mechanism of economic systems.* London: Heinemann, 1953.

Vickers, Sir G. Control, Stability and choice. *General Systems*, 1957, **2**, 1–8.

von Bertanlanffy, L. The theory of open systems in physics and biology. *Science*, 1950, **111**, 23–29.

Walker, C. R., & Guest, R. *The man on the assembly line.* Cambridge, Mass.: Harvard University Press, 1952.

Walter, W. G. *The living brain.* London: Duckworth, 1953.

Weber, M. *The theory of social and economic organization.* Glencoe: Free Press, 1947.

Weiner, N. *Cybernetics.* New York: Wiley, 1948.

Whyte, W. F. *Human relations in the restaurant industry.* New York: McGraw-Hill, 1948.

Whyte, W. H. *The organization man.* New York: Simon & Schuster, 1956.

Wilson, S. A sociological case-study of operator training. *Occupational Psychology*, 1959, **3**, 166–173, 244–254.

Woodward, J. *Management and technology.* London: Her Majesty's Stationery Office, 1958.

Woodward, J. *Industrial organization: Theory and practice.* Oxford: Oxford University Press, 1965.

Wrong, D. The oversocialized conception of man in modern sociology. *American Sociological Review*, 1961, **26**, 183–193.

Reading 7

A Diagnostic Model for Organizational Behavior

David A. Nadler
Michael L. Tushman

Managers perform their jobs within complex social systems called "organizations." In many senses, the task of the manager is to influence behavior in a desired direction, usually toward the accomplishment of a specific task or performance goal. Given this definition of the managerial role, skills in the diagnosis of patterns of organizational behavior become vital. Specifically, the manager needs to be able to *understand* the patterns of behavior that are observed, to *predict* in what direction behavior will move (particularly in the light of managerial action), and to use this knowledge to *control* behavior over the course of time.

The understanding, prediction, and control of behavior by managers occurs, of course, in organizations every day. The problem with managerial control of behavior as frequently practiced is that the understanding-prediction-control sequence is based on the intuition of the individual manager. This intuitive approach is usually based on models of behavior or organization which the manager carries around in his or her head—models that are often naïve and simplistic. One of the aims of this paper will be to develop a model of organizations, based on behavioral science research, that is both systematic and useful.

The model to be discussed will serve two ends. It will provide a way of systematically thinking about behavior in organizations as well as provide a framework within which the results of research on organizational behavior can be expressed.

Effective managerial action requires that the manager be able to diagnose the system in which he or she is working. Since all elements of social behavior cannot be dealt with at once, the manager facing this "blooming, buzzing" confusion must simplify reality—that is, develop a model of organizational functioning. The diagnostic model will present one way of simplifying social reality that still retains the dynamic nature of organizations. The model will focus on a set of key organizational components (or variables) and their relationships as the primary determinants of behavior. The diagnosis of these key components will provide a concise snapshot of the organization. However, organizations do not stand still. The diagnostic model will preserve the changing nature of organizations by evaluating the effects of feedback on the nature of the key components and their relationships.

While the diagnostic model is a potentially powerful managerial tool, it must be seen as a developing tool. Parts of the model are less well developed than others (e.g., the informal organization). As research in organizational behavior advances, so should the development of this diagnostic model. Finally, no claim is made that this diagnostic model is the most effective way of organizing reality. It is suggested, however, that models of organizational behavior are important and that they ought to (a) deal with several variables and their relationships, and (b) take into account the dynamic nature of organizations.

In conclusion, the premise of this paper is that effective management requires that the manager be able to systematically diagnose, predict, and control behavior. The purpose of this paper is to present a research-based (as opposed to intuitive) model of oganizational behavior which can be used to diagnose organizations as well as integrate behavioral science research results. The model should therefore be of use to practitioners in organizations, as well as to students in the classroom.

BASIC ASSUMPTIONS OF THE MODEL

The diagnostic model which will be discussed here is based on a number of assumptions about organizational life. These assumptions are as follows:

Organizations Are Dynamic Entities Organizations exist over time and space, and the activities which make up organizations are dynamic. There are many definitions of organizations like Schein's statement (1970) that

> an organization is the rational coordination of the activities of a number of people for the achievement of some common explicit purpose or goal, through division of labor and function, and through a hierarchy of authority and responsibility.

While definitions like this are adequate to define what an organization is, they are static in nature and do not enable one to grasp how the different components of organization interact with each other over time. An adequate model of organizations must reflect the dynamic nature of organizational behavior.

Organizational Behavior Exists at Multiple Levels There are different levels of abstraction at which organizational behavior can be examined. Specifically, behavior occurs at the *individual*, the *group*, and the *organizational systems* levels. Behavior that is attributable to each of these levels can be identified and isolated (that is, one can see the behavior of individuals as different than the behavior of groups or of organizations themselves). At the same time, these three levels interact with each other, behavior at the organizational level being affected by the behavior of individuals, behavior at the group level being affected by phenomena at the organizational level, etc.

Organizational Behavior Does Not Occur in a Vacuum Organizations are made up of both social and technical components and thus have been characterized as sociotechnical systems (Emery & Trist, 1960). The implication of this is that any approach to looking at behavior must also take into account the technical components of the organization—such issues as the nature of the task, and the technology. Since the organization is dependent on inputs, knowledge, and feedback from the environment, our model must also take into account the constraints of the organization's task environment (e.g., to what extent is the market changing).

Organizations Have the Characteristics of Open Social Systems Organizations have the characteristics of systems which are composed of interrelated components and conduct transactions with a larger environment. Systems have a number of unique behavioral characteristics and thus a model of organizational behavior must take into account the systemic nature of organizations.

OPEN-SYSTEMS THEORY

The point made above about open-systems theory is a crucial one, which needs to be explored in more depth. The basic premise is that the characteristics of systems which are seen in both the physical and social sciences (Von Bertalanffy, 1962; Buckley, 1967) are particularly valuable when looking at organizations. Social organizations, it is claimed, can be viewed as systems (Katz & Kahn, 1966) with a number of key systems characteristics.

What is a system and what are systems characteristics? In the simplest of terms, a system is a "set of interrelated elements." These elements are interdependent, so that changes in the nature of one component may lead to changes in the nature of the other components. Further, because the system is embedded within larger systems, it is dependent on the larger environment for resources, information, and feedback. Another way of looking at a system is to define it as "a mechanism that imports some form of energic input from the environment, which submits that input to some kind of transformation process, and which produces some kind of energic output back to the environment."

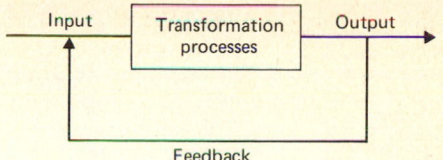

Figure 7-1 The elementary systems model.

(Katz & Kahn, 1966.) The notion of open systems also implies the existence of some boundary differentiating the system from the larger environment in which it is embedded. These system boundaries are usually not rigid. This familiar view of a system can be seen in Figure 7-1. Closed systems, on the other hand, are not dependent on the environment and are more deterministic in nature. Closed systems tend to have more rigid boundaries, and all transactions take place within the system, guided by unitary goals and rationality. (An example approaching a closed system would be a terrarium, completely self-contained and insulated from the larger environment.)

A more extensive definition of open systems has been presented by Katz and Kahn (1966) in the form of a listing of characteristics of open social systems. An adapted list of these characteristics follows:

1 *Importation of energy* A system functions by importing energy (information, products, materials, etc.) from the larger environment.

2 *Throughput* Systems move energy through them, largely in the form of transformation processes. These are often multiple processes (i.e., decision, material manipulation, etc.)

3 *Output* Systems send energy back to the larger environment in the form of products, services, and other kinds of outcomes which may or may not be intended.

4 *Cycles of events over time* Systems function over time and thus are dynamic in nature. Events tend to occur in natural repetitive cycles of input, throughput, and output with events in sequence occurring over and over again.

5 *Equilibrium seeking* Systems tend to move toward the state where all components are in equilibrium—where a steady state exists. When changes are made which result in an imbalance, different components of the system move to restore the balance.

6 *Feedback* Systems use information about their output to regulate their input and transformation processes. These informational connections also exist between system components. Thus, changes in the functioning of one component will lead to changes in other system components (second-order effects).

7 *Increasing differentiation* As systems grow, they also tend to increase their differentiation; more components are added, more feedback loops, more transformation processes. Thus, as systems get larger, they also get more complex.

8 *Equifinality* Different system configurations may lead to the same end point, or conversely, the same end state may be reached by a variety of different processes.

9 *System survival requirements* Because of the inherent tendency of systems to "run down" or dissipate their energy, certain functions must be performed (at least at minimal levels) over time. These requirements include goal achievement and adaptation (the ability to maintain balanced successful transactions with the environment)

A SPECIFIC SYSTEMS MODEL

Open-systems theory is a general framework for conceptualizing organizational behavior over a period of time. It sensitizes the manager to a basic model of organizations (i.e., input-throughput-output-feedback) as well as to a set of basic organizational processes (e.g., equilibrium, differentiation, equifinality). While systems concepts are useful as an overall perspective, they do not help the manager systematically diagnose specific situations or help him or her apply research results to specific problems. A more concrete model

must be developed that takes into account system-theory concepts and processes and helps the manager deal with organizational reality.

According to Figure 7-1, organizations (or some other unit of interest; e.g., a department or factory) take some set of inputs, work on these inputs through some sort of transformation process, and produce output which is evaluated and responded to by the environment. While managers must attend to the environment and input considerations, they must specifically focus on what the organization does to produce output. That is, managers are intimately involved in what systems theory terms the *transformation processes*. It is the transformation processes, then, on which the model will specifically focus. Given the cycle of processes from input to feedback, the model will focus on the more specific variables and processes that affect how the organization takes a given set of inputs and produces a set of organizational outputs (e.g., productivity, innovation, satisfaction). While the diagnostic model will specifically focus on the determinants of the transformation processes and their relationships to outputs, it must be remembered that these processes are part of a more general model of organizational behavior that takes inputs, outputs, and the environment into account.

One approach to thinking about organizational behavior is to focus on the organization as a system made up of key variables or components that have relationships with each other. These components exist in states of relative balance or consistency. Leavitt (1965), for example, identifies four major components of organization as being people, tasks, technology, and structure. The model presented here builds on this view, and is based specifically on models developed and used by Seiler (1967) and by Lorsch and Sheldon (1972).

The model is based on the systems assump-

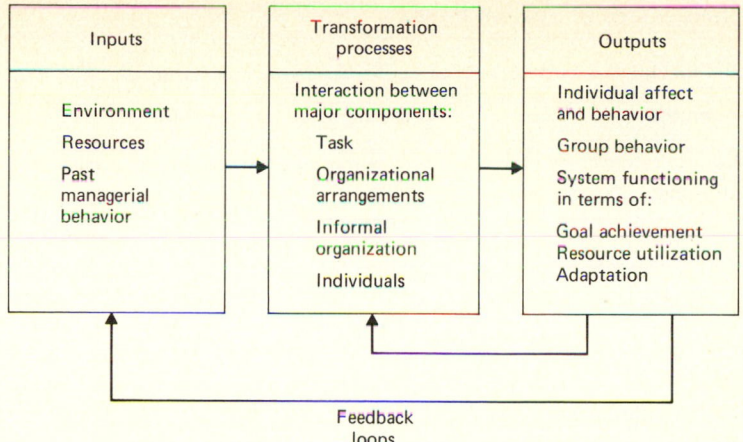

Figure 7-2 The systems model as applied to organizational behavior.

tions outlined above. The inputs to the system (see Figure 7-2) are those factors that at any one point in time are relatively fixed or given. Three major classes of inputs can be identified, including (1) the environment of the system, (2) the resources available to the system, and (3) the behavior of managers in the past, including predetermined strategies, policies, and goals.

The transformation process of the system is seen as the interaction between four major components of the organizational system: (1) the tasks of the organization, (2) the individuals in the organizational system, (3) the organizational arrangements, and (4) the informal organization.

The outputs are the results of the interactions among the components, given the inputs. Several major outputs can be identified, including individual affect and behavior, group behavior, and the effectiveness of total system functioning. Looking at the total system, particular attention is paid to the system's ability to attain its goals, to utilize available resources, and to successfully adapt over periods of time. Explicit in the model are feedback loops running from the outputs and the transformation process. The loops represent the flow of information about the nature of the

system output and the interaction of system components. The information is available for use to make modifications in the nature of systems inputs or components.

In understanding the model, it is important to understand what makes up the system inputs, components, and outputs, and how they relate to each other. In particular, it is important for the manager to understand how system components relate to each other since these relationships are particularly critical for influencing behavior.

The Nature of Inputs

Inputs are important since at any point in time they are the fixed or given factors which influence organizational behavior. The inputs provide both constraints and opportunities for managerial action. While the diagnosis of organizational behavior is focused primarily on the understanding of the interactions among system components, an understanding of the nature of the inputs is important. The major classes of inputs which constrain organizational behavior are listed in Table 7-1. A brief description of these inputs is as follows:

Environmental Inputs Organizations as open systems carry on constant transactions

Table 7-1 Dimensions of System Inputs

Environment	Resources	Past managerial behavior
External environment: Markets Government Financial institutions Competitors Suppliers Labor unions The larger culture, etc. **Internal environment:** Immediate suprasystems **Environmental characteristics:** Stability Homogeneity	Capital Raw materials Technologies People Intangibles	**Goals:** Explicit goals Implied goals of the managerial 　subsystem **Plans and policies:** Strategies **Critical decisions in the past**

with the environment. Specifically, three factors in the environment of the specific organization are important. First, there are the various groups, organizations, and events which make up the external environment. Second, the organization may be embedded within another larger, formal system. For example, a factory which is being considered may be part of a larger, multinational corporation or of a larger, corporate division, Third, both the internal and the external environment can be described according to a number of dimensions (such as stability and homogeneity) which appear to affect the functioning of organizations (Emery & Trist, 1965).

Resources   Another important input is composed of the resources available to the organization. Any organization has a range of resources available as inputs. Major categories for classifying resources would include capital resources (including liquid capital, physical plant, property, etc.), raw materials (the material on which the organization will perform the transformation process), technologies (approaches or procedures for performing the transformation), people, and various intangible resources.

Past Managerial Behavior   Finally, another given, in the short term, is the critical choices that have been made by managers in the past. Most important are those choices that relate to the distinctive competence or competitive advantage of the organization and approaches that relate to realizing the potential of the organization. These decisions form a set of precedents which set the conditions within which current organizational behavior takes place.

The above listed inputs therefore provide opportunities, provide constraints, and may even make demands upon the organization. The issue of how the organization functions to make use of these opportunities and constraints is perhaps the most central issue of managerial and organizational behavior.

The Nature of Organizational Components

Assuming a set of inputs, the transformation process occurs through the interaction of a number of basic components of organization. The major components (listed with their subdimensions in Table 7-2) are as follows:

Task Component   This component concerns the nature of the tasks or jobs which

Table 7-2 Dimensions of System Components

Task	Individuals	Organizational arrangements	Informal organization
Extent and nature of interdependence	**Demographics:** Education	**Leadership practices:** Functional behavior	**Group functioning:** Informal as distinct from formal structures
Level of complexity (required skill)	Age	Participation	Communication patterns
Certainty	Skill levels	**Microstructure:**	Norms, values
Autonomy; control	Ethnic background	Task allocation	Informal goals
Extent of feedback	Urban or rural	Reward allocation	Actual decision making
Variability	Etc.	Formal goals	
Meaningfulness		Planning systems	**Intergroup relations:**
Informational requirements	**Personality differences:**	Control and information systems	Information flow (quality)
	Strength of needs	Selection and placement systems	Conflict or cooperation
	Self-esteem		Perceptions
	Internal or external orientation	**Macrostructure:**	
	Perceptual biases	Division of labor	**Political processes and structures:**
	Etc.	Grouping of tasks and individuals	Networks, cliques, coalitions
		Anatomical dimensions of organization	
		Centralization	
		Formalization	
		Decision making	
		Integrating mechanisms	
		Physical location of areas	

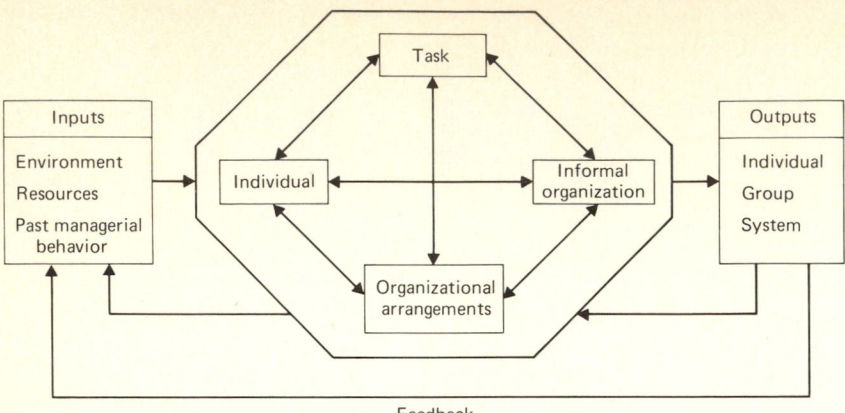

Figure 7-3   The diagnostic model.

must be performed by the organization, by groups, and by individuals. Major dimensions of tasks include the extent and nature of interdependence between task performers, the level of required skill, the degree of autonomy, the extent of feedback, the variability of the task, the potential meaningfulness of the task, and the types of information needed to adequately perform the task.

Individuals Component   This component obviously refers to the individuals who are members of the organization. The major dimensions of this component relate to the systematic differences in individuals which have relevance for organizational behavior. Such dimensions include background or demographic variables such as skill levels, levels of education, etc., and individual differences in strength of need, personality, or perceptual biases.

Organizational Arrangements   This component includes all formal mechanisms used by the organization to direct structure or control behavior. Major dimensions include leadership practices, microstructure (how specific jobs, systems, or subcomponents are structured), and macrostructure (how whole units,

departments, and organizations are structured).

Informal Organization   In addition to the formal prescribed structure which exists in the system, there also is an informal social structure which tends to emerge over time. Relevant dimensions of the informal organization include the functioning of informal group structures, the quality of intergroup relations, and the operation of various political processes throughout the organization.

Organizations therefore can be looked at as a set of components including the task, the individuals, the organizational arrangements, and the informal organization. (For the complete model see Figure 7-3). To be useful, however, the model must go beyond the simple listing and description of these components, and must describe the dynamic relationship that exists among the various components.

The Concept of Fit

Between each pair of inputs there exists a degree of consistency or inconsistency. Specifically, the fit between two components is defined as follows:

The degree to which the needs, demands, goals, objectives, and structures of one component are consistent with the needs, demands, goals, objectives, and structures of another component.

Thus, fit (indicated by the double-headed arrows in the model in Figure 7-3) is a measure of the mutual consistency between pairs of components. Because components cover a range of different types of phenomena, however, fit can be more clearly defined only by referring to specific fits between specific pairs of components. In each case, research results can be used as a guide to evaluate whether the components are in a state of high consistency or high inconsistency. An awareness of these fits is critical since inconsistent fits will be related to dysfunctional behavior.

Specific definitions of fit are presented in Table 7-3. For each of the six fits among the components, more information is provided about the specific issues which need to be examined in order to determine the level of consistency between the components. In addition, a seventh relationship—that between the organizational components and the environmental inputs—is presented along with relevant citations.

The Fit Hypothesis

Just as each pair of components has a degree of high or low consistency, so does the aggregate model display a relatively high or low total system "fit." Underlying the model is a basic hypothesis about the nature of fits and

Table 7-3   Definitions of Fits

Fit	Issues
Individual-organization	To what extent individuals' needs are met by the organizational arrangements. To what extent individuals hold clear or distorted perceptions of organizational structures. The convergence of individual and organizational goals.
Individual-task	To what extent the needs of individuals are met by the tasks. To what extent individuals have skills and abilities to meet task demands.
Individual-informal organization	To what extent individual needs are met by the informal organization. To what extent does the informal organization make use of individual resources, consistent with informal goals.
Task-organization	Whether the organizational arrangements are adequate to meet the demands of the task. Whether organizational arrangements tend to motivate behavior consistent with task demands.
Task-informal organization	Whether the informal organization structure facilitates task performance or not. Whether it hinders or promotes meeting the demands of the task.
Organization-informal organization	Whether the goals, rewards, and structures of the informal organization are consistent with those of the formal organization.
Component-environment fits	Whether the structure of the components are consistent with the demands of the environment, particularly the relationship between organizational arrangements and environment.

their relationship to behavior. This hypothesis is as follows:

> Other things being equal, the greater the total degree of consistency or fit between the various components, the more effective will be organizational behavior at multiple levels. Effective organizational behavior is defined as behavior which leads to higher levels of goal attainment, utilization of resources, and adaptation.

The implications of the fit hypothesis in this model are that the manager needs to adequately diagnose the system, determine the location and nature of inconsistent fits, and plan courses of action to change the nature of those fits without bringing about dysfunctional second-order effects. The model also implies that different configurations of the key components can lead to effective behavior (consistent with the systems characteristic of equifinality). Therefore, the question is not finding the "one best way" of managing, but of determining effective combinations of inputs that will lead to consistent fits.

This process of diagnosing fit and identifying combinations of inputs to produce consistency is not necessarily an intuitive process. A number of situations which lead to consistent fits have been defined in the research literature. Goodness of fit, therefore, is based upon theory and research rather than intuition. In most cases, the theory provides considerable guidance about what leads to consistent relationships (although in some areas the research is more abundant than in others; the research on informal organization, for example, has been sparse in recent years). The implication is that any manager, attempting to diagnose behavior, needs to become familiar with critical findings of the relevant research so that he or she can evaluate the nature of fits in a particular system.

The Nature of Outputs

The model indicates that the outputs flow out of the interaction of the various components.

Any organizational system produces a number of different outputs. For general diagnostic purposes, however, four major classes of outputs are particularly important:

Individual Behavior and Affect A crucial issue is how individuals behave, specifically with regard to their behavior as members of an organization (for example, absenteeism, lateness, turnover) and with regard to their performance of designated tasks. Individuals also have affective responses to the work environment (levels of satisfaction, for example) which are of consequence. Other individual behaviors, such as nonproductive behavior, drug usage, off-the-job activities, etc., are also (in many cases) outputs of the organization.

Group and Intergroup Behavior Beyond the behavior of individuals, the organization is also concerned with the performance of groups or departments. Important considerations would include intergroup conflict or collaboration and the quality of intergroup communication.

System Functioning At the highest level of abstraction is the question of how well the system as a whole is functioning. The key issues here include (1) how well the system is attaining its desired goals of production, output, return on investment, etc.; (2) how well the organization is utilizing available resources; and (3) how well the organization is adapting (i.e., maintaining favorable transactions with the environment over a period of time).

USING THE DIAGNOSTIC MODEL

Given the diagnostic model, the final question to be addressed here is how the model can be put to use. A number of authors have observed that the conditions facing organizations are always changing, and that managers must therefore continually engage in problem identification and problem-solving activities (e.g., Newman, Summer, & Warren, 1972; Schein, 1970). These authors suggest that managers must gather data on the performance of their organization, compare the ideal with the actual performance levels, develop and choose action plans, and then implement and evaluate these action plans. These problem-solving phases link together to form a *problem-solving process* if the evaluation phase is seen as the beginning of the next diagnostic phase. For long-term organizational viability, this problem-solving process must be continually reaccomplished (Schein, 1970; Weick, 1969). The basic phases of this problem-solving process are outlined in Figure 7-4.

How does the diagnostic model relate to this problem-solving process? The problem-solving process requires diagnosis, the generation of action plans, and the evaluation of the action plans. *Each of these steps requires a way of looking at organizations to guide the analysis.* To the extent that the diagnostic model integrates system-theory concepts and presents a specific model of organizations, then the model can be used as the core of the problem-solving process. The model can, therefore, be used as a framework to guide the diagnosis, the evaluation of alternative actions, and the evaluation and feedback of the results of a managerial action. Further, to the extent that the manager is familiar with the

research results bearing on the different fits in the model, he or she will be better able both to diagnose the situation and evaluate alternative action plans. In short, the problem-solving process—along with the research-based use of the diagnostic model—can be used as an effective managerial tool.

Given the problem-solving process and the diagnostic model, it is possible to identify and describe a number of discrete steps in the problem-solving cycle. These steps can be organized into three phases: (1) diagnosis; (2) alternative solutions–action; and (3) evaluation-feedback.

Diagnosis

This phase is premised on the idea that any managerial action must be preceded by a systematic diagnosis of the system under investigation. This phase can be broken into four distinct, but related, steps.

1. *Identify the system.* Before any detailed analysis can begin, it is important to identify the system being considered. The unit of analysis must be clearly specified (i.e., project, division, organization).

2. *Determine the nature of the key variables.* Having defined the system, the next step is to use the data in the situation (or case) to determine the nature of the inputs and the four key components. The analyst should focus on the underlying dimensions of each variable. The diagnosis should not focus on an exhaustive description of each component, but rather should focus on the dimensions which the analyst considers most important in the particular situation.

3. *Diagnose the state of fits and their relationship to behaviors (i.e., outputs).* This step is the most critical in the diagnosis phase. It really involves two related stages; (a) diagnosing fits between the components, and (b) considering the link between the fits and system output.

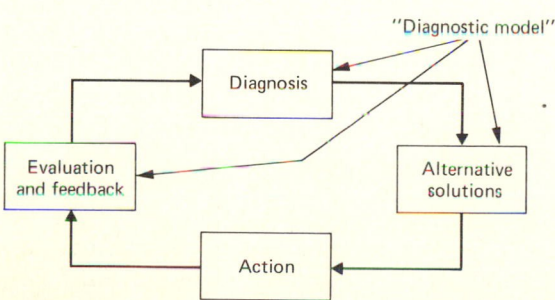

Figure 7-4 Basic phases of using the diagnostic model.

a. Using experience, observations, and relevant research knowledge, the manager must evaluate each of the fit lines in the model. The analyst must focus on the extent to which the key components are consistent (or fit) with each other.

b. Fits (or lack of fits) between the key components have consequences in terms of system behavior. This step makes the fit-to-behavior link explicit. That is, given the diagnoses of the various fits, the analyst must then relate the fits to behaviors observed in the system (e.g., conflict, performance, stress, satisfaction). This is a particularly key step since managerial action will be directed at these inconsistent fits.

4. *Identify critical system problems.* Based on the diagnosis of fits and their behavioral consequences, the final diagnostic step is to relate the set of behaviors to system outputs (goal achievement, resource utilization, and adaptation). Given these outputs, the manager must then evaluate which system behaviors require managerial attention and action.

The diagnostic phase forces the analyst to make a set of decisions. The analyst must decide the unit of analysis, make decisions as to the most salient characteristics of each of the key variables, and make decisions as to the relationships between the key components and their effects on behavior. Finally, the manager must relate the observed behaviors to system outputs and decide on the system's most pressing problems. None of the above decisions are clearcut—each involves managerial discretion. It follows that there is no one best diagnosis of any set of organizational conditions.

Alternative Solutions–Action

Diagnosis leads to a consideration of potential managerial actions. This evaluation-action phase can be separated into three stages.

5. *Generate alternative solutions.* Having identified critical problems and the relationship between fits and behavior, the next step is to generate a range of possible managerial actions. These actions or interventions will be directed at the inconsistent fits which will in turn affect the behaviors under consideration.

Action plans for a particular situation may differ. There may be different diagnoses or there may be a number of interventions or organizational arrangements leading to the same end point (following from the system characteristic of equifinality). In short, there is not likely to be one most appropriate set of managerial actions to deal with a particular set of conditions.

6. *Evaluate alternative strategies.* While there usually is not one single most appropriate managerial action to deal with a particular situation, the various alternatives can be evaluated for their relative merits. To what extent do the solutions deal with the inconsistent fits? Does one solution deal with the inconsistent fits more comprehensively? Are there dysfunctional second-order (i.e., latent) consequences of the action—for instance, will changing the task dimensions deal with an inconsistent fit between tasks and the informal organization but adversely affect the fit between tasks and the individual? In short, given the highly interdependent nature of open systems, the manager must systematically evaluate the alternative actions. On the basis of theory, research, and experience, the manager must make predictions about the possible effects of different strategies. The manager should focus on the extent to which the intervention deals with the critical system problem *as well as* with the possibilities of latent consequences of the intervention. This exercise of prediction should provide a way of evaluating the relative strengths and weaknesses of the alternative actions.

7. *Choose strategies to be implemented.* Given the explicit evaluation of the different approaches, the final step in this phase is to weigh the various advantages and disadvantages of the alternative actions and choose an action plan to be implemented.

Evaluation and Feedback

The two preceding phases leave the manager with an action plan to deal with the critical system problem(s). The final phase in using the diagnostic model deals with the implementation of the action plan and with the importance of evaluation, feedback, and adjustment of strategy to meet emergent system requirements.

8. *Implement strategies.* This step deals explicitly with issues that arise in introducing change into an ongoing system. It recognizes the need to deal with the response of organizations to change. To what extent will the intervention be accepted and implemented (as opposed to resisted and sabotaged)?

9. *Evaluate and examine.* After implementing a strategy it is important to continue the diagnostic activity and to explicitly evaluate the actual versus the ideal (or predicted) impact of the intervention on the system. Feedback concerning the organization's or the environment's response to the action can then be used to adjust the intervention to better fit the system's requirements and to deal with any unanticipated consequences of the change. In a sense then, step 9 closes the loop and starts the diagnosis-alternatives-action-evaluation cycle again (see Figure 7-4).

In conclusion, we have discussed a number of discrete, though related, steps for using the diagnostic model. The model provides a way of systematically diagnosing organizations. This diagnosis can then be used as an integral part of a problem-solving strategy for the organization. Further, the model can assist the manager in evaluating alternative solutions (i.e., what fits are dealt with) as well as evaluating the effects of the managerial actions (i.e.,

what fits were affected). Since organizations are made up of processes that must recur, the manager must continuously go through the kind of problem-solving strategy indicated in Figure 7-4. If this adaptive-coping kind of scheme is critical for organizational viability over time (see Schein, 1970), then the diagnostic model can be seen as a concrete research-based tool to facilitate the diagnosis of the system *and* to provide a base for evaluating alternative actions and the consequences of those actions.

The diagnostic model and the problem-solving cycle are ways of structuring and dealing with the complex reality of organizations. Given the indeterminate nature of social systems, there is no one best way of handling a particular situation. The model and the problem-solving cycle do, however, force the manager to make a number of decisions and to think about the consequences of those decisions. If the diagnostic model and problem-solving process have merit, then it is up to the manager to use these tools along with his or her experiences to make the appropriate set of diagnostic, evaluative, and action decisions over a period of time.

REFERENCES

Buckley, W. *Sociology and modern systems theory.* Englewood Cliffs: Prentice-Hall, 1967.

Emery, F. E., & Trist, E. L. Socio-technical systems. In *Management sciences models and techniques.* Vol. W. London: Pergamon Press, 1960.

Emery, F. E., & Trist, E. L. The causal texture of organizational environments. *Human Relations,* 1965, **18**, 21–32.

Katz, D., & Kahn, R. L. *The social psychology of organizations.* New York: Wiley, 1966.

Leavitt, H. J. Applied organizational change in industry. In J. G. March (Ed.), *Handbook of organizations.* Chicago: Rand-McNally, 1965.

Lorsch, J. W., & Sheldon, A. The individual in the organization: A systems view. In J. W. Lorsch & P. R. Lawrence (Eds.), *Managing group and intergroup relations*. Homewood, Ill.: Irwin-Dorsey, 1972.

Newman, W. H., Summer, C. E., & Warren, E. K. *The process of management* (3d ed.). Englewood Cliffs: Prentice-Hall, 1972.

Schein, E. H. *Organizational psychology*. Englewood Cliffs: Prentice-Hall, 1970.

Seiler, J. A. *Systems analysis in organizational behavior*. Homewood, Ill: Irwin-Dorsey, 1967.

Von Bertalanffy, L. *General systems theory: Foundations, development, applications* (Rev. ed.) New York: Braziller, 1968.

Weick, K. E. *The social psychology of organizing*. Reading, Mass.: Addison-Wesley, 1969.

Part Two

Development of Individual-Organization Relationships

Chapter 3

Choice Processes

The relationship between an individual and an organization begins with a process of mutual choice. The entry of an individual into an organization requires that two choices be made. The individual must choose to join the organization and the organization must choose to admit the individual. Organizations differ substantially in the permeance of their boundaries. In some organizations, entry is easily accomplished and the selection process is of no consequence. However, in most work organizations the reverse is true. The boundaries are not permeable and the choice process both from the individual's and the organization's point of view is a major decision, since it involves the commitment of considerable time and money and may constitute the beginning of a lifetime relationship.

Because most of past research has been directed toward helping organizations do a better job of choosing individuals, a great deal is known about how this decision best can be made. For example, a considerable body of knowledge exists about the effectiveness of different selection approaches, and an extensive technology is available for assessing the effectiveness of these approaches. The reading by Zedeck and Blood reviews these findings and methods. It provides a good description of just what selection instruments can and cannot be expected to accomplish, and it provides an introduction to these basic methods used to assess the validity of different selection approaches.

The area of selection has become increasingly complex and controversial in the last ten years. For example, legislation now requires that organizations use only selection approaches that are demonstrably valid. Zedeck and Blood make this point in their discussion of "unfair discrimination." There also is a rising concern about the degree to which testing constitutes an unfair invasion of privacy. Because testing and selection have become so controversial, more and more organizations are reevaluating their selection procedures. In some cases they are even deciding to stop testing because the costs and problems involved are simply too great. Unfortunately, few firms actually go to the trouble of assessing the cost effectiveness of their selection program. The Janz and Dunnette article is particularly useful in this regard. It represents one of the first attempts to systematically relate selection decision to financial outcomes, and it suggests that decisions relative to selection strategy might be made on a more rational basis.

Compared with the amount of attention that has been given to how *organizations* can make better selection decisions, relatively little has been directed toward how *individuals* can make better decisions. However, there has been some interesting recent research on entering organizations from the individual's viewpoint. This research suggests that organizations may be able to help both themselves and the individual by providing applicants with better data upon which to base their decisions about employment. It also suggests that individual choices are based upon the kind of motivation model described in Chapter 1 of this book. The article by Wanous summarizes the research conducted so far, and makes some interesting points about future research needs and about needed changes in organizational employment practices.

Reading 8

Selection and Placement

Sheldon Zedeck
Milton R. Blood

Selection involves accepting or rejecting applicants for membership in the organization, usually for a specific job. The usual form of the problem would be 26 applicants for 18 openings for machine operators. How do we decide which to accept? Occasionally, a selection process is used to promote current members of the organization. *Placement* is more complex because it requires the matching of several persons to several jobs. Placement decisions usually involve persons who have been accepted into the organization. We must decide what function each should fulfill. It is necessary, then, to specify clearly the goals of the placement decision—maximizing production, maximizing worker satisfaction, minimizing interpersonal conflict, and so on. Since the selection problem is more often encountered than the placement problem, we will consider selection in greater detail.

Before discussing some of the procedures for regulating selection and placement processes, one assumption of these procedures should be pointed out. The reader should consider carefully the implications and bear them in mind in any applied situation. Statistical procedures assume a measurable criterion which our selection decisions will maximize. Those persons will be chosen for each job who are predicted to perform best on the criterion for that job. The measure which is used as a criterion for the development of selection procedures can be [a] performance evaluation measure. . . . It can be whatever we would like to maximize. There will be jobs for which we would like to choose those who are predicted to have the greatest tenure. In other situations it may be appropriate to choose individuals on the basis of their trainability. Whatever we choose as our criterion measure, there is an assumption in the statistical decision process that it is to be maximized.

DEVELOPMENT OF A GENERAL SELECTION SYSTEM

In the following sections we discuss the considerations necessary to developing a general selection system. We begin by identifying the personnel needs of the organization. Then we present the selection techniques. Finally, we discuss how to evaluate the usefulness of our selection procedures.

Manpower Planning

A complete program of new-member acquisition begins with a plan for manpower utilization which includes much more than the specifications of current openings in the organization. The first step in the program is the specification of expected short-term and long-term manpower needs. Using information about expansion or reduction plans and usual turnover rates for various jobs, reasonable forecasts can be made about future work force deficiencies and surpluses.

Once we estimate future manpower conditions, policy decisions can be made and the consequences of various selection and training schemes considered. These considerations should include the costs of training, the costs of recruiting, the costs of a selection system, the benefits of transferring workers from one job to another, the benefits of promoting within the organization, and so on. From careful deliberation on these points it is often possible to plan career ladders or progressive paths for members. Thus members are encouraged to stay in the organization without being locked into dead-end positions. A possible career ladder for ORG [a hypothetical organization that is to be staffed] may consist of hiring workers in a production unit with the intention of moving them up through the staff foreman position or into the salesman position.

Career ladders often imply that training will be carried out in the organization; that is, while at one step, members will be preparing for the next. A career-ladder strategy will mean that the most appropriate selection criterion will not necessarily be performance on the immediate task for which a person is hired. Selection procedures should instead consider how trainable the new members are and how readily they will adapt to later (probably more important) duties.

Though all forecasting is subject to error, intelligent planning can avoid shortages of persons with critical skills. Advance planning is the rule in administering production materials and facilities. The most important resource, manpower, should not be administered less thoughtfully.

Recruiting

The initial problem is to interest persons in becoming members. There are many ways to accomplish this—ads in newspapers and magazines, visits to college campuses, employment agencies, word of mouth, and so on. The technique should match the job available and the labor market. If an E.D.P. consultant is desired for ORG, an ad in a local newspaper will be less effective than a visit (or telephone call) to a college computer-science department. The methods of recruitment and publicity *do* influence the applicant population from which new members can be chosen. If one wishes, for example, to increase the number of applicants from minorities (or with high school degrees, sales experience, or money to invest), it is necessary to recruit in the locations and media which are most accessible to those special populations.

Recruitment costs should always be included in an assessment of the effectiveness of personnel policies. If qualified applicants regularly apply to the organization without solicitation, recruiting expenses are unnecessary. Because rare and valuable skills are more expensive to recruit, it is sometimes better to recruit and hire persons with lesser skills and to train them. There are few general rules for a ready-made recruiting policy, however, and policies usually should be tailored to the applicant population, the task, and the needs of the organization.

The characteristics of the applicant population are determined by the mode of recruitment, which in turn limits the appropriateness of the selection model and the information it provides for decision making in the specific situation. If the selection procedure is based on an applicant sample recruited in a specific manner, the results are appropriate only if succeeding applicants are recruited similarly.

Job Choice

Finally, before discussing the procedures of personnel selection, there is the matter of job choice. Job choice is personnel selection from the perspective of the potential employee rather than the organization. The selection problem is quite different from these two viewpoints. From the perspective of the organization, statistics can estimate the number (or percentage) of errors which will be made in the long run or over a large number of decisions ("How many of our 100 new production workers will perform at the minimum criterion level?"). For the individual, however, statistical methods estimate the risk involved in a single decision ("How likely is it that I will be successful if I take that job?").

Job choice has been discussed in terms of the developmental process of a personal career, the satisfaction of personal needs, and the grouping of persons with similar orientations in similar kinds of work (Crites, 1969; Holland, 1966; Roe, 1956; Super & Bohn, 1970). The two mose popular instruments used in job counseling are the Kuder Preference Record (Kuder, 1960) and the Strong Vocational Interest Blank (Strong, 1966). It is not our intention to provide an introduction to the field of job choice; interested readers are encouraged to pursue the topic in the sources indicated above. All readers, however, are encouraged to recognize the difference in the individual and organizational approaches to selection problems and to understand that we deal here almost exclusively with the latter perspective. This does not imply that the individual perspective is less important, only that it is different.

VALIDITY

Since we are concerned with hiring employees who will be successful in ORG, it is necessary to establish a selection system. Stage 1 in the development of our selection system requires job analyses . . . and then determination of what we will consider as "success" in ORG and how it will be measured. . . .

Stage 2 requires formulating hypotheses which state the expected relationship between our criterion (criteria) and potential predictor(s). The results of hypotheses testing will be expressed by correlation coefficients. When correlation coefficients are used to show the relationship between predictors and criteria they are called validity coefficients. What information sources (tests, biographical information, and so on) can we use as possible predictors of the criteria? What information will reflect differences among the applicants? What information can be obtained from or about the applicant that is related to our criteria?

The initial formulation of these hypotheses is based on systematic job analyses, experience, information from other organizations with respect to the predictors they use, literature reviews, and "educated guesses." The latter are usually based on the *face validity* of the information source. That is, some sources, as judged from their items, questions, or content, "look as if" they are related to the criterion.

Our guesses, experience, and so on also may indicate that there are some abstract concepts related to the behavior we are trying to predict. If we have measures of these concepts, we can hypothesize that they will be potential predictors of the criterion behavior. For example, it has been assumed that general intelligence influences performance of many jobs. Before we can test the hypothesis that general intelligence is related to job performance, we must develop a measure of general intelligence. The ultimate assessment of whether, in fact, we have a measure of general intelligence is a judgmental decision inferred from research evidence that is accumulated over many studies. If our measure of general intelligence is related to concepts that we expect it to be related to *and* unrelated to concepts we expect it not to be related to, we may conclude that we have developed *construct validity* for our measure. . . .

Even though the choice of our potential predictor is based on construct validity, we must test the relationship between the construct and the criterion empirically, just as we would empirically test the relationship between any other potential predictor (picked on the basis of experience, face validity, and so on) and the criterion. Before we review the empirical validation, however, we should consider Stage 3 in our development of a selection system—possible information sources or predictors.

Information Sources

One of the most popular and frequently used sources of information is the *interview*. It is used primarily to obtain specific information about the applicant's character, personality, job knowledge, and attitude. If these aspects are assessed, weighted, or scored, the interview becomes a predictor which can and should be empirically validated. The interview also fulfills other functions. If it is the first step in the recruitment procedure (on the college campus, for example), it may serve a public relations function. The organization has an opportunity to "sell itself." Facts pertaining to the specific job, company policy, types of benefits, and so on can be presented to the interviewee. These facts should facilitate his decision as to whether he desires to pursue employment with the company. Initial interviews also serve a screening function. The organization can eliminate from further selection procedures applicants who have very little chance of being selected. If the interview is conducted after collecting other types of information, all predictor information may be combined to clarify and resolve any inconsistencies.

In some cases, the interviewer is required to examine all the data and make a decision to hire or reject. This decision making is based on the *clinical prediction* selection model in which the decision maker uses an intuitive strategy to combine and evaluate information. Evidence indicates that clinical prediction is not as good as systematic empirical prediction (Meehl, 1954). Because clinical prediction is an individual intuitive strategy, it is almost impossible to generalize from one decision maker to another or even to generalize from one situation to another for the same decision maker.

As a screening or decision-making device, the primary concern of the interview is negative information. Evidence indicates that interviews are particularly attentive to negative facts or information about the applicant, and this information contributes most to the interviewer's assessment (Mayfield, 1964).

In general, the interview, as a decision-making device, is unreliable and not highly related to the criterion measure. The usefulness of the interview depends on its relative structure and the idiosyncracies of the interviewer. If the interview is relatively unstructured, reliable assessments are unlikely. If one applicant were interviewed twice, different questions might be asked each time and, consequently, different information given and different decisions made. On the other hand, if the interview were highly structured and interviewers asked the same questions, reliability would be increased. The totally structured interview, however, can be replaced with a questionnaire which saves time and money though diminishing the opportunity to pursue and develop responses. One strategy, thus, is the semistructured interview: ask a few prepared questions, but allow time to discuss and pursue points as they develop.

The problem of idiosyncracy cannot be alleviated by adjusting the format of the interview. Evidence indicates that interviewers' decisions are influenced by their stereotypes of good applicants, by biases formed early in the interview, by negative information, personal appearance, information already available to the interviewer (application blank or test scores), and even impressions of preceding applicants (Webster, 1964). Experienced interviewers can control how much the interviewee talks. The reactions of the interviewer—leaning forward or backward in the chair, sighing, frowning, or smiling—will influence the interviewee and are particularly important since they affect the interviewee's motivation (which he wants to maximize to present a favorable impression).

All these characteristics of the interview situation tend to restrict its reliability. Interviews do have value, however, as a public relations function and, with respect to selection, interviews are valuable as preliminary screening, when it is impossible to develop relatively good empirical procedures (the small company or small applicant sample), and when traits *can* be better assessed by the interview than other means. One special use of the interview is that it permits us to obtain and use as a predictor specific information about the job applicant's knowledge. Such interviews, *oral trade tests*, consist of questions which are phrased in the language of the worker and job.

Another information source which is a potential predictor is the *biographical information blank* (BIB) or *application blank*. Biographical information or application blanks contain personal, demographic, and situational information: age, sex, address, marital status, number of dependents, military status, past work experience, and so on. (See Glennon, Albright, & Owens, 1966, for a comprehensive catalog of potential items.) In addition, attitudes, preferences, and interests are frequently assessed. From this information one can obtain a systematic picture of the applicant which indirectly reflects his personal and motivational characteristics. One assumption underlying the use of questions pertaining to past work experience is that they may be the best predictor of future performance. In essence, BIBs are measures of those personal characteristics which are least susceptible to faking.

The essential point, however, is that the items comprising the BIB can and should be weighted and scored for use as a predictor. The easiest way to construct a predictor from a BIB is to select discriminatory items—that

is, those which distinguish between successful and nonsuccessful workers on the performance criterion. For example, if 85 percent of our successful workers have two or more dependents whereas only 15 percent of those with zero or one dependent are successful, we obviously should prefer an applicant with two or more dependents. (Hypotheses pertaining to responsibility, mobility, and so on might explain this relationship.) The end result of an individual BIB is a sum of weighted scores on all items which is used as a predictor. (For a detailed discussion of weighting application blanks, see Guion, 1965.)

If items are used for decision making without evidence that they are related to the criterion, there may be evidence of unfair, illegal discrimination. Also, since many of the items can be more personal than a request for the applicant's age, the problem of invasion of privacy is very real. If the item does not help you to make a decision, why ask it?

References often are requested on application blanks. The information obtained often concerns the applicant's responsibility and motivation. Scoring reference information is difficult and requires a subjective evaluation or weighting.

Usually, previous employers and personal friends are listed as references. The lack of value to the employer of the latter source is obvious; it is not difficult to find a friend who will say a few good things in your behalf. References from a former boss are more difficult to evaluate. Does he really know enough about the applicant to write about him; can he evaluate the abilities that are necessary for the new job and the applicant's talent in relation to them? Then there are more cynical concerns. Some bosses will write a "great" letter so that the applicant will get the job and the present boss will be rid of him. Also, from the point of view of the new organization, "If he's so good, why don't you try to keep him?" Perhaps the best way to use a reference is as a screening device with emphasis on negative information.

The most obvious predictors are *tests*. Achievement tests measure how well an individual can presently perform; aptitude tests measure his potential. Tests can be differentiated into paper and pencil or performance; speed (how much you can do in a given time) or power (how much do you know); or verbal or nonverbal.

Tests of intellectual ability can measure general intelligence, verbal ability, numerical ability, convergent and divergent reasoning, creativity, and so on; psychomotor skill tests will measure dexterity, eye-hand or -finger coordination, and so on. Personality and motivation tests also can be used. The *job sample* is a specific test which requires the applicant to demonstrate that he possesses the necessary skills by actually doing the tasks. The job sample test is a simulation; it is representative of the work actually performed on the job and includes all of the important aspects of performance. If the job involves computations on an adding machine, the test would require the applicant to make similar computations. (For a general discussion of tests and testing see Cronbach, 1970. For a discussion of available tests see Buros, 1972.)

Basic Validation Procedures

Stage 4 in the selection process involves the examination of the relationship between one or more information sources (predictors) and the criterion or criteria. Because the purpose of a selection system is to facilitate selection of an applicant for a position, it is essential that we emphasize here, as we did when discussing manpower analysis, that the recruiting sample not only restricts the degree of generalization possible but, in effect, dictates the validation model. Validity, generally speaking, is the degree to which one measure is related to another. In employment situations, validity reflects the degree to which a predictor or information source is related to performance on the job, the criterion.

One appropriate validation model involves *predictive validity*. The purpose of administering a predictor, or collecting information from an applicant, is to predict how that person will perform on the job. The process of examining the relationship between the predictor and subsequent performance, the criterion, is referred to as predictive validity or the follow-up method of validation.

An ideal predictive validity design would involve administration of a potential predictor (we will discuss multiple predictors below) to a group of applicants. Based on chance, lottery, or any other random procedure, but *not* on the basis of their predictor scores, these applicants would join the organization. Though this procedure would maximize the information from the predictive validity study only rarely is an organization willing to hire randomly. In actual practice, applicants are chosen on the basis of the existing selection system which the investigators hope to improve upon. The problem with this procedure is that the validation sample (the applicants who are *hired*) will not include persons who are rejected by the current system. Since we may not know the validity of the current system, some of the applicants may be rejected unfairly or potentially excellent workers may be rejected. We could never discover this if the current selection system is used as a screening device to determine who is hired into the validation sample.

In the ideal or actual case, if we are trying to validate a job knowledge test as a predictor, we would administer the test to the applicants and file the results without using the test scores for decision making. The results are filed because we have no justification for using them; at this point, we do not know if the test is valid in this application. After the applicants who were hired (the validation sample) have been on the job for a specified length of time, performance measures are obtained. The relationship between the scores on the potential predictor and the performance measure is examined and indicates the potential usefulness of the predictor.

Examine this procedure closely. It involves investing time and money in a predictor which may eventually prove to have no relationship to the criterion. The information necessary to determine the validity of the predictor may not be obtained until a year later, and then there is no guarantee that it will be valid. In addition to the cost and time, there is reluctance to hire anyone without using a "mystical" test score. In other words, the most appropriate validation model in its purest form is not that which most organizations would be willing to apply.

An alternative to the predictive validity model is *concurrent validity*, or present-employee validation. Concurrent validity involves the administration of the predictor to a group of incumbent workers, simultaneously obtaining criterion measures on them. Criterion measures can be obtained the day following predictor administration, the same day, or even a day before.

Now recall the purpose of validation and our discussion of recruitment. We are concerned with hiring new workers. What happens if we apply what we know about the relationship between the predictor and criterion for the incumbent workers to a group of applicants? First, the motivation level differs for the two groups. Our present workers will be told that the test scores "do not count," that they are being used for research. If the predictor is "valid," the new applicants will be told that test scores will be used to decide whether or not they are hired. The different instructions will affect motivation which in turn will affect results. Second, present workers have the advantage of experience when they provide potential predictor information. Their scores might be substantially different

from those they would have obtained as applicants. Many applicants lack job experience. Consequently, the incumbent's experience will influence predictor results and affect any generalization to an applicant group. Furthermore, since those individuals who had performed poorly would no longer be on the job, the range of the criterion scores would be restricted. This would influence (lower) the predictor-criterion relationship. Concurrent validity is not appropriate for most situations. Unfortunately, however, many industries employ the model because it gives instant results! Concurrent validity, because of the problems mentioned above, and contrary to popular belief, is not an estimate (over or under) of predictive validity!

Concurrent validity may be appropriate for validating job sample tests, however. When we use job sample tests, we are concerned with whether the applicant can do the job *now*, today. That is, can the applicant type, operate the machine, and so on. Through a careful job analysis we would identify the important components of the job and how they are performed. We should attempt to validate a job sample test empirically. The concurrent validation model can be used to determine successful incumbents' performance level which, in turn, gives us a job sample standard for applicants. However, the predictive validation model again may be more appropriate. Because of organizational, situational, and personal characteristics, how someone *can* do the job may differ from how he *will* do the job.

Content validity is another alternative validation procedure, one which does not involve statistical relationships. Content validity is based on the judgment of the developer (a professional tester trained in the area of test construction) of the predictor measure. But it is important to distinguish between content and face validity. Content validity is established by a judgment that *the predictor is job-related*. Face validity means that *the pre-*

dictor seems appropriate to the person being tested. Though face validity may be useful in obtaining cooperation with the testing procedure or in convincing organization officials that the test is appropriate, it is not a sufficient (or necessary) condition for using a test as a predictor.

The judgment of content validity should be based on a careful and detailed analysis of the criterion which is to be predicted. This analysis will be either a total job analysis or, in the case of preparing predictors for part of a set of multiple criteria, an analysis of those job elements to be predicted. The developer of the predictor then constructs a test which will (in his judgment) representatively sample the skills, attitudes, or behaviors required by the job.

Content validity, therefore, is no better (or worse) than the trained judgment of the test builder. In some cases a predictive validity study may be appropriate for a predictor which has content validity. However, content validity frequently must be used if a predictive validity study is unfeasible: (1) there may be too few applicants to carry out the statistical analyses of predictive validity; (2) time constraints may prohibit waiting for the establishment of criteria performance levels; or (3) the job may be so critical or the consequences of poor performance so severe that one would not want to risk using the wide-range performance criteria required to establish predictive validity.

Results of Validation

We have mentioned *results of validation.* Whether predictive or concurrent validations, these results usually are correlation coefficients that are interpreted as *validity coefficients.* The validity coefficient r_{CP} ranges from -1.00 to $+1.00$, where the absolute value indicates the strength of relationship between the criterion (C) and the predictor (P), and the sign indicates the direction of the relation-

ship. The coefficient can be tested for statistical significance.

Several precautions must be observed when interpreting a validity coefficient. First, most correlation statistics are appropriate for linear relationships between the predictor and criterion. If a nonlinear relationship exists, the traditional Pearson correlation coefficient will provide an underestimation of validity.

Second, if we do not have the full range of possible scores on either the predictor or criterion, again we will get an underestimate of validity. This restriction of range might occur in concurrent validation with current workers, who are likely to be relatively successful, whereas those who were unsuccessful would no longer be with the organization. Consequently, we do not have the full range of possible scores on the criterion. Restriction of range on the potential predictor may occur in the predictive validation model if applicants are hired on a nonrandom basis. This may decrease the range of the potential predictor in the validation sample.

Third, reliability of both the predictor and criterion limit validity. If the predictor and/or criterion is unreliable and therefore inconsistent in assessing its own characteristic, we cannot expect one to measure the other. Thus, if we have poor reliabilities in the predictor and/or criterion we will get underestimates of validity. We can correct for this attenuation and obtain an estimate of validity that is based on the assumption of perfect reliabilities (see Guion, 1965, pp. 31–33). This estimate will indicate whether it is advantageous to improve upon the reliability of the predictor and/or criterion.

In addition to a validity coefficient, we also obtain a regression or prediction equation. The regression equation, in the form of $C' = a + bP$ (where P is the predictor score, a and b are statistical weights, and C' is a predicted criterion score), is that which we use to make predictions for individual applicants. This equation and the validity coefficient are computed on the data from our validity sample. The data are the predictor score and criterion score for each member of the validity sample. If we are satisfied with the strength of the validity coefficient and decide to use the predictor in selection, we administer the predictor to a new applicant. We can obtain the predicted criterion score, C', for the new applicant by substituting his score on the predictor in the regression equation. Suppose the regression equation developed on our validity sample is $C' = 10 + 2P$. If an applicant scores 40 on the predictor his predicted criterion or performance level would be 90 ($C' = 10 + 2(40)$). Another applicant with a predictor score of 33 would have a predicted criterion score of 76. We would use this information in selection decisions by hiring the applicants with the highest scores or by hiring all who score above a specified level. (See Ghiselli, 1964, for a detailed discussion of the statistics involved in validation and reliability.)

The results of validation also may be expressed in *expectancy charts* and *tables*. Expectancy charts express results in terms of probabilities. The *individual expectancy* chart (Figure 8-1) indicates the probabilities of applicant success on the criterion given their predictor score ranges. For example, if an applicant scores 18 on the predictor, he has a

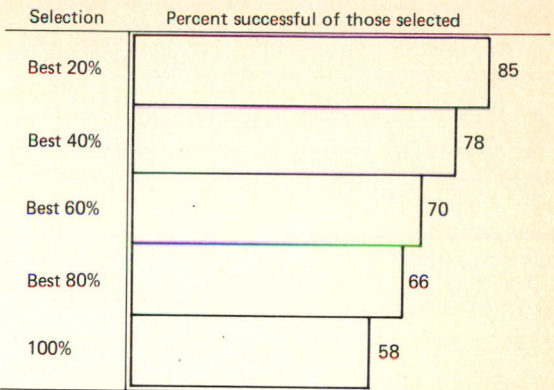

Figure 8-2 Institutional expectancy chart.

63 percent chance of being successful on the criterion. The *institutional expectancy* chart (Figure 8-2) indicates to the organization the percentage of those selected who will be successful on the criterion, given that the organization selects certain percentages of the best "scores" on the predictor. For example, if the organization selects the top 40 percent scorers on the predictor, 78 percent of these will be successful on the criterion. (Procedures to construct these charts are described in Guion, 1965.)

Extension of the Basic Validation Procedure: Multiple Prediction and Multiple Cutoff

To this point, our discussion of validity has been restricted to the situation with one predictor and one criterion. However, as already indicated, there are several sources of predictor information. Using more than one type of predictor can increase our understanding and ability to predict the criterion.

With one predictor and one criterion, we are dealing with simple correlation (validity), r. If we decide to form a "test battery"—for example, use a BIB and an aptitude test as predictors—we can employ a model of validation which simultaneously uses more than one predictor. Multiple correlation, R, provides an estimate of the relationship between the criterion and the composite of, in this case, two

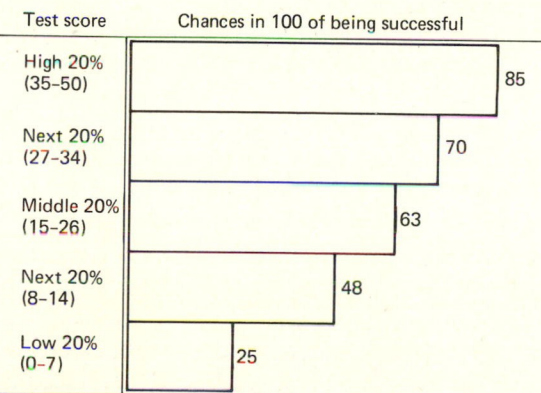

Figure 8-1 Individual expectancy chart.

predictor scores. If the aptitude test is correlated + .30 with the criterion and the addition of BIB "scores" indicates a multiple correlation of + .40, we may conclude that two predictors are better than one. The resulting prediction equation would be of the form $C' = a + b_1P_1 + b_2P_2$ (where a, b_1 and b_2 are weights, P_1 and P_2 are two predictors, and C' the predicted criterion value). Suppose the multiple regression equation developed on our validity sample is $C' = 5 + 3P_1 + 1.5P_2$ (where P_1 and P_2 represent aptitude test scores and BIB scores, respectively). If an applicant scores 40 on the aptitude test and 6 on the BIB, his predicted criterion would be 134 ($C' = 5 + 3(40) + 1.5(6)$). Another applicant with an aptitude test score of 30 and a BIB score of 26 would also have a predicted criterion of 134.

The essential characteristic of multiple correlation is the composite of the two predictors; it is possible for one predictor to compensate for another. That is, a deficiency or low score by the second applicant on the aptitude test was overcome by his high score (favorable responses) on the BIB. The combination of the two predictors and its relationship to the criterion is the essence of a *compensatory model of validation*.

An alternative to multiple correlation, or the compensatory model, is a *multiple cutoff* approach. Rather than permitting high scores on one predictor to compensate for low scores on another, the multiple cutoff model requires that a minimum score be obtained on *each* valid predictor. All predictor information is crucial; all characteristics, abilities, and so on are considered essential for successful performance. A decision to hire an applicant is made only if he scores at or above the cutoff on all predictors.

Two points should be made about multiple predictors. First, our examples have been restricted to two predictors. If three or more are used in either the compensatory or cutoff

model, nothing changes conceptually (only more computer time is required); it is just an extension of the one or two predictor cases. Second, we have referred to the relationship between two predictors and one criterion. We do not mean to suggest that prediction of one criterion is an adequate basis for suitable selection systems. When more than one criterion is used, a battery or set of predictors is validated independently for each criterion.

Cross-Validation

In the discussion on validity, we have implied that if we have (for example) 100 applicants for a job, we administer a set of predictors to all applicants, hire all applicants, and finally evaluate their performance. We then compute a multiple correlation and prediction equation which is evaluated for statistical significance; if the significance is satisfactory, we subsequently use the predictors for selection decisions on new applicant samples.

This validation procedure is not complete. If we employ the procedure as described, there is the problem that the statistical results (prediction weights—a's and b's) may be biased or distorted due to capitalization on chance factors in that specific sample of 100. The regression equation may be unique to that specific validity sample and would not be useful in new but similar applicant samples. Consequently, it is necessary to *cross-validate*, or determine how effective the prediction equation is. We need to know whether the same equation would occur in similar samples.

Cross-validation usually involves splitting the *total initial sample* (100) into two subsamples (subsample sizes are arbitrary). The regression equation is computed for one subsample ($N = 67$) and then applied to the other subsample, the holdout group ($N = 33$). For this *first subsample*, we might obtain an equation such as $C' = 6 + 4P_1 + 3P_2$. If the predictor scores for the *holdout* group are substituted in this equation, we obtain a *pre-dicted criterion score* for each member of the holdout group. However, we do know the *actual* criterion scores for the members of the holdout group. The correlation between the predicted and the actual scores for the holdout subsample is an indication of the *validity of the predictor battery*. If this coefficient is statistically significant, the prediction equation is potentially useful.

There is, however, a dilemma to cross-validation. By splitting the total sample into two subgroups we obtain an unbiased estimate of predictor validity for future samples. But the subsample regression equation itself is more likely to be in error than one based on a larger, total sample. Several researchers have investigated this dilemma (Campbell, 1967; Chandler, 1964; Gollob, 1967, 1968; Mosier, 1951; Norman, 1965), but there is no statistically satisfactory resolution.

We should emphasize that cross-validation is not independent of or in addition to the validity procedure previously described. Validation involves cross-validation; it is a simultaneous procedure. Validity results that do not include cross-validation should be regarded with caution.

Utility of Selection Systems

Cross-validation provides evidence of the *statistical* significance of prediction equations. Another consideration is *practical* significance, or utility, which is Stage 5 in our validation procedure. Does a valid selection system result in the hiring of a percentage of workers who will eventually be considered successful greater than the percentage of successful workers hired without the selection system? The basic parameter in a discussion of utility is the decision maker's value judgment in relation to the relative worth of various decision results, payoff matrices. These value judgments or statements are difficult to measure. The basic strategy is to maximize the average gain for the organization in obtaining satisfactory workers. The preferred selection strategy is that which provides the greatest gain or utility value. In evaluating the strategies, we consider the gain in hiring with a selection system as opposed to no selection system, one system as opposed to another, and cost and time of systematic selection. With respect to costs, we are concerned with recruiting, training, and material costs and costs due to incorrect decisions. If the company hires someone who turns out to be unsuccessful, the costs are obvious. However, we must consider the other possibility—the costs of rejecting someone who would have been successful. Not only does the organization lose, but the effects on the applicant may be severe. (See Cronbach & Gleser, 1965, for a discussion of utility in terms of decision theory.)

The simplest way to evaluate the utility of a selection system is to examine a scatterplot (Figure 8-3). The data used to form the scatterplot are obtained from the members of the validity sample.

Suppose Score C on the criterion is the point dividing successful and unsuccessful workers. Suppose, also, that score P on the predictor is the cut-off point that determines who is hired and rejected. This point can be

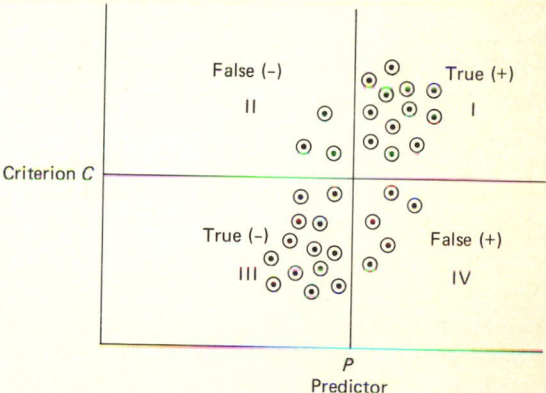

Figure 8-3 Scatterplot of criterion and predictor data.

determined so that the least number of errors is made—that is, the fewest number of unsuccessful workers would be hired and the fewest number of successful workers would be rejected. Unless the validity coefficient is one, there will be errors. Separating the group at P and C on the predictor and criterion respectively results in the division of the scatterplot into quadrants.

Quadrants I and III reveal the number of workers correctly identified, as either successful (*true positive*) or unsuccessful (*true negative*). Quadrant II indicates the number of workers that the test indicates will do poorly (because they score below P) but who are evaluated eventually as successful (the *false negatives*). Quadrant IV indicates the number of workers who would be hired on the basis of their predictor score but who are subsequently evaluated as unsuccessful (the *false positives*).

To determine if the selection system is useful, the percentage of workers who would be considered successful if chosen on the basis of the selection system can be compared with the percentage considered successful and chosen without systematic predictor information. The latter percentage is the *base rate*. The base rate is determined by the ratio

$$\frac{I + II}{I + II + III + IV}$$

To determine the gain or percentage increase in successful workers if a new selection system is used, we can use the formula

$$\frac{I}{I + IV} - \frac{I + II}{I + II + III + IV}$$

The first part of the formula indicates the percentage of workers who are hired on the basis of the selection system and who are considered successful on the criterion. The second part of the formula is the base rate. The difference is the percentage improvement, or gain.

Taylor-Russell tables (1939) present the gain in using a selection system where a new predictor is added to existing selection procedures. The gain depends on validity coefficients, base rates, and selection ratios. The selection ratio is the number of people to be hired, divided by the number of applicants. If the validity coefficient and the base rate are held constant as the selection ratio is increased (the greater the percentage of people hired), the gain will decrease. If the validity coefficient and selection ratio are held constant, the greater the base rate, the less the gain. If the base rate and the selection ratio are held constant, as the validity coefficient increases so does the gain.

Reevaluation

Stage 6, the final stage in validation, requires that validity coefficients be reassessed periodically. Criteria and performance are dynamic. The job itself, the way tasks are performed, and the characteristics of the people performing the tasks change over time; thus, we also should expect validity coefficients to change. If we continuously use a predictor or set of predictors, we should regularly check the validity for any changes.

PLACEMENT

Placement problems arise after a decision has been made to hire an applicant. The basis for this initial decision may have been that the applicant possesses "general" abilities that the company likes to see in its workers, or that he is number one in his class, or that he is returning to the organization after a leave of absence and his previous job has been filled. Regardless of the reason, the organization has a member without a specific position in mind.

The objectives of placement are to place each applicant in a position in which he will do his best work, *or* in a position so that each position is filled by someone who meets at least minimum requirements, *or* in a position so that the organization will receive maximum performance from the group of applicants as a whole. If we are trying to accomplish the first objective, we need to predict how well the applicant will do in each of the available positions. To accomplish this objective we could use regression analysis to obtain a predicted criterion score for each of the positions for which he is considered. The decision then would be to place the applicant on the job for which he has the highest predicted criterion value. Or, with *pattern analysis* we use the predictor information of those workers who

are presently considered successful. Pattern analysis requires comparison of the applicant's predictor scores with the average predictor score values of successful workers in each position. Similarity between these scores is the basis for the placement decisions. The similarity is assessed by profile statistics, profile coefficients, or "distance from the standard" scores (Nunnally, 1967). A simple example of a decision based on similarity is illustrated in Figures 8-4 and 8-5. The average predictor score values for successful production workers are shown by the bold line in Figure 8-4; the values for successful salesmen are shown in Figure 8-5. The predictor scores

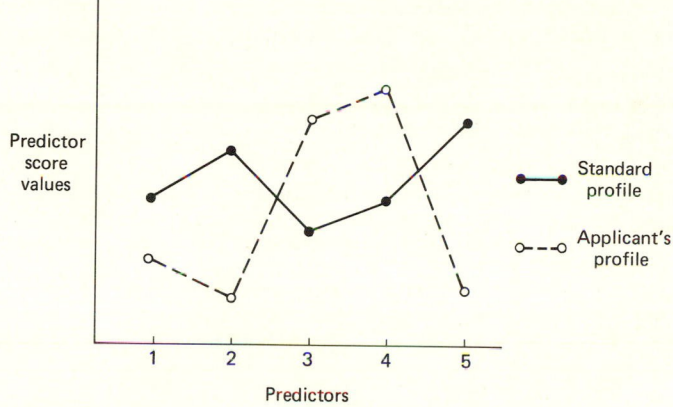

Figure 8-4   Pattern of predictor scores for workers.

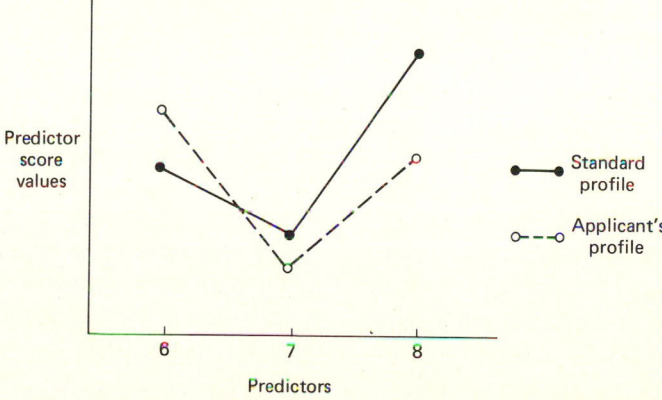

Figure 8-5   Pattern of predictor scores for salesmen.

of a single applicant have been superimposed as a dotted line on each figure. From the figures it is clear that the applicant is more like successful salesmen than successful workers.

If we are trying to accomplish the second objective (filling each position with an applicant who meets minimum requirements), we need to set a cutoff for the predictors of each position and place applicants in any position for which they meet the multiple cutoff requirements.

To accomplish the third objective (the organization will receive maximum performance from the group of applicants as a whole), we can use a combination of the previous strategies. We can use regression and profile analysis to place each applicant in such a position that the total result of all placement decisions yields maximum performance for the organization. In other words, we may not place an applicant in the position for which he is predicted to do his best work if this meant that either another position would not be filled because there was no applicant or another applicant might be without a suitable position. For example, if Allan Allaround is predicted to perform very successfully as a worker and adequately as a salesman, whereas Mike Minimal is predicted to perform adequately as a worker but poorly as a salesman, Allan is best placed as a salesman and Mike as a worker.

PREDICTION FOR PROMOTION AND TRANSFER DECISIONS

We mentioned previously that predictor information sources could be used when we want to promote or transfer current workers. If we were considering a worker in ORG who has applied for the position of salesman, we might administer the same predictor battery to him as we would to an applicant from outside ORG. There is nothing different about the validation procedures whether the predictors are being used for promotion or transfer decisions or for initial selection.

Some organizations have established career ladders for their workers. If the interval of time between someone's entry into one position and promotion to the next is relatively brief, initial gathering of information may include predictors for the second step position. Again, there is nothing different about validation in this situation.

Another approach to promotions which is currently receiving considerable emphasis is the use of *assessment centers* (Bray & Grant, 1966). Those employees being considered for promotion receive extensive examination with a variety of techniques. This usually involves one to three days of testing, interviewing, and participating in simulated job activities. All workers at managerial levels often participate in assessment centers regardless of their level of interest in promotions. The information obtained is used to identify candidates with promotion potential and to provide feedback to the participants about their strengths and weaknesses. If information from assessment center examinations is used for promotion decisions it should be validated as in any other situation.

UNFAIR DISCRIMINATION AND SELECTION SYSTEMS

Recent legislation (Civil Rights Act of 1964, Title VII), Supreme Court rulings (*Griggs vs. Duke Power*, March 1971) and guidelines (Equal Employment Opportunity Commission, 1970; Office of Federal Contract Compliance, 1971) have emphasized the problem of unfair discrimination towards minority groups and sexes with respect to selection and hiring. Unfair discrimination exists when applicants with equal probabilities of success on the job have unequal probabilities of being hired for the job (Guion, 1966).

One way to assess whether unfair discrimination exists is to divide the validity sample into groups on the basis of the variable of concern (race or sex) and compare the validity coefficients and the regression equations for each group. For example, Figure 8-6 illustrates the scatterplot for a case where two groups differ on average score on both the predictor and criterion, yet the regression equations are equal. In this case there is no unfair discrimination for there is equally good prediction for the two groups; the group that has the higher predictor scores (Group 1) also is more successful on the criterion.

In contrast, the two groups in Figure 8-7 are equally successful on the criterion, but Group I scores higher on the predictor than Group II. Though the validity coefficients are equal, the regression equations are different. Consequently, if P_1 is chosen as the cutoff, there would be unfair discrimination against Group II. One solution would be to have two cutoffs—P_1 if the applicant is a member of Group I and P_{11} if the applicant is a member of Group II. Another solution would be to establish a separate regression equation for each group and to use the predicted criterion scores from the appropriate equation for each appli-

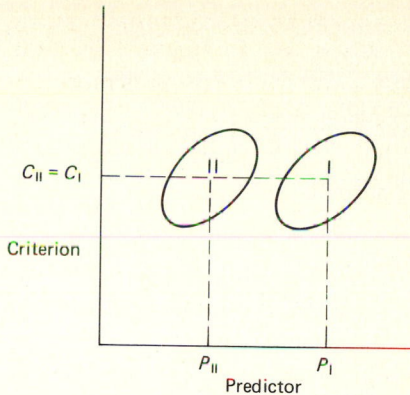

Figure 8-7 Comparison of two groups that differ in performance on the predictor, but perform similarly on the criterion.

cant. (An excellent article which illustrates interactions between predictor and criterion scores and their effect on heterogeneous or socially mixed groups is presented by Bartlett and O'Leary, 1969.)

With respect to whether discrimination exists, the burden of proof is on the employer. He must show that his predictor is related to performance and that the predictor is not differentially valid. To do this, the organization must conduct careful job analyses; develop reliable, relevant, and practical criterion measures; and perform appropriate and complete validity analyses.

REFERENCES
Job Choice

Crites, J. O. *Vocational psychology.* New York: McGraw, 1969.

Holland, J. L. *Psychology of vocational choice.* New York: Ginn, 1966.

Kuder, G. F. *Manual for the Kuder preference record—Vocational.* Chicago: Science Research Associates, 1960.

Roe, A. *Psychology of occupations.* New York: Wiley, 1956.

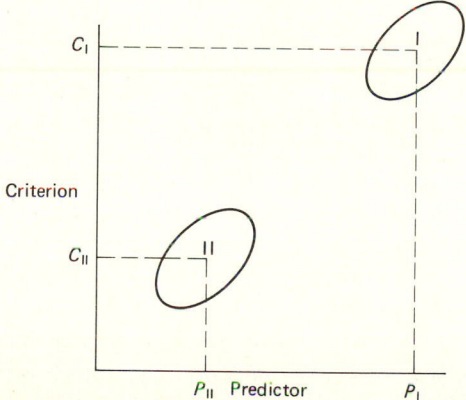

Figure 8-6 Comparison of two groups (I and II) that differ on average score on the predictor (*P*) and criterion (*C*).

Strong, E. K., Jr. revised by D. P. Campbell. *Strong vocational interest blank: Manual.* Stanford, Calif.: Stanford University Press, 1966.

Super, D. E., & Bohn, M. J. *Occupational psychology.* Belmont, Calif.: Wadsworth, 1970.

Information Sources

Bray, D. W., & Grant, D. L. The assessment center in the measurement of potential for business management. *Psychological Monographs.* 1966, **80** (17, Whole No. 625).

Buros, O. K. (Ed.) *The seventh mental measurements yearbook.* Highland Park, N.J.: Gryphon, 1972.

Cronbach, L. J. *Essentials of psychological testing.* New York: Harper & Row, 1970.

Ghiselli, E. E. *The validity of occupational aptitude tests.* New York: Wiley, 1966.

Glennon, J. R., Albright, L. E., & Owens, W. A. *A catalog of life history items.* Reproduced by the Richardson Foundation, 1966.

Guion, R. M., & Gottier, R. F. Validity of personality measures in personnel selection. *Personnel Psychology*, 1965, **18**, 135–164.

Huck, J. R. Assessment centers: A review of the external and internal validities. *Personnel Psychology*, 1973, **26**, 191–212.

Mayfield, E. C. The selection interview—A re-evaluation of published research. *Personnel Psychology*, 1964, **17**, 239–260.

Meehl, P. E. *Clinical vs. statistical prediction.* Minneapolis: University of Minnesota Press, 1954.

Webster, E. C. *Decision making in the employment interview.* Montreal: Industrial Relations Centre, McGill University, 1964.

Wernimont, P. R., & Campbell, J. P. Signs, samples and criteria. *Journal of Applied Psychology*, 1968, **52**, 372–376.

Validation

American Psychological Association. *Standards for educational and psychological tests and manuals.* Washington: 1966.

Campbell, J. P. Cross validation revisited. Paper presented at the meeting of the Midwestern Psychological Association, Chicago, 1967.

Chandler, R. E. Validity, reliability, baloney—and a little mustard. Paper presented at the meeting of the Midwestern Psychological Association, 1964.

Cronbach, L. J., & Gleser, G. C. *Psychological tests and personnel decisions.* Urbana, Ill., University of Illinois Press, 1965.

Dunnette, M. D. *Personnel selection and placement.* Belmont, Calif.: Wadsworth, 1966.

Ghiselli, E. E. *Theory of psychological measurement.* New York: McGraw-Hill, 1964.

Gollob, H. F. Cross-validation in fixed effects analysis of variance. Paper presented at the meeting of the American Psychological Association, San Francisco, 1968.

Gollob, H. F. Cross-validation using samples of size one. Paper presented at the meeting of the American Psychological Association, Washington, D.C., 1967.

Guion, R. M. *Personnel Testing.* New York: McGraw-Hill, 1965.

Mosier, C. I. Symposium. The need and means of cross-validation I. Problems and designs of cross-validation. *Educational and Psychological Measurement.* 1951, **11**, 5–11.

Naylor, J. C., & Shine, L. C. A table for determining the increase in mean criterion score obtained by using a selection device. *Journal of Industrial Psychology*, 1965, **3**, 33–42.

Norman, W. T. Double-split cross-validation. An extension of Mosier's design, two undesirable alternatives, and some enigmatic results. *Journal of Applied Psychology*, 1965, **49**, 348–357.

Nunnally, J. C. *Psychometric theory.* New York: McGraw-Hill, 1967.

Taylor, H. C., & Russell, J. T. The relationship of validity coefficients to the practical effectiveness of tests in selection: Discussion and tables. *Journal of Applied Psychology*, 1939, **23**, 565–578.

Zedeck, S. Problems with the use of "moderator" variables. *Psychological Bulletin*, 1971, **76**, 295–310.

Unfair Discrimination

Bartlett, C. J., & O'Leary, B. S. A differential prediction model to moderate the effects of heterogeneous groups in personnel selection and classification. *Personnel Psychology*, 1969, **22**, 1–17.

Equal Employment Opportunity Commission.

Guidelines on employee selection procedures. *Federal Register*, 1970, **35**, 12333 (1–3).

Guion, R. M. Employment tests and discriminatory hiring. *Industrial Relations*, 1966, **5**, 20–37.

Office of Federal Contract Compliance Employee testing and other selection procedures. *Federal Register*, 1971, **36**, 19307–19310.

Reading 9

An Approach to Selection Decisions: Dollars and Sense

J. Thomas Janz
Marvin D. Dunnette

The utility of different approaches for selecting people and of particular selection decisions can be evaluated according to estimated costs. Brogden and Taylor (1950) suggested such an approach, Cronbach and Gleser (1965) spelled out a theoretical basis for a cost-accounting approach, and Dunnette (1966) gave examples of how it might be applied to practical personnel selection decisions.

At the level of the organization, institutional decisions about hiring or rejecting job candidates can be aided by determining the actual dollar values of different kinds of job behavior (both effective and ineffective) and applying those values to equations which have been developed to predict those behaviors. At the level of individual applicants or job candidates, individual decisions can be aided by determining relative probabilities for the occurrence of different facets of job performance and degrees of certainty for various predictions of particular individual job-performance outcomes.

Figure 9-1 shows a sequence of steps to guide researchers in evaluating both the potential and actual cost effectiveness of different selection systems. Such estimates may then be used to help decide whether or not to conduct selection research and how worthwhile such research is.

Stage 1 involves a careful behavioral job analysis and estimation of dollar values or costs associated with different facets and levels of job performance. Results from stage 1 form a basis for deciding whether or not the *potential* cost advantages of a new selection system are sufficient to warrant doing the research to develop a system. During stage 2, a new selection system is developed and the degree of relationship between decisions made with it and the occurrence of different facets and levels of job performance is determined. Results from stage 2 form a basis for deciding whether or not the *actual* cost advantages of the new selection system are sufficient to warrant implementing it for making actual selection decisions. Stage 3 involves a period of time over which the selection system is implemented and used to aid in making selection decisions. Stage 4 involves a program review and evaluation of results obtained during stage 3.

STAGE 1: BEHAVIORAL ANALYSIS OF THE JOB

A clear understanding of workers' behaviors and their organizational consequences is essential as a basis for improving on investments in personnel. A picture of the job must be

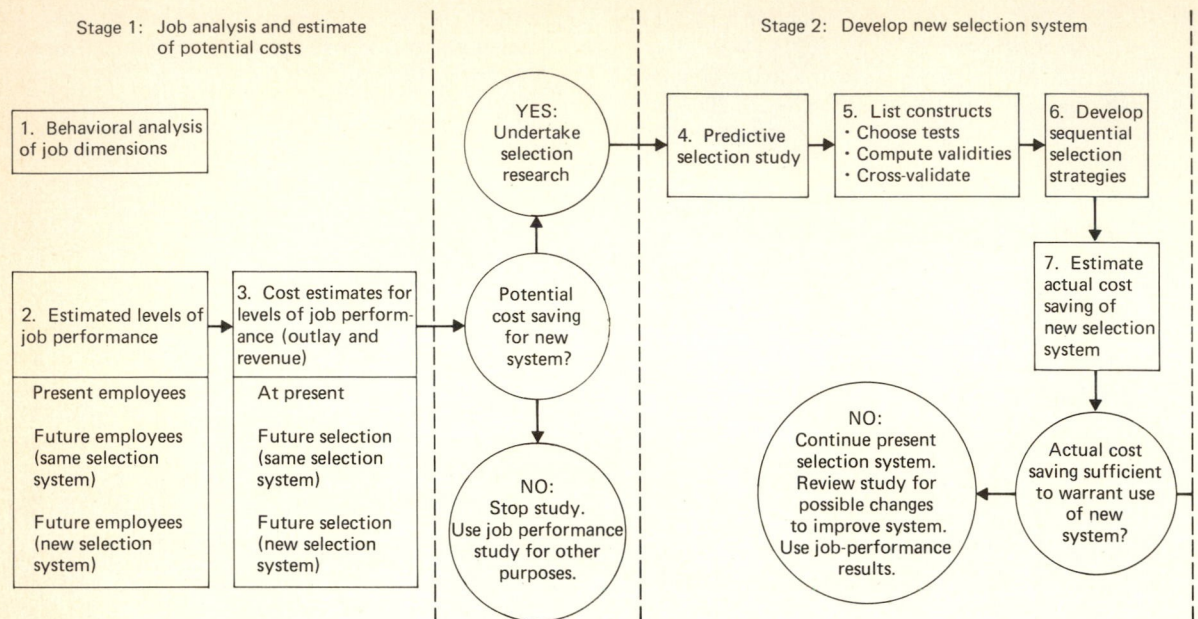

Figure 9-1 Stages involved in undertaking, evaluating, implementing, and reviewing selection research programs.

constructed from the complex jigsaw puzzle that it may, at first, appear to be. Clearly defined job dimensions can be discovered and used to simplify the puzzle and to bring clarity to the picture. Such job dimensions are best derived by generating and analyzing critical incidents, task statements, or behavioral summaries of actual job performance episodes (Smith & Kendall, 1963; Campbell, Dunnette, Lawler, & Weick, 1970, p. 118). The episodes or incidents can be grouped by a number of methods ranging from a subjective sorting by job experts to statistical factoring or clustering of a similarities matrix between all possible incident or task pairs (Brown, 1967). Once behavioral dimensions have been developed, the separate question of criterion *measurement* must be considered. Some quantitative dimensions such as productivity may be measured by objective methods, but most will need to be measured by developing rating scales. All measures, whether objective or

subjective, must, of course, be evaluated according to redundancy and reliability.

Next, some number of knowledgeable persons must consider the relative dollar costs or values associated with different levels of effectiveness on each of the various job-performance dimensions. As mentioned, Brogden and Taylor (1950) advocated a "dollar criterion," but they presented only limited guidelines for estimating the organizational "end result" factors of performance. The impact of different levels of performance can be estimated with two types of end result variables: outlay costs and revenues. "Outlay costs" refer to expenses incurred. "Revenue" refers to the market value of goods or services produced by a unit.

For example, consider aspects of job performance involving equipment maintenance. Consequences of poor performance on this job dimension are such things as equipment breakdowns causing costly repairs (an outlay

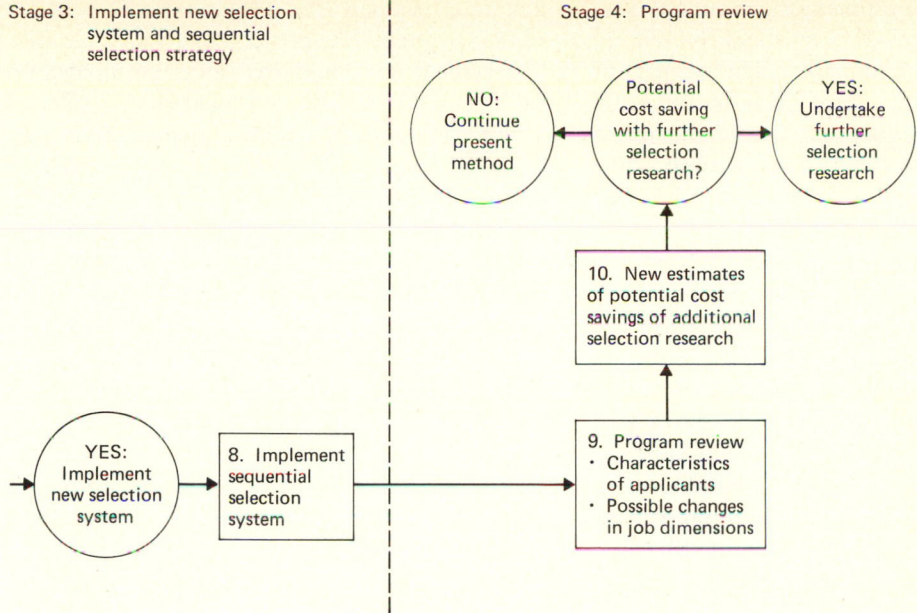

Stage 3: Implement new selection system and sequential selection strategy

Stage 4: Program review

cost) or lost production time leading to less of the product available for sale (a revenue effect). Company statistics and the experience of supervisors may be used to derive outlay costs stemming from equipment maintenance for some specified time period (two to three years), and the annual costs computed. The procedure would be similar but more challenging for revenues. While close records are kept of expenses, the impact of performance on revenues requires subjective judgment.

Continuing our example of equipment maintenance, a first step toward developing cost estimates would require that supervisors estimate the total lost production time due to equipment failure. Though such estimates may, at first glance, seem virtually impossible, we can obtain a feeling for their accuracy by examining the degree of agreement between supervisors who have made independent estimates. Moreover, lower, upper, and middle values of the range of estimates may be used to derive the outer bounds of such cost esti-

mates. After estimates have been made of the revenue losses induced by lost production time related to equipment failure, supervisors would estimate that part of the lost revenues that is probably associated with different levels of the operator's performance in the area of equipment maintenance.

To illustrate, consider the task of estimating what proportion, if any, of such revenue losses might be due to such exemplary job behaviors as the following:

Regularly checks all important fluid levels and moving parts.

Remedies minor problems before they become serious.

Always handles delicate equipment such as sensors and samplers carefully.

Cleans such items carefully before putting them away.

Acts quickly during malfunctions to prevent further damage.

As should be apparent, the above job behaviors constitute descriptions of top performance on the equipment maintenance job-performance dimensions. It is highly unlikely that supervisors would believe that any part of costs related to equipment breakdown would be due to these highly effective patterns of performance. In contrast, poor or ineffective behaviors would, of course, be judged as being implicated in some fraction of the over-all costs involved in equipment breakdown.

Finally, the dollar value associated with each performance level would be computed as the estimated fraction multiplied by the total cost related to that performance dimension divided by the number of persons exhibiting that type of performance. Note that supervisors would never be asked to judge directly a dollar value. They (a) detail outlay and revenue impacts of the dimension, and (b) judge what fraction of the capitalized total impact is due to a particular level of job performance.

Two more kinds of information are required before one is ready to decide whether or not to proceed with developing a new selection system. One is the estimated outlay costs of selection for (a) random selection; (b) the current selection system; and (c) the proposed new selection system. The second is a careful estimation of the selection ratio which has been used and which will presumably continue to be used over the life of the program. Once again, upper, lower, and middle values provide more information than simply a single estimate. For purposes of illustration in Table 9-1, only the middle value is utilized for the hypothetical data shown therein. Table 9-1 shows possible cost implications for two performance dimensions: maintenance and job persistence. The potential utility of different selection systems is computed separately for each dimension according to various levels of job performance. This information is then combined from the two separate sets of computations. The column labeled "I" is the hypothetical ideal case where top performance would be obtained from *all* persons selected. The column labeled "Reas" is more difficult to

generate because estimates must take account of base rates, the projected selection ratio, and typical test validities obtained in comparable situations. The purpose of the "Reas" column is not to provide a precise estimate of outcomes for the new system but merely to point up those instances where a new selection system would probably not be warranted.

The crucial information for deciding whether to proceed with the investment in selection research is shown at the bottom of Table 9-1 under "Potential savings." We suggest that a minimum potential saving of at least two or three times the outlay costs of the new selection system would be necessary to warrant proceeding. Even when results force one to abandon further selection research, the time spent on developing performance measures will in no sense have been wasted. These measures would, of course, be used for regular employee-performance appraisal and feedback, to aid in making promotion and placement decisions, and to guide supervisors in setting group and individual goals.

STAGE 2: DEVELOPING A NEW SELECTION SYSTEM

Stage 2 requires, first of all, that a list of likely psychological constructs be compiled for predicting the areas of job performance found to be important. The list of possible constructs is then used to select tests and inventories to measure them. Ideally, more than one measure should be chosen for each construct. Individuals' scores on the various tests and inventories should, of course, be consistent across a period of time (test-retest reliability), across methods (convergent validity), and relatively independent of measures of different constructs by similar methods (discriminant validity).

The choice between concurrent and predictive validation strategies should lean toward *predictive*. The reduced short-term costs of concurrent validation have resulted in its fre-

Table 9-1 Computations Showing Cost Implications of Job Performance on an Assembler Job in Relation to Possible Use of Different Selection Strategies*

Performance Dimension 1: Maintenance						Performance Dimension 2: Job Persistence				
Performance		Number of Persons at Each Performance Level				Performance	Number of Persons at Each Performance Level			
Level	Value	PR	P	I	Reas	Value	PR	P	I	Reas
(Best) 1	− 100	40	49	500	130	5,000	38	46	500	135
2	− 200	60	73	−	165	4,200	52	63	−	155
3	− 300	85	104	−	105	3,550	81	99	−	105
4	− 500	112	137	−	60	2,950	114	139	−	65
5	− 800	69	84	−	30	2,200	72	88	−	25
6	− 1,000	28	32	−	8	1,280	32	39	−	15
(Worst) 7	− 1,500	16	21	−	2	550	21	26	−	0
		410	500		500		410	500		500

PR = present performance distribution in the incumbent population.
 P = projected performance distribution in the selected population given continuation of present practice.
 I = performance distribution in the selected population given an ideal outcome.
Reas = performance distribution given a reasonable outcome.
 U = unit vector, 7×1.

Criterion 1 (Maintenance):
Potential values associated with the above selection outcomes
 1. Ideal outcome: $I'V = -\$50,000$
 2. Random outcome: $U'V \times (500/7) = -\$134,285$
 3. Present practice outcome: $P'V = -\$249,900$
 4. Reasonable outcome: $Reas'V = -\$142,000$

Criterion 2 (Job Persistence):
Potential values
 1. Ideal outcome: $+ \$2,500,000$
 2. Random outcome: $+ \$1,409,116$
 3. Present practice outcome: $+ \$1,513,920$
 4. Reasonable outcome: $+ \$1,964,700$

Probable returns on investment for the above selection outcomes
 1. Ideal: (values/costs) − outlays = $2,500,000 − $50,000 − $100,000 = $2,350,000
 2. Random: $1,409,116 − $314,285 − $10,000 = $1,084,831
 3. Present practice: $1,513,920 − $249,900 − $25,000 = $1,239,020
 4. Reasonable: $1,964,700 − $142,000 − $100,000 = $1,722,700
Savings: (Reasonable − Present) = $483,680
       (Ideal − Present) = $1,110,980

*Outlay costs for developing and implementing each selection system are assumed to be as follows: Random: $10,000
Present Practices − $25,000
New System = $100,000

quent use, but this is unwise. Results from concurrent studies may be underestimates of the true validities of a new selection system because restriction of range on both perform- ance and test measures may have attenuated the magnitude of statistical relationship be- tween them. The sample of incumbents availa- ble for the usual concurrent study will typically not include either the least effective (those who have failed on the job) or the most effective (those who have been promoted to better jobs).

The validity of a new selection system must be evaluated according to its actual advantages in cost savings. The cost advantages of correct selection decisions and the relative costs due to selection errors of both types (i.e., selecting persons who later fail or rejecting persons who would actually have succeeded) can be estimated by methods similar to those illustrated by Dunnette (1966; pp. 175–183). The cost superiority of the new selection system must, of course, be tested for statistical significance and the estimates must be based on cross-validated validity coefficients. How big an advantage justifies using a new selection system? Demonstration of statistical significance is not the final answer, even though it does possess desirable legal properties. If the new selection system showed either little or negative return, it would obviously not be a desirable choice.

STAGE 3: IMPLEMENTING A NEW SELECTION SYSTEM

The major decision required for implementing a new selection system involves how to use individuals' scores on the new system to make selection decisions. This matter will, of necessity, have already been considered in order to provide information for developing cost estimates during stage 2. Nonetheless, we comment briefly on the process here for the purpose of making more explicit how such selection decisions may be implemented with the new system.

Deciding what a given score means for a particular applicant involves a choice between (a) hiring the applicant, (b) rejecting the applicant, or (c) obtaining more information about the applicant before making a final decision. Figure 9-2 shows how decision points might be

chosen according to the results of the validation study. An applicant may either be accepted with at least confidence Ca, or rejected with at least confidence Cr. Or, he or she may be conditionally accepted until additional information can be gathered to make a decision at a sufficiently high degree of confidence. In Figure 9-2, this higher degree of confidence might be obtained from some later information, such as how well the person does on a test measuring his or her level of learning during early training for the job. Other sources of additional information might include how well he or she performs during a standardized probationary period on the job (a job-sample test) or some other type of validated test or behavioral information. The selection process can, in fact, be viewed as a sequence of decision points ranging all the way from decisions based on test scores at the time of application, job tryouts, training results, early job performance, etc., to decisions eventually made on the basis of the actual job performance or criterion measurement itself.

Viewed in this way, a predictive validation study is actually a never-ending series of selection decisions based on an accumulation of information from early test performance right up to and including the ultimate measure of performance on the job. In effect, then, once the actual selection program begins, not *all* applicants need to take *all* tests initially. For example, Joe Cool may be shown to have such good potential on the basis of his score on a single ability test that an immediate prediction may be made for him with the required level of confidence. In contrast, another applicant, scoring lower, may be in a range where the test does not yield a good level of confidence for making decisions. Then, we might need to administer several tests and a job simulation before we could confidently make a decision about that applicant. Common practice is to assess confidence in selection decisions for all persons. This

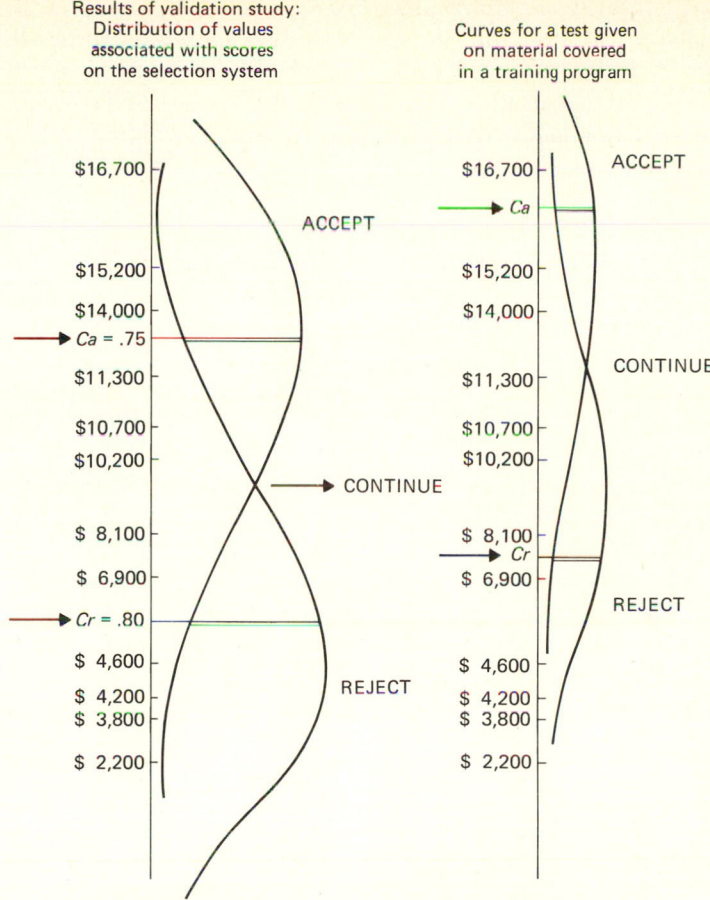

Results of validation study:
Distribution of values
associated with scores
on the selection system

Curves for a test given
on material covered
in a training program

$16,700

$16,700   ACCEPT

→ Ca

ACCEPT

$15,200

$15,200

$14,000

$14,000

→ Ca = .75

$11,300

$11,300   CONTINUE

$10,700
$10,200

$10,700
$10,200

→ CONTINUE

$ 8,100

$ 8,100
→ Cr

$ 6,900

$ 6,900

→ Cr = .80

REJECT

$ 4,600

$ 4,600

$ 4,200
$ 3,800

$ 4,200
$ 3,800

REJECT

$ 2,200

$ 2,200

Figure 9-2 Selection decisions based on validity results.

practice provides no guarantee of minimum acceptable confidence for decisions to select or reject. The approach we suggest ensures that no one is either accepted or rejected until some specified minimum level of confidence is demonstrated. Different values for Ca and Cr can be tried to determine their effect on overall selection returns.

In short, decisions are less costly for the initially more predictable persons and more costly (but still just as accurate) for the initially less predictable persons. This sequential strategy of decision making serves the goals of both the institutional decision maker and the individual applicant. The notion that different

kinds of individuals have different testing costs leads to a change in calculating return. Return for a given alternative is the sum of overall value for all those selected *minus* the sum of testing costs (including materials, time of test administrators, and salary paid the applicant up to the time of decision) for all applicants *minus* such general recruitment and administrative costs as advertising, maintenance of facilities, etc.

STAGE 4: PROGRAM REVIEW

Nothing lasts forever, and the effectiveness of selection programs is no exception. Both the characteristics of the applicant population and the behavioral makeup of the job need planned, systematic review. Selection programs should have an assigned life, after which a thorough examination and overhaul is made. There is no point in either letting valuable new potential go unnoticed or in continuing with selection programs having insignificant or negative returns. The possibility of such review and the possible need for beginning the entire selection research and development cycle anew is shown in Figure 9-1.

REFERENCES

Brogden, H. E., & Taylor, E. K. The dollar criterion: Applying the cost accounting concept to criterion construction. *Personnel Psychology*, 1950, **3**, 133–154.

Brown, K. R. Job analysis by multidimensional scaling. *Journal of Applied Psychology*, 1967, **51**, 469–475.

Campbell, J. P., Dunnette, M. D., Lawler, E., & Weick, K. *Managerial behavior, performance, and effectiveness*. New York: McGraw-Hill, 1970.

Cronbach, L. J., & Gleser, G. C. *Psychological tests and personnel decisions*. Urbana, Ill.: University of Illinois Press, 1965.

Dunnette, M. D. *Personnel selection and placement*. Belmont, Calif.: Wadsworth, 1966.

Schmidt, F. L., & Kaplan, L. B. Composite vs. multiple criteria: A review and a resolution of the controversy. *Personnel Psychology*, 1971, **24**, 419–434.

Smith, P. C., & Kendall, L. M. Retranslation of expectations: An approach to the construction of unambiguous anchors for rating scales. *Journal of Applied Psychology*, 1963, **47**, 149–155.

Reading 10

Organizational Entry: The Individual's Viewpoint

John P. Wanous

All organizational systems import various types of energy: people, money, raw materials, information, and so forth. This paper is concerned with *human* energy sources, in particular new employees in organizations. Fundamentally, the "organizational entry process" can be viewed in two ways: (1) from the individual's viewpoint, and (2) from the organization's perspective. This paper focuses exclusively on the individual's viewpoint during the entry process and has four objectives. The first is to define the individual's view of organizational entry in general, and then identify four components of this process. The second objective is to describe why new employees are an important group to study. The third is to review what we know about each of the topic areas in organizational entry. The final objective is to point out what remains to be done for a better understanding of newcomers in organizations.

WHAT IS ORGANIZATIONAL ENTRY?

Organizational entry concerns how individuals move from outside to inside a new organization. Viewed from the perspective of the individual who enters, the entry process begins outside the organization as people think about possible entry. The process continues throughout the phase where an effort is made to join, when there is an acceptance of the individual by the organization, and when the individual makes the final decision to enter.

The topic of organizational entry continues to be important even after entry itself. In particular, it is important to consider the "aftereffects" of the entry process on both the individual and the organization. An examination of these entry consequences does *not* include what some have called "organizational socialization" (Bakke, 1953; Schein, 1968) or the "personalizing process" (Bakke, 1953). Both of these processes occur *after* entry, but are *not* necessarily *direct* consequences of the entry itself. Organizational socialization refers to how individuals learn: (1) the basic values and goals of the organization, (2) the means for attaining them, (3) individual job responsibilities, (4) acceptable behavior patterns for effective job performance, and (5) other guiding principles for maintaining the organization (Schein, 1968). The personalizing process refers to how each individual leaves his or her "mark" on the organization. Together these describe the character of mutual-influence processes that are set in motion when newcomers enter organizations.

Organizational entry does not focus on these two active processes, but it does include that postentry behavior of newcomers which has been caused by the entry process itself. It can perhaps be best understood by listing four specific components, each of which has become a question for research.

1   How do individuals choose new organizations?
2   How accurate and complete is the information that "outsiders" have about new organizations?
3   What is the impact of organizational recruitment on the "matching" of individual and organization?

4   What are the consequences of matching or mismatching individuals and organizations?

NEW EMPLOYEES AS AN IMPORTANT TOPIC

Implied by the above questions is a view of organizational entry from the individual's viewpoint, not the organization's. Viewing entry from an organizational perspective changes the way such questions are asked. For example, the selection and testing research in industrial psychology is the "flip side" of the first area. Concern over getting lots of data about job applicants is the organizational analogue of the second question. For the third area, organizations have been concerned with making themselves appear attractive for recruitment purposes, but have not investigated the impact of this recruitment strategy on newcomers. Thus, one reason why the study of new employees has merit is that we know so little about it from the individual's viewpoint. The second reason is closely related. Because organizations and researchers have viewed new employees primarily as passive figures, they have tended to concentrate on abilities and skills in the context of predicting job performance. This emphasis overlooks the fact that individuals choose new organizations and that the satisfaction of the individual's need is a crucial element in keeping effective employees from leaving.

A third reason for the significance of this area is that turnover in most organizations tends to be highest during the first six months or so of work experience. This varies from situation to situation, but tends to be fairly characteristic of most business organizations. In many cases this is quite costly to an organization, when there is a "revolving-door" effect for certain jobs. That is, there can be high turnover for some entry-level jobs because the newcomers are "testing" the work environment to see if it will be satisfactory. If it is not, they often leave quickly; hence the revolving-door phenomenon. A fourth point is that people who join new organizations are probably more open to influence than they will be at any other time spent in that particular organization. For example, the formation of a "psychological contract" (Schein, 1968) may revolve around how well matched are personal versus organizational values.

MATCHING INDIVIDUAL AND ORGANIZATION: A GENERAL FRAMEWORK FOR ORGANIZATIONAL ENTRY

Most organizations are constantly involved in a "matching process" between the individual and the organization. On the one hand, newcomers to an organization come with their own *individual talent* (such as skills, abilities, and knowledge), as well as important *human needs*. On the other hand, the typical organization can be viewed as having *talent requirements* for various jobs as well as its own particular *climate characteristics*. Thus, there are two important "match-ups" which occur during the process of new employees entering an organization: (1) individual talent with organizational talent requirements, and (2) human needs with organizational climate. This general process of matching individual and organization is *continuous* because both people and jobs change over time, and because there is constant labor force movement (hires, promotions, quits, and fires).

It is fair to say that most organizations strongly emphasize the match between employees' talents and job demands. On the other hand, matching the needs of employees and the characteristics of jobs is typically underemphasized. In fact, rarely are efforts made to match newcomers to a specific job in a particular organization in terms of human needs and the job climate.

While both matches are probably important

for motivation, performance, and job satisfaction, the match between employee's talent and job-talent requirements probably has a more immediate and powerful effect on job performance than it does on job satisfaction or job tenure (Lofquist & Dawis, 1969). A poor match typically results in poor job performance. Sometimes, however, a mismatch of this first type can affect job tenure (i.e., absenteeism, turnover, or tardiness), especially when an individual is *over*-qualified for a job.

On the other hand, the match between human needs and organizational climate usually has a more immediate and potent effect on job satisfaction and tenure than on job performance. A poor matching can produce employees' dissatisfaction which results in tardiness, absenteeism, and turnover. There are exceptions to this, of course, because some individuals may use ineffective job performance as a way to "get back" at an organization for a job which is not psychologically rewarding (Argyris, 1964).

Two selection processes operate in the matching of people and jobs. One of these involves the organization selecting the individual and the other involves the individual selecting the organization. Research pertaining to the former abounds in industrial psychology, as it has been a major focus there. When the organization is selecting an individual the tendency has been to assess the *talents* of an applicant for placement on an appropriate type of job. On the other hand, when individuals select an organization they often look for a potentially satisfying climate in which to work (in a business organization), or study (in a university).

Thus, there has been a historical tendency for the matching of individual talent and organizational requirements to be associated with the organization's selection of individuals rather than vice versa. It is obvious that a complete treatment of organizational entry necessarily includes *both* match-ups, and should stress organizational selection of individuals as well as the individuals' choices of organizations. However, the present paper is intentionally slanted toward the relatively underresearched topics concerning organizational entry from the individual's viewpoint.

EXAMPLES OF RESEARCH ON ORGANIZATIONAL ENTRY

Although our present knowledge about organizational entry is highly asymmetrical, we do have a good start in all four of the areas listed on page 127. Below are examples of what has been done to date.

How Do Individuals Choose New Organizations?

About one dozen studies of organizational choice can be found in today's literature. The procedures of each study vary. For example, one long-term study investigated how a group of forty-nine people studying for the master's degree at Carnegie-Mellon University chose their first full-time jobs (Vroom, 1966; Vroom & Deci, 1971). This study "tracked" the job expectations and goals these students held concerning the organizations they interviewed. For most students there was a very close correspondence between their *overall* ratings of "organizational attractiveness" and an *index* composed of their *specific expectations* (about each organization) multiplied by their *personal goals* for the job. When it came time to choose a particular job offer, 76 percent of them picked the organization which had been rated the highest on the index of "expectations × goals." This was felt to be strong confirmation of the "expectancy theory" of motivation (Vroom, 1964), upon which the study was based.

A number of other studies have also found that individuals tend to select those organizations which have the greatest personal attractiveness based on an index of their *expecta-tions* multiplied by their *goals*. Perhaps the best way to characterize these studies is to distinguish among the various stages in the individual's choice of organization:

Stage 1: Initial Attractiveness of an Organization Most studies indicate that people are attracted to those organizations which are rated highest on a psychological index based on *both* an individual's *expectations* about what the organization will be like *and* each person's own values or goals (Huber, Daneshgar, & Ford, 1971; Lawler, Kuleck, Rhode, & Sorenson, 1975; Vroom, 1966; Wanous, 1975a).

Stage 2: Effort to Join a Particular Organization After deciding what organizations are most attractive, the field of possibilities is somewhat narrowed. From among those remaining, certain ones seem to be more highly sought out than others. An individual's greatest efforts to join a particular organization seem to be directed to those which not only are attractive, but which are seen as likely to offer an opening. In a nutshell, studies have shown that one's *expectations* of gaining entry *and* the *attractiveness* of an organization determine how hard most individuals try to join certain organizations (Glueck, 1974; Lawler et al., 1975; Wanous, 1975a).

Stage 3: Choice from among Organizations Offering Entry In between stages 2 and 3 the initiative returns to the organization, which selects or rejects the individual. Every organization that one tries to enter will not necessarily offer admission. Once again the range of possibilities is limited. From among those which do extend offers, most people choose the one which has the greatest attractiveness (Ford, Huber, & Gustafson, 1972; Huber et al., 1971; Lawler et al., 1975; Pieters, Hundert, & Beer, 1968; Soelberg, 1967; Vroom, 1966; Wanous, 1975a).

Although the art of organizational choice seems to be quite rational, and well understood, research has uncovered two interesting "twists." For example, the *act of choosing* seems to *distort* the perceptions of those engaged in the process. Immediately after deciding which organization to enter, most people tend to perceive it as even *more* attractive than before the choice. They also tend to perceive the rejected alternatives as even less attractive (Lawler et al., 1975; Soelberg, 1967; Vroom, 1966). This is an example of a basic human need to *justify* one's own choices, although it may not always occur (Sheridan, Richards, & Slocum, 1975).

The second "twist" to be found is that newcomers in organizations tend to be *less* satisfied with their choice than either before making it or immediately after choosing (Vroom & Deci, 1971; Wanous, 1975a). This result raises many questions, but especially those concerning the quality of information outsiders have when making choices and the impact of typical recruitment programs on such expectations. Both of these are taken up in the next two component areas of the organizational entry process.

How Accurate and Complete Is the Information of Outsiders about New Organizations?

Until recently, problems of misinformation were not considered serious enough to warrant much attention. The subsequent disappointment after entry clearly implies that some people were led to expect the wrong things about new organizations. The research to be discussed under topic 3 (see page 131) also points in the direction of inaccurate—especially inflated—expectations held by outsiders before entry.

A study of Harvard M.B.A. students (Ward & Athos, 1972) indicated that recruiters from various companies gave "glowing" rather than "balanced" descriptions, and glossed over details of organizational life. Research at an automotive manufacturer (Dunnette, Arvey, & Banas, 1973) examined two groups of employees: those who left within their first four years, and those who remained longer than four years. They found that most people's expectations were *not* realized in actual job situations. The problem of unfulfilled expectations was much more severe for those who "terminated early." Only such concrete expectations as pay levels were confirmed by actual experience, a finding documented by Wanous (1972b) earlier in a study of University of Minnesota graduating seniors.

The American Telephone and Telegraph study of newly entered managers (Bray, Campbell, & Grant, 1974) shows that expectations decline with increasing years in the same company. This study did not begin until after entry, but found that employees' expectations about the future continued to decline for the first seven years of AT&T work experience. This decline was about equal for both effective and ineffective performers.

A recent study of M.B.A. students in three New York City graduate business schools (Wanous, 1976) provides the most detailed information on the quality of information that outsiders have about new organizations. Students were asked to complete questionnaires about their school choices at three points in time: (1) outsiders—before entry, (2) newcomers—shortly after entry in the fall semester, and (3) insiders—during the spring after the first academic year. There was a *decline* from naive (inflated) expectations of outsiders to realistic (lower) beliefs on the part of insiders. Interestingly enough, the decline occurred only for those aspects "intrinsic" to the educational process itself (e.g., quality of teaching, school status, competition), and not for those "extrinsic" to learning (e.g., location, tuition, transfer credit, etc.). The Wanous (1976) study also looked at a smaller group of telephone operators who moved from outside to inside the Southern New England Telephone Company. As with the M.B.A. students, there was a decline for intrinsic job characteristics. Unlike the M.B.A. study, a decline also occurred for extrinsic factors, but it was not as strong as the decline for intrinsic job characteristics.

As the M.B.A. data from the Wanous (1976) study indicate, there may *not* be a problem of "total inaccuracy" on the part of outsiders. Nevertheless, those aspects considered intrinsic in this study, and in other studies (e.g., Dunnette, Campbell, & Hakel, 1967), are the ones *most* important to individuals. This poses a very serious and interesting problem for organizational recruitment. Namely, outsiders tend to have inaccurately inflated expectations about those organizational characteristics (i.e., the intrinsic ones) which are the hardest ones to describe because they are the most abstract. Even if an organization tried to describe itself accurately to new recruits, it would not be easy. The next section discusses a series of studies where a variety of organizations tried to recruit newcomers with as much realism as possible.

What Is the Impact of Organizational Recruitment on the "Matching" of Individual and Organization?

One way to deal with the inflated expectations of outsiders is to give recruits a "realistic job preview" (Wanous, 1975b, c) to "set" initial expectations at a realistic level and to help individuals make better organizational choices. Over the last twenty years six experimental studies in organizations have compared the effectiveness of a realistic job preview with a more "traditional" approach.

The basic difference between the two strategies is that the realistic one emphasizes *specific* facts which are typical of *both* desirable *and* undesirable aspects of the organization. The traditional approach tries to maximize the number of recruitees for each opening by "selling" the job in its most positive light. Recruitment by the traditional approach also tends to overlook the costs associated with high quit rates.

The six experiments involved a variety of techniques to present a realistic job preview: four studies used a booklet, one a film, and another a two-hour "practice session." They involved a variety of individuals and jobs: insurance salesmen, West Point cadets, telephone operators, and sewing machine operators. The first two groups were all male, while the latter were all female.

A number of criteria were used to assess the impact of these realistic job previews. First, was the ability to recruit newcomers impaired by the use of realism? Four of the six studies directly addressed this issue and three show no impairment at all (Wanous, 1973; Weitz, 1956; Youngberg, 1963). A fourth study (Farr, O'Leary, & Bartlett, 1973) found a slightly higher rate of job offer refusals for those seeing the realistic job preview. Second, were initial job expectations really lowered due to the realistic preview? Two of the six directly addressed this issue, and the answer is clearly affirmative (Wanous, 1973; Youngberg, 1963). In fact, Wanous found that the preview was "selective," i.e., it lowered *only* those initial expectations that were discussed in the preview, and did not "spill over" to other aspects of the job.

A third question is whether realistic recruitment results in more positive attitudes on the part of newcomers. Two of the six studies did address this issue and both found such beneficial effects as higher satisfaction after three months (Youngberg, 1963) and fewer thoughts of quitting (Wanous, 1973). The fourth, and final, question is whether realism resulted in lower turnover. For many organizations this is the "bottom line" question concerning the effectiveness of realistic job previews. The typical way to assess it has been to compare the percentage of newcomers who "survive" (i.e., do *not* leave) with a similar percentage for those in the control group. The higher the survival percentage, the lower the turnover, and the more effective the preview. These results are listed below in chronological order, showing the realistic preview's percentage first, followed by the job survival rate of the control group.

- At Life and Casualty Insurance Company of Tennessee, 68 percent versus 53 percent over five months for life insurance agents (Weitz, 1956).
- At Prudential Insurance Company, 71 percent versus 57 percent over six months for life insurance agents (Youngberg, 1963).
- At West Point, 91 percent versus 86 percent over one year for first year cadets (Macedonia, 1969).
- At the Southern New England Telephone Company, 62 percent versus 50 percent over three months for telephone operators (Wanous, 1973).
- At Manhattan Industries, Inc., 88.9 percent versus 68.8 percent over six weeks for white sewing machine operators. No differences were found for Black operators, however.
- At West Point, 94 percent versus 88.5 percent over a three-month summer training period for first year cadets (Ilgen & Seely, 1974).

What Are the Consequences of Matching or Mismatching Individuals and Organizations?

Thus far we have seen that individuals *try* to "match" themselves to organizations, but they often make such decisions on the basis of incomplete and inaccurate information. A few organizations, however, have consciously tried to recruit newcomers using realistic job previews to effect better match-ups between human needs and organizational climate. The majority of organizations, whether bueinesses or universities, have not attempted systematic, realistic recruiting. Thus it is important to ask what the consequences are when mis-

matches between individuals and organizations occur.

Guiding this brief review are two assumptions. First, based on the "matching model" presented earlier, it is expected that the match between individual and organization will have a greater impact on job *satisfaction* and *tenure* than on actual job performance. Second, in most cases a good, or "close," match between an individual's needs and the organizational climate is desirable. The exceptions to these assumptions will be discussed last.

The match-up between individual and organization takes place in two related "levels": (1) the immediate job or task, and (2) general aspects of the climate other than the immediate job, such as pay, relationships with co-workers, the status of the organization, etc. (Schneider, 1975). This distinction is similar to the one Herzberg et al. have drawn between job content and the job's context (Herzberg, Mausner, & Snyderman, 1959).

Studies of the relationship between job characteristics and individual differences are good examples of research falling into the first type of matching category. Early studies in the area of task (or job) characteristics sought to identify the most important ones which influence employees' motivation, performance, tenure and satisfaction (e.g., Herzberg et al., 1959). Recent studies have gone beyond the mere identification of important job characteristics to include the influence of individual differences (in desires or needs). Several recent studies have shown that matching *actual* job characteristics to *desired* characteristics leads to high levels of employee's motivation and satisfaction, but not necessarily to performance (Hackman & Lawler, 1971; Wanous, 1974).

Besides the individual's match-up to the immediate job, studies have examined the consequences of the match-up between individuals and the broader context of organizational climate. Most of these do, in fact, support the assumption that organizational climate has a greater impact on satisfaction than on actual job performance (Friedlander & Margulies, 1969; Lawler, Hall, & Oldham, 1974; Pritchard & Karasick, 1973).

A recent study by Schneider (1975) tried to relate the match-up (or "fit," as he called it) between individual and organization to both performance and tenure among 1,125 life insurance agents. Initially he was unable to find any sizeable relationships. Further analysis revealed that some of the agencies studied had far "better" climates than others. That is, they were higher on supportiveness, concern, morale, and autonomy, and lower on conflict than other agencies. By then examining the match-up between individual and organization for both the "good" and "bad" agencies, he found differences which had been hidden when he examined all the agencies together. Among the "good" agencies the expected relationship was found (i.e., the closer matched individuals and organizations were, the higher the sales and the lower the turnover). On the other hand, in the "bad" (or "negative") climates the reverse was true. The *less* the individual was similar to the climate, the better were sales and turnover was lower. Although Schneider's study is one of the first to separate out the *type* of climate, it does suggest that a strict interpretation of matching individual to organization may have to be slightly modified. This is especially true for those organizations with basically "negative" climates.

WHERE DO WE GO FROM HERE?

For the future study of organizational entry, the greatest single need is for an *integrated conceptual overview* of the entire process. The present paper should be considered as only suggestive in this regard. What needs to be done is to adopt a general "systems view" of this process by drawing on the relevant research from industrial, organizational, social, and vocational psychology, as well as from the relevant areas of other disciplines such as industrial sociology, labor economics, and industrial relations. In one way or another all these areas of research have something of relevance for the study of organizational entry.

Certainly, future efforts in this direction should look at organizational entry from *both* sides of the matching process, and should consider both organizational selection of individuals as well as organizational choice by individuals. The present paper did *not* do this because it was considered more urgent to emphasize the underdeveloped research areas.

The future may also hold different views of organizational entry depending on the *type* of organization concerned. Most of what we know today has been obtained from studies in business organizations, and less so from colleges, universities, or the military. The basic problem of matching individual and organization is common to all these organization types, but shows up in quite different ways. For example, some businesses experience high turnover in certain entry-level jobs. In university programs, however, students pay for the opportunity to study (rather than being paid for their services), and they can be influenced by the magnet of "sunk costs." That is, the length of time for getting a degree is predictable. Thus, the longer a student remains in a school, the greater is the investment in it, and the harder it is to leave before graduation. In the military, the situation is still different. Given the legal nature of commitment to such service, the major problem is to retain qualified personnel at reenlistment time.

REFERENCES

Argyris, C. *Integrating the individual and the organization.* New York: Wiley, 1964.

Bakke, E. W. *The fusion process*. New Haven: Labor and Management Center, Yale University, 1953.

Bray, D. W., Campbell, R. J., & Grant, D. L. *Formative years in business*. New York: Wiley, 1974.

Dunnette, M. D., Arvey, R. D., and Banas, P. A. Why do they leave? *Personnel*, 1973, **3**, 25–39.

Dunnette, M. D., Campbell, J. P., & Hakel, M. D. Factors contributing to job satisfaction and job dissatisfaction in six occupational groups. *Organizational Behavior and Human Performance*, 1967, **2**, 143–174.

Farr, J. L., O'Leary, B. S., & Bartlett, C. J. Effect of a work sample test upon self-selection and turnover of job applicants. *Journal of Applied Psychology*, 1973, **58**, 283–285.

Ford, D. L., Huber, G. P., & Gustafson, D. H. Predicting job choices with models that contain subjective probability judgments: An empirical comparison of five models. *Organizational Behavior and Human Performance*, 1972, **7**, 397–416.

Friedlander, F., & Margulies, N. Multiple impacts of organizational climate and individual value systems upon job satisfaction. *Personnel Psychology*, 1969, **22**, 171–183.

Glueck, W. F. Decision-making: Organizational choice. *Personnel Psychology*, 1974, **27**, 77–93.

Hackman, R. J., & Lawler, E. E., III. Employee reactions to job characteristics. *Journal of Applied Psychology*, 1971, **55**, 259–286.

Herzberg, F., Mausner, B., & Snyderman, B. *The motivation to work*. New York: Wiley, 1959.

Huber, G. P., Daneshgar, R., & Ford, D. L. An empirical comparison of five utility models for predicting job preferences. *Organizational Behavior and Human Performance*, 1971, **6**, 267–282.

Ilgen, E. W., & Seely, W. Realistic expectations as an aid in reducing voluntary resignations. *Journal of Applied Psychology*, 1974, **59**, 452–455.

Lawler, E. E., III, Hall, D. T., & Oldham, G. R. Organizational climate: Relationship to organizational structure, process, and performance. *Organizational Behavior and Human Performance*, 1974, **11**, 139–155.

Lawler, E. E., III, Kuleck, W. J., Rhode, J. G., & Sorenson, J. E. Job choice and post decision dissonance. *Organizational Behavior and Human Performance*, 1975, **13**, 133–145.

Lofquist, L. H., & Dawis, R. V. *Adjustment to work*. New York: Appleton-Century-Crofts, 1969.

Macedonia, R. M. "Expectations—press and survival." Unpublished doctoral dissertation, New York University, Graduate School of Public Administration, 1969.

Pieters, G. R., Hundert, A. T., & Beer, M. Predicting organizational choice: A post hoc analysis. *Proceedings of the 76th Annual Convention of the American Psychological Association*, 1969, 573–574.

Prichard, R. D., & Karasick, B. The effects of organizational climate on managerial job performance and job satisfaction. *Organizational Behavior and Human Performance*, 1973, **9**, 126–146.

Schein, E. H. Organizational socialization and the profession of management. *Industrial Management Review*, 1968, **9**, 1–16.

Schneider, B. Organizational climate: Individual preferences and organizational realities revisited. *Journal of Applied Psychology*, 1975, **60**, 459, 465.

Sheridan, J. E., Richards, M. D., & Slocum, J. W. Comparative analysis of expectancy and heuristic models of decision behavior. *Journal of Applied Psychology*, 1975, **60**, 361–368.

Soelberg, P. Unprogrammed decision making. *Industrial Management Review*, 1967, **8**, 19–29.

Vroom, V. H. *Work and motivation*. New York: Wiley, 1964.

Vroom, V. H. Organizational choice: A study of pre and post decision processes. *Organizational Behavior and Human Performance*, 1966, **1**, 212–225.

Vroom, V. H., & Deci, E. L. The stability of post decisional dissonance: A follow-up study of the job attitudes of business school graduates. *Organizational Behavior and Human Performance*, 1971, **6**, 36–49.

Wanous, J. P. Occupational preferences: Perceptions of valence and instrumentality, and objective data. *Journal of Applied Psychology*, 1972, **56**, 152–155.

Wanous, J. P. Effects of a realistic job preview of job acceptance, job attitudes, and job survival.

Journal of Applied Psychology, 1973, **58**, 327–332.

Wanous, J. P. Individual differences and reactions to job characteristics. *Journal of Applied Psychology*, 1974, **59**, 616–622.

Wanous, J. P. *Organizational entry: The transition from outsider to newcomer to insider* (Working Paper 75-14). New York University, Graduate School of Business Administration, 1975a.

Wanous, J. P. Tell it like it is at realistic job previews. *Personnel*, 1975b, **52** (4), 50–60.

Wanous, J. P. A job preview makes recruiting more effective. *Harvard Business Review*, 1975c, **53** (5), 16, 166–8.

Wanous, J. P. Organizational entry: From naive expectations to realistic beliefs. *Journal of Applied Psychology*.

Ward, L. B., & Athos, A. G. *Student expectations of corporate life.* Boston: Division of Research, Graduate School of Business Administration, Harvard University, 1972.

Weitz, J. Job expectancy and survival. *Journal of Applied Psychology*, 1956, **40**, 245–247.

Youngberg, C. F. "An experimental study of job satisfaction and turnover in relation to job expectations and self expectations." Unpublished doctoral dissertation, New York University Graduate School of Arts and Sciences, 1963.

Chapter 4

Adaptation and Developmental Processes

After individuals and organizations have chosen each other, the processes of adaptation and development begin. As in any type of social situation, the new member must learn about the group (in this case, the organization) he or she has joined, and the group (organization) will need to integrate the new member. These reciprocal processes start when the initial choices are made, but they never completely end. The member and the organization are continually influencing each other, both during the initial months of adaptation to each other, and later. The organization is attempting to make the individual into as valuable a member as possible, and the individual, in turn, is attempting to utilize the organization for personal satisfaction in the work situation. Each party, as it were, helps to "develop" the other. When the processes work correctly, both gain in relation to what they started with at the time of the individual's entry into the organization.

The four readings presented in this chapter provide both conceptual views of these processes and examples of actual organizational practices in the development of human resources. In the first article, Schein describes and analyzes the "individual's movement through an organization"—in effect, the organizational career. The fundamental point in this article is that each career movement is an interaction of attributes of the person and of the organization. Given this, there is emphasis on the concepts of both "socialization" (the influence of the organization on the individual) and "innovation" (the reciprocal process). Particularly crucial in this article is the way organizations are conceptualized. Schein puts forth a very useful way of thinking about them as "cones"—that is, structured vertically, horizontally, and circumferentially. This permits him to describe types of movements through the organization, the types of boundaries crossed, the attributes of boundaries, and the relation of boundary crossing to careers. The individual's adaptation and development in the organization is then logically viewed as a set of career steps or stages. Finally, the article puts forth several provocative hypotheses concerning career development. These hypotheses are useful not only in relation to this specific article, but also for the general issues they raise about organizational behavior.

The article by Van Maanen, Schein, and Bailyn also uses the career as a key concept. Here, in contrast to the Schein article, considerable emphasis is placed on factors outside (as well as inside) the organization that affect careers. The focus is on how an individual's view of career development interacts with the organization's view and with society's view. The article stresses that there are multiple career patterns (with no obvious "best" pattern) when individual career histories are examined. The article begins by reviewing the current situational context of careers, and then proceeds to propose and examine some new perspectives. It concludes with a set of predictions regarding the future. Throughout, it is clear the authors believe that individuals do not need to be passive with respect to what happens to them in organizations as far as their careers are concerned, and that there are distinct roles for both the organization and

society's institutions to play in helping facilitate career development.

In the next article, Gomersall and Myers describe how one company experimented with a new way to integrate new members into the organization. The experiment describes the very real state of anxiety that any of us feels when entering a new organization, and it shows how attention by the organization can help reduce the problem considerably. The innovative approach detailed in the article is one that could be adapted by a wide variety of organizations to suit particular job circumstances, and thus the lessons learned from this one experiment could be applied to many other "new member" situations. As will be seen from the article, the results of this approach not only aided the new members in their adaptation, but also provided some beneficial effects for their supervisors.

The final article in this chapter, by Byham, provides a description of an approach utilized for assisting organizations in determining the managerial capabilities of individuals in lower levels. This approach, termed the "assessment center," not only gives organizations valuable and relevant information about their members, but also provides the individuals who are assessed with useful feedback concerning their own managerial skills. The article outlines in detail the assessment-center methods and also discusses the usefulness of assessment centers in predicting future managerial success. It seems clear that such assessment approaches can help both the individual and the organization in improving the processes of adaptation and development.

Reading 11

The Individual, the Organization, and the Career: A Conceptual Scheme

Edgar H. Schein

INTRODUCTION

The purpose of this paper is to present a conceptual scheme and a set of variables which make possible the description and analysis of an individual's movement through an organization. We usually think of this set of events in terms of the word "career," but we do not have readily available concepts for describing the multitude of separate experiences and adventures which the individual encounters during the life of his organizational career. We also need concepts which can articulate the relationship between (a) the career seen as a set of attributes and experiences of the *individual* who joins, moves through, and finally leaves an organization and (b) the career as defined by the *organization*—a set of expectations held by individuals inside the organization which guide their decisions about whom to move, when, how, and at what "speed." It is in the different perspectives which are held toward careers by those who act them out and those who make decisions about them that one may find some of the richest data for understanding the relationship between individuals and organizations.

The ensuing discussion will focus first on structural variables, those features of the organization, the individual, and the career which are the more or less stable elements. Then we will consider a number of "process" variables which will attempt to describe the dynamic interplay between parts of the organization and parts of the individual in the context of his ongoing career. Basically there are two kinds of processes to consider: (1) the influence of the organization on the individual, which can be thought of as a type of *acculturation* or *adult socialization*, and (2) the influence of the individual on the organization, which can be thought of as a process of *innovation* (Schein, 1968).

Both socialization and innovation involve the relationship between the individual and the organization. They differ in that the former is initiated by the organization and reflects the relatively greater power of the social system to induce change in the individual, whereas the latter is initiated by the individual and reflects his power to change the social system. Ordinarily these two processes are discussed as if they were mutually exclusive of each other and as if they reflected *properties* of the organization or the individual. Thus certain organizations are alleged to produce conformity in virtually all of their members, while certain individuals are alleged to have personal strengths which make them innovators wherever they may find themselves. By using the concept of career as a process over time which embodies many different kinds of relationships between an organization and its members, I hope it can be shown that typically the same person is both influenced (socialized) and in turn influences (innovates), and that both processes coexist (though at different points in the life of a career) within any given organization.

Reproduced by special permission from *Journal of Applied Behavioral Science*, 1971, **7**, 401–426. The ideas in this paper derive from research conducted from 1958 to 1964 with funds from the Office of Naval Research, Contract NONR 1841 (83), and subsequently with funds from the Sloan Research Fund, M.I.T.

THE STRUCTURE OF THE ORGANIZATION

Organizations such as industrial concerns, government agencies, schools, fraternities, hospitals, and military establishments which have a continuity beyond the individual careers of their members can be characterized structurally in many different ways. The particular conceptual model one chooses will depend on the purposes which the model is to fulfill. The structural model which I should like to propose for the analysis of careers is not intended to be a general organizational model; rather, it is designed to elucidate that side of the organization which involves the movement of people through it.

My basic proposition is that the organization should be conceived of as a three-dimensional space like a cone or cylinder in which the external vertical surface is essentially round and in which a core or inner center can be identified. What we traditionally draw as a pyramidal organization on organization charts should really be drawn as a cone in which the various boxes of the traditional chart would represent adjacent sectors of the cone but where movement would be possible within each sector toward or away from the center axis of the cone. Figure 11-1 shows a redrawing of a typical organization chart according to the present formulation.

Movement within the organization can then occur along three conceptually distinguishable dimensions:

1 *Vertically*—corresponding roughly to the notion of increasing or decreasing one's *rank* or *level* in the organization;

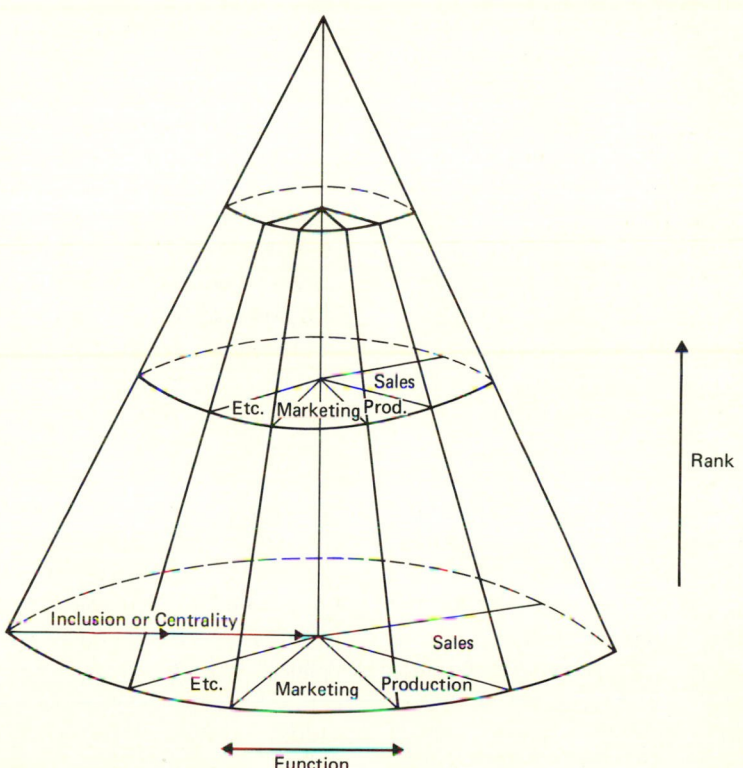

Figure 11-1 A three-dimensional model of an organization.

2 *Radially*—corresponding roughly to the notion of increasing or decreasing one's *centrality* in the organization, one's degree of being more or less "on the inside";

3 *Circumferentially*—corresponding roughly to the notion of changing one's function or one's division of the organization.

Whether movement along one of these dimensions is ever independent of movement along another one is basically an empirical matter. For present purposes it is enough to establish that it would be, in principle, possible for an individual to move along any one of the dimensions without changing his position on either of the other ones, with one exception. Vertical movement usually produces some radial movement, i.e., increased rank increases centrality unless one posits a cylinder or some other *basic* shape.

Corresponding to the three types of movement one can identify three types of *boundaries* which characterize the internal structure of the organization:

1 *Hierarchical boundaries*—which separate the hierarchical levels from one another;

2 *Inclusion boundaries*—which separate individuals or groups who differ in the degree of their centrality;[1]

3 *Functional or departmental boundaries*—which separate departments, divisions, or different functional groupings from one another.

Boundaries can vary in (a) *number*, (b) *degree of permeability*, and (c) type of *filtering properties* which they possess. For example, in the military there are a great many functional boundaries separating the different line and staff activities; but the overall policy of rotation and keeping all officers highly flexible makes these boundaries highly permeable in

[1]The organization as a multilayered system corresponds to Lewin's (1948) concept of the personality as a multilayered system comparable to an onion.

the sense that people move a great deal from function to function. On the other hand, a university would also have many functional boundaries corresponding to the different academic departments; but these would be highly impermeable in the sense that no one would seriously consider the movement of an English professor to a Chemistry department, or vice versa. A small family-run business, to take a third example, is an organization with very few functional boundaries in that any one manager may perform all of the various functions.

Similarly, with respect to hierarchical or inclusion boundaries one can find examples of organizations in which there are many or few levels, many or few degrees of "being in," with the boundaries separating the levels or inner regions being more or less permeable. The external inclusion boundary is, of course, of particular significance, in that its permeability defines the ease or difficulty of initial entry into the organization. Those companies or schools which take in virtually anyone but keep only a small percentage of high performers can be described as having a highly permeable external inclusion boundary but a relatively impermeable inclusion boundary fairly close to the exterior. On the other hand, the company or school which uses elaborate selection procedures to take in only very few candidates, expects those taken in to succeed, and supports them accordingly can be described as having a relatively impermeable external inclusion boundary but no other impermeable boundaries close to the exterior.

Further refinement can be achieved in this model if one considers the particular types of filters which characterize different boundaries, i.e., which specify the process or set of rules by which one passes through the boundary. Thus, hierarchical boundaries filter individuals in terms of attributes such as seniority, merit, personal characteristics, types of attitudes held, who is sponsoring them, and so on.

Functional boundaries filter much more in terms of the specific competencies of the individual or his "needs" for broader experience in some scheme of training and development (the latter would certainly not be considered in reference to a hierarchical boundary). Inclusion boundaries are probably the most difficult to characterize in terms of their filtering characteristics in that the criteria may change as one gets closer to the inner core of the organization. Competence may be critical in permeating the external boundary, but factors such as personality, seniority, and willingness to play a certain kind of political game may be critical in becoming a member of the "inner circle."[2] Filter properties may be formally stated requirements for admission or may be highly informal norms shared by the group to be entered.

With reference to individual careers, organizations can be analyzed and described on the basis of (a) number of boundaries of each type, (b) the boundary permeability of the different boundaries, and (c) the filtering system which characterizes them. For example, most universities have two hierarchical boundaries (between the ranks of assistant, associate, and full professor), two inclusion boundaries (for initial entry and tenure), and as many functional boundaries as there are departments and schools. Filters for promotion and tenure may or may not be the same depending on the university but will generally involve some combination of scholarly or research publication, teaching ability, and "service" to the institution. Organizations like industrial ones which do not have a formal tenure system will be harder to diagnose as far as inclusion filters go, but the inclusion boundaries are just as much a part of their system. The variables identified thus far are basically intended as a set of categories in terms of

which to describe and compare different types of organizations in respect to the career paths they generate.

A final variable which needs to be considered is the *shape* of the three-dimensional space which characterizes the organization. The traditional pyramidal organization would presumably become in this scheme a cone. An organization with very many levels could be thought of as a very steep cone, while one with few levels could be thought of as a flat cone. The drawing of the organization as a cone implies, however, that the person at the highest level is also the most central, which, of course, is not necessarily the case. If the top of the organization is a management team, one might think of a truncated cone; if there is a powerful board of directors who represent a higher level but a wider range of centrality, one might think of an inverted cone, the point of which touches the apex of the main cone and which sits on top of the main one. In universities where the number of full professors is as large as the number of assistant professors, one might think of the organization more as a cylinder with a small cone on top of it representing the administration.

I am not stating any requirements that the shape of the organization be symmetrical. If a certain department is very large but peripheral, it might best be thought of as a large bulge on an otherwise round shape. If one considers internal inclusion boundaries, one may have some departments which are in their entirety very central and thus reach the vertical axis (core), while other departments do not contain anyone who is very central in the organization and thus do not reach the core at all. The shape of the inner core is also highly variable. It may be an inverted cone, which would imply that the number of central people *increases* with rank. Or it might be a cylinder, which would imply that there are equal numbers of central people at all ranks. Or it might be some highly asymmetrical shape reflecting

[2]One of the best descriptions of such filters in an organization can be founded in Dalton's (1959) discussion of career advancement in the companies studied.

the reality that the number of central people varies with length of service, department, political connections with higher ranks, access to critical company information, and the like.[3]

Some Problems of Measuring Organizational Structure

The problem of measurement varies greatly as a function of the degree in which boundaries and their filtering characteristics are explicitly acknowledged by a given organization and by the wider society. Thus, hierarchical boundaries which separate levels are a widely accepted fact of organizational life, and the rules for permeating them tend to be fairly explicit. To the extent that implicit informal factors do operate it becomes more difficult to measure the filtering properties of the hierarchical boundaries in any given organization.

Functional boundaries are generally the easiest to identify because our typical analysis of organizations emphasizes different functions and departments. Similarly, the rules of entry to a function or department tend to be fairly explicit.

The inclusion boundaries are the hardest to identify and measure because to a considerable extent their very existence usually remains implicit. While it may be clear to everyone in a company that there is an inner circle (which may cut across many rank levels), this fact may be denied when an outsider probes for the data. The filtering mechanism may be that more difficult to identify because even the willing informant, including members of the inner circle, may be unclear about the actual mechanisms by which people move toward the center. Even the *concept* of centrality is unclear in that it does not discriminate between (a) an individual person's *feeling* of being central or peripheral and (b) some *objec-*

tive criterion of his actual position in the organization's social structure.

In my discussion thus far, the term "centrality" denotes the person's objective position as measured by the degree to which company secrets are entrusted to him, by ratings of others of his position, and by his actual power. His subjective rating of himself might correlate highly with these other measures and thus might prove to be a simpler measuring device, but it does not basically define centrality because a person may misperceive his own position.

It may be argued that I have overstated the assumption that the organization is an integrated, unified entity. After all, it may be only a group of individual people or subgroups who are coordinating their activities in some degree but operating from quite different premises. Therefore, there are no "organizational" boundaries; there are only individual approaches to the movement and promotion of their subordinates.

There is ample evidence for the assertion that persons who associate with one another around a common task for any length of time *do* develop group boundaries of various sorts and a set of norms which define their permeability and filtering properties (e.g., Homans, 1950). But it is quite possible that several such groups coexist within a larger social system and that they develop different norms. In applying the concepts which I am outlining in this paper it is therefore necessary to identify as the "organization" a group which has interacted for a sufficient length of time to have developed some common norms. Later, in analyzing the progress of a career, it will of course be necessary to consider the difficulties which are created for the individual as he moves from a group with one set of norms about boundaries to another group with a different set of norms about boundaries, even though both groups are part of the same larger organization.

[3] Dalton (1959) has identified what he calls "vertical cliques" which cover different ranks as well as departments of an industrial organization.

THE STRUCTURE OF THE INDIVIDUAL

Any given individual can be thought of as a more or less integrated set of social selves organized around a basic image or concept of self. His basic temperament, intellectual equipment, learned patterns of feeling expression, and psychological defenses underlie and partially determine this self-image and the kinds of social selves which the individual constructs for himself to deal with his environment. But our focus is on the "constructed" selves which make it possible for the individual to fulfill various role expectations in his environment, not on the more enduring underlying qualities or the basic self-image learned in childhood.

I am using the concept of a constructed social self in the sense of Mead (1934) and more recently of Becker, Geer, Hughes, and Strauss (1961) and Goffman (1955, 1957, 1959), as the person's assumptions about, perceptions of, and claims on a given social situation in which role expectations may be more or less well defined. The basic rules of conduct and interaction in terms of which the person orients himself to any social situation are largely culturally determined, but these basic rules still leave each individual a wide latitude in how he will choose to present himself in any given situation (the "line" he will take) and how much social value or status he will claim for himself (his "face").

This conception of the individual places primary emphasis on those aspects of his total being which are the most immediate product of socialization, which most immediately engage other persons in daily life, and which are most dependent on the reinforcement or confirmation of others. For example, at a *basic* level, a person may be temperamentally easily frustrated, may have developed a character structure around the repression of strong aggressive impulses, and may rely heavily on denial and reaction-formation as defense mechanisms. These characteristics describe his basic underlying personality structure but they tell us little of how he presents himself to others, what his self-image is, how he behaves in occupational or social roles, how much value he places on himself, and what kind of interaction patterns he engages in with others.

Focusing on his constructed selves, on the other hand, might show us that this person presents himself to others as very even tempered and mild mannered, that in group situations he takes a role of harmonizing any incipient fights which develop between others, that he tries to appear as the logical voice of reason in discussions and is made uneasy by emotions, that he prefers to analyze problems and advise others rather than getting into action situations (i.e., he prefers some kind of "staff" position), and that he does not get too close to people or depend too heavily upon them. None of the latter characteristics are inconsistent with the basic personality structure, but they could not have been specifically predicted from that structure. Persons with the same kind of underlying character structure might enter similar interactive situations quite differently. In other words, I am asserting that it is not sufficient to describe a person in terms of basic personality structure if we are to understand his relationship to organizations. Furthermore, I am claiming that it is possible to analyze the person's functioning at the social self level; and that this level of analysis is more likely to be productive for the understanding of career patterns and the reciprocal influence process between individual and organization.

Each of us learns to construct somewhat different selves for the different kinds of situations in which we are called on to perform and for the different kinds of roles we are expected to take. Thus, I am a somewhat different person at work than at home; I present myself somewhat differently to my superior than to my subordinate, to my wife than to my children, to my doctor than to a salesman, when I am at a party than when I am at work, and so on. The long and complex process of socialization teaches us the various norms, rules of conduct, values and attitudes, and desirable role behaviors through which one's obligations in situations and roles can be fulfilled. All of these patterns become part of us, so that to a large extent we are not conscious of the almost instantaneous "choices" we make among possible patterns as we "compose ourselves" for entry into a new social situation. Yet these patterns can be immediately brought to consciousness if the presented self chosen is one which does not fit the situation, that is, fails to get confirmation from others. Failure to get confirmation of a self which involves a certain claimed value is felt by the actor as a threat to his face; he finds himself in a situation in which he is about to lose face if he and the others do not take action to re-equilibrate the situation (Goffman, 1955).

The various selves which we bring to situations and among which we choose as we present ourselves to others overlap in varying degrees in that many of the attributes possessed by the person are relevant to several of his selves. Thus, emotional sensitivity may be just as relevant when a person is dealing with a customer in a sales relationship as it is with his wife and children in a family relationship. The person's attributes and underlying personality structure thus provide some of the common threads which run through the various social selves he constructs, and provide one basis for seeking order and consistency among them.

Another basis for such order and consistency is to be found in the role demands which the person faces. That is, with respect to each role which the person takes or to which he aspires, one can distinguish certain central expectations, certain essential attributes which the person must have, or certain behaviors he must be willing to engage in, in order to fulfill the role minimally (*pivotal* attributes or norms). Other attributes and behaviors are desirable and relevant though not necessary (*relevant* attributes or norms), while still another set can be identified as irrelevant with respect to the role under analysis although it includes various "latent" role capacities the person may have (*peripheral* attributes or norms).[4] The pivotal, relevant, and peripheral attributes of a role will define in some degree the filters which operate at the boundary guarding access to that role.

The changes which occur in a person during the course of his career as a result of adult socialization or acculturation are changes in the nature and integration of his social selves. It is highly unlikely that he will change substantially in his basic personality structure and his pattern of psychological defenses, but he may change drastically in his social selves in the sense of developing new attitudes and values, new competencies, new images of himself, and new ways of entering and conducting himself in social situations. As he faces new roles which bring new demands, it is from his repertoire of attributes and skills that he constructs or reconstructs himself to meet these demands.

A final point concerns the problem of locating what we ordinarily term as the person's beliefs, attitudes, and values at an appropriate level of his total personality. It has been adequately demonstrated (e.g., Adorno, Frenkel-Brunswick, Levinson, & Sanford, 1950; Smith, Bruner, & White, 1956; Katz, 1960) that beliefs, attitudes, and values are intimately related to basic personality structure and psychological defenses. But this relationship differs in different persons according to the functions which beliefs, attitudes, and values serve for them. Smith et al. (1956) distinguish

---

[4]This analysis is based on the distinction made by Nadel (1957) and utilized in a study of out-patient nurses by Bennis (1959).

three such functions: (1) *reality testing*—where beliefs and attitudes are used by the person to discover and test the basic reality around him; (2) *social adjustment*—where beliefs and attitudes are used by the person to enable him to relate comfortably to others, express his membership in groups, and his social selves; and (3) *externalization*—where beliefs and attitudes are used to express personal conflicts, conscious and unconscious motives, and feelings.

The kind of function which beliefs and attitudes serve for the individual and the kind of flexibility he has in adapting available social selves to varying role demands will define for each individual some of his strengths and weaknesses with respect to organizational demands and the particular pattern of socialization and innovation which one might expect in his career.

For example, a given individual might well have a number of highly labile social selves in which his beliefs and attitudes serve only a social adjustment function. At the same time, he might have one or more other highly stable selves in which he shows great rigidity of belief and attitude. The process of socialization might then involve extensive adaptation and change on the part of the person in his "labile" social selves without touching other more stable parts of him. He might show evidence of having been strongly influenced by the organization, but only in certain areas.[5] Whether this same person would be capable of innovating during his career would depend on whether his job would at any time call on his more stable social selves. The activation of such stable selves might occur only with promotion, the acquisition of increasing responsibility, or acceptance into a more central region of the organization.

[5]For a relevant analysis of areas which the organization is perceived to be entitled to influence, *see* Schein and Ott (1962) and Schein and Lippitt (1966).

When we think of organizations as infringing on the private lives of their members we think of a more extensive socialization process which involves changes in more stable beliefs and attitudes which are integrated into more stable social selves. Clearly, it is possible for such "deeper" influence to occur, but in assessing depth of influence in any given individual-organizational relationship we must be careful not to overlook adaptational patterns which *look* like deep influence but are only the activation of and changes in relatively more labile social selves.

Some Problems of Measuring Individual Structure

I do not know of any well-worked-out techniques for studying a person's repertoire of social selves, their availability, lability, and associated beliefs and attitudes. Something like rating behavior during role playing or sociodrama would be a possible method, but it is difficult to produce in full force the situational and role demands which elicit from us the social selves with which we "play for keeps." Assessment techniques which involve observing the person in actual ongoing situations are more promising but more expensive. It is possible that a well-motivated person would be able to provide accurate data through self-description, i.e., he might tell accurately how he behaves in situations that he typically faces.

If observation and interview both are impractical, it may be possible to obtain written self-descriptions or adjective checklist data (where the adjectives are specifically descriptive of interactional or social behavior) in response to hypothetical problem situations which are posed for the individual. The major difficulty with this technique stems from the likelihood that much of the "taking" of a social self is an unconscious process which even a well-motivated subject could not reconstruct accurately. Hence his data would be limited to his conscious self-perceptions. Such conscious self-perceptions could, of course, be supplemented by similar descriptions of the subject made by others. Some recent research using a similar formulation has been reported by Hall (1968, 1971).

THE STRUCTURE OF THE CAREER

The career can be looked at from three points of view: (1) The individual moving through an organization builds certain perspectives having to do with advancement, personal success, nature of the work, and so on (Becker et al., 1961). (2) Those individuals who are in the organization as managers take the "organizational" point of view, build perspectives in terms of the development of human resources, allocation of the right people to the right slots, optimum rates of movement through departments and levels, and so on. (3) The outside observer of the whole process is struck by certain basic similarities between organizational careers and other transitional processes which occur in society such as socialization, education, the acculturation of immigrants, or initiation into groups. If one takes this observer perspective one can describe the structure and process of the career in terms of a set of basic *stages* which create transitional and terminal *statuses* or *positions* and involve certain psychological and organizational processes (*see* Table 11-1).

In the first column of the table, I have placed the basic stages as well as the key transitional events which characterize movement from one stage to another. The terminology chosen deliberately reflects events in organizations such as schools, religious orders, or fraternities where the stages are well articulated. These same stages and events are assumed to exist and operate in industrial, governmental, and other kinds of organizations even though they are not so clearly defined or labeled. Where a stage does not exist for a given organization, we can ask what the functional equivalent of that stage is. For example, the granting of tenure and the stage of permanent membership is not clearly identified in American business or industrial concerns, yet there are powerful norms operating in most such organizations to retain employees who have reached a certain level and/or have had a certain number of years of service. These norms lead to personnel policies which on the average guarantee the employee a job and thus function as equivalents to a more formal tenure system.

It should be noted that the kinds of stages and terminology chosen also reflect the assumption that career movement is basically a process of learning or socialization (during which organizational influence is at a maximum), followed by a process of performance (during which individual influence on the organization is at a maximum), followed by a process of either becoming obsolete or learning new skills which lead to further movement. These are relatively broad categories which are not fully refined in the table. For example, in the case of becoming obsolete, a further set of alternative stages may be provided by the organizational structure—(a) retraining for new career; (b) lateral transfer and permanent leveling off with respect to rank, but not necessarily with respect to inclusion; (c) early forced exit ("early retirement"); or (d) retention in the given stage in spite of marginal performance (retaining "dead wood" in the organization).

In the second column of the table are found the kinds of terms which we use to characterize the statuses or positions which reflect the different stages of the career. In the third column I have tried to list the kinds of interactional processes which occur between the individual and the organization. These processes can be thought of as reflecting preparation of the incumbent for boundary transition; preparation of the group for his arrival; actual

Table 11-1 Basic Stages, Positions, and Processes Involved in a Career

Basic stages and transitions	Statuses or positions	Psychological and organizational processes: Transactions between individual and organization
1. Pre-entry	Aspirant, applicant, rushee	Preparation, education, anticipatory socialization
Entry (transition)	Entrant, postulant, recruit	Recruitment, rushing, testing, screening, selection, acceptance ("hiring"); passage through external inclusion boundary; rites of entry; induction and orientation
2. Basic training, novitiate	Trainee, novice, pledge	Training, indoctrination, socialization, testing of the man by the organization, tentative acceptance into group
Initiation, first vows (transition)	Initiate, graduate	Passage through first inner inclusion boundary, acceptance as member and conferring of organizational status, rite of passage and acceptance
3. First regular assignment	New member	First testing by the man of his own capacity to function; granting of real responsibility (playing for keeps); passage through functional boundary with assignment to specific job or department
Substages 3a. Learning the job 3b. Maximum performance 3c. Becoming obsolete 3d. Learning new skills, et cetera		Indoctrination and testing of man by immediate workgroup leading to acceptance or rejection; if accepted, further education and socialization (learning the ropes); preparation for higher status through coaching, seeking visibility, finding sponsors
Promotion or leveling off (transition)		Preparation, testing, passage through hierarchical boundary, rite of passage; may involve passage through functional boundary as well (rotation)
4. Second assignment	Legitimate member (fully accepted)	Processes under no. 3 repeat
Substages 5. Granting of tenure	Permanent member	Passage through another inner inclusion boundary
Termination and exit (transition)	Old-timer, senior citizen	Preparation for exit, cooling the mark out, rites of exit (testimonial dinners, and so on)
6. Post-exit	Alumnus, emeritus, retired	Granting of peripheral status, consultant or senior advisor

transition processes such as tests, rites of passage, and status-conferring ceremonies; and post-transition processes prior to preparation for new transitions.[6]

Boundary Passage

Basically the dynamics of the career can be thought of as a *sequence of boundary passages*. The person can move up, around, and in; and every career is some sequence of moves along these three paths. Thus it is possible to move primarily inward without moving upward or around as in the case of the janitor who has remained a janitor all of his career but, because of association with others who have risen in the hierarchy, enjoys their confidences and a certain amount of power through his opportunities to coach newcomers.

It is also possible to move primarily upward without moving very far inward or around, as in the case of the scarce and highly trained technical specialist who must be elevated in order to be held by the organization but who is given little administrative power or confidential information outside his immediate area. Such careers are frequently found in universities where certain scholars can become full professors without ever taking the slightest interest in the university as an organization and where they are not seen as being very central to its functioning.

The problem of the professional scientist or engineer in industry hinges precisely on this issue, in that the scientist often feels excluded in spite of "parallel ladders," high salaries, frequent promotions, and fancy titles. Moving in or toward the center of an organization implies increase in power and access to information which enables the person to influence his own destiny. The "parallel ladder" provides rank but often deprives the professional in industry of the kind of power and sense of influence which is associated with centrality.

[6]*See* Strauss (1959) for an excellent description of some of these processes.

Finally, movement around without movement in or up is perhaps most clearly exemplified in the perpetual student, or the person who tries some new skill or work area as soon as he has reasonably mastered what he had been doing. Such circumferential or lateral movement is also a way in which organizations handle those whom they are unwilling to promote or get rid of. Thus they are transferred from one job to another, often with the polite fiction that the transfers constitute promotions of a sort.

In most cases, the career will be some combination of movement in all three dimensions: the person will have been moved up, will have had experience in several departments, and will have moved into a more central position in the organization. Whether any given final position results from smooth or even movement or represents a zigzagging course is another aspect to consider. Because subcultures always tend to exist within a large organization, one may assume that any promotion or transfer results in some *temporary* loss of centrality, in that the person will not immediately be accepted by the new group into which he has been moved. In fact, one of the critical skills of getting ahead may be the person's capacity to regain a central position in any new group into which he is placed.[7] In the military service, whether a person is ultimately accepted as a good leader or not may depend upon his capacity to take a known difficult assignment in which he temporarily loses acceptance and centrality, and in spite of this loss, to gain high productivity and allegiance from the men.

The attempt to describe the career in terms of sequential steps or stages introduces some

[7]In a fascinating experiment with children, Merei (1941) showed that a strong group could resist the impact of a strong leader child and force the leader child to conform to group norms; but that the skillful leader child first accepted the norms, gained acceptance and centrality, and then began to influence the group toward his own goals.

possible distortions. For example, various of the stages may be collapsed in certain situations into a single major event. A young man may report for work and be given as his first assignment a highly responsible job, may be expected to learn as he actually performs, and is indoctrinated by his experiences at the same time that he is using them as a test of his self. The whole assignment may serve the function of an elaborate initiation rite during which the organization tests the man as well. The stages outlined in Table 11-1 all occur in one way or another, but they may occur simultaneously and thus be difficult to differentiate.

Another distortion is the implication in Table 11-1 that boundaries are crossed in certain set sequences. In reality it may be the case that the person enters a given department on a provisional basis before he has achieved any basic acceptance by the organization so that the functional boundary passage precedes inclusion boundary passage. On the other hand, it may be more appropriate to think of the person as being located in a kind of organizational limbo during his basic training, an image which certainly fits well those training programs which rotate the trainee through all of the departments of the organization without allowing him to do any real work in any of them.

A further complexity arises from the fact that each department, echelon, and power clique is a suborganization with a subculture which superimposes on the major career pattern a set of, in effect, subcareers within each of the suborganizations. The socialization which occurs in subunits creates difficulties or opportunities for the person in the degree that the subculture is well integrated with the larger organizational culture. If conflicts exist, the person must make a complex analysis of the major organizational boundaries to attempt to discover whether subsequent passage through a hierarchical boundary (promotion) is more closely tied to acceptance or rejection of subcultural norms; i.e., does the filter operate more in terms of the person's capacity to show loyalty even in the face of frustration or in terms of disloyalty for the sake of larger organizational goals even though this entails larger personal risks?

IMPLICATIONS AND HYPOTHESES

Thus far I have tried to develop a set of concepts and a model of the organization, the individual, and the career. The kinds of concepts chosen were intended to be useful in identifying the interactions between the individual and the organization as he pursues his career within the organization. We need concepts of this sort to make it possible to compare organizations with respect to the kinds of career paths they generate, and to make it possible to describe the vicissitudes of the career itself. Perhaps the most important function of the concepts, however, is to provide an analytical frame of reference which will make it possible to generate some hypotheses about the crucial process of organizational influences on the individual (socialization) and individual influences on the organization (innovation). Using the concepts defined above, I would not like to try to state some hypotheses as a first step toward building a genuinely sociopsychological theory of career development.

Hypothesis 1

Organizational socialization *will occur primarily in connection with the passage through hierarchical and inclusion boundaries; efforts at education and training will occur primarily in connection with the passage through functional boundaries. In both instances, the amount of effort at socialization and/or training will be at a maximum just prior to boundary passage, but will continue for some time after boundary passage.*

The underlying assumption behind this hy-

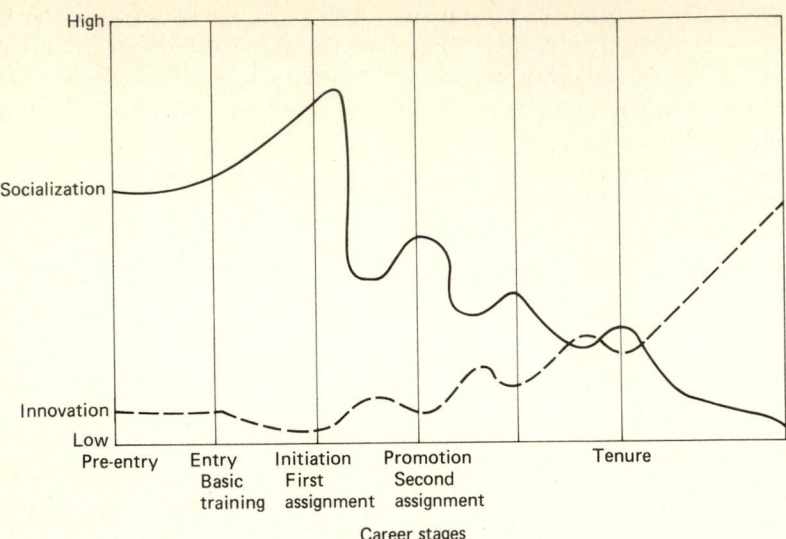

Figure 11-2 Socialization and innovation during the stages of a career.

pothesis is that (a) the organization is most concerned about correct values and attitudes at the point where it is granting a member more authority and/or centrality, and (b) the individual is most vulnerable to socialization pressures just before and after boundary passage. He is vulnerable before because of the likelihood that he is anxious to move up or in and is therefore motivated to learn organizational norms and values; he is vulnerable after boundary passage because of the new role demands and his needs to reciprocate with correct attitudes and values for having been passed. It is a commonly observed organizational fact that a griping employee often becomes a devoted, loyal follower once he has been promoted and acquired responsibility for the socialization of other employees.[8]

Hypothesis 2

Innovation, *or the individual's influence on the organization, will occur* in the middle *of a*

[8]*See also* Lieberman (1956) for an excellent research study demonstrating attitude change after promotion.

given stage of the career, at a maximum distance from past or future boundary passage.

The person must be far enough from the earlier boundary passage to have learned the requirements of the new position and to have earned centrality in the new subculture, yet must be far enough from his next boundary passage to be fully involved in the present job without being concerned about preparing himself for the future. Also, his power to induce change is lower if he is perceived as about to leave (the "lame duck" phenomenon). Attempts to innovate closer to boundary passage either will meet resistance or will produce only temporary change.

Hypothesis 3

In general, the process of socialization will be more prevalent in the early stages of a career and the process of innovation late in the career, but both processes occur at all stages.

Figure 11-2 attempts to diagram the relationships discussed above. The boundaries that are most relevant to these influence processes are the hierarchical ones in that the power of the organization to socialize is most intimately tied to the status rewards it can offer. One cannot ignore, however, the crucial role which inclusion boundaries and centrality may play in affecting the amount of socialization or innovation. If it is a correct assumption that genuinely creative innovative behavior can occur only when the person is reasonably secure in his position, this is tantamount to saying that he has to have a certain amount of acceptance and centrality to innovate. On the other hand, if the acceptance and centrality involve a subculture which is itself hostile to certain organizational goals, it becomes more difficult for the person to innovate (except in reference to subcultural norms). This is the case of the men in the production shop with fancy rigs and working routines which permit them to get the job done faster and more comfortably (thus innovating in the service of subgroup norms), yet which are guarded from management eyes and used only to make life easier for the men themselves. One thing which keeps these processes from being shared is the subgroup pressure on the individual and his knowledge that his acceptance by the subgroup hinges on his adherence to its norms. Innovation by individuals will always occur in some degree, but it does not necessarily lead to any new ideas or processes which are functional for the total organization.

Whether or not organizational innovation occurs, then, becomes more a function of the degree in which subgroup norms are integrated with the norms and goals of the total organization. In complex organizations there are many forces acting which tend to make groups defensive and competitive, thus increasing the likelihood of their developing conflicting norms (Schein, 1965). Where this happens the process of innovation can still be stimulated through something akin to the "heroic cycle" by which societies revitalize themselves. Campbell (1956) shows how the myth of the hero in many cultures is essentially similar. Some respected member of the total organization or society is sent away (freed from the subgroup norms) to find a magic gift which he must bring back to revitalize the organization. By temporarily stepping outside the organization the person can bring back new ideas and methods without directly violating subgroup norms and thus protect his own position as well as the face of the other group members.

Hypothesis 4

Socialization or influence will involve primarily the more labile social selves of the individual, while innovation will involve primarily the more stable social selves of the individual, provided the individual is not held captive in the organization.

I am assuming that if socialization forces encounter a stable part of the person which he is unable or unwilling to change, he will leave the organization if he can. On the other hand, if a given way of operating which flows from a stable portion of the individual is incompatible with other organizational procedures or norms, i.e., if innovation is impossible, the individual will also leave. The only condition under which neither of these statements would hold is the condition in which the individual is physically or psychologically unable to leave.

Hypothesis 5

A change in the more stable social selves as a result of socialization will occur only under conditions of coercive persuasion, i.e., where the individual cannot or does not psychologically feel free to leave the organization.

Conditions under which coercive persuasion (Schein, 1961) would operate can be produced by a variety of factors: a tight labor market in which movement to other organizations is constrained; an employment contract which involves a legal or moral obligation to remain with the organization; a reward system which subtly but firmly entraps the individual through stock options, pension plans, deferred compensation plans, and the like.

If conditions such as those mentioned above do operate to entrap the individual, and if he, in turn, begins to conform to organizational norms even in terms of the more stable parts of his self, he will indeed become unable to innovate. It is this pattern which has been identified by Robert K. Merton as operating in bureaucratic frameworks and which writers like W. H. Whyte have decried with the label of "organizational man." It should be noted, however, that this pattern occurs only under certain conditions; it should not be confused with normal processes of socialization, those involving the more labile parts of the person's self and the more pivotal role requirements or norms of the organization.

An important corollary of this hypothesis is that if organizations wish to ensure a high rate of innovation, they must also ensure highly permeable external boundaries; i.e., they must ensure that employees feel free to leave the organization. The less permeable the exit boundary, the greater the pressures for total conformity.

In conclusion, I have tried to show with this conceptual scheme and the hypotheses which can be derived from it that the concept of career and its attendant processes of socialization and innovation can be usefully employed as an analytical tool for exploring the complex relationship between the individual and the organization.

REFERENCES

Adorno, T. W., Frenkel-Brunswick, Else, Levinson, D. J., & Sanford, R. N. *The authoritarian personality.* New York: Harper, 1950.

Becker, H. S., Geer, Blanche, Hughes, E. C., & Strauss, A. S. *Boys in white.* Chicago, Ill.: Univer. of Chicago Press, 1961.

Bennis, W. G. The role of the nurse in the OPD. Boston Univer. Research Rep. No. 39, 1959.

Campbell, J. *The hero with a thousand faces.* New York: Meridian, 1956.

Dalton, M. *Men who manage.* New York: Wiley, 1959.

Goffman, E. On face work. *Psychiatry*, 1955, **18**, 213–231.

Goffman, E. Alienation from interaction. *Human Relat.*, 1957, **10**, 47–60.

Goffman, E. *The presentation of self in everyday life.* Garden City, N.J.: Doubleday Anchor, 1959.

Hall, D. T. Identity changes during an academic role transition. *School Rev.*, Dec. 1968, 445–469.

Hall, D. T. A theoretical model of career subidentity development in organizational settings. *Organization behavior and human performance*, 1971, **6**, 50–76.

Homans, G. C. *The human group.* New York: Harcourt, Brace, 1950.

Katz, D. (Ed.) Attitude change. *Pub. Opinion Q.*, 1960, **24**, 163–365.

Lewin, K. *Resolving social conflicts.* New York: Harper, 1948.

Lieberman, S. The effects of changes in roles on the attitudes of role occupants. *Human Relat.*, 1956, **9**, 385–402.

Mead, G. H. *Mind, self, and society.* Chicago, Ill.: Univer. of Chicago Press, 1934.

Merei, F. Group leadership and institutionalization. *Human Relat.*, 1941, **2**, 23–39.

Nadel, F. *The theory of social structure.* Glencoe, Ill.: Free Press, 1957.

Schein, E. H. *Coercive persuasion.* New York: Norton, 1961.

Schein, E. H. *Organizational psychology.* Englewood Cliffs. N.J.: Prentice-Hall, 1965.

Schein, E. H. Organizational socialization and the profession of management. *Indust. Mgmt. Rev.*, 1968, **9**, 1–15.

Schein, E. H., & Lippitt, G. L. Supervisory attitudes toward the legitimacy of influencing subordinates. *J. Appl. Behav. Sci.*, 1966, **2** (2), 199–209.

Schein, E. H., & Ott, J. S. The legitimacy of organizational influence. *Amer. J. Sociol.*, 1962, **6**, 682–689.

Smith, M. B., Bruner, J. S., & White, R. W. *Opinions and personality.* New York: Wiley, 1956.

Strauss, A. S. *Mirrors and masks.* Glencoe, Ill.: Free Press, 1959.

Reading 12

The Shape of Things to Come: A New Look at Organizational Careers

John Van Maanen

Edgar H. Schein

Lotte Bailyn

People have always had careers. But only recently has serious attention been directed to the way careers actually develop, and to the forces—individual, organizational, and societal—that shape this development. Yet, managers in organizations need the results of such inquiry if they are to utilize their human resources most effectively and deal with such recurrent topics of managerial concern as turnover, morale, motivation, and productivity from both a long- and short-term point of view. It is our contention that by using the career as a fundamental unit of study and action, we will be able to learn substantially more about why people in organizations behave as they do and, more critically, discover how to do something about it.

The key to our developing framework on careers is found not in the person, the organization, or the work task itself, but rather in the ways in which cultural, organizational, and occupational demands interact with individual aspirations, family concerns, and work demands across time. Throughout this paper we will try to spell out the implications of this perspective and to make clear why we believe the study of careers must encompass this complex whole. We begin in section I with some examples of current issues and problems in organizational careers. In section II, we extract from these examples the requirements for the systematic study of careers if that inquiry is to have the far-reaching consequences we believe possible. And, finally, in section III, we discuss the implications of this view for career development systems and for what we see to be the shape of things to come.

I THE SHAPE OF THINGS PRESENT

We live in an era in which a great variety of life-styles is realistically available. But as the possibilities expand, so do the painful necessities for choosing, and so also do the difficulties that individuals have in meshing various, and often conflicting, needs and desires. As people introduce more intricate considerations into their personal career choices, managers of organizations are faced with new and unexpected complexities in their traditional ways of mobilizing and directing human resources.

The evidence is everywhere, Individuals refuse to be promoted or to move to another

This paper is based on the ongoing theoretical and empirical work of a group of faculty members in the Organizations Studies Group of the Sloan School of Management at M.I.T. The goal of this effort is to develop a conception of occupational and organizational careers that can encompass the full range of contemporary social and psychological issues. It is based on the belief, as this paper is meant to suggest, that only if future career research is guided by such a synoptic view will its results be able to assist individuals in their choice of and within a career, as well as help organizations develop more humane and ultimately more productive personnel policies. For previous products of this effort see Van Maanen (ed.), 1977; Schein, 1975a; Van Maanen and Schein, 1976; and Bailyn and Schein, 1976.

city. Young couples will not accept job offers unless *both* are placed satisfactorily. The problems of mid-life are increasingly met not by a quiet, internal crisis, but by a radical, external change in life-style, including, at times, permanent career transformations. Organizations report having problems with young workers who are not responding in the time-honored fashion to traditional assignments and rewards. Some companies seem to be having enormous difficulties in successfully recruiting and upgrading the careers of women and minority employees. And tales regarding the ineffectiveness of "plateaued" personnel with long service are multiplying. Things have been moving so rapidly that some firms have even gone so far as to hire outside consultants to advise their own employees on whether, in light of personel needs, the employees in question should or should not accept an offered transfer or promotion within the organization.[1]

In general, our cultural understandings of the "proper" organization of work are undergoing change. More and more people, for instance, are ignoring the traditional conception that professional work is more valuable or worthwhile than nonprofessional work. Indeed, very talented people are taking jobs for which they are overeducated. Take, for example, the growing number of trained and licensed architects who are becoming involved in the "hands-on" jobs such as stonemasonry or carpentry, in the construction trades. Or consider also the many students who are avoiding certain professions—such as engineering and other applied sciences—because

the work is viewed as potentially harmful to society. Further, numerous employees are putting a positive value on staff, technical, and skilled craft positions which involve responsibility and influence through the practice of certain occupational skills but which explicitly do *not* involve managing others. The idea of rising in an organization is no longer limited to the idea of "getting into management" but is increasingly associated with having more influence through one's practical competence.

At the same time, we see more people who put little effort into their jobs and great effort into their hobbies, sports, social life, or other leisure-time activities in which they feel they can more fully express themselves. In other words, the concept of work itself has undergone a considerable transition from something sacred and unquestioned in a bygone society to a set of activities whose "meaning" has become a major concern in today's society (Berger, 1964). People now have many choices about their work and career, and it is no longer possible to make uniform assumptions about how any person will approach his or her work.

In some occupations and organizations, which almost invariably promote tension between work, self, and family concerns of employees, this uncertainty about the meaning of work is particularly evident. There is the Willy Loman syndrome of social isolation common to the proverbial traveling salesman; there is the confusion that accompanies the jet-set, "if-it's-Tuesday-it-must-be-Belgium" international executive; there is the rootlessness of the geographically mobile corporate manager of whom it is asked, if not demanded, that he shift communities time and time again, disturbing, in the process, his family and coterie of friends and acquaintances.[2]

Difficulties also arise when organizational

---

[1]Career development appears to be at least one area in which practical applications have outrun supportive research. Indeed, research seems to be playing "catch up" to the new programs which are being implemented with increasing frequency. While this is in many ways a happy state of affairs, it does beg the question of the worth of these programs, not to mention the perhaps unintended consequences of such a quick leap from *problem* identification to *program* solution.

[2]At least one writer has suggested that it is, in part, the brutalizing effects of rootlessness arising from corporate mobility that has led to a significant increase in the suicide rates among the middle-aged (Seidenberg, 1975).

rewards are perceived by individuals to be inappropriate to their particular career phase or stage. Indeed, many organizations are learning that for some people in mid-career, financial rewards are not enough to maintain commitment and motivation. Nor is "job enlargement" or an increase in work challenge welcomed by all. What many people require at this stage is an opportunity to engage their abilities in something new. In fact, some executives have turned down generous bonuses and promotions just for the opportunity to try their hand at something different (Beckhard, 1977). And some technical people at mid-career (as well as the organizations that employ them) are better served by being allowed to place their work in a secondary role than by attempts to rekindle their involvement in work (Bailyn, 1977).

A new order of complexity is also introduced by the changing role of women. A wife can no longer be viewed merely as an appendage to her husband: the foreign service no longer "requires" wives to follow orders from the wives of officers at higher positions than their husbands; companies no longer automatically evaluate wives when their husbands are up for promotion. And yet the supportive roles that a woman does play in her husband's career—in what has been called the "two-person career" (Papanek, 1973)—are beginning to be seen as more important, as is evident in the expense some multinational firms incur when entire families are sent on trial visits to countries in which the husband may someday be asked to work. Further, as more women enter the higher work ranks on their own, these changes are likely to accelerate. If the husband of a female college president is given a title, salary, and function, it seems likely that sooner or later the important ancillary roles that wives play will also come to be recognized formally by the institutions that employ their husbands. Finally, for the growing number of "dual-career families"

(Rapoport & Rapoport, 1969), work decisions made by one member of the family obviously have a significant impact on the other. Without question, organizations will have to recognize that such "extraneous" forces play a powerful role in the careers of their employees.

What all these examples suggest is that careers must be examined within the total life space of a person. Personal and family constraints cannot be viewed as unrelated to work concerns. People do not live neat, compartmentalized lives in which each separate concern operates within a closed system. For too many years we have studied and made proclamations about such issues as work satisfaction and job motivation as if they existed somehow outside of an individual's full and rich life in progress. It is clear that a broadening of perspective is required.

II A NEW PERSPECTIVE ON ORGANIZATIONAL CAREERS

This contextual emphasis—the realization that one cannot look at work and career in isolation from other aspects of people's lives—is the basic element of our perspective. From the point of view of the individual, this may seem obvious—though it has more often been paid lip service than incorporated into systematic investigation. But we are saying more than this: we are implying also that this contextual element is crucial to employing organizations and to the larger social institutions that affect all our lives.

Educational programs and opportunities, for example, which create and subsequently sustain many of the available career paths in society, will not be successful in their professed goals if they are not matched to the overall goals of the people they are designed to help. Moreover, if federal and state statutes governing such diverse topics as manpower training, welfare assistance, unemployment insurance, affirmative action programs, and day-care centers are to be effective, they must rest on an understanding of this broader context.

Nor can employing organizations afford to ignore the role that work plays in the total lives of their employees. The growth and productivity of organizations is now, more than ever, dependent on the effectiveness of human performance, which is less and less likely to be predictable in traditional ways. Organizations that cannot respond to their employees as total human beings may stagnate, and become less efficient than those organizations better able to manage their employees' careers.

A second major attribute of our perspective is its emphasis on *development*, on the *changes* that occur in all aspects of a person's life throughout the adult years. Every person goes through a series of stages in his or her career, each of which may require different involvements and capacities. This "career cycle," further, evolves side by side with a "personal cycle" of changing needs and abilities and with a "family cycle." The latter is determined both by the structural stages of the family (as defined primarily by the number and ages of children) and by the developmental needs of spouse and children. At any given point in time, each of these cycles makes its particular demands upon the individual in the form of growth opportunities to be seized, vulnerabilities to be dealt with, and constraints with which the person must cope. It is the *interaction* of these opportunities, areas of vulnerability, and constraints that creates the particular life issues that the person must resolve at any given time.

If individuals and the organizations that employ them are not sensitive to these complex realities, they may find themselves in trouble. For example, if management decides to deal with an alienated engineer by giving him a more "people-oriented job," it may be helping him personally with his problem of low job motivation, but the new role may also require increased commitment to his organization. If this happens at a time when his children are leaving home and his wife requires more of his time, this seemingly "obvious" solution to his work problem may backfire. Or, to take another example, consider the manager who has worked very hard to attain a high position in his organization, but at a certain stage in his life begins to question the value of career advancement as his major life goal. He is perhaps ready to become, in Erickson's (1959) words, more "generative" to others in the organization, more desirous to act as a guide and mentor to younger employees, and more willing to meet the previously ignored needs of his family. On the other hand, his wife, who has been generative or supportive of others all her life, may be ready to enter an independent and autonomous phase of life no longer centered solely on the family. Thus, what might have been an integrative move by either one at an earlier phase now merely reverses the sources of strain in their lives.

But the lack of congruence of cycles need not only occur between husband and wife, or between employee and organization. It may also occur *within* the individual. It is an intriguing hypothesis, for instance, that strain in one area can be handled by a person provided he or she is not simultaneously under strain in any of the other areas. "Failure"—broadly defined as a problem that is not dealt with effectively and which has led to more or less irreversible consequences—may, therefore, be partially explained by the coming together of periods of vulnerability in more than one cycle, causing more stress than the person can handle.

These considerations make it clear why it is important to distinguish between those issues that have to do with a career as defined externally by society and organizations, and those that have to do with a career as it is perceived and lived internally. This "internal" career evolves from the particular combination of forces, out of the many possible, that impinge on a person at a given point in time. These forces emanate from a person's "career anchor,"[3] from the needs and tasks associated with the particular life stage which the individual has reached, and from the circumstances of the immediate family, particularly the needs and stages of spouse and children. Because of the uniqueness of these forces, it is obvious that people will experience the same external career events (such as a raise, a promotion, or a geographical move) in very different ways. Thus one must be prepared to find multiple patterns in the way people live out and experience their careers, and in the manner in which they balance career concerns with other life concerns.

Our research has confirmed the existence of such multiple patterns at every point. A longitudinal study of alumni of the Sloan School of Management, for example, showed that this group exhibited five different career anchors: managerial competence, technical-functional competence, autonomy, creativity, and security (Schein, 1977). Engineers at mid-career, to take another case, were found to be people-oriented, or technically and professionally oriented, or not very strongly oriented to work at all but more accommodative to families (Bailyn, 1977). If such pluralism in the "human resources pool" is not recognized by multiple

reward systems and multiple career ladders within an organization, difficulties are bound to occur.

A vivid example of the lack of recognition of such multiple patterns occurred in a career workshop held in a large financial organization for its general managers. Among this group of managers, there turned out to be three distinct patterns of "ambition," even though the company value system clearly put the emphasis on only one of these patterns. Some of the managers, all currently at the regional level, did want to climb the corporate ladder to positions of group vice-president, executive vice-president, and ultimately president—the traditional pattern. However, some equally talented managers in the group wanted to remain at the regional level because they wanted the autonomy that this level of management made possible. These men saw movement up into corporate headquarters as undesirable and were willing to trade rank for autonomy and the ability to really run their own show. They wanted to be promoted to larger regions but not into headquarters. Finally, a third group of managers wanted to leave line management responsibilities and enter corporate headquarters in senior staff roles where they would have an opportunity to influence policy through conceptualizing how certain areas of the business should be handled. Of greatest interest was the fact that these men were surprised to discover the diversity within their own group (their initial assumption had been that they all wanted to be president), and were shocked and dismayed to find that the second and third groups did not feel free to tell their bosses what they wanted from their careers because it would violate traditional career expectations.

It is such mismatches between employers and employees that have prompted us to argue that the central problem of career development in organizations is how to match internal career needs and external career opportunities

[3]Schein's notion of career anchors is a way of summarizing those factors that might be said to "drive" the internal career. Career anchors are seen as syndromes of personal interests, abilities, needs, values, talents, and motives that organize and give stability to the career. Such anchors may be latent or unconscious in the person when he or she first chooses a career, but become manifest both to the individual and to others as actual work experience accumulates. They are clearly "inside" the person, functioning as a set of driving and constraining forces. Hence, if people move into settings in which they are likely to fail, or move into settings in which their values are compromised, they will be "pulled back" into something more congruent with their skills and beliefs; thus, the metaphor of "anchor." (See Schein, 1975b, 1977.)

(Schein, 1975a, Van Maanen & Schein, 1976). It is to the implications of our perspective for the success of such an endeavor that we now turn.

III THE SHAPE OF THINGS TO COME

An adequate matching of individual needs and organizational opportunities will not occur unless individuals, organizations, and other social and governmental institutions *all* take some responsibility for the things they can control. For example, no successful matching can occur unless both employee and employer know what the needs and opportunities of the other actually are. Yet, the prevailing practice in many organizations is for decision makers to guess at or assume the needs and values of their employees and then simply move them about at will (Alfred, 1967). Clearly, such a practice can never assure success. To be sure, employees themselves may not know their own desires, but in many work settings they are made to feel that to ask for or to initiate a career shift, however slight, will bring suspicion of disloyalty and hence adversely affect the course of their entire future. Thus, one of the first and most important changes to be made is to alter this unilateral concept of career development—the organization must define its available career paths, the employee must learn more about his or her internal career needs, and a climate of mutual trust necessary for the sharing of this information must be established and maintained.

But one must further assume that government will have to play a key role in this matching process as well, because some mismatches will not be resolvable within a given organization. For example, if an organization has to terminate employees because they have the wrong mix of talents or needs, or if employees discover that a given organization cannot provide them with the opportunities they seek, they may well need help of an institutional sort in making a career shift, particularly if such a shift requires additional education and training or a period of extensive search for new opportunities. The creation of mechanisms to aid this process may be particularly important during mid- and late-career periods because so many organizations are biased against investing in older employees (Fogarty, 1975).

Only by the joint action of individuals, the organizations that employ them, and government will it be possible to achieve an optimal utilization of human resources. In the remainder of this paper we outline some specific actions and directions for the future that we feel are necessary to reach this goal. First, we examine the sorts of things that government and other societal institutions might be expected to undertake. Second, we suggest several directions in which organizations might move. And third, we consider the kinds of issues individuals will have to deal with to further develop their own careers.

A What Government and Other Social Institutions Can Do

It is becoming obvious that as political, economic, social, and technological conditions change, so do the needs for different kinds of talent within a society. Societies differ with regard to the extent to which they centralize planning, both economic and social, but the interrelated issues of what kinds of competence are needed and how they are to be stimulated and controlled are major problems no society can long ignore. We would expect, therefore, that the future will bring improved procedures for forecasting manpower needs and the creation of various mechanisms to recruit and train talent pools.

At present, the dissemination of career information has become a multi-million dollar governmental activity in this country. But along with information dispersal must come appropriate institutional structures to support and promote entrance into various career paths. Job fairs, work-study programs, and support for education and on-the-job training represent the beginnings of such governmental support systems.

At another institutional level, what is now primarily a private activity—aptitude testing and vocational counseling—will perhaps come to be offered on a much broader scale through the public educational system. Already the counseling function as practiced in the high schools is undergoing significant alterations as an increasing number of employing organizations are taking a more active part—particularly in minority communities. We would hope also that counseling, in general, will shed the "classification of people" approach and pay more attention to the classification of the actual features of work careers, allowing more and more students to make their own career choices on more realistic grounds, unencumbered by restricting labels regarding what they are or are not "fit" to do. Thus, counseling in educational institutions must begin to emphasize "process consultation" models in helping people *enact* better career decisions rather than rely on the traditional "expert consultation" models in which a young person is implicitly or explicitly *told* what he or she should do on the basis of a profile of interest and attitude tests (Schein, 1969).

Yet, no matter how carefully people choose their careers, there will inevitably be mistakes. People may misread their needs, or their needs may change; job opportunities may be inaccurately perceived or may undergo actual transformations. It is too much to expect that employees and employers can, by themselves, solve all the problems of mismatch. New mechanisms that permit people to reassess and change their careers and to obtain additional education or training are necessary. Such mechanisms are in fact already becoming available (Pascal, Bell, Dougharty, Dunn,

& Thompson, 1975). The job corps, teacher corps, and subsidized adult education are recent examples of governmental support in this area. Relatedly, we would also expect to see governmental restrictions placed on such organizational practices as coercive pension plans that discourage employees from leaving their present organizations except at great financial cost. And, insofar as schooling is concerned, we expect that the present bias of graduate schools against those people who are ten or more years out of college will slowly disappear, resulting in an easing of the problems associated with career shifts.

In summary, it should be clear that many different sorts of institutional support systems and policy changes are needed if we are to improve significantly utilization of our human resources. Not only must we as a society assist people in selecting, preparing, and entering into appropriate lines of work, but we must also be prepared to aid those people who wish to redirect their work efforts at later points in their careers.

B What Organizations Can Do

Organizations will have to grow increasingly sophisticated in the design and implementation of human resource planning and forecasting systems. They will have to learn to identify correctly the career needs of their employees, and match them with organizational requirements. The procedures and systems to achieve this matching will necessarily be complex and will have to be carefully monitored and evaluated. Such systems are likely, also, to increase the sharing of responsibility for career development between organizations and individuals since effective manpower 'forecasting and planning cannot be carried out without such sharing. Organizations need information not only about their own manpower requirements, but also about employees' aspirations. Mechanisms such as job posting elicit such information, and also stimulate employees' initiative to develop their own careers by actively seeking new assignments. Job posting also stimulates the organization to do more honest performance appraisal, because employees who do not qualify for a particular job must be told precisely why they did not qualify and what they would have to do to rectify the situation.

Career counseling, in the widest sense, is likely to be expanded and closely linked to performance appraisal. This will require a variety of activities designed to help employees identify their own job needs and aid the organization in finding positions to fit them. Such counseling will increasingly be conducted within the confines of internal or external "assessment centers" (Bray & Grant, 1966). Such centers, instead of trying to infer future performance from personality traits as revealed on projective or other tests, make the assumption that assessment can be improved by putting candidates into situations that simulate the actual jobs to be performed. Evaluators, in most situations, are people who are familiar with the job because they have performed it themselves. Feedback relates assessment to observed behavior and thus permits candidates to perceive themselves more accurately and to develop a more realistic sense of their career chances. Whereas in the past such centers have primarily served the needs of the organization, increasingly their focus will have to shift to considering the needs of the individual employee as well. They will become *development centers* instead of assessment centers.

Special temporary assignments and job-rotation programs which help employees make career choices and help the organization assess their talents are also likely to become more salient in the future. This kind of program is broader than the assessment center approach because an individual spends time in a consequential situation and is thus provided with a more elaborate taste and test of his or her abilities.

Another form of "counseling" lies in the adoption of a workshop program to aid people in thinking about their careers. Such programs were initially focused on improving the process of bringing new employees into the organization by smoothing the transition from school to work (Kotter, 1973). But they also provided opportunities for larger career issues to be raised. Mid-career workshops are logical extensions of the "joining-up" workshops and have already been tried in a number of organizations. These workshops can help people learn how to make a life plan, how to think about the role of their work career within that plan, and how to develop concrete action steps toward implementing the plan.

Finally, a whole series of innovations will have to be introduced to make organizational reward systems more flexible, and more responsive to the wide range of needs of employees. For example, organizations in the future will have to become more involved in supporting educational and training activities at all levels in the firm. Further, it is likely that they will have to offer time off and financial support for such training if they are to keep their best workers from leaving the organization. One can even see prospective employees evaluating particular job opportunities on the basis of the kinds of educational opportunities promoted by several competing companies. Very clearly, educational and training activities are becoming more and more important elements of an organization's overall reward system.

Organizations will also have to provide support such as sabbaticals and flexible working hours for off-work activities. Extended leaves to pursue community service or teaching activities, already available for senior people, may well become the norm for employees at all levels. Law firms, for instance, are already finding that they must promise time for public service work (*pro bono publico*) in order to attract top law students. And, in the case of plateaued employees, such policies may actually come to represent the major rewards for individuals throughout the remainder of their careers. With the growing emphasis on self-awareness, leisure, and social relevance, "time off" may well become one of the most important benefits a company can offer its employees.

In the financial area, giving employees a choice among several forms of rewards (such as salary, bonus plans, benefit packages, stock options, or paid leave) will have to become a central feature of personnel policies. In terms of promotional policies, organizations in the future will need to develop multiple promotional ladders to reflect the fact that not all employees want to be supervisors or general managers, nor, given the flattening out of organizational growth curves, can all employees reasonably expect to be supervisors or general managers. Hence, the increasing importance of developing multiple tracks in the effort to reward the horizontal as well as the vertical careers. Little attention, for example, has yet been given to upgrading such roles as financial analyst, computer programmer, staff specialist, purchasing agent, secretary, or the skilled and unskilled worker on the factory floor.

The objective of all these activities is to widen options so that employees can make more meaningful career choices, and so that organizations can allocate their human resources more effectively.

C What Individuals Can Do

It would be a mistake, however, to assume that government and employing organizations can sweep away all the career problems confronting individuals. Organizations promoting change are vulnerable. Businesses can lose money, educational innovations may fall by the wayside, and governmental agencies can undergo major budget cuts. One might hypothesize, therefore, that the movement toward and through change will not be linear, but uneven: the forces of change and resistance will probably interact continually. The

result may be a kind of seesawing between tradition and originality as various forces gain temporary advantage. What are the issues facing individuals as a result of this situation? What tensions are likely to arise?

We suspect that there will be a growing sentiment toward increased personal accountability for careers: individuals are likely to become more directly answerable for the incompetent performance of their duties as well as more demanding of more appropriate rewards for competent performance. In other words, with increasing choice will come increasing responsibility. While we recognize that individuals can never control all the forces that determine their careers from the outside, we expect that people will be forced into doing more about their own careers than they are now doing.

Toward this end, it will be necessary for people to become more attuned to their own needs, their values, and their personal goals. In this, they are supported by other trends in the society, including the so-called personal growth movement—which has created a desire in people to understand themselves more completely—and the general tendency to decrease the arbitrary power of organizations over people. In such a climate, particularly if employers continue to offer more options to their employees, it is not unrealistic to assume that people will develop considerably more insight into their own particular career experiences and desires. To the extent that they do so, their future career accomplishments, experiences, and work circumstances will benefit.

The aim of career development for individuals, therefore, is to increase their awareness of their beliefs and preferences about a career, and to have them expose themselves to personal examination. As this happens, individuals will require more varied career paths, and organizations will have to respond to the resulting pluralism. It is primarily the impetus of employees themselves, pushing for increased options and for more control over their own career destinies, that will lead organizations and other social institutions to respond in the ways we have outlined above. And, ultimately, no equitable allocation of employment opportunities will be possible without the joint efforts of government, employing organizations, and individual employees.

REFERENCES

Alfred, T. Checkers and choice in manpower management. *Harvard Business Review*, January–February 1967, 157–167.

Bailyn, L. Involvement and accommodation in technical careers: An inquiry into the relation to work at mid-career. In J. Van Maanen (Ed.), *Organizational careers: Some new perspectives.* London: Wiley International, 1977.

Bailyn, L., & Schein, E. H. Life/Career considerations as indicators of quality of employment. In A. D. Biderman & T. F. Drury (Eds.), *Measuring work quality for social reporting.* Beverly Hills, California: Sage, 1976, 151–168.

Beckhard, P. Managerial careers in transition: Dilemmas and directions. In J. Van Maanen (Ed.), *Organizational careers: Some new perspectives.* London: Wiley International, 1977.

Berger, P. Some general observations on the problem of work. In P. Berger (Ed.), *The human shape of work.* Chicago: Regnery, 1964, 211–241.

Bray, D. W., & Grant, D. L. The assessment center in the measurement of potential business management. *Psychological Monographs*, **80**, 1966.

Erickson, E. H. Identity and the life cycle. *Psychological Issues*, **1**, 1959, 1–171.

Fogarty, M. *Forty to sixty: How we waste the middle aged.* London: Centre for Studies in Social Policy, 1975.

Kotter, J. The psychological contract. *California Management Review*, Spring 1973, 156–165.

Papanek, H. Men, women, and work: Reflections on the two-person career. *American Journal of Sociology*, **78**, 1973, 852–872.

Pascal, A. H., Bell D., Dougharty, L. A., Dunn, W. L., & Thompson, V. M. *An evaluation of policy related research on programs for mid-life redirection.* Santa Monica, California: The Rand Corporation, R-1582, 1975.

Rapoport, R., & Rapoport, R. N. The dual career family: A variant pattern and social change. *Human Relations*, **22**, 1969, 3–30.

Schein, E. H. *Process consultation.* Reading, Massachusetts: Addison-Wesley, 1969.

Schein, E. H. Career development: Theoretical and practical issues for organizations. Paper read at Conference on Career Development, International Labor Office. Budapest, Hungary, April, 1975a.

Schein, E. H. How career anchors hold executives to their career paths. *Personnel*, **52**, May–June 1975b, 11–24.

Schein, E. H. Career anchors and career paths: A panel study of management school graduates. In J. Van Maanen (Ed.), *Organizational careers: Some new perspectives.* London: Wiley International, 1977.

Seidenberg, R. *Corporate wives—Corporate casualties?* New York: Doubleday, 1975.

Van Maanen, J. (Ed.) *Organizational careers: Some new perspectives.* London: Wiley International, 1976.

Van Maanen, J., & Schein, E. H. Career development. In J. R. Hackman & L. Suttle (Eds.), *Improving life at work.* Pacific Palisades, California: Goodyear, 1977.

Reading 13

Breakthrough in On-the-Job Training

Earl R. Gomersall
M. Scott Myers

In this article we shall describe and analyze the results of an unusual study just completed at Texas Instruments Incorporated (TI). The study dealt with the relationship between organization climate and job performance. One of the objectives was to find out what would happen in a large manufacturing department if the causes of anxiety among new employees were reduced. The following gains were accomplished:

- Training time was shortened by one half.
- Training costs were lowered to one third of their previous levels.
- Absenteeism and tardiness dropped to one half of the previous normal.
- Waste and rejects were reduced to one fifth of their previous levels.
- Costs were cut as much as 15% to 30%!

We feel that similar gains can be realized in other organizations, in and out of manufacturing, if they use the approach to be described. If so, the TI study should lead to significant improvements in the efficiency of U.S. industry. Moreover, the gains are not limited to the categories just listed. In the TI manufacturing department, for instance, the results are stimulating managers to try other innovations which, in a circular fashion, are touching off chains of events leading to still more innovations and bringing about basic changes in the job and in the values of the supervisor.

SETTING OF THE STUDY

The study resulted from our cooperative efforts—one of us is a manufacturing manager and the other an industrial psychologist—in what was initially intended to be an application of motivational techniques through job enlargement. . . . Although job enlargement replicated from other TI experiments was successful, this article primarily describes innovations by line management to improve job performance through deliberate changes in the organizational climate of the manufacturing department.

The setting for the study was a rapidly growing TI department which, at the time of the experiment, included over 1,400 persons spread throughout three shifts. The department manufactured integrated circuits (microminiature circuitry units). The subjects of the study were women operators who collectively performed approximately 1,850 different operations (the most numerously replicated of these operations having only 70 operators per shift). Approximately 57% of the operators worked with microscopes, and all jobs placed a premium on visual acuity, eye-hand coordination, and mechanical aptitude. Selection standards for operators included high school education and passing scores on the General Aptitude Test Battery of the Texas Employment Commission.

The work reported here commenced with a

meeting of the authors to plan the application of job-enlargement programs as practiced by other areas of the corporation. Despite the fact that all first- and second-line supervisors had attended the TI motivation seminars and knew the principles of job enlargement, the department manager felt that, in practice, these principles were not being successfully implemented. Part of the answer seemed to lie in the fact that both the supervisors and the employees were in a continuous process of adapting to rapid expansion and technological change. For this and other reasons, as will be discussed later, supervisors and employees were experiencing anxiety. This anxiety appeared to have an effect on their work.

Operations were typified by a continuous training process—training new people hired for expansion and replacement purposes and retraining transferees and the technologically displaced. The consequences of this training program can be illustrated with the classical growth curve shown in Figure 13-1. As this curve shows:

The ball bonders required approximately three months to reach what we term the "competence" level. (The competence level is the stage at which assemblers can independently manufacture the product, but have not yet achieved the speed and accuracy ultimately expected of them

to reach the labor standards set by industrial engineering. The competence level is about 85% of labor standards; a position about 115% of standard is termed the "mastery" level.)

The learning curve of ball bonders was fairly typical of production operations in the department (and, for that matter, of learning in many other companies and industries).

Competence and Creativity

A need was recognized to find out at what stage in the learning process assemblers could be meaningfully involved in the problem-solving, goal-setting process. Were they ready, for example, at one month, at which time they were halfway to the competence level? Or must they have fully reached the competence level before creative involvement in problem solving could be expected?

To answer this question, two experimental groups were selected, one comprised of individuals of one-month tenure, and the other of individuals who had been with the organization three or more months:

The one-month group, when involved in the problem-solving process, came up with maintenance-type suggestions such as:

- We need more coat racks.
- Standards not set right.
- We don't have enough time to eat.
- There aren't enough maintenance technicians around to fix machines.
- Too much confusion at shift breaks.

The more seasoned group came up with over two pages of specific, technically oriented suggestions to improve the quality of operations, many not previously considered from a management standpoint. Following are examples of suggestions from the seasoned group:

- Do not split manufacturing lots between operators.
- Assign the same quality inspector to a given group of operators to assure continuity.

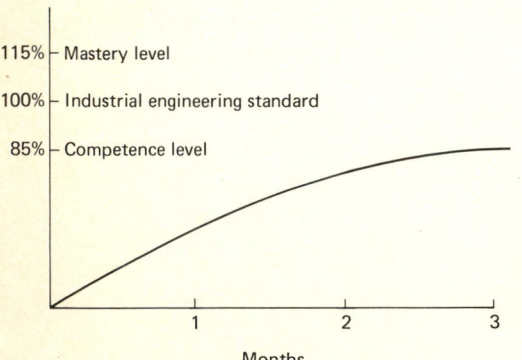

Figure 13-1 Learning curve for ball bonders.

- Print wiring diagrams on the backs of all lot travelers (operation sequence sheets).
- Give each girl a capillary punch for capillary repair.
- Technicians should always repair burnt-out electrical heaters, and girls should always change own capillaries.

This experiment corroborates earlier observations that minimal job competence is a requisite to creative problem solving. The finding seems to have quite general application. Not only do untrained employees impair the problem-solving efforts of skilled workers, but they themselves are frustrated by their inability to participate in the problem-solving activities. So there is added reason to seek ways to accelerate on-the-job learning.

EXPERIMENTS CONDUCTED

Why did the one-month group fail in the problem-solving experiment? The reason, we postulated, was not only lack of familiarity with hardware and processes, but also debilitating anxieties associated with lack of job competence during the early days of employment. These relationships were not mere conjecture. The department manager had, during the past year, followed a systematic program for interviewing individuals during the morning coffee break. The results of 135 interviews with 405 operators yielded the following facts:

- Their first days on the job were anxious and disturbing ones.
- "New employee initiation" practices by peers intensified anxiety.
- Anxiety interfered with the training process.
- Turnover of newly hired employees was caused primarily by anxiety.
- The new operators were reluctant to discuss problems with their supervisors.
- Their supervisors had been unsuccessful in translating motivation theory into practice.

Similar interviews conducted with the supervisors and middle managers yielded these additional conclusions:

- They experienced as much anxiety as new assemblers.
- They felt inadequate with seasoned, competent subordinates.
- They cut off downward communication to conceal ignorance.
- Supervisory defensiveness discouraged upward communication.
- Motivation principles learned in the classroom were not being implemented on the assembly line.

Preliminary Analysis

Facts uncovered through these interviews underscored the importance of anxiety in inhibiting job effectiveness for both operators and supervisors. It seemed obvious that anxiety dropped as competence was achieved. The relationship between the learning curve and what was believed to be the anxiety curve of operators is illustrated in Figure 13-2.

To supplement information obtained through personal interviews and to gain a better understanding of the characteristics of the anxiety to be reduced, we developed a 92-item questionnaire to measure the following possible causes of tension or anxiety: supervision; job knowledge and skill; social

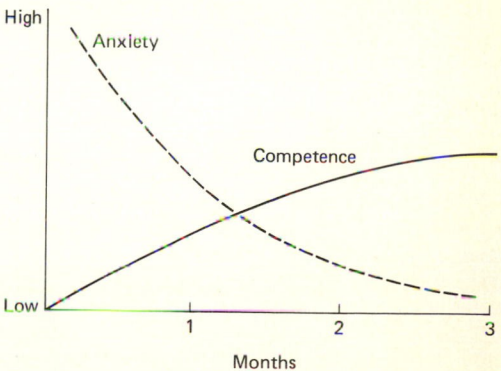

Figure 13-2 Relationship of anxiety to competence.

acceptance; physical condition; orientation; job pressure; regimentation; vocational adjustment; personal problems; financial worries; outside social factors; and opportunities for the satisfaction of growth, achievement, responsibility, and recognition needs.

Administration of this questionnaire to short-tenure and seasoned employees identified three types of tension in the job situation—the first two harmful and the third helpful:

1 One form of anxiety, mentioned previously, stemmed from the unpredictable and sometimes threatening new world of work and, as illustrated in Figure 13-2, was higher among *new* trainees.

2 Another type of tension resulted from anxieties about non-job factors such as personal finances, domestic problems, professional status, and outside social relationships. This type existed in equal amounts in *both* groups.

3 The third type of tension was identified as a positive, inner-directed desire for constructive self-expression. This creative tension found constructive expression best in an atmosphere of approval and self-confidence after job competence was reached.

Anxiety versus Performance

Assuming the validity of Figure 13-2, we posed the following question: "Is it possible to accelerate achievement to the competence level by reducing anxiety at a faster rate?" In other words, we wanted to know if it were possible to achieve the relationships illustrated by the dotted lines in Figure 13-3.

Anxiety on the job is characteristically assumed to be the dependent variable, gradually dropping as competence is acquired. Might not the reverse be true? Might not competence increase as a result of anxiety being decreased? With such questions in mind, we decided to design an orientation program to reduce the anxieties of experimental groups of new employees:

The next group of ten girls hired for bonding work on the second shift was chosen as the first experimental group. A control group was selected from the first and third shifts. Precautions were taken to avoid the "Hawthorne effect" of influencing behavior through special attention. (The "Hawthorne effect" was first reported by Elton Mayo and F. J. Roethlisberger in their experiments at Western Electric. They noticed that improvements in operators' performance often followed simply from outsiders' taking an interest in them.) The control group was oriented in the customary manner and the experimental group through a revised approach. Neither group was told of the experiment, and members of both groups had no reason to think they were being subjected to special treatment.

Conventional Indoctrination

The control group went through the usual first-day orientation, which consisted of a two-hour briefing on hours of work, insurance, parking, work rules, and employee services. This session included warnings of the consequences of failure to conform to organization expectations and, though not intended as a threat, tended to raise rather than reduce anxieties.

Following this orientation, it was customary for a bonder to be introduced to her friendly but very busy supervisor, who gave her fur-

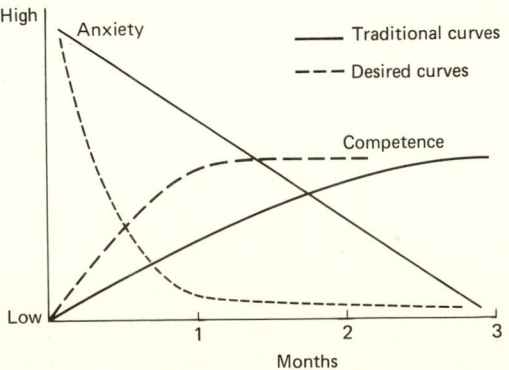

Figure 13-3 Postulated consequence of anxiety reduction.

ther orientation and job instruction. Unfortunately, the supervisor's detailed familiarity with the operations had desensitized him to the technological gap between them, and the following might be typical of what the operator heard him say:

> "Alice, I would like you to take the sixth yellow chair on this assembly line, which is in front of bonding machine #14. On the left side of your machine you will find a wiring diagram indicating where you should bond your units. On the right-hand side of your machine you will find a carrying tray full of 14-lead packages. Pick up the headers, one at a time, using your 3-C tweezers and place them on the hot substrate below the capillary head. Grasp the cam actuator on the right-hand side of the machine and lower the hot capillary over the first bonding pad indicated by the diagram. Ball bond to the pad and, by moving the hot substrate, loop the wire to the pin indicated by the diagram. Stitch bond to this lead, raise the capillary, and check for pigtails. When you have completed all leads, put the unit back in the carrying tray.
>
> "Your training operator will be around to help you with other details. Do you have any questions?"

Overwhelmed by these instructions and not wanting to offend this polite and friendly supervisor to look stupid by telling him she did not understand anything he said, the operator would go to her work station and try to learn by watching her peers on either side of her. But they, in pursuit of operating goals, had little time to assist her. Needless to say, her anxieties were increased and her learning ability was impaired. And the longer she remained unproductive, the more reluctant she was to disclose her wasted effort to her supervisor and the more difficult her job became.

Experimental Approach

The experimental group participated in a one-day program especially designed to overcome anxieties not eliminated by the usual process of job orientation. Following the two-hour orientation by Personnel, they were isolated in a conference room before they could be "initiated" by their peers. They were told there would be no work the first day, that they should relax, sit back, and have a coke or cigarette, and use this time to get acquainted with the organization and each other and to ask questions. Throughout this one-day anxiety-reduction session, questions were encouraged and answered. This orientation emphasized four points:

1 "Your opportunity to succeed is very good" Company records disclosed that 99.6% of all persons hired or transferred into this job were eventually successful in terms of their ability to learn the necessary skills. Trainees were shown learning curves illustrating the gradual buildup of competence over the learning period. They were told five or six times during the day that all members of this group could expect to be successful on the job.

2 "Disregard 'hall talk'" Trainees were told of the hazing game that old employees played—scaring newcomers with exaggerated allegations about work rules, standards, disciplinary actions, and other job factors—to make the job as frightening to the newcomers as it had been for them. To prevent these distortions by peers, the trainees were given facts about both the good and the bad aspects of the job and exactly what was expected of them.

The basis for "hall talk" rumors was explained. For example, rumor stated that more than one half of the people who terminated had been fired for poor performance. The interviews mentioned earlier disclosed the fact that supervisors themselves unintentionally caused this rumor by intimating to operators that voluntary terminations (marriage, pregnancy, leaving town) were really performance terminations. Many supervisors felt this was a good negative incentive to pull up the low performers.

3 "Take the initiative in communication" The new operators were told of the natural reluctance of many supervisors to be talkative and that it was easier for the supervisor to do his job if they asked him questions. They were told that supervisors realized that trainees needed continuous instruction at first, that they would not understand technical terminology for a while, that they were expected to ask questions, and that supervisors would not consider them dumb for asking questions.

4 "Get to know your supervisor" The personality of the supervisor was described in detail. The absolute truth was the rule. A description might reveal that—

> . . . the supervisor is strict, but friendly;
>
> . . . his hobby is fishing and ham radio operation;
>
> . . . he tends to be shy sometimes, but he really likes to talk to you if you want to;
>
> . . . he would like you to check with him before you go on a personal break, just so he knows where you are.

Following this special day-long orientation session, members of the experimental group were introduced to their supervisor and their training operators in accordance with standard practice. Training commenced as usual, and eventually all operators went on production.

SIGNIFICANT GAINS

A difference in attitude and learning rate was apparent from the beginning in the progress of the two groups. By the end of four weeks, the experimental group was significantly outperforming the control group, as shown in Figure 13-4. Note that the experimental group excelled in production and job attendance as well as in learning time.

Figure 13-5 compares the learning curves

	Experimental group	Control group
Units per hour	93	27
Absentee rate	0.5%	2.5%
Times tardy	2	8
Training hours required	225	381

Figure 13-4 One-month performance levels of experimental and control groups.

of the two groups. It is interesting to note that when anxiety is minimized, learning appears to be almost a straight-line function of time, suggesting that the area between the experimental curve and the control curve represents learning time lag caused by anxiety.

When the experimental study began showing significant results, the anxiety-reduction process was used on additional groups. Figure 13-6 shows performance curves reflecting similar results for more than 200 members of experimental and control groups for assembling, welding, and inspection; their absenteeism rates are also compared. It is interesting to note that the third week's methods change in the inspection department depressed the performance of the experimental group more than that of the control group, but the experimental group made a more rapid recovery.

Attaining Mastery

Now let us make a general observation: after an operator achieves an acceptable level of competence, further improvement depends on the nature of the incentive. The usual practice is to set labor standards somewhat in excess of the plateau which an operator can comfortably achieve in the short run. As noted earlier, standards traditionally impose an expectation about 15 percentage points above the competence plateau. However, there is a more positive incentive for surpassing the competence plateau. This is the opportunity for self-initiated creative effort. Let us look at some

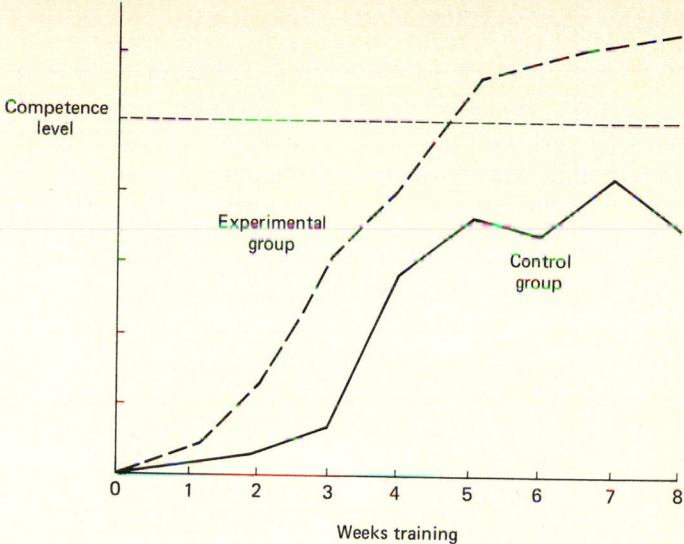

Figure 13-5 Learning curves of experimental and control groups.

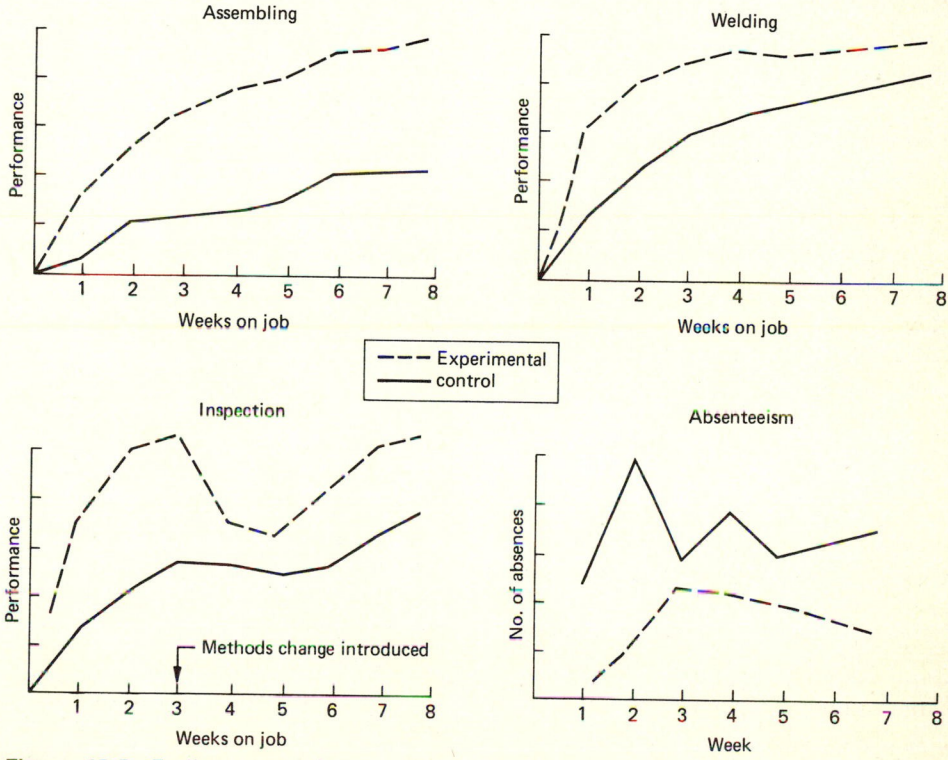

Figure 13-6 Further comparisons of experimental and control groups.

aspects of the TI experiment which bear on this.

In the integrated circuits groups without methods improvement, the motivated assemblers exceeded labor standards by about 15% to achieve what we term the "mastery level." Since the mastery level is usually attained after plateauing at the competence level, members of the control group seldom reached the mastery level before the fifth month.

But in the experimental group, by contrast, the mastery level was achieved in two to three months.

As illustrated in the smoothed curves of Figure 13-7, the area between control group and experimental group curves represents an improvement in performance of approximately 50%. For 100 new hires in this department at TI, that gain was equivalent to net first-year savings of at least $50,000. On the basis of reduced turnover, absenteeism, and training time, additional annual savings of $35,000 were estimated.

Spread of Confidence

As trainees with less anxiety gradually became members of the regular work force, their attitudes began influencing the performance of the work groups they joined. The greater confidence of the new members seemed to inspire greater confidence among their older peers; also, their higher performance estab-lished a new reference point for stimulating the natural competitiveness which existed among members of work groups. Old peers were sometimes hard pressed to maintain a superiority margin between themselves and the rapidly learning newcomers. There was evidence of improvements in quality and quantity, not only among immediate peer groups, but also among adjacent work groups who were influenced through the informal social system in the plant.

The performance of an entire shift was difficult to measure because of changing methods and standards, but Figure 13-8 shows the results of putting 10 operators trained under the system among 60 workers on the second shift. The second shift, which for the previous seven weeks had had the lowest productivity, became clearly the highest producer five weeks after the experiment began. Although transferring some of the 10 experimentally trained operators to the first shift in the thirteenth week dropped the performance level of the second shift, the transfusion appeared to raise the performance level of the first shift.

Quality Improvement

The new training system influenced performance in more ways than one. For example, in analyzing the causes of defects management noted that, contrary to common assumptions,

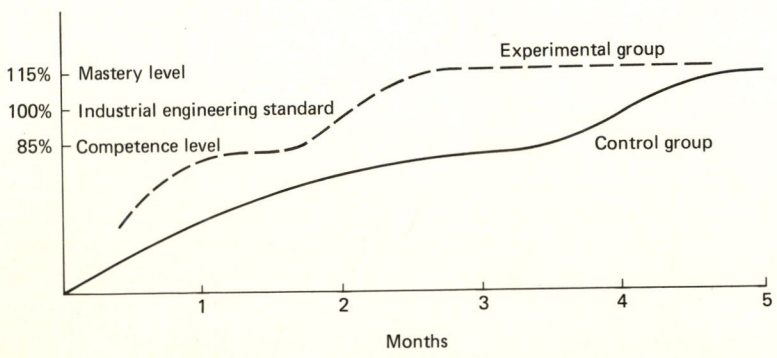

Months

Figure 13-7 Mastery attainment by experimental and control groups.

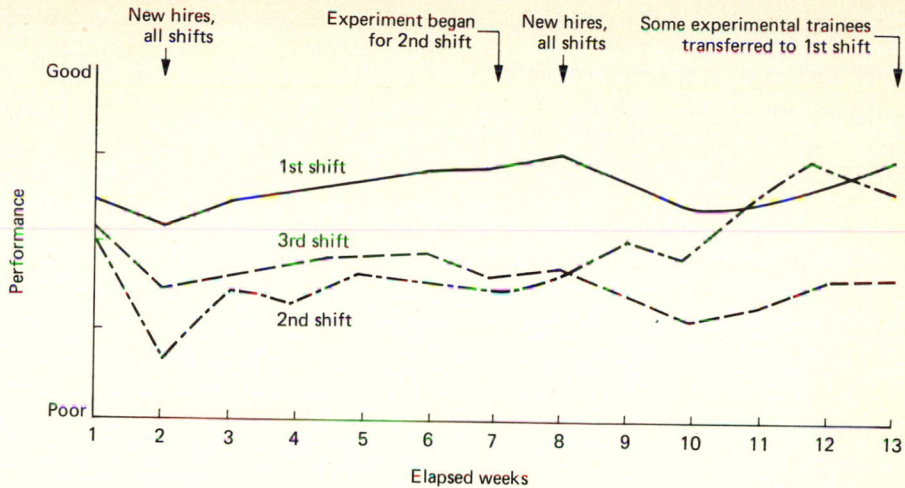

Figure 13-8 Comparative performance of three shifts.

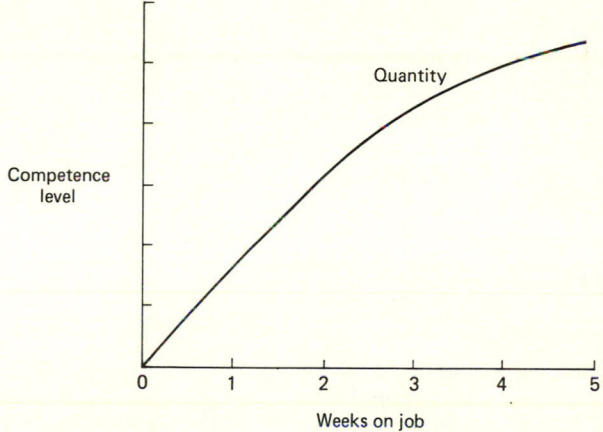

Figure 13-9 Quantity-quality relationships.

the faster operators (by definition, master operators) were making fewer errors. The relationship of output to defects is shown in Figure 13-9; note that those trainees who exceeded the competence level within four weeks were usually making products with practically no defects.

It had been the practice to subject all units to 100% inspection for nine specific reject criteria. This required one inspector for every two assembly operators. Master operators, whose defects were close to zero, were now permitted to submit completed units to quality assurance inspectors for lot inspection, thus bypassing the normal 100% inspection. The pride which these operators felt because of their accomplishment and because of being identified with the master operator group actually improved their product quality over the standards achieved through 100% inspection. The lot rejection rate dropped by a factor of five, and labor costs were lowered by 30%. Not only was pride in workmanship returned to the job, but an old manufacturer's axiom was validated: "Quality cannot be *inspected* into a product; it must be *built* into it."

BROADER IMPLICATIONS

The results of this experiment are significant to the operating manager in terms of the criteria most important to him—reduced costs, higher quality, satisfied customers, and increased profits. Without improvements in these measures, no matter how noble the other motives, experiments of this type generally have low priority.

At the same time, because this experiment has led to improvements in terms of these traditional management criteria at TI, managers have become enthusiastically involved in its implementation and, in the process, have become the agents for other changes. Now let us look at some of these effects.

New Understanding

As managers have gradually become more sensitive to the relationship between attitudes and behavior, they have begun to seek a better understanding of the causes of attitude change. Motivation theory, which they had learned as an intellectual process in a company motivation seminar, has become meaningful for them as they observe its implementation in the work situation. Job enlargement and increased motivation through the application of behavioral theory in other groups has become interesting to them; and systems for measuring attitudes, teaching problem solving, goal setting, and providing performance feedback are now seen in new perspective. These new perspectives constitute a foundation for greater managerial effectiveness at all levels and in all functions.

Improved Training

It is interesting to note that, as managers reviewed the results of anxiety reduction for production personnel, they would observe, "You know, managers have anxieties, too. . . ." And many would volunteer descriptions of their own debilitating anxieties.

Why do supervisors have anxieties about their competence as supervisors? Primarily because of mistaken concepts of the proper role of a supervisor. This error is understandable in the light of the typical man's background:

Approximately 60% of the first-line supervisory positions are filled by new college graduates. They reach industry after a life of conditioning in "superior-subordinate" relationships. After a long background of parent-child, teacher-student, officer-enlisted man experiences, it is normal for them to come to their first supervisory job with the notion that a leader is someone who "can do everything his subordinates can, only better."

Because of this traditional image of infallibility of leaders, the new supervisor understandably feels inadequate in his new role of supervising large numbers of individuals, most of whom know the operations better than he does. He does not realize that the operators recognize and accept his limitations and that it is futile and self-defeating for him to try to conceal them.

To help new supervisors gain early acceptance of their limitations and a better understanding of their supervisory role, TI developed a plan for having operators train the supervisor! Working in pairs, operators (who have received trainer training) give the new or transferred supervisor his first orientation to the assembly line, acquainting him with the pitfalls traditionally encountered by new supervisors and defining his role as it is perceived by the operators. This innovative approach serves three basic purposes:

1   It provides a supervisor with valid information directly from the persons who have the greatest knowledge of the operations.

2   It provides assurance to the operators

that the supervisor is properly qualified and acquainted with their problems. Because they get personally involved in his training, they will seek to make him successful.

3   Most importantly, this approach to training is significant because of its impact on the values of the supervisor. A supervisor who, in his first experience as a manager, learns to expect and seek information from subordinates, and discovers that they are creative and responsible, is conditioned or permanently "programmed" to look to, and rely on, subordinates for assistance in solving problems. And, as Douglas McGregor and many others have pointed out, people tend to rise to properly delegated expectations of supervision. Supervisors who are programmed to have high expectations of subordinates are ideally suited for pursuing job enlargement.

Fluid Communication

A significant effect of the new orientation program is the encouragement of upward communication. In the final analysis, communication depends upon the behavior of supervisors who, through the language of action, provide a climate conducive to natural and informal exchange of information. It was as a result of sensitizing supervisors to the importance of listening and maintaining fluid communication channels at all levels that the following incident took place:

> An operator approached a manager during coffee break and casually struck up a conversation about the "units with little white specks on them that leaked after welding." The supervisor asked, "What little white specks?" The operator pointed out that almost all of the units that leaked after welding had little specks on them, a fact unnoted before. Verifying and investigating this fact revealed that units were placed in plastic trays while still hot from a previous process; their heat caused many of them to fuse to the plastic container. Pulling them from the container caused the units to pull away a small amount of plastic, thus insulating them during the welding process.

> Once this was discovered, the problem was solved simply by delaying the placing of units in the plastic trays until they had cooled sufficiently. This single suggestion reduced rejects by a factor of four for this product—a projected cost prevention of hundreds of thousands of dollars.

The point we want to emphasize here is that casual questions and observations of the type described take place only in an atmosphere of approval, genuine respect, and interest.

CONCLUSION

As the principles of the new approach have been adopted and adapted by other departments at TI, we have been able to gain new appreciation of the respective roles of managers and behavioral scientists. The manager should look to behavioral scientists not to solve his problems, but only to provide needed information about them. To ask the scientists to do more robs the manager of his charter and violates the very principle which he is expected to implement through job enlargement.

However, the behavioral scientist is operating within his proper realm of responsibility if he serves as a change agent by assisting managers in planning the application of theories and principles and by giving visibility to their achievements. Incidentally, there should be broader recognition that, as the previous discussion indicates, behavioral science applications can be measured in traditional production indexes as well as in the more nebulous criteria of morale and attitudes.

Important Effects

The approach described in this article has had important effects on TI's manufacturing department:

1   It has made the department more effective by reducing costs and waste and by improving quality and profitability.

2 It has made the workplace more attractive for the employees by reducing anxiety and making work more challenging. This has resulted in less reactive behavior, better attendance, and better utilization of talent.

3 Supervisors are becoming more effective managers. As their involvement in anxiety reduction and job enlargement results in more responsible and creative behavior on the part of operators, supervisors learn to delegate with greater confidence. This in turn frees them from details which heretofore seemed oppressively inescapable so they can spend more time on higher level developmental work.

These gains do not, of course, happen independently but, rather, in a mutually reinforcing and circular way.

The new approach can, if applied broadly, reduce the costs of personnel administration. Outside their staffing responsibilities, personnel departments traditionally devote most of their efforts to administering supplemental benefits, working on collective bargaining, settling grievances, and, in general dealing with causes of dissatisfaction. Dissatisfaction and preoccupation with so-called "maintenance" factors (that is, parking arrangements, fringe benefits, vacation schedules, and so on) are not usually a consequence of inadequacy of these factors but a symptom of thwarted motivation needs. People in jobs which offer opportunity for growth, for achievement, responsibility, and recognition, have little incentive to get sidetracked with peripheral issues and feel no need to seek the intervention of a labor union to "police" management. In fact, on a properly designed and delegated job in a suitable organizational climate, the employee is in a real sense a manager himself. His proprietary interest in managing his job gives him a sense of company identification that causes him to see unionism as a deterrent to his effectiveness. Hence, meaningful work eliminates the wastefulness of uninspired and reactive behavior and the cost of elaborate systems for dealing with dissatisfaction.

The rate of technological displacement—and hence the need for effective training—is increasing. This fact, in combination with the current labor shortage, the entry of more young people and minority groups into industrial employment, and the development of new plants domestically and internationally, means that management should place more emphasis on training and other personnel management innovations than ever before. Lessened turnover and accelerated learning curves constitute a significant advantage to companies that are able to achieve them.

U.S. business has been hard pressed to match international competition. Handicapped by the pay differential, American companies have met the challenge primarily through technical innovation and superior quality. They can also meet it with management innovation. A great deal can be accomplished in this way, as our experiences with accelerated learning and job enlargement demonstrate.

Reading 14

Assessment Centers for Spotting Future Managers

William C. Byham

Deciding whom to promote to management from the rank and file is a classic difficulty. There is a great difference between the skills and talents required for rank and managerial positions, and a man's performance in the ranks provides scant basis for judging how well he would do if he were promoted to first-level management. Companies have learned from bitter experience that the best salesman or the finest mechanic does not necessarily make the best supervisor.

Usually, it is just about as hard to judge whether a man who is working well at one level of management will "take hold" at a higher level. The skills required may be more nearly alike in this case, but even experienced executives find it hard to assess the exact scope of a man's ability and the breadth of his shoulders. Previously developed yardsticks for measuring management potential have not really been worth their salt. Batteries of written tests, for example, cannot assess the way a man works with people; supervisors' ratings can be highly biased; and so on.

To obtain a basis for making promotion decisions, a score or more of companies have resorted to the corporate assessment center approach. This assessment procedure simulates "live" the basic situations with which a man would be faced if he *were* moved up and develops information about how well he will cope at the higher level before the decision to promote him is actually made. AT&T, IBM, General Electric, J.C. Penney, Standard Oil (Ohio), and Sears, Roebuck, are a few of the companies that have established such centers.

In these centers, specially trained managers (and occasionally psychologists) act as "assessors" who evaluate candidates for promotion—either into management or within management—on their potential and their areas of weakness. Groups of men pass through series of standardized exercises such as management games, in-basket tests, and leaderless discussion sessions, while the assessors observe their behavior closely. . . .

The assessors discuss each candidate's performance separately and then generate a comprehensive report on each candidate which management can combine with current performance information as it sees fit. As well as identifying the men most likely to succeed, the assessment reports spell out the individual deficiencies of each candidate and suggest guidelines for management to use in developing him.

These reports constitute powerful planning tools for management: it can use the reports to plan the orderly progression of management within the company; it can adjust its hiring patterns; if necessary, it can direct that jobs be designed which match and give growing space to particular men's abilities and potential; and, most important, the company can plan a rational, sensible route for the candidate to follow as he moves up the ladder.

Reports have proved to be remarkably valid. Longitudinal studies of thousands of employees assessed over the last few years indicate that this assessment method is much more accurate than traditional appraisal procedures, and these seem to be the reasons:

- The exercises used are designed to bring out the specific skills and aptitudes needed in the position(s) for which a group of candidates is being assessed.
- Since the exercises are standardized, assessors evaluate the candidates under relatively constant conditions and thus are able to make valid comparative judgments.
- The assessors usually do not know the candidates personally; so, being emotionally disengaged, they are unbiased.
- The assessors are shielded from the many interruptions of normal working conditions and can pay full attention to the candidates' behavior in the exercises.
- The procedures focus their attention on the primary kinds of behavior they ought to observe in evaluating a promotion candidate.
- They have been trained to observe and evaluate these kinds of behavior.

THE FIRST EXPERIMENTS

American Telephone & Telegraph first applied the assessment center idea 14 years ago as part of the data collection procedures for its Management Progress Study, a study of Bell System personnel the company undertook to gain insight into the management development process and to identify the variables related to success.[1]

Over four years, AT&T processed 422 men from six Bell Systems through a three-and-a-half day assessment center to obtain basic data on their experimental population. AT&T had got the idea for assessment centers from the pioneering work of the Office of Strategic

Services, which used the method for selecting agents during World War II. Descriptions of the ingenious exercises used by the OSS make both interesting and enjoyable reading.[2]

Some Bell executives who took part in the Management Progress Study assessment centers recognized the possibility that the technique could aid them with one of their critical problems—i.e., identifying potential among candidates for first-line management. They invited the AT&T researchers to set up an assessment center for them, and as a result the first nonresearch application of the method was made in 1958 by Michigan Bell. It achieved immediate and widespread acceptance throughout AT&T. Today, AT&T affiliates operate 50 centers all over the country, processing 10,000 candidates a year. The Bell centers are still used primarily to evaluate the management potential of men being considered for first-level management positions.

TODAY'S APPLICATIONS

Other companies that have observed the success of the Bell System centers have also used the method primarily to identify candidates for first-level management. Today, however, there seems to be a trend toward using the method with higher levels of management. While still concentrating their primary use at the lower levels, companies such as Standard Oil (Ohio), IBM, General Electric, and AT&T have established middle-management centers for promotion and development purposes. Penney, for instance, is experimenting in how to assess middle-level managers in its retail stores to determine their aptitude for large- or medium-sized store management.

---

[1]See Douglas W. Bray and Donald Grant, "The Assessment Center in the Measurement of Potential for Business Management," *Psychological Monographs*, 1966, Vol. 80, 1110–17.

[2]OSS Assessment Staff, *Assessment of Men* (New York, Rinehart, 1948), and *Fortune*, "A Good Man Is Hard to Find," March 1946, p. 92.

At these higher levels, centers usually focus on stimulating a man's self-development and career planning through increasing his self-knowledge. After the games and exercises, a participant is given time to critique his own performance and also that of his teammates. A "T-group" atmosphere is often created to increase self-learning. Conditions in such a center are sufficiently well controlled, however, that none of the negative effects which have occasionally characterized the T-group session have been noted here.

Middle-management assessment is already exerting profound impact on organizational planning. In meshing the company's projected manpower needs with its manpower resources as described in its assessment and development reports, Standard Oil (Ohio) goes so far as to consider, for each likely man, the kind of supervision under which he works at his best, the kinds of pressures he can tolerate, and so on, to find the best possible place for him to work and grow. The company also tries to tailor specific job responsibilities to the individual through changes in organization and areas of responsibility.

The concept has yet to be applied at the top level of management, and perhaps it never will be. Promotion and development decisions near the top are highly sensitive and highly personal, and a mechanical procedure for assessing candidates, however excellent, may not be suited to the situation.

So far as screening applicants for new employment at lower and middle levels is concerned, the assessment center method has little value for most companies, since there is seldom a large enough group of prospects at a given time to justify the expense of operating a program. Because of their great size, AT&T and Sears have been able to use the method in initial hiring. Sears operates a very short assessment program for college prospects in its eastern region, and college students who pass the campus interview are brought in large groups to Philadelphia for a day and a half of orientation and assessment. AT&T flies candidates for its "communications consultant" school to New York for assessment. Although this is expensive, research has shown that selection based on assessment pays off.

To my knowledge, 20 companies have been responsible for assessing more than 70,000 candidates in the last 10 years, but at least 100 more companies are developing centers or are in an advanced stage of center planning. Many others are "looking into the idea." As an indication of this interest, I might cite the fact that more than 200 company representatives attended conferences on the assessment center method during 1969.

Applications of the method have multiplied almost every year since the first industrial application of assessment centers by AT&T 14 years ago, and, within the limits I have outlined, these applications vary widely. . . . Some centers process only 6 candidates at a time, while a few process more than 12. The ratio of assessors to candidates ranges from 3-to-1 to 1-to-1. While centers with a two-and-a-half consecutive day cycle are most common, some cycles are only two days long and these days are not necessarily consecutive. Others are five or six days long because assessment is integrated with training activities.

Obviously, there is no right or wrong way to structure a center—the specific application must be designed to meet specific company needs and operating requirements. This flexibility is reflected particularly in the variety and combinations of exercises used in centers. Each company chooses exercises that bring out the behaviors they desire to assess. . . . I shall say more about the appropriate choice of exercises later.

Centers typically find that 30% to 40% of

the candidates in a group fall into their acceptable outstanding category, 40% into their questionable category, and 20% to 30% into their unacceptable category.

Figures like these are often viewed askance by executives, and consequently I should like to discuss the question of validity next, before going into such topics as the "extra" benefits that centers bring and how centers are constructed and managed.

ARE THE ASSESSMENTS VALID?

In brief—yes, they *can* be. Unlike many other management development techniques that industry has widely accepted, the assessment center method has been well received partly because properly controlled research has shown it to be of value. This research has reassured both business executives and professional psychologists working in the personnel area that the assessment center method is almost certainly more valid than any other means of identifying and analyzing a candidate's management potential.

Four Kinds of Studies

Existing validity studies are of four kinds. Three of them focus on centers that are new or experimental, and the fourth focuses on the operational center that has existed for some period of time. To begin with, let me describe the three kinds of study that focus on the new centers.

First, where an assessment center is purely experimental and set up only for research purposes, a study usually compares assessment predictions with the candidates' later performance. Ordinarily, in these circumstances, the assessment reports are not released to management.

The work of Douglas W. Bray and Donald Grant on the original, experimental AT&T centers is of this kind, and it indicates that these centers' predictions were highly accurate. For instance, 64% of the candidates predicted to enter middle management had done so by the eighth year after assessment, while only 32% of those candidates predicted not to achieve middle-management positions had done so.

Second, a study may compare assessments made at a new, but "real life" center—that is, one that generates reports that are meant to be used—with candidates' later performance. An AT&T study of its new-salesman selection center reflects this pattern. The reports on the first 78 candidates who passed through this center were withheld from line management. All these men were subsequently hired as salesmen, and six months later their performance in the field was evaluated by trained observers who accompanied them on their calls. The results of both the original assessments and the performance review are shown in Table 14-1. This exhibit shows, for example, that of the 32 salesmen assessed as "acceptable" at the center, 19 were still judged "acceptable" when their field performance was reviewed.

In this study, the correlation between assessment ratings and performance is .51. Interestingly, when these men's performance in the field was compared with the ratings of the men made by their supervisors, no significant correlation emerged. Similarly, no significant correlation was found between their field performance and the ratings given them by training personnel who worked with them in a sales training program.

(These two AT&T studies are somewhat unusual in that management was not notified of the assessment findings in either case. When management *is* notified of the findings and uses them in planning promotions and development activity, as in the next two kinds of study, bias is introduced and validity is harder to estimate.)

Third, a study may compare the success of a company's executive development program

Table 14-1   Validity Study of Assessment of Sales Representatives

	Number of candidates		
Findings	**Original assessment**	**Field review**	**Validity of assessment**
More than acceptable	9	9	100%
Acceptable	32	19	60
Less than acceptable	16	7	44
Unacceptable	21	2	10

Source: Douglas W. Bray and Richard J. Campbell, "Selection of Salesmen by Means of an Assessment Center," *Journal of Applied Psychology*, Vol. 52, No. 1, 1968, p. 38.

before and after a center has been set up. For example, one can contrast the "success" of the last 50 or 100 people promoted before the center's installation with the first 50 or 100 people promoted thereafter with the aid of assessment reports. Several studies of this kind report substantial improvement, and these are the ones executives find hardest hitting and most convincing.

From the executive's point of view, the basic question vis-à-vis validity is this: Is the assessment center a definite improvement over other means of identifying management potential—and, notably, is it a definite improvement over supervisory judgment? Once again, the answer is "Yes, it *can* be."

Of all studies, those of the third kind are the ones that can convince managers that the center approach really does work, because it allows them to contrast the effectiveness of relying on supervisory judgment alone (or even assisted by simple testing) with the superior effectiveness of using assessment reports to develop their people. Studies comparing the success of candidates promoted with assessment to those promoted without it consistently show a 10% to 30% improvement.

The *fourth* and most common kind of validity check is the follow-up study of candidates who have been assessed at an operating center

and then promoted and developed by a management that is aware of the assessment findings.

Six such studies (some unpublished) report correlation between assessment findings and subsequent performance, the correlations ranging between .27 and .64. For instance, an IBM study of lower-level and middle-level managers reveals a correlation of .37. In general, assessments of potential for positions *above* the first level are more valid than assessments for positions *at* the first level.

Management Gains Better Judgments

While the weight of research is heavily on the side of the assessment center, this alone does not account for the method's phenomenal acceptance by management, which is less influenced by correlation coefficients than by evidence of the adequacy and fairness of a procedure. And a manager has only to act as an assessor or even sit through the assessors' deliberations to be convinced of the fairness, adequacy, and the accuracy of the method.

First timers observing an assessor discussion are always amazed by the extent and depth of information brought out. Like putting together a mosaic, assessors are able to integrate observations from various exercises to build a picture of how the candidate will perform in higher management. . . .

Accurate judgments also convince management. In one instance, management insisted on "testing out" its center by putting through several candidates whom it considered "stars" and "bums." The assessors had no trouble spotting the bums, but in discussing a man that management considered a superstar, the assessors found their evaluations were all negative. After hours of discussion of possible extenuating circumstances, the assessors prepared a verdict of "low potential." The man was promoted anyway. He proved totally unable to handle the job and was replaced after two months. Management needed no more convincing.

In sum, it would appear that the validity of certain assessment centers can be established. But, of course, this does not mean that all assessment centers are valid, for, by their very nature, each company's center is and should be substantially different from any other company's. Still, the accumulation of research findings from a variety of types of centers lends considerable credibility to the general validity of the technique.

In a survey of the 20 companies that operated centers, I uncovered some 22 studies in all that showed assessment *more* effective than other approaches and only one that showed it exactly *as* effective as some other approaches. None showed it *less* effective. As I suggested before, these studies exhibit correlations between center predictions and achievement criteria such as advancement, salary grade, and performance ratings that range as high as .64. The companies appear satisfied that they are on the right track.

MANY INDIRECT BENEFITS

Over and above the explicit goals of assessment, companies have consistently found that a number of added dividends accrue from centers.

The first and most obvious of these dividends is candidate training. Even when candidate training is not a defined objective of a center, it does take place. Completing an in-basket, participating in group discussions, and playing management games are genuine training exercises, even if there is no immediate feedback of results. After all, such exercises were used as training exercises long before they were used in assessment centers.

Second, passing through an assessment center has a positive influence on morale and job expectations. Candidates see the center as a chance to show their ability in fair and realistic situations. They also obtain a realistic idea of the requirements of the positions for which they are being considered. After doing an in-basket, for example, some candidates from the ranks have withdrawn themselves from consideration because of their new understanding of the volume of paperwork involved in a manager's job.

Third, by designing the exercises carefully, it is possible to improve candidates' understanding and attitudes subtly while they are being assessed. For example, one company that routinely assessed service technicians for management potential designed a group discussion exercise that concentrated the candidates' attention on a service-facility staffing problem. This exercise was structured to lead the candidates logically to the conclusion that management sometimes has no alternative but to increase the overtime of the present staff. By participating in this exercise, the candidates who were incumbent technicians gained sympathetic insight into management's reasons for occasionally asking them to work overtime.

Fourth, by far the most valuable fringe benefit is assessor training. The actual training of an assessor prior to his assignment parallels a management training program. During training, assessors participate in management games, in-baskets, and group discussions, followed by reviews of their performance in each of the activities.

An even more important training experience is actual participation as an assessor. In a normal work situation it is rare for managers to have the opportunity to spend uninterrupted time observing behavior and then comparing their observations with others. General Electric feels so strongly about the benefits of the assessment center to assessors that it has established a policy of a 1-to-1 assessor-candidate ratio to expose a substantial percentage of management to this experience.

Almost all of an assessor's training and experience is transferable to his job and should improve his ability to interview and appraise his subordinates. It is also possible for an assessor-manager to transfer some of the actual exercises from an assessment center to the everyday work situation. This has been done very successfully by managers in one company division, who use the in-basket and two exercises from the corporate assessment center as a screening device for hiring at the management level. These managers have found these procedures to be extremely useful in bringing out information not easily obtained through a personal interview with an applicant or a check on his background.

While these fringe benefits are important individually, they are even more important as an integral whole, since they indicate what may be the crucial advantage of the assessment center method over other, supplementary methods of identifying management potential. When a company uses psychological tests alone, or sends candidates to an outside psychologist for evaluation, it is in reality weakening itself because its executives are becoming dependent on others. Serving as assessor strengthens management skills. In addition, developing a center forces a company to focus on and resolve issues of job goals and define appropriate sources of manpower, things companies ought to do but frequently do not do.

BUILDING AND MANAGING CENTERS

The first and most important task in developing a center is establishing its goals and priorities. Management might ask itself these questions: Whom will we assess? Who will do the assessing? How will center reports be used—especially for manpower development? Who will see them? Will the reports be discussed with candidates? If so, how? The following discussion will develop some perspective on how these questions might be answered.

Identifying the Candidates

Candidates are commonly nominated for assessment by their supervisors. Usually supervisors are instructed to nominate employees who are performing adequately in their current jobs and who, in their estimation, have potential for advancement.

However, relying on supervisors' nominations represents a major philosophical inconsistency. One of the reasons for using the assessment center technique in the first place is to overcome some of the prejudices and biases inherent in supervisory judgment; yet the supervisor is ordinarily made the sole judge of whether a person should be assessed.

Companies can circumvent this potential bias by allowing candidates to nominate themselves or by establishing a rule that assessment will be automatic for all candidates who reach certain levels in the company. Both these alternatives mean that more candidates must be assessed, and this involves additional expense. Hence, they have been tried only on a limited basis.

Choosing the Assessors

Typically, assessors are line managers working two or three levels above the man being assessed. A group of junior foremen, for example, might be assessed by a team that includes division superintendents to whom the senior foremen report. These are the individuals who are responsible for promotion and who know most thoroughly the job requirements of the positions one level above the candidate's.

The job background of the assessor, of course, depends on the purpose of the specific assessment center. Where broader management aptitudes are being assessed, it is common for the assessors to be drawn from a number of areas in a company. This not only brings in a number of viewpoints, but exposes the candidate to representatives of a number of areas where he may find promotional opportunity. Having representatives of different areas also increases the acceptance of the findings throughout the company.

Assessors from management, like the candidates themselves, are usually nominated by their superiors (although in a few companies the center administrator makes an effort to recruit them). Naturally, the practice has its dangers. After a center has passed from the experimental to the operational phase, "purity" controls may be relaxed somewhat, and senior management may be tempted to send "cooperative" managers to centers to act as assessors. This temptation is particularly strong where the assessors serve for extended terms.

Center administrators have chosen to react to this problem in various ways. Some companies rely on their assessor training programs to screen out assessors who are unacceptable in the role, for one reason or another. The rationale here is that it is easy to spot an unqualified assessor during training and ease him out without bloodshed. As a fine point of strategy, for example, many center administrators suggest that it is wise to establish a pool of assessors, rather than train assessors for specific assignments. With the pooling arrangement, it is easy for the administrator to bypass unqualified assessors.

A major point of controversy among operators of assessment centers is the desirability of using professional psychologists rather than specially trained managers as assessors. Most arguments for using psychologists are based on their skills in observation; they are trained to recognize behavior not obvious to the untrained eye. While this argument is plausible, it has yet to be demonstrated in an operational center. Three studies have found no differences.

However, the superiority of psychologists over completely untrained managers is well established. Because of this superiority, companies often use psychologists as assessors in experimental or pilot programs, where training management accessors would be difficult. Psychologists are also used extensively for assessing higher levels of company management; at high levels, it is difficult to get and train managers who do not know the candidates personally, and the objective, independent psychologist is seen as the fairest evaluator.

By and large, companies now prefer to establish a pool of trained manager-assessors, each of whom serves more than once. Individual assessors are usually drawn from the pool to serve once or twice a year—a few companies ask assessors to serve only once. AT&T's practice is exceptional—it assigns assessors for six-month terms and center administrators for one year.

There are advantages and disadvantages to brief assignments. On the one hand, brief assignments usually mean that better men can be recruited, their enthusiasm and effort will be greater, more managers will benefit from the training involved in becoming an assessor, and more managers will be well prepared, after their tour of duty is over, to make judicious use of assessment reports. On the other hand, more managers must be trained and kept off their jobs; and those who serve briefly will not have as comprehensive an experience as assessors as they would if they had served a longer period.

Where the appointment is for an extended period of six months or so, of course, more rigorous and lengthy assessor training is feasible—AT&T trains managers for a month—and longer experience in the role is very valuable to an assessor. One substantial disadvantage of the long assignment is that assessment becomes a routine matter, which it never should. Reports from fatigued assessors read like computer output, and it is hard to think of them as anything more. Currently, only AT&T appoints assessors for prolonged periods.

Training the Assessors

In the companies now operating assessment centers, there is a notable difference in the emphasis placed on training assessors. Some companies give new assessors as little as one hour of training, which really amounts to just an orientation to the whole procedure, while most others spend three or four days.

One can argue that the task of an assessor is similar to the requirements of most managers' jobs—a manager must interview individuals, observe groups, and evaluate presentations. Assessing requires skill in these same areas, and hence many feel that there is little justification for further training.

The principal rebuttal to these arguments is this: because a man has been doing something, he has not necessarily been doing it well. Companies report marked improvements in the reliability of supervisory ratings after the supervisors have been trained to work as assessors. Nonprofessionals need to be shown what to look for in observing group discussions and individual presentations, or they may focus on purely surface characteristics. While rigid scientific studies are lacking, it is obvious from comparing the reports presented by experienced and inexperienced assessors that training makes a very big difference in the quality of performance.

The most common method of training is by understudy. In the usual situation, an assessor-in-training sits through an entire assessment cycle as a nonvoting member. Another method of assessor training, particularly when assessment centers are being introduced, is to have the assessors go through the assessment experience first as candidates. Everything is the same except that there are no assessors present. In a typical training situation, the assessors go through an activity such as group discussion and then critique the discussion and identify possible areas of observation afforded by the situation. Several companies videotape activities to give assessors practice in making observations.

Selecting the Exercises

A center's success rests in large part on the thoughtful, accurate selection of assessment exercises, for they stimulate the behavior to be observed. Thus, the first step is to define the behavior one wants to observe. Key managers familiar with the positions for which the candidates are to be assessed should discuss this among themselves, and the center developer should ask them questions like these: "Can you describe the behavior of successful and unsuccessful people in the positions in question?" "How do you evaluate people for this position?" "What are the tasks to be performed?" "What characteristics will be needed in our managers 10 years from now?"

After a list has been compiled and agreed on, another meeting should be held to determine which of these characteristics can be assessed adequately on a man's current job. After eliminating these from the list, the characteristics that remain become the objectives of the assessment center program, and the assessment exercises should be selected to bring out these behaviors.

Because certain key forms of behavior, such as leadership, delegation, control, motivation, selling ideas, organization, and operation under time stress, are important to many companies, exercises that bring them out are common to many centers. Almost all centers have an in-basket, one or two leaderless group discussion exercises, and a management game. While these activities may be similar in type from center to center, the specific content may be quite different depending on the educational and organizational level of the candidates.

The whom-to-promote leaderless group discussion described earlier is more appropriate, for instance, for lower-level candidates because the decision to be made is relatively simple and straightforward. One higher-level variation puts the candidate in the role of a member of a school board. The board has just received a bequest of $100,000. Each candidate is told to advocate a different point of view, and he is given adequate time and information to develop his arguments. Unlike the promotion exercise, where only one decision can be reached, the board can allocate the money to one or any combination of the members' projects. The points of view specified for the candidates are rather weakly defined, and hence there is considerable opportunity for them to develop their arguments in a creative fashion.

Many jobs have a unique but highly important aspect, and if this can be simulated, the company ought to develop a special exercise. Here are two interesting examples of such special exercises:

□ Penney has developed an effective exercise called the Irate Customer Phone Call. During dinner on the first night of the program, the candidates are told that they are to play the role of a manager during the evening, and that they may receive a phone call between 8:00 and 10:00 that night. This phone call is from an assessor playing an irate customer who makes several unreasonable demands on the candidate, after thoroughly convincing him of how upset he is about a service matter. The candidate's ability to handle this situation is evaluated along several dimensions, such as tact under stress.

□ The Peace Corps puts individual volunteers into a mock community development meeting with host nationals. The volunteer has been briefed in writing by the previous Peace Corps volunteer for the area, who has stated that the most important thing for the community is to bring in fresh, uncontaminated water from the nearby mountain. The purpose of this exercise is to determine the extent to which the new man will follow and push the ideas of the previous volunteer and the extent to which he will listen to the host nationals and form his own judgments.

At the meeting, the host nationals propose their own pet (and conflicting) projects. Depending on the characteristics of the people of the particular country being simulated, they ignore the volunteer's proposals, demonstrate impatience, pretend lack of understanding, exhibit hostility, and so on. They demand that the volunteer raise money or redesign plans, and a national might try to win over the volunteer to his own schemes through subtle persuasion or flattery.

Tests can also make a significant contribution to assessment if they are selected and used wisely. Intelligence, reading, arithmetic, and personality tests have all been found to increase the accuracy of certain assessment decisions. Tests should only be used under the direction of a psychologist, however, and great care should be taken in communicating test results lest they bias observations. Results are best reported to the assessors working at a center in broad terms such as "superior," "average," or "below average," since they can easily misinterpret numbers or percentiles. It is good practice to hold back giving test findings until the very end of the assessment discussion of the candidate.

Management must also take extreme care in generalizing about the relative importance of various exercises. Depending on the objectives of the center and the content of the exercises (all games are not equally effective or appropriate), the relative importance of various assessment activities may vary greatly. One thing does seem clear: where it is included, the in-basket is usually the most important exercise in an assessment center.

Informing Candidates of Results

One of the most important, yet most hazardous, aspects of assessment center operation is feeding the reports back to the candidates. Companies handle this in widely different ways, depending on the purpose of their centers. Three companies offer candidates the option of receiving or not receiving feedback. Between 60% and 90% ask for it. These companies find that candidates who do very well and those who do very poorly usually know where they stand and do not request feedback, whereas those in the middle want to find out how they did and get hints for self-improvement. Some companies give feedback to all candidates automatically.

In almost all cases, and certainly in companies that are strongly concerned about management development, results are carefully couched in terms of the directions that a candidate's personal development should take in the future. The candidate's impact on his fellow candidates may be communicated to him to make him more objective about himself. His performance on individual tasks may be discussed with an eye to establishing a plan to overcome noted deficiencies.

When assessment and training are combined, it is possible to provide some feedback to candidates prior to their leaving the center.

In some companies, a candidate must wait weeks for a feedback interview. Obviously, the sooner the feedback interview takes place, the more impact the training and development recommendations will have.

If a psychologist is available, he usually has the responsibility of discussing the center's result with the candidate. Otherwise, assessors or former assessors are given the responsibility.

The Place of Professionals

An industrial psychologist working in a large company was asked by a senior manager to aid in selecting supervisors for a newly created division. The psychologist suggested the assessment center method and submitted a report describing the technique and various exercises frequently used. The psychologist waited a month without receiving any reaction and finally telephoned the manager—who, to his surprise, reported that the assessment center was a big success and that he was very pleased with the outcome. Along with his subordinates, this manager had developed an assessment center for his own specific purpose, created his own exercises, and was running the center to his own satisfaction.

This vignette not only proves that managers can create assessment centers for their own specific purposes, but indicates also that a professional may not be needed. Yet psychologists do play an important role in center development. Psychologists are particularly valuable in these areas:

- Aiding managers to identify kinds of behavior that are critical to success.
- Developing or selecting assessment center exercises to bring out these kinds of behavior in the candidates.
- Training assessors.
- Administering pilot programs.
- Reviewing, critiquing, and improving the program.
- Researching the program's effectiveness.

Often psychologists' major contribution is to speed up the development of assessment centers. Some companies have spent as long as a year going through the various steps leading to the operation of their first center; with professional aid, other companies have accomplished the same thing in one month. As in so many areas, the difference seems to be in knowing what you are doing and benefiting from the experiences of others.

Just as there is no evidence that psychologists necessarily make better assessors than line managers, there is no evidence that psychologists make better assessment center administrators than line managers. Nevertheless, with the exception of AT&T, the majority of companies' centers are operated by industrial psychologists. This is partly the result of the newness of assessment centers in many companies. The appropriate role of the industrial psychologist seems to be that of developing and installing centers, rather than their continual operation. Psychologists should, however, retain responsibility for quality control and, in some cases, assessor training as well.

Negative Effects of Centers

When assessment centers are first explained to them, most managers immediately ask two questions: "What happens to the men who are not chosen for the center?" and, "What happens to the men who do not do well in the center?"

The Effect of Not Being Chosen   This depends primarily on how the center has been set up within a company. In some companies, centers have achieved the status of management development programs, and here, just as a young executive may feel he must go through T-group or grid training, he may feel he must be assessed. In these situations, anxiety develops among the ones not chosen, but to no greater extent than from failure to be chosen for any other development activity.

The Effect of Doing Poorly   Candidates who do poorly in assessment centers are usually quite aware of their performance. A logical response from a candidate who has done poorly would be to start looking around for another job. Whether this actually happens is unclear: one study indicates a higher turnover among poorly rated candidates, but other studies find no differences.

Turnover among weak candidates may be viewed in different ways. Some companies see a moderate amount of turnover as beneficial, in that "dead wood" disappears and opportunities for advancement are increased. Of course, if the candidate represents a sizable investment in terms of company experience or technical knowhow, losing him may be a disaster. The key to preventing turnover is the method and content of the feedback of results to the candidate.

WHAT DO CENTERS COST?

It is obvious that assessment centers are not inexpensive. The costs vary, naturally, depending on the length of the program, its location, and whether the candidates' and assessors' time is counted. Considering only out-of-the-pocket expenses, Wolverine Tube estimates that the cost of assessing 12 men is equivalent to 12 lunches. AT&T, which has regional centers and usually must transport and house most of its candidates and assessors, figures total cost (including candidate and assessor salaries) as approximately $500 per candidate. A division of IBM which uses motels for its centers roughly figures $5,000 per 12 candidates exclusive of staff salary.

While these costs may appear high, they are probably quite small compared with the cost of executive failure. In general, the cost of operating an assessment center should be proportionate to the importance of the assessment decision to be made. Companies should be willing to spend much more money and time on assessing candidates for middle- or top-management positions than they are for assessing candidates for first-level positions.

Savings in Small Organizations

Many companies feel that they must have 10,000 or more employees to use assessment centers. This is not true. In the last two or three years, I have seen several effective applications in small organizations. There are many ways that costs and time requirements can be shaved:

- A center can be run on company property, instead of taking men away to a motel or other expensive facility.
- A center can be designed to fit into the normal workday, which cuts overtime costs. To avoid disrupting work, assessment can take place all in one day or in two or more separated days. Even Saturday and Sunday have been used.
- To shorten time requirements, candidates may be required to do many exercises before coming to the center. For example, candidates may complete a personal information form, take tests, and go through an in-basket exercise before coming to the center. In one Penney center, the personal interview and in-basket interview are conducted at the common convenience of assessor and candidate; only group exercises are held on the one day allocated for assessment.
- It is often possible to combine assessment activities with an existing training program without lengthening the training program. For instance, a two-day assessment center was integrated into a two-week training program for Junior Achievement professional staff by merely restructuring training activities already a part of the program.

The resulting training was more effective because of the increased self-awareness provided by the assessment and took no longer to accomplish. The one new activity added was an in-basket, which proved to be a needed addition to the training program. The only added costs were expenses for assessors, but

there was a secondary payoff to this because the assessors' presence added greatly to the effectiveness of the training.

- Using commercially available exercises instead of specifically modeled exercises is a significant source of savings, but sound judgment must be used in selecting them. The only company offering exercises specifically designed for assessment centers is Assessment and Development Designs of New York City.

The major problem reported by small organizations is that the assessors know the candidates and sometimes are their immediate superiors. While this kind of contamination is not ideal, most problems can be controlled by careful training of assessors coupled with judicious assignment of assessors to candidates.

CONCLUSION

The assessment center method may not be appropriate for many companies, even where the cost of operation is manageable. Particularly at higher level positions, most companies do not have enough candidates to warrant the operation of an assessment center. For these companies, a possibility may be the operation of multi-company centers where a number of companies send one or two individuals to a center operated by a consultant, a university, or another company.

Three such centers have been operated on an experimental basis with seemingly good results. One center used psychologists and other professionals as assessors, while the other two relied on their managers. The latter seems preferable because it trains the managers, orients them to the proceedings, and helps them understand the use of the assessment center report.

While the effectiveness of an assessment center has not been proved beyond a shadow of a doubt, all the research, both published and unpublished, seems to indicate that the method has more validity than other existing methods. It is in this comparison that the strength of an assessment center lies. Granted that it is not perfect, it seems that using an assessment center for identifying management potential is a sounder and fairer method than those traditionally used by management.

Part Three

Influences on Work Behavior: Structural Factors

Chapter 5

Organizational Structure and Design

All of us, at one time or another, have participated in a variety of types of organizations—schools, companies, government agencies, the armed forces, hospitals, and so forth. Such experiences should have served to demonstrate—perhaps dramatically so in some instances—that the way organizations are designed and structured influences the behavior of their members. The same individual may behave quite differently in two organizations that serve the same function in society (e.g., two business firms or two city governments) but that are designed and structured differently. The issue that has to be kept in mind, however, is not just that design and structure impact behavior; rather, the issue is *in what ways* do structural factors influence the behavior of members? An equally important issue is the following: Can management alter and change the design of organizations in ways that benefit both members and the organizations? To what extent is such change feasible, even if desirable? These are some of the kinds of issues that are dealt with in this chapter.

The opening article, by Pugh, addresses the broad question of whether there are general "principles" of organization structure that can be put into practice irrespective of specific contextual conditions, or whether structures must be closely adapted to particular environmental and external circumstances. In attempting to deal with this issue, Pugh and his colleagues have collected considerable research data, which are summarized nontechnically. The conclusions that are reached represent the results of an ambitious research program carried out over many years. Using these findings, Pugh and his associates have extracted six primary dimensions of organization structure; furthermore, they have been able to design scales to measure these dimensions. The article describes the structural profiles of six organizations on these six dimensions, and also provides a categorization of types of structures. The major conclusion is that context is quite important in affecting organizational design—perhaps more important than has been previously realized—but that there is still a fair amount of freedom for the organization to make design decisions within these contextual constraints.

The following article, by Galbraith, presents a particular perspective on organization design: namely, an information-processing viewpoint. In this selection the emphasis is on how the organization can deal with uncertainties in its task environment. Obviously, the more turbulent and dynamic the environment, the greater the necessity for the organization to design strategies for coping with certainty. As Galbraith points out, organizations can try to preplan, they can attempt to "increase their flexibility to adapt to their inability to preplan," or they can try to decrease the level of performance required for continued existence. In design terms, four options are listed by Galbraith for dealing with uncertainty: (1) creation of slack resources, (2) creation of self-contained tasks, (3) investment in vertical information systems, and (4) creation of lateral relationships. Each option, of course, has its associated set of benefits and costs. The important goal, for Galbraith, is the matching of information requirements and the capacity of the organization to process information. If the organization does not make conscious attempts to get the best match possible, it will "receive" a match in the form of severe organizational problems.

The final article in the chapter, by Cammann and Nadler, discusses the design of a major operational feature of organizations: control systems. The authors view this issue from the perspective of the manager, and ask how management can best adapt control systems to particular needs and circumstances. The article defines two major categories of control systems: "external controls" and "internal motivation." The costs and presumed benefits of each are outlined, and the choice between them (or of a modified combination of them) is examined in terms of four key issues: (1) the consistency between strategy choice and the manager's style; (2) the relation of the system to the organization's climate, structure, and reward system; (3) the reliability of measures of job performance; and (4) individual differences among subordinates. Throughout this analysis, the authors make the basic assumption that managers *can* make informed choices among various control strategies, and that such choices really do make a difference in affecting behavior in organizations.

Reading 15

The Measurement of Organization Structures: Does Context Determine Form?

D. S. Pugh

This article will give some answers, admittedly partial and preliminary, to the following questions: Are there any general principles of organization structure to which all organizations should adhere? Or does the context of the organization—its size, ownership, geographical location, technology of manufacture—determine what structure is appropriate? Last, how much leeway does the management of a company have to design the organization initially and tamper with it later on? Obviously, the questions are interdependent. If the context of the organization is crucial to determining the suitable structure, then management operates within fairly rigid constraints; it can either recognize the structure predetermined by the context and make its decisions accordingly or it can fail to recognize the structure indicated by the context, make the wrong decisions, and impair the effectiveness or even the survival of the organization. This assumes, of course, that management retains the latitude to make the wrong decisions on structure.

Even more obviously, these questions are difficult to answer. Let's begin with the fact that systematic and reliable information on organizational structure is scarce. We have a plethora of formal organization charts that conceal as much as they reveal and a quantity of unsynthesized case material. What we need is a precise formulation of the characteristics of organization structure and the development of measuring scales with which to assess differences quantitatively.

We do know something about the decisions that top managers face on organizations. For example, should authority be centralized? Centralization may help maintain a consistent policy, but it may also inhibit initiative lower down the hierarchy. Again, should managerial tasks be highly specialized? The technical complexity of business life means that considerable advantages can accrue from allowing people to specialize in a limited field. On the other hand, these advantages may be achieved at the expense of their commitment to the overall objectives of the company.

Should a company lay down a large number of standard rules and procedures for employees to follow? These may ensure a certain uniformity of performance, but they may also produce frustration—and a tendency to hide behind the rules. Should the organization structure be "tall" or "flat"? Flat structures—with relatively few hierarchical levels—allow communications to pass easily up and down, but managers may become overloaded with too many direct subordinates. Tall structures allow managers to devote more time to subordinates, but may well overextend lines of command, and distort communications.

All these choices involve benefits and costs. It also seems reasonable to suppose that the extent and importance of the costs and benefits will vary according to the situation of the company. All too often in the past these issues have been debated dogmatically in an "either/or" fashion, without reference to size,

Reprinted by permission of the publisher from *Organizational Dynamics*, Spring 1973, 19–34, © 1973 by AMACOM, a division of American Management Association.

technology, product range, market conditions, or corporate objectives. Operationally, the important question is: In what *degree* should organizational characteristics such as those above be present in different types of companies? To answer this question there must obviously be accurate comparative measures of centralization of authority, specialization of task, standardization of procedure, and so on, to set beside measurements of size, technology, ownership, business environment, and level of performance. A program of research aimed at identifying just such measurements—of organization structure, operating context, and performance—was inaugurated in the Industrial Administration Research Unit of the University of Aston a number of years ago, and continues in the Organizational Behaviour Research Group at the London Business School and elsewhere. The object of the research is threefold:

a To discover in what ways an organization structures its activities,

b To see whether or not it is possible to create statistically valid and reliable methods of measuring structural differences between organizations,

c To examine what constraints the organization's context (i.e., its size, technology of manufacture, diffusion of ownership, etc.) imposes on the management structure.

FORMAL ANALYSIS OF ORGANIZATION STRUCTURE

Measurement must begin with the ideas on what characteristics should be measured. In the field of organization structure the problem is not the absence of such ideas to distill from the academic discourse, but rather variables that can be clearly defined for scientific study.

From the literature we have selected six primary variables or dimensions of organization structure:

Specialization—the degree to which an organization's activities are divided into specialized roles.

Standardization—the degree to which an organization lays down standard rules and procedures.

Standardization of employment practices—the degree to which an organization has standardized employment practices.

Formalization—the degree to which instructions, procedures, etc., are written down.

Centralization—the degree to which the authority to make certain decisions is located at the top of the management hierarchy.

Configuration—the "shape" of the organization's role structure, e.g., whether the management chain of command is long or short, whether superiors have limited span of control—relatively few subordinates—or broad span of control—a relatively large number of subordinates, and whether there is a large or small percentage of specialized or support personnel. Configuration is a blanket term used to cover all three variables.

We need to distinguish between the two forms of standardization because they are far from synonymous. High standardization of employment practices, for example, is a distinctive feature of personnel bureaucracies but not of workflow bureaucracies.

In our surveys, we have limited ourselves to work organizations employing more than 150 people—a work organization being analyzed as one that employs (that is, pays) its members. We constructed scales from data on a first sample of fifty-two such organizations, including firms making motor car bumpers and milk chocolate buttons, municipal organizations that repaired roads or taught arithmetic, large department stores, and small insurance companies, and so on. Several further samples duplicated the original investigation and increased the number of organizations to over two hundred.

Our problem was how to apply our six

dimensions—how to go beyond individual experience and scholarship to the systematic study of existing organizations. We decided to use scales in measuring the six dimensions of any organization—so that the positions of a particular organization on those scales form a profile of the organization.

Our approach to developing comparative scales also was guided by the need to demonstrate that the items forming a scale "hang together," that is, they are in some sense cumulative. We can represent an organization's comparative position on a characteristic by a numerical score, in the same way as an I.Q. score represents an individual's comparative intelligence. But just as an I.Q. is a sample of a person's intelligence taken for comparative purposes and does not detract from his uniqueness as a functioning individual, so our scales, being likewise comparative samples, do not detract from the uniqueness of each organization's functioning. They do, however, indicate limits within which the unique variations take place.

We began by interviewing at length the chief executive of the organization, who may be a works manager, an area superintendent, or a chairman. Then followed a series of interviews with department heads of varying status, as many as were necessary to obtain the information required. Interviews were conducted with standard schedules listing what had to be found out.

We were concerned with making sure that variables concerned both manufacturing and nonmanufacturing organizations. Therefore we asked each organization, for example, for which of a given list of potentially standardized routines it had standardized procedure. (See Figure 15-1 for sample questions in the six dimentions.)

On the other hand, because this was descriptive data about structure, and was personal to the respondent, we made no attempt to standardize the interview procedures themselves. At the same time, we tried to obtain documentary evidence to substantiate the verbal descriptions.

ANALYSIS OF SIX STRUCTURAL PROFILES

For purposes of discussion we have selected six organizations and have constructed the structural profiles for each one. Two are governmental organizations. The other four are in the private sector of the economy but the nature of the ownership varies drastically— one is family owned; another is owned jointly by a family and its employees; the third is a subsidiary of a large publicly owned company; the fourth is a medium-size publicly held company. The number of employees also varies widely from 16,500 in the municipal organization to only 1,700 in the manufacturing organization owned by the central government. We selected these six from the many available in order to demonstrate the sort of distinctive profiles we get for particular organizations and to underscore the way in which we can make useful comparisons about organizations on this basis.

With all this diversity, it is not too surprising that no two profiles look alike. What is surprising, and deserves further comment, are the similarities in several of the six dimensions between several of the six organizations (see Figure 15-2).

Organization A is a municipal department responsible for a public service. But it is far from being the classic form of bureaucracy described by Weber. By definition, such a bureaucracy would have an extremely high-score pattern on all our scales. That is, it would be highly specialized with many narrowly defined specialist "officers," highly standardized in its procedures, and highly formalized; with documents prescribing all activities and recording them in the files as

Specialization

1 Are the following activities performed by specialists—i.e., those exclusively engaged in the activities and not in the line chain of authority?
    a activities to develop, legitimize, and symbolise the organizational purpose (e.g., public relations, advertising).
    b activities to dispose of, distribute, and service the output (e.g., sales, service).
    c activities to obtain and control materials and equipment (e.g., buying, stock control).
    d activities to devise new outputs, equipment, processes (e.g., R&D, development).
    e activities to develop and transform human resources (e.g., training, education).
    f activities to acquire information on the operational field (e.g., market research).
2 What professional qualifications do these specialists hold?

Standardization:

1 How closely defined is a typical operative's task (e.g., custom, apprenticeship, rate fixing, work-study)?
2 Are there specific procedures to ensure the perpetuation of the organization (e.g., R&D programs, systematic market research)?
3 How detailed is the marketing policy (e.g., general aims only, specific policy worked out and adhered to)?
4 How detailed are the costing and stock control systems (e.g., stock taking: yearly, monthly, etc.; costing: historical job costing, budgeting, standard cost system)?

Standardization of employment practices

1 Is there a central recruiting and interviewing procedure?
2 Is there a standard selection procedure for foremen and managers?
3 Is there a standard discipline procedure with set offenses and penalties?

Formalization

1 Is there an employee handbook or rulebook?
2 Is there an organization chart?
3 Are there any written terms of reference or job descriptions? For which grades of employees?
4 Are there agenda and minutes for workflow (e.g., production) meetings?

Centralization

Which level in the hierarchy has the authority to
    a decide which supplies of materials are to be used?
    b decide the price of the output?
    c alter the responsibilities or areas of work of departments?
    d decide marketing territories to be covered?

Configuration

1 What is the chief executive's span of control?
2 What is the average number of direct workers per first-line supervisor?
3 What is the percentage of indirect personnel (i.e., employees with no direct or supervisory responsibility for work on the output)?
4 What is the percentage of employees in each functional specialism (e.g., sales and service, design and development, market research)?

Figure 15-1 Sample questions in six dimensions.

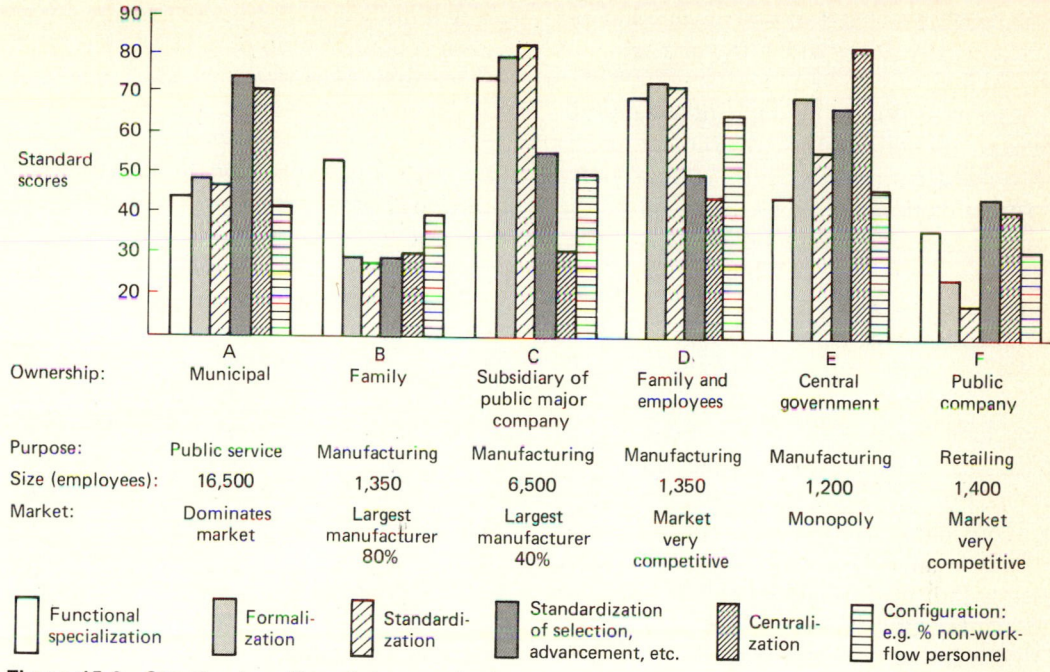

Figure 15-2 Structural profiles of six organizations.

precedents. If everything has to be referred upward for decision, then it would also score as highly centralized. In configuration it would have a high proportion of "supportive" or administrative or "non-workflow" personnel. But clearly this example does not fit this pattern completely; it is below standard in both specialization and configuration, which demonstrates the effectiveness of this method of determining empirically what profile actually exists in overcoming stereotyped thinking.

Organization B represents a relatively unstructured family firm, relying more on traditional ways of doing things. Although it has the specialities usual in manufacturing industry (and hence a comparatively high specialization score) it has minimized standardized procedure and formalized paperwork.

Organization C represents "big business." It is the subsidiary of a very large company, and its profile shows the effects of size: generally, very high scores on specialization, standardi-

zation, and formalization, but decentralized. The distinctively different relationship of centralization is typical. Centralization correlates *negatively* with almost all other structural scales. The more specialized, standardized, and formalized the organization, the *less* it is centralized, or to put it the other way around, the more it is decentralized. Therefore these scales do not confirm the common assumption that a large organization and the routines that go with them "pass the buck" upward for decision with elaborate staff offices; in fact, such an organization is relatively decentralized.

But it is not only a question of size, as the profile of Organization D shows. It has the same number of employees as Organization B, yet its structure is in striking contrast and is more nearly that of a much larger firm. Clearly the policies and attitudes of the management of an organization may have a considerable effect on its structure, even though factors like size, technology, and form of ownership set the framework within which the management must function.

Organization E is an example of a manufacturing unit owned by the government and is characterized by a high centralization and a high formalization score. Comparison of the profiles of D and E brings home the fact that two organizations may be "bureaucratic" but in quite different ways.

Organization F is included as an example of the relatively low scores often found in retailing.

If we look closely at all the profiles, we can spot several that have pronounced features in common. For example, organizations C and D both score high on functional specialization, formalization, and standardization. Moreover, by using the statistical method of principal components analysis, we emerge with a comparatively few composite scores that sum up the structural characteristics of each organization. Plotting the composite scores reveals several closely related clusters, four of which

we will discuss in detail. (See Figure 15-3 for a visual representation of the clusters.)

The first cluster the reader may already have recognized from studying the six profiles in Figure 15-2. It indicates that high specialization, high standardization, and high formalization are a pattern that prevails in large-scale manufacturing industry. Among the examples are factories in the vehicle accessory and vehicle assembly industry, those processing metals, and those mass-producing foodstuffs and confectionery. Organizations like this have gone a long way in regulating their employees' work by specifying their specialized roles, the procedures they are to follow in carrying out these roles, and the documentation involved in what they have to do. In short, the pattern of scores among specialization, standardization, and formalization denotes the range and pattern of structuring. So manufacturing industry tends to have highly structured work activities—production schedules, quality inspection procedures, returns of output per worker and per machine, forms

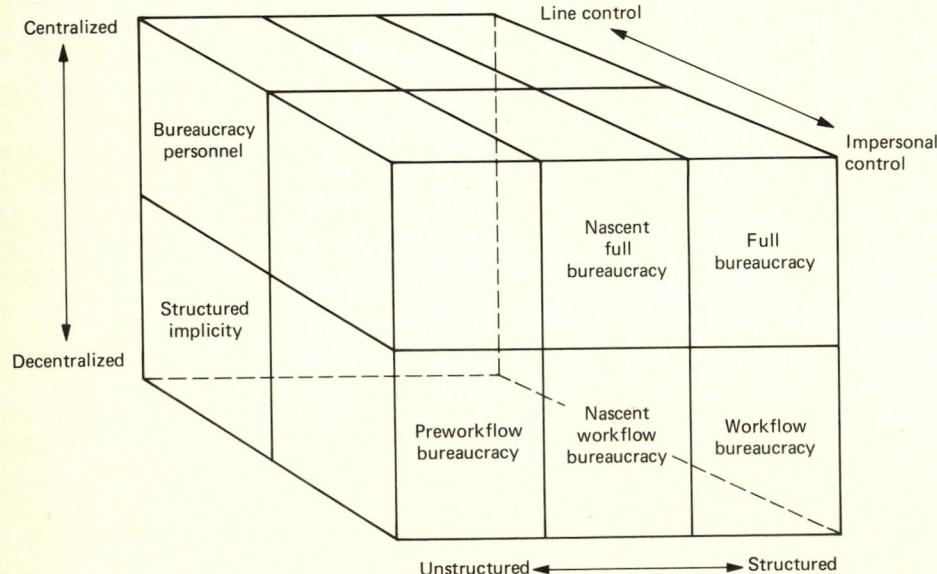

Figure 15-3 Relationships between the clusters.

recording maintenance jobs, etc. We can call this the *workflow bureaucracy* kind of organization. In Figure 15-2, Organizations C and D follow this pattern. This kind of organization (placed in the lower right front box in Figure 15-3) usually has a high percentage of "non-workflow" personnel (employees not directly engaged in production). Many of these are in the large specialized sections such as production planning and scheduling, quality inspection and testing, work-study, and research and development, which generate standardization and formalization.

To some it may be surprising that the workflow structured organization is relatively decentralized. The explanation appears to be that when the responsibilities of specialized roles are laid down, and activities are regulated by standardized procedures records, top management can afford to decentralize because the organizational machine will run as it has been set to run, and decisions will be made in the way they were intended with less need to refer them to the top.

Grouped in the upper left back box are organizations with a high centralization of authority and low structuring of activities. The authority of these organizations is centralized, usually concentrated in a controlling committee outside and above the unit itself, and in most cases, such organizations do not structure daily work activities very much. However, their scores on a scale of procedures for standardization of selection, advancement, and so on indicate that they do standardize or structure the employment activity. They have central recruiting, selecting, disciplining and dismissing procedures, conducted by formally constituted boards, appeal procedures, and the like. Such an organization is called a *personnel bureaucracy*, since it bureaucratizes everything relating to employment, but not the daily work activity to anything like the same degree. Personnel bureaucracies are typically local or central government departments (for

example, a municipal education department or the regional division of a government ministry) and the smaller branch factories of large corporations.

In general, there is less formal structuring of activities in service organizations than in manufacturing industries. Also, when service organizations are geographically dispersed over many sites or are publicly owned, the concentration of authority increases and they become personnel bureaucracies. An example of the influence of public ownership is the difference between one motorbus organization owned by a local government authority and another, one of the largest remaining "private" transport organizations in the country. The central government, through a holding corporation, owns 50 percent of the equity of the private company, but takes no direct part in its operations. They have identical technologies (scores of 6 each on the scale of workflow integration) and are in the same size range (8,618 and 6,300 employees); therefore they are very close in structural profile, except for the higher concentration of authority of the municipal undertaking that reflects its high dependence on local government.

A cluster of organizations can be seen in the lower left back box, which at first glance are low on both structuring and centralization. This minimal structuring and dispersed authority suggests unregulated chaos. Not so; instead, this indicates that such organizations score low on the structural characteristics because the scales reflect overt regulation. Such an organization we call an *implicitly structured organization*. These organizations are run not by explicit regulation but by implicitly transmitted custom, a common condition in small organizations where management and ownership overlap. On investigation, this hypothesis was supported. These implicitly structured organizations are comparatively small factories (within the size range of the sample); they tend to be independent of external links and they have scores on concentration of ownership that indicate that the operating control of the organization has remained with the owning directors.

The upper right front box of Figure 15-3 includes those organizations that are high on both structuring and centralization, and therefore show the characteristics of a workflow bureaucracy (for example, standardization of task control procedures), as in large manufacturing corporations, together with the characteristics of personnel bureaucracy (for example, centralized authority for decision making), as in government departments. This was in fact found to be the case. A central government branch factory, government-owned public services, and nationalized industries fit this pattern. Thus, we may regard them as examples of *full bureaucracy.*

ANALYSIS OF ORGANIZATIONAL CONTEXT

Once we have measured organization structure, the question arises, "Do organizations of different size have different kinds of structure?" Similarly, organizations can range from being technologically very advanced to being very simple, or from being owned and controlled by one man to being owned by many people and controlled (i.e., actually run) by none of them. Clearly we must employ as much vigor in measuring the nonstructural or contextual aspects of organizations as we did in measuring the structural factors. To guide the measuring, we have identified the principal dimensions of context as follows:

Origin and History—whether an organization was privately founded, and the kinds or changes in ownership, location, etc. it has experienced.

Ownership and Control—the kind of ownership (e.g. private or public) and its concentration in a few hands or dispersion into many.

Size—number of employees, net assets, market position, etc.

Charter—the nature and range of goods and services.

Technology—the degree of integration achieved in an organization's work process.

Location—the number of geographically dispersed operating sites.

Interdependence—the extent to which an organization depends on customers, suppliers, trade unions, any owning groups, etc. Figure 15-4 lists some examples of the information that was obtained.

EXPLORING STRUCTURE AND CONTEXT

Now it has become possible to explore in a wide range of diverse work organizations the relationship between structural and contextual characteristics. How far, for example, is specialization a function of size? Note that the question is not "Is specialization a result of large size or is it not?" Now we are in a position to rephrase the question: *To what extent* is size associated with specialization? The correlation between size and overall role specialization in the first sample was 0.75—thus size is the most important single element. But what part do other factors play? The correlation of "Workflow Integration"—a scale that has been developed for measuring comparative technology (see Figure 15-4)—and overall specialization was 0.38. This is not very large in itself, but since there is no relationship between size and technology (correlation of 0.08), we should expect an analysis using both dimensions to produce a higher relationship than size alone. This is in fact what happens, and the multiple correlation of size with technology and specialization is 0.81. Thus knowing an organization's score on our scales of size *and* technology, we can predict to within relatively close limits what its specialization score will be. Likewise, knowing an organization's dependence on other organizations and its geographical dispersion over sites tells a great deal about the

Workflow integration

A highly workflow-integrated technology is signified by:

1 Automatic repeat-cycle equipment, self-adjusting.
2 Single-purpose equipment.
3 Fixed "line" or sequence of operations.
4 Single input point at commencement of "line."
5 No waiting time between operations.
6 No "buffer stocks" between operations.
7 Breakdown anywhere stops workflow immediately.
8 Outputs of workflow (production) segments/departments become inputs of others, i.e., flow from department to department throughout.
9 Operations evaluated by measurement techniques against precise specifications.

A technology low in workflow integration is at the opposite extremes on these items.

Vertical integration (component scale of dependence)

1 Integration with suppliers: ownership and tied supply/long contracts/single orders.
2 Sensitivity of outputs volume to customer influence: outputs for schedule and call off/order/stock.
3 Integration with customers: ownership and tied market/long-term contracts/regular contracts/single orders.
4 Dependence of organization on its largest customer: sole/major/medium/minor outlet.
5 Dependence of largest customer on organization: sole/major/medium/minor supplier.

Dependence

1 Status of organizational unit: branch/head branch/legal subsidiary/principal unit.
2 Unit size as a percentage of parent-group size.
3 Representation on policy-making boards.
4 Number of specialist services contracted out.
5 Vertical integration.

Figure 15-4 Some contextual scales.

likely centralization of authority in its structure (multiple correlation of 0.75).

These relationships of context and structure we have found to be reasonably stable in surveys of different samples. Where differences in the relationships have been found they have been easily related to the varying characteristics of the samples studied. In general, the framework has been adequate for thinking about the degree of constraint that contextual factors place on the design of organizational structures. The degree of constraint appears to be substantial (about 50 percent of the variability between structures may be directly related to contextual features such as size, technology, interdependence,

etc.) but it allows considerable opportunities for choice and variation in particular organizations based on the attitudes and views of the top management.

In other words, context is a determining factor—perhaps overall the determining factor—designing, shaping, and modifying the structure of any organization. But within these contextual limits, top management has plenty of leeway left to make its influence felt—50 percent is a major margin of freedom. With this approach, we can discuss a number of basic issues of organizational design, such as those indicated at the beginning of this article. And we can conduct the discussion on the basis of a number of comparative empirical findings—which inevitably underline the range of variation possible—rather than merely on individual views and experiences—which inevitably tend to dogmatic overgeneralization. The two issues we'll focus on are the relationship between size and formalization (paperwork procedures) and the effects of technology on organization structure.

FORMALIZATION OF PROCEDURES

Using the measures that we have developed, we can explore systematically the relationship between a structural feature of organization, such as the degree of formalization of paperwork procedures, and a contextual one, such as size of operation—indicated by the number of personnel employed.

Formalization indicates the extent to which rules, procedures, instructions, and communications are written down. How does the weight of documentation vary from organization to organization? Definitions of thirty-eight documents have been assembled, each of which can be used by any known work organization. They range from, for example, organization charts, memo forms, agendas, and minutes to written terms of reference, job descriptions, records of maintenance performed, statements of tasks done or to be done on the output, handbooks, and manuals of procedures. Scores range from four in a single-product foodstuffs factory where there are few such documents to 49 in a metals processing plant where each routine procedure is documented in detail.

A large range of differences in paperwork usage is found in all our surveys. What relation does this have to the size of organization? The correlations found range from 0.55 to 0.83 in different samples, demonstrating a strong tendency for the two to go together but still allowing many exceptions. Figure 15-5 gives examples of three typical organizations and also of two organizations that have considerably less paperwork, and two that have considerably more, than would be expected from their size alone.

The four unusual organizations emphasize the range of variation possible and lead us to look for factors other than size in explanation. Ownership patterns may play a part, the government-owned plant having more formalization than would be expected, the family retail firm having less. But the family manufacturing firm has considerably more, so the attitudes of its top management and their belief in the necessity for formal procedures becomes relevant. Similarly, the presence of a large number of professional staff in the municipal service is accompanied by the belief that they do not require such a high degree of control on their jobs because of their professional training.

One further important factor relating to formalization is clear: In our comparative surveys of international samples we have found that formalization is the one aspect of structure that clearly distinguishes U.S. and Canadian organizations from British ones. Size for size, North American organizations have a formalization score that is, on the average, 50 percent greater than their British counterparts. Since the relationship with size holds up in both cultures, and since in general, American organizations are bigger than British ones, the average American manager is subjected to considerably more control through paperwork procedures than his British opposite number. The reason for this cultural difference we can only speculate on. It may be that in the more homogeneous British culture more things can be taken for granted, whereas in the more heterogeneous American culture, controls even in smaller organizations must be spelled out formally to be effective.

THE EFFECTS OF TECHNOLOGY ON ORGANIZATIONS

Does technology determine organization? Is the form of organization in a chemical plant,

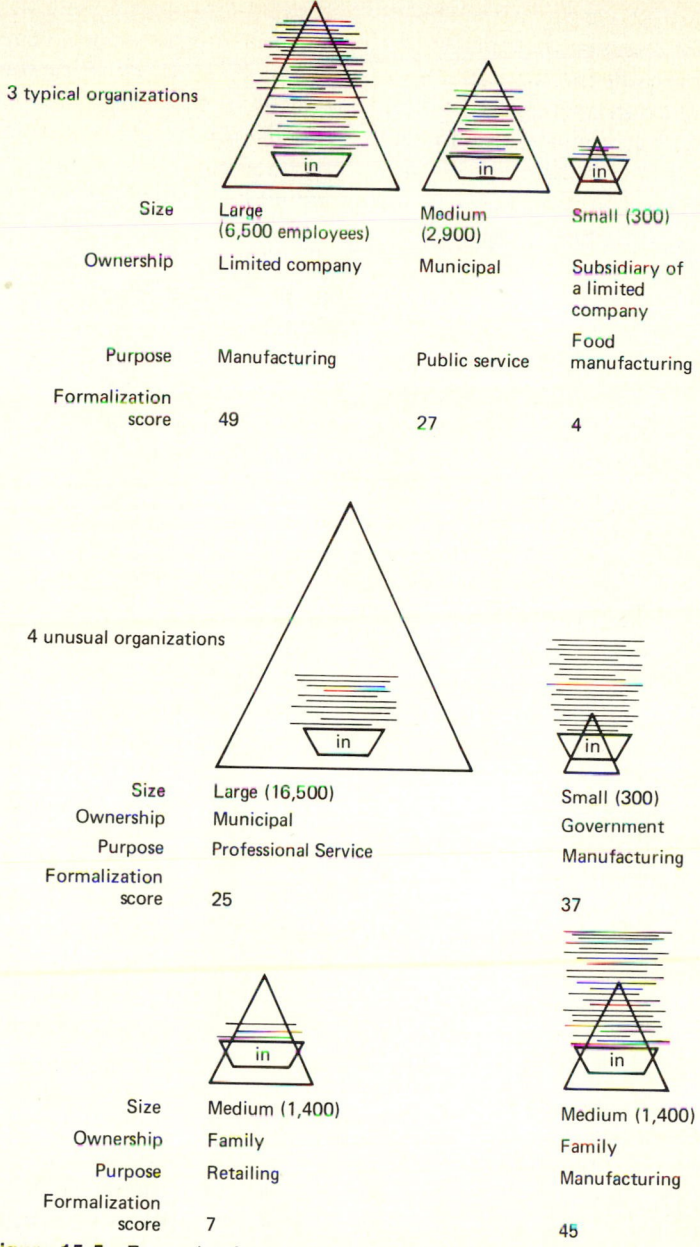

Figure 15-5 Examples from seven organizations.

for instance, dictated by the fact that it is a chemical plant—that is, by its highly automated equipment and continuous flow process? And is the organization of a batch production engineering factory shaped by the way its work is done—that is, by its rows of machine tools and its varying batches?

This is a contentious question. It also asks how far the number of levels of management, the centralization of major decisions, the proliferation of standard procedures, the development of specialist "service" sections, and the many other features of the structure of an organization depend on its technology.

In a study that has had considerable impact both on management and behavioral science writers, Joan Woodward in *Management and Technology* maintains that "It was possible to trace a cause and effect relationship between a system of production and its associated organizational pattern and, as a result, to predict what the organizational requirements of a firm are likely to be, given its production system."

Woodward took this view as a result of comparing as many as 80 firms on a unit and small batch, large batch and mass, and flow process classification. She found, for example, that the line of command from the chief executive of each firm was shortest in unit and small batch firms, lengthened in large batch and mass, and was longest in process firms. Another example of this relationship was the ratio of managers to total personnel, which also increased from unit up to process technology.

In contrast, it appeared that the spans of control of the first-line production supervisors were widest in large batch and mass production (average 46), but dropped away in unit and small batch on the one side (to average 22) and in process industries to an average of 14. Other suggested examples of this pattern were clear definition of duties and amount of paperwork, which were also greatest in large batch/mass technology.

Woodward's study immediately raised the question of whether it was possible to develop general management principles of organization, as advocated by such writers as Fayol, Urwick, Gulick, and Brown. Woodward maintained that this was now no longer possible. The principles that they had advocated—such as the necessity of clear lines of authority and responsibility (one man, one boss, etc.) and limited spans of control for effective supervision—might well apply in large batch and mass production forms, for they rested primarily on the experience of managers and consultants in this range of technology. But outside this range, in unit/jobbing and process technologies, different principles probably would be required.

The studies that we have carried out include replications of the Woodward work, since technology is one of a range of contextual factors that we examined. Equipped with a much more comprehensive analysis of organization structure than Woodward we can explore much more systematically what the *relative* effects of technology are on organization structure.

In addition to using Woodward's categories, the present research program also developed a measure of technology based on the items in Figure 15-4 and labeled "Workflow Integration." This discriminates among organizations on the basis of the rigidity or flexibility of the sequence of operations carried out by the equipment on the work. This has affinities with the Woodward classification but is not equivalent to it. Thus it was possible to examine the relationships of these two measures with the dimensions of organization structure.

Did the organizations with the most process-oriented technologies have the largest scores on specialization of management roles, standardization of procedures, etc.? In the first study, taking manufacturing organizations only, a correlation of 0.52 was found between Woodward technology and standardization. This would suggest considerable support for the proposition that the technology of manufacture has considerable bearing on the management structure. But the advantage of a survey that takes a range of factors into account becomes immediately apparent when we consider the relationship of other factors. The correlation of size with specialization is 0.83, and with standardization it is 0.65, both of which are considerably higher than the technology relationships. When we recall that size and technology are correlated among manufacturing organizations, and the effects of size are discounted by the technique known as partial correlation, then the remaining relationships of technology to structure are slight indeed (0.26 with specialization, 0.07 with standardization). In general, our studies have confirmed that the relationship of technology to the main structural dimensions in manufacturing organizations are always very small and play a secondary role relative to other contextual features such as size and interdependence with other organizations (such as owning group, customers, suppliers, etc.).

Where technology is shown to be related to manufacturing organization structures is in a number of highly specific jobs ratios that we consider under the heading of "configuration" (see Figure 15-1).

The ratio of subordinates to first-line supervisors is the only point at which the Woodward results and the present results agree exactly. Supervisors have most subordinates in large batch/mass production. This is where each foreman often has forty or fifty workers turning out large quantities of standard items, whereas in jobbing or in process plants he has a smaller group.

Hence the proportion of employees in inspection work and in maintenance work is also greatest at the large batch stage, and lower in both unit production and processing.

The proportions in production control are highest from unit or jobbing to the mass stage, dropping away in process technologies where production control is built into the processes themselves and does not require the clerical and progress-chasing effort imposed by complex assemblies.

The detailed examination of these features is interesting, but it is of much less consequence than their implications taken as a whole. What is distinctive about them, as against the range of organizational characteristics not related to technology?

The first-mentioned characteristic, ratio of subordinates to first-line supervisors, is an element of organization at the level of the operative and his immediate boss. Obviously, the number of men a supervisor requires to run a row of lathes differs from the number he requires to run the more continuous integrated workflow of an automatic transfer machine. Thus, subordinate/supervisor ratio is an aspect of organization that reflects activities directly bound up with the technology itself. Also, it is the variety of equipment and products in batch production that demands larger numbers of inspectors and of maintenance personnel; unit and process technologies are less demanding in this respect. It is the complexity of technology both in variety of equipment and in sequences of operations that requires relatively large numbers of production control personnel outside the more automatic process-type technologies.

The point is made more clearly by the contrast with, say, activities such as accounting or market research that are not directly implicated in the work technology itself—where research results show no connection with the technological factors.

In this light, it may be suggested that the connections between the workflow integration measure of technology and the numbers engaged in employment and in purchasing and warehousing may be due to the intermediate position of these activities. They are closer to the production work itself than, for example, accounting, but not as close as inspection.

So among the extensive range of organizational features studied, only those directly centered on the production workflow itself show any connection with technology; these are all "job-counts" of employees on production-linked activities. Away from the shop floor, technology appears to have little influence on organization structure.

FURTHER DEVELOPMENTS

Our on-going research program is exploring new areas. For example, what changes in organization structure take place over time? In one small study that we have already undertaken, 14 organizations were restudied after a period of four to five years. The organizations were all manufacturing firms and workflow bureaucracies in terms of Figure 15-3. There was an overall decrease in size of 5 to 10 percent, as measured by number of employees, but the other contextual features remained constant. In spite of this stability there was a clear tendency for structuring scores to increase (more specialization, standardization, formalization), but with a decrease in centralization. If within certain limits—imposed by the organization's context—top management may be able to accentuate one of two broad strategies of control, *either* to retain most decision making at the top and put up with wider spans of control *or* to delegate decisions to lower-level specialists and rely on procedures and forms to maintain control, then on this evidence they are consistently choosing the second alternative, at least in manufacturing.

Clearly, more evidence is required before the significance of this trend can be evaluated. And evidence is also required on the *processes* by which organization structures get changed. What are the interdepartmental power struggles, the interpersonal conflicts, the pressures for and resistance to proposed changes that make up the evolving structure as it responds to changes in the organization's context? Studies have already been carried out that show a clear relationship of structure to organizational climate and morale. One study, for example, has shown that greater structuring of activities is accompanied by more formal interpersonal relationships, and greater centralization of authority leads to a greater degree of "social distance" between the levels in an organization—social distance being the degree to which a manager regards his supervisor as boss only and not as a colleague as well. These important concomitants of structure need to be more fully investigated.

IMPLICATIONS OF THE RESEARCH

It has long been realized that an organization's context is important in the development of its structure. What is surprising is the magnitude of the relationships outlined above. People often speak as if the personalities of the founder and directors of a business had been the most important influence in creating the present organization. Other people point to historical crises or to the vagaries of government policy as being the stimuli that caused the business to develop in a particular way. Though we would certainly expect personality, events, and policies to play their part, the fact that information relating solely to an organization's context enables us to make such good predictions indicates that context is more important than is generally realized.

The manager of the future will have available to him ever increasing amounts of information, and will be anxious to know what signals he should primarily attend to. If he knows what is crucial to organization functioning he can manage by exception. What types and amounts of environmental change can occur before internal adjustments must be made to maintain performance?

The fact that there are now valid and reliable comparative measures of organization context and structure placed in a generalizable framework of relationships enables the many managers who have collaborated in these surveys to do a better job of placing their organizations in relation to others and to work toward evaluating the costs and benefits of the forms of management structure that could be developed to enable them to meet the challenges of the future.

Reading 16

Organization Design: An Information Processing View

Jay R. Galbraith

THE INFORMATION PROCESSING MODEL

A basic proposition is that the greater the uncertainty of the task, the greater the amount of information that has to be processed between decision makers during the execution of the task. If the task is well understood prior to performing it, much of the activity can be preplanned. If it is not understood, then during the actual task execution more knowledge is acquired which leads to changes in resource allocations, schedules, and priorities. All these changes require information processing *during* task performance. Therefore *the greater the task uncertainty, the greater the amount of information that must be processed among decision makers during task execution in order to achieve a given level of performance.* The basic effect of uncertainty is to limit the ability of the organization to preplan or to make decisions about activities in advance of their execution. Therefore it is hypothesized that the observed variations in organizational forms are variations in the strategies of organizations to 1) increase their ability to preplan, 2) increase their flexibility to adapt to their inability to preplan, or, 3) to decrease the level of performance required for continued viability. Which strategy is chosen depends on the relative costs of the strategies. The function of the framework is to identify these strategies and their costs.

THE MECHANISTIC MODEL

This framework is best developed by keeping in mind a hypothetical organization. Assume it is large and employs a number of specialist groups and resources in providing the output. After the task has been divided into specialist subtasks, the problem is to integrate the subtasks around the completion of the global task. This is the problem of organization design. The behaviors that occur in one subtask cannot be judged as good or bad *per se*. The behaviors are more effective or ineffective depending upon the behaviors of the other subtask performers. There is a design problem because the executors of the behaviors cannot communicate with all the roles with whom they are interdependent. Therefore the design problem is to create mechanisms that permit coordinated action across large numbers of interdependent roles. Each of these mechanisms, however, has a limited range over which it is effective at handling the information requirements necessary to coordinate the interdependent roles. As the amount of uncertainty increases, and therefore information processing increases, the organization must adopt integrating mechanisms which increase its information processing capabilities.

1 Coordination by Rules or Programs

For routine predictable tasks March and Simon have identified the use of rules or programs to coordinate behavior between interdependent subtasks [March and Simon, 1958, Chap. 6]. To the extent that job related situations can be predicted in advance, and behaviors specified for these situations, programs allow an interdependent set of activities to be performed without the need for inter-unit communication. Each role occupant sim-

Reprinted from "Organizational Design: An Information Processing View," by Jay R. Galbraith, *Interfaces*, vol. 4, no. 3, May 1974, pp. 28–36, published by the Institute of Management Sciences.

ply executes the behavior which is appropriate for the task related situation with which he is faced.

2 Hierarchy

As the organization faces greater uncertainty its participants face situations for which they have no rules. At this point the hierarchy is employed on an exception basis. The recurring job situations are programmed with rules while infrequent situations are referred to that level in the hierarchy where a global perspective exists for all affected subunits. However, the hierarchy also has a limited range. As uncertainty increases the number of exceptions increases until the hierarchy becomes overloaded.

3 Coordination by Targets or Goals

As the uncertainty of the organization's task increases, coordination increasingly takes place by specifying outputs, goals or targets [March and Simon, 1958, p. 145]. Instead of specifying specific behaviors to be enacted, the organization undertakes processes to set goals to be achieved and the employees select the behaviors which lead to goal accomplishment. Planning reduces the amount of information processing in the hierarchy by increasing the amount of discretion exercised at lower levels. Like the use of rules, planning achieves integrated action and also eliminates the need for continuous communication among interdependent subunits as long as task performance stays within the planned task specifications, budget limits and within targeted completion dates. If it does not, the hierarchy is again employed on an exception basis.

The ability of an organization to coordinate interdependent tasks depends on its ability to compute meaningful subgoals to guide subunit action. When uncertainty increases because of introducing new products, entering new markets, or employing new technologies these

subgoals are incorrect. The result is more exceptions, more information processing, and an overloaded hierarchy.

DESIGN STRATEGIES

The ability of an organization to successfully utilize coordination by goal setting, hierarchy, and rules depends on the combination of the frequency of exceptions and the capacity of the hierarchy to handle them. As the task uncertainty increases the organization must again take organization design action. It can proceed in either of two general ways. First, it can act in two ways to reduce the amount of information that is processed. And second, the organization can act in two ways to increase its capacity to handle more information. The two methods for reducing the need for information and the two methods for increasing processing capacity are shown schematically in Figure 16-1. The effect of all these actions is to reduce the number of exceptional cases referred upward into the organization through hierarchical channels. The assumption is that the critical limiting factor of an organizational form is its ability to handle the non-routine, consequential events that cannot be anticipated and planned for in advance. The non-programmed events place the greatest communication load on the organization.

1 Creation of Slack Resources

As the number of exceptions begin to overload the hierarchy, one response is to increase the planning targets so that fewer exceptions occur. For example, completion dates can be extended until the number of exceptions that occur are within the existing information processing capacity of the organization. This has been the practice in solving job shop scheduling problems [Pounds, 1963]. Job shops quote delivery times that are long enough to keep the scheduling problem within the computational and information processing limits of the orga-

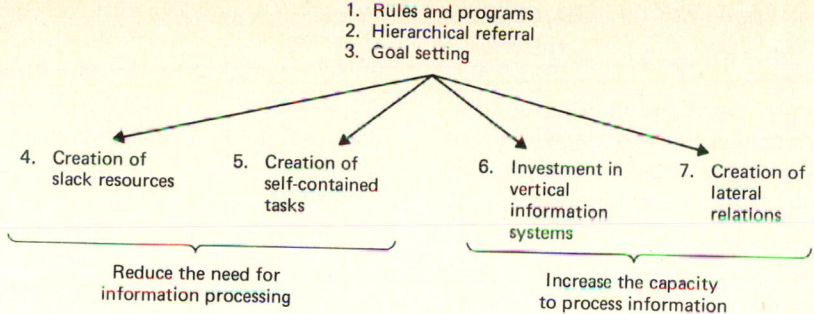

Figure 16-1 Organization design strategies.

nization. Since every job shop has the same problem standard lead times evolve in the industry. Similarly budget targets could be raised, buffer inventories employed, etc. The greater the uncertainty, the greater the magnitude of the inventory, lead time or budget needed to reduce an overload.

All of these examples have a similar effect. They represent the use of slack resources to reduce the amount of interdependence between subunits [March and Simon, 1958, Cyert and March, 1963]. This keeps the required amount of information within the capacity of the organization to process it. Information processing is reduced because an exception is less likely to occur and reduced interdependence means that fewer factors need to be considered simultaneously when an exception does occur.

The strategy of using slack resources has its costs. Relaxing budget targets has the obvious cost of requiring more budget. Increasing the time to completion date has the effect of delaying the customer. Inventories require the investment of capital funds which could be used elsewhere. Reduction of design optimization reduces the performance of the article being designed. Whether slack resources are used to reduce information or not depends on the relative cost of the other alternatives.

The design choices are: (1) among which factors to change (lead time, overtime, ma-

chine utilization, etc.) to create the slack, and (2) by what amount should the factor be changed. Many operations research models are useful in choosing factors and amounts. The time-cost trade off problem in project networks is a good example.

2 Creation of Self-Contained Tasks

The second method of reducing the amount of information processed is to change the sub-task groupings from resource (input) based to output based categories and give each group the resources it needs to supply the output. For example, the functional organization could be changed to product groups. Each group would have its own product engineers, process engineers, fabricating and assembly operations, and marketing activities. In other situations, groups can be created around product lines, geographical areas, projects, client groups, markets, etc., each of which would contain the input resources necessary for creation of the output.

The strategy of self-containment shifts the basis of the authority structure from one based on input, resource, skill, or occupational categories to one based on output or geographical categories. The shift reduces the amount of information processing through several mechanisms. First, it reduces the amount of output diversity faced by a single collection of resources. For example, a professional organization with multiple skill specialties providing service to three different client groups must schedule the use of these specialties across three demands for their services and determine priorities when conflicts occur. But, if the organization changed to three groups, one for each client category, each with its own full complement of specialties, the schedule conflicts across client groups disappear and there is no need to process information to determine priorities.

The second source of information reduction occurs through a reduced division of labor. The functional or resource specialized structure pools the demand for skills across all output categories. In the example above each client generates approximately one-third of the demand for each skill. Since the division of labor is limited by the extent of the market, the division of labor must decrease as the demand decreases. In the professional organization, each client group may have generated a need for one-third of a computer programmer. The functional organization would have hired one programmer and shared him across the groups. In the self-contained structure there is insufficient demand in each group for a programmer so the professionals must do their own programming. Specialization is reduced but there is no problem of scheduling the programmer's time across the three possible uses for it.

The cost of the self-containment strategy is the loss of resource specialization. In the example, the organization foregoes the benefit of a specialist in computer programming. If there is physical equipment, there is a loss of economies of scale. The professional organization would require three machines in the self-contained form but only a large time-shared machine in the functional form. But those resources which have large economies of scale or for which specialization is necessary may remain centralized. Thus, it is the degree of self-containment that is the variable. The greater the degree of uncertainty, other

things equal, the greater the degree of self-containment.

The design choices are the basis for the self-contained structure and the number of resources to be contained in the groups. No groups are completely self-contained or they would not be part of the same organization. But one product divisionalized firm may have eight of fifteen functions in the division while another may have twelve of fifteen in the divisions. Usually accounting, finance, and legal services are centralized and shared. Those functions which have economies of scale, require specialization or are necessary for control remain centralized and not part of the self-contained group.

The first two strategies reduced the amount of information by lower performance standards and creating small autonomous groups to provide the output. Information is reduced because an exception is less likely to occur and fewer factors need to be considered when an exception does occur. The next two strategies accept the performance standards and division of labor as given and adapt the organization so as to process the new information which is created during task performance.

3 Investment in Vertical Information Systems

The organization can invest in mechanisms which allow it to process information acquired during task performance without overloading the hierarchical communication channels. The investment occurs according to the following logic. After the organization has created its plan or set of targets for inventories, labor utilization, budgets, and schedules, unanticipated events occur which generate exceptions requiring adjustments to the original plan. At some point when the number of exceptions becomes substantial, it is preferable to generate a new plan rather than make incremental changes with each exception. The issue is then how frequently should plans be revised—yearly, quarterly, or monthly? The greater the frequency of replanning the greater the resources, such as clerks, computer time, input-output devices, etc., required to process information about relevant factors.

The cost of information processing resources can be minimized if the language is formalized. Formalization of a decision-making language simply means that more information is transmitted with the same number of symbols. It is assumed that information processing resources are consumed in proportion to the number of symbols transmitted. The accounting system is an example of a formalized language.

Providing more information, more often, may simply overload the decision maker. Investment may be required to increase the capacity of the decision maker by employing computers, various man-machine combinations, assistants-to, etc. The cost of this strategy is the cost of the information processing resources consumed in transmitting and processing the data.

The design variables of this strategy are the decision frequency, the degree of formalization of language, and the type of decision mechanism which will make the choice. This strategy is usually operationalized by creating redundant information channels which transmit data from the point of origination upward in the hierarchy where the point of decision rests. If data is formalized and quantifiable, this strategy is effective. If the relevant data are qualitative and ambiguous, then it may prove easier to bring the decisions down to where the information exists.

4 Creation of Lateral Relationships

The last strategy is to employ selectively joint decision processes which cut across lines of authority. This strategy moves the level of decision making down in the organization to where the information exists but does so without reorganizing around self-contained groups. There are several types of lateral decision processes. Some processes are usually referred to as the informal organization. However, these informal processes do not always arise spontaneously out of the needs of the task. This is particularly true in multinational organizations in which participants are separated by physical barriers, language differences, and cultural differences. Under these circumstances lateral processes need to be designed. The lateral processes evolve as follows with increases in uncertainty.

4.1 Direct Contact between managers who share a problem. If a problem arises on the shop floor, the foreman can simply call the design engineer, and they can jointly agree upon a solution. From an information processing view, the joint decision prevents an upward referral and unloads the hierarchy.

4.2 Liaison Roles When the volume of contacts between any two departments grows, it becomes economical to set up a specialized role to handle this communication. Liaison men are typical examples of specialized roles designed to facilitate communication between two interdependent departments and to bypass the long lines of communication involved in upward referral. Liaison roles arise at lower and middle levels of management.

4.3 Task Forces Direct contact and liaison roles, like the integration mechanisms before them, have a limited range of usefulness. They work when two managers or functions are involved. When problems arise involving seven or eight departments, the decision making capacity of direct contacts is exceeded. Then these problems must be referred upward. For uncertain, interdependent tasks such situations arise frequently. Task forces are a form of horizontal contact which is designed for problems of multiple departments.

The task force is made up of representatives from each of the affected departments. Some are full-time members, others may be part-time. The task force is a temporary group. It exists only as long as the problem remains. When a solution is reached, each participant returns to his normal tasks.

To the extent that they are successful, task forces remove problems from higher levels of the hierarchy. The decisions are made at lower levels in the organization. In order to guarantee integration, a group problem solving approach is taken. Each affected subunit contributes a member and therefore provides the information necessary to judge the impact on all units.

4.4 Teams The next extension is to incorporate the group decision process into the permanent decision processes. That is, as certain decisions consistently arise, the task forces become permanent. These groups are labeled teams. There are many design issues concerned in team decision making such as at what level do they operate, who participates, etc. [Galbraith, 1973, Chapters 6 and 7]. One design decision is particularly critical. This is the choice of leadership. Sometimes a problem exists largely in one department so that the department manager is the leader. Sometimes the leadership passes from one manager to another. As a new product moves to the market place, the leader of the new product team is first the technical manager followed by the production and then the marketing manager. The result is that if the team cannot reach a consensus decision and the leader decides, the goals of the leader are consistent with the goals of the organization for the decision in question. But quite often obvious leaders cannot be found. Another mechanism must be introduced.

4.5 Integrating Roles The leadership issue is solved by creating a new role—an integrating role [Lawrence and Lorsch, 1967, Chapter 3]. These roles carry the labels of product managers, program managers, project managers, unit managers (hospitals), materials managers, etc. After the role is created, the design problem is to create enough power in the role to influence the decision process. These roles have power even when no one reports directly to them. They have some power because they report to the general manager. But if they are selected so as to be unbiased with respect to the groups they integrate and to have technical competence, they have expert power. They collect information and equalize power differences due to preferential access to knowledge and information. The power equalization increases trust and the quality of the joint decision process. But power equalization occurs only if the integrating role is staffed with someone who can exercise expert power in the form of persuasion and informal influences rather than exert the power of rank or authority.

4.6 Managerial Linking Roles As tasks become more uncertain, it is more difficult to exercise expert power. The role must get more power of the formal authority type in order to be effective at coordinating the joint decisions which occur at lower levels of the organization. This position power changes the nature of the role which for lack of a better name is labeled a managerial linking role. It is not like the integrating role because it possesses formal position power but is different from line managerial roles in that participants do not report to the linking manager. The power is added by the following successive changes:

a The integrator receives approval power of budgets formulated in the departments to be integrated.

b The planning and budgeting process starts with the integrator making his initiation in budgeting legitimate.

c Linking manager receives the budget for the area of responsibility and buys resources from the specialist groups.

These mechanisms permit the manager to exercise influence even though no one works directly for him. The role is concerned with integration but exercises power through the formal power of the position. If this power is insufficient to integrate the subtasks and creation of self-contained groups is not feasible, there is one last step.

4.7 Matrix Organization The last step is to create the dual authority relationship and the matrix organization [Galbraith, 1971]. At some point in the organization some roles have two superiors. The design issue is to select the locus of these roles. The result is a balance of power between the managerial linking roles and the normal line organization roles. Figure 16-2 depicts the pure matrix design.

The work of Lawrence and Lorsch is highly consistent with the assertions concerning lateral relations [Lawrence and Lorsch, 1967, Lorsch and Lawrence, 1968]. They compared the types of lateral relations undertaken by the most successful firm in three different indus-

tries. Their data are summarized in Table 16-1. The plastics firm has the greatest rate of new product introduction (uncertainty) and the greatest utilization of lateral processes. The container firm was also very successful but utilized only standard practices because its information processing task is much less formidable. Thus, the greater the uncertainty the lower the level of decision making and the integration is maintained by lateral relations.

Table 16-1 points out the cost of using lateral relations. The plastics firm has 22% of its managers in integration roles. Thus, the greater the use of lateral relations the greater the managerial intensity. This cost must be balanced against the cost of slack resources, self-contained groups and information systems.

CHOICE OF STRATEGY

Each of the four strategies has been briefly presented. The organization can follow one or

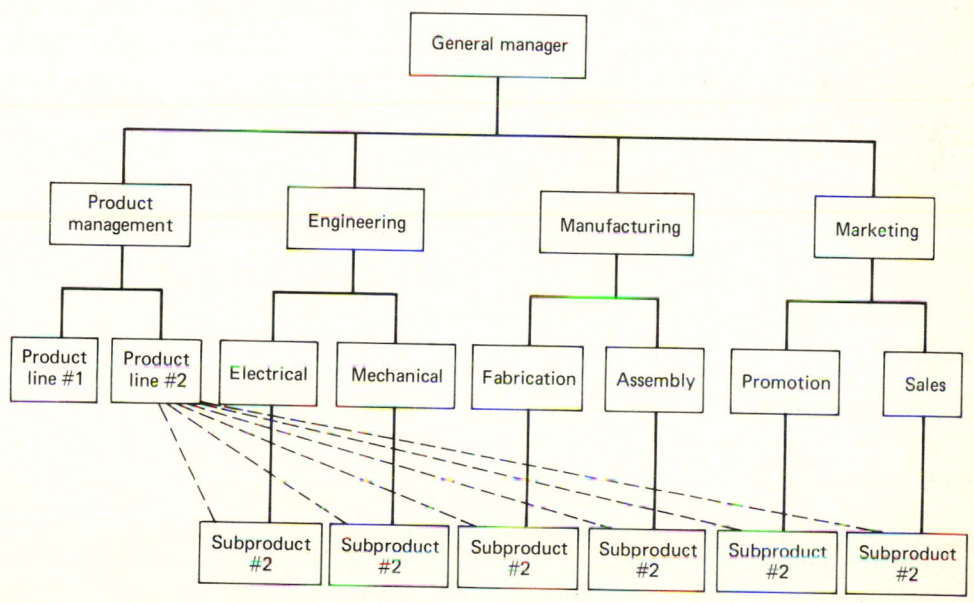

    - - - = Technical authority over the product
    ———— = Formal authority over the product (in product organization, these relationships may be reversed)

Figure 16-2 A pure matrix organization.

Table 16-1

	Plastics	Food	Container
% new products in last ten years	35%	20%	0%
Integrating Devices	Rules Hierarchy Planning Direct Contact Teams at 3 levels Integrating Dept.	Rules Hierarchy Planning Direct Contact Task forces Integrators	Rules Hierarchy Planning Direct Contact
% Integrators/Managers	22%	17%	0%

[Adopted from Lawrence and Lorsch, 1967, pp. 86–138 and Lorsch and Lawrence, 1968].

some combination of several if it chooses. It will choose that strategy which has the least cost in its environmental context. [For an example, see Galbraith, 1970.] However, what may be lost in all of the explanations is that the four strategies are hypothesized to be an exhaustive set of alternatives. That is, if the organization is faced with greater uncertainty due to technological change, higher performance standards due to increased competition, or diversifies its product line to reduce dependence, the amount of information processing is increased. *The organization must adopt at least one of the four strategies when faced with greater uncertainty.* If it does not consciously choose one of the four, then the first, reduced performance standards, will happen automatically. The task information requirements and the capacity of the organization to process information are always matched. If the organization does not consciously match them, reduced performance through budget and schedule overruns will occur in order to bring about equality. Thus the organization should be planned and designed simultaneously with the planning of the strategy and resource allocations. But if the strategy involves introducing new products, entering new markets, etc., then some provision for increased infor-

mation must be made. Not to decide is to decide, and it is to decide upon slack resources as the strategy to remove hierarchical overload.

There is probably a fifth strategy which is not articulated here. Instead of changing the organization in response to task uncertainty, the organization can operate on its environment to reduce uncertainty. The organization through strategic decisions, long term contracts, coalitions, etc., can control its environment. But these maneuvers have costs also. They should be compared with costs of the four design strategies presented above.

SUMMARY

The purpose of this paper has been to explain why task uncertainty is related to organizational form. In so doing the cognitive limits theory of Herbert Simon was the guiding influence. As the consequences of cognitive limits were traced through the framework, various organization design strategies were articulated. The framework provides a basis for integrating organizational interventions, such as information systems and group problem solving, which have been treated separately before.

BIBLIOGRAPHY

Cyert, Richard, and March, James, *The Behavioral Theory of the Firm*, Prentice-Hall, Englewood Cliffs, N. J., 1963.

Galbraith, Jay, "Environmental and Technological Determinants of Organization Design: A Case Study" in Lawrence and Lorsch (ed.) *Studies in Organization Design*, Richard D. Irwin Inc., Homewood, Ill., 1970.

Galbraith, Jay, "Designing Matrix Organizations," *Business Horizons*, (Feb. 1971), pp. 29–40.

Galbraith, Jay, *Organization Design*, Addison-Wesley Pub. Co., Reading, Mass., 1973.

Lawrence, Paul, and Lorsch, Jay, *Organization and Environment*, Division of Research, Harvard Business School, Boston, Mass., 1967.

Lorsch, Jay, and Lawrence, Paul, "Environmental Factors and Organization Integration," Paper read at the Annual Meeting of the American Sociological Association, August 27, 1968, Boston, Mass.

March, James, and Simon, Herbert, *Organizations*, John Wiley & Sons, New York, N. Y., 1958.

Pounds, William, "The Scheduling Environment" in Muth and Thompson (eds.) *Industrial Scheduling*, Prentice-Hall Inc., Englewood Cliffs, N. J., 1963.

Simon, Herbert, *Models of Man*, John Wiley & Sons, New York, N. Y., 1957.

Reading 17

Making Effective Use of Control Systems

Cortlandt Cammann
David A. Nadler

Organizations spend large amounts of money, time, and effort designing and maintaining control systems. These systems are intended to increase the ability of organizations to coordinate the actions of their members and to identify problems as they arise. Often, however, instead of increasing organizational control, these systems end up motivating dysfunctional behavior on the part of employees and managers. They spend their time and energy "beating the system," "managing their results," and finding ways to subvert the effects of the control system (e.g., Argyris, 1964; Jasinsky, 1956; Hopwood, 1973). When organization members respond to control systems in these ways, the systems reduce rather than increase the amount of effective control that the organization exercises.

Why does this happen? Our research and the research of others indicate that the problem often lies with the ways that control systems are used by managers (Jasinsky, 1956; Nadler, Mirvis, & Cammann, in press). Most control systems (including budgets, management information systems, and financial accounting systems) are essentially systems of management. They collect information about specific aspects of organizational performance on a regular basis and feed this information back to a network of people in the organization. The systems themselves are not capable of directly controlling organizational performance. Rather, they are capable of getting information about organizational performance to the managers who are in a position to exercise control. If these managers use the system

A later version of this paper was published under the title "Fit Control Systems to Your Management Style," *Harvard Business Review*, January–February 1976.

well, the control system works. If they use it poorly, the system may produce unintended and dysfunctional effects.

In light of this, it is interesting that organizations seldom invest much effort in training their managers to use their control systems. Most organizations spend a lot of time designing, constructing, and refining the systems themselves, but generally these efforts are directed toward improving the *technical* aspects of the system. The result is that organizational control systems are continually becoming more precise, more accurate, and more technologically sophisticated. However, in this rush for technical sophistication, two questions are often overlooked:

1 How effective is the system (and the way it is being used) in doing what it is supposed to do?
2 How could the system be better used to increase its effectiveness?

Recent research in a number of different organizations has provided some answers to these questions. This research indicates that control systems influence the way organization members direct their energy on their jobs. They are more likely to put time and effort into areas covered by control systems. The research has also shown that the way organization members respond to control systems depends largely on the way the systems are used by the managers they report to. Finally, the research indicates that different managers develop different strategies for using control systems, and that each strategy has costs and benefits associated with it.

Only when managers understand the way in which these systems influence the behavior of their subordinates, and the trade-offs involved in using different control strategies, can they learn to use control systems effectively. In the remainder of this article we will discuss the factors which managers should consider when they choose the control style they will use. We will start by examining the ways in which control systems influence the behavior of managers. Then we will describe some of the strategies which managers develop for using control systems, the factors which managers ought to consider when they choose their control style, and the implications of their choice for the effectiveness of the organization's control system.

HOW DO CONTROL SYSTEMS INFLUENCE SUBORDINATES' BEHAVIOR?

When an area of performance is covered by the organization's control system, organization members direct time and energy into improving their performance in the measured area. There are three reasons for this direction of energy:

1 Measurement of an area of activity indicates that top management feels that area is important and is watching.
2 Managers generally use control system measures in some way when they evaluate a subordinate's performance. Since the subordinates usually feel that their managers' evaluation of their performance influences their rewards, they tend to put energy into measured areas.
3 It is easy for organization members to see changes in performance measures which are part of the control system. If their performance is improving, this can be a source of personal satisfaction.

Figure 17-1 provides an example of how measurement directs energy. In two different organizations—a northeastern public utility and a midwestern bank—employees were asked to indicate to what degree different areas of activity were measured. At another point they were also asked how much time and effort they put into each area. As can be seen, the general pattern is that the more an area is seen as measured, the more time and effort people put into it. This time and effort repre-

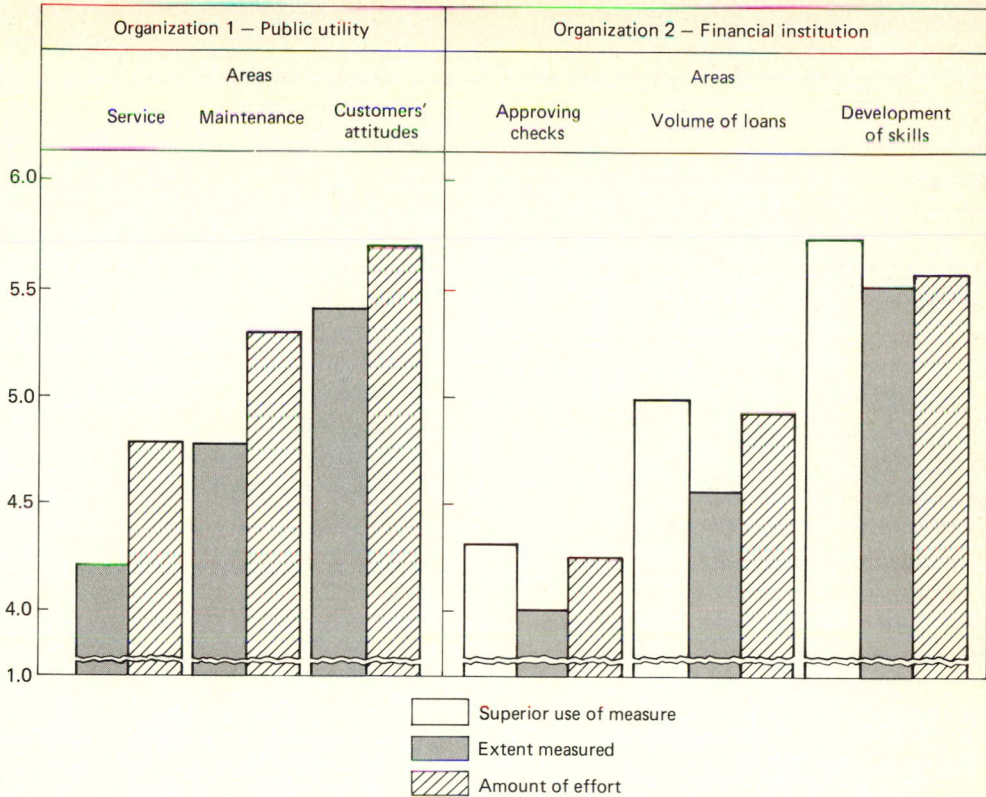

Figure 17-1 Area measurement and effort in two organizations.

sents a direction of energy into areas that the subordinates perceive as being measured, as opposed to those areas that are not perceived as being measured.

In the financial institution, an additional piece of information was obtained. Subordinates were asked how much their manager used the measures in evaluating their performance. As can be seen in Figure 17-1, the manager's use of the measures also is related to the amount of effort that subordinates put into an area.

WHAT DO CONTROL SYSTEMS MOTIVATE?

It appears that control systems can direct energy into an area, but how is this energy used? On one hand, subordinates can be motivated to increase the level of performance, to produce larger quantities or higher quality work. On the other hand, measurement can produce the dysfunctional consequences often observed by researchers. The energy is directed into "game playing" where subordinates' efforts are aimed at "beating the system" rather than performing well. Game playing often includes such behaviors as setting low goals that can be easily met, manipulating measures to come out with the desired results, and actually sabotaging the system.

One of the authors observed an example of this in a large government organization where, in an attempt to control and direct the behavior of employees, all employees were required to fill out a form accounting for the way they spent their time in twenty-minute blocks. The intent was to motivate employees to manage their time and to generate valid information about how much time was being allocated to different tasks. The result, however, was vastly different. The employees saw the system as an attempt to regiment their lives and activities. Instead of being a useful tool, the time sheets became a recreational activity; Friday afternoons (at the coffee break), employees got together to fill out their time sheets, each competing to see who could come up with the most preposterous record of activities. Needless to say, these records had no relation to actual work that was done. The system did not motivate people to increase performance; it motivated people to play games with the system.

Figure 17-2 presents a model which summarizes the effects of control systems. The existence of measures in an area has an effect on behavior, but measurement by itself is not the only factor. The measures have to be reasonably accurate, and they have to be used by managers. If reasonable measures exist, and are used, they will motivate subordinates to direct their energy to that area. This energy can either be directed in ways which are productive or counterproductive for the organization, depending on the way measures are used.

STRATEGIES OF CONTROL

What does this model of control mean to the manager? It means that a manager must give serious thought to use of control system measures in any one area. The manager must consider the consequences of his or her actions in terms of the kind of behavior that is motivated in his or her subordinates. Although there is a range of strategies for control, two major approaches seem to have proven most useful for many managers. As can be seen in Figure 17-3, each of these strategies requires different behaviors on the part of the manager and can result in different outcomes (both desirable and undesirable) related to subordinates' behavior.

External Control

One control strategy can be named "external control." It is based on the assumption that subordinates in the particular situation are motivated primarily by external rewards and need to be controlled by their supervisors. To effectively use the control system in this way requires a number of steps. First, the goals and standards associated with the system need to be made relatively difficult in order to

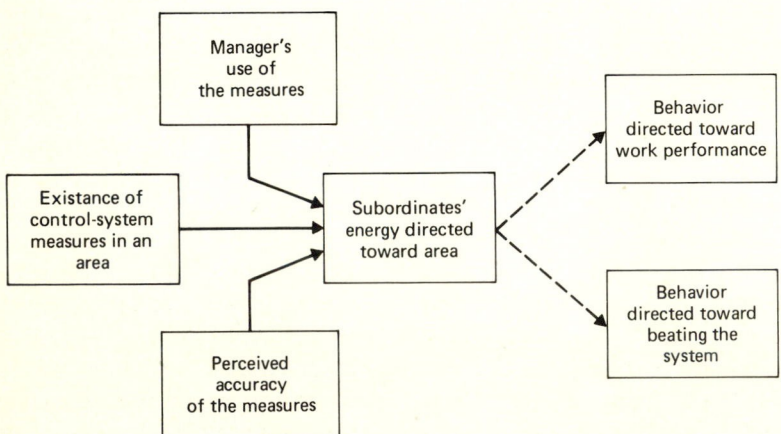

Figure 17-2 Model of how control systems and their use affect behavior.

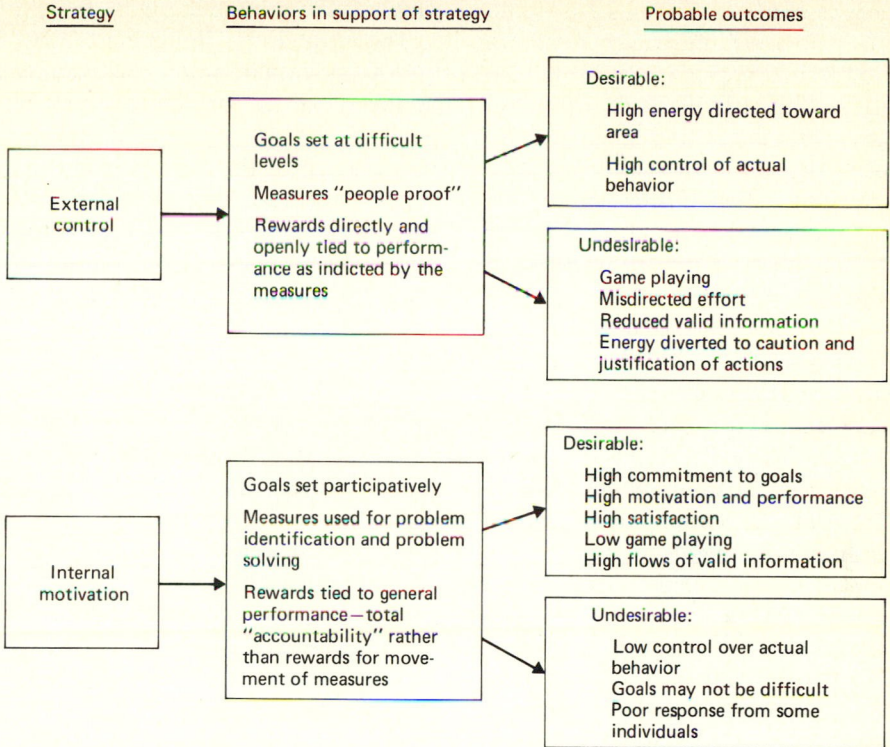

Figure 17-3 Two different strategies of control.

"stretch" subordinates and leave little room for slack (Hofstede, 1967). Second, the measures need to be constructed so that they are "people proof" to prevent individuals from being able to manipulate the measures. Third, rewards need to be directly and openly tied to performance, as indicated by the measures in the control system, in order to ensure that the subordinates have an incentive to work hard. An example of this approach would be to evaluate a manager solely on the basis of the performance of his or her profit center, with relatively high levels of profit being budgeted and with compensation tied primarily and directly to the number of dollars of profit.

This kind of strategy can have different effects. On one hand, subordinates will channel a great deal of energy into measured areas and will try hard to make their measures

move, since they can gain rewards by doing so (Lawler, 1971, 1973). Where the system is very tightly structured, this results in a high degree of control of the actual behavior of subordinates. On the other hand, several undesirable results can result from this approach. First, this use of the control system will motivate an organization's members to improve their performance measures, but will not create any commitment to doing a better job. The subordinates will begin to develop an instrumental orientation toward performance and doing well will begin to mean doing well on the performance measures, not necessarily doing their jobs more effectively. As a result, if they can increase their measured performance by manipulating the measures, providing false information, intentionally setting low goals and standards, or sabotaging the system, the organization's members can be expected to do so. Second, such a strategy may result in misdirected effort. Subordinates may put all their energy into the particular behaviors that are measured, while forgetting those unmeasured behaviors that are also vital. For example, all efforts may become directed toward increasing sales volume with the effect of decreasing the amount of effort devoted to ongoing customer service. In this case, the result is short-term maximization in the measured area with possible negative long-term effects because of the lack of attention to unmeasured areas. Third, such an external control strategy may tend to reduce the flow of valid information, particularly negative information. If people are directly rewarded for positive movement of measures, they may become motivated to withhold other information from higher-level managers: information which would negate the meaning of those measures, or negative information needed for making decisions. Finally, such an approach may bring about excessive caution and direct energy toward justification of all actions. Subordinates may be motivated to ensure that the measures either continue to look good (by not taking any risks), or justify measures that have decreased by putting a lot of energy into assembling "just in case" files filled with information rationalizing or justifying a decrease in measured performance. In either case, energy is being directed toward coping with the system, rather than toward the larger goal of organizational effectiveness.

Internal Motivation

Another control strategy is "internal motivation." It is based on the assumption that subordinates in a particular situation can be motivated by building a commitment to organizational goals and involvement in the tasks to be done. It assumes that they will be motivated by the feelings of accomplishment, achievement, recognition, and self-esteem that come from having performed a job well.

This strategy is implemented by using the control system in a very different manner than in the external control strategy. First, while goals are set using the system, the most important feature of these goals is not their difficulty, but the fact that they are set participatively. Those people who are responsible for achieving goals are given some influence over the nature of those goals. Second, the measures are used for joint problem identification and solution rather than for punishment or blame. When a measure begins to move in an undesired direction, it is not the time for heads to roll. It is time for managers and subordinates to meet together (1) to determine the reasons for the movement of the measures and (2) to develop solutions to the problems that are brought to the surface by the measures. Thus, the system takes on a function as an "early warning system," bringing problems to the surface and beginning the problem-solving process before problems become crises. Finally, while rewards are tied to performance, they are not tied to one or two specific measures. Rather, the reward structure should emphasize "accountability" for the entire job performance, only part of which may be represented by the measures in a control system. In general, the role of the control system becomes future-oriented and problem-based (Newman, 1975). The system controls behavior by directing future efforts rather than punishing past actions.

Again, this kind of strategy can also have different kinds of effects. On one hand, it can generate high commitment to goals that are developed because an organization's members participate in setting them and feel responsible for seeing that they are achieved. This commitment can lead to high levels of energy directed toward task performance. As performance increases and individuals monitor their progress through the measures of the control system, such a strategy can also enhance feelings of satisfaction which subordinates feel as a result of performing their jobs well. The open nature of the control system and its general, rather than specific, accountability also means that there is little incentive for subordinates to play games with the system or to behave dysfunctionally. More important, it encourages and rewards the flow of valid information, and—in particular—negative information.

At the same time, such a strategy may have some undesirable effects. The looser nature of the system means that the manager will have less control over the actual behavior of his subordinates. Because the manager gives up total control over the specific goals to be set, less ambitious goals may be set through the participative process. In addition, since the information provided by the control system is being used for problem solving and not for evaluation, it becomes difficult to use this information as a basis for giving rewards. Thus, the manager is forced to give up some of the value of the control system as a tool for external motivation in order to build internal motivation on the part of subordinates. Finally, some persons may not respond to the open and relatively participative process because of differences in working style or personality. These people will not be motivated to perform well with this kind of strategy.

Choice of Strategies

Neither of these two strategies is necessarily the "right" strategy to use in all cases. Each has its costs and benefits. The important thing is for a manager to consciously and carefully choose the strategy that is appropriate for his or her particular situation. In making that choice, several issues need to be considered:

Managerial Style In choosing a control strategy, a manager must examine the consistency between that strategy and the other behaviors that make up his or her style as a manager. In choosing, a manager may have to modify either style or control strategy so that the total approach to managing is consistent. To take a specific example, when a manager generally makes all important decisions without involving subordinates, it would be a mistake to use an internal motivation approach to control. The subordinates will be accustomed to following the manager's lead; they may not be capable of setting realistic goals of their own; or worse, they may use their influence to set easy goals which they know they can achieve. It is only in the context of a generally participative manager-subordinate relationship that an internal-motivation approach to control is likely to be effective (Cammann, 1974).

The Larger Organizational Climate, Structure, and Reward System A control strategy, to be most effective, should be consistent with other factors in the organization that determine employees' behavior. A control strategy is only one of a number of devices to influence behavior in an organization; in an effective organization, those devices are designed to be consistent. For example, a very tight control system in an organization which normally provides a great deal of discretion and freedom for its employees would soon run into a number of problems.

The Reliability of Job-Performance Measures In some cases, control-system measures accurately reflect job performance. In others, the measures are unreliable or do not adequately indicate how well the job is being done. When the control system is an unreliable indicator of performance, it is hard to implement a tight external control strategy: the use of inaccurate or unreliable measures as a basis for evaluation and reward could have disastrous consequences. Under such conditions, a looser and more internally oriented control strategy is required.

Individual Differences   Different people are motivated by different sets of needs, and respond differently to the same organizational structures. The choice of a control strategy assumes that the manager knows something about the nature of his or her subordinates. Persons who are primarily involved in their work because of their commitment to the work that is being done (for example, in many professional occupations) are probably going to be less responsive to an external control strategy than persons whose primary motivation for being a member of the organization is financial rewards or promotion. Another important issue is how much employees desire to participate in decision making. Some employees may respond well to the opportunity for participation, while others may not want to become more involved or assume the responsibility that goes along with participation (Vroom & Yetton, 1973). Thus, the types of people who work for the manager should be a factor influencing his or her choice of a control strategy.

AN INFORMED CHOICE

The process of choosing a control strategy needs to be one of informed choice. At first glance, it may appear that a manager has too many factors to juggle to allow an effective choice. One way around this problem is to lay out sequentially the key decisions and choice points as a manager goes through the process of deciding what kind of control strategy to use.

As a first step, the manager needs to ask himself or herself a number of questions. These questions are listed in Figure 17-4. Basically, managers need to determine what kind of managerial style they generally use, what kind of organization they are in, how accurate and reliable are the important performance measures, and how much their subordinates want to participate in decision making.

The next step is to apply the answers to these questions in a systematic way in order to determine what kind of strategy is most appropriate. One way of doing this is a decision-tree approach, presented in Figure 17-5. As indicated by the chart, different combinations of answers to the key questions lead the manager to different recommended strategies with different issues concerning the implementation of the strategy.

In addition to the decision steps outlined in Figure 17-5, the manager also needs to consider the trade-offs between different strategies in his or her particular situation. The most obvious question is, "What are the consequences of different desirable or undesirable outcomes (as listed in Figure 17-3) for my particular group of subordinates?" For example, if in the particular situation, the opportunities for game playing are few and the costs of game playing are low, a tight control strategy may be more feasible than in other kinds of situations. In most organizations, however, the potential costs of game playing are high, and managers should give serious consideration to an intrinsic control strategy if the basic decision-making process indicates that such a strategy is feasible.

SUMMARY

Control systems constitute one important implement in a manager's "tool kit" of approaches to building an effective organization. Control is a central dimension of the manager's job, and the choice of a control strategy is a crucial one. Managers need to balance the costs and benefits of different control strategies by making informed choices.

Control systems and the way that they are used constitute a potentially powerful tool to influence the behavior of individuals in organi-

1 In general, what kind of managerial style do I have?

Participative
I frequently consult my subordinates on decisions, encourage them to disagree with my opinion, share information with them, and let them make decisions whenever possible.

Directive
I usually take most of the responsibility for and make most of the major decisions, pass on only the most necessary job relevant information, and provide detailed and close direction for my subordinates.

2. In general, what kind of climate, structure, and reward system does my organization have?

Participative
Employees at all levels of the organization are urged to participate in decisions and influence the course of events. Managers are clearly rewarded for developing employees' skills and decision-making capacity.

Nonparticipative
Most important decisions are made by a few people at the top of the organization. Managers are not rewarded for developing employees' competence or for encouraging employees to participate in decision making.

3 How accurate and reliable are the measures of key areas of subordinate performance?

Accurate
Measures are reliable; all major aspects of performance can be adequately measured; changes in measures accurately reflect changes in performance; measures cannot be easily sabotaged or faked by subordinates.

Inaccurate
Not all critical aspects of performance can be measured; measures often don't reflect important changes in performance; good performance cannot be adequately defined in terms of the measures; measures can be easily sabotaged.

4. Do my subordinates want to participate and respond well to opportunities to take responsibility for decision making and performance?

High desire to participate
Employees are eager to participate in decisions, are involved in the work itself, can make a contribution to decision making, and want to take more responsibility.

Low desire to participate
Employees do not want to be involved in many decisions, don't want additional responsibility, have little to contribute to decisions being made, and are not very involved in the work itself.

Figure 17-4 Questions a manager should ask when choosing a control strategy.

zations. Just as individual managers need to make careful and informed choices among control strategies, organizations need to be conscious of the alternative approaches to designing and using control systems. Becoming aware of the potential effects of control

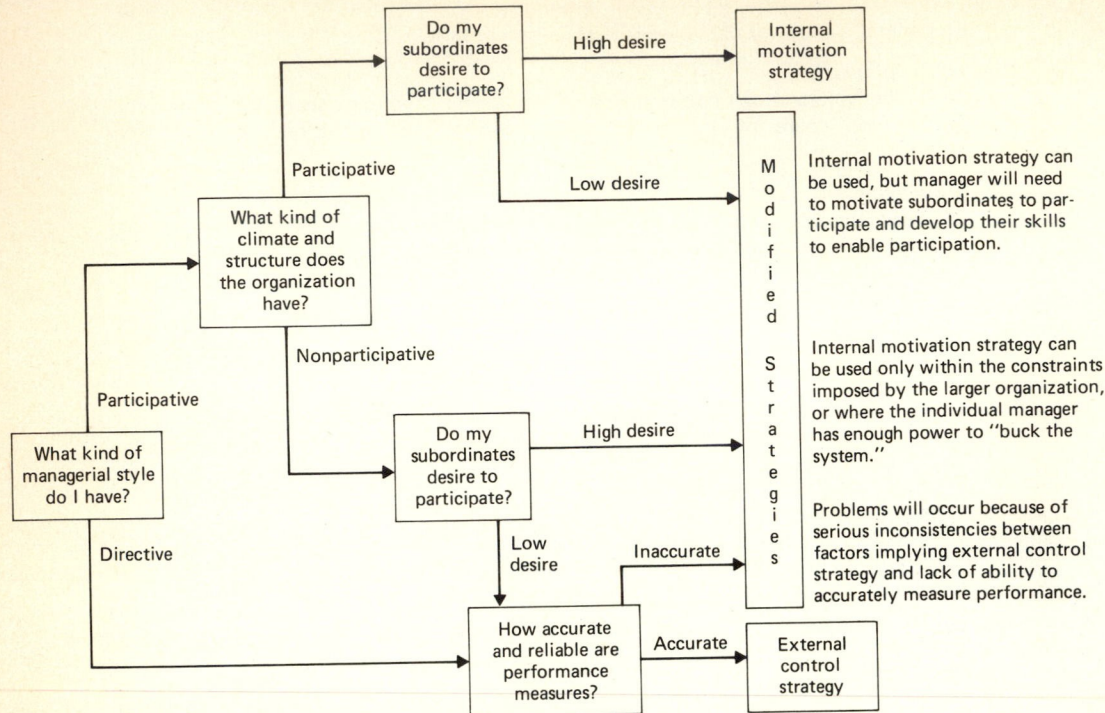

Figure 17-5 A decision tree for choosing a control strategy.

systems and the great importance of the *process* of control (as opposed to the technology of control) is one step that organizations can take to make themselves and the people that work for them more productive and more effective.

REFERENCES

Argyris, C. *Integrating the individual and the organization.* New York: Wiley, 1964.

Cammann, C. *Can accounting systems produce change?* Paper presented at the 82d annual meeting of the American Psychological Association, New Orleans, 1974.

Hofstede, G. H. *The game of budget control.* Assen, Netherlands: Van Gorcum, 1967.

Hopwood, A. G. *An accounting system and managerial behavior.* Lexington, Mass.: Lexington Books, 1973.

Jasinsky, F. J. Use and misuse of efficiency controls. *Harvard Business Review*, 1956, **34**(4), 105–112.

Lawler, E. E. *Pay and organizational effectiveness: A psychological view.* New York: McGraw-Hill, 1971.

Lawler, E. E. *Motivation in work organizations.* Monterey, Calif.: Brooks/Cole, 1973.

Nadler, D. A., Mirvis, P. H., & Cammann, C. The ongoing feedback system: Experimenting with a new managerial tool, *Organizational Dynamics*, in press.

Newman, W. H. *Constructive control: Design and use of control systems.* Englewood Cliffs, N. J.: Prentice-Hall, 1975.

Vroom, V. H., & Yetton, P. W. *Leadership and decision making.* Pittsburgh: University of Pittsburgh Press, 1973.

Chapter 6

Work Design

What constitutes a well-designed job? Until relatively recently, most guidelines for how work should be designed emphasized simple considerations of organizational efficiency: smooth workflow, minimal wasted effort, direct managerial control over the work, minimal training requirements, and so on. Industrial engineers conducted studies to determine the "best" job design (which often turned out to be the simplest possible job), time and motion analysts identified the most efficient way for the job to be performed, and management provided close supervision to ensure that the work was being done exactly as it was supposed to be done. Behavioral scientists had little to say about the design of work other than to be sure that jobs did not make demands on people that exceeded human capabilities, and to help in the selection of individuals who were qualified for the jobs.

In recent years, these guidelines have been undergoing change. In this country, the pioneering work of Frederick Herzberg and Louis Davis on the psychological and social aspects of job design has led to an increased awareness of the human part of person-job relationships. Numerous organizations have undertaken projects aimed at enriching jobs, and in many cases these experiments have improved both the quality of work life for employees and organizational productivity. Overseas, even broader changes in jobs and work systems have been carried out, in the spirit of "industrial democracy."

The readings in this chapter were chosen to reflect current thought and practice of behavioral science about the design of work— including discussion of some of the problems that have appeared as increasing numbers of organizations have undertaken activities to redesign work. The chapter begins with an article by Dowling, describing job redesign as it applies to the assembly line. Dowling reports extensively on his investigations of design innovations in three European plants, with special emphasis on the idea of designing work for groups rather than for individuals. In addition, some interesting observations are provided about the circumstances under which job redesign is most likely to be a useful and effective intervention—and those under which it may be inappropriate.

In the next article, Hackman provides a new way of understanding why many employees respond positively to "enriched" work. On the basis of this conceptualization, Hackman then provides some specific guidelines for proceeding with the redesign of work for individuals and for teams. Included is a discussion of ways to diagnose a work system before redesigning jobs, and some cautions regarding differences among people in their "readiness" for enriched work.

The theme of individual differences is explored in more detail in the next article, by Wanous, who provides a down-to-earth examination of the question "Who wants job enrichment?" Wanous explores three different methods for identifying employees who are likely to prosper on enriched jobs, and concludes his reading with a set of guidelines for dealing effectively with differences among people when jobs are redesigned.

The chapter ends with an article by Hackman in which he reports on his observations of job enrichment projects being carried out around the country, and concludes that the rate of failure for such projects is distressingly high. The reasons for these failures, however, appear to have less to do with the merits of enriched work per se than with the way changes entailed by job enrichment are planned and carried out. Hackman identifies a number of common problems that occur when work is redesigned, and then points out some practices of implementation that characterized the most successful projects he observed. The article ends with a discussion of several ways that job redesign is unique among behavioral approaches to organizational change—and therefore potentially worth the considerable effort required to carry it out competently.

Reading 18

Job Redesign on the Assembly Line: Farewell to Blue-Collar Blues?

William F. Dowling

The authors of the much-quoted, much-praised, and much-criticized HEW report *Work in America* wound up their study with a rhetorical bang: "Albert Camus wrote that 'without work life goes rotten. But when work is soulless, life stifles and dies.' Our analysis of work in America leads to much the same conclusion: Because work is central to the lives of so many Americans, either the absence of work or employment in meaningless work is creating an increasingly intolerable situation."

Most who argue that the rhetoric in the report is exaggerated and the thesis overstated would exempt the assembly line, particularly the auto assembly line, from their dissent. The auto assembly line epitomizes the conditions that contribute to employee dissatisfaction: fractionation of work into meaningless activities, with each activity repeated several hundred times each workday, and with the employees having little or no control over work pace or any other aspect of working conditions.

Two generations of social scientists have documented the discontent of auto workers with their jobs. Yet the basic production process hasn't changed since Ford's first Highland Park assembly plant in 1913. We read a lot about the accelerating pace of technology: Here's a technology that's stood still for 60 years despite the discontent.

The social explanations are easy. The automakers—when they thought about the problem at all—dismissed it. The economic advantages of the assembly line seemingly outweighed any possible social costs—including the high wages, part of which might properly be considered discontentment pay. In short, the cash register rang more clearly than the gripes.

Recently, the situation has changed. The advent of an adversary youth culture in the United States, the rising educational levels, with a concomitant increase in employee expectations of the job, the expansion of job opportunities for all but the least skilled and the most disaffected, have raised the level of discontent. One of the big three automakers, for example, now has an annual turnover rate of close to 40 percent. G.M.'s famous Lordstown Vega plant, the latest triumph of production engineering—with the average time per job activity pared to 36 seconds and workers facing a new Vega component 800 times in each eight-hour shift—has been plagued with strikes, official and wildcat, slowdowns, and sabotage. At times, the line has shut down during the second half of the day to remedy the defects that emerged from the line during the first half.

IS JOB REDESIGN THE ANSWER?

Much has been written about the two automobile plants in Sweden, Volvo and Saab-Scania, that have practiced job redesign of the assembly line on a large scale. The results, variously reported, have appeared in the world press. Also receiving wide press coverage have been

Reprinted by permission of the publisher of *Organizational Dynamics*, Autumn 1973, 51–67. © 1973 by AMACOM, a division of American Management Association.

the efforts of Philips N.V. in The Netherlands to redesign jobs on the lines assembling black-and-white and color TV sets. So much for instant history!

We visited the three companies during a recent trip to Europe and shall attempt to evaluate and compare them. But first a caveat: We eschew chic terms, such as job enrichment, autonomy, job rotation, and employee participation, in favor of the drabber job redesign for several reasons. First, the other terms have taken on emotional connotations; they've become the rallying ground for true believers who view them as a partial answer or panacea to the problem of employee alienation in an industrial society. The term job redesign, by contrast, has no glamor and no followers. Second, most efforts at job redesign, certainly the three we're going to write about, include elements of job enrichment, autonomy, job rotation, and employee participation in varying degrees at different times, but none of the competing terms affords a sufficiently large umbrella to cover what's happened and what's planned in the three organizations. Last, true believers passionately define their faiths differently; using any of the other terms as central would involve us in tiresome and trivial questions of definition. Hence, our choice of job redesign. It's comprehensive, and noncontroversial.

"Job redesign—the answer to what?" might have been a more descriptive subhead than one implying that our sole concern would be the question of employee discontent and its converse, employee satisfaction. Ours is a wider net. We're going to ask and answer (the answers, of course, being partial and tentative) these questions:

1 What conditions on the assembly line are economically favorable to which forms of job redesign?

2 Do many employees resent and resist job redesign? Do they prefer monotonous, repetitive work?

3 Are the "best" results from job redesign obtained when it's at its most thorough (job rotation plus job enrichment plus autonomy plus employee participation)?

4 Is there any single element in job redesign that seems to account for the biggest increase in employee satisfaction?

5 What are the benefits of job redesign— both those we can measure and monetize and those that can only be described?

6 On balance, does management gain as much from job redesign as the employee whose job is redesigned?

7 Last, what's the impact of the overall culture and political system on job redesign? What's the evidence, pro or con, that the success of job redesign at Volvo, Saab-Scania, or Philips—or the lack of it—would be replicated on similar assembly lines in the United States?

A tall order, but remember that we promised only tentative and partial answers to the seven questions.

JOB REDESIGN AT PHILIPS

First Generation, 1960–1965

We start with Philips because, of our three companies, Philips is the pioneer; its experience with job redesign goes back to 1960. We use the term first generation, second generation, and so on to mark the stages of the Philips program because this is Philips' terminology—obviously appropriated from computer lingo.

In the first experiment, concern was more with the deficiencies of long assembly lines than it was with improving job satisfaction. Breaking up the existing line of 104 workers into five shorter assembly lines, installing buffer stocks of components between groups, and placing inspectors at the end of each group instead of the whole assembly line reduced waiting times by 55 percent, improved feedback, and improved the balance of the system—various short chains being stronger than one long chain because the line can never travel faster than the worker with the longest average time per operation.

Almost incidentally, morale also improved: Only 29 percent of the workers on the assembly line responded positively to the survey question "I like doing my job," versus a 51 percent positive response from the test line. Furthermore, when the test line was restructured with half the number of workers, so that each one performed twice the original cycle and workplaces alternated with empty seats, production flowed more smoothly and quality improved. Dr. H. G. Van Beek, a psychologist on the original study team, drew a dual lesson from the experiment: "From the point of view of production, the long line is very vulnerable; from the point of view of morale—in the sense of job satisfaction—downright bad."

Subsequent experiments in several plants involved rotating workers between different jobs on the assembly line, enriching jobs by having employees set their own pace within overall production standards, and enlarging them by making employees responsible for inspecting their own work. Most of the gains from the experiments Philips entered under the heading of "social profit." In other words, morale and job satisfaction improved but bread-and-butter items such as productivity and scrap showed little improvement.

Second Generation, 1965–1968

The key feature of the second phase, a program that involved a few thousand employees scattered over 30 different locations, was the abolition of foremen. With supervisors' enlarged span of control, the men on the assembly line acquired autonomy and more control over their jobs. Even an authoritarian supervisor would find that he was spread too thin to exercise the same amount of control as the previous foreman had.

Once again, the bulk of the profits were social. The bill for waste and repairs dropped slightly, and, of course, Philips pocketed the money that had been paid to the foremen. Otherwise, the gains to Philips were nonmonetary.

Third Phase, 1968

This phase, one that is ongoing, has focused on giving various groups of seven or eight employees total responsibility for assembling either black-and-white TV sets or color selectors for color TV sets, a task equivalent in complexity to assembling a black-and-white set from scratch.

We want to emphasize the word *total:* The group responsible for assembling the black-and-white sets, for example, not only performs the entire assembling task but also deals directly with staff groups such as procurement, quality, and stores, with no supervisor or foreman to act as intermediary or expediter. If something is needed from another department or something goes wrong that requires the services of another department, it's the group's responsibility to deal with the department.

"This third phase has had its problems," concedes Den Hertog, staff psychologist. "Typically, it's taken about six months for the groups to shake down—adjust to the increased pressures and responsibilities." Establishing effective relationships with unfamiliar high-status employees in staff departments has proved the biggest single problem. On the other hand, anyone in an experimental group can opt out at any time—an option that has yet to be taken up. Of course, it may be the satisfaction of being a member of a select group, even physically separated from other work groups by a wall of green shrubbery, that accounts for no employee's having made a switch. Hertog, however, believes that the increase in intrinsic job satisfactions has more than compensated for any pains of adjustments and accounts for the lack of turnover.

What about results? What's the measurable

impact of the program? There have been additional costs, such as increased training costs; more important, small autonomous groups require new and smaller machines to perform traditional assembly line tasks. On the other hand, there have been measurable benefits. Overall, production costs in man-hours have dropped 10 percent, while waiting times have decreased and quality levels have increased by smaller but still significant amounts.

To restructure work and redesign jobs in ways that increase employee job satisfaction at no net cost to the company over the long run is all that Philips, as a matter of policy, requires of such programs. Short-term deficits caused by purchases of new equipment are something it's prepared to live with.

Where is Philips going from here? Obviously, the potential for effective job redesign is large. With 90,000 workers in 60 plants, Philips has barely scratched the surface. Part of the answer would seem to lie in the future strength of the movement for employee participation and power equalization that is particularly strong in Norway and Sweden and is gaining adherents in The Netherlands.

At Philips the primary response has been the establishment of worker consultation in some 20 different departments. Worker consultation is just what it sounds like: Employees meet with first- and second-level supervision to discuss problems of joint interest. Worker consultation exists at different levels in different departments, stresses Hertog, who attributes the difference to the level of maturity of the group itself: "In some groups we're still at the flower pot phase, talking about what should be done to improve meals in the cafeteria, while at other extremes we have departments where we have left the selection of a new supervisor for the group up to the workers."

It's significant that those groups who have considered the question of job redesign con-sistently have criticized Philips for not doing more of it. The expansion of job redesign, in part, would seem to depend on the expansion of work consultation and the pressures exerted by the workers themselves to get job redesign extended.

JOB REDESIGN AT SAAB-SCANIA

To claim that Saab-Scania has abolished the auto assembly line would misrepresent the facts. Saab-Scania, or to speak more precisely, the Scania Division, has instituted small-group assembly of auto engines—not the whole car—in its new engine plant. Even so, this effort is limited to 50 employees in a plant with a workforce of approximately 300, most of whom monitor automatic transfer machines that perform various machining tasks. (See Figure 18-1). There's only one manual loading operation in the entire machining process.

More important, the humanization of the auto assembly line is the most dramatic single instance in a series starting in 1969 that Palle Berggen, the head of the industrial engineering department, characterized as "one phase in the development of enhanced industrial democracy."

We won't quarrel with his description, although we think he succumbed to the rhetoric of public relations. Scania, in its actions from 1969 on, has responded to some problems for which the best word is horrendous. Employee turnover was running around 45 percent annually, and in the auto assembly plant, 70 percent. Absenteeism was also extraordinary—close to 20 percent. Under such conditions, the maintenance of an even flow of production, something crucial in an integrated work system like Scania's, presented insuperable problems. Also, it was increasingly difficult to fill jobs on the shop floor at all. A survey taken in 1969 indicates what Scania was up against: Only four out of 100 students graduating from high school in Sweden indicated their willing-

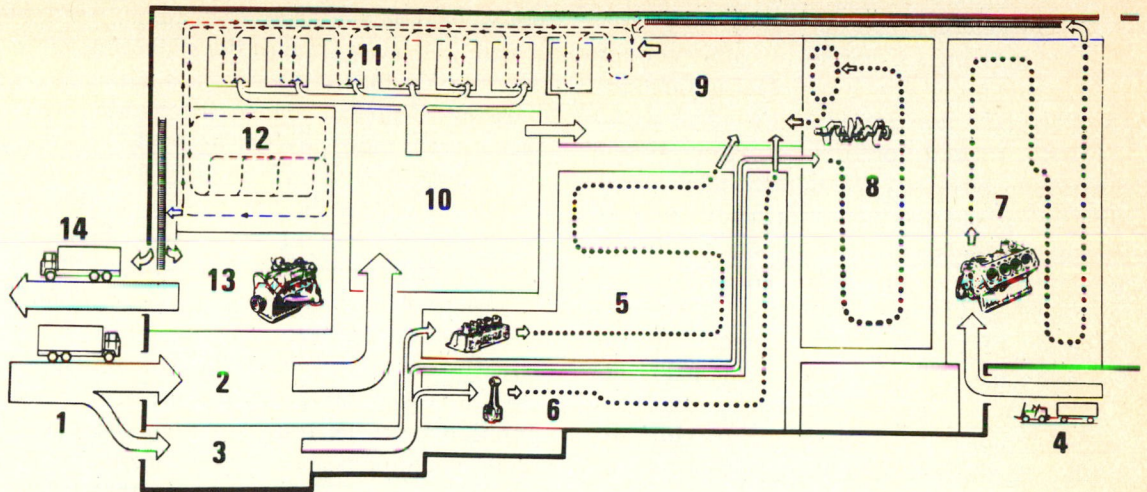

Figure 18-1 Diagram of engine plant, Saab-Scania.

ness to take a rank-and-file factory job. In consequence, Scania became heavily dependent on foreign workers—58 percent of the current workforce are non-Swedes. This in turn created problems, both expected and otherwise—among the former problems of training and communications, among the latter an epidemic of wildcat strikes, previously unknown in Sweden, that largely resulted from the manipulation by extreme left elements of foreign workers ignorant of the tradition among Swedish employees of almost total reliance upon the strong trade union organization to protect their interests.

Any response to these conditions *had* to have as its number one objective the maintenance of productivity. To assert anything else is window dressing—unconvincing as well as unnecessary. No one can fault an industrial organization for undertaking a program whose primary goal is the maintenance of productivity.

This is not to deny that one byproduct of the program has been "enhanced industrial democracy." What happened is that the pursuit of productivity led to an examination of the conditions that created job satisfactions; these, in turn, suggested the series of actions "that enhance industrial democracy"—a term subject to almost as many definitions as there are interpreters.

Production Groups and Development Groups

Employee representation is nothing new at Scania. Like every company in Sweden with more than 50 employees, it's had an employee-elected Works Council since 1949. However, these bodies have no decision-making function; their role is limited to receiving and responding to information from top management, and their effectiveness depends on the willingness of top management to seriously consider suggestions from the Works Council. David Jenkins, in his recent book *Job Power*, tells of asking a company president if he had ever been influenced by worker suggestions. His reply: "Well, yes. We were going to build a new plant and we showed the workers the plans at one of the meetings. They objected very much to the fact that the plant would have no windows. So we changed the plans and had some windows put in. It doesn't cost much more and, actually, the building looks better. And the workers feel better."

The production and development groups initiated in the truck chassis assembly plant in 1969, by contrast, have real decision-making power. Production groups of five to 12 workers with related job duties decide among themselves how they will do their jobs, within the quality and production standards defined by higher management; they can rotate job assignments—do a smaller or larger part of the overall task. At the same time, the jobs of all members of the production group were enlarged by making them jointly responsible for simple service and maintenance activities, housekeeping, and quality control in their work area, duties formerly performed by staff personnel.

Development groups, a parallel innovation, consist of foremen, industrial engineers, and two representatives of one or more production groups whose function is to consider ideas for improving work methods and working conditions. Representatives of the production groups are rotated in a way that guarantees that every member of a production group will serve each year on a development group.

Employee reception of the production group has been mixed but largely positive. The results appear to be favorable, although Scania has done little or nothing to measure them quantitatively. However, impressions have been sufficiently favorable so that within four years production and development groups have expanded to include 2,200 out of the 3,600 employees in the main plant at Södertälje, and within the year they will be extended throughout the company.

Work Design in the Engine Plant

The four machine lines for the components in the engine factory—the cylinder block, the cylinder head, the connecting rod, and the crankshaft—mainly consist of transfer machines manned or monitored by individual operations. Group assembly is restricted to the seven final assembly stations, each of which contains a team of fitters that assemble an entire engine.

Team members divide the work among themselves; they may decide to do one-third of the assembly on each engine—a ten-minute chore—or follow the engine around the bay and assemble the entire engine—a 30-minute undertaking. In fact, only a minority prefer to do the total assembly job. (Using traditional assembly line methods, each operation would have taken 1.8 minutes.) The team also decides its own work pace, and the number and duration of work breaks within the overall requirement of assembling 470 engines in each ten-day period, a specification that allows them a good deal of flexibility in their pacing. Incidentally, over half the employees in the engine plant are women, while the assembly teams are over 80 percent female. We personally saw four assembly teams with only a single man in the lot.

Benefits and Costs

Kaj Holmelius, who is responsible for planning and coordination of the production engineering staff, ticked off the principal credits and debits, along with a few gray areas in which it would be premature to estimate results. On the plus side, he cited the following:

1 Group assembly has increased the flexibility of the plant, making it easier to adjust to heavy absenteeism.

2 The group assembly concept is responsible for a lower balancing loss due to a longer station time.

3 Less money is invested in assembly tools. Even allowing for the fact that you have to buy six or seven times as many tools, the simpler tools make for a smaller overall cost.

4 Quality has definitely improved, although by how much it's hard to estimate.

5 Productivity is higher than it would have been with the conventional assembly line—

although once more, there is no proof. Lower production speed per engine, because it's not economical to use some very expensive automatic tools, is outweighed by higher quality and reduced turnover.

6 Employee attitudes have improved, although there have been no elaborate surveys taken. To Holmelius the best indication of job satisfaction is that it's impossible to fill all the requests to transfer from other parts of the plant to the assembly teams.

On the negative side, in addition to the reduced production speed, group assembly takes up considerably more space than the conventional assembly line.

In the neutral corner is the impact on absenteeism and turnover. Absenteeism is actually higher in the engine plant—18 percent versus 15 percent for overall plant operations at Södertälje. However, Holmelius attributes the difference to the fact that the engine plant employs a heavier percentage of women. As for turnover, with the plant in operation for a little more than a year, it's too early to tell. Because of an economic slowdown, turnover generally is down from the 45 percent crisis level of 1969 to 20 percent, and it's Holmelius' belief that turnover in the assembly teams will prove significantly lower than average.

What's the Future of Group Assembly?

It's easier to point out the directions in which Scania does *not* plan to extend group assembly. An experiment with having employees assemble an entire truck diesel engine—a six-hour undertaking involving 1,500 parts—was abandoned at the employees' request; they couldn't keep track of all the parts. Similarly, group assembly wouldn't work with the body of the trucks—truck bodies are too complex, and group assembly would require twice the space currently needed. The moot question at the moment is car assembly. So far, group assembly has been applied only to assem-

bling doors. We suspect that in any decision, economic calculations will predominate, including, of course, the inherently fuzzy calculation about the economic value of job satisfaction.

JOB REDESIGN AT VOLVO

Job redesign at Volvo began, almost accidentally, in the upholstery shop of the car assembly plant during the mid-1960s, but a companywide effort had to wait until 1969, when Volvo faced the same problems that plagued Scania—wildcat strikes, absenteeism, and turnover that were getting out of hand and an increasing dependence on foreign workers. Turnover was over 40 percent annually; absenteeism was running 20 to 25 percent, and close to 45 percent of the employees of the car assembly plant were non-Swedes. One other event in 1971 made a difference: Volvo acquired a young, hard-driving new managing director. Pehr Gyllenhammar, who developed a keen interest in the new methods of work organization.

Ingvar Barrby, head of the upholstery department, started job redesign by persuading production management to experiment with job rotation along the lines he had read about in Norway. The overwhelmingly female workforce complained frequently about the inequity of the various jobs involved in assembling car seats; some jobs were easier than others, while still others were more comfortable and less strenuous, and so on. To equalize the tasks, Barrby divided the job into 13 different operations and rotated the employees among tasks that were relatively arduous and those that were relatively comfortable. Jealousy and bickering among employees disappeared: First, jobs were no longer inequitable; second, employees perceived that they had exaggerated the differences between jobs anyway—the grass-is-greener syndrome. More important, turnover that had been running 35 percent quickly fell to 15 percent, a gain that has been maintained over the years.

Job Alternation and "Multiple Balances"

Volvo uses these phrases instead of the more commonly used job rotation and job enrichment, but the concepts are the same. In job alternation or job rotation, the employee changes jobs once or several times daily, depending on the nature of the work in his group. Take Line IV A, for example, whose function is to do the external and internal sealing and insulation of car bodies. Because internal sealing is such uncomfortable work—employees work in cramped positions inside the car body—the work is alternated every other hour. The remaining jobs are rotated daily.

"Multiple balances" is our old friend, job enrichment, under another name. One example involves the overhead line where the group follows the same body for seven or eight stations along the line for a total period of 20 minutes—seven or eight times the length of the average job cycle.

Not all employees have had their jobs rotated or enriched—only 1,500 out of 7,000 in the car assembly at Torslanda are affected by the program. Because participation is strictly voluntary, the figures at first glance seem to indicate a massive show of disinterest on the part of Volvo employees. Not so. True, some employees prefer their jobs the way they are. The bigger problem is that Volvo has, to date, lacked the technical resources to closely scrutinize many jobs to determine whether and how they can be enlarged or enriched, or it has scrutinized them and determined that it isn't economically feasible to enlarge or enrich them. A company spokesman gave the job of coating under the car body to prevent rust as an example of a thoroughly unpleasant job that so far has defied redesign.

Production Teams at Volvo Lundbyverken

In the truck assembly plant at Lundbyverken, Volvo has carried job redesign several steps further, with production teams who, in form and function, roughly duplicate the production groups previously described at Scania. The production team, a group of five to 12 men with a common work assignment, elects its own chargehand, schedules its own output within the standards set by higher management, distributes work among its members, and is responsible for its own quality control. In these teams, group piecework replaces individual piecework and everyone earns the same amount, with the exception of the chargehand. Currently, there are 23 production teams involving 100 out of the plant's 1,200 employees. Plans call for the gradual extension of the production team approach to cover most, if not all, of the factory workforce.

The Box Score at Volvo

Have the various forms of job redesign, job rotation, job enrichment, and production teams paid off for Volvo? If so, what forms have the payoff taken? Anything we can measure or monetize? Or are we reduced to subjective impressions and interesting although iffy conjectures about the relationship between factors such as increased job satisfaction and reduced turnover?

The two plants deserve separate consideration: Absenteeism and turnover traditionally have been lower at the truck assembly plant than at the car assembly plant. The jobs are inherently more complex and interesting—even before job enrichment, some individual jobs took up to half an hour. The workers, in turn, are more highly skilled and tend to regard themselves as apart from and above the rank-and-file auto worker. They see themselves more as junior engineers. Within this context, it's still true that the introduction of production teams has led to further improvement: less labor turnover, less absenteeism, an improvement in quality, and fewer final adjustments.

At the auto assembly plant the picture isn't clear. Turnover is down from 40 to 25 percent. However, an economic slowdown undoubtedly accounts for some of the decline, while other actions unrelated to job redesign may account for part of the remainder. When Volvo surveyed its employees to probe for the causes of turnover and absenteeism, most of the causes revealed were external—problems with housing, child care, long distances traveling to the plant, and so on. Volvo responded with a series of actions to alleviate these causes, such as extending the bus fleet, together with the community, to transport employees, loaning money to employees to purchase apartments at very favorable rates of interest, putting pressure on the community to expand day care centers, and so on. Such measures presumably contributed to the decline of turnover. Nevertheless, Gyllenhammar is convinced that "we can see a correlation between increased motivation, increased satisfaction on the job, and a decrease in the turnover of labor." Absenteeism is a sadly different picture: It's double what it was five years ago, a condition that Gyllenhammar attributes to legislation enabling workers to stay off the job at practically no cost to themselves.

As for output in that part of the auto assembly plant covered by job enrichment or job enlargement, there was no measurable improvement. Quality, on balance, has improved, and the feeling is that improved quality and decreased turnover had more than covered the costs of installing the program.

The Future of Job Redesign at Volvo

Despite the relatively ambiguous success of Volvo's job redesign efforts, whatever Volvo has done in the past is a pale prologue to its future plans. In about nine months, Volvo's new auto assembly plant at Kalmar will go on stream. And, for once, that overworked term "revolutionary" would seem justified.

Physically, the plant is remarkable. Gyllenhammar describes it as "shaped like a star and on each point of the star you have a work group finishing a big share of the whole automobile—for example, the electrical system or the safety system or the interior." Assembly work takes place along the outer walls, while component parts are stored in the center of the building. Architecturally, the building has been designed to preserve the atmosphere of a small workshop in a large factory, with each work team having its own entrance, dressing room, rest room, and so on. Each team is even physically shielded from a view of the other teams. (See Figures 18-2 and 18-3.)

Each work team, of 15 to 25 men, will distribute the work among themselves and determine their own work rhythm, subject to the requirement of meeting production standards. If the team decides to drive hard in the morning and loaf in the afternoon, the decision is theirs to make. As with production teams in the truck assembly plant, the team will choose its own boss, and deselect him if he turns out poorly.

The new plant will cost about 10 percent more—some 10 million Swedish kroner—than a comparable conventional auto assembly plant. Time alone will tell whether the extra investment will be justified by the decreased turnover, improved quality, and even reduced absenteeism that its designers confidently expect at the new facility. In announcing the plan for the new factory, Gyllenhammar's economic objectives were modest enough, his social objectives more ambitious. "A way must be found to create a workplace that meets the needs of the modern working man for a sense of purpose and satisfaction in his

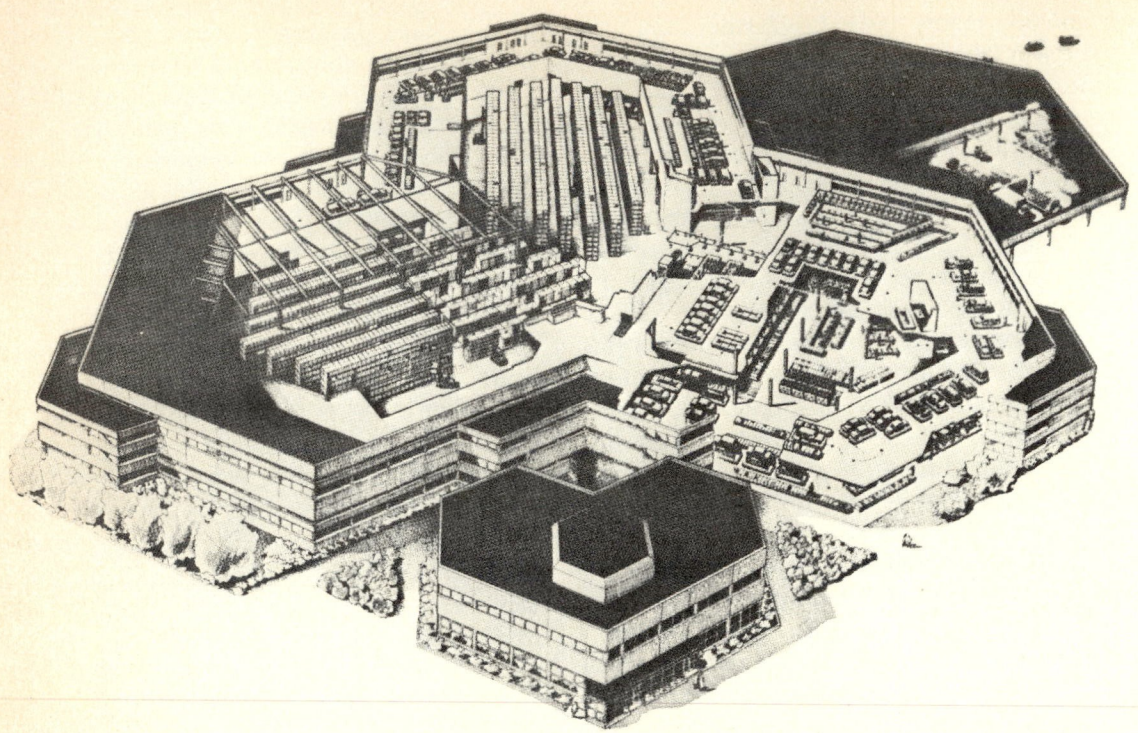

Figure 18-2   Exploded drawing of Volvo auto assembly plant at Kalmar.

daily work. A way must be found of attaining this goal without an adverse effect on productivity." With luck, he may achieve both.

WHAT DOES IT ADD UP TO?

On the basis of what we learned at Philips, Saab-Scania, and Volvo, what answers—tentative and partial—do we have to the seven questions that we raised earlier in the article? Or are the results of the programs so ambiguous and inconclusive that, as long as we restrict ourselves to the context of these three companies, we must beg off attempting to answer some of the questions at all? That none of the companies answered all of the questions, and that many of the answers rely on subjective impressions haphazardly assembled, rather than on quantitative

data systematically collected, of necessity, limit our answers, but they don't prevent us from presenting them—with the appropriate caveats.

1   What Conditions on the Assembly Line Are Economically Favorable to Which Forms of Job Redesign?

The basic question here is under what conditions can a man-paced assembly line replace a machine-paced assembly line? Unless this is economically feasible, no form of job redesign is likely to be adopted. Even allowing for rhetoric, none of our three companies—and no other organization of which we are aware—has indicated a willingness to suffer economic losses in order to increase the satisfactions employees might feel if they switched over from machine-paced to man-paced as-

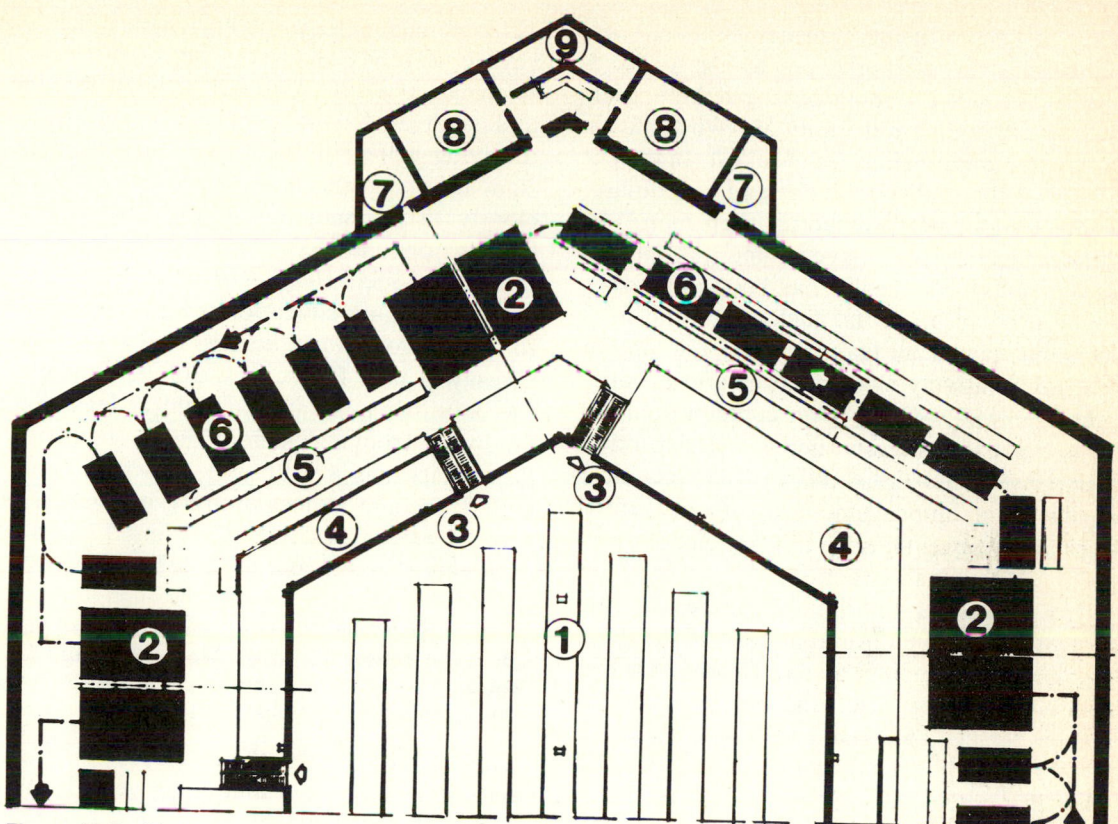

Figure 18-3 Diagram of small workshop at Volvo assembly plant at Kalmar.

sembly lines. Take the case of manufacturing a pair of man's pants in a garment factory. Give the job to one man and he will take half a day; divide the work among many people on a line with each one using advanced technical equipment, and it takes one man-hour to produce a pair of trousers. The future of job redesign is not bright in a pants factory.

The man-paced assembly line, however, has a couple of widely recognized advantages over the machine-paced line: First, it's much less sensitive to disruption; the whole line doesn't have to stop because of one breakdown—human or technical; second, extensive and costly rebalancing need not be undertaken every time production is increased

or decreased. You simply add more people or groups. Of course, there are advantages to machine-paced production, the outstanding one being speed of production, which depends, in turn, on an even flow of production.

There's the rub—and there's the number one cause for job redesign, certainly at Volvo and Saab-Scania. Absenteeism and turnover had risen to the point where they canceled out the economic advantages of machine-paced production. At the same time, evidence had accumulated that job redesign organized around a man-paced assembly line might strike at the root causes of inordinate turnover and absenteeism.

If you look at the design of the new engine

plant at Scania, it incorporates Drucker's insight that "the worker is put to use to use a poorly designed one-purpose machine tool, but repetition and uniformity are two qualities in which human beings are weakest. In everything but the ability to judge and coordinate, machines can perform better than man." In the new engine plant, everything that can be automated economically has been—probably 90 percent of the total task—with the final assembly paced by teams on the assumption that the relatively slight increases in production time will be more than compensated for by better balancing and decreased disruption —improvements inherent in the technical change—and improvements in quality, turnover, and absenteeism, the anticipated by-products of job satisfaction.

The results, as you have seen, are sketchy. However, we can affirm that none of the three organizations, by their own testimony, has lost economically by the changeover from a machine-paced to a man-paced assembly line. How much they have gained is decidedly a more iffy question.

2 Do Many Employees Resent and Resist Job Redesign? Do They Prefer Monotonous, Repetitious Work?

A flip answer might be "God only knows—and he isn't talking." Any answer, at best, is based largely on conjecture. Joseph E. Godfrey asserts that "workers may complain about monotony, but years spent in the factories lead me to believe that they like to do their jobs automatically. If you interject new things you spoil the rhythm of the job and work gets fouled up." As head of the General Motors Assembly Line Division he is qualified, but biased. But even Fred Herzberg, whose bias is obviously in the other direction, concedes that "individual reaction to job enrichment is as difficult to forecast in terms of attitudes as it is in terms of performance. Not all persons

welcome having their job enriched." The Survey Research Center at The University of Michigan in a 1969 study concluded that factors such as having a "nutrient supervisor, receiving adequate help, having few labor standard problems all seem to relate at least as closely to job satisfaction as having a challenging job with 'enriching demands.'" One things does seem clear: Assuming the job level is held constant, education is inversely related to satisfaction. And when Pehr Gyllenhammar foresaw a near future in which 90 percent of the Swedish population would at least have graduated from high school, he was realistically anticipating a situation in which Volvo would become almost entirely dependent on foreign employees unless it found ways of enriching the auto assembly jobs.

3 Are the "Best" Results from Job Redesign Obtained When It's at Its Most Thorough (Job Rotation Plus Job Enrichment Plus Autonomy Plus Employee Participation)?

Work in America flatly endorses the thesis that "it is imperative that employers be made aware of the fact that thorough efforts to redesign work, not simply 'job enrichment' or 'job rotation,' have resulted in increases of productivity from 5 to 40 percent. In no instance of which we have evidence has a major effort to increase employee participation resulted in a long-term decline in productivity." Obviously, in this context "best" results mean increased productivity.

Before we can answer the question and respond to the claims asserted in *Work in America* a few definitions are necessary. Most descriptions of the elements that enter into a satisfying job concentrate on three: (1) variety, (2) responsibility, and (3) autonomy. Variety defines itself. Responsibility is more complex; it involves both working on a sufficiently large part of the total job to feel that it is a meaningful experience, and also having a sufficient amount of control over what you are doing to feel personally responsible.

Companies responding to this need for more responsibility may add set-up and inspection to the employee's duties or ask him to assemble one-third of an engine instead of a single component—both examples of horizontal job enrichment; and the employee may be permitted to control the pace at which he works—an example of vertical job enrichment. Everything that is subsumed under vertical job enrichment is included in autonomy but it also means something else and something more—giving to the employee himself some control over how his job should be enlarged or enriched—a clear demarcation point between almost all American approaches to job enrichment and some European.

We're describing a circular process; the worker in Sweden and The Netherlands places a higher value on autonomy than the worker in the United States. Therefore, job redesign that incorporates increased autonomy for the employee will be more appreciated and lead to more job satisfaction than comparable efforts would in the United States. Here, Huey Long's concept of a satisfying job, with allowances for the regional overtones, and the hyperbole, still makes sense: "There shall be a real job, not a little old sowbelly black-eyed pea job, but a real spending money beefsteak, and gray Chevrolet Ford in the garage, new suit, Thomas Jefferson, Jesus Christ, red, white, and blue job for every man." The employee did then and still does define, although to a progressively decreasing degree, a satisfying job in terms of how much it pays. For a measure of the difference, take the definition of a dissatisfying job by Malin Lofgren, a 12-year-old Swedish schoolboy: "A bad job is one where others make all the decisions, and you have to do what others say."

Now that the tedious, although necessary, business of definition is out of the way, how do we answer the question with reference to our three companies? Inconclusively. If we define "best" results in terms of gains in productivity, the only certifiable gain occurred with the Philips production groups that scored high on both horizontal and vertical job enrichment, and in which employees were consulted in advance about the ways in which their job should be enriched. In the body of the article, we didn't go into their institutional arrangements, but suffice it to say that both Saab-Scania and Volvo have comparable consultative institutions. Thus, the autonomy factor assumes less significance. The only significant differences would appear to be: (1) The increased status caused by making the production groups at Philips wholly responsible for liaison with other departments, (2) the Hawthorne, or, as the Philips personnel call it, the "Princess" effect—the groups having been visited and complimented by such dignitaries as Queen Juliana and Marshal Tito. On the other hand, the groups at Volvo that chose their own supervisors—certainly a measure of autonomy—have not increased their productivity. Quality, turnover, attendance had improved. But with productivity, there was no measurable impact.

4 Is There Any Single Element in Job Redesign That Seems to Account for the Biggest Increase in Employee Satisfaction?

In a word—no. But that requires an explanation. Our failure to respond principally reflects lack of evidence; none of the organizations concerned asked themselves the question. None tried on any systematic basis to relate what they were doing in redesigning jobs to what they were accomplishing in increased job satisfaction. Word-of-mouth testimony and more cheerful figures—as in the case of Volvo and Saab-Scania with turnover—seemed sufficient to confirm the efficacy of past efforts and sanction future ones, on similar although expanded lines.

5 What Are the Benefits of Job Redesign—Both Those We Can Measure and Monetize and Those That Can Only Be Described?

We begin with a proposition shared by a generation of social scientists who have studied the problem and attempted to answer the question: Employee attitudes and job satisfaction are correlated much more clearly with factors such as absenteeism, turnover, and quality than they are with productivity.

The three companies reinforce this finding. Only one experiment at Philips establishes a positive correlation between job satisfaction and productivity, while several—Philips with productivity groups in Phase III, Saab-Scania in the engine plant and the truck assembly plant, and Volvo in its truck plant—all report improvements in quality, the problem in each case being the absence of quantifiable data. Turnover is another area in which the responses are positive, but suggestive rather than conclusive—"probably lower" in the Scania engine plant; lower in the truck assembly plant; down in both the truck assembly and auto assembly plant at Volvo—but there are no firm figures at the Volvo truck assembly line, while the decrease in turnover at the auto assembly plant is partly attributed to causes unrelated to job redesign. Philips proffers no comparisons of absenteeism or turnover before and after job redesign. All we know is that so far no one in the production groups has decided to quit. In short, the evidence—what there is of it—is positive, but fragmented and based more on impressions than on data.

6 On Balance, Does Management Gain as Much from Job Redesign as the Employee Whose Job Is Redesigned?

A two-headed question that logically requires both extensive employee attitude surveys be-fore and after job redesign, along with firm measurements that demonstrate the impact of job redesign on factors such as quality, output, absenteeism, and turnover. As we have seen, we have very little of either. The only attitude surveys were first, the one conducted at the Volvo auto assembly plant to determine the causes of excessive absenteeism and turnover—most of which had nothing to do with job satisfaction and where the subsequent substantial drop in turnover at best could only partially be ascribed to job redesign—and the survey at Philips, where the switchover from machine-paced to man-paced assembly line improved employees' satisfaction with their jobs.

On balance, as previously stated, management has achieved at least an economic draw from its efforts at job redesign, along with a measure of insurance against a fretful future in which employee expectations will become increasingly difficult to fulfill and the job redesign carried out or contemplated will, it is hoped, help to meet those expectations.

As for the satisfactions the employees have gained from the collective efforts at enlarging and enriching their jobs, we can only guess. We have a few pieces of anecdotal evidence, such as the flood of applications to work in the final assembly at Scania's engine plant, or the absence of turnover among the production groups at Philips. In short, we know too little to generalize.

7 Last, What's the Impact of the Overall Culture and Political System on Job Redesign? What's the Evidence, Pro or Con, That the Success of Job Redesign at Volvo, Saab-Scania, or Philips—or Lack of It—Would Be Replicated in Similar Assembly Lines in the United States?

Technologically, there are no convincing reasons why assembly lines in new automobile factories or television plants in the United States couldn't be redesigned along lines similar to what has been done at Philips, Saab-

Scania, and Volvo. It might prove prohibitively expensive in existing plants—after all, job redesign at Volvo's auto assembly plant was largely restricted, on economic grounds, to job rotation. However, new plants in the United States should present no more inherent problems of job redesign than new plants in Sweden. Yet auto executives in the United States have gone on record as feeling that the situation is hopeless. A 1970 report of the Ford Foundation found that none of the corporation executives interviewed "really believe that assembly line tasks can be significantly restructured," and "no one really believes that much can be done to make the assembly jobs more attractive."

Not that all the features of job redesign at Philips, Saab-Scania, and Volvo are equally exportable. The three companies exist in a different political and social ethos, one in which both management and the workers have gone much further in accepting the idea of employee participation in decision making than all but a handful of managers and a small minority of workers in the United States. A survey of Swedish managers in 1970, for example, showed that 75 percent favored more employee decision making in all departments. Even the idea of replacing the decision of the supervisor with collective employee decisions elicited a favorable response from 11 percent of the managers. Given this different ethos, it is not surprising that all three companies have experimented with what would be in the United States the radical step of either dispensing with first-level supervision or leaving it up to the employees to choose their own supervisor. It is a form of autonomy that few managements in the United States would consider for an instant, and one in which few employees would take much interest.

But why not consider it, as long as management continues to set overall standards of production and quality and to hold the group responsible for meeting them? The experiment of having employees choose their own bosses with the experimental groups in the truck assembly plant at Volvo works so well that it has been incorporated as one of the basic design features in the new auto assembly plant. Employees demonstrated that, given the opportunity, they would choose as leaders men who could organize the work and maintain order and discipline.

Let's indulge in speculation. The single quality that most clearly distinguishes between the efforts at job enrichment here and in the three companies we visited is the emphasis abroad on letting the employees have a part—and sometimes a decisive part—in deciding how their jobs should be enriched. By contrast, most exponents of job enrichment in the United States take the "papa-knows-best" approach. Fred Herzberg, the best-known work psychologist, asserts that when people took part in deciding how to change their own jobs, "the results were disappointing." We suspect that Herzberg's real objection is not to the results themselves, but to the difficulty of selling most managements on the idea that employee participation should be an integral part of any process of job enrichment. The experiences at Volvo, Saab-Scania, and Philips suggest that the objection to the employee's participating in how his own job should be enriched or redesigned has its roots in symbolism, rather than substance, in the irrational preoccupation with management prerogatives, rather than in any real or potential threat to productivity or profits.

What about the future? Technologically, there seem to be no compelling reasons why Ford, G.M., and Chrysler cannot take a leaf from Volvo and Saab-Scania. Whether they will is another question. The combination of inertia, custom, and commitment is a formidable one. So far the automakers have chosen to move in the opposite direction: shorter work cycles, smaller jobs, more rapidly moving lines. We should recall that it took a crisis—

nothing less than the probability that most people would refuse to work at all or only for uneconomic periods on the jobs the organization had to offer them—to "break the cake of custom" at Volvo and Saab-Scania. Even today, it is clear that there are limits to which auto assembly jobs can be enriched, a limitation obvious in Gyllenhammar's bitter observation that "'absenteeism with pay' is based on the very utopian hypothesis that people love to work, and no matter what happens they will strive to go to their job every morning." Still, the situation he is in is preferable to the situation he faced. And some of the difference is due to job redesign.

We suspect that it will take a crisis of similar magnitude, together with the belief that they have no choice, to unfreeze the attitudes of automakers in the United States and get them moving in the direction of man-paced assembly lines and the forms of job redesign they facilitate. That such a development, over the long run, is in the cards we strongly believe, but how long it will take for the cards to show up, we leave to the astrologers.

Reading 19

Designing Work for Individuals and for Groups

J. Richard Hackman

As yet there are no simple or generally accepted criteria for a well-designed job, nor is a single technology acknowledged as the proper way to go about redesigning work. Moreover, it often is unclear in specific circumstances whether work should be structured to be performed by individual employees, or whether it should be designed to be carried out by a *group* of employees working together.

The first part of this selection reviews one current model for work design that focuses on the individual performer. In the second part, discussion turns to a number of issues that must be dealt with when work is designed for interacting teams of employees.

DESIGNING WORK FOR INDIVIDUALS

A model specifying how job characteristics and individual differences interact to affect the satisfaction, motivation, and productivity of individuals at work has been proposed by Hackman and Oldham (1976). The model is specifically intended for use in planning and carrying out changes in the design of jobs. It is described below, and then is used as a guide for a discussion of diagnostic procedures and change principles that can be used in redesigning the jobs of individuals.

The Job Characteristics Model

The basic job characteristics model is shown in Figure 19-1. As illustrated in the figure, five core job dimensions are seen as creating three critical psychological states which, in turn, lead to a number of beneficial personal and work outcomes. The links among the job dimensions, the psychological states, and the outcomes are shown to be moderated by the strength of individuals' growth needs. The

Adapted from J. R. Hackman, Work design. In J. R. Hackman & J. L. Suttle (Eds.), *Improving life at work: Behavioral science approaches to organizational change.* Santa Monica, Calif.: Goodyear Publishing Company, 1977. Portions of this material have been adapted from articles by Hackman and Oldham (1975) and Hackman, Oldham, Janson and Purdy (1975).

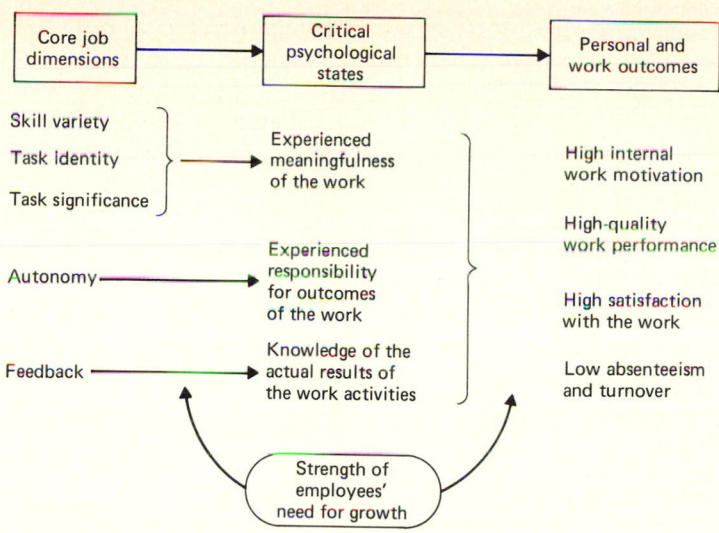

Figure 19-1 The job characteristics model of work motivation.

major classes of variables in the model are reviewed briefly below.

Psychological States The three following psychological states are postulated as critical in affecting a person's motivation and satisfaction on the job:

1 Experienced meaningfulness: The person must experience the work as generally important, valuable, and worthwhile.
2 Experienced responsibility: The individual must feel personally responsible and accountable for the results of the work he or she performs.
3 Knowledge of results: The individual must have understanding, on a fairly regular basis, of how effectively he or she is performing the job.

The more these three conditions are present, the more people will feel good about themselves when they perform well. Or, following Hackman and Lawler (1971), the model postulates that internal rewards are obtained by individuals when they *learn* (knowledge of results) that they *personally* (experienced responsibility) have performed well on a task that they *care about* (experienced meaningful-

ness). These internal rewards are reinforcing to the individual, and serve as incentives for continued efforts to perform well in the future. When the persons do not perform well, they do not experience a reinforcing state of affairs, and may elect to try harder in the future so as to regain the rewards that good performance brings. The net result is a self-perpetuating cycle of positive work motivation powered by self-generated rewards, that is predicted to continue until one or more of the three psychological states is no longer present—or until the individual no longer values the internal rewards that derive from good performance.

Job Dimensions Of the five job characteristics shown in Figure 19-1 as fostering the emergence of the psychological states, three contribute to the experienced meaningfulness of the work, and one each contributes to experienced responsibility and to knowledge of results.

The three job dimensions that contribute to a job's *meaningfulness* are:

1 *Skill variety* The degree to which a job requires a variety of different activities in carrying out the work, which involve the use of a number of different skills and talents of the person.

When a task requires a person to engage in activities that challenge or stretch his or her skills and abilities, that task almost invariably is experienced as meaningful by the individual. Many parlor games, puzzles, and recreational activities, for example, achieve much of their fascination because they tap and test the intellective or motor skills of the people who do them. When a job draws upon several skills of an employee, that individual may find the job to be of very high personal meaning—even if, in any absolute sense, it is not of great significance or importance.

2 *Task identity* The degree to which the job requires completion of a "whole" and identifiable piece of work—that is, doing a job from beginning to end with a visible outcome.

If an employee assembles a complete product or provides a complete unit of service he or she should find the work more meaningful than if he or she were responsible for only a small part of the whole job—other things (such as skill variety) being equal.

3 *Task significance* The degree to which the job has a substantial impact on the lives or work of other people—whether in the immediate organization or in the external environment.

When individuals understand that the results of their work may have a significant effect on the well-being of other people, the experienced meaningfulness of the work usually is enhanced. Employees who tighten nuts on aircraft brake assemblies, for example, are much more likely to perceive their work as meaningful than are workers who fill small boxes with paper clips—even though the skill levels involved may be comparable.

The job characteristic predicted to prompt feelings of personal *responsibility* for the work outcomes is autonomy. "Autonomy" is defined as the degree to which the job provides substantial freedom, independence, and discretion to the individual in scheduling the work and in determining the procedures to be used in carrying it out.

To the extent that autonomy is high, work outcomes will be viewed by workers as depending substantially on their *own* efforts, initiatives, and decisions, rather than on the adequacy of instructions from the boss or on a manual of job procedures. In such circumstances, individuals should feel a strong personal responsibility for the successes and failures that occur on the job.

The job characteristic that fosters *knowledge of results* is "feedback," which is defined as the degree to which carrying out the work activities required by the job results in the individual's obtaining direct and clear information about the effectiveness of his or her performance.

It often is useful to combine the scores of a job on the five dimensions described above into a single index reflecting the overall potential of the job to prompt self-generated work motivation on the part of job incumbents. Following the model diagramed in Figure 19-1, a job high in motivating potential must be high on at least one (and hopefully more) of the three dimensions that lead to experienced meaningfulness, *and* high on autonomy and feedback as well—thereby creating conditions for all three of the critical psychological states to be present. Arithmetically, scores of jobs on the five dimensions are combined as follows to meet this criterion:

Motivating potential score (MPS) =

$$\left(\frac{\text{skill variety} + \text{task identity} + \text{task significance}}{3} \right)$$

$$\times \text{ autonomy } \times \text{ job feedback}$$

As can be seen from the formula, a near-zero score of a job on either autonomy or feedback will reduce the overall MPS to near-zero; whereas a near-zero score on one of the three job dimensions that contribute to experienced meaningfulness cannot, by itself, do so.

Strength of the Individual's Need for Growth   The strength of a person's need for growth is postulated to moderate how people react to complex, challenging work at two points in the model shown in Figure 19-1: first, at the link between the objective job dimensions and the psychological states, and again between the psychological states and the outcome variables. The first link means that persons with a high need for growth are more likely (or better able) to *experience* the psychological states when an objective job is enriched than persons with a low need for growth. The second link means that individuals with a high need for growth will respond more positively to the psychological states, when they are present, than persons with a low need for growth.

Outcome Variables   Also shown in Figure 19-1 are several outcomes that are affected by the level of self-generated motivation experienced by people at work. Of special interest as an outcome variable is internal work motivation (Lawler & Hall, 1970; Hackman & Lawler, 1971), because it taps directly the contingency between effective performance and self-administered affective rewards. Typical questionnaire items measuring internal work motivation include: (1) I feel a great sense of personal satisfaction when I do this job well; (2) I feel bad and unhappy when I discover that I have performed poorly on this job; and (3) My own feelings are *not* affected much one way or the other by how well I do on this job (reversed scoring).

Other outcomes listed in Figure 19-1 are the quality of work performance, job satisfaction (especially satisfaction with opportunities for personal growth and development on the job), absenteeism, and turnover. All these outcomes are predicted to be affected positively by a job high in motivating potential.

Validity of the Job Characteristics Model

Empirical testing of the job characteristics model of work motivation is reported in detail elsewhere (Hackman & Oldham, 1976). In general, results are supportive, as suggested by the following overview:

1   People who work on jobs high on the core job characteristics are more motivated, satisfied, and productive than people who work on jobs that score low on these characteristics. The same is true for absenteeism, although less strongly so.

2   Responses to jobs high in objective motivating potential are more positive for people who have strong needs for growth than for people with weak needs for growth. The moderating effect of an individual's need for growth occurs both at the link between the job dimensions and the psychological states and at the link between the psychological states and the outcome measures, as shown in Figure 19-1. (This moderating effect is not, however, obtained for absenteeism.)

3   The job characteristics operate *through* the psychological states in influencing the outcome variables, as predicted by the model, rather than influencing the outcomes directly. Two anomalies have been identified, however: (1) results involving the feedback dimension are in some cases less strong than for those obtained for the other dimensions (perhaps in part because individuals receive feedback at work from many sources—not just the job), and (2) the linkage between autonomy and experienced responsibility does not operate exactly as specified by the model in affecting the outcome variables (Hackman & Oldham, 1976).

Diagnostic Use of the Model

The job characteristics model was designed so that each major class of variables (objective job characteristics, mediating psychological states, strength of the individual's need for growth, and work motivation and satisfaction) can be directly measured in actual work situations. Such measurements are obtained using the Job Diagnostic Survey (JDS), which is described in detail elsewhere (Hackman & Oldham, 1975). The major intended uses of the JDS are (1) to diagnose existing jobs before planned work redesign, and (2) to evaluate the effects of work redesign—for example, to determine which job dimensions did and did not change, to assess the impact of the changes on the motivation and satisfaction of employees, and to test for any possible alterations after the change in the need for growth of people whose jobs were redesigned.

In the paragraphs to follow, several steps are presented that might be followed by a change agent in carrying out a diagnosis using the JDS.

Step 1: Are Motivation and Satisfaction Really Problems? Sometimes organizations undertake job enrichment or work redesign to improve work motivation and satisfaction when in fact the real problem with work performance lies elsewhere—for example, in the equipment or technology of the job. It is important, therefore, to examine the level of employees' motivation and satisfaction at an early stage in a job diagnosis. If motivation and satisfaction are problems, and are accompanied by documented problems in work performance, absenteeism, or turnover as revealed by independent organizational indices, the change agent would continue to step 2. If not, the agent presumably would look to other aspects of the work situation (e.g., the technology, the workflow) to identify and understand the reasons for the problem which gave rise to the diagnostic activity.

Step 2: Is the Job Low in Motivating Potential? To answer this question, the change agent would examine the Motivating Potential

Score of the target job, and compare it with the MPS scores of other jobs to determine whether or not the *job itself* is a probable cause of the motivational problems documented in step 1. If the job turns out to be low on MPS, he would continue to step 3; if it scores high, he would look for other reasons for the motivational difficulties (e.g., the pay plan, the nature of supervision, and so on).

Step 3: What Specific Aspects of the Job are Causing the Difficulty? This step involves examination of the job on each of the five core job dimensions, to pinpoint the specific strengths and weaknesses of the job as it currently exists. It is useful at this stage to construct a profile of the target job, to make visually apparent where improvements need to be made. An illustrative profile for two jobs (one "good" job and one job needing improvement) is shown in Figure 19-2.

Job A is an engineering maintenance job, and is high on all of the core dimensions; the MPS of this job is very high: 260.[1] Job enrichment would not be recommended for this job; if employees working on the job are unproductive and unhappy, the reasons probably have little to do with the design of the work itself.

Job B, on the other hand, has many problems. This job involves the routine and repetitive processing of checks in a bank. The MPS of 30—which is quite low—would be even lower if it were not for the moderately high task significance of the job. (Task significance is moderately high because the people are handling large amounts of other people's money, and their efforts potentially have important consequences for the unseen clients.) The job provides the individuals with very little direct feedback about how effectively they are performing; the employees have little autonomy in how they go about doing the job; and the

---

[1]MPS scores can range from 1 to 343. The average is about 125.

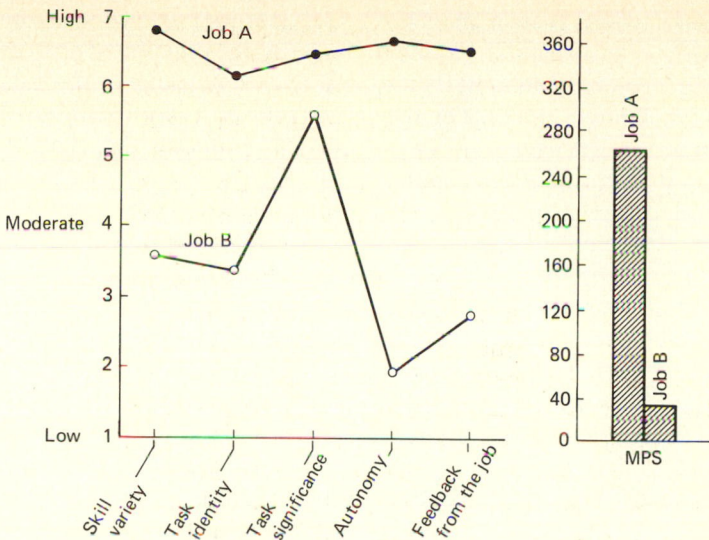

Figure 19-2 JDS profile of a "good" job and a "bad" job.

job is moderately low in both skill variety and task identity.

For Job B, then, there is plenty of room for improvement, and many avenues to consider in planning job changes. For still other jobs, the avenues for change may turn out to be considerably more specific: for example, feedback and autonomy may be reasonably high, but one or more of the core dimensions which contribute to the experienced meaningfulness of the work (i.e., skill variety, task identity, and task significance) may be low. In such a case, attention would turn to ways to increase the standing of the job on these latter three dimensions.

Step 4: How Ready Are the Employees for Change? Once it has been documented that there is need for improvement in the focal job, and the particularly troublesome aspects of the job have been identified, then it is appropriate to begin planning the specific action steps which will be taken to enrich the job. An important factor in such planning is determining the strength of the employees' needs for growth, since employees whose needs for growth are strong should respond more readily to job enrichment than employees whose needs are weak. The measure of the need for growth provided by the JDS can be helpful in identifying which employees should be among the first to have jobs changed (i.e., those whose needs for growth are strong), and how such changes should be introduced (e.g., perhaps with more caution for individuals whose needs for growth are weak).

Step 5: What Special Problems and Opportunities Are Present in the Existing Work System? Before undertaking actual job changes, it is always advisable to search for any special roadblocks that may exist in the organizational unit as it currently exists, and for special opportunities that may be built upon in the change program.

Frequently of special importance in this regard is the level of *satisfaction* employees currently experience with various aspects of their organizational life. For example, the JDS provides measures of satisfaction with pay, job security, co-workers, and supervision. If the diagnosis reveals high dissatisfaction in one or more of these areas, then it may be very difficult to initiate and maintain a successful job redesign project (Oldham, 1976; Oldham, Hackman & Pearce, 1976). On the other hand, if satisfaction with supervision is especially high, then it might be wise to build an especially central role for supervisors in the initiation and management of the change process.

Other examples could be given as well. The point is simply that such supplementary measures (especially those having to do with aspects of employee satisfaction) may be helpful in highlighting special problems and opportunities that deserve explicit recognition and attention as part of the diagnosis of an existing work system.

Principles for Enriching Jobs

The core job dimensions specified in the job-characteristics model are tied directly to a set of action principles for redesigning jobs (Hackman, Oldham, Janson & Purdy, 1975; Walters & Associates, 1975). As shown in Figure 19-3, these principles specify what types of changes in jobs are most likely to lead to improvements in each of the five core job dimensions, and thereby to an increase in the motivating potential of the job as a whole.

Principle 1: Forming Natural Work Units A critical step in the design of any job is the decision about how the work is to be distributed among the people who do it. Consider, for example, a typing pool—consisting of one su-

pervisor and ten typists—that does all the typing for one division of an organization. Jobs are delivered in rough draft or dictated form to the supervisor, who distributes them as evenly as possible among the typists. In such circumstances the individual letters, reports, and other tasks performed by a given typist in one day or week are randomly assigned. There is no basis for identifying with the work or the person or department for whom it is performed, or for placing any personal value upon it.

By contrast, creating natural units of work increases employees' "ownership" of the work, and therefore improves the chances that employees will view it as meaningful and important rather than as irrelevant and boring. In creating natural units of work, one must first identify what the basic work items are. In the typing pool example, that might be "pages to be typed." Then these items are grouped into natural and meaningful categories. For example, each typist might be assigned continuing responsibility for all work requested by a single department or by several smaller departments. Instead of typing one section of a large report, the individual will type the entire piece of work, with knowledge of exactly what the total outcome of the work is. Furthermore, over a period of time the typist will develop a growing sense of how the work affects co-workers or customers who receive the completed product. Thus, as shown in Figure 19-3, forming natural units of work increases two of the core job dimensions that

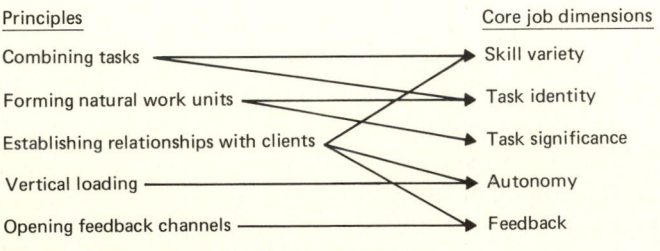

Figure 19-3   Principles for changing jobs.

contribute to experienced meaningfulness—task identity and task significance.

It is still important that work be distributed so that the system as a whole operates efficiently, of course, and workloads must be arranged so that they are approximately equal among employees. The principle of natural work units simply requires that these traditional criteria be supplemented so that, insofar as possible, the tasks that arrive at an employee's work station form an identifiable and meaningful whole.

Principle 2: Combining Tasks The very existence of a pool made up entirely of persons whose sole function is typing, reflects a fractionalization of jobs that sometimes can lead to such hidden costs as high absenteeism and turnover, extra supervisory time, and so on. The principle of combining tasks is based on the assumption that such costs often can be reduced by simply taking existing and fractionalized tasks and putting them back together again to form a new and larger module of work. At the Medfield, Massachusetts plant of Corning Glass Works, for example, the job of assembling laboratory hotplates was redesigned by combining a number of previously separate tasks. After the change, each hotplate was assembled from start to finish by one operator, instead of going through several separate operations performed by different people.

Combining tasks (like forming natural work units) contributes in two ways to the experienced meaningfulness of the work. First, task identity is increased. The hotplate assembler, for example, can see and identify with a finished product ready for shipment—rather than a nearly invisible junction of solder. Moreover, as more tasks are combined into a single worker's job, the individual must use a greater variety of skills in performing the job, further increasing the meaningfulness of the work.

Principle 3: Establishing Relationships with Clients By establishing direct relationships between workers and their clients, jobs often can be improved in three ways. First, feedback increases because additional opportunities are created for the employees to receive direct praise or criticism of their work outputs. Second, skill variety may increase, because of the need to develop and exercise one's interpersonal skills in managing and maintaining the relationship with the client. Finally, autonomy will increase to the degree that individuals are given real personal responsibility for deciding how to manage their relationships with the people who receive the outputs of their work.

Creating relationships with clients can be viewed as a three-step process: (1) identification of who the client actually is; (2) establishing the most direct contact possible between the worker and the client; and (3) establishing criteria and procedures so that the client can judge the quality of the product or service received and relay his judgments directly back to the worker. Especially important (and, in many cases, difficult to achieve) is identification of the specific criteria by which the work output is assessed by the client—and ensuring that both the worker and the client understand these criteria and agree with them.

Principle 4: Vertical Loading In vertical loading, the intent is to partially close the gap between the "doing" and the "controlling" aspects of the job. Thus, when a job is vertically loaded, responsibilities and controls that formerly were reserved for management are given to the employee as part of the job. Among ways this might be achieved are the following:

Giving job incumbents responsibility for deciding on work methods, and for advising or helping train less experienced workers.

Providing increased freedom in time management, including decisions about when to start and stop work, when to take a break, and how to assign work priorities.

Encouraging workers to do their own trouble-shooting and manage work crises, rather than calling immediately for a supervisor.

Providing workers with increased knowledge of the financial aspects of the job and the organization, and increased control over budgetary matters that affect their own work.

When a job is vertically loaded, it inevitably increases in *autonomy*. And, as shown in Figure 19-1, this should lead to increased feelings of personal responsibility and accountability for the work outcomes.

Principle 5: Opening Feedback Channels   In virtually all jobs there are ways to open channels of feedback to individuals to help them learn not only how well they are performing their jobs, but also whether their performance is improving, deteriorating, or remaining at a constant level. While there are various sources from which information about performance can come, it usually is advantageous for workers to learn about their performance *directly as they do the job*—rather than from management on an occasional basis.

Feedback provided by the job itself is more immediate and private than feedback provided by its supervisor, and can also increase workers' feelings of personal control over their work. Moreover, it avoids many of the potentially disruptive interpersonal problems which can develop when workers can find out how they are doing only by means of direct messages or subtle cues from the boss.

Exactly what should be done to open channels for feedback from the job varies from job to job and organization to organization. In many cases, the changes involve simply removing existing blocks which isolate the individual from naturally occurring data about performance, rather than generating entirely new feedback mechanisms. For example:

Establishing direct relationships with clients (discussed above) often removes blocks between the worker and natural external sources of data about the work.

Quality control in many organizations often eliminates a natural source of feedback, because all quality checks are done by people other than the individuals responsible for the work. In such cases, feedback to the workers, if there is any, may be belated and diluted. By placing most quality-control functions in the hands of workers themselves, the quantity and quality of data available to them about their own performance will dramatically increase.

Tradition and established procedure in many organizations dictate that records about performance be kept by a supervisor and transmitted up (not down) the organizational hierarchy. Sometimes supervisors even check the work and correct any errors themselves. The worker who made the error never knows it occurred and is therefore denied the very information which can enhance both internal work motivation and the technical adequacy of his performance. In many cases, it is possible to provide standard summaries of performance records directly to the workers (and perhaps also to their superiors), thereby giving employees personally and regularly the data they need to improve their effectiveness.

Computers and other automated machines sometimes can be used to provide individuals with data now blocked from them. Many clerical operations, for example, are now performed on computer consoles. These consoles often can be programed to provide the clerk with immediate feedback in the form of a CRT display or a printout indicating that an error has been made. Some systems even have been programed to provide the operator with a positive feedback message when a period of error-free performance has been sustained.

Conclusion   The principles for redesigning jobs reviewed above, while illustrative of the kinds of changes that can be made to improve the jobs of individuals in organizations, obviously are not exhaustive. They were selected for attention here because of the links (Figure

19-3) between the principles and the core job dimensions in the motivational model presented earlier. Other principles for enriching jobs (which, although often similar to those presented here, derive from alternative conceptual frameworks) are presented by Ford (1969), Glaser (1975), Herzberg (1974), and Katzell and Yankelovich (1975, chap. 6).

DESIGNING WORK FOR TEAMS

Often it is easier or more appropriate, given the nature of the work to be done and the organizational circumstances under which it is to be done, to design work for interacting teams rather than for individuals working alone. In such cases, the ultimate aim generally is similar to that sought when individual job enrichment is carried out: that is, to improve the quality of the work experience of the people involved, and simultaneously to increase the quality and quantity of the work produced. The difference is that the work is defined and implemented as a *group* task, rather than as an interconnected set of individual tasks. Because of this, a larger chunk of work can be included within the boundaries of the task, thereby increasing the intrinsic meaningfulness of the work. Moreover, the possibility is increased for the development of close, socially satisfying work relationships among team members. Such relationships are highly valued by many people, but difficult or impossible to achieve by means of redesign of individual jobs in such work settings as assembly lines, where individual work stations may be fixed and so widely separated that meaningful social interaction with others is (for all practical purposes) precluded.

Until relatively recently, most work design for teams has been carried out from the perspective of sociotechnical systems theory, and has involved the creation of autonomous or semi-autonomous work groups. Specific arrangements (e.g., how the group task itself is designed, the size and composition of the work group, the nature of the reward system) have varied from project to project, but the following attributes are characteristic of most autonomous work groups:[2]

1 A "whole" task for the group, in which the mission of the group is sufficiently identifiable and significant that members find the work of the group meaningful.

2 Workers who each have a number of the skills required for completion of the group task, thereby increasing the flexibility of the group in carrying out the task. When individuals do not have a robust repertoire of skills initially, procedures are developed to encourage cross-training among members.

3 Autonomy for the group to make decisions about the methods by which the work is carried out, the scheduling of various activities, the assignment of different individuals to different tasks, and (sometimes) the selection of new group members.

4 Compensation based on the performance of the group as a whole, rather than on the contributions of individual group members.

It should be emphasized that these four ingredients are simply summary statements of the kinds of changes that often are made when work is redesigned for interacting teams. They do not represent the only way to design work for groups, nor are these ingredients necessarily the most appropriate ones for any given instance. Therefore, it may be useful to step back from specific change principles and attempt to identify the major *general* criteria for the design of work for teams—and then to explore alternative strategies for attempting to achieve those criteria.

Design Criteria for Interacting Work Groups

The two criteria listed below appear to be the minimum requirements for the design of interacting work teams if high productivity by the

[2]See, for example, Bucklow (1966), Davis (1966, p. 44), Davis and Trist (1974), Gulowsen (1972, pp. 375–378), and Trist, Higgin, Murray, and Pollock (1963, chap. 9).

team and the satisfaction of its members are to be achieved simultaneously.

1. The team itself should be a cohesive group, in which members feel committed to the goals of the group, and in which they can experience significant personal satisfaction through their interactions with teammates.

In a highly cohesive group, members greatly value the rewards (usually interpersonal) that fellow members can provide. This means that the quality of the social experience of members in cohesive groups is likely to be high rather than low. It also means that cohesive groups usually have considerable leverage in enforcing member compliance with group norms. That is, since members of cohesive groups strongly value the rewards controlled by their peers, they are especially likely to engage in behavior that is congruent with group norms. Failure to do so can result in those rewards being made unavailable to them (e.g., being "frozen out") or can lead other group members to negatively sanction their actions (Hackman, 1976).

The problem is that while cohesive groups have been shown to generate a high degree of uniformity of behavior in terms of group norms, the *direction* of those norms is unrelated to the level of cohesiveness of the group (Berkowitz, 1954; Schachter, Ellertson, McBride, & Gregory, 1951; Seashore, 1954). Sometimes highly cohesive groups enforce a norm of low performance; at other times they encourage and support members' efforts toward high performance. Relatively little is known about what factors determine whether group norms will encourage high or low performance (e.g., Lawler & Cammann, 1972; Vroom, 1969, pp. 226–227). It is necessary, therefore, to propose an additional criterion for the design of work teams in organizations.

2. The environment of the work group, including its task, must be such that the group norms that emerge and are enforced are consistent with the two aims of high productivity and satisfying interpersonal relationships.

Approaches to Work Design for Interacting Groups

Meeting the two design criteria identified above requires, at minimum, attention to (1) the composition and dynamics of the group itself, (2) reward contingencies in the organizational environment, and (3) the structure of the group task. These matters are explored below.

Design and Maintenance of the Group qua Group It is important that members of an interacting work team be able to experience themselves as part of a group that is *psychologically meaningful* to them. Usually this requires that the group be moderately small (usually less than fifteen members, although apparently successful autonomous work groups of larger size have been reported), and that members occupy a single workplace (or at least contiguous workplaces with easy access to one another). Merely calling a set of people a "group" for reasons other than the nature of their relationships with each other (e.g., a set of flight attendants who have the same supervisor but who literally fly all over the country and rarely see one another) does not meet the conditions for creation of an effective work team.

Moreover, while reasonably close and meaningful interpersonal relationships can be important to the success of interacting work teams, group process interventions (e.g., "team building") that focus *exclusively* on relationships among group members—or on the social climate of the group as a whole—should be used with caution. Direct interpersonal interventions can be quite powerful in altering social behavior in a group, and for this reason they may be very useful in increasing the capability and willingness of members to share with one another special skills that are needed for work on the group task. Yet research also shows that when such interventions are used alone, the group's task effectiveness rarely is enhanced (and often suffers) as a result (cf. Hackman & Morris, 1975; Herold, in press). Thus, while process interventions can be of great use as part of a broader intervention package aimed at creating effective work teams, total reliance on such interventions appears inappropriate if the goal is to work toward simultaneous improvement of the social experience of the members *and* their collective task productivity.

Design of Environmental Contingencies The way the organizational environment of the group is arranged can affect whether or not it is in the best interest of group members to work together effectively and, indeed, whether or not it is *possible* for them to do so. Especially important in this regard are the compensation system and the role of the first-line supervisor.

In almost every case in which autonomous work groups have been successfully created in organizations, pay systems have been arranged so that members were paid on a basis of the performance of the group as a whole, rather than in terms of the level of performance of individual employees. Moving to a group-based compensation system increases the chances that internal cooperation and cohesiveness will increase as members work together to obtain the group-level rewards. Moreover, dysfunctional group interaction that grows from the fear (or the fact) of pay inequities among members should diminish when compensation is tied directly to the output of the group as a whole. It should be noted, however, that simply moving to a group-level compensation system does *not* eliminate the possibility of less than optimal productivity norms. When group members mistrust management, for example, norms enforcing low productivity may emerge to protect the group against possible changes of performance standards by management. Thus, while group-level compensation plans play an important part in the design of work for

interacting teams, they in no way guarantee high group productivity.

Also critical to the design of work for teams is the new role that first-line supervisors play under such arrangements. In many applications, the supervisor moves from having day-to-day (even minute-to-minute) responsibility for the work behavior and productivity of individual employees to a role that primarily involves managing the *boundaries* of the group—not what goes on within those boundaries (Taylor, 1971). Thus, the supervisor assists the group in liaison with other groups, and may serve as the advocate of the group in discussion with higher management, but routine decision-making about the work and management of work crises is left to the group. Under such conditions, group members should experience substantially more ownership of their work activities and output, thereby creating the conditions required for members to experience collective responsibility for—and commitment to—their shared task.

Design of the Group Task One of the greatest determinants of whether a group develops a norm of high or low productivity is the design of the group task itself. What task characteristics are likely to prompt high group commitment to effective performance? As a start, the five core dimensions used in the job characteristics model of individual work motivation would seem useful (i.e., skill variety, task identity, task significance, autonomy, and feedback). There is no reason why such dimensions could not be applied to the analysis of group tasks just as they are to individual tasks.

If group tasks were designed to be high on these or similar job dimensions, then an increase in the task-relevant motivation of group members would be expected—and, over time, group norms about productivity should become consistent with the increased motivation of individual group members. Yet, such positive outcomes should come about only (1) if the individual group members identify with and feel commitment to the group as a whole (it is, after all, a *group* task), and (2) if the internal process of the group facilitates and reinforces (rather than impairs) concerted action toward shared group goals.

The core job dimensions have little to offer toward the creation of these two conditions. How, for example, could a group task be designed so that all members see it as providing high autonomy—and therefore experience substantial *personal* responsibility for the outcomes of the *group*? Moreover, given that it is now well documented that how group tasks are designed affects not only the motivation of group members, but also the patterns of social interaction that develop among them (Hackman & Morris, 1975), how can group tasks be structured so that they prompt task-effective rather than dysfunctional interaction among members?

Such questions have no simple answers. And while task design *per se* potentially can contribute to their solution, the issues raised also are affected by the environmental contingencies that are operative, and by the design and composition of the group itself. Thus, once again, it must be concluded that no single approach can create an effective design for work to be done by interacting teams. Instead, such a goal requires simultaneous use of a number of different handles for change—some of which have to do with the group, some with the task, and some with the broader organizational context.

Group versus Individual Task Design: Which When?

Choices for designing work for individuals or for groups are complex, and in many cases depend on factors idiosyncratic to a given situation. In general, however, a group-based design seems indicated when one or more of the following conditions is present:

1 When the product, service, or technology is such that meaningful individual work is not realistically possible (e.g., when a large piece of heavy equipment is being produced). In such cases it often is possible for a group to take autonomous responsibility for an entire product or service—while the only possible job design for individuals would involve small segments of the work (cf. Walton, 1975).

2 When the technology or physical work setting is such that high interdependence among workers is required. For example, Susman (1970) has suggested that one effect of increased automation (especially in continuous process production) is to increase interdependence among workers. The creation of autonomous work groups under such circumstances would seem to be a rather natural extension of the imperatives of the technology itself. When, on the other hand, there are no required interdependencies (e.g., telephone installers who operate their own trucks, coordinating only with a foreman or dispatcher), then there would seem to be no real basis on which meaningful work teams could be formed, and enrichment of individual jobs might be a better alternative.

3 When individuals have strong social needs—and the enrichment of individual jobs would run significant risk of breaking up existing groups of workers that provide social satisfactions to their members. In such cases, designing work for teams would capitalize on the needs of employees, whereas individual-oriented job enrichment might require that individuals give up important social satisfactions to obtain a better job (Reif & Luthans, 1972).

4 When the overall motivating potential of employees' jobs would be expected to be *considerably* higher if the work were arranged as a group task rather than as a set of individual tasks. Probably in most cases the standing of a job on the core dimensions would increase if the job were designed as a group task, simply because a larger piece of work can be done by a group than by an individual. This should not, however, automatically tilt the decision toward group work design—there are numerous interpersonal factors that must be attended to in effectively designing work for interacting groups. Sometimes the risk or effort required to deal with such factors may make it more appropriate to opt for individual task design, even though a group task might be expected to be somewhat better *as a task* than would be any of the individual tasks.

Cautions in Designing Work for Groups

In conclusion, three caveats about the design of work for groups are suggested:

1 Existing evidence suggests that the work must provide group members with *substantial* autonomy if they are to experience high responsibility for it. Just as "pseudo-participation" in organizations may be worse than no participation at all, so it is that autonomous work groups should not be formed unless there is reasonable assurance that the result will not be a potentially frustrating state of "pseudo-autonomy." This, of course, requires careful attention to issues of management and supervision, to ensure that managers are both willing and able to provide the group with sufficient real autonomy to carry out the proposed group task (cf. Gulowsen, 1972).

2 The needs of employees who will make up the groups must be carefully attended to, because work in interacting teams on a complex task will not be satisfying or motivating to all people. Optimally, the need of group members for both social interaction and growth should be rather high. If the social needs of group members are high but their needs for growth are low, then there is risk that the group members will use the group solely as a source of social satisfaction. Even if the task were very high in objective motivating potential, members might find the group so much more involving than the task that productivity would suffer. When, on the other hand, members have a high need for growth but low needs for social interaction, then it might be better to consider designing the work for individuals, if technology permits. If employees have both low social needs and low needs for growth, then prospects for creating teams in which members work together effectively and productively on a challenging task would appear very dim indeed.

3 Finally, it should be noted that virtually all of the above discussion has focused on characteristics of groups and of tasks that are likely to generate high *motivation* to perform the task effectively. For some group tasks, the level of motivation (or effort) of group members is not critical to the success of the group; instead, the effectiveness of the performance varies simply with the level of knowledge and skill of the members, or with the performance strategies utilized by the group (cf. Hackman & Morris, 1975). In such circumstances, the attributes of the group, the task, and the environment that would be required for a high degree of group effectiveness would be quite different from those proposed here.

REFERENCES

Berkowitz, L. Group standards, cohesiveness and productivity. *Human Relations*, 1954, **7**, 509–519.

Bucklow, M. A new role for the work group. *Administrative Science Quarterly*, 1966, **11**, 59–78.

Davis, L. E. The design of jobs. *Industrial Relations*, 1966, **6**, 21–45.

Davis, L. E., & Trist, E. L. Improving the quality of work life: Sociotechnical case studies. In J. O'Toole (Ed.), *Work and the quality of life*. Cambridge, Mass.: MIT Press, 1974.

Ford, R. N. *Motivation through the work itself*. New York: American Management Association, 1969.

Glaser, E. M. *Improving the quality of worklife . . . And in the process, improving productivity*. Los Angeles: Human Interaction Research Institute, 1975.

Gulowsen, J. A measure of work group autonomy. In L. E. Davis & J. C. Taylor (Eds.), *Design of jobs*. Middlesex, England: Penguin, 1972.

Hackman, J. R. Group influences on individuals in organizations. In M. D. Dunnette (Ed.), *Handbook of industrial and organizational psychology*. Chicago: Rand McNally, 1976.

Hackman, J. R., & Lawler, E. E. Employee reactions to job characteristics. *Journal of Applied Psychology Monograph*, 1971, **55**, 259–286.

Hackman, J. R., & Morris, C. G. Group tasks, group interaction process, and group performance effectiveness: A review and proposed integration. In L. Berkowitz (Ed.), *Advances in experimental social psychology* (Vol. 8). New York: Academic Press, 1975.

Hackman, J. R., & Oldham, G. R. Development of the Job Diagnostic Survey. *Journal of Applied Psychology*, 1975, **60**, 159–170.

Hackman, J. R., Oldham, G. R. Motivation through the design of work: Test of a theory. *Organizational Behavior and Human Performance*, 1976, **16**, 250–279.

Hackman, J. R., Oldham, G., Janson, R., & Purdy, K. A new strategy for job enrichment. *California Management Review*, 1975, **17** (4), 57–71.

Herold, D. M. Group effectiveness as a function of task-appropriate interaction processes. In J. L. Livingstone (Ed.), *Managerial accounting: The behavioral foundations.* Columbus, Ohio: Grid Publishers, in press.

Herzberg, F. The wise old Turk. *Harvard Business Review*, 1974, **52**, 70–80.

Katzell, R. A., Yankelovich, D., et al. *Work, productivity and job satisfaction.* New York: The Psychological Corporation, 1975.

Lawler, E. E., & Cammann, C. What makes a work group successful? In A. J. Marrow (Ed.), *The failure of success.* New York: Amacom, 1972.

Lawler, E. E., & Hall, D. T. The relationship of job characteristics to job involvement, satisfaction and intrinsic motivation. *Journal of Applied Psychology*, 1970, **54**, 305–312.

Oldham, G. R. Job characteristics and internal motivation: The moderating effect of interpersonal and individual variables. *Human Relations*, 1976, **29**, 559–569.

Oldham, G. R., Hackman, J. R., & Pearce, J. L. Conditions under which employees respond positively to enriched work. *Journal of Applied Psychology*, 1976, **61**, 395–403.

Reif, W. E., & Luthans, F. Does job enrichment really pay off? *California Management Review*, 1972, **15**, 30–37.

Schachter, S., Ellertson, N., McBride, D., & Gregory, D. An experimental test of cohesiveness and productivity. *Human Relations*, 1951, **4**, 229–238.

Seashore, S. *Group cohesiveness in the industrial work group.* Ann Arbor: University of Michigan, 1954.

Susman, G. I. The impact of automation on work group autonomy and task specialization. *Human Relations*, 1970, **23**, 567–577.

Taylor, J. C. Some effects of technology in organizational change. *Human Relations*, 1971, **24**, 105–123.

Trist, E. L., Higgin, G. W., Murray, H., & Pollock, A. B. *Organizational choice.* London: Tavistock, 1963.

Vroom, V. H. Industrial social psychology. In G. Lindzey & E. Aronson (Eds.), *Handbook of social psychology* (2d ed.). Reading, Mass.: Addison-Wesley, 1969.

Walters, R. W., & Associates. *Job enrichment for results.* Reading, Mass.: Addison-Wesley, 1975.

Walton, R. E. From Hawthorne to Topeka and Kalmar. In E. L. Cass & F. G. Zimmer (Eds.), *Man and work in society.* New York: Van Nostrand-Reinhold, 1975.

Reading 20

Who Wants Job Enrichment?

John P. Wanous

People are different. They have different motives and goals for the jobs they hold. Nevertheless, such an obvious assertion as this is far too often forgotten when it comes to climbing aboard a currently fashionable managerial practice. When a new technique for better organization begins to show promise, it runs the risk of being implemented somewhat indiscriminately on large numbers of employees.

Job enrichment is a good case in point. This technique has a track record of producing substantial dollar savings in a wide variety of situations, but there have been failures.

The premise of this article is that some of these failures could have been avoided with currently existing behavioral science technology. The main problem has not been with the theory of how to change work procedures. Rather, the problem is that job enrichment has been thrust upon the *wrong types of people.* Future failures will continue to crop up unless *both the individual and the job* are considered. We need to assess people as well as jobs when considering any effort at job enrichment. Currently, we know much more about the characteristics of *jobs* that make them enriched, but far less about the characteristics of *people* who really want such jobs.

Despite this imbalance, the situation is not at all hopeless. My review of the research concerning individual differences relevant for job enrichment revealed the following:

- The most successful cases of job enrichment were those where the employees themselves had high desires for jobs with increased variety, responsibility, challenge, feedback, and so forth.

- It is possible to measure pertinent individual differences quickly and inexpensively, and obtain positive results by "matching" the right people to newly enriched jobs.

- Currently, there are three ways to identify those individuals who want job enrichment.

- All three techniques have been used successfully, but there are important differences among them. They cannot be considered completely substitutable for one another.

- Only one research study to date has used all three techniques simultaneously, so that a direct comparison could be made among them.

MATCHING UP INDIVIDUAL NEEDS AND JOB CHARACTERISTICS

The accumulated research evidence clearly shows that both individual and job characteristics need to be "matched." The individual characteristics relevant for job enrichment are sometimes called "needs," "desires," or "motives." Regardless of what terminology is used, the important point is that—psychologically speaking—people differ. Not everyone shares a high desire for the challenge and responsibility which come with job enrichment. Table 20-1 shows the consequences of both matches and mismatches between employees and jobs.[1]

[1]This table is adapted from one prepared by L. W. Porter, E. E. Lawler III, and J. R. Hackman, *Behavior in Organizations.* New York: McGraw-Hill, 1975.

Table 20-1 Matching Individuals and Jobs

Degree of job enrichment	Intensity of desire for job enrichment	
	High	**Low**
Enriched	"Match" 1 Performance quality is high. 2 Satisfaction is high. 3 Absenteeism and turnover are low.	"Mismatch" 1 Employee is overwhelmed and possibly confused. 2 Performance is poor. 3 Absenteeism and turnover are high.
Simple	"Mismatch" 1 Employees feel underutilized. 2 Job satisfaction is low. 3 Absenteeism and turnover are high.	"Match" 1 Employees can be motivated by pay incentives in the absence of intrinsic motivation. 2 Performance is high.

Measuring Desires for Job Enrichment

Within the last five to ten years behavioral research in organizations has produced three different techniques for measuring the differences among employees in their desires for job enrichment. These could be considered relatively new, but actually have coexisted almost as long as job enrichment. Despite this coexistence, the theory and practice of *job enrichment* has received more attention then the theory and method of differentiating among employees who will perform well and be better satisfied on enriched jobs.

The three ways to assess employees who want job enrichment are: (1) demographics, (2) work values, and (3) need strength. The theory behind each of these is described first,

followed by an illustration of the technique, and finally by the advantages and pitfalls of each one.

Demographics   This method of assessment uses two types of demographic information which are easily available: urban versus rural location and white-color versus blue-collar work (Table 20-2).

In the cell representing "urban–blue-collar" are those employees most likely to be *alienated* from "middle-class" working norms, sometimes referred to as the "Protestant work ethic," or simply the "work ethic." These are employees *least* likely to be motivated by job enrichment approaches which offer increased challenge, responsibility, participation, and

Table 20-2 Demographic Method

Type of job	Location: (1) Plant or (2) Area where the person grew up	
	Rural	**Urban**
Blue-collar	O.K.	Alienated
White-collar	O.K.	O.K.

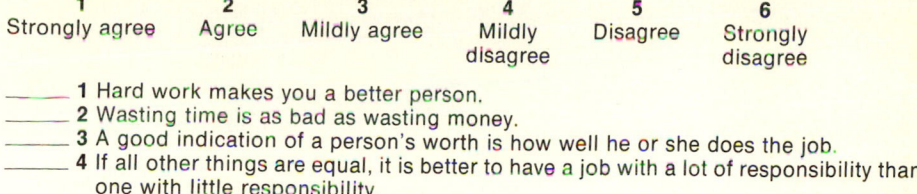

Please indicate your agreement or disagreement with each of the statements below. There are no right or wrong answers. The important thing is to state how you feel about each item. Please use the 6-point scale to rate your agreement or disagreement.

1	**2**	**3**	**4**	**5**	**6**
Strongly agree	Agree	Mildly agree	Mildly disagree	Disagree	Strongly disagree

_____ **1** Hard work makes you a better person.
_____ **2** Wasting time is as bad as wasting money.
_____ **3** A good indication of a person's worth is how well he or she does the job.
_____ **4** If all other things are equal, it is better to have a job with a lot of responsibility than one with little responsibility.

Figure 20-1 Work-values method.

feedback. They are most likely to be workers who seek satisfaction *off* the job, believing that "work is work" and *not* a major source of satisfaction in one's life. On the other hand, those in the remaining three cells can be included in efforts at job enrichment, because they presumably believe in the work ethic.

Since the development of this taxonomy in 1968,[2] researchers have discovered an ambiguity in how to define the urban–rural difference. Results congruent with this classification scheme have been found using both plant location and the area where employees grew up (i.e., where they were "socialized"). In many cases, these areas are the same (i.e., people grow up and go to work nearby). This ambiguity has plagued some efforts to use this approach.

The major advantages of the demographic approach are its simplicity, ease of implementation, and low cost. The advantage of simplicity is double-edged, however. The demographic method is admittedly a crude approximation for determining the basic work values of employees. As such it will always be more error-prone than a more direct method for measuring the work values of employees. However, the advantages must be balanced against the drawbacks. On the one hand, this method is very unobtrusive. Employees would not even realize they were being considered for possible work changes, and expectations would not be unduly raised.

Work Values This method is similar to the previous one: i.e., both attempt to measure the basic work values of employees. While the demographic approach does this indirectly, the work-values method is straightforward. A short questionnaire is used to identify persons who strongly believe in the (Protestant) work ethic. To date, two such instruments have been developed, one of which is shown in Figure 20-1.[3]

The questionnaire method is a very direct way to get at the basic work values of employees. However, the time required of employees to complete the questionnaire must be considered, and there is always the possibility that some people will fake their answers. Using a questionnaire may also sensitize employees to impending changes. As a consequence, the hopes of individuals may be raised beyond the organization's capacity to fulfill them.

[2]C. L. Hulin and M. R. Blood, Job enlargement, individual differences, and worker responses. *Psychological Bulletin*, 1968, **69**, 41–55.

[3]The longer version, not shown, is by S. Wollack, J. G. Goodale, J. Wijting, and P. C. Smith, Development of the survey of work values, *Journal of Applied Psychology*, 1971, **55**, 331–338. The shorter one, shown here, is by M. Blood, Work values and job satisfaction. *Journal of Applied Psychology*, 1969, **53**, 456–459.

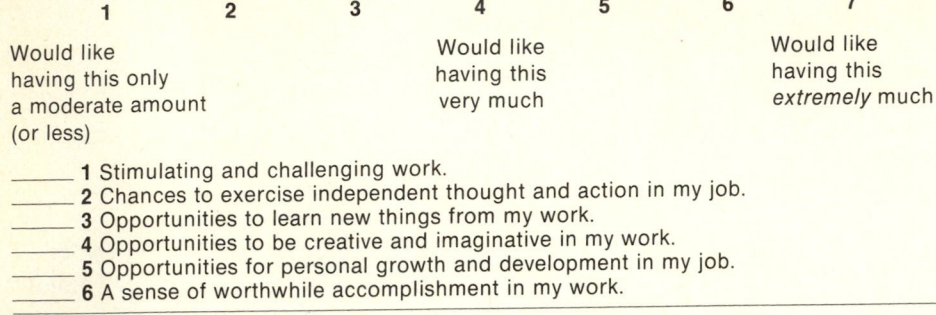

Listed below are a number of characteristics which could be presented on any job. People differ about how much they would like to have each one present in their own jobs. We are interested in learning *how much you personally would like* to have each one present in your job.

Using the scale below, please indicate the *degree* to which you *would like* to have each characteristic present in your job.

1	2	3	4	5	6	7

Would like
having this only
a moderate amount
(or less)

Would like
having this
very much

Would like
having this
extremely much

_____ 1 Stimulating and challenging work.
_____ 2 Chances to exercise independent thought and action in my job.
_____ 3 Opportunities to learn new things from my work.
_____ 4 Opportunities to be creative and imaginative in my work.
_____ 5 Opportunities for personal growth and development in my job.
_____ 6 A sense of worthwhile accomplishment in my work.

Figure 20-2   Need strength method.

Need Strength   This procedure also uses a questionnaire, but different and more specific types of questions are asked. The theory behind this approach is that the most pertinent information concerns the *specific job needs* of people. In contrast to measuring *general* work values, this method asks individuals to rate the *strength* of their *specific desires* for job characteristics. Included are those typically associated with highly enriched jobs; a few representative items are shown in Figure 20-2.[4]

The need strength approach has been used more than the work values technique, and has been found to be highly effective in correctly identifying employees who really want job enrichment. Thus far it has been employed in at least five published accounts, involving more than 100 different jobs and 2,000 people.

Which Approach Is Most Effective?

The whole point of measuring these individual differences is identifying those people who are most likely to be motivated by enriched jobs, and who will be satisfied with increases in responsibility, challenge, and so forth. Thus, the "test" of which method is most effective rests on an assessment of the *relationship* between *job characteristics* and *personal reactions* to the characteristics. If a particular technique "works," then those who want job enrichment should experience a strong relationship between enriching job characteristics and their satisfaction with those characteristics, as shown in Figure 20-3.

Surprisingly, only one research study used all three simultaneously so that a direct comparison could be made among the various methods.[5] Using a group of eighty telephone operators, all three methods were used to divide the total group into good and poor

[4]The rationale for selecting the job characteristics to be included was developed by J. R. Hackman and E. E. Lawler III, in their article Employee reactions to job characteristics, *Journal of Applied Psychology*, 1971, **55**, 259–286. An updated version, the one shown here, is from J. R. Hackman and G. R. Oldham, Development of the job diagnostic survey, *Journal of Applied Psychology*, 1975, **60**, 159–170.

[5]John P. Wanous, Individual differences and reactions to job characteristics. *Journal of Applied Psychology*, 1974, **59**, 616–622.

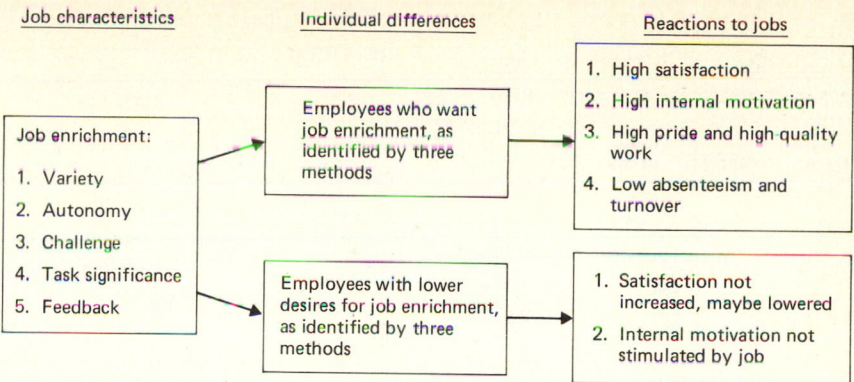

Figure 20-3 How individual differences among employees should work.

prospects for job enrichment. Thus need strength and belief in the Protestant work ethic could be classified as "strong" or "weak," and operators could also be classified as "urban" or "rural," according to where they had grown up (i.e., had been socialized).

The results showed that classification by need strength revealed the clearest differences. Those designated as having strong needs for job enrichment experienced a strong relationship between enriching job characteristics and their own job satisfaction. On the other hand, those identified as having weaker needs for such jobs reported they saw little or no relationship between enriching job characteristics and their satisfaction. These results meant that the need strength method was working properly.

Similar, but not as strong, results were obtained when using the Protestant work ethic, but the demographic approach proved to be quite ineffective. Since the demographic approach has been useful in other instances, however, its ineffectiveness in this particular study should not be considered definitive.

GUIDELINES FOR IMPLEMENTATION

A number of considerations should be incorporated in any decision to assess individual differences for job enrichment projects. These include effectiveness, cost, the quality of management-employee relationships, use of interviews, and combination of techniques.

Effectiveness

In *Theory* the need strength method should be the best way to measure these individual differences because it is aimed directly at the heart of the issue, i.e., desires for job characteristics associated with job enrichment. The work values method is a bit further removed because it is focused on one's general orientation to working. Using the demographic approach to approximate work values is even further removed, theoretically speaking.

In *practice*, the results nearly parallel what would be expected theoretically. Clear and consistent results have been obtained with the need strength method. Consistent and encouraging results have also been found using work values. The demographic technique has had inconsistent success.

The issue of effectiveness goes deeper because one must also consider the extensiveness of previous testing for each method. For example, the demographic approach has been the most widely scrutinized, followed closely by the need strength approach. Only the work values approach still lacks adequate testing. Considering both effectiveness and extensiveness of testing, the need strength method appears to be the best choice at the present time.

Cost

In terms of both direct and indirect costs of obtaining the information, the demographic approach is the least expensive. If one used plant location to assess the urban–rural difference, the choice is easy. If area of early socialization is used instead, costs go up a bit, but not too much. A personnel department clerk could obtain the necessary information from the forms that employees completed when applying for work.

Both work values and need strength require the administration of questionnaires. Here costs go up because care must be taken to design the instruments, administer them, and analyze them. This may or may not involve giving employees time off from work, but the efforts of others to conduct and administer the project must be considered.

Typically, one would *not* administer only those items pertaining to the Protestant work ethic or to need strength. These would normally be included with other items about job attitudes in a longer questionnaire. Despite the fact that this raises the costs of obtaining pertinent information, there are advantages to giving these particular items along with other questions. One is that the purpose of the questionnaire is not so obviously geared toward singling out particular employees, thus reducing the tendency for individuals to bias their responses. A second reason for doing this is that the other questions can focus on the diagnosis of current personnel problems or early detection of potential difficulties.

Quality of Employee-Management Relationships

One theme running through the three methods is the degree to which the purpose of a particular procedure is transparent to employees. Clearly, the demographic approach is the least obvious of all three, and the need strength approach is the most direct.

The quality of employee-management relationships may sometimes be a consideration in the choice of which method to use. Where there is mistrust and suspicion, the risk of employees' giving "bad data" on questionnaires is much higher. Despite this, valid data have been collected, but primarily by outside university researchers who were able to convince employees of their sincerity and their intent and ability to maintain confidentiality. Thus, it has been possible to collect reasonably accurate data when the purposes were primarily research-oriented. Doing the same for managerial action is more difficult, because individual names must be obtained and because company personnel (rather than outsiders) will probably collect the data. Under these conditions the demographic approach may be a better alternative.

Using Interviews

One variation of the strength-of-needs and work-values methods would be to obtain the information from talking to employees. This could be done informally or formally, and it offers the advantage of being able to follow up on questions by probing into the underlying reasons for an employee's attitudes. Since supervisors and employees interact constantly, relevant information could be collected in a rather unobtrusive way—a clear advantage over the questionnaire method. However, the success of this method depends on the skill of the interviewer and the degree of trust between supervisor and employee. Furthermore, it may be quite difficult to quantify the results of an interview so that comparisons among employees can be made.

Combining Techniques

Because each method offers something unique, it might be wise to combine all three to cope with different situations. For example, the speed and low cost of the demographic approach makes it a good first step as a "screening" device to select locations or find those people most receptive to job enrichment. Since research shows that the need strength method is effective, questionnaires could then be used at a later stage. This would cut costs and reduce the danger of elevating employees' expectations because a smaller, more select group of employees would be involved in the administration of questionnaires.

What about those plants located in urban areas that employ mostly blue-collar employees, personnel who also grew up in urban areas? The demographic method recommends extreme caution in undertaking job enrichment. However, using the need strength (or perhaps the work values) technique would enable a company to identify those employees who do not fit into the mold of the alienated, uninvolved worker solely on the basis of demographic background.

Reading 21

Is Job Enrichment Just a Fad?
J. Richard Hackman

Every five years or so, a new behavioral science "solution" to organizational problems emerges. Typically one or two organizations try out the newly conceived solution with great success. Then management journals and the popular press pick up the success stories and spread word of them wildfirelike across the country. And finally, after a few years, disillusioned managers and employees conclude—sometimes reluctantly, sometimes angrily—that the solution really does not solve much of anything, and it fades away.

It looks as if work redesign (or job enrichment, or job enlargement—call it what you will) is to be the darling of the mid-1970s. Job enrichment began in the United States with the pioneering research of people like Frederick Herzberg and Louis Davis.[1] Early tests of the technique, such as the studies at AT&T

shepherded by Robert Ford, were highly successful.[2] Now, programs for change involving the redesign of work are flooding the country, stories showing "how we profited from job enrichment" are appearing in management journals, and the labor community is struggling to determine how it should respond to the tidal wave that seems to be forming.

The question of the moment, then, is whether work redesign can be developed into a robust and powerful tool for organizational change—or whether it, like so many of its predecessors from behavioral science, will fade into disuse as managers experience failure and disillusionment in its application. Despite the recent fervor, job enrichment seems to be failing at least as often as it is succeeding, and because of this failure, the answer to the question is by no means clear.

[1] Frederick Herzberg, "One More Time: How Do You Motivate Employees?" HBR January–February 1968, p. 53.

[2] Robert N. Ford, "Job Enrichment Lessons from AT&T," HBR January–February 1973, p. 96.

This article reports on some applications of work design as a strategy for change that some colleagues and I have observed in about 20 organizations over the last two years. We have watched job enrichment projects being planned, implemented, and/or recovered from, and we have talked with hundreds of employees, managers, and consultants. We have identified a number of practices that often lead to job enrichment failures and other factors that are common to many of the more successful projects. With the hope that debunking can be halted before it obscures the real value of job enrichment, I discuss some of these issues here.

WHAT GOES WRONG

Is the whole philosophy of job enrichment off base? Or does the problem lie in how it is being carried out? I propose that the basic idea of job enrichment is sound but that the way projects are planned and installed in many organizations almost guarantees poor results.

Here, then, are six major things that go wrong when organizations redesign work.

1   Rarely Are the Problems in the Work System Diagnosed before Jobs Are Redesigned

It is now reasonably clear that job enrichment does not work in all organizational circumstances. Yet rarely does top management insist that a systematic study of the jobs and the people to be affected be carried out before the project begins. As a result, faulty initial assumptions often go undetected, and the project may be doomed from the start.

In some organizations studied, the jobs to be enriched appeared to have been chosen according to no definite scheme. Some may have "seemed right" for enrichment. Others may have seemed peripheral to the major work done in the organization and, thus, safe to work on. Still other jobs seemed to have everything wrong with them: the work was not getting done on time or correctly; employees were furious about their pay, the cleanliness of the rest rooms, and scores of other grievances. The managers in these organizations apparently hoped that somehow job enrichment would fix everything all at once.

Such near-random selection will not work, of course. Given existing technological constraints, some jobs are about as good as they ever can be. In such cases, job enrichment is at best a waste of time. Other jobs have so much wrong with them (faulty engineering, poor supervision, inequitable pay) that how "enriched" they are is irrelevant. Job enrichment might add even more complexity to an already chaotic situation. When the people responsible for a project overlook job suitability in job enrichment, the project often fails, simply because it is aimed at an inappropriate target.

Also, in many organizations, no one had assessed the differences in employees' "readiness" to handle job changes before the projects were installed. Assuming that all employees were alike, line managers often expressed doubt that their employees could handle the proposed new responsibilities, as well as skepticism that employees would enjoy working on enriched jobs. Sometimes, as planning for work redesign proceeded, managers dropped these stereotyped views, but only rarely did they make sure that the projects were designed with the recognition that employees may differ in their psychological readiness for enriched work.

Furthermore, managers themselves were frequently not ready to deal with the kinds of problems that inevitably arose when a major organizational change was made. For example, in one service organization, the management team responsible for enriching the jobs of some clerical employees nearly collapsed when initial assessments showed a drop-off in productivity shortly after the change was installed. Discussion of possible reasons for the problem quickly deteriorated into attempts to assign blame for the difficulty to one or another of the managers. Prior diagnosis of the management team's readiness for change would have increased the chance that their problems might have been resolved *before* the job changes themselves were made. Instead, another "job enrichment failure" had occurred and was added to the tally.

Finally, in the unsuccessful projects, top management had often failed to assess its own commitment to job enrichment. This failure sometimes spelled disaster later. A high-level executive in one company had agreed to sponsor a project without really understanding that the changes would create a good deal of uncertainty in the organization. When he began hearing complaints from some of his subordinates about the "chaos" the project was causing, he concluded that he had been misled and put the project outside the protective umbrella he had provided and into serious organizational jeopardy. In another company, only one vice president was counted on to protect a fledgling project from "meddling" by others, who favored alternative approaches to organizational change. When the vice president departed from the organization to attend an executive development program of several months' length, his temporary replacement terminated the job enrichment activities and substituted a program more to his own liking.

2 Sometimes the Work Itself Is Not Actually Changed

Redesigning a job often appears seductively simple, and some managers underestimate how much time and effort a project can take. In practice, job redesign is a rather challenging undertaking, requiring a good deal more energy than do most other organizational development activities, such as attitude improvement programs, training courses, and objectives-setting practices.

There are many reasons that is is hard to redesign jobs. At the purely bureaucratic level, often the entire personnel and job description apparatus must be engaged to get the changes approved, documented, and implemented. If the organization is unionized, frequently the planned changes must be negotiated beforehand—sometimes a formidable task. Simple inertia can tempt some managers to add window dressing to make things appear different rather than to actually change what people *do* on their jobs. Finally, when even one job in an organization is changed, many of the interfaces between that job and related ones must be dealt with as well. In even moderately complex work systems, that is no small matter.

Because of such forces against change, job enrichment projects that have very little impact on the work itself are frequently carried out. A case in point is a project that involved clerical employees who worked in the stock transfer department of a large bank. It was clear that before the change some jobs in the department were already more "enriched" than others. Legal clerks, for example, had considerable autonomy in handling problems involving death inheritance taxes, testamentary letters, and so on. The job required a great deal of skill, and most people who held it found the work both challenging and satisfying. Other jobs were highly routine—for example, those of operators, who entered names and addresses of stock transferees on a console for computer processing, and those of typists, who typed and mailed correspondence composed by others. Research data collected before the change showed that the people who held the "better" jobs were more motivated, productive, and satisfied and were less likely to be absent from the job.

But it turned out that the people who had held the "good" jobs before the change also held them afterwards—and those people whose jobs had originally been routine, repetitive, and virtually without feedback had essentially identical jobs after the work was redesigned. After about six months, there was even a slight deterioration in worker satisfaction and motivation. One manager concluded: "We tried job enrichment, and it failed."

All that had actually happened was that employees had been put into small groups and encouraged to train one another in the various tasks required to carry out the transfer of securities. A supervisor had been assigned to each group and given responsibility for coordinating a more diverse set of functions than had previously been the case. The office had been physically rearranged, the names of some jobs altered, and without question a great stirring about had taken place. But the jobs themselves had remained virtually untouched.

3 Even When the Work Itself Is Substantially Changed, Anticipated Gains Are Sometimes Diminished or Reversed Because of Unexpected Effects on the Surrounding Work System

When people do behave differently at work because of job redesign, the changes may create shock waves that reverberate throughout adjacent parts of the organization. If insufficient attention is given to such spin-off effects, job changes may backfire.

The site of the backfire varies from case to case. In one company, employees who prepared customer accounts for computer processing were given increased autonomy in scheduling their work and in determining their own work pace. These job changes resulted in a less predictable schedule of data input to the computer system. As a result, while data-processing managers struggled to figure out how to respond to the new and irregular flow of work, excessive computer delays occurred. The net result of the project was a decrease in the promptness of customer service and an increase in antagonism between computer operators and the employees whose jobs had been enriched.

In another case, rank-and-file employees who dealt with customers by telephone were given a number of responsibilities that their supervisors had previously handled. At first, the employees seemed to prosper with their new responsibilities of handling emergency requests and deciding when deviation from standard company practice was called for. But later it became clear that there was a deterioration of morale and an increase in tension between supervisors and subordinates.

Apparently the supervisors had found themselves with little work to do after the change (the employees were doing much of what their supervisors used to do), and when they turned to higher management for instructions, they were told to "develop your people—that's what a manager's job is." The supervisors had little idea of what "developing your people" involved, and in many cases they implemented that instruction by standing over their employees' shoulders and correcting each error they could find. Resentment quickly developed between the supervisor and the employee groups, and more than overcame any positive benefits that had accrued from the changes in the job itself.

4 Rarely Are the Work Redesign Projects Systematically Evaluated

The evaluation done for enrichment projects often consists only of reports like "Well, let me tell you, only one week after we did the actual job enrichment, this guy who had been on the lathe for 15 years came up to me and said, 'For the first time I'm proud of my job.'"

Sometimes, however, staff members point to "harder" data, such as the reduction in personnel in the unit where job enrichment took place. Surely such data reflect higher productivity per worker, but even they are of little help to the manager who is trying to understand exactly what caused it. And, of great importance in unionized organizations, they are hardly the kind of data that will engage the enthusiasm of the bargaining unit for broader application of work redesign.

There are many good reasons that decent evaluations of work redesign projects do not get done. First, there are no ways to translate human gains into dollars and cents that people agree on using. Second, it is hard to determine what proportions of measured productivity and unit profitability are caused by job redesign. Third, many accounting systems are not designed to handle the costs of absenteeism, turnover, training, and extra supervisory time. And, fourth, a lot of managers do not trust the job satisfaction measures to which they do have access.

These reasons can be convincing, until one asks what was done to try to overcome the problem of evaluating job design and finds, for instance, that the accountants were not even asked to help. One is then left with several unhappy hypotheses: nobody knows how to do a decent evaluation; management does not know that systematic evaluation is an essential part of job enrichment; or the desire of the people responsible for the program to have it appear successful is so strong that they cannot afford the risk of an explicit evaluation.

In a retailing organization, for example, job enrichment was "sold" to top management by a single individual and soon came to be known throughout the organization as "Joe's program." Understandably, Joe developed a considerable personal interest in the image of the program. When he was given the chance to do a systematic evaluation of the project's contribution to productivity, Joe showed considerable hesitation and finally declined the offer. Later discussions with him revealed that although he recognized the usefulness of the information he might gain from an evaluation, he felt that the benefits to be gained would be more than countered by the risk of his losing control over the image of the program.

Whatever the reasons for avoiding an evaluation, the frequent result of not having one is that little is learned from the work redesign project that would be helpful in doing it better another time. And few trustworthy data are provided to help management consider whether or not the activity is worthy of further experimentation and more investment of managerial time and organizational resources. "Let me tell you what this guy said. . . ." just is not the sort of data on which thoughtful decisions about the allocation of organizational resources can be based.

5 Line Managers, Consulting Staff Members, and Union Officers Do Not Obtain Appropriate Education in the Theory, Strategy, and Tactics of Work Redesign

In some organizations, line managers and their staff receive no educational preparation for job enrichment projects other than what they pick up in routine reading of management journals. In other organizations, key personnel visit only one or two companies where work redesign projects have been carried out successfully before beginning to plan their own program. Sometimes a group of managers attends a workshop to learn the basics of job design.

But for the most part, unfortunately, managers tend to learn just enough about job enrichment to become comfortable with the basic ideas and principles of work design. Once this level is reached, their commitment to learning drops and/or they become overwhelmed by the day-to-day pressures of getting the project planned and installed. And in many cases, this disinterest lasts throughout the life of the project and beyond. A manager in one organization, for example, suffered through what was clearly a rather unsuccessful job enrichment project and then, a few months later, began planning a new one—doing everything exactly the way he had done it before.

The role of the internal consultant is of special importance in conducting any organization development activity—and job enrichment is no exception. I have often heard such individuals complain that they are not sufficiently respected as professionals in their organizations and that they constantly have to fight to gain "field credibility." This is understandable. If I were a line manager or a union officer, I would very much want to see evidence that the person who will bear primary professional responsibility for the project about to be done in my unit is competent.

It is also true, however, that top managers sometimes want altogether unrealistic amounts of reassurance about the competence of the staff consultants who will be carrying out the project. And managers often seek unrealistically high estimates of the probability of success of the project being contemplated. Understandably, lower-level managers and staff consultants often collude in hand-holding activities. This collusion can provide comfort and reassurance to everyone involved, but it may also cover up the need for additional education about the redesign of work. Top managers need to take the initiative in encouraging reeducation and updating in the theory, strategy, and tactics of work redesign.

Traditional Bureaucratic Practice Creeps into Work Design Activities

Job enrichment projects offer employees a chance to become more autonomous and self-directed in carrying out the work of the organization. According to job enrichment theory, managers assume that employees have the competence and sense of responsibility to seek appropriate assistance when they need it and thus that they can work with a minimum of interference. Far too often, however, the *process* of implementing job enrichment is strikingly incongruent with this intended end.

Expecting to achieve a flexible, employee-oriented work system with rigid, bureaucratic procedures that operate strictly from the top down is unrealistic. At the least, such procedures will raise questions in employees' minds about the genuineness of the change. The

employees may no longer put any trust in the project or commit themselves to it.

In a manufacturing organization, for instance, planners followed standard company practice and wrote extremely detailed, step-by-step descriptions of the new jobs in their job enrichment program, which they passed down to the employees through company foremen. The employees were not exactly overwhelmed with gratitude at these job improvements. As one machine operator put it, "They're dictating to me again, but this time about how I should enjoy taking more responsibility and initiative in getting *their* work out!"

Yet, again and again in the organizations studied, standard, traditional organizational practices were being used to install work redesign. More often than not, the employees were the last to know what was happening, and only rarely were they given any real opportunity to participate actively in the change or to influence it. In many cases, the employees were never told why the changes were being made. One manager said, "I don't understand why they didn't respond more enthusiastically. Don't they realize how we're going to put a lot more responsibility into their work and make it more interesting?" Apparently he did not see the basic incongruence between the goals being aspired to and the means, between "what we want to achieve" and "how we're going to do it."

HOW IT CAN BE DONE

For all these reasons and undoubtedly for more, job enrichment projects are failing. Moreover, they are leaving a bad taste in the mouths of both managers and employees. Even though the failures may be relatively unobtrusive now, they may soon become overwhelming.

What can managers do to avoid such problems and to increase the chances that work redesign projects will be carried out effectively in their own organizations? Successful projects have one or more of the following ingredients.

1 Key Individuals Responsible for the Work Redesign Project Attack the Especially Difficult Problems Right from the Start

In many organizations, there seems to be a great temptation to "sell" a job enrichment project and only then to begin negotiations on the difficult problems that must be solved to carry it out. If such problems are raised before the project is agreed to, the chances that it will never get off the ground are increased. Nevertheless, it appears that in the long run it may be wiser not to start a project for which the tough issues cannot be resolved beforehand than to start one under circumstances that require compromise after compromise to keep the project alive after it has begun.

The vigilance of management can help ensure that the tough issues are not swept under the rug while the project is still being considered. Issues too often reserved for later discussion are:

- The nature and extent of the commitment of management and union leaders, including the circumstances under which a decision to terminate the project may be made. Both management and union leaders need to realize that protecting and nurturing the project during its early stages may require a good deal of energy.
- The criteria by which the project will ultimately be evaluated and how the evaluation will be made. Since there are serious measurement difficulties in assessing any work redesign project, all parties—top management as well as union sponsors—must be aware of these difficulties and committed to the evaluation methodology at the outset.
- The method of communicating the experiences gained in the project as guidelines for others. It is especially critical for manage-

ment to abandon a punitive stance and to encourage free discussion and analysis of the project as it develops.

2 Management Makes Sure That a Diagnosis of the Changes Needed in the Target Jobs, Based on Some Articulated Theory of Work Redesign, Is Conducted before Implementation

Until recently, most work redesign projects have been based on either the motivator-hygiene theory of Herzberg or some version of the sociotechnical systems theory. Now, however, a number of new approaches to work redesign, some of which specify explicit principles for improving jobs have appeared and are giving people responsible for job enrichment considerable choice about the conceptual basis for their programs.

Some of the theories are probably better than others. Yet, in practice, it may not be of enormous importance which particular theory is used. Having a theory is important primarily because it facilitates the development of specific objectives for the change project and because it specifies the kinds of data about the job, the people, and the situation that are required for planning the changes and, later, for evaluating them.

A manager responsible for a work redesign project, regardless of its theoretical framework, might wish to make sure that explicit consideration is given to each of the following issues:

- Can the jobs under consideration be *meaningfully* changed? That is, will job enrichment make enough of a difference in the jobs to affect the people who do them? Would meaningful job redesign involve unrealistically high expenditures of capital or changes in technology? What specific aspects of the work are especially problematic at present?
- Are the employees reasonably ready for change and capable of handling their new duties afterward? Are they reasonably satis-

fied with bread-and-butter issues of pay, supervision, and job security, or would an attempt to improve jobs run into resistance and hostility because of existing dissatisfaction with these items? Managers frequently overestimate their employees' satisfaction with such bread-and-butter issues and underestimate their technical competence as well as their psychological readiness to take on added responsibility and challenge in their work.

• Is management itself ready to handle the extra burdens and challenges that will be created by the change? It is better to find out before changing than to risk a major breakdown during the first week of the project.

• How are supervisors, related peer groups, and clients likely to be affected by the change? Are these individuals ready and able to handle the changes, or is developmental work required before beginning work on the target jobs themselves?

Such diagnoses are not easy to make. They arouse anxiety about whether the organization is flexible enough to tolerate a loss in managerial control over the hour-by-hour activities of employees and whether managers themselves are competent enough to establish and nurture the changes. Although the answers that emerge are not always easy to digest, the diagnostic task may be one of the most crucial of all in work redesign projects. And ensuring that an adequate diagnosis takes place may be among the most important contributions a manager can make to such projects.

3 Management Ensures That Specific Changes Are Publicly Discussed and Based Explicitly on the Diagnosis

There are at least three major advantages to being public and explicit in moving from the theory to the diagnosis and then to the steps undertaken to modify jobs.

First, if plans are explicitly based on the diagnostic results, the project is protected from boiling over into irrelevancies like the perennial "parking problem" and the occa-

sional "washroom problem." This is not to say that such problems should not be dealt with; but if one is undertaking the redesign of work, the changes should have to do with the work itself. Actions planned according to a theory-based diagnosis of the work situation are much less likely to miss the mark than those stemming from a more undirected probing like "What can we do here to improve things?"

Second, when the diagnosis is carried out and discussed publicly, all parties involved have the chance to influence the redesign activities and become familiar with them. In one telephone company, for instance, the level of personal threat experienced by employees dropped significantly when they became involved in the project. Management was subsequently surprised by the amount of energy employees contributed to the project and by the quality of their ideas.

Finally, by tying changes explicitly to the diagnostic results, managers can increase the chances that principles helpful to future development of effective work redesign will emerge from the project because it will be easier to trace the reasons various changes were tried and to discern where things went wrong or right.[3]

4 The People Responsible for the Work Project Prepare Contingency Plans Ahead of Time to Deal with Both the Problems and the Opportunities That Emerge from Work Redesign Activities

One of the most crucial times in a job enrichment project occurs when the first really significant problem emerges. For example, in a large bank, the first set of unexpected difficulties led many to conclude that the project was

---

[3]The links between theory, diagnosis, and action are explored in more detail in an article entitled "A New Strategy for Job Enrichment," by J. Richard Hackman, Greg R. Oldham, Robert Janson, and Kenneth Purdy, *California Management Review*, Summer 1975, p. 57.

failing. This conclusion was premature, but the doubts caused such high losses in staff energy and morale that it appeared for a while the project might actually fail.

For comparison, consider what happened in a manufacturing company when problems having to do with compensation for people performing "enriched" work developed. Before the employees' surprise and dismay at what seemed an unfair system rose to unmanageable levels, the managers produced some alternative compensation arrangements, which they had worked out in rough form beforehand. The employees were reassured by the existence of alternate plans, only moderate amounts of managerial energy had to be taken away from the maintenance of the project itself to deal with the compensation problem, and a workable solution was found.

It is not possible, of course, to plan ahead for all the problems that come up when work is redesigned. Indeed, until a project is well under way, it is often not possible to know what the most pressing difficulties will be. But managers can be ready to deal with some of the more common problems.

For example, the training department can be alerted that its services may be required if first-line managers find themselves in difficulty supervising the employees after the work is redesigned; those responsible for selection and placement can be asked to engage in some contingency planning on the chance that the new work system may require untraditional placement procedures. One does not begin with such matters, but a thoughtful manager will anticipate them and be prepared to deal with them if they develop.

5 Those Responsible for the Work Redesign Project Are Prepared to Evaluate the Project Continuously throughout Its Life

There is no neat package available for installing work redesign projects in an organization,

and there may never be. People responsible for job enrichment must learn as they go.

Because of the pressure on lower-level managers to make job enrichment programs at least appear successful, top management must often insist on having meaningful evaluations of such programs. And for the evaluations to be valid and useful, top management needs to create an organizational climate in which the evaluation is viewed as an occasion for *learning* rather than for criticizing the performance and competence of those who actually install the changes.

To do an evaluation well is a costly proposition. It is expensive to adopt an open, evaluative stance that involves active experimentation with different ways of changing jobs. It is painful to learn from failure and to try again.

Yet such prices may be more than worthwhile to an organization contemplating job enrichment; paying them may be the only realistic way the organization can develop the considerable knowledge and expertise it will need to utilize the redesign of work as a full-fledged strategy for organizational change.

JOB ENRICHMENT—WORTH THE EFFORT?

Clearly, discovering how to effectively implement job enrichment is a substantial managerial challenge. But the gains that can be realized are also substantial and among behavioral science approaches to changing organizations they are in some ways unique.

Job Redesign Can Improve the Basic Relationship between a Person and His or Her Work

When all the outer layers are stripped away, most organizational problems—and most of the opportunities for organizational change—come to rest in the relationship between a person and his job. Industrial psychologists have offered numerous strategies for adjusting people to jobs and propping up their waning motivation to carry out their work. The human relations movement, the design of piece-rate incentive systems, and the experimentation with various managerial styles were all more or less aimed at overcoming the natural disenchantment of the worker with his work that results from automation and "scientific management."

Job enrichment raises the possibility of rearranging the work itself so as to move from extrinsic motivational props toward genuinely internal work motivation. An employee will work because the work interests and challenges him and when he performs effectively will reward himself for doing well.

Effective Work Redesign Changes Behavior Directly and Does So in a Way That Maintains the Change

People do the tasks they are given either well or poorly, but they do them. How well they do them depends on many factors, including how the tasks themselves are designed. People do not, however, always behave consistently with their attitudes, their level of job satisfaction, or what they "know" they should do. Effective work redesign, then, does not rely on changing attitudes first by trying, for example, to induce the worker to care more about the work outcomes, as in zero-defect programs. Instead, the strategy is to change the behavior itself, and to change it so that the employee gradually acquires a positive attitude about his work, the organization, and himself.

Moreover, after jobs have been changed, the structure of the new tasks reinforces the changes that have taken place. One need not worry much about the kind of backsliding that occurs so often after training or attitude modification activities. The stimuli that most powerfully affect how a person behaves on the job are the ones that come from the job itself. And once those stimuli are changed, they are likely

to stay that way—at least until the job is once again redesigned.

Work Redesign Offers the Chance to Initiate Other Organizational Changes and to Alter Managerial Style

As I noted earlier, work redesign invariably creates some turbulence in other parts of the work system. Such turbulence can create special opportunities for initiating organizational changes in areas like supervision, training, reward systems, and career paths, where previously no one had felt a pressing need for developmental work.

Managers sometimes view personnel problems as simply a matter of finding the right pegs to fit existing holes in the organizational pegboard and of shaving and hammering those pegs to make them fit. Work redesign can lead managers to take the alternative view that both the pegs and the holes are fair game for change in attempting to achieve the best possible fit between the organization and the people who carry out its work.

In the Long Run, Work Redesign Can Help Organizations Rehumanize Rather Than Dehumanize the People Who Work in Them

Despite the fact that the work-ethic issue might have been overemphasized in recent years, there is, nonetheless, convincing evidence that organizations can and sometimes do stamp out part of the humanity of their members. In particular, companies often discourage the natural motivation toward growth and personal development that is so clearly present in infants.

Work redesign can help individuals regain the kick that comes from doing a job well and encourage them to care enough about their work to develop the competence to do it even better. These payoffs from work redesign go well beyond simple job satisfaction. Cows grazing in the field may be satisfied, and organizations can keep employees just as satished by paying them well, keeping bosses off their backs, and arranging things so that the days pass without undue stress or strain.

This is not the kind of satisfaction at issue here. It is a satisfaction that develops only when an individual is stretching and growing as a human being and increasing his sense of competence and worth. Whether creation of opportunities for personal growth is a legitimate goal for work redesign activities is a value issue I cannot deal with here. I hope the case for the value of work redesign strictly in terms of organizational health can rest on the points I have already discussed. But the potential personal impact of work redesign on the people who do the actual work should neither be overlooked nor underemphasized.

This description of work redesign's potential to change jobs effectively may sound absolutely glowing. It should. The evidence—although scattered and unsystematic—demonstrates that job redesign really can work. It can lead to the kinds of positive outcomes I have suggested. The emphasis for now, however, must be carefully placed on the word *potential* because that potential is not often realized in work redesign projects being undertaken today. And unless managers and their staffs begin to take the challenge of implementation with the seriousness it demands, the opportunity to realize that potential may slip away for many years. Job enrichment will indeed have become "just another behavioral science fad," and organizations will lose a valuable tool for change.

Part Four

Influences on Work Behavior: Organizational Practices and Social Processes

Chapter 7

Evaluating and Rewarding Work Effectiveness

The measurement of performance and the giving of rewards are very visible and important features of almost every organization. They also are among the most controversial. The literature is full of debates about how performance should be appraised and how pay should be administered. "New" approaches are constantly being suggested, but the basic issues remain the same. In the area of performance appraisal, they concern how performance can best be measured; in the area of rewards they concern how rewards (such as pay) should be related to performance, and how rewards can be distributed equitably.

Performance appraisal is intended to serve a number of important functions in most organizations: it is supposed to provide feedback to employees about their performance, identify employees' development needs, form the basis for the giving of rewards, and aid in planning and control. The debates about which approach to performance appraisal is the best have been many and long. At present, there is no one approach that is unanimously acclaimed as the best. However, it does seem that there is agreement that approaches which rely solely on ratings (e.g., "How friendly is the person?" [low] 1 2 3 4 5 [high]) are inferior to systems which rely on agreed-to objectives and which are clearly based on work behavior. There also is general agreement that it is difficult simultaneously to appraise performance for the purposes of giving rewards and discussing the developmental needs of employees. Probably the key article in producing general acceptance of this view is Reading 22, by Meyer, Kay and French. It is one of those articles which have become classics at a young age. It has spawned a number of performance appraisal systems in organizations which are more oriented toward objectives, and which try to tie the appraisal process to the accomplishment of specific goals. Much recent writing in the field has been primarily concerned with elaborating the basic points originally made by Meyer, Key, and French.

Although there is a great deal of debate about how pay can best be related to performance and distributed equitably, there is little disagreement about the desirability of doing so. Most agree that when pay and other rewards are related to performance, motivation is increased, and that when pay is equitably distributed, turnover and absenteeism tend to be low. However, this is where the agreement ends. As the reading by Hamner points out, it is one thing to get agreement on the principle but it is another to successfully operationalize the principle. Hamner points out that organizations frequently end up administering pay in ways that prevent pay from being an important motivator—despite the avowed intention

to have it function as a motivator. In the article which follows, Lawler notes that relatively few new pay practices have been developed recently, and suggests some new approaches that are being tried with success in a few organizations.

The last few years have seen an increased interest in the application of Skinnerian behavior-modification techniques to organizations. The reading by Luthans and White is illustrative of the recent writing in this area. It contends that a tremendous potential improvement in organizational effectiveness can be gained by the application of behavioral-modification techniques. In the next article, Whyte presents a very different view of the usefulness of Skinnerian theory in organizations. He feels that much of the theory is *not* applicable to the real world of work, and he supports this view with a number of examples from his own extensive research on pay incentive plans.

Reading 22

Split Roles in Performance Appraisal

Herbert H. Meyer

Emanuel Kay

John R. P. French, Jr.

In management circles, performance appraisal is a highly interesting and provocative topic. And in business literature, too, knowledgeable people write emphatically, pro and con, on the performance appraisal question.[1] In fact, one might almost say that everybody talks and writes about it, but nobody has done any real scientific testing of it.

At the General Electric Company we felt it was important that a truly scientific study be done to test the effectiveness of our traditional performance appraisal program. Why? Simply because our own experience with performance appraisal programs had been both positive and negative. For example:

- Surveys generally show that most people think the idea of performance appraisal is good. They feel that a man should know where he stands and, therefore, the manager should discuss an appraisal of his performance with him periodically.
- In actual practice, however, it is the extremely rare operating manager who will employ such a program on his own initiative. Personnel specialists report that most managers carry out performance appraisal interviews only when strong control procedures are established to ensure that they do so. This is surprising because the managers have been told repeatedly that the system is intended to help them obtain improved performance from their subordinates.

We also found from interviews with employees who have had a good deal of experience with traditional performance appraisal programs that few indeed can cite examples of constructive action taken—or significant improvement achieved—which stem from suggestions received in a performance appraisal interview with their boss.

TRADITIONAL PROGRAM

Faced with such contradictory evidence, we undertook a study several years ago to determine the effectiveness of our comprehensive performance appraisal process. Special attention was focused on the interview between the subordinate and his manager, because this is the discussion which is supposed to motivate the man to improve his performance. And we found out some very interesting things—among them the following:

- Criticism has a negative effect on achievement of goals.
- Praise has little effect one way or the other.
- Performance improves most when specific goals are established.
- Defensiveness resulting from critical appraisal produces inferior performance.
- Coaching should be a day-to-day, not a once-a-year, activity.

[1]Douglas McGregor, "An Uneasy Look at Performance Appraisal," HBR May–June 1957, p. 89; Harold Mayfield, "In Defense of Performance Appraisal," HBR March–April 1960, p. 81; and Alva F. Kindall and James Gatza, "Positive Program for Performance Appraisal," HBR November–December 1963, p. 153.

- Mutual goal setting, not criticism, improves performance.
- Interviews designed primarily to improve a man's performance should not at the same time weigh his salary or promotion in the balance.
- Participation by the employee in the goal-setting procedure helps produce favorable results.

As you can see, the results of this original study indicated that a detailed and comprehensive annual appraisal of a subordinate's performance by his manager is decidedly of questionable value. Furthermore, as is certainly the case when the major objective of such a discussion is to motivate the subordinate to improve his performance, the traditional appraisal interview does not do the job.

In the first part of this article, we will offer readers more than this bird's-eye view of our research into performance appraisal. (We will not, however, burden managers with details of methodology.) We will also describe the one-year follow-up experiment General Electric conducted to validate the conclusions derived from our original study. Here the traditional annual performance appraisal method was tested against a new method we developed, which we called Work Planning and Review (WP&R). As you will see, this approach produced, under actual plant conditions, results which were decidedly superior to those afforded by the traditional performance appraisal method. Finally, we will offer evidence to support our contention that some form of WP&R might well be incorporated into other industrial personnel programs to achieve improvement in work performance.

APPRAISING APPRAISAL

In order to assure a fair test of the effectiveness of the traditional performance appraisal method, which had been widely used throughout General Electric, we conducted an intensive study of the process at a large GE plant where the performance appraisal program was judged to be good; that is, in this plant—

> . . . appraisals had been based on job responsibilities, rather than on personal characteristics of the individuals involved;

> . . . an intensive training program had been carried out for managers in the use of the traditional appraisal method and techniques for conducting appraisal interviews;

> . . . the program had been given strong backing by the plant manager and had been policed diligently by the personnel staff so that over 90% of the exempt employees had been appraised and interviewed annually.

This comprehensive annual performance appraisal program, as is typical, was designed to serve two major purposes. The first was to justify recommended salary action. The second, which was motivational in character, was intended to present an opportunity for the manager to review a subordinate's performance and promote discussion on needed improvements. For the latter purpose, the manager was required to draw up a specific program of plans and goals for the subordinate which would help him to improve his job performance and to qualify, hopefully, for future promotion.

Interview Modifications

Preliminary interviews with key managers and subordinates revealed the salary action issue had so dominated the annual comprehensive performance appraisal interview that neither party had been in the right frame of mind to discuss plans for improved performance. To straighten this out, we asked managers to split the traditional appraisal interview into two sessions—discussing appraisal of performance and salary action in one interview and performance improvement plans in another to be held about two weeks later. This split provided us with a better opportunity to conduct our experiment on the effects of participation in goal planning.

To enable us to test the effects of participation, we instructed half the managers to use a *high participation* approach and the other half to use a *low participation* technique. Thus:

• Each of the "high" managers was instructed to ask his appraisee to prepare a set of goals for achieving improved job performance and to submit them for the manager's review and approval. The manager also was encouraged to permit the subordinate to exert as much influence as possible on the formulation of the final list of job goals agreed on in the performance improvement discussion.

• The "low" managers operated in much the same way they had in our traditional appraisal program. They formulated a set of goals for the subordinate, and these goals were then reviewed in the performance improvement session. The manager was instructed to conduct this interview in such a way that his influence in the forming of the final list of job goals would be greater than the subordinate's.

Conducting the Research

There were 92 appraisees in the experimental group, representing a cross section of the exempt salaried employees in the plant. This group included engineers; engineering support technicians; foremen; and specialists in manufacturing, customer service, marketing, finance, and purchasing functions. None of the exempt men who participated as appraisees in the experiment had other exempt persons reporting to them; thus they did not serve in conflicting manager-subordinate roles.

The entire group was interviewed and asked to complete questionnaires (a) before and after the salary action interview, and (b) after the delayed second discussion with their managers about performance improvement. These interviews and questionnaires were designed to achieve three objectives:

1 Assess changes in the attitudes of individuals toward their managers and toward the appraisal system after each of the discussions.
2 Get an estimate from the appraisee of the degree to which he usually participated in decisions that affected him. (This was done in order to determine whether or not previous lack of participation affected his response to participation in the experiment.)
3 Obtain a self-appraisal from each subordinate before and after he met with his manager. (This was done in order to determine how discrepancies in these self-appraisals might affect his reaction to the appraisal interview.)

Moreover, each salary action and performance improvement discussion was observed by outsiders trained to record essentially what transpired. (Managers preferred to use neither tape recorders nor unseen observers, feeling that observers unaffiliated with the company—in this case, graduate students in applied psychological disciplines—afforded the best way of obtaining a reasonably close approximation of the normal discussions.) In the appraisal for salary action interviews, for example, the observers recorded the amount of criticism and praise employed by the manager, as well as the reactions of the appraisee to the manager's comments. In the performance improvement discussions, the observers recorded the participation of the subordinate, as well as the amount of influence he seemed to exert in establishing his future success goals.

Criticism and Defensiveness

In general, the managers completed the performance appraisal forms in a thorough and conscientious manner. Their appraisals were discussed with subordinates in interviews ranging from approximately 30 to 90 minutes in length. On the average, managers covered 32 specific performance items which, when broken down, showed positive (praise) appraisals on 19 items, and negative (criticism) on 13. Typically, praise was more often related to *general* performance characteristics, while criticism was usually focused on *specific* performance items.

The average subordinate reacted defensively to seven of the manager's criticisms during the appraisal interview (that is, he reacted defensively about 54% of the time when criticized). Denial of shortcomings cited by the manager, blaming others, and various other forms of excuses were recorded by the observers as defensive reactions.

Constructive responses to criticism were *rarely* observed, In fact, the average was less than one per interview. Not too surprising, along with this, was the finding that the more criticism a man received in the performance appraisal discussion, the more defensively he reacted. Men who received an above-average number of criticisms showed more than five times as much defensive behavior as those who received a below-average number of criticisms. Subordinates who received a below average number of criticisms, for example, reacted defensively only about one time out of three. But those who received an above-average number reacted defensively almost two times out of three.

One explanation for this defensiveness is that it seems to stem from the overrating each man tended to give to his own performance. The average employee's self-estimate of performance *before* appraisal placed him at the 77 percentile. (Only 2 of the 92 participants estimated their performance to be below the average point on the scale.) But when the same men were asked *after* their performance appraisal discussions how they thought their bosses had rated them, the average figure given was at the 65 percentile. The great majority (75 out of 92) saw their manager's evaluation as being less favorable than their self-estimates. Obviously, to these men, the performance appraisal discussion with the manager was a deflating experience. Thus, it was not surprising that the subordinates reacted defensively in their interviews.

Criticism and Goal Achievement

Even more important is the fact that men who received an above-average number of criticisms in their performance appraisal discussions generally showed *less* goal achievement 10 to 12 weeks later than those who had received fewer criticisms. At first, we thought that this difference might be accounted for by the fact that the subordinates who received more criticisms were probably poorer performers in general. But there was little factual evidence found to support this suspicion.

It was true that those who received an above-average number of criticisms in their appraisal discussions did receive slightly lower summary ratings on over-all performance from their managers. But they did not receive proportionally lower salary increases. And the salary increases granted were *supposed* to reflect differences in job performance, according to the salary plan traditionally used in this plant. This argument, admittedly, is something less than perfect.

But it does appear clear that frequent criticism constitutes so strong a threat to self-esteem that it disrupts rather than improves subsequent performance. We expected such a disruptive threat to operate more strongly on those individuals who were already low on self-esteem, just as we expected a man who had confidence in his ability to do his job to react more constructively to criticism. Our group experiment proved these expectations to be correct.

Still further evidence that criticism has a negative effect on performance was found when we investigated areas which had been given special emphasis by the manager in his criticism. Following the appraisal discussion with the manager, each employee was asked to indicate which one aspect of his performance had been most criticized by the manager. Then, when we conducted our follow-up investigation 10 to 12 weeks later, it revealed that improvement in the most-criticized aspects of performance cited was considerably *less* than improvement realized in other areas!

Participation Effects

As our original research study had indicated, the effects of a high participation level were also favorable in our group experiment. In general, here is what we found:

• Subordinates who received a high participation level in the performance interview reacted more favorably than did those who received a low participation level. The "highs" also, in most cases, achieved a greater percentage of their improvement goals than did their "low" counterparts. For the former, the high participation level was associated with greater mutual understanding between them and their managers, greater acceptance of job goals, a more favorable attitude toward the appraisal system, and a feeling of greater self-realization on the job.

• But employees who had traditionally been accustomed to low participation in their daily relationship with the manager did not necessarily perform better under the high participation treatment. In fact, those men who had received a high level of criticism in their appraisal interviews actually performed better when their managers set goals for them than they did when they set their own goals, as permitted under the high participation treatment.

In general, our experiment showed that the men who usually worked under high participation levels performed best on goals they set for themselves. Those who indicated that they usually worked under low levels performed best on goals that the managers set for them. Evidently, the man who usually does not participate in work-planning decisions considers job goals set by the manager to be more important than goals he sets for himself. The man accustomed to a high participation level, on the other hand, may have stronger motivation to achieve goals he sets for himself than to achieve those set by his manager.

Goal-Setting Importance

While subordinate participation in the goal-setting process had some effect on improved performance, a much more powerful influence was whether goals were set at all. Many times in appraisal discussions, managers mentioned areas of performance where improvement was needed. Quite often these were translated into specific work plans and goals. But this was not always the case. In fact, when we looked at the one performance area which each manager had emphasized in the appraisal interview as most in need of improvement, we found that these items actually were translated into specific work plans and goals for only about 60% of our experiment participants.

When performance was being measured 10 to 12 weeks after the goal-planning sessions, managers were asked to describe what results they hoped for in the way of subordinate on-the-job improvement. They did this for those important performance items that had been mentioned in the interview. Each manager was then asked to estimate on a percentage scale the degree to which his hoped-for changes had actually been observed. The average percent accomplishment estimate for those performance items that *did* get translated into goals was 65, while the percent estimate for those items that *did not* get translated into goals was about 27! Establishing specific plans and goals seemed to ensure that attention would be given to that aspect of job performance.

Summation of Findings

At the end of this experiment, we were able to draw certain tentative conclusions. These conclusions were the basis of a future research study which we will describe later. In general, we learned that:

Comprehensive Annual Performance Appraisals Are of Questionable Value Certainly a major objective of the manager in traditional appraisal discussions is motivating the subordinate to improve his performance. But the evidence we gathered indicated clearly that praise tended to have no effect, perhaps because it was regarded as the sandwich which surrounded the raw meat of criticism.[2] And criticism itself brought on defensive reactions that were essentially denials of responsibility for a poor performance.

Coaching Should Be a Day-to-Day, Not a Once-a-Year, Activity   There are two main reasons for this:

1   Employees seem to accept suggestions for improved performance if they are given in a less concentrated form than is the case in comprehensive annual appraisals. As our experiment showed, employees become clearly more prone to reject criticisms as the number of criticisms mount. This indicates that an "overload phenomenon" may be operating. In other words, each individual seems to have a tolerance level for the amount of criticism he can take. And, as this level is approached or passed, it becomes increasingly difficult for him to accept responsibility for the shortcomings pointed out.

2   Some managers reported that the traditional performance appraisal program tended to cause them to save up items where improvement was needed in order to have enough material to conduct a comprehensive discussion of performance in the annual review. This short-circuited one of the primary purposes of the appraisal program—that of giving feedback to the subordinates as to their performance. Studies of the learning process point out that feedback is less effective if much time is allowed to elapse between the performance and the feedback. This fact alone argues for more frequent discussions between the manager and the subordinate.

Goal Setting, Not Criticism, Should Be Used to Improve Performance   One of the most significant findings in our experiment was the

[2]See Richard E. Farson, "Praise Reappraised," HBR September–October 1963, p. 61.

fact that far superior results were observed when the manager and the man *together* set specific goals to be achieved, rather than merely discussed needed improvement. Frequent reviews of progress provide natural opportunities for discussing means of improving performance *as needs occur*, and these reviews are far less threatening than the annual appraisal and salary review discussions.

Separate Appraisals Should Be Held for Different Purposes   Our work demonstrated that it was unrealistic to expect a single performance appraisal program to achieve every conceivable need. It seems foolish to have a manager serving in the self-conflicting role as a counselor (helping a man to improve his performance) when, at the same time, he is presiding as a judge over the same employee's salary action case.

NEW WP&R METHOD

This intensive year-long test of the performance appraisal program indicated clearly that work-planning-and-review discussions between a man and his manager appeared to be a far more effective approach in improving job performance than was the concentrated annual performance appraisal program.

For this reason, after the findings had been announced, many GE managers adopted some form of the new WP&R program to motivate performance improvement in employees, especially those at the professional and administrative levels. Briefly described, the WP&R approach calls for periodic meetings between the manager and his subordinate. During these meetings, progress on past goals is reviewed, solutions are sought for job-related problems, and new goals are established. The intent of the method is to create a situation in which manager and subordinate can discuss job performance and needed improvements in detail without the subordinate becoming defensive.

Basic Features

This WP&R approach differs from the traditional performance appraisal program in that:

- There are more frequent discussions of performance.
- There are no summary judgments or ratings made.
- Salary action discussions are held separately.
- The emphasis is on mutual goal planning and problem solving.

As far as frequency is concerned, these WP&R discussions are held more often than traditional performance appraisal interviews, but are not scheduled at rigidly fixed intervals. Usually at the conclusion of one work planning session the man and manager set an approximate date for the next review. Frequency depends both on the nature of the job and on the manager's style of operating. Sometimes these WP&R discussions are held as often as once a month, whereas for other jobs and/or individuals, once every six months is more appropriate.

In these WP&R discussions, the manager and his subordinate do not deal in generalities. They consider specific, objectively defined work goals and establish the yardstick for measuring performance. These goals stem, of course, from broader departmental objectives and are defined in relation to the individual's position in the department.

Comparison Setting

After the findings of our experiment were communicated by means of reports and group meetings in the plant where the research was carried out, about half the key managers decided they would abandon the comprehensive annual performance appraisal method and adopt the new WP&R program instead. The other half were hesitant to make such a major change at the time. They decided, consequently, to continue with the traditional performance appraisal program and to try to make it

more effective. This provided a natural setting for us to compare the effectiveness of the two approaches. We decided that the comparison should be made in the light of the objectives usually stated for the comprehensive annual performance appraisal program. These objectives were (a) to provide knowledge of results to employees, (b) to justify reasons for salary action, and (c) to motivate and help employees do a better job.

The study design was simple. Before any changes were made, the exempt employees who would be affected by these programs were surveyed to provide base-line data. The WP&R program was then implemented in about half of the exempt group, with the other half continuing to use a modified version of the traditional performance appraisal program. One year later, the identical survey questionnaire was again administered in order to compare the changes that had occurred.

Attitudes and Actions

The results of this research study were quite convincing. The group that continued on the traditional performance appraisal showed no change in *any* of the areas measured. The WP&R group, by contrast, expressed significantly more favorable attitudes on almost all questionnaire items. Specifically, their attitudes changed in a favorable direction over the year that they participated in the new WP&R program with regard to the—

. . . amount of help the manager was giving them in improving performance on the job;

. . . degree to which the manager was receptive to new ideas and suggestions;

. . . ability of the manager to plan;

. . . extent to which the manager made use of their abilities and experience;

. . . degree to which they felt the goals they were shooting for were what they *should* be;

. . . extent to which they received help from the manager in planning for *future* job opportunities;

. . . value of the performance discussions they had with their managers.

In addition to these changes in attitudes, evidence was also found which showed clearly that the members of the WP&R group were much more likely to have taken specific actions to improve performance than were those who continued with the traditional performance appraisal approach.

CURRENT OBSERVATIONS

Recently we undertook still another intensive study of the WP&R program in order to learn more about the nature of these discussions and how they can be made most effective. While these observations have not been completed, some interesting findings have already come to light—especially in relation to differences between WP&R and traditional performance appraisal discussions.

Perceived Differences

For one thing, WP&R interviews are strictly man-to-man in character, rather than having a father-and-son flavor, as did so many of the traditional performance appraisals. This seems to be due to the fact that it is much more natural under the WP&R program for the subordinate to take the initiative when his performance on past goals is being reviewed. Thus, in listening to the subordinate's review of performance, problems, and failings, the manager is automatically cast in the role of *counselor*. This role for the manager, in turn, results naturally in a problem-solving discussion.

In the traditional performance appraisal interview, on the other hand, the manager is automatically cast in the role of *judge*. The subordinate's natural reaction is to assume a defensive posture, and thus all the necessary ingredients for an argument are present.

Since the WP&R approach focuses mainly on immediate, short-term goals, some managers are concerned that longer range, broader plans and goals might be neglected. Our data show that this concern is unfounded. In almost every case, the discussion of specific work plans and goals seems to lead naturally into a consideration of broader, longer range plans. In fact, in a substantial percentage of these sessions, even the career plans of the subordinates are reviewed.

In general, the WP&R approach appears to be a better way of defining what is expected of an individual and how he is doing on the job. Whereas the traditional performance appraisal often results in resistance to the manager's attempts to help the subordinate, the WP&R approach brings about acceptance of such attempts.

CONCLUSION

Multiple studies conducted by the Behavioral Research Service at GE reveal that the traditional performance appraisal method contains a number of problems:

1 Appraisal interviews attempt to accomplish the two objectives of—
. . . providing a written justification for salary action;
. . . motivating the employee to improve his work performance.
2 The two purposes are in conflict, with the result that the traditional appraisal system essentially becomes a salary discussion in which the manager justifies the action taken.
3 The appraisal discussion has little influence on future job performance.
4 Appreciable improvement is realized only when specified goals and deadlines are mutually established and agreed on by the subordinate and his manager in an interview split away from the appraisal interview.

This evidence, coupled with other principles relating to employee motivation, gave rise to the new WP&R program, which is proving to be far more effective in improving job performance than the traditional performance appraisal method. Thus, it appears likely that companies which are currently relying on the comprehensive annual performance appraisal process to achieve improvement in work performance might well consider the advisability of switching to some form of work-planning-and-review in their industrial personnel programs.

Reading 23

How to Ruin Motivation with Pay

W. Clay Hamner

MERIT PAY—SHOULD IT BE USED?

Most behavioral scientists believe in the "law of effect," which states simply that behavior which appears to lead to a positive consequence tends to be repeated. This principle is also followed by most large organizations which have a merit pay system for their management team. Merit pay or "pay for performance" is so widely accepted by compensation managers and academic researchers that criticizing it seems foolhardy.

Despite the soundness of the principle of the law of effect on which merit pay is based, academic researchers have criticized the merit system as being detrimental to motivation rather than enhancing motivation as designed. These criticisms generally fall into one of two categories. The first group of researchers criticize the failure of the merit plan to increase the motivation of the work force because of mismanagement or lack of understanding of the merit program by managers. The second group of researchers criticize the use of merit pay because it utilizes externally mediated rewards rather than focusing on a system where individuals can be motivated by the job itself. This second criticism centers on the proposition that employees who enjoy their job (i.e., are intrinsically motivated) will lose interest in the job when a merit pay plan is introduced because they soon believe they are doing the job for the money and not because they enjoy their job. Therefore, for the first group of researchers, the recommendation is that compensation managers need to examine ways to improve the introduction of merit plans, while the second group of researchers, albeit fewer in number, would recommend that compensation managers need to deemphasize the merit pay plan system and concentrate on improving other aspects of the job.

The purpose of this presentation will be to examine the research behind both of these positions and then present recommendations which, it is hoped, will enable the compensation manager to utilize a "pay performance" plan as a method of improving the quality and quantity of job performance. Let's begin the discussion by examining possible reasons why merit pay systems fail.

REASONS WHY MERIT PAY SYSTEMS FAIL

As noted earlier, one group of researchers has concluded that the failure of merit pay plans is

Adapted by permission of the publisher from *Compensation Review*, Third Quarter, 1975. © 1975 by AMACOM, a division of American Management Association.

due not to a weakness in the law of effect, but to a weakness in its implementation by compensation managers and the line managers involved in the merit increase recommendations. For example, after reviewing pay research from General Electric and other companies, H. H. Meyer (1975) concluded that despite the apparent soundness of the simple principle on which merit pay is based, experience tells us that it does not work with such elegant simplicity. Instead, managers typically seemed to be inclined to make relatively small discriminations in salary treatment among individuals in the same job regardless of perceived differences in performance. As a matter of fact, Meyer notes, when discriminations are made, they are likely to be based on factors other than performance—such as length of service, future potential, or perceived need for "catch up," where one employee's pay seems low in relation to others in the group.

Michael Beer (see Beer & Gery, 1972), Director of Organizational Development at Corning Glass, explains why the implementation of the merit system has lost its effectiveness when he states that pay systems evolve over time and administrative considerations and tradition often override the more important considerations of behavioral outcomes in determining the shape of the system and its administration. Therefore, both of these researchers seem to say that it is not the merit pay theory that is defective. Rather, the history of the actual implementation of the theory is at fault. Let us look at the shortcomings—noted in the literature—that may cause low motivation to result from a merit pay program.

Pay Is Not Perceived As Being Related to Job Performance

Edward E. Lawler, III, a leading researcher on pay and performance, has noted that one of the major reasons managers are unhappy with their wage system is that they do not perceive the relationship between how hard they work (productivity) and how much they earn. Lawler (1966), in a survey of 600 middle and lower level managers, found virtually no relationship between their pay and their rated performance. Of the managers studied, those who were most highly motivated to perform their jobs effectively were characterized by two attitudes: (1) they said that their pay was important to them and (2) they felt that good job performance would lead to higher pay for them.

There are several reasons why managers do not perceive their pay as being related to performance even when the company claims to have a merit pay plan. First, many rewards (e.g., stock options) are *deferred payments*, and the time horizon is so long that the employee loses sight of its relationship to performance. Second, the *goals* of the organization on which performance appraisals are based are either unclear, unrealistic, or unrelated to pay. W. H. Mobley (1974) found only 36 percent of the managers surveyed from a company using an MBO program saw goal attainment as having considerable bearing on their merit increase, while 83 percent of their bosses claim that they used the goal attainments to determine their pay increase recommendations. Third, the *secrecy* of the annual merit increases may lead managers to conclude that their recommended pay increase has no bearing on their past year's performance. R. L. Opsahl and M. D. Dunnette (1966) claimed that secrecy is due in part to a fear by salary administrators that they would have a difficult time mustering convincing arguments in favor of many of their practices. E. E. Lawler (1971) summarized his extensive research on secrecy of pay by stating that managers did not have an accurate picture of what other managers were earning. There was a general tendency for the managers to overstate the pay of managers at their own level (thereby reducing their own pay, relatively speaking) and at one level below them (again reducing their own pay, relatively speaking), while they tended to underestimate the pay of managers one level above them (thus reducing the value of future promotions).

Performance Ratings Are Seen As Biased

While many managers working under a merit program believe that the program is a good one, they are dissatisfied with the evaluation of their performance given them by their immediate superior. A merit plan is based on the assumption that managers can make objective (valid) distinctions between good and poor performance. Unfortunately, most evaluations of performance are subjective in nature, and consist of a "summary score" from a general (and sometimes dated) performance evaluation form. As H. H. Meyer (1975) notes, the supervisor's key role in determining pay creates a problem in that it reminds the employee very clearly that he or she is dependent on the supervisor for rewards. Therefore, the merit plan should, whenever possible, be based on objective measures (e.g., group sales, cost reduction per unit, goal obtainment, etc.) rather than subjective measures (e.g., cooperation, attitude, future potential, etc.).

As an aside, it should be noted that in the area of fair employment of minorities, both the courts (e.g., see *Rowe v. General Motors Corporation*, 1972) and the new EEOC (1974) guidelines recognize the potential of bias in subjective performance appraisals, and organizations must begin examining the validity of their performance ratings to see if they are, in fact, job related. My recent research has shown that, even when objective measures of job performance are clearly spelled out, supervisors have a tendency to rate blacks differently than whites and females differently than males even though their performance levels are identical (e.g., see Scott & Hamner, 1975; Hamner, Kim, Baird, & Bigoness, 1974). E. E. Lawler, III, feels that the complaints of managers and employees about the subjective nature of their performance evaluations may be a sign of a system of poor leadership.

Lawler (1971) notes that many plans seem to fail not because they are mechanically defective, but because they are ineffectively introduced, there is a lack of trust between superiors and subordinates, or the quality of the supervisor is too low. He adds that no plan can succeed in the face of low trust and poor supervision, no matter how well-constructed it may be. L. W. Gruenfeld and P. Weissenberg (1966) reported support for this theory of poor leadership espoused by Lawler when they found that good managers are much more amenable than poor managers to the idea of basing pay on performance.

Rewards Are Not Viewed As Rewards

A third problem in administering a merit increase deals with management's inability to communicate accurately to the employee the information that they are trying to communicate through the pay raise. There is no doubt that the pay raise is more than money; it tells the employee "You're loved a lot," "You're only average," "You're not appreciated around here," "You'd better get busy," etc. Often management believes it is communicating a positive message to the employee, but the message being received by the employee is negative. This may have a detrimental effect on his or her future potential. Opsahl and Dunnette (1966) warn us that the relation between performing certain desired behaviors and attainment of the pay-incentive must be explicitly specified.

The reasons that the reward message may not be seen as a reward include the following: (1) Conflicting reward schedules may be operating. (2) A problem of inequity among employees is perceived to exist. (3) The merit increase is threatening to the self-esteem of the employee. All three of these problems center on the fact that the pay increases are generally kept secret—thus causing the employees to draw erroneous conclusions—or on the fact that there is little or no communication in the form of coaching and counselling coming from the supervisor during the year, or following the performance appraisal. Instead, the employee is "expected to know" what the supervisor thinks about his or her performance. As Beer and Gery (1972) stated, the more frequent the formal and informal reviews of performance and the more the individual is told about reasons for an increase, the greater his preference for a merit increase and the lower his preference for a seniority system.

Conflicting Reward Schedules   Such schedules come about because of a defect in the merit plan itself. For example, individual rewards (e.g., the best manager will get a free trip to Hawaii) are set up in such a way that cooperation with other managers is discouraged, or perhaps a cost-reduction program is introduced at the expense of production, and one department (sales) suffers while another department (manufacturing) benefits in the short run. As Kenneth F. Foster, Manager of Composition at Xerox, has noted (see *Harvard Business Review*, July-August 1974), pay plans must be constantly changing because of general business conditions, shifts in management philosophy, competitive pressures, participant feedback, and modification in the structure and objectives of the organization. Nevertheless, these changes should be designed in such a way that the negative side effect of reduced cooperation does not result. For this reason, many companies are using a company-wide merit plan (e.g., the Scanlon Plan; see Frost, Wakeley, & Ruh, 1974) where there is a financial incentive to everyone in the organization based on the performance of the total organization.

Inequity   Inequity in pay can come about for one of two reasons. First, the employee perceives the merit increase to be unfair relative to his own past year's performance. That is, he is dissatisfied with the performance evaluation, or else feels the performance evaluation is fair, but believes his supervisor failed to reward him in a manner consistent with his rating. A much more common problem is that while the employee may agree with the dollar amount of his pay, he perceives that others who are performing at levels below him are receiving as large an increase as he, or else those who are performing at his same level are receiving higher raises. For example, an employee who was rated as above average receives an 8 percent pay increase. He perceives this to be low since he believes that the average increase was 9 percent, when in fact it was $6^1/_2$ percent. In order to avoid the feeling of inequity, which will contribute to dissatisfaction with pay and possible lower job performance, Lawler (1973) recommends that managers tell their employees how the salary raises were derived (e.g., 50 percent based on cost of living and 50 percent on merit) and tell them the range and mean of raises given in the organization for people at their job level. Lawler advocated the abandonment of secrecy policies: "There is no reason why organizations cannot make salaries public information" (1965, p. 8).

Threat to Self-Esteem   H. H. Meyer, in an excellent paper, argues that the problem with merit pay plans may be more than a problem of equity. Drawing on his previous research (Meyer, Kay, & French, 1965), he concluded that 90 percent of the managers at General Electric rated themselves as above average. Bassett and Meyer (1968) and Beer and Gery (1972) found similar results. Meyer concludes that the inconsistency in the information of the merit raise with the employee's evaluation of his or her performance will be a threat to the manager's *self-esteem*, and the manager may cope with this threat by either denying the importance of hard work or disparaging the source. Meyer concludes:

> The fact that almost everyone thinks he is an above average performer probably causes most

of our problems with merit pay plans. Since the salary increases most people get do not reflect superior performance (as determined by interpersonal comparisons, or as defined in the guide book for the pay plan), the effects of the actual pay increases on motivation are likely to be more negative than positive. The majority of the people feel discriminated against because, obviously, management does not recognize their true worth (1975, p. 13).

Managers of Merit Increases Are More Concerned with Satisfaction with Pay than Job Performance

Most studies which survey managers' satisfaction with their pay have shown high levels of dissatisfaction. Porter (1961) found that 80 percent of the managers surveyed from companies throughout the United States reported dissatisfaction with their pay. These same findings have been reported in surveys at General Electric (Penner, 1967) and a cross-section of managers from many companies (Lawler, 1965). Beer (Beer & Gery, 1972) points out that too often dissatisfaction with pay is assumed to mean dissatisfaction with amount. However, his research suggests that a change to a merit system with no increase in amount paid out by the company will increase satisfaction if the reasons for the increases are explained.

Opsahl and Dunnette (1966) noted that while there is a great deal of research on satisfaction with pay, there is less solid research in the area of the relationship between pay and job performance than any other field. Because of this failure to deal with the role of pay, Lawler (1966) notes that many managers have come to the erroneous conclusion that the experts in "human relations" have shown that pay is a relatively unimportant incentive.

In fact, Cherrington, Reitz, and Scott (1971) found that the magnitude of the relationship between satisfaction and performance depends primarily upon the performance-reinforcer contingencies that have been arranged (i.e., people who were appropriately reinforced were satisfied with their pay, while those people who were dissatisfied with their pay were those who were inappropriately rewarded). Likewise, Hamner and Foster (1974) found that the best performers working under a contingent (piece rate) pay plan were more satisfied than the poorer performers, but that there was no relationship between satisfaction and performance for those paid under a noncontingent (across the board) pay plan.

Managers need to be concerned with two questions. First, *is the merit raise being based on performance?* Numerous studies (e.g., see Lee, 1969; Belcher, 1974) show that pay is not closely related to performance in many organizations that claim to have merit ranges. Typically, these studies show that pay is much more closely related to job level and seniority than performance. In fact, Belcher (1974) reports that low, zero, and even negative correlations between pay and supervisory ratings of performance occur even among managers where the correlation would be expected to be high.

Second, *who is doing the complaining?* Donald Finn, Compensation Manager at J. C. Penney, says we are often "hung up" as managers about the satisfaction of employees with our pay recommendations. He says:

> So who is complaining and why? If low producers are low earners, the pay plan is working—but there will be complaints. If a company wants an incentive plan in which rewards are commensurate with risk, it must be willing to accept a relatively broad range of earnings and corresponding degrees of manager satisfaction. (*Harvard Business* Review, July-August, 1974, p. 8.)

Beer agrees with Finn when he says:

> A merit system can probably be utilized effectively by management in motivating employees. This concept has been in disfavor lately, but our findings indicate that more might be done with money in motivating people, particularly those who are work and achievement oriented in the first place.

While a merit system would seem to be less need satisfying to the security-oriented individual and, therefore, potentially less motivating, there is probably a net gain in installing a merit system. Those who are high in achievement-oriented needs will be stimulated by such a system to greater heights of performance, while those high in security-oriented needs will become more dissatisfied and it is hoped, will leave. (Beer & Gery, 1972, p. 330.)

Trust and Openness about Merit Increases Is Low

A merit system will not be accepted and may not have the intended motivational effects if managers do not actively administer a performance appraisal system, practice good human relations, explain the reasons for the increases and ensure that employees are not forgotten when eligibility dates come and go. The organization must provide an open climate with respect to pay, and an environment where work and effort are valued (Beer & Gery, 1972).

The Xerox Corporation has recognized the problem of trust and openness and states a philosophy that "If pay and satisfaction is to be high, pay rates must vary according to job demands in such a way that each perceived increment in a job demand factor will lead to increased pay" (*Xerox Compensation Planning Model*, June 1972). This same document at Xerox notes that organizations expect extremely high levels of trust on the part of their employees, in that:

(a) Only 72% of 184 employing organizations had a written statement of the firm's basic compensation policy covering such matters as paying competitive salaries, timing of wage and salary increases, and how raises are determined.

(b) Only 51% of these same organizations communicate their general compensation policies directly to all employees, while 21% communicate the policy only to managers.

(c) Contrarily, 69% of the firms do not provide their employees with wage and salary schedules or progression plans that apply to their own categories, thus indicating a low trust level toward employees.

(d) Over 50% of the firms do not tell their employees where this information is available.

(e) In only 48% of the firms do managers have access to salary schedules applying to their own level in the organization, and in only 18% of the companies do managers have knowledge of the salaries of other managers at their own level or higher levels. (*Xerox Compensation Planning Model*, June, 1972, pp. 68–69.)

Some Organizations View Money As the Primary Motivator, Ignoring the Importance of the Job Itself

The first five shortcomings deal with the criticism of researchers that the failure of the merit plan is due to poor implementation, and not due to a weakness in the theory of the "law of effect." However, the sixth shortcoming under discussion now centers on the second criticism that employees who have intrinsically interesting jobs will lose interest in the job when a merit pay plan is introduced. An intrinsically motivating job can be defined as one that is interesting and creative enough that certain pleasures or rewards are derived from completing the task itself. Until recently, most theories dealing with worker motivation (e.g., Porter & Lawler, 1968) have assumed that the effects of intrinsic and extrinsic reinforcement (e.g., merit pay) are additive; i.e., a worker will be more motivated to complete a task which combined both kinds of rewards than a task where only one kind of reward is present.

Deci (1971, 1972a, b), among others (Likert, 1967; Vroom & Deci, 1970), criticizes behavioral scientists who advocate a system of employee motivation that utilizes externally mediated rewards, i.e., rewards such as money administered by someone other than the employee. In so doing, according to Deci, management is attempting to control the employee's behavior so he or she will do as told. The limitations of this method of worker motivation, for Deci, is that it only satisfies a person's "lower order" needs (Maslow, 1943) and does not take into account "higher order" needs for self-esteem and self-actualization.

Deci recommends that we should move away from a method of external control, and toward a system where individuals can be motivated by the job itself. He says that this approach will allow managers to focus on higher-order needs where the rewards are mediated by the recipient (intrinsically motivated). To motivate employees intrinsically, tasks should be designed which are interesting, creative, and resourceful, and workers should have some say in decisions which concern them "so they will feel like causal agents in the activities which they engage in" (Deci, 1972a, p. 219).

Deci has introduced evidence which reportedly shows that a person's intrinsic motivation to perform an activity decreases when he or she receives contingent monetary payment for performing an interesting task. Deci concludes from these findings that:

> Interpreting these results in relation to theories of work motivation, it seems clear that the effects of intrinsic motivation and extrinsic motivation are not additive. While extrinsic rewards such as money can certainly motivate behavior, they appear to be doing so at the expense of intrinsic motivation; as a result, contingent payment systems do not appear to be compatible with participative management systems. (1972b, pp. 224–225.)

Deci brings out an important point: Managers should not use pay to offset a boring or negative task. However, like Herzberg before him, his results don't appear to completely support his conclusion about the effect of money as a motivator. Research by both Hamner and Foster (1974) and Calder and Staw (1975) has shown that the effect of intrinsic and extrinsic monetary rewards is additive and that even Deci's results themselves, on close examination, support this more traditional argument. In addition, I am not sure that merit pay plans are incompatible with a participative management system. The noted psychologist B. F. Skinner offers advice to managers on both of these last two arguments.

Skinner recommends that the organization should design feedback and incentive systems in such a way that the dual objective of getting things done and making work enjoyable are met. He says:

> It is important to remember that an incentive system isn't the only factor to take into account. How pleasant work conditions are, how easy or awkward a job is, how good or bad tools are— many things of that sort make an enormous difference in what a worker will do for what he receives. One problem of the production-line worker is that he seldom sees any of the ultimate consequences of his work. He puts on left front wheels day in and day out and he may never see the finished car. . . . (1973, p. 39.)

Skinner also suggested that people be involved in the design of the contingencies of reinforcements (in this case, merit pay plans) under which they live. This way the rewards come from the behavior of the worker in the environment, and not the supervisor. Both Kenneth F. Foster at Xerox and Joe W. Rogers, Chairman of the Board of Waffle House, agree. Foster, commenting on the McDonald pay plan, said, "McDonald's management is to be commended for recognizing a number of important incentive reward axioms. Foremost, the reward system must be meaningful to the recipient. They must also see it as equitable and its financial outcomes and rewards as within their power to control." (*Harvard Business Review*, July-August 1974, p. 5.) Rogers agreed, saying, "In the restaurant industry, a bonus system must be self-monitoring and deal only with the facts. All areas of judgment by a friendly or unfriendly superior should be absent in a bonus system. . . . let people participate in the design of the new pay. Credibility with the participants is much more critical." (Ibid., p. 6.)

Deci's recommendation that jobs be designed so that they are interesting, creative, and resourceful should be wholeheartedly supported by proponents of a merit pay plan. Skinner warns managers that too much dependency on force and a poorly designed monetary reward system may actually reduce performance, while designing the task so that it is automatically reinforcing can have positive effects on performance. He says:

> The behavior of an employee is important to the employer, who gains when the employee works industriously and carefully. How is he to be induced to do so? The standard answer was once physical force: men worked to avoid punishment or death. The by-products were troublesome however, and economics is perhaps the first field in which an explicit change was made to positive reinforcement. Most men now work, as we say, "for money."
>
> Money is not a natural reinforcer; it must be conditioned as such. Delayed reinforcement, as in a weekly wage, raises a special problem. No one works on Monday morning because he is reinforced by a paycheck on Friday afternoon. The employee who is paid by the week works during the week to avoid losing the standard of living which depends on a weekly system. Rate of work is determined by the supervisor and special aversive contingencies maintain quality. The pattern is therefore still aversive. It has often been pointed out that the attitude of the production-line worker toward his work differs conspicuously from that of the craftsman, who is envied by workers and industrial managers alike. One explanation is that the craftsman is reinforced by more than monetary consequences, but another important difference is that when a craftsman spends a week completing a given set object, each of the parts produced during the week is likely to be automatically reinforcing because of its place in the completed object. (Skinner, 1969, p. 18.)

RECOMMENDATIONS FOR OVERCOMING FAILURES IN MERIT PAY SYSTEM

In the discussion of the shortcomings of merit pay plans, my suggestions for overcoming these deficiencies have been implied or suggested. Let us briefly review and outline several of these suggestions as a point of departure for our discussion.

1 *Openness and trust should be stressed by the compensation manager.* As a minimum, employees should know the formula for devising the merit increases and should be told the range and mean of the pay increases for people at their job level. This alone should reduce some of the feeling of low self-esteem and inequity present in many organizations today.

2 *Supervisors should be trained in rating and feedback techniques.* Compensation managers should help personnel design and carry out training programs which emphasize the necessity of having consistency between performance ratings, other forms of feedback, and pay increases. In addition, managers should be trained to emphasize objective rather than subjective areas of job performance. Skinner sees one of the greatest weaknesses in the motivation of workers through reinforcement principles as due to poor training of managers. He says that what must be accomplished, and what he believes is currently lacking, is an effective training program for managers. "In the not too distant future, a new breed of industrial managers may be able to apply the principles of operant conditioning effectively." (*Organizational Dynamics*, 1973, p. 40.)

3 *Components of the annual pay increase should be clearly and openly specified.* Compensation managers need to allocate a certain percentage for a cost-of-living increase (not to cover the total cost of living, however) and a percentage for merit. The percentage for merit should be an average and not a maximum, and the manager should be able to distribute this percentage in anyway he or she deems appropriate. In other words, it should not be an either-or situation where the worker either gets the full amount of the merit increase or none at all. Any pay increase due to an adjustment for past inequities and pay increases due to promotions should come out of the payroll increase first, but should not be included in the stated average pay increase. Frequently, if the organization can afford a 10 percent increase in wages and benefits, it might take 2 percent of wages and benefits to use for the adjustments mentioned above, and then allocate an 8 percent average increase to cost of living (e.g., 4 percent) and merit (e.g., 4 percent). Therefore, the range of pay increases would be from 4 percent to 12 percent—not including adjustments—where the average for the department would be 8 percent. Along these same lines, I feel it is important to give the increases in percentages and not dollar amounts since managers have a tendency to "cheat" long-term good performers (i.e., high pay managers) when a dollar amount is used.

4 *Each organization should tailor its pay plan to the needs of the organization and individuals therein—with participation a key factor in the merit pay plan design.* One of the reasons the Scanlon plan has been so successful is that it combines participation with the company's ability to afford a merit increase. Workers understand how they get the increase they do and why it is the amount it is. In addition each company using a Scanlon approach has a unique pay plan designed especially for that organization by the members of the organization.

5 *Don't overlook other rewards.* Compensation managers should work with other staff people in the organization to improve the climate of the organization, the task design, and other forms of feedback to ensure that an employee has as much chance of success as possible.

ETHICAL IMPLICATIONS: EXCHANGE, NOT CONTROL

No discussion of effective uses of merit pay plans would be complete without a discussion of the compensation manager's ethical responsibilities in using pay as a motivator. There is no doubt that poorly designed reward structures can interfere with the development of spontaneity and creativity. Reinforcement systems which are deceptive and manipulative are an insult to everyone's integrity. The employee should be a willing party to any attempt to influence, with both parties benefiting from the relationship.

Nord (1974), referring to a well designed incentive plan, says:

> I would add that to the degree that such approaches increase the effectiveness of man's exchanges with his environment, the potential for expanding freedom seems undeniable. To me these outcomes seem highly humanistic, although, for some reason this approach is labeled anti-humanistic and approaches which appear to have less potential and human advancement are labeled humanistic.

I concur with Nord, and think the ethical responsibility of compensation managers is clear. The first step in the ethical use of monetary control in organizations is the understanding by managers of the determination of behavior (see Hamner, 1974). Since reinforcement is the single most important concept in the learning process, managers must learn how to design effective reinforcement programs that will encourage productive and creative employees. This presentation has attempted to outline the knowledge and research available for this endeavor.

REFERENCES

Bassett, G. L., & Meyer, H. H. Performance appraised based on self review. *Personnel Psychology*, 1968, **21**, 421–430.

Belcher, D. W. *Compensation Administration.* Prentice-Hall., Englewood Cliffs, N.J., 1974.

Beer, M., & Gery, G. J. Individual and organizational correlates of pay system preferences. In H. L. Tosi, R. House, & M. D. Dunnette (Eds.), *Managerial Motivation and Compensation.* East Lansing, Michigan: Michigan State University Press, 1972.

Blood, M. R. Applied behavioral analysis from an organizational perspective. Paper presented at the 82nd Annual Convention of the American

Psychological Association, New Orleans, August 1974.

Calder, B. J. & Staw, B. M. The interaction of intrinsic and extrinsic motivation: Some methodological notes. *Journal of Personality and Social Psychology*, 1975, **31**, 599–605.

Case of Big Mac's pay plans. *Harvard Business Review*, July–August 1974, 1–8.

Cherrington, D. L., Reitz, H. J., & Scott, W. E. Effects of reward and contingent reinforcement on satisfaction and task performance. *Journal of Applied Psychology*, 1971, **55**, 531–536.

Deci, E. L. Effects of externally mediated rewards on intrinsic motivation. *Journal of Personality and Social Psychology*, 1971, **18**, 105–115.

Deci, E. L. Work: Who does not like it and why? *Psychology Today*, August 1972(a), **92**, 57–58.

Deci, E. L. The effects of contingent and non-contingent rewards and controls on intrinsic motivation. *Organizational Behavior and Human Performance*, 1972(b), **8**, 217–229.

Drucker, P. F. Beyond the stick and carrot: Hysteria over the work ethic. *Psychology Today*, November 1973, **87**, 89–93.

Employee survey finds most like their work. *Equinews*, March 18, 1974 (Vol. III, No. 6).

Equal Employment Opportunity Commission Guidelines (Rev. ed.). Washington, D.C.: U.S. Government Printing Office, 1974.

Frost, C. F., Wakeley, J. H., & Ruh, R. A. *The Scanlon Plan for Organization Development: Identity, Participation and Equity.* East Lansing: Michigan State University Press, 1974.

Gruenfeld, L. W., & Weissenberg, P. Supervisory characteristics and attitudes toward performance appraisals. *Personnel Psychology*, 1966, 143–152.

Hamner, W. Clay. Reinforcement theory and contingency management in organizational settings. In H. L. Tosi & W. C. Hamner (Eds.), *Management and Organizational Behavior: A Contingency Approach.* St. Clair Press, 1974.

Hamner, W. Clay, Kim, J., Baird, L., & Bigoness, W. Race and sex as determinants of ratings by "potential" employees in a simulated work sampling task. *Journal of Applied Psychology*, 1974, **59**, 705–711.

Hamner, W. Clay, & Foster, L. W. Are intrinsic and extrinsic rewards additive? A test of Deci's cognitive evaluation theory. Paper presented at the National Academy of Management, Seattle, 1974.

Lawler, E. E. Managers' perceptions of their subordinates' pay and of their superiors' pay. *Personnel Psychology*, 1965, **18**, 413–422.

Lawler, E. E. The mythology of management compensation. *California Management Review*, 1966, **9**, 11–22.

Lawler, E. E. *Pay and Organizational Effectiveness.* New York: McGraw-Hill, 1971.

Lawler, E. E. *Motivation in Work Organization.* Monterez, Calif.: Brooks/Cole, 1973.

Lee, S. M. Salary equity: Its determination, analysis and correlates. Unpublished doctoral dissertation, University of Georgia, 1969.

Likert, R. *New Patterns of Management* (2nd ed.). New York: McGraw-Hill, 1967.

Maslow, A. H. A theory of human motivation. *Psychological Review*, 1943, **50**, 370–396.

Meyer, H. H. The pay for performance dilemma. *Organizational Dynamics*, 1975, **3**(3), 39–50.

Meyer, H. H., Kay, E., & French, J. R. P. Split roles in performance appraisals. *Harvard Business Review*, January-February 1965.

Mobley, W. H. The link between MBO and merit compensation. *Personnel Journal*, June 1974, 423–427.

Nord, W. R. Some issues in the application of operant conditioning to the management of organizations. Paper presented at the National Academy of Management, Seattle, 1974.

Opsahl, R. L., & Dunnette, M. D. The role of financial compensation in industrial motivations. *Psychological Bulletin*, 1966, **66**, 94–118.

Penner, D. D. A study of the causes and consequences of salary satisfaction. General Electric Company, *Behavioral Research Service Report*, 1967.

Porter, L. W. A study of perceived need satisfactions in bottom and middle management jobs. *Journal of Applied Psychology*, 1961, **45**, 1–10.

Porter, L. W., & Lawler, E. E. *Managerial attitudes and Performance.* Homewood, Ill.: Irwin-Dorsey, 1968.

Rowe vs. General Motors Corporation, 457 F 2d. 348 (5th Cir. 1972).

Scott, W. E., & Hamner, W. Clay. The influence of

variations in performance profiles on the performance evaluation process: An examination of the validity of the criteria. *Organizational Behavior and Human Performance*, 1975.

Skinner, B. F. *Contingencies of Reinforcement.* New York: Appleton-Century-Crofts, 1969.

Skinner, B. F. Conversations with B. F. Skinner.

Organizational Dynamics, Winter 1973, 31–40.

Vroom, V. H., & Deci, E. L. An overview of work motivation. In V. H. Vroom & E. L. Deci (Eds.), *Management and Motivation.* Baltimore.: Penguin Press, 1970.

Xerox Compensation Planning Model. Rochester, N.Y.: Xerox Corporation, June 1972.

Reading 24

New Approaches to Pay Administration

Edward E. Lawler III

Significant improvements can be made in the way most organizations administer pay. This conclusion is suggested by the experiences of a few organizations that have been willing to innovate in the area of pay administration. Such practices as cafeteria-style fringe-benefit programs, lump-sum salary increases, and participation of employees in pay decisions are yielding improvements in both productivity and the quality of work life. Although these and other innovative pay practices probably aren't right for all organizations, they apparently will yield improvements in the quality of work life and organizational effectiveness in many.

Despite the potential advantages of these new pay practices, most organizations seem hesitant to abandon the traditional approaches to wage and salary administration. Because of this hesitancy, they are failing to get the maximum return possible on the money they spend on pay. The reasons for this are many and involve some basic misunderstandings about how pay can affect employee behavior. Thus, before we discuss some of the new approaches to pay administration, it is necessary to briefly deal with two issues concerned with how pay influences behavior in organizations.

PAY IS IMPORTANT

The writings of behavioral scientists like Herzberg and Maslow seem to have convinced many executives that pay is not all that important to employees and that it can only be a source of dissatisfaction. Thus, when executives seek ways to increase motivation and productivity, they tend to forget about changes in the pay system and to concentrate on such things as job enrichment programs, team-building sessions, and management training. The research evidence on the effects of pay does not support the view that it is unimportant or just a source of dissatisfaction (Lawler, 1971). Quite the opposite seems to be true. Pay seems to have a strong impact on satisfaction, and therefore can affect absenteeism and turnover. When pay is tied to performance it also has been shown to contribute to motivation. Thus, the evidence suggests that pay is important to employees and that it can significantly affect their behavior.

PAY IS PART OF A TOTAL SYSTEM

All too often executives fail to take a system viewpoint when they consider approaches to improving organizational effectiveness. Be-

Another version of this article appeared in *Personnel*, September-October 1976, **53**(5), 11–23. Used by permission of the publisher, AMACOM, a division of American Management Associations.

cause of this, they think it is possible to install such things as management by objectives and job enrichment in their organizations without changing the pay system. Nothing could be farther from the truth. New practices in other areas usually require new pay practices. Organizations are complex, interrelated systems and, to operate effectively, all the subsystems must be in harmony. If changes are made in one important area (e.g., job or organization design), changes are required in others so that all the subsystems will be in balance. Thus, even though an organizational change begins by altering the nature of jobs, it cannot stop there if it is to be effective. It must go on to alter all the other relevant systems in the organization.

Because pay is important and pervasive in organizations, almost any important organizational change is likely to require a change in the pay system. The reverse of this is also true; that is, almost any change in the pay system requires changes in other aspects of the organization if it is to be effective. Because of the great importance of the fit between pay system practices and other management practices, the discussion of new pay practices which follows emphasizes the kinds of organizational conditions under which they will work best. It starts by describing five new pay practices and then it shows how to decide whether they will be effective in your organization.

CAFETERIA FRINGE BENEFITS

The typical fringe-benefit program provides equal amounts of such benefits as life insurance and health insurance to all members of the organization who are at similar levels in the organization. Typically, there is one fringe-benefit package for hourly employees, one for salaried employees, and a third for the top levels of management. This approach emphasizes the differences between levels of the organization and fails to emphasize the significant differences among people who are at the same organizational level. Research quite clearly shows that what is a valued benefit to one employee is not always a valued benefit to another (Nealey, 1963). When studies ask employees to allocate a hypothetical raise among a number of benefits, such things as age, marital status, and number of children influence which benefits a person prefers. For example, young unmarried men want more vacation time, while young married men are willing to give up vacation for higher pay. Older employees want greater retirement benefits, and younger employees want more cash.

These findings are hardly surprising: it stands to reason that people in different life situations have different needs. The fact that many people do not get the fringe benefits they want has some interesting implications for the degree to which fringe-benefit programs contribute to the quality of work life a person experiences and hence to organizational effectiveness. Essentially, it means that most fringe-benefit programs fail to contribute optimally to both. They end up costing the organization money for benefits that are not valued by the employees and that do not contribute to their satisfaction and desire to work for the organization.

One way to improve employees' satisfaction with fringe benefits at virtually no cost to the organization is to introduce a "cafeteria-style" fringe-benefit compensation plan. This plan involves giving employees the amount of money the organization is willing to spend on their total pay package and allowing them to spend this money as they wish. They can choose to take it all in cash or they can choose to take some in cash and use the rest to buy the fringe benefits they actually want. The choice brings home to the employees rather clearly just how much the organization is spending to compensate them, and it assures that the money will be spent only on the fringe benefits they want. Thus, it can increase employees' perceptions of the value of their pay package and it can also increase their pay satisfaction. These in turn contribute to organizational effectiveness because they decrease absenteeism and turnover, and generally allow the organization to attract a more competent work force.

There are some practical problems with the cafeteria approach, but they are far from insurmountable. One obvious difficulty is that the plan will complicate the bookkeeping aspects of wage and salary administration. With the assistance of a computer, this difficulty can be overcome, however. Probably the most serious practical problem with the cafeteria approach stems from the fact that the cost and availability of many fringe benefits (e.g., life insurance plans) is based upon the number of people who subscribe to them. Thus, it is difficult to price a benefit plan and to determine its availability in advance so that an employee can make an intelligent decision about whether or not he or she wants to participate in it. In large companies, this is not likely to be a serious problem since a minimum number of participants probably can be guaranteed in advance. Smaller companies may have to try to negotiate special agreements with insurance companies and others who underwrite aspects of the benefit package, or they may simply have to take some losses when the plan first goes into effect. After some experience with the plan, an organization should be able to judge in advance the number of employees who will select different benefits and be able to price them accordingly.

Despite the practical problems with cafeteria-style plans, two organizations, the Systems Group of the TRW Corporation and the Educational Testing Service, have put them into effect. The largest and first plan was put into effect at TRW (Fragner, 1975). It started with a series of surveys designed to get an estimate of how many people would choose different benefit options. The plan, as implemented in the fall of 1974, is far from a full cafeteria plan, since it only allows for a limited number of choices and requires everyone to take minimum levels of the important benefits. It does, however, put all 12,000 employees in the organization on the plan, it does allow for new choices each year, and it does give employees choices among significantly different benefit plans (over 80 percent of the employees took advantage of this opportunity and changed their benefit packages). At the present time, for example, the employees can choose among four hospital plans. It should be noted that the plan is supported by an extensive computer software program, that its introduction was preceded by more than a year of development work, and that it was tried in an organization that has a record of communicating effectively with its employees. The ETS plan covers a smaller number of employees (less than 3,000) but it provides more opportunities for choice than does the TRW plan.

SKILL EVALUATION PAY PLANS

The pay systems of most organizations are built upon job-evaluation programs which first describe a job and then assess the characteristics of it. Once a job has been evaluated, it is compared with a survey of what other organizations pay for jobs with similar characteristics in order to set the pay for the job at a level that is in line with the outside market. This approach has many weaknesses, including the fact that it fails to reward individuals for all the skills they have; and it fails to encourage individuals to learn new job-related skills. Most of these problems occur because job-evaluation plans treat employees not as individuals but as jobholders.

In an attempt to improve on traditional job-evaluation plans, some organizations in the United States and abroad have recently introduced skill-evaluation pay plans. In these plans, people are paid according to what they can do rather than what job they do. Most of these plans pay people according to the number of jobs in the organization they can perform and do not take into account the job the person actually does at a given time. This has the effect of focusing on the individual more than the job, and of encouraging individuals to learn more skills.

As with most new approaches to management, it isn't clear when or where skill-evaluation pay plans were first used. They have been most frequently used in plants which are structured around work groups that practice a high level of job rotation. Evaluations based on skills seem to fit well here because effective job rotation *requires* individuals who have a variety of skills. At this point, this approach has enjoyed limited acceptance in the United States. Proctor and Gamble has used it in some of its new plants, and General Foods has used it in its Topeka, Kansas, plant (Walton, 1972).

The pay plan at Topeka provides a good example of how this type of plan works. It is based upon the starting rate given to all non-management employees when they are hired. After they have mastered five different jobs, they move up to the next higher pay rate. After they have mastered all the production jobs in the plant, which usually takes a minimum of two years, they move to the top or plant rate. Employees are given encouragement and support to learn new skills. The members of the person's work team decide when a person has actually mastered a new set of skills. After people learn all the jobs, they continue to rotate among the same jobs. At this point, their only opportunity for additional pay lies in acquiring a specialty rate which is given to individuals who have gained expertise in a skilled trade (e.g., plumbing or electricity).

There are several ways in which plans based on skills seem to contribute to organizational effectiveness. They increase the flexibility of the work force and give employees a broader perspective on how the plant operates. This seems to lead to a more adaptive production system and to better decision making by all members of the work force. An attitude survey which I recently did at Topeka showed, in addition, that the plan there contributes to a spirit of personal growth and development and is seen as a very fair way to administer pay.

Despite having a high degree of promise, such plans are not without their problems. These plans require a large investment in training. This investment can take many costly forms, including formal classroom education and having inexperienced individuals doing jobs. It is interesting to note that most of the plants where these plans have been successfully used are essentially process production plants (e.g., chemicals, bulk food). This seems to be a production technology where it is particularly advantageous to use skill evaluation plans. With process production there is a definite advantage to having individuals know a number of jobs, since it creates a flexible work force that understands the total plant as a system. This is particularly important in process plants, since the jobs are so highly interrelated. This is in marked contrast to many service and unit production organizations where jobs are very independent. It is also important to note that these plans usually lead to high wage levels. Because of the plan, employees become more valuable and they have to be paid accordingly. Finally, there is the danger that the organization will end up with a highly trained work force that wants to continue to develop but has nowhere to go. This problem can be overcome by such things as group incentive plans and interplant transfers, but it needs to be anticipated.

LUMP-SUM SALARY INCREASES

In most organizations, there is no flexibility with respect to when raises are distributed to employees. Although organizations speak in terms of annual salary increases, in fact, all but a few organizations actually give raises by adjusting the regular pay checks of employees. For example, if the person is paid weekly, then his or her weekly pay check is increased to reflect the amount of the "annual salary increase." This approach allows employees no flexibility with respect to when they receive their raises. To get the full amount of their "annual increase," they have to wait a full year. It also often has the effect of perceptually "burying" a raise so that after it is divided up among the regular pay checks—and the tax deductions are made—very little change occurs in the take-home pay.

Recognizing these problems, some organizations have instituted plans for lump-sum salary increases, in order to make their salary increases more flexible and visible, and at the same time, communicate to their employees that they are willing to do innovative things in the area of pay administration. Under these programs, individuals are given the opportunity to decide when they will receive their annual increase. Just about any option is available including receiving *all* of it in one lump sum at the beginning of the year. Employees can also choose to have it folded into their regular salary check, as has been done in the past. Each year, the employees can make a new choice. They are not bound by any of their past choices, and each year they have the opportunity to allocate not only the current year's raise but the raises from all the years since the program began.

The money which is advanced to employees is treated as a loan so that if they quit before the end of the year, they have to pay the company back for the proportion of their pay increase they have not yet earned. Also, since the money is advanced to employees before they earn it, they are charged interest at a low rate to offset the cash-flow problems this causes the companies. This has the effect of somewhat reducing the attractiveness of taking the money in advance, but practice indicates that most persons still prefer to take the money early.

Unfortunately, there is little research evidence on how effective the lump-sum program is. All that can be reported so far is that it appears to be a practice which helps both the organization and the individual employee. It costs individuals nothing, and they gain the opportunity to shape their income to fit their unique needs and desires. The costs involved to an organization are minimal. The administration of a lump-sum increase plan does involve some small extra costs for the organization. Like a cafeteria fringe-benefit program, it requires extra bookkeeping and record keeping. There also will undoubtedly be some situations where money will be lost because employees will quit and won't pay back the advances they received. On the plus side, all other things being equal, organizations which give individuals the choice of when they will receive their increases should have a competitive advantage in attracting and retaining employees. Like other practices which make organizations more attractive, it can pay off in a number of ways—better selection ratios, lower turnover, and lower absenteeism. These, in turn, will result in lower personnel costs and a more talented group of employees.

Giving lump-sum increases also serves to increase the visibility and saliency of the amount of a salary increase. A large raise tends to come across clearly as a large amount of money and a small raise tends to come across as just what it is—a small increase. Increasing the saliency of the amount of a raise may or may not be functional for an organization. It depends on how well pay is administered by the organization. If pay is administered arbitrarily and not based on performance, then it is hardly functional to increase the saliency of the size of an increase. On the other hand, if an organization does a "good" job of administering pay, then increasing the saliency of raises can be functional.

For example, if the increases are based on performance, then the lump-sum approach has the potential of making pay a more effective motivator because pay will be more clearly tied to behavior. If pay increases are equitably distributed, lump-sum increases can make it clear that this is true, thereby increasing pay satisfaction and reducing the tendency of individuals who perform at a high level to look for another job. On the other hand, if pay increases are inequitably distributed, lump-sum increases can highlight this and lead to problems.

COMMUNICATING ABOUT PAY

Secrecy about pay rates seems to be an accepted practice in most business organizations. Most executives, when asked why they favor secrecy, argue that everyone is more satisfied when the pay is secret and they point out that most individuals prefer secret pay. They don't point out, however, that secrecy also gives pay administrators greater latitude in administering pay, since they don't have to explain their actions. Despite the apparent advantages of secrecy, some organizations are making information about pay more public (e.g., Corning Glass, Bell Laboratories). The reasons for this are significant and suggest that many organizations can profit from greater openness.

Research I have conducted shows that secrecy tends to lead people to overestimate the pay of individuals at the same levels in the organization, and it shows that the greater the overestimation, the greater the dissatisfaction (Lawler, 1971). This finding suggests that pay secrecy may do more to cause pay dissatisfaction than to reduce it, because it encourages misperceptions that contribute to dissatisfaction. There is also reason to believe that secrecy can reduce motivation. The motivating power of pay depends on the rather delicate perception that performance will lead to a pay increase. This perception requires a belief in the honesty of the organization and a trust in its future behavior. Secrecy does not contribute to trust; openness does, because it allows people to test for themselves the validity of an organization's statements, and it communicates to individuals that the organization has nothing to hide (Steele, 1975).

Making pay information public will not in itself establish the belief that pay is based upon performance. All it can do is clarify those situations where pay actually *is* based upon performance, but where it is not obvious because salary information is not available. This point was recently demonstrated in one organization that had a merit-based plan and kept pay secret. Data collected several years ago showed that the employees said there was only a moderate relationship between pay and performance. Data collected after the company became more open about pay showed a significant increase in the employee's perceptions of the degree to which pay and performance were related. The crucial factor in making this change to openness successful was that pay was actually tied to performance. Making pay rates public where pay is not tied to performance will only serve to emphasize more dramatically that pay and performance are not related, thereby further reducing the power of pay to motivate.

In addition to making the relationship between pay and performance clear, openness can have another important effect. It can motivate managers to make better pay decisions. With secrecy it is difficult for individuals to obtain the kind of factual information that is needed to question the salary or the raise they have received, and the validity of what supervisors tell them about the relative size of their raise. Thus, supervisors, in a sense, are protected from challenges to their pay decisions. Making pay public can change this and can increase the motivation of managers to do a good job of pay administration.

There is a danger in making pay public, however. For example, superiors may simply decide to give everyone the same pay in order to avoid the uncomfortable situation of telling some employees why they are receiving less than others.

One question which always arises whenever greater openness about pay is discussed is, How much information about pay should be made public? Should everyone's salary be made public, or only pay ranges for the various kinds of jobs? The answer depends on the situation. Consideration needs to be given to how well performance can be measured. If it is difficult to measure—as it often is in high level jobs—then open pay needs to be approached carefully because it will be difficult to administer pay in a way that will clearly tie it to performance. If the organization has always had strict secrecy concerning pay, then it would be foolish to try to make pay completely open overnight. As a beginning, an organization might release some information on pay ranges and median salaries for various jobs. Most individuals do want at least this amount of information to be public. Next, organizations might give out information on the size of raises and on who is getting them. Finally, the organization could move to complete openness, but only when it has, as a whole, become more open, and is characterized by a high level of trust among superiors, subordinates, and peers. Few organizations at the present time are ready for complete openness; it simply goes too much against the political climates and power politics that exist.

PARTICIPATION IN PAY DECISIONS

There are a number of decisions that need to be made about pay. The most important include those concerning pay-system design and those concerning operating decisions about how much particular individuals are to be paid. Although these decisions are typically made by top management, some organizations are experimenting with having them made by the individuals who are affected by the decisions.

The results of these efforts have often been quite positive. For example, a building maintenance company which was concerned about absenteeism asked several groups of employees to design an attendance bonus plan for themselves. The same plan was then installed in other areas in the company. The results showed the importance of participation in the design process. Attendance increased in all groups where it was applied, but it increased the most in the groups that developed it (Lawler & Hackman, 1969).

As part of another study, the employees of a small manufacturing plant were asked to design their own pay system. The result was a new pay program calling for an 8 percent increase in the organization's salary costs and a significant realignment of employee salaries. A survey of the company six months after the new system went into effect showed significant improvements in turnover, job satisfaction, and satisfaction with pay and its administration. Why did this occur? The workers seemed to feel better about their pay because the additional information they received gave them a clearer, more accurate picture of how it compared with that of others. Further, the participation led to feelings of ownership of the plan, and produced a plan where the actual decisions about pay were made by their peers. These factors led to feelings that the pay system was fair and trustworthy. It also seemed that the new pay rates themselves were more in line with the workers' perceptions of what was fair, and that pay satisfaction would have increased somewhat even if the employees hadn't developed a commitment to the plan. This is not surprising, of course, since what constitutes fair pay exists only in the mind of the person who perceives the situation, and in this situation the plan allowed the people with the relevant feelings to control the pay rates directly. Thus, in this case, not only did participation by employees lead to more understanding and commitment, it seemed to lead to better decisions. This line of reasoning is summarized in Figure 24-1, which shows that, under some conditions, participation leads to higher-quality decisions, and that it usually leads to favorable perceptions of pay.

In yet another situation, a company has asked its executives to redesign their own bonus system. It is too early to report on the long-term effectiveness of this move, but it is not too early to report that the executives worked hard to develop a new plan and that the new plan was seen as reasonable by top management.

The situation with respect to decisions about how individuals will be treated within an established pay structure is different from the one concerning pay-system design. In the Topeka plant of General Foods, and others around the world, this decision is made by peers. The limited research which has been done so far suggests that when peers are given the opportunity to make decisions, they behave responsibly and make decisions that result in a high degree of satisfaction with pay and commitment to the organization. There

typically are problems, however. Probably the most important of these is the difficulty peer groups have in saying no to a request for a pay raise when there are no limits on how many individuals can get raises or good performance ratings. This is a particular problem when there are no clear-cut objective standards for what constitutes doing a job well. Some organizations have tried to solve this problem by giving the group a lump sum of money to allocate among the group members. This prevents the group from deciding that everyone is doing well and deserves the maximum increase the organization can offer. It doesn't, however, prevent the group from deciding to give everyone the same raise. This often is not functional because it means that pay isn't related to performance in a motivating way, and yet it seems to be a frequent outcome. The reason this decision is so often reached is that individuals have trouble talking about each other's performance, particularly when no standards are agreed upon. Most groups which have handled this issue successfully not only have agreed upon standards, but have also engaged in considerable group process work and have expert process consultation. Finally, it is important to note that participation in decisions about pay takes up employees' production time and that this has a cost.

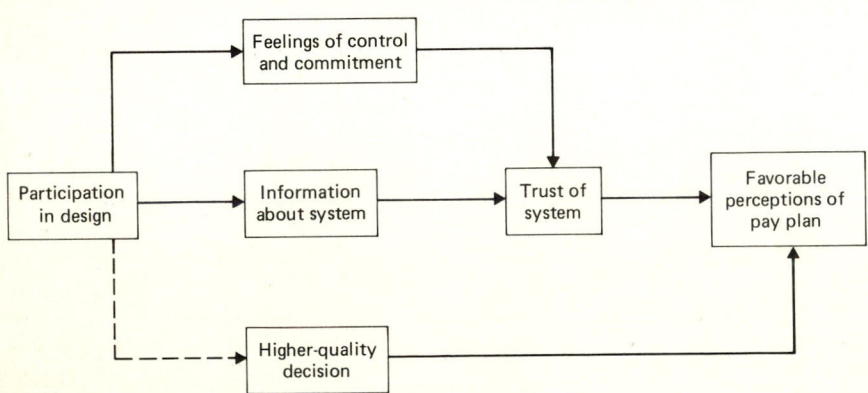

Figure 24-1 Effects of participation on perceptions of pay.

DECIDING WHAT WILL WORK FOR YOU

At this point, the reader is probably thinking, "All these new approaches are interesting, but will they work in my organization? How can I decide which ones to try?" Table 24-1 was designed to give the interested reader an overview of the different practices. It lists the advantages and disadvantages of each. A major advantage of most of them is increased satisfaction and job attractiveness. Although this may not have an immediate direct impact on profit or organizational effectiveness, it nevertheless is a significant advantage since it can reduce absenteeism, turnover, and tardiness. These, in turn, have significant impacts on profits and organizational effectiveness. Also shown in Table 24-1 are some of the situational factors which favor each of the new approaches. It is impossible to emphasize too strongly the importance of these situational factors. The potential advantages of these practices can be realized only if they are installed in a situation that is favorable to them.

Two factors in particular need to be given a great deal of weight in decisions concerning new pay practices: the management style of the organization and the condition of the present pay system. The executive who is interested in trying these pay practices in his or her organization should first ask, "What management style do I want to see used in my organization?" If the answer to this is participative or democratic, a different set of pay practices are applicable than if the answer is

Table 24-1 Summary of New Pay Practices

	Major advantages	Major disadvantages	Favorable situational factors
Cafeteria-style fringe benefits	Increased satisfaction with pay and benefits	Cost of administration	Well-educated, heterogeneous work force
Lump-sum salary increases	Increased satisfaction with pay; greater visibility of pay increases	Cost of administration	Fair pay rates
Skill-based evaluation	More flexible and skilled work force; increased satisfaction	Cost of training and higher salaries	Employees who want to develop themselves; jobs that are interdependent
Open salary information	Increased satisfaction with pay; greater trust, and motivation; better salary administration	Pressure to pay all employees the same; complaints about pay rates	Open climate, fair pay rates, pay based on performance
Participative pay decisions	Better pay decisions; increased satisfaction, motivation, and trust	Time consumed	Democratic management climate; work force that wants to participate and that is concerned about organizational goals

authoritative or top down. The second question which should be asked is, "Are the present pay rates in my organization basically fair and equitable?" If the answer to this is yes, then several new practices are applicable which are not applicable if the answer is no.

Figure 24-2 presents a detailed analysis of how the answers to the questions concerned with management style and pay fairness affect the applicability of pay practices. It assumes that an effort is being made to use pay as a motivator and that a clear, visible relationship between pay and performance is desired. Basically, it suggests that most of the new practices are best applied where there is a participative management style. In most cases these practices have been implemented after a participative management style has been adopted, but this needn't be. A few organizations have experimented (e.g., the manufacturing company mentioned earlier) with using changes in pay administration practices as a way of moving the organization toward a more participative management style. In these situations changes in the pay system have been used as an important lever in a larger program of change. It is also apparent that most of these practices are applicable only when a good, basic pay structure is in place. Openness, salary information, and cafeteria benefit programs are not substitutes for a good basic salary system that sets fair salaries. They can, however, often lead to significant advantages when a good, basic salary plan is in place.

SUMMARY AND CONCLUSIONS

It seems clear that some useful new approaches to an old problem, pay administration, have been developed and used by a few organizations. These new approaches vary widely in their applicability to other organizations and in their potential impact. The thoughtful executive should take a diagnostic approach toward these practices. That is, each should be considered in light of the conditions which exist in his or her organization. Chances are, most executives will find that some are applicable while others are not. The crucial thing is that each be given careful consideration, for each potentially can have a favorable impact. But it certainly is true that, with respect to changes in the pay system, the buyer must be aware.

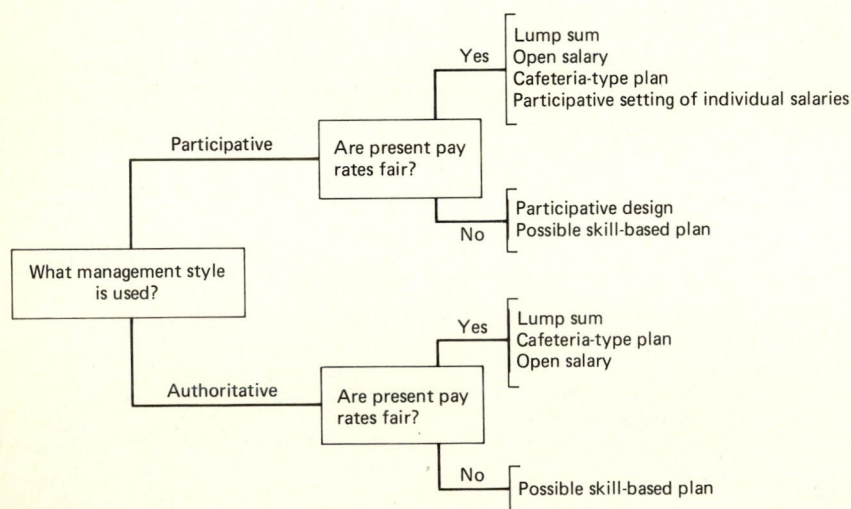

Figure 24-2   Guide to choosing among the new approaches to pay administration.

REFERENCES

Fragner, B. N. Employee's "cafeteria" offers insurance options. *Harvard Business Review,* 1975, **53**(6) 7–10.

Lawler, E. E. *Pay and organizational effectiveness.* New York: McGraw-Hill, 1971.

Lawler, E. E., & Hackman, J. R. The impact of employee participation in the development of pay incentive plans: A field experiment. *Journal of Applied Psychology,* 1969, **53,** 467–471.

Nealey, S. Pay and benefit preferences. *Industrial Relations,* 1963, **3,** 17–28.

Steele, F. *The open organization.* Reading, Mass.: Addison-Wesley, 1975.

Walton, R. E. How to counter alienation in the plant. *Harvard Business Review,* November–December 1972, **50**(6), 70–81.

Reading 25

Behavior Modification: Application to Manpower Management

Fred Luthans

Donald D. White, Jr.

Sophisticated quantitative tools to improve organizational effectiveness have been developed in recent years. The behavioral approach to management also has contributed to the better understanding of human behavior in organizations.

However, by comparison, fresh ideas and new techniques from behavioral science have not kept pace with technical advances made in management practice. Too often, knowledge in behavioral science is rarely applied to manpower management. Can the gap between behavioral science theory and research and practical application to manpower management be bridged?

One new application was recently inferred in Owen Aldis' lighthearted article, "Of Pigeons and Men."[1] He used the concepts from learning theory, as applied to pigeons in the laboratory, for analyzing improved employee performance in the workplace.

The recent upsurge of interest in behavior

[1] Owen Aldis, "Of Pigeons and Men," *Harvard Business Review,* July-August, 1961, pp. 59–63.

modification or behavior therapy has stimulated the authors to attempt a meaningful application to manpower management. Behavior modification may provide managers on all levels with a practical tool for shaping, improving, and motivating behavior of organizational participants.

WHAT IS BEHAVIOR MODIFICATION?

Behavior modification is not new and is relatively simple to understand. In the literature, behavior modification is sometimes equated with learning itself, *i.e.,* any change in behavior. In more popular usage, it is a specific technique and form of therapy that is being extensively used in the treatment of mental patients and for the behavioral control of school children. Its roots are in the behaviorist school of psychological thought.

More directly, behavior modification is derived from B. F. Skinner's operant conditioning. The basic process involves systematically reinforcing positive behavior while at the

Personnel Administration, 1971, **34,** 41–47. Reprinted by permission of the International Personnel Management Association, 1313 East 60th Street, Chicago, Illinois 60637.

same time ignoring or exercising negative reinforcements to eliminate unwanted behavior. The end result is the creation of a more acceptable response to the given stimulus situation. Before direct applications are discussed, some of the key elements of behavior modification should be clarified.

The technique concentrates on a person's overt behavior and not on the underlying causes of behavior. The behavioral approach to management has taken an opposite approach by attempting to determine why an individual behaves in a given way. Consequently, a good deal of effort has been devoted to "looking beneath the surface." Unfortunately, pinpointing the cause of behavior is very difficult because of many independent or related causal factors which affect behavior. Behavior modification eliminates this difficulty by dealing with overt symptoms only. Concentration on outward behavior allows the manpower manager to try realistically to modify behavior. This does not imply that the "obvious" is always the "actual." However, under behavior modification, managers are not required to psychoanalyze workers. Managers need only to have the ability to observe and deal with outward manifestations of behavior.

Success of behavior modification depends on acute awareness of the behavior variables that are subject to manipulation and change. The first step is for managers to be familiar with the total behavior patterns of subordinates or workers. From the standpoint of goal attainment, they must then decide which patterns are acceptable, which are not, and what new behavior patterns are needed. Overt patterns may be altered immediately. In time, attitudes may also be affected by a behavior modification program.

BEHAVIOR REPLACEMENT

There are two primary aspects of behavior modifications programs. First, an attempt is made to eliminate unwanted behavior that detracts from organizational goal attainment. Extinction may be accomplished in two ways. Learning theory states that " . . . when the response is followed by punishment . . . the frequency of probability of recurrence decreases."[2] Therefore, punishment may be applied to cause specified behavior to be abandoned. The difficulty with negative reinforcement is the possibility of "backlash" reaction and a short duration of extinction. In other words, another undesirable reaction may result, or the punished behavior may reappear in a short time. One analysis concludes that, "Under punishment, the behavior is only temporarily suppressed, only to emerge again when the aversive consequence no longer follows."[3] The following situation illustrates this point.

Consider the case of a group of workers gathered around the timeclock, listening to Joe's off-color story. Joe's boss walks by and gives Joe a disgusted look. This act by the boss is a negative reinforcement of his behavior, and the story stops. When the boss leaves the area, the negative reinforcement disappears, and Joe's story is finished.

Extinction of behavior may also be accomplished through the withholding of positive reinforcement. If customary rewards for the action in question are no longer granted, then extinction will occur. A simple example would be the "office jokester" who tells one of his typically non-humorous stories during the coffee break. For this effort, he receives no positive reinforcement from the group, and

[2]Bernard Berelson and Gary A. Steiner, *Human Behavior*, Second edition, (New York: Harcourt, Brace, & World, Inc., 1967), p. 132.

[3]Halmuth H. Schaefer, "Investigations in Operant Conditioning Procedures for a Mental Hospital," found in *Reinforcement Theory in Psychological Treatment: A Symposium*, Jerome Fisher and Robert E. Harris, editors, California Mental Health Research Monograph, No. 8, p. 28.

they immediately turn to another topic. If reward is repeatedly withheld, the bad jokes eventually will be eliminated. "This is not passive disappearance, but rather there is learned an inhibition or tendency not to respond."[4] Since the use of punishment may only temporarily suppress and not totally extinguish behavior, a logical alternative would be to withhold positive sanctions.

A second major goal of behavior modification is to create *acceptable new responses* to an environmental stimulus. As in eliminating behavior, reinforcement techniques play the vital role in developing new behavioral responses. The process is often very complex. For example, some responses which are producing wanted behavior unwittingly may be provoking negative sanctions. Removal of the negative sanctions for the wanted behavior is obviously a prerequisite before the positive reinforcement can be applied.

Direct reward of responses is the best method to stabilize intended behavior patterns. The consensus of learning theory states that, ". . . when a response is followed by a reward (or 'reinforcement'), the frequency of probability of its recurrence increases."[5] This statement implies a treatment for both wanted and unwanted behavior. Eliminating undesirable behavior without providing a new substitute pattern leaves the worker open to learn another undesirable set of responses. The entire procedure may have to be repeated. The substitution of new desirable responses in place of behavior that is being eliminated is often referred to as behavior replacement, or, more commonly, behavior modification. Thus, the overall purpose of behavior modification is to leave the individual with new or modified behavioral patterns in place of behavior that was deemed to be not wanted or needed.

[4]Leonard P. Ullmann and Leonard Krasner, *Case Studies in Behavior Modification* (New York: Holt, Rinehart and Winston, Inc., 1965), p. 16.
[5]Berelson and Steiner, *op. cit.*

TYPES OF REINFORCEMENT

Perhaps the most important ingredient in the successful application of behavior modification is the administration of the program. Every discussion of learning theory carefully explains that reinforcement must be applied according to a detailed, systematic plan. The reinforcement schedule that is used depends on the nature and degree of behavior that the person presently demonstrates. If the overt symptoms of the desired behavior pattern exist, it follows that no reinforcement of the behavior is possible. One avenue would be to inform the individual what response would lead to a reward. For example, "Tom, if you perform in the following manner, you will be given a raise." Tom is now aware of the response that is required of him to obtain the reinforcement, and his expectancy of the reinforcement will cause him to act.

An alternative approach to reinforcement would require new behavior to be shaped from existing behavior. Assume that the desired pattern does not currently exist and, therefore, cannot be reinforced. To move toward the new behavior, a reward may be applied to responses which closely approximate the desirable behavior. Modification or shaping can be accomplished by discriminately employing reinforcement to basic elements of approximate behavior. A closely controlled reinforcement schedule is applied when the wanted end behavior appears.

Many types of reinforcement schedules are available. Generally they are classified into a combination of fixed or variable and interval or ratio. A fixed schedule, i.e., reinforcement each time the desired behavior occurs, might be employed until the pattern is at an acceptable level. Later, rewards may be administered on a variable basis. A decision to use a fixed or variable schedule and whether this schedule should be based on time (interval) or the number of performances (ratio) must be carefully analyzed. For example, jobs that can be performed and measured by each piece produced are easily adaptable to ratio schedules. On the other hand, administrative positions may be better suited to interval scheduling. When conditions permit, variable schedules of reinforcement should be used because they tend to provide the greatest resistance to extinction.

ORGANIZATIONAL REWARD SYSTEMS

Systems of rewards, which are currently being used by industry and other types of organizations, can be adapted to a behavior modification program. Money, status, promotion, public recognition, and personal praise are all valid reinforcements of behavior. Under behavior modification, these commonly used rewards are administered from a well-planned, systematic program. It allows manpower managers to concentrate on needed behavior patterns and determines what schedule of reinforcement will most effectively bring out the new or eliminate the old behavior.

In the typical organizational reward system, no restrictions are placed on the number of stimuli (rewards) which may be used to elicit a desired response. Learning theory would state that once an organizational participant is conditioned to one stimulus, a similar stimulus also will evoke the response. On the other hand, the less similar the two stimuli are to one another, the less frequent will be the probability of the desired response. This concept, known as "generalization," is significant to organizational reward systems in that it provides a basis for using a variety of similar rewards to reinforce wanted behavior.

A properly administered reward system must determine exactly what behavior is being reinforced. Here, an interesting observation was made by Ferster and Perrott:

Superficially, the salary might be considered on a fixed-interval schedule of reinforcement, in the sense that the money is a reinforcing event which is delivered every fourteen or thirty days. In the technical sense of reinforcement, however, money reinforces only the behavior of accepting the paycheck. This performance is reinforced every time it occurs.[6]

Accordingly, the supposition that the paycheck is reinforcing the *job performance* is not necessarily valid. A solution to this problem would be to use another type of reward or schedule which may be more appropriately applied to actual job behavior. For example, salary increments granted according to attainment of specific predetermined objectives would incorporate a ratio schedule that would provide more direct reinforcement than salary administered on an interval basis. An innovative method of administering reward to assembly line workers was suggested by Aldis in his article, "Of Pigeons and Men."

Let us take, for example, a worker whose job consists of installing a taillight on an automobile as it passes along the assembly line. He might attach a small device similar to a taximeter to the machine the worker employs. This behavior would ring a bell after the man has made a sufficient number of responses and the amount he has earned would flash before him. Under a setup like this, he might have to be pulled away from the line for a coffee break.[7]

Many questions and problems naturally arise when implementing behavior modification. For example, one criticism may be that the speed of the assembly line, not the method of reinforcement, actually controls the number of worker responses. However, it is the authors' contention that these types of problems can be overcome by innovative refinements and applications of behavior modification. For instance, one possible refinement of the Aldis proposal might call for reinforce-

[6]C. B. Ferster and Mary Carol Perrott, *Behavior Principles* (New York: Appleton-Century-Crofts, 1968), p. 328.
[7]Aldis, *op. cit.*, p. 61.

ment to be administered on the basis of a variable ratio schedule, as opposed to the fixed ratio schedule. This would eliminate the boring and possibly frustrating effect resulting from hearing the bell every "x" number of units and having the same reward payment flashed before him time after time.

APPLICATIONS TO MANPOWER MANAGEMENT

Simple application of behavior modification may be made in training workers to use certain methods, perform specific tasks, or to increase their knowledge in a particular area. These techniques are currently being used in programmed learning materials. The theoretical basis for programmed learning is that a response on the part of the reader, i.e., filling in a word or answering a question, evokes a stimulus from the learning environment. The stimulus of a correct answer or verbal praise becomes a positive reinforcement.

Most manpower situations are not subject to the high degrees of control that are characteristic of programmed learning. On-the-job training for specific operations or general behavior adaptation is complicated by more complex environmental factors. Accordingly, specific types of rewards that are to be used and the schedules by which they are to be administered must be thoroughly planned and communicated. For instance, if more than one superior has significant influence on the behavior of the worker, they should all participate in the program. Although the immediate superior undoubtedly has the most effect on an employee's actions, others in the organization may also be in a position to reinforce, either positively or negatively, the behavior exhibited. Conflicts and inconsistencies in the type of reinforcement given or in the schedule itself will have an adverse effect on the program.

Initially, programs designed to modify or adapt behavior would probably be used in training new workers. However, it must be emphasized that behavior modification techniques are mainly designed to *replace* one behavior pattern with another. This replacement factor has implications for the retraining of experienced, as well as new, employees. Similarly, behavior modification may be an important tool in overcoming the many problems associated with training minority workers and hardcore unemployed.

Realistic examples are probably necessary to illustrate the application of behavior modification to manpower management. Suppose the cultural backgrounds of a group of hardcore-unemployed tend to increase the probability of tardiness or absenteeism. A competitive situation might be established where trainees are awarded points or monetary credits for their attendance or promptness. If the man is absent or tardy, his cumulative points or credit totals would be lowered. Monetary bonus payments, gifts, such as small appliances, or even personal or public praise can be administered on an interval schedule. In this case, reinforcement in the form of points or symbolic dollars, made immediately upon the recognition of positive or negative behavior, reinforces getting to work on time. Carryover to job performance may be accomplished by generalizing the reward, i.e., changing its form, and by continuing to deliberately reinforce behavior that leads to goal attainment.

Another example could apply to white collar employees. An objective of the sales department is to increase the volume of sales. In terms of manpower management, the individual salesman becomes the critical variable in obtaining this objective. Each salesman might be given a book in which he records only the amount of his monetary commission and/or points toward a desirable bonus gift. The entry would be made *immediately* following each sale. In order to assure that the instructions are being carried out in practice, the district manager would communicate to his salesmen that the record book would be examined first on a continuous (perhaps daily) basis and later intermittently. The reinforcement that the examination provides will cause the salesman to make entries immediately after each sale and not at a later time. Recording the monetary commission in the record book will directly reinforce each sale that is made, and each sale would, in turn, serve as a stimulus for each subsequent selling situation. Finally, his recognition that sales are increasing will motivate him to continue making entries and would become a self-generating reward. This example is significantly different from incentive programs currently used by many sales organizations. The commission that is recorded reinforces the sale, not the act of making the entry. The desired benefit of commission or bonus systems is often lost when the reward becomes "just another entry" on a daily or weekly sales report.

Application of the principle of reinforcement is not restricted to individual task performance. An aircraft company used an innovative technique in the final assembly hangar of a repair and overhaul operation. A large sign visible to all was placed on the wall. This sign indicated the number of planes that had passed final inspection and the number which still remained unfinished. When word was released that a plane had passed the final inspection phase, bells rang throughout the plant. All work temporarily stopped while employees observed the numerical changes which were made on the wall sign. The workers were observed to turn to one another to nudge or voice approval concerning their accomplishment. In this case the reward served to reinforce participation in the final product and enabled the employee to see himself as a contributor to overall organizational objectives.

DEVELOPMENT AND RESOCIALIZATION

The most far-reaching implication for behavior modification lies in the area of manpower development and resocialization. A worker may achieve higher productivity or may even demonstrate more acceptable social behavior in terms of variables, such as absenteeism or tardiness, but can his total relationship to the organization be altered? Is it possible for organizational participants' total development, from the standpoint of attitudes, degree of commitment, or conflict with the formal organization be significantly adapted or resolved by behavior modification?

Douglas McGregor and Chris Argyris, widely accepted management theorists, argue that most organizational participants are mature persons, who under proper conditions, seek self-direction and self-control. To those who point out the opposite characteristics observable in many workers, the reply is that most of man's activities are merely a product of the pattern of socialization to which he has been subjected. For example, McGregor's Theory Y states that, under proper conditions, workers will exercise self-direction, seek responsibility, and show the capacity to use creative approaches to daily tasks.[8]

The authors basically agree with these widely held assumptions of the behavioral approach to management. However, some expansion and refinement seem to be in order. The generally accepted theories imply that workers who seem to have no desire to make a meaningful contribution to the organization are "products of the system." They have been socialized into their present role. In other words, the process of socialization has *trained* them to accept undesirable behavior patterns as a "way of life." If this is the case, how can a manager hope to modify or reverse stabilized patterns of behavior? Can on-the-job life styles developed over many years be changed? It is in this context that behavior modification may have tremendous implications for manpower management.

[8]Douglas McGregor, *The Human Side of Enterprise* (New York: McGraw-Hill Book Company, Inc., 1960), pp. 47–48; Chris Argyris, *Personality and Organization* (New York: Harper & Brothers, 1957).

In classical conditioning, a conditioned stimulus elicits a conditioned response.[9] Analogous to manpower management, the worker is told by his boss to work harder, and he responds by increasing his output. However, another outcome may be the creation of conflict between the worker and his superior. Frustration manifested through defense mechanisms, such as aggression or withdrawal (sabotage and apathy) may result. As a counter to classical conditioning, behavior modification allows the worker to emit a response which will affect the nature of the environmental stimulus. The subordinate is not acted upon by his environment as in classical conditioning. Instead, his environment is being affected by his own activities. A properly conceived behavior modification program allows the individual to assert self-direction and self-control.

Manpower managers can utilize behavior modification techniques to generate goal direction and self-control among all levels of personnel. The popular management system, Management by Objectives (M.B.O.), provides an excellent vehicle for such a program. M.B.O., first described by Peter Drucker and later popularized by George Odiorne, provides an opportunity for all personnel to contribute to job goals and encourages the setting of checkpoints to measure progress.[10] M.B.O. is ends rather than means oriented. Such a system facilitates achievement motivation, particularly for jobs that can be designed and controlled by the subordinate. Positive reinforcement is inherent in the achievement of objectives. Material rewards, in terms of salary increase, bonus, and promotion, also come from the appraisal by results.

The long range potential for behavior modification seems limitless. Behavioral scientists conclude that once behavior patterns have been changed, attitudes and opinions may follow.[11] This implies that behavior modification may transcend mere performance objectives. Organizational participants' feelings, attitudes and morale may be affected. For example, when dealing with the hard-core unemployed, manpower managers may go further than just concentrating on improved performance. Positive attitudes towards attendance, quality of work, and the organization in general may result from a behavior modification program. It is potentially a technique to accomplish organizational resocialization.

Behavior modification is a technique which may enable manpower management to modify or eliminate undesirable employee behavior and replace it with behavior that is more compatible with goal attainment. The technique is built around the use of rewards for observable behavior. The rewards are administered systematically through a predetermined reinforcement schedule. The process allows the individual whose behavior is being modified to elicit an environmental stimulus as a result of his prior response. Although the rewards discussed in this paper are generally familiar to manpower managers, the *systematic application* of reinforcement schedules is the new difference provided by behavior modification. The other major difference from traditional techniques is the emphasis that is given to observable performance response as opposed to reward stimulus.

Many scholars, humanitarians, and practitioners are undoubtedly troubled by the apparent manipulative aspects of behavior modification and the moral question of who has the right to determine desirable or undesirable behavior. A typical accusation may be that under behavior modification, organizational participants are being manipulated and molded into someone's conception of the ideal

[9]Ullmann and Krasner, *op. cit.*, p. 16.
[10]Peter F. Drucker, *The Practice of Management* (New York: Harper & Row, Publishers, 1954), Chapter 7; and George S. Odiorne, *Management By Objectives* (New York: Pitman Publishing, 1965).

[11]Berelson and Steiner, *op. cit.*, pp. 96; 115.

"organization man." Manipulation in itself is not the end. "The psychology of tomorrow will involve the development of clear and explicit value judgments as to what kinds of human behavior are most desirable under specific sets of circumstances and will offer technical recommendations about how to effect these behaviors."[12] Behavior modification is a recommended technique to adapt behavior to the cooperative system and to organizational goal attainment.

Behavior modification is not untested. It is being used quite extensively in mental hospitals, clinics, group therapy, schoolrooms, and even in the home. "Its origin, growth, and development illustrate an important point about applied psychology: although the applications grow out of basic laboratory research, they may take unique directions." [13] Manpower management is a unique but appropriate direction for behavior modification.

As early as 1965 Ullmann and Krasner stated:

> We think that one likely future development will be work with larger units of behavior with increasingly general social application. If behavior can be reliably categorized by observers and if subjects' responses can be generalized to physically dissimilar but functionally equivalent exemplars, then new and broader areas of behavior will become suitable foci for behavior modification techniques.[14]

Direct applications to manpower management include training, retraining, compensation, absenteeism, tardiness and motivation of organizational participants. On a more grandiose scale, behavior modification may provide the missing link to the fusion of individual and organizational goals.

[12] *Psychology Today: An Introduction* (Del Mar, California: CRM Books, 1970), p. 667.
[13] *Ibid.*, p. 654.

[14] Ullmann and Krasner, *op. cit.*, p. 61.

Reading 26

Skinnerian Theory in Organizations

William F. Whyte

As a long-time consultant and researcher in industry, I often come in contact with the executive who has just discovered the importance of "the human element."

"What we must do is change people's attitudes," he usually says.

As politely as I can, I tell him to forget attitudes. The problem is to change the conditions to which people are responding. If he does that, people will behave differently and he will find that attitudes—if they still interest him—will adjust themselves to the new situation.

Problems

My line of argument sounds purely Skinnerian, of course. And I do, in fact, agree with B. F. Skinner's basic formulation [see "Beyond Freedom and Dignity," *Psychology Today*, August 1971]. Behavioral scientists should abandon their preoccupation with the inner life of man and concentrate on the relations between man and environment, Skinner argues. Behavior is shaped and maintained by its consequences; these consequences (or reinforcers, as Skinner calls them) can be either positive or negative, but positive reinforcers generally are more effective than negative reinforcers in the production and maintenance of behavior.

Despite this basic agreement, however, my experiences in industry have led me to conclude that when we move out of the laboratory into the complexities of real life, Skinner's operant-conditioning theory tells us very little about the prediction and control of behavior. As I see it, Skinner fails to deal with four crucial elements in real-life behavior: 1) the cost-benefit ratio and the social-comparison process; 2) the problem of conflicting stimuli; 3) the problem of time lag and trust; and 4) the one-body problem.

Control

In the industrial field, incentive systems provide a useful focus for analyzing these four elements because such systems are explicit attempts by management to control behavior through reinforcement: more production, more pay. I am aware, of course, that Skinner himself is no advocate of piece-rate pay, but I believe that the system nevertheless can be used to illustrate the problems we face in attempting to apply Skinner's basic theory to real-life situations. My studies of incentive systems in U.S. industry point to some of the necessary qualifications that we must build into the Skinner schema.

1 THE COST-BENEFIT RATIO AND THE SOCIAL-COMPARISON PROCESS

Laboratory experimenters, from Pavlov with his dogs to Skinner with his pigeons, could disregard the costs of the action to the actor, for they were trifling compared to the benefits the experimental animal received as a consequence of his action. That is generally not the case in human affairs. The important rewards a person seeks usually involve substantial effort.

In analyzing individual piece-rate incentive systems, we can ignore the question of whether the person will produce more if he gets more money for putting out additional effort

and applying superior skill. Other things being equal, most persons would rather have more money than less and will make some effort to get more. The important question is: How much effort in relation to how much more money?

More

This question focuses on the rate-setting problem. Management commonly assumes that workers on piece rates will produce 25 to 30 percent more than they would produce if they were paid a flat, hourly rate. In the abstract, the rate-setting problem is simple: if we determine the number of pieces the average worker produces on time or hourly rates and call this number 100 percent, then the worker on piece rates will produce more and get about 130 percent of his hourly rate. For example, if a time-study man determines that a worker with a base pay of $2.00 an hour should produce 10 units an hour, the equation yields a price of 20 cents per unit produced. At an incentive pace, therefore, the worker should average 13 pieces an hour, raising his pay to $2.60.

But this assumption depends on the accuracy of the time-study man's estimates, which he makes by observing and measuring the work of fast, average, and slow workers under normal working conditions, and by throwing in adjustments for such factors as personal time and fatigue. Workers are well aware that if they can get the time-study man to decide that eight units an hour is a fair nonincentive pace, making the price per piece 25 cents instead of 20 cents, they can make more money with the same effort or the same amount of money with less effort.

Motion

The rate-setting process leads to elaborate charades played by workers for the benefit of the time-study man. Experienced workers learn how to slow down while appearing to work with maximum effort. They add extra motions that appear to be necessary but that can be eliminated after the rate has been set. If the time-study man demands that a worker operate his machine at a faster speed, the worker can find ways to damage the machine to prove that the speed demanded was excessive.

Of course, these maneuvers do not entirely fool the time-study man. He knows that workers try to mislead him, but he does not know how much. To the measurements he makes, he plugs in an estimate of how much he is being fooled. Thus he combines scientific observation and measurement with a guessing game.

If the worker fools the time-study man more than the time-study man allows for, the result is a loose rate on which the worker can make high earnings without excessive effort. If the time-study man overcompensates for the amount he thinks he is being fooled, the result is a tight rate on which the worker finds it difficult or impossible to make the incentive pay he seeks. If the rate is loose, workers are happy; but management is unhappy because it is paying too high a price for the units produced. If the rate is tight, workers are unhappy because they cannot make their expected earnings without excessive effort.

Levels

In more general terms, we are dealing with what George Homans calls the relationship between investments and rewards. Out of their experience, persons develop ideas about an equitable level of rewards in terms of their personal investments (level of education or training, years of service, skill, effort). If the person is not receiving rewards that he considers comparable to the investments he has made, he becomes dissatisfied and searches for ways to achieve a better balance.

The person also judges the equity of his investment-reward (or cost-benefit) ratio in terms of what another person with similar investments is getting in the way of rewards. If the other person seems to be getting more than the person is getting for similar investments, the person complains or reduces the

level of his investments (producing less, giving less attention to quality, and so on).

In other words, providing positive reinforcers for production in the industrial situation is a highly complex problem that involves observation-and-measurement procedures embedded in a network of relationships among the person, the time-study man, the supervisor, and other workers.

2   CONFLICTING STIMULI

The problem of conflicting stimuli has not escaped the attention of stimulus-response or operant-conditioning psychologists. In fact, Ivan Pavlov entered into this field when he conditioned dogs to respond, in anticipation of food, to a light in the shape of a full moon, and to cringe, in anticipation of an electric shock, in response to a light in the shape of a new moon. By varying the shapes of the lights so that the stimuli came to resemble each other ever more closely, Pavlov produced experimental neuroses in his animals. With these experiments the question was whether a given stimulus stood for a potential reward or a potential penalty—a situation that occurs frequently outside the laboratory. However, situations in which a given behavior of a person may yield both rewards and penalties probably are even more frequent.

Conflict

One such case, passed on to me by Robert Kahn, involved the incentive system and the suggestion system in a factory. By itself, the suggestion system would appear to have no aversive consequences, but the conflicting stimuli become apparent when the suggestion system is combined with the incentive system.

Those who do research on incentive systems find that workers, out of their experience and skill on the job, often devise improved work methods or tools that enable them to increase their output or to produce the same amount with less effort. Since the rate set on the particular job is based on methods described by the time-study man, and since any official change in job methods or tools or machines entitles management to make a new study and set a new rate, workers naturally keep these improvements to themselves. They also keep an eye out for the time-study man and revert to the official job methods or hide their inventions when he comes by.

Prowl

In the plant studied by Kahn and his associates, the time-study man, well aware of worker customs, often went on the prowl, hoping to discover a hidden invention and thereby gain the right to restudy the job. If the workers lost out in this hide-and-seek game, the improvements they themselves had invented would become part of the official job methods, a new piece rate would be set, and their earnings on the job would be reduced or they would have to work harder to maintain the same level of earnings. In this way, the workers could lose all the benefits of their own ingenuity.

Gain

Through the suggestion system, workers could gain rewards for their inventions. If a person wrote up a new job method and put it into the suggestion box before the time-study man had observed it, management would study the economic gains involved in the improvement and present a reward to the person—possibly a substantial fraction of the gains that would accrue to management. But management also would invoke the time-study and rate-setting procedures, just as it would have done if the time-study man had invented the improvement, and the result would be a piece-rate cut. The person might well gain a financial reward substantially greater than what he would lose through the reduction of the rate on the job, but for his fellow workers the consequences would be entirely aversive.

Workers who face the conflicting stimuli of the incentive system and the suggestion sys-

tem find that any action offers prospects of both rewarding and aversive consequences. If they conceal the invention successfully from management, they all are rewarded; but if management discovers it they all lose. If the person puts in his suggestion, he gains but the others lose.

This case illustrates the complexities that human beings find in many real-life situations. They do indeed respond, as Skinner argues, in terms of the consequences of past behavior. But many situations provide such conflicting stimulus conditions that we cannot predict any response simply by analyzing the relationship between the person and the anticipated reinforcement.

3 TIME LAG AND TRUST

Few of a person's acts bring immediate reward to him. The time span between behavior and reinforcement may be only a few minutes—but it also may be many months. Psychologists and sociologists, interpreting the problems caused by time lag in terms of deferred gratification, have noted that individuals differ in their responsiveness to delayed rewards and that middle-class persons generally are more responsive to them than are lower-class persons.

Time lag also involves the problem of the predictability of the environment—and for a person, other human beings are a major part of that environment. If another person tells the person to do something to gain a reward a year later, the person bases his decision to act only in part on his estimate of the probability that the actions proposed will produce the reward promised. He also asks himself: Can I trust the other person? His answer depends in part upon his past experiences with the other person (and with personnel in like positions).

Cuts

The piece-rate field again provides a useful illustration. It is standard practice for management to promise that it will not cut piece rates on a given job no matter how much workers earn on the job. Nevertheless, workers widely fear rate cuts, and they restrict their output to conceal loose rates. Why? Does management violate its pledges? No doubt such abuses sometimes happen, but much more common are the problems of interpreting rights and procedures. Union contracts generally allow management to make a new time study and set a new rate when it has introduced a "major" or "substantial" change in methods, tools, or equipment used on a job. Between workers and management, we find frequent disagreements as to what constitutes a "major" change.

Furthermore, a series of minor changes over a period of months or years could well add up to a major change; but at what point does management intervene to change the rate? How can we expect workers to respond if, as in the case I described earlier, the workers themselves introduced the changes?

Workers tell us that exceptionally high earnings on a given incentive job are sure to attract attention. Time-study men who note deviations from expected results are likely to restudy a job to determine whether changes have occurred that would justify new time studies and new rates. If they cannot show that the nature of the job has changed substantially, they have still another option: to "re-engineer" the job on management's initiative to such an extent that there can no longer be any question that a major change has been introduced.

Such responses by time-study men are to be expected under the conditions prevailing in most piece-rate operations. The existence of a job that produces out-of-line earnings demonstrates to management that the time-study man has made mistakes in his fundamental task of rate-setting. In other words, the behavior of workers in responding to positive reinforcement produces aversive consequences for the time-study man.

Further, the requirements of the wage-and-salary system push management to seek ways to get around its pledge against rate-cutting. In the experimental laboratory, the psychologist can isolate the experimental animal from all other tasks, reinforcements, and experimental animals. In the factory situation such isolation is impossible. Both workers and management see each rate as part of a total system of payments. A major change in one element of the system can have disturbing effects on other parts of the system.

Up

For example, let's look at two hypothetical jobs, A and B. A pays \$2.00 an hour, B pays \$2.25 an hour, and the line of promotion runs from A to B. The two jobs are now put on piece rates. A turns up with a loose rate that yields earning of \$3.00 an hour, whereas B has a tight rate on which earnings average \$2.65 an hour.

In these conditions workers quite naturally do not want to take "promotions" from A to B. If management requires them to do so, as it can in some contracts, the workers are likely to respond with actions that prove aversive to management. In other words, as management acts to keep rates in line, the workers have good reason to believe that while responding strongly to a given rate will bring short-term positive reinforcement, in the long run it will have aversive consequences: the rate will be cut so that they will get less money for their work or will have to do more work for the same money. How strongly workers feel and how decisively they act to create aversive consequences for management when they have grievances will depend also upon the nature of their past relations with management—which is another way of expressing the degree of trust that workers will have about management's future behavior.

4   THE ONE-BODY PROBLEM

In studying the laboratory experiments of Pavlov or Skinner, we are interested only in the environmental conditions that induce the dog or the pigeon to behave in a certain way. We are not concerned with the motivation of Ivan Pavlov or B. F. Skinner, who are manipulating these environmental conditions. When we deal with human beings outside the laboratory, however, we will be able to predict and control very little if we limit our concern to the contingencies affecting the behavior of the individual. Since many if not most of the contingencies to which a person responds are provided by another person (or by several others), we must learn to deal simultaneously and systematically with the contingencies affecting the behavior of both the person and the other person.

Part

In a sense this point involves a restatement of the issues I have already raised. In discussing the cost-benefit ratio, the problem of conflicting stimuli, and the time-lag and trust problem, I have not been able to limit our attention to the person. The worker is part of a social system in which he interacts with the time-study man, the foreman, other workers, union officers, and management. We cannot explain his behavior except in terms of the behavior of others with whom he interacts. More importantly, for practical purposes, if we want to change his behavior we cannot limit ourselves to a strategy designed simply to change the contingencies to which he is exposed. We must include in our strategy plans for changing the contingencies affecting the behavior of the principal other persons with whom he is interacting.

Vacuum

It may appear that all I am saying is that social psychology is better than individual psychology, but there is much more to be said than that. We do indeed have to deal with interpersonal relations, but those relations do not occur in a social or technological vacuum. Relations among persons tend to be structured through organizations, and within these organizational

contexts behavior is linked to reinforcements in structured ways.

In industry we find many situations in which the behavior that produces rewards for a person also produces aversive consequences for another person and frequently such conflicts are built into the functional differences between departments or work groups. Salesmen who often get rewards solely on the basis of their sales volumes naturally try to sell as much as possible, and they give little attention to the credit ratings of potential customers. On the other hand, management evaluates the performance of the credit department in terms of its experience in collecting bills, so credit people naturally tend to disallow orders from customers who appear to be poor credit risks. By vetoing an order, the credit man deprives the salesman of a reward and produces further aversive consequences on the customer relations the salesman is trying to develop. Yet, if the credit man approves the order and the bill goes unpaid, the credit man suffers aversive consequences.

Tension

Friction-causing problems also crop up frequently in work-flow relations, in which work passes regularly from one group to another. In studies of busy restaurants, for instance, we observed a common friction point: the service counter where waitresses give food orders to countermen and pick up food when it is ready. Tension always mounts as the rush hour advances, with waitresses competing to place orders and yelling at countermen to hurry up, while countermen yell back at waitresses.

In such situations we can understand readily that concentrating on the behavior of the individual salesman, credit man, waitress, or counterman will yield little useful knowledge. But, while recognizing the need to examine interpersonal relations, we should not see these relations simply as the interplay of personalities. They occur in a highly patterned structure. Unless we can change the pattern, we can do little to change the behavior.

Network

At its simplest level, the problem of the prediction and control of behavior involves creating conditions in which the behavior that positively reinforces one person also positively reinforces the other person (in the same group or organization)—or at least does not produce aversive consequences for the other person. To do this, we can examine the current interpersonal behavior of the person and the other person, noting how the behavior of one rewards or penalizes the other. Then, on the basis of this analysis, we can seek to devise a more rewarding task structure and network of interpersonal relations.

In some cases, the introduction of changes in the immediate interpersonal situation can produce decisive changes in the balance of positive and negative reinforcers. Often we can accomplish such changes in interpersonal relations by changing the technology or work flow. For example, we found that some restaurants had eliminated the aversive conflict between waitresses and countermen by erecting a service counter high enough to provide a physical barrier and introducing a spindle on which waitresses placed their written orders. Countermen pulled orders off in sequence and set out filled trays with order slips in the same sequence.

Plan

We should also recognize that we cannot resolve many problems of human conflict and frustration by tinkering at the immediate interpersonal level. Here again the individual piece-rate incentive system provides a convenient example. While students of incentive problems have devised ways to alleviate some of the more severe conflicts, we have had to realize that the system itself operates so as to produce tensions and frustrations and that only a far-reaching system change can get at the basic problem.

Various innovators have tried to meet the problems of reinforcement for work performance through a broad-based collective-reward system, which eliminates the problems of individual work measurement, rate-setting and their attendant conflicts. Such is the approach of the Scanlon Plan, which provides for a plant-wide sharing in the fruits of increased productivity, supported by worker and supervisor participation in a series of departmental and plant-wide committees that generate, evaluate and recommend changes leading to increased productivity. A similar rationale underlies profit-sharing plans, though the link between profits and work performance is much less direct than in the Scanlon Plan, and profit-sharing plans do not always involve worker participation in the development of ideas for improving performance.

We also need to examine even more fundamental structural changes whereby the workers in an enterprise, through their representatives, control policies and procedures on wages, bonuses, production, and so on. Such changes have arisen in isolated instances in the United States, particularly in the plywood industry on the West Coast. The system exists on a national scale in Yugoslavia, and its apparent success in both human and physical terms has led increasing numbers of social scientists and politicians from other countries to examine the theory and practice of the Yugoslav approach.

Rhetoric

In examining these broader structural changes, we should not let the current rhetoric regarding Marxism versus capitalism mislead us. The Yugoslavs say they are Communists—in fact, they claim to be the only ones who are acting out the authentic Marx—but their industrial system is distinctly different from that of the Soviet Union—or of the United States. Given what we know about the expectable characteristics of large-scale organizations, we are likely to find, in the government-run enterprises of the Soviet Union as in the privately owned enterprises of the United States, many of the same situations in which a person and another person characteristically find themselves on collision-course reinforcement schedules. If we are to devise new organizational systems that maximize both performance and positive reinforcement for organizational members, we need to come down from the sphere of political ideology and undertake detailed analyses of the sociotechnical system: the system of interpersonal relations that is linked with a structure of technology, work flow, and task organization.

Let us not abandon Skinner, but let us not assume either that his schema carries us beyond the beginning point in the prediction and control of human behavior. Until we shift our attention from the one-body problem and develop formulations in terms of two or more bodies interacting together within an organizational framework and with specified tasks, we will not be able to devise strategies that will effectively control the contingencies of reinforcement for both a person and another person.

Chapter 8

Group and
Interpersonal Processes

Many factors combine to determine what happens in an organization: the characteristics of organization members, the structure and technology of the organization itself, various organizational policies and practices, and so on. The other chapters of this book provide abundant testimony about the importance of such factors in affecting behavior in organizations. Yet because organizations involve people working collectively toward some shared goals, *relationships among people* always serve as the basic vehicle for carrying out the work, and for carrying on the organization.

Relationships in organizations tend to be clustered into groups, of which there are many varieties. At one extreme, a group can be a collection of workers in a shop, each carrying out his or her own tasks, aware of one another but not interacting with each other for any work-related purpose. Or a group can be several individuals working together temporarily to solve a problem, make a decision, or carry out a specific task. Or a group can be a set of people who work together intensively, day in and day out, with substantial and continuing responsibility for some aspect of the overall organizational task. Indeed, some organizations have established an "office of the presidency" in which the top management of the organization is handled by a group.

The nature of the relationships that occur within and between groups has a major impact on the quality of life of people at work—and significantly influences the productive effectiveness of the organization. Because of the simultaneous diversity and ubiquity of groups in organizations, however, it sometimes is difficult to determine just why some groups are more effective than others, and why some groups provide their members with positive and growthful experiences while others rigidly enforce norms to maintain the status quo. The readings in this chapter shed some light on such questions.

The chapter opens with a classic paper by Whyte which describes and documents how groups monitor and control the productivity of group members—even though members work as individuals, and are paid financial incentives based on individual productivity. Whyte shows that "goldbricking" and quota restriction are very well-organized within work groups, and that the effects on individual work behavior are profound. In the next article, Lawler and Cammann address the opposite side of the same coin. They located a work group in which group norms supported *high* productivity, and attempted to discern why that group differed from a less effective comparison group. Their explanation extends well beyond the boundaries of the group itself: group norms about productivity were found to be affected not only by the motivation of group members, but also by the nature (and clarity) of the reward system, the amount of autonomy workers had in their jobs, and the nature of the group's relationship to management. Both these articles deal with groups in which members are coacting—that is, members perform their individual tasks in the presence of one another, but there is no single outcome generated interactively by the group as a whole.

The next two articles address the task effectiveness of groups in which members *do* work together on a common task. Janis describes and explores a phenomenon he calls "groupthink," in which highly cohesive groups composed of talented members develop and im-

plement plans of action that turn out to be grossly inappropriate and ineffective. Janis identifies some of the causes and indicators of groupthink, illustrates the phenomenon by reviewing cases of policy-making fiascos executed by groups of high-level governmental officials, and then offers some guidelines for avoiding the groupthink trap.

In the next article, Hackman and Morris focus on the role of group interaction process as a key in determining how effectively a group will perform its task. They suggest that what is an "appropriate" way for group members to interact will vary from task to task: different tasks require different patterns of group process if the group is to be highly effective. A number of interventions that can be used to improve the quality (and the task-appropriateness) of group interaction process are suggested, discussed, and evaluated.

The chapter closes with an article by Smith that proposes an entirely different way of viewing groups in organizations. Whereas most discussions of groups (including the earlier articles in this chapter) emphasize what happens *within* groups, Smith proposes that what happens *between* different groups may be as important—or more so—in understanding individual perceptions of reality, patterns of emergent leadership, and even the personal "identity" of group members. Smith illustrates these phenomena with case materials drawn from a school system, an experiential "power laboratory," and a group of survivors from an aircraft crash. By examining the nature of intergroup dynamics, he concludes, one can gain significantly greater understanding of group and interpersonal processes than can be obtained from looking only at the characteristics of individual group members or at phenomena that take place within the group.

Reading 27

Quota Restriction and Goldbricking

William Foote Whyte

Restriction of output is not a simple, uniform phenomenon. It occurs, with different sorts of behavior, on different types of jobs.

To see the pattern in restriction, let us examine the experience of Donald Roy on the drill line. Here we can confine ourselves to the last six months of his eleven-month employment period, for this represents a time when he was sufficiently skilled to make bonus on approximately two jobs out of every three (65.6 per cent). And, of course, he had the skill to go well beyond the quota if he had cared to do so.

In this situation, anything beyond the guaranteed day rate of 85 cents per hour represents making bonus. Roy worked on a wide variety of jobs, and each one had its own rate set by time study. Throughout the period he kept a record of his earnings on each job run.

If we assume that the operator is working with uniform effort on jobs with rates varying randomly from loose to tight, then we would expect a distribution of earnings in something like a normal, bell-shaped curve. That is, we would find that the operator who earned over the day rate two-thirds of the time would have the peak number of his jobs perhaps in the earnings interval $1.05-$1.14, with steadily diminishing numbers of jobs below and above that, going as low as 55 cents and as high as $1.54.

Instead, we find a radically different distribution as illustrated in Figure 27-1. As the graph indicates, we have here two distributions of jobs. Below the "make out" line, the distribution is irregular, but the peak of 9.1 per cent of jobs run falls in the 45-54 cent interval. It is noteworthy here that only 1.1 per cent of

the jobs fall in the 75-84 cent interval where the operator had almost "made out."

On the "make out" side of the graph, we find less than two per cent of the jobs falling into each of the first three earnings intervals. The line then jumps up to 8.4 per cent for $1.15-1.24 and soars to 52.3 per cent for $1.25-1.34. The line then dips back to zero for the next three intervals and records .2 per cent for $1.65-1.74—representing apparently a job on which Roy had miscalculated his earnings.

We have systematic figures only upon Roy in this case, but he frequently was able to record the earnings of the day shift man on his own machine and to check the earnings of other fellow workers. In all cases, they conformed to the pattern we see here.

What does this pattern mean? Roy interprets it in this way: There are two types of restriction, which he terms "goldbricking" and "quota restriction." In the eyes of the operators there were two types of jobs: "stinkers" and "gravy jobs," with anything in between being only a transitory phenomenon.

With 85 cents an hour as the guaranteed day wage, earnings of $1 an hour seemed to be the dividing line between a good job and a poor job. If the workers felt that $1 an hour was the most they could possibly earn with the utmost skill and effort, then they refused to try for the incentive. In that case they did not just relax to an easy, comfortable pace that might have yielded something close to 85 cents. They actively put on the brakes to hold production down to between 20 and 50 cents below the guaranteed day rate. That behavior Roy classifies as "goldbricking."

On the other hand, if the job seemed to

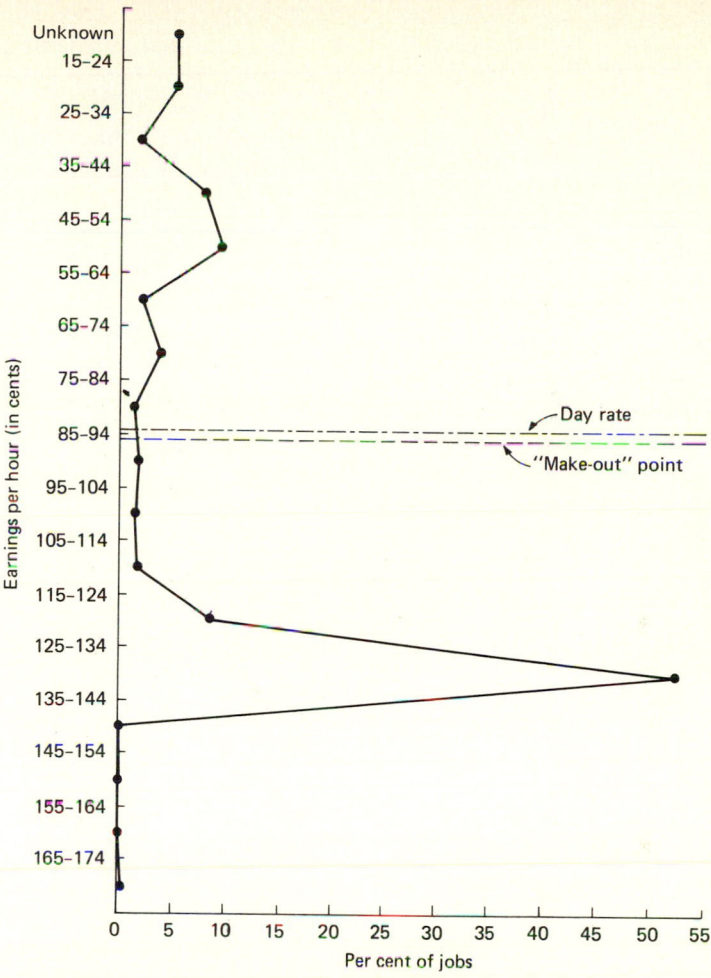

Figure 27-1 A pattern of piece work earnings.

promise $1 and a little more, then the operators went to work with skill and ingenuity to exploit its possibilities to the utmost. Thus a job that promised earnings of, say, $1.04 did not remain for long at that figure. The workers soon found ways to build it up to somewhere between $1.15 and $1.29. On some jobs this would be the top production they could possibly reach. Other jobs would promise earnings of up to $2 or even $3 per hour. On these, however, they held back production so as not to go over $1.29 per hour. This Roy classifies as "quota restriction."

QUOTA RESTRICTION

When the operator is new on the job he may not receive explicit instructions from fellow workers as to how much he is to make. To be sure, he hears of the dangers of rate cutting and the evil practices of the time-study men as he joins in the conversation with other workers. But at first he may be so lacking in skill that there is no chance of his exceeding the quota.

When the new man gains skill, so that it looks as though it will soon be possible for him to go beyond the quota, he then receives more specific and detailed instructions. Roy reports the situation in this way:

> From my first to my last day at the plant I was subject to warnings and predictions concerning price cuts. Pressure was the heaviest from Joe Mucha, day man on my machine, who shared my job repertoire and kept a close eye on my production. On November 14, the day after my first attained quota, Joe Mucha advised:
>
> "Don't let it go over $1.25 an hour, or the time-study man will be right down here! And they don't waste time, either! They watch the records like a hawk! I got ahead, so I took it easy for a couple of hours."
>
> Joe told me that I had made $10.01 yesterday and warned me not to go over $1.25 an hour. He told me to figure the setups and the time on each operation very carefully so that I would not total over $10.25 in any one day.
>
> Jack Starkey defined the quota carefully but forcefully when I turned in $10.50 for one day, or $1.31 an hour.
>
> Jack Starkey spoke to me after Joe left. "What's the matter? Are you trying to upset the applecart?"
>
> Jack explained in a friendly manner that $10.50 was too much to turn in, even on an old job. "The turret-lathe men can turn in $1.35," said Jack, "but their rate is 90 cents, and ours 85 cents."
>
> Jack warned me that the Methods Department could lower their prices on any job, old or new, by changing the fixture slightly or changing the size of the drill. According to Jack, a couple of operators (first and second shift on the same drill) got to competing with each other to see how much they could turn in. They got up to $1.65 an hour, and the price was cut in half. And from then on they had to run that job themselves, as none of the other operators would accept the job.
>
> According to Jack, it would be all right for us to turn in $1.28 or $1.29 an hour, when it figured out that way, but it was not all right to turn in $1.30 an hour.
>
> Well, now I know where the maximum is—$1.29 an hour.

In this situation Roy did not observe any

"rate busters," workers who refused to abide by the informally established ceiling. How they would have been dealt with is indicated in the story about the men who competed with each other until they were making $1.65 an hour. When the job was reengineered and the price cut, the other men refused to work on it, thus forcing the former competitors to stay with the "stinker." It is also clear from the story that such behavior was distinctly frowned upon and men who violated the group's standards would at least be ostracized from the group if not more severely punished.

GOLDBRICKING

Goldbricking behavior was equally well organized. In effect the workers were bargaining with management over the rate.

Roy gives this report based on his work diary:

> The hinge-base fight is an example of deliberate restriction on a major job that was regarded as poorly priced. This fight went on for at least nine months at the machine operated by Jack Starkey. During this period three men worked second shift on Jack's machine in the following sequence: Ed Sokolsky, Dooley, and Al McCann.
>
> *December 19.* Ed Sokolsky and Jack Starkey have not been doing well. Ed cusses intermittently and leaves his machine for long periods of time. The foremen find the machine idle, and Steve bellows about it. Ed calls the price he is working on a "stinker." I know it is, because Ed is free with his advertising of the "gravy" he finds.
>
> Ed seems to have constant trouble with his jig, a revolving piece attached to the side of the table. Two disks seem to stick together, and Ed is constantly (every day or so) using the crane to dismantle the jig (a very heavy one). He sands the disks and oils them, taking several hours for the cleaning operation. Steve saw the dismantled jig again tonight and bellowed, "Again?" Steve does not like it.
>
> Paul, the setup man, gets concerned, too, when he finds the jig torn down and Ed away

somewhere. He says, "Where the hell's Ed?" in a provoked manner.

February 10. I noticed that Ed was poking along and asked him if he had a good job. He shook his head, saying that he was making but 46 cents an hour, turning out 2 pieces an hour that paid 23 cents each.

February 26 Jack Starkey told me tonight that, although his job on the hinge bases was retimed, there was no raise in price. The price is still 23 cents.

I said, "All you've got to turn out is 5 an hour to make $1.15."

"I'd just like to see anybody turn out 5 of these an hour," said Jack, "with a tolerance of 0.0005!"

Later, Ed Sokolsky said that he and Jack were turning out about 24 pieces in a 10-hour period (2.4 an hour), that the job had been retimed several times, but no raise in price had been given.

Ed and Jack asked for a price of 38 cents. Ed said that they could turn out 3 an hour, but, until they got a decent price, they were turning out 2 an hour.

Toward the end of the evening I noticed that Ed's machine was idle, and Ed was sitting on a box, doing nothing.

"What's the matter, did they stop the job on you?" I asked.

"I stopped it," said Ed. "I don't feel like running it."

March 20 Dooley worked on the hinge bases again tonight. He admitted that he could barely make out on the job, but "Why bust my ass for day rate? We're doing 3 an hour or less until we get a better price!"

This 3-an-hour-or-less business has been going on several months. The price is 23 cents; so Dooley and Jack turn in 69 cents an hour (or less).

May 15 McCann said that Starkey was arguing all day over the price of the hinge bases. The methods men maintain that they can't raise the price "because the jacks that the parts go on sell for $14 apiece." They plan to retool the job and lower the price. According to McCann, Jack told them that if he didn't get a decent price he was going to make out on the job but scrap every one of the pieces.

"Jack fights it out with them," said McCann.

"He'll stay right with the machine and argue. I get disgusted and walk away.

"Jack turned out 28 today," McCann went on. "That's too many, nearly 3 an hour. He'll have to watch himself if he expects to get a raise in price."

Starkey was running the hinge bases again tonight. I remarked, "I see you're in the gravy again."

His reply was, "Yeah! 69 cents an hour!"

McCann did not seem to enjoy the hinge bases either. He looked bored, tired, and disgusted all evening. His ten hours is a long stretch at day work. He cannot make out early and rest after eleven o'clock (for four hours), but has to keep on the machine until three.

August 14. Al McCann was working on the hinge bases tonight, one of the jobs that he and Jack are protesting as to price. Gil (the foreman) sat and stood behind Al for at least an hour, and I could see that Al did not like it. He worked steadily, but with deliberate slowness, and did not look at Gil or speak to him. Al and Jack have agreed to restrict production on the hinge bases until they get a better price, and Gil was probably there to see what Al could really do. I think that Al and Jack could make out on the job, but not at $1.25 an hour, and they cut production to less than 80 cents an hour.

August 16. Al told me that they had won a price raise on the hinge bases, from 23 to 28 cents, and another raise to 31 cents.

"But it's still not high enough. As it is now we can make exactly 93 cents an hour. We're trying to get 35 cents. We can turn out 1 in exactly 16 minutes. That's not 4 an hour. We've been giving them 3 an hour."

At the 31-cent price and at the output rate of 3 pieces per hour the men were turning in 93 cents per hour or $7.44 per 8-hour day. Since the special base rate as experienced operators on a machine handling heavy fixtures was $1.10 per hour, they were earning 17 cents an hour less than they were paid.

Roy reports the end of the hinge-base fight in these words from his diary:

Al said tonight that he was making out on the hinge bases, that he got disgusted Friday, speeded up the tools, and turned in 31 pieces for earnings of $9.60 ($3^7/_8$ pieces per hour, or $1.20 per hour earnings).

"It was easy, just as easy as the frames. Now I'm kicking myself all over for not doing it before. All I did was to change the speed from 95 to 130. I was sick of stalling around all evening, and I got mad and decided to make out and let the tools burn up. But they made it all right, for 8 hours. What's the use of turning in 93 cents an hour when you can turn in $1.25 just as easy? They'd never raise a price you could make 93 cents on anyhow. Now maybe they'll cut it back."

Tonight Al made out easily in 6 hours, though he stretched the last few pieces to carry him until 10:30.

We can make two observations on the basis of this case. We see, in the first place, the war of conflicting pressures regarding the piece-rate price. Convinced that the piece rate is too low, the workers stand together to hold down production to hurt management and thus force an increase in the price. After many months the pressure is eventually successful in raising the price from 23 up to 31 cents apiece. Even this does not seem to be enough to the men, but now the price has risen to a point where they realize that if they really work at it they can make more than their base rate. How long, then, should they go on holding back production and fighting for a still better price? They now have to weigh the chances of getting a further adjustment from management against the losses that they are suffering in their pay envelope. The point is finally reached where some individual tires of the struggle over rates and decides to see what he can do on the job. If he is successful in making quota earnings or near quota earnings, then the fight is over and the new rate has in effect been accpeted.

It is also instructive to note that the private estimates of the operators as to the production they could achieve were on the conservative side. When they were holding back production they did not really believe it possible to turn out a piece in less than 16 minutes. When they once decided that there was no further point in holding back, when they went ahead and bent all their efforts toward production, they found that they could make quota earnings—and not in eight hours but in six. Apparently men are not good estimators as to what they can do on a machine when the estimates are made at a time when they are not really trying for production.

In this situation we see the conflict fought out directly with management by the workers themselves. In other situations we might find the union prominently involved in the struggle, pressing grievances against piece rates. In this situation, while the men were represented by a union, they had no faith in it and preferred to handle their problems themselves. But even in cases where union stewards and officers are active in the struggle against management's administration of the incentive program, it is evident that the union has not created the conflict. The union is simply one important channel through which the conflict is expressed.

Reading 28

What Makes a Work Group Successful?

Edward E. Lawler III
Cortlandt Cammann

In 1970, the chairman of Harwood Companies came to us with a most unusual request: Why, he wanted to know, was one of their work units so extraordinarily productive? Usually when firms seek out behavioral science researchers it is because they are having problems. Consequently, specialists in the field of organization behavior usually analyze groups or institutions that are not working right. A lot can be learned from observing groups that are having troubles, but it is refreshing and very useful to study successful groups, too. Only in this way can hard evidence be obtained on what distinguishes effective from ineffective groups.

The work group singled out was the warehousing, order packing, and shipping unit in one of Harwood's Virginia plants. At the time, the unit consisted of eleven employees and a supervisor. All lived in rural Virginia. Their mean age was thirty-seven. Only six of them had high school diplomas. Their average length of time in the group was fifteen years, and their average service in the company seventeen years. All were married, and most had children.

The department assembles the products manufactured in several of the company's nearby plants, stores them until needed, fills customer orders as they come in, and ships them out. Though the work does not require a high level of skill, it can be physically tiring. Alertness is required, as the inventory contains more than 3,000 separate styles and sizes. There are several thousand separate accounts, and requirements for quantities, sizes, and colors vary widely from order to order. During some periods of the year the men can put in a great deal of overtime if they wish. At other times the workload is relatively light.

Our first task was to determine whether this group was, in fact, as productive and effective as management said it was. We quickly discovered, from the records and from interviews, that the group had not always been thought of so highly. Indeed, between 1950 and 1958, its productivity was abysmal. In those years as many as twenty-one men worked in the department during seasonal peaks. Because of clerical chaos, many of the orders that reached the shipping department were for products that were out of stock. Floors were cluttered with partially filled orders.

Understandably, turnover, absenteeism, and grievances were high. Annual turnover ranged from 20 to 50 percent. Personal relationships in the department were marked by arguing and fighting rather than by teamwork. Each man had a specific job, and since the flow of orders from customers was not controlled, it frequently happened that some of the men were extremely busy while others had little to do. The attitude was every man for himself.

The shipping department supervisor was beset by difficulties. It was his job to maintain the rate of shipment, to accept responsibility for the accuracy of shipments, and to oversee the workforce. In carrying out these responsibilities, he had to work under the direction of the plant manager, the production manager, and five men connected with sales in the New

York office. He found himself pulled in many directions at the same time, and he was never able to perform to the satisfaction of all his bosses.

In 1958, an inventory and order control system was introduced, and the layout of the plant was changed. Soon after these changes were instituted the supervisor was transferred, and his assistant became the new supervisor. The role of the supervisor was changed. He no longer received instructions directly from New York. Since a new computer had begun to produce "clean orders," his role was primarily to organize and maintain the force necessary to ship the orders that came to him each day. All instructions and changes in the daily routine of shipping came from the plant customer relations office and from a plant staff member who was assigned responsibility in this area.

At about the same time, a bonus plan was proposed to the work group by management. This included a sharing by the company and the group of any reductions in cost from the previous year. After thoroughly discussing the proposal with management, the group unanimously agreed to accept the plan. Several days later group members requested that their number be cut from seventeen to eleven. The six who left were placed in other jobs within the company, and the size of the group has remained at about eleven ever since. With the exception of some minor improvements in the packaging of merchandise, there have been no significant technological changes since 1958. Thus the production figures for the years from 1958 to the present are comparable.

During this period the shipping department's output has climbed sharply. Data on average productivity per man-hour are pre-

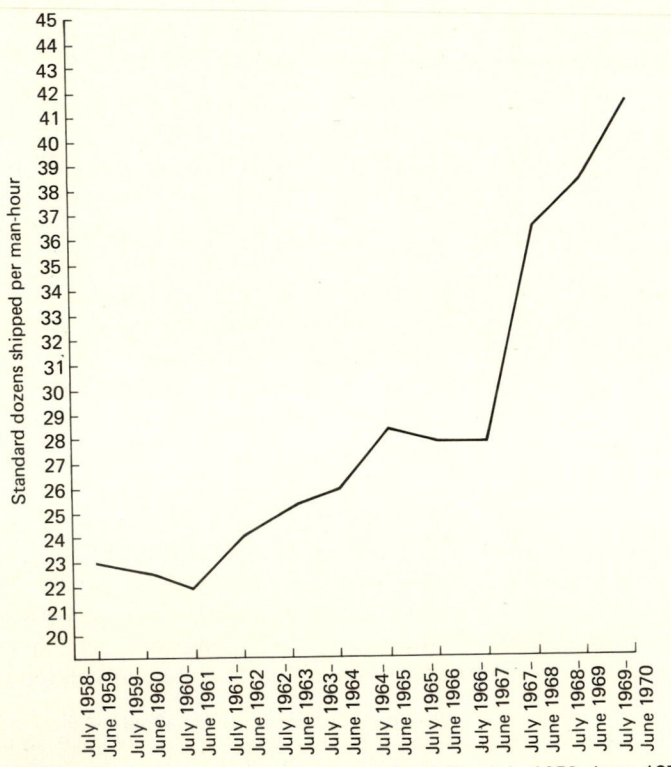

Figure 28-1   Change in average productivity, July 1958–June 1970.

sented in Figure 28-1 and show a gradual increase from 1958 to 1967, and a sharp rise since then. Over all, the average worker was turning out twice as much in 1970 as he was in 1958, even though there were no changes in technology or equipment.

Two other measures of this unit's effectiveness were available. During the twelve years from June 1958 to June 1970, only three people chose to quit the group. This represents a voluntary turnover of under 2 percent per year, compared with a turnover for the entire plant of 25 percent per year. Also, from June 1969 to June 1970, the only year for which it was calculated, absenteeism was less than one percent of the total possible man-days, compared with 5 percent for the total work population. So, not only has this become a decidedly productive group—it is one in which people seem to want to participate.

Any group's productivity is influenced by a variety of forces, not all of which by any means are related to technology. Some forces—for example, poor equipment, group pressures to restrict output—hold production down, while others serve to push it up—individual motivation, new equipment, group norms *favoring* increased output.

Researchers have found five factors that strongly influence group productivity: technology, intrinsic motivation, extrinsic motivation, group norms about cooperation and productivity, and the abilities of the group members. To discover why the productivity of the Virginia shipping department was higher than that of other groups, we needed to learn how each of these five factors was affecting it. This was accomplished in a comparative study.

The first group to be compared with the shipping department was also in the Virginia plant. It performed a different kind of work (cutting and spreading fabric) and was considered to be about average in efficiency.

The second group chosen for comparison was the shipping department in another factory in another state. This department was chosen because it did the same kind of work, operated under a similar pay plan, was part of the same corporation, but had lower productivity. The researchers had to accept management's assessment of relative productivity, since the actual figures were not comparable. Turnover and absenteeism were much higher in this department than in either of the Virginia groups. The average seniority was 5.2 years, in contrast to 15 years and 18 years in the Virginia groups.

While the study focused on both similarities and differences among the three groups, the differences naturally were of most interest to us, because they were the characteristics more likely to explain the Virginia shipping department's better record. Some of the characteristics it *shares* with other groups probably do contribute to its productivity; but the comparative analysis is unlikely to pinpoint those.

We began our research informally by interviewing several workers in the Virginia shipping department. On the basis of these interviews, a "structured" interview was prepared and a questionnaire developed to measure group norms, intrinsic (that is, self-generated) motivation, and extrinsic (externally induced) motivation. All members of the three work groups completed the questionnaire. Interviews were conducted with all members of the Virginia shipping unit and with six members of the other shipping department.

There were no significant differences in technology between the Virginia shipping group and the other shipping group. Unusual physical or mental abilities were also ruled out in accounting for the record of the Virginia group. Any physically fit man with average intelligence can perform shipping-department tasks. We had no reason to doubt that the employees in all the company's shipping departments possessed the requisite ability.

By elimination, we were left with the probability that the clue was to be found in psychological factors. Specifically, it seemed likely to rest in the Virginia group's desire to produce at a high level and in the kind of personal relationships and group pressures, or norms, that existed.

What a group accepts as normal in matters such as productivity and cooperation can have a strong impact on its performance. A number of studies have shown that when groups adopt anti-productivity norms, individual members tend to restrict their output. It is also true that when groups develop pro-productivity norms, production tends to rise.

Our questionnaire and interview data clearly indicated that the Virginia shipping department had developed pro- rather than anti-productivity norms. This is undoubtedly *one* of the main reasons its output was so high. However, its norms about productivity were not significantly different from those of the comparison groups. Therefore the pro-productivity norms alone could not explain why it surpassed the other groups.

When groups perform tasks that require cooperative effort, productivity is influenced by their norms about teamwork. The work of the shipping department demands mutual help. Boxes and cartons are passed from one person to another, a process that must go smoothly. All the groups studied tended to have norms strongly favoring cooperation. But these norms, and in particular the feeling of team spirit, were strongest in the Virginia shipping department group, as illustrated by the following comments made by its members:

We all try to work as one team. It's a good bunch of boys to work with.

We have a lot of fun . . . nobody gets mad.

They're all nice fellows. They work well together.

Two of the workers used the analogy of the family to describe the atmosphere of the group. On the other hand, the shipping group in the other plant described itself in different terms:

There could be a lot better cooperation. Sometimes the fellows get to work together and other times they just don't.

They don't work together . . . not a hundred percent like they should.

The clearly superior team spirit of the Virginia group appeared to be at least partially responsible for its greater efficiency.

The norms of the Virginia department seemed ideal from many points of view. Members were promanagement, supported and encouraged high productivity, and favored cooperation. How do such norms develop? Supervisory style, trust of management, and the reward system all contribute to the making of high-spirited morale. In the Virginia group, these three factors seem to have combined to encourage high productivity.

The Harwood management has been using a participative approach for a number of years and appears to have won the trust of its employees, who told us:

I think they would look out for my interest.

They [the top plant management] will speak to you if they see you outside the plant. Now I think that goes a long way with people working for them. Something like that means a lot to me. I'd go out of my way if I could do anything for a person like that.

Other employees stressed that management had never harmed them and had always shown concern for them. They also trust Harwood not to do what so many companies do: change the incentive plan when the employees start to earn more.

The Virginia shippers were much more satisfied with their supervisor than were the members of the other two groups.

I haven't got anything I can say against him— taken all the way 'round he is a good supervisor.

I don't believe they have any better here at the plant. He's a good fellow.

This supervisor didn't push the men; he didn't supervise them closely. He told them what had to be done and expected that it would be accomplished. As he himself described it, he would rather lead than push. He was prepared to exert influence if something was not getting done, but he wouldn't ride the men about it.

In the shipping department of the other plant, the employees complained that their supervisor was at first too strict, later too lenient. He is gone now. The new supervisor was promoted from the work group and has yet to prove himself. Some of the men lack confidence in him. Some say he supervises too closely. These differences in leadership style seem to contribute to the better team spirit in Virginia.

The kind of incentive plan used in the Virginia plant supported the development of favorable norms. When this plan was started in 1958, job classifications were abolished. All members of the group were free to perform all tasks, so the workload could be distributed evenly. This encouraged cooperation. Almost certainly, part of the increase in productivity since 1958 has resulted from the increased ability of the work group to use its labor where it could be most effective.

At the same time the job classifications were tossed out, a group incentive bonus was introduced to tie the individual worker's pay to his group's performance. The plan created a "reward situation" where it was to the advantage of each member to keep his fellow workers on their toes.

Provided that workers trust management and have a participatory relationship with their supervisors, group plans generally tend to encourage favorable norms about productivity. This seems to be precisely what happened in the Virginia shipping group.

It has often been observed that some people work hard, under any conditions, because of their values about work. Jobholders who are committed to the Protestant work ethnic, and who strongly believe in self-control, are said to have high intrinsic motivation. High intrinsic motivation may be a factor in the superior productivity of the Virginia shipping department. Measures of this variable were included in the questionnaire and the employees did tend to score high.

Intrinsic motivation is reinforced when a good fit occurs between the needs of the worker and the characteristics of his job so that good performance leads to inner rewards, such as a feeling of competence. Lawler and Hackman argue that this occurs when workers who value such intrinsic rewards hold jobs that provide them with feedback, autonomy, and wholly meaningful tasks.

An analysis of the shipping jobs suggests that they are capable of generating some intrinsic motivation. Feedback and autonomy are high, but opportunities to work on challenging, meaningful tasks are limited. Interestingly, on our questionnaire measure the Virginia group had higher intrinsic motivation scores than the other groups. This seems to stem from a feeling that they have more autonomy than the other groups. It does not appear that the higher degree of autonomy they report is owing to any basic difference in the nature of the job itself. Rather it seems due to the different styles used by the supervisors. It is an interesting example of how the supervisor can have an important influence on his subordinates' perceptions of the nature of their jobs. Again in part, the higher motivation of the shipping group can apparently be explained by a greater intrinsic motivation.

Any external reward can be a source of motivation if it is valued by the employees and if earning it is seen as being related to performance.

The external reward most frequently used is money; indeed, incentive plans that tied dollar reward to superior performance were used by all the groups studied. The employees in all the groups valued money very highly and clearly saw a connection between their pay and their performance.

The Virginia shipping department, however,

differed from the others in one important respect: The workers saw a much closer connection between their productivity and their pay than did the members of the other groups. The Virginia shippers felt that they could actually figure out what their earnings would be in a given week and clearly understood the basis on which they were paid. The other shipping group workers could not clearly grasp how their pay was determined. Both the questionnaire and the interview data suggested that they were unsure about the calculations. Their plan was more complicated; it is not surprising that they were unable to understand it.

Lawler and Hackman have shown that when employees participate in the design of a pay plan it is likely to be more successful because they understand it better and are more committed to making it work effectively. The Virginia shipping group had participated in the development of its plan. Members had been given a voice in drawing it up, and they had a chance to accept or reject it. In the other shipping department, this procedure was not followed; the employees clearly had less comprehension of their incentive plan and were less committed to it.

One other piece of evidence strongly indicates that dollar reward is a strong motivation in the Virginia work group. Until June 1967, the incentive system included a ceiling on the bonus that the men could receive. This ceiling was removed in the summer of 1967. Figure 29-1 shows the obvious results: Average productivity rose about 30 percent, and the higher level of output has been consistently maintained since then, This rise seems to be attributable almost entirely to the nature of the pay system. Accordingly, a strong case can be made that a major reason for the Virginia group's higher productivity is the unique pay incentive system.

Why is the Virginia shipping department highly productive? The answer now seems clear. The men who work in it have high intrinsic and extrinsic motivation, and have group norms that promote cooperation and productivity. The high motivation and positive group norms have been encouraged by a number of favorable conditions. These include good supervision, trust of management, an acceptable pay system, and work that allows some autonomy. The other groups studied had generally positive norms and reasonably high motivation. However, these factors simply did not interact to create the strong forces for productivity that developed in the Virginia group.

The reasons for this seem to lie in two important factors: First, the pay system in the Virginia shipping department makes a clear connection between pay and performance, and the employees are committed to it. Second, the supervisor in the Virginia group generally uses a participative style and is respected by his men. These elements were missing in the other groups, and because of it they turned out less work.

One way to determine the validity of our diagnosis would be to try to change the other groups. Specifically, the pay plan and type of supervision could be revised in the other shipping department—and, indeed, the management is planning to try this. If our analysis is correct, the change should result in better performance there. The kind of comparative study we have done can produce valuable indications about why a group is productive, but final proof can come only from experiments in which changes are introduced.

Reading 29

Groupthink

Irving L. Janis

"How could we have been so stupid?" President John F. Kennedy asked after he and a close group of advisers had blundered into the Bay of Pigs invasion. For the last two years I have been studying that question, as it applies not only to the Bay of Pigs decision-makers but also to those who led the United States into such other major fiascos as the failure to be prepared for the attack on Pearl Harbor, the Korean War stalemate and the escalation of the Vietnam War.

Stupidity certainly is not the explanation. The men who participated in making the Bay of Pigs decision, for instance, comprised one of the greatest arrays of intellectual talent in the history of American Government—Dean Rusk, Robert McNamara, Douglas Dillon, Robert Kennedy, McGeorge Bundy, Arthur Schlesinger Jr., Allen Dulles and others.

It also seemed to me that explanations were incomplete if they concentrated only on disturbances in the behavior of each individual within a decision-making body: temporary emotional states of elation, fear, or anger that reduce a man's mental efficiency, for example, or chronic blind spots arising from a man's social prejudices or idiosyncratic biases.

I preferred to broaden the picture by looking at the fiascos from the standpoint of group dynamics as it has been explored over the past three decades, first by the great social psychologist Kurt Lewin and later in many experimental situations by myself and other behavioral scientists. My conclusion after poring over hundreds of relevant documents—historical reports about formal group meetings and informal conversations among the members—is that the groups that committed the fiascos were victims of what I call "groupthink."

"Groupy"

In each case study, I was surprised to discover the extent to which each group displayed the typical phenomena of social conformity that are regularly encountered in studies of group dynamics among ordinary citizens. For example, some of the phenomena appear to be completely in line with findings from social-psychological experiments showing that powerful social pressures are brought to bear by the members of a cohesive group whenever a dissident begins to voice his objections to a group consensus. Other phenomena are reminiscent of the shared illusions observed in encounter groups and friendship cliques when the members simultaneously reach a peak of "groupy" feelings.

Above all, there are numerous indications pointing to the development of group norms that bolster morale at the expense of critical thinking. One of the most common norms appears to be that of remaining loyal to the group by sticking with the policies to which the group has already committed itself, even when those policies are obviously working out badly and have unintended consequences that disturb the conscience of each member. This is one of the key characteristics of groupthink.

1984

I use the term groupthink as a quick and easy way to refer to the mode of thinking that persons engage in when *concurrence-seeking* becomes so dominant in a cohesive ingroup that it tends to override realistic appraisal of alternative courses of action. Groupthink is a term of the same order as the words in the newspeak vocabulary George Orwell used in his dismaying world of *1984*. In that context, groupthink takes on an invidious connotation. Exactly such a connotation is intended, since the term refers to a deterioration in mental efficiency, reality testing and moral judgments as a result of group pressures.

The symptoms of groupthink arise when the members of decision-making groups become motivated to avoid being too harsh in their judgments of their leaders' or their colleagues' ideas. They adopt a soft line of criticism, even in their own thinking. At their meetings, all the members are amiable and seek complete concurrence on every important issue, with no bickering or conflict to spoil the cozy, "we-feeling" atmosphere.

Kill

Paradoxically, soft-headed groups are often hard-hearted when it comes to dealing with outgroups or enemies. They find it relatively easy to resort to dehumanizing solutions—they will readily authorize bombing attacks that kill large numbers of civilians in the name of the noble cause of persuading an unfriendly government to negotiate at the peace table. They are unlikely to pursue the more difficult and controversial issues that arise when alternatives to a harsh military solution come up for discussion. Nor are they inclined to raise ethical issues that carry the implication that *this fine group of ours, with its humanitarianism and its high-minded principles, might be capable of adopting a course of action that is inhumane and immoral.*

Norms

There is evidence from a number of social-psychological studies that as the members of a group feel more accepted by the others, which is a central feature of increased group cohesiveness, they display less overt conformity to group norms. Thus we would expect that the more cohesive a group becomes, the less the members will feel constrained to censor what they say out of fear of being socially punished for antagonizing the leader or any of their fellow members.

In contrast, the groupthink type of conformity tends to increase as group cohesiveness increases. Groupthink involves nondeliberate suppression of critical thoughts as a result of internalization of the group's norms, which is quite different from deliberate suppression on the basis of external threats of social punishment. The more cohesive the group, the greater the inner compulsion on the part of each member to avoid creating disunity, which inclines him to believe in the soundness of whatever proposals are promoted by the leader or by a majority of the group's members.

In a cohesive group, the danger is not so much that each individual will fail to reveal his objections to what the others propose but that he will think the proposal is a good one, without attempting to carry out a careful, critical scrutiny of the pros and cons of the alternatives. When groupthink becomes dominant, there also is considerable suppression of deviant thoughts, but it takes the form of each person's deciding that his misgivings are not relevant and should be set aside, that the benefit of the doubt regarding any lingering uncertainties should be given to the group consensus.

Stress

I do not mean to imply that all cohesive groups necessarily suffer from groupthink. All ingroups may have a mild tendency toward groupthink, displaying one or another of the symptoms from time to time, but it need not be so dominant as to influence the quality of the group's final decision. Neither do I mean to imply that there is anything necessarily inefficient or harmful about group decisions in general. On the contrary, a group whose members have properly defined roles, with traditions concerning the procedures to follow in pursuing a critical inquiry, probably is capable of making better decisions than any individual group member working alone.

The problem is that the advantages of having decisions made by groups are often lost because of powerful psychological pressures that arise when the members work closely together, share the same set of values and, above all, face a crisis situation that puts everyone under intense stress.

The main principle of groupthink, which I offer in the spirit of Parkinson's Law, is this:

The more amiability and esprit de corps there is among the members of a policy-making ingroup, the greater the danger that independent critical thinking will be replaced by groupthink, which is likely to result in irrational and dehumanizing actions directed against outgroups.

Symptoms

In my studies of high-level governmental decision-makers, both civilian and military, I have found eight main symptoms of groupthink.

1 Invulnerability Most or all of the members of the ingroup share an *illusion* of invulnerability that provides for them some degree of reassurance about obvious dangers and leads them to become overoptimistic and willing to take extraordinary risks. It also causes them to fail to respond to clear warnings of danger.

The Kennedy ingroup, which uncritically accepted the Central Intelligence Agency's disastrous Bay of Pigs plan, operated on the false assumption that they could keep secret the fact that the United States was responsible for the invasion of Cuba. Even after news of the plan began to leak out, their belief remained unshaken. They failed even to consider the danger that awaited them: a worldwide revulsion against the U.S.

A similar attitude appeared among the members of President Lyndon B. Johnson's ingroup, the "Tuesday Cabinet," which kept escalating the Vietnam War despite repeated setbacks and failures. "There was a belief," Bill Moyers commented after he resigned, "that if we indicated a willingness to use our power, they [the North Vietnamese] would get the message and back away from an all-out confrontation. . . . There was a confidence— it was never bragged about, it was just there—that when the chips were really down, the other people would fold."

A most poignant example of an illusion of invulnerability involves the ingroup around Admiral H. E. Kimmel, which failed to prepare for the possibility of a Japanese attack on Pearl Harbor despite repeated warnings. Informed by his intelligence chief that radio contact with Japanese aircraft carriers had been lost, Kimmel joked about it: "What, you don't know where the carriers are? Do you mean to say that they could be rounding Diamond Head (at Honolulu) and you wouldn't know it?" The carriers were in fact moving full-steam toward Kimmel's command post at the time. Laughing together about a danger signal, which labels it as a purely laughing matter, is a characteristic manifestation of groupthink.

2 Rationale As we see, victims of groupthink ignore warnings; they also collectively construct rationalizations in order to discount warnings and other forms of negative feedback that, taken seriously, might lead the group members to reconsider their assumptions each time they recommit themselves to past decisions. Why did the Johnson ingroup avoid reconsidering its escalation policy when time and again the expectations on which they based their decisions turned out to be wrong?

James C. Thompson Jr., a Harvard historian who spent five years as an observing participant in both the State Department and the White House, tells us that the policymakers avoided critical discussion of their prior decisions and continually invented new rationalizations so that they could sincerely recommit themselves to defeating the North Vietnamese.

In the fall of 1964, before the bombing of North Vietnam began, some of the policymakers predicted that six weeks of air strikes would induce the North Vietnamese to seek peace talks. When someone asked, "What if they don't?" the answer was that another four weeks certainly would do the trick.

Later, after each setback, the ingroup agreed that by investing just a bit more effort (by stepping up the bomb tonnage a bit, for instance), their course of action would prove to be right. *The Pentagon Papers* bear out these observations.

In *The Limits of Intervention*, Townsend Hoopes, who was acting Secretary of the Air Force under Johnson, says that Walt W. Rostow in particular showed a remarkable capacity for what has been called "instant rationalization." According to Hoopes, Rostow buttressed the group's optimism about being on the road to victory by culling selected scraps of evidence from news reports or, if necessary, by inventing "plausible" forecasts that had no basis in evidence at all.

Admiral Kimmel's group rationalized away their warnings, too. Right up to December 7, 1941, they convinced themselves that the Japanese would never dare attempt a full-scale surprise assault against Hawaii because Japan's leaders would realize that it would precipitate an all-out war which the United States would surely win. They made no attempt to look at the situation through the eyes of the Japanese leaders—another manifestation of groupthink.

3 Morality Victims of groupthink believe unquestioningly in the inherent morality of their ingroup; this belief inclines the members to ignore the ethical or moral consequences of their decisions.

Evidence that this symptom is at work usually is of a negative kind—the things that are left unsaid in group meetings. At least two influential persons had doubts about the morality of the Bay of Pigs adventure. One of them, Arthur Schlesinger Jr., presented his strong objections in a memorandum to President Kennedy and Secretary of State Rusk but suppressed them when he attended meetings of the Kennedy team. The other, Senator J. William Fulbright, was not a member of the group, but the President invited him to express his misgivings in a speech to the policymakers. However, when Fulbright finished speaking the President moved on to other agenda items without asking for reactions of the group.

David Kraslow and Stuart H. Loory, in *The Secret Search for Peace in Vietnam*, report that during 1966 President Johnson's ingroup was concerned primarily with selecting bomb targets in North Vietnam. They based their selections on four factors—the military advantage, the risk to American aircraft and pilots, the danger of forcing other countries into the fighting, and the danger of heavy civilian casualties. At their regular Tuesday luncheons, they weighed these factors the way school teachers grade examination papers, averaging them out. Though evidence on this point is scant, I suspect that the group's ritualistic adherence to a standardized procedure induced the members to feel morally justified in their destructive way of dealing with the Vietnamese people—after all, the danger of heavy civilian casualties from U.S. air strikes was taken into account on their checklists.

4 Stereotypes Victims of groupthink hold stereotyped views of the leaders of enemy groups: they are so evil that genuine attempts at negotiating differences with them are unwarranted, or they are too weak or too stupid to deal effectively with whatever attempts the ingroup makes to defeat their purposes, no matter how risky the attempts are.

Kennedy's groupthinkers believed that Premier Fidel Castro's air force was so ineffectual that obsolete B-26s could knock it out completely in a surprise attack before the invasion began. They also believed that Castro's army was so weak that a small Cuban-exile brigade could establish a well-protected beachhead at the Bay of Pigs. In addition, they believed that Castro was not smart enough to put down any possible internal uprisings in support of the exiles. They were wrong on all three assumptions. Though much of the blame was attributable to faulty intelligence, the point is that none of Kennedy's advisers even questioned the CIA planners about these assumptions.

The Johnson advisers' sloganistic thinking about "the Communist apparatus" that was "working all around the world" (as Dean Rusk put it) led them to overlook the powerful nationalistic strivings of the North Vietnamese government and its efforts to ward off Chinese domination. The crudest of all stereotypes used by Johnson's inner circle to justify their policies was the domino theory ("If we don't stop the Reds in South Vietnam, tomorrow they will be in Hawaii and next week they will be in San Francisco," Johnson once said). The group so firmly accepted this stereotype that it became almost impossible for any adviser to introduce a more sophisticated viewpoint.

In the documents on Pearl Harbor, it is clear to see that the Navy commanders stationed in Hawaii had a naive image of Japan as a midget that would not dare to strike a blow against a powerful giant.

5 Pressure Victims of groupthink apply direct pressure to any individual who momentarily expresses doubts about any of the group's shared illusions or who questions the validity of the arguments supporting a policy alternative favored by the majority. This gambit reinforces the concurrence-seeking norm that loyal members are expected to maintain.

President Kennedy probably was more active than anyone else in raising skeptical questions during the Bay of Pigs meetings, and yet he seems to have encouraged the group's docile, uncritical acceptance of defective arguments in favor of the CIA's plan. At every meeting, he allowed the CIA representatives to dominate the discussion. He permitted them to give their immediate refutations in response to each tentative doubt that one of the others expressed, instead of asking whether anyone shared the doubt or wanted to pursue the implications of the new worrisome issue that had just been raised. And at the most crucial meeting, when he was calling on each member to give his vote for or against the plan, he did not call on Arthur Schlesinger, the one man there who was known by the President to have serious misgivings.

Historian Thomson informs us that whenever a member of Johnson's ingroup began to express doubts, the group used subtle social pressures to "domesticate" him. To start with, the dissenter was made to feel at home, provided that he lived up to two restrictions: 1) that he did not voice his doubts to outsiders, which would play into the hands of the opposition; and 2) that he kept his criticisms within the bounds of acceptable deviation, which meant not challenging any of the fundamental assumptions that went into the group's prior commitments. One such "domesticated dissenter" was Bill Moyers. When Moyers arrived at a meeting, Thomson tells us, the President greeted him with, "Well, here comes Mr. Stop-the-Bombing."

6 Self-censorship Victims of groupthink avoid deviating from what appears to be group consensus; they keep silent about their misgivings and even minimize to themselves the importance of their doubts.

As we have seen, Schlesinger was not at all hesitant about presenting his strong objections to the Bay of Pigs plan in a memorandum to the President and the Secretary of State. But he became keenly aware of his tendency to suppress objections at the White House meetings. "In the months after the Bay of Pigs I bitterly reproached myself for having kept so silent during those crucial discussions in the cabinet room," Schlesinger writes in *A Thousand Days*. "I can only explain my failure to do more than raise a few timid questions by reporting that one's impulse to blow the whistle on this nonsense was simply undone by the circumstances of the discussion."

7 Unanimity   Victims of groupthink share an *illusion* of unanimity within the group concerning almost all judgments expressed by members who speak in favor of the majority view. This symptom results partly from the preceding one, whose effects are augmented by the false assumption that any individual who remains silent during any part of the discussion is in full accord with what the others are saying.

When a group of persons who respect each other's opinions arrives at a unanimous view, each member is likely to feel that the belief must be true. This reliance on consensual validation within the group tends to replace individual critical thinking and reality testing, unless there are clear-cut disagreements among the members. In contemplating a course of action such as the invasion of Cuba, it is painful for the members to confront disagreements within their group, particularly if it becomes apparent that there are widely divergent views about whether the preferred course of action is too risky to undertake at all. Such disagreements are likely to arouse anxieties about making a serious error. Once the sense of unanimity is shattered, the members no longer can feel complacently confident about the decision they are inclined to make. Each man must then face the annoying realization that there are troublesome uncertainties and he must diligently seek out the best information he can get in order to decide

for himself exactly how serious the risks might be. This is one of the unpleasant consequences of being in a group of hardheaded, critical thinkers.

To avoid such an unpleasant state, the members often become inclined, without quite realizing it, to prevent latent disagreements from surfacing when they are about to initiate a risky course of action. The group leader and the members support each other in playing up the areas of convergence in their thinking, at the expense of fully exploring divergencies that might reveal unsettled issues.

"Our meetings took place in a curious atmosphere of assumed consensus," Schlesinger writes. His additional comments clearly show that, curiously, the consensus was an illusion—an illusion that could be maintained only because the major participants did not reveal their own reasoning or discuss their idiosyncratic assumptions and vague reservations. Evidence from several sources makes it clear that even the three principals—President Kennedy, Rusk and McNamara—had widely differing assumptions about the invasion plan.

8 Mindguards   Victims of groupthink sometimes appoint themselves as mindguards to protect the leader and fellow members from adverse information that might break the complacency they shared about the effectiveness and morality of past decisions. At a large birthday party for his wife, Attorney General Robert F. Kennedy, who had been constantly informed about the Cuban invasion plan, took Schlesinger aside and asked him why he was opposed. Kennedy listened coldly and said, "You may be right or you may be wrong, but the President has made his mind up. Don't push it any further. Now is the time for everyone to help him all they can."

Rusk also functioned as a highly effective mindguard by failing to transmit to the group the strong objections of three "outsiders" who had learned of the invasion plan— Undersecretary of State Chester Bowles,

USIA Director Edward R. Murrow, and Rusk's intelligence chief, Roger Hilsman. Had Rusk done so, their warnings might have reinforced Schlesinger's memorandum and jolted some of Kennedy's ingroup, if not the President himself, into reconsidering the decision.

Products

When a group of executives frequently displays most or all of these interrelated symptoms, a detailed study of their deliberations is likely to reveal a number of immediate consequences. These consequences are, in effect, products of poor decision-making practices because they lead to inadequate solutions to the problems being dealt with.

First, the group limits its discussions to a few alternative courses of action (often only two) without an initial survey of all the alternatives that might be worthy of consideration.

Second, the group fails to reexamine the course of action initially preferred by the majority after they learn of risks and drawbacks they had not considered originally.

Third, the members spend little or no time discussing whether there are nonobvious gains they may have overlooked or ways of reducing the seemingly prohibitive costs that made rejected alternatives appear undesirable to them.

Fourth, members make little or no attempt to obtain information from experts within their own organizations who might be able to supply more precise estimates of potential losses and gains.

Fifth, members show positive interest in facts and opinions that support their preferred policy; they tend to ignore facts and opinions that do not.

Sixth, members spend little time deliberating about how the chosen policy might be hindered by bureaucratic inertia, sabotaged by political opponents, or temporarily derailed by common accidents. Consequently, they fail to work out contingency plans to cope with foreseeable setbacks that could endanger the overall success of their chosen course.

Support

The search for an explanation of why groupthink occurs has led me through a quagmire of complicated theoretical issues in the murky area of human motivation. My belief, based on recent social psychological research, is that we can best understand the various symptoms of groupthink as a mutual effort among the group members to maintain self-esteem and emotional equanimity by providing social support to each other, especially at times when they share responsibility for making vital decisions.

Even when no important decision is pending, the typical administrator will begin to doubt the wisdom and morality of his past decisions each time he receives information about setbacks, particularly if the information is accompanied by negative feedback from prominent men who originally had been his supporters. It should not be surprising, therefore, to find that individual members strive to develop unanimity and esprit de corps that will help bolster each other's morale, to create an optimistic outlook about the success of pending decisions, and to reaffirm the positive value of past policies to which all of them are committed.

Pride

Shared illusions of invulnerability, for example, can reduce anxiety about taking risks. Rationalizations help members believe that the risks are really not so bad after all. The assumption of inherent morality helps the members to avoid feelings of shame or guilt. Negative stereotypes function as stress-reducing devices to enhance a sense of moral righteousness as well as pride in a lofty mission.

The mutual enhancement of self-esteem and morale may have functional value in enabling the members to maintain their capacity to take action, but it has maladaptive consequences insofar as concurrence-seeking tendencies interfere with critical, rational capacities and lead to serious errors of judgment.

While I have limited my study to decision-making bodies in Government, groupthink symptoms appear in business, industry and any other field where small, cohesive groups make the decisions. It is vital, then, for all sorts of people—and especially group leaders—to know what steps they can take to prevent groupthink.

Remedies

To counterpoint my case studies of the major fiascos, I have also investigated two highly successful group enterprises, the formulation of the Marshall Plan in the Truman Administration and the handling of the Cuban missile crisis by President Kennedy and his advisers. I have found it instructive to examine the steps Kennedy took to change his group's decision-making processes. These changes ensured that the mistakes made by his Bay of Pigs ingroup were not repeated by the missile-crisis ingroup, even though the membership of both groups was essentially the same.

The following recommendations for preventing groupthink incorporate many of the good practices I discovered to be characteristic of the Marshall Plan and missile-crisis groups:

1   The leader of a policy-forming group should assign the role of critical evaluator to each member, encouraging the group to give high priority to open airing of objections and doubts. This practice needs to be reinforced by the leader's acceptance of criticism of his own judgments in order to discourage members from soft-pedaling their disagreements and from allowing their striving for concurrence to inhibit criticism.

2   When the key members of a hierarchy assign a policy-planning mission to any group within their organization, they should adopt an impartial stance instead of stating preferences and expectations at the beginning. This will encourage open inquiry and impartial probing of a wide range of policy alternatives.

3   The organization routinely should set up several outside policy-planning and evaluation groups to work on the same policy question, each deliberating under a different leader. This can prevent the insulation of an ingroup.

4   At intervals before the group reaches a final consensus, the leader should require each member to discuss the group's deliberations with associates in his own unit of the organization—assuming that those associates can be trusted to adhere to the same security regulations that govern the policy-makers—and then to report back their reactions to the group.

5   The group should invite one or more outside experts to each meeting on a staggered basis and encourage the experts to challenge the views of the core members.

6   At every general meeting of the group, whenever the agenda calls for an evaluation of policy alternatives, at least one member should play devil's advocate, functioning as a good lawyer in challenging the testimony of those who advocate the majority position.

7   Whenever the policy issue involves relations with a rival nation or organization, the group should devote a sizable block of time, perhaps an entire session, to a survey of all warning signals from the rivals and should write alternative scenarios on the rivals' intentions.

8   When the group is surveying policy alternatives for feasibility and effectiveness, it should from time to time divide into two or more subgroups to meet separately, under different chairmen, and then come back together to hammer out differences.

9   After reaching a preliminary consensus about what seems to be the best policy, the group should hold a "second-chance" meeting at which every member expresses as vividly as he can all his residual doubts, and rethinks the entire issue before making a definitive choice.

How

These recommendations have their disadvantages. To encourage the open airing of objections, for instance, might lead to prolonged and costly debates when a rapidly growing crisis requires immediate solution. It also could cause rejection, depression and anger. A leader's failure to set a norm might create cleavage between leader and members that could develop into a disruptive power struggle if the leader looks on the emerging consensus as anathema. Setting up outside evaluation groups might increase the risk of security leakage. Still, inventive executives who know their way around the organizational maze probably can figure out how to apply one or another of the prescriptions successfully, without harmful side effects.

They also could benefit from the advice of outside experts in the administrative and behavioral sciences. Though these experts have much to offer, they have had few chances to work on policy-making machinery within large organizations. As matters now stand, executives innovate only when they need new procedures to avoid repeating serious errors that have deflated their self-images.

In this era of atomic warheads, urban disorganization and ecocatastrophes, it seems to me that policymakers should collaborate with behavioral scientists and give top priority to preventing groupthink and its attendant fiascos.

Reading 30

Improving Group Performance Effectiveness

J. Richard Hackman
Charles G. Morris

When decision makers in public and private institutions in this society are faced with genuinely important tasks, it is likely that they will assign those tasks to groups for solution. Sometimes the reason is simply that one individual could not be expected to handle the task by himself (e.g., formulating a new welfare policy, which requires a diversity of knowledge and skills). Other times it is because decision makers assume that the added human resources available in a group will lead to a product higher in *quality*—or at least lessen the chances that the product will be grossly defective.

Given current knowledge about group effectiveness, the state of affairs described above is not an occasion for optimism. Although literally thousands of studies of group performance have been conducted over the last several decades, we still know very little about why some groups are more effective than others. We know even less about what to do to improve the performance of a given group working on a specific task.

Excerpted and adapted from Hackman, J. R., & Morris, C. G. Group tasks, group interaction process, and group performance effectiveness: A review and proposed integration. In L. Berkowitz (Ed.), *Advances in experimental social psychology* (Vol. 8). New York: Academic Press, 1975. The research reported in this paper was supported, in part, by the Organizational Effectiveness Research Program of the Office of Naval Research.

GROUP PROCESS AS A POSSIBLE KEY

We suggest that one key to understanding the effectiveness of small groups is to be found in the ongoing *interaction process* that takes place among members as they work on a task. At one extreme, for example, group members may work together so badly that members do not share with one another uniquely held information that is critical to the problem at hand; in this case, the quality of the group outcome surely will suffer. On the other hand, group members may operate in great harmony, with the comments of one member prompting quick and sometimes innovative responses in another, which then leads a third to see a synthesis between the ideas of the first two, and so on; in this case, a genuinely creative outcome may result.

In general, social psychologists have tended toward a rather pessimistic view of group process, describing it as something that, for the most part, impairs task effectiveness. One well-known theory of group performance, for example, deals with interaction process almost exclusively in terms of "process losses" that prevent a group from approaching its optimal or potential productivity (Steiner, 1972). And it turns out that predictions of group productivity based on this view of group process are, for many tasks, reasonably accurate.

Other social psychologists suggest that the interaction among group members helps to catch and remedy errors which might slip by if individuals were doing the task by themselves. Thus, the argument goes, although groups may be slow and inefficient because of process problems, their use is more than justified when the *quality* of a solution (i.e., freedom from errors) is of paramount importance (cf. Taylor & Faust, 1952). Recent work by Janis (1972), however, calls into question the efficacy of group interaction for finding and correcting errors, at least under some circumstances. Janis shows that as members become exces-

sively close-knit and generate a clubby feeling of "we-ness," there may be a marked decrease in the exchange of discrepant or unsettling information, and a simultaneous unwillingness to deal seriously with such information even when it is forced to their attention. Janis suggests that the principles of "groupthink" help to explain a number of highly significant and unfortunate decisions made by top-level government officials, such as the Bay of Pigs invasion, and Britain's "appeasement" policy toward Hitler before World War II. Apparently even for some very important decisions, patterns of group interaction can develop which allow large and significant errors of fact and judgment to "slip through" and seriously impair group effectiveness.

A more optimistic view of the role of group process is offered by Collins and Guetzkow (1964), who propose that, in some circumstances, interaction can result in "assembly-effect bonuses." That is, patterns of interaction may develop in which the individual inputs of group members combine to yield an outcome better than that of any single person—or even than the sum of individual products. The literature reviewed by Collins and Guetzkow, however, offers little help in understanding how to create such bonuses. The "brainstorming" fad of the late 1950s seemed to offer one clear instance in which the assembly-effect bonus led to group outcomes of higher creativity than those obtained by pooling the products of individuals; yet subsequent research failed to reveal any creative bonuses which were attributable to the group interaction process per se.

Organizational psychologists involved with experiential "training groups" or with "team-building" activities also tend to be optimistic about the possibility of enhancing the effectiveness of groups by alternating group processes. In general, they assume that members of many task groups are inhibited from exchanging ideas and information and from working together in a concerted fashion to complete the task. Interpersonal training activities are intended, at the least, to remove some of the emotional and interpersonal obstacles to effective group functioning and thereby to permit group members to devote a greater proportion of their energies toward actual work on tasks. Unfortunately, while there is substantial evidence to show that such interpersonal training activities do alter what goes on among group members (and how members feel about that), it remains unclear whether or not such training improves the effectiveness of the group.

In sum, there is substantial agreement among researchers and observers of task-oriented groups that something important happens in group interaction that can affect performance outcomes. There is little agreement about just what that "something" is, when it will enhance (or when it will impair) group effectiveness, and how it can be monitored, analyzed, and altered. It is to these questions that we now turn.

HOW GROUP INTERACTION PROCESS AFFECTS GROUP PERFORMANCE

We suggest that the impact of group interaction on group effectiveness is *not* direct, but instead operates by affecting three "summary variables" that do directly determine how well a group does on its task. These variables can be used to summarize the causes of task effectiveness. The influence of group interaction process on performance effectiveness, then, can be understood by examining how process affects:

1 The level of *effort* the group applies to carrying out its task

2 The adequacy of the *task performance strategies* used by the group in carrying out the task

3 The level and appropriateness of the *knowledge and skills* brought to bear on the task by group members

To the extent that interaction processes control or influence these three summary variables, we believe, then the performance of a group working on almost any task will be substantially affected. The remainder of this section extends and elaborates this proposition.

Summary Variable 1: Members' Efforts

For most group tasks, effort counts heavily in determining how well the group performs. Group interaction can affect the level of effort actually brought to bear on the task in two ways: (1) by influencing how well the efforts of individual members are *coordinated*, and (2) by influencing the *level* of effort members choose to expend working on the task (i.e., their task motivation).

Coordination of Members' Efforts When task effectiveness is affected by the amount of effort group members apply to their work, then it is important that members coordinate their activities in a way that minimizes the amount of effort that is "wasted." In a tug-of-war, for example, a group will do quite poorly unless some means is devised to ensure that its members all pull at the same time.

Whenever the efforts of individual group members must be coordinated to accomplish some task, there always is some "slippage" that keeps the group from achieving its potential productivity (i.e., that which would be obtained if the efforts of each member were fully useable by the group). Moreover, the larger the group, the greater the process loss, simply because the job of getting all members functioning together in a coordinated fashion becomes increasingly difficult as the number of members increases (Steiner, 1972).

Raising or Lowering the Level of Members' Efforts While individual members usually approach a given group task with some notion about how hard they expect to work on it, what happens in the group can radically alter that expectation in either direction. Presumably, an individual will increase his level of effort to the extent that working hard with the other group members leads to the satisfaction of his personal needs or the achievement of his personal goals. If his task-oriented efforts are reinforced, he should work harder on the task; but if his efforts are ignored or punished, his effort should decrease. Thus, social interaction can importantly affect how much effort an individual chooses to expend in work on the group task.

The depression of members' efforts has been explored by Steiner (1972) in terms of a "motivation decrement" that becomes more of a problem as the size of the group increases. Members presumably feel that their own efforts are less critically needed in larger groups, because there are many other people available to do the work. Moreover, individuals may find it increasingly difficult to obtain satisfaction of their own needs because of the limited amount of "air time" available to individual members of large groups.

Little research has been conducted on how motivation *increments* might be created—i.e., patterns of interaction in the group that would prompt members to work especially hard on the group task. The feasibility of creating such increments in task-oriented groups is explored later in this paper.

Summary Variable 2: Task Performance Strategies

As used here, "strategy" refers to the choices made by group members about how the group will go about performing the task. For example, a group might decide to opt for a very high quality product at the expense of quantity of production (a strategy choice about outcomes); or members might decide to free-associate about ideas for proceeding with the task before actually starting work on it (a strategy choice about procedure).

Strategy choices can be very important in determining how well a group does its task (cf.

Hackman & Morris, 1975), and group interaction can affect the strategies actually used by a group in two ways: (1) by influencing how preexisting notions about "appropriate" strategy are actually *implemented* in doing the task, and (2) by affecting the *development* of strategies for proceeding with the task that are new to the group and uniquely suited to its task.

Implementing Existing, Shared Strategies   As people gain experience with various tasks in the course of their everyday lives, strategies for working on these tasks become well-learned. When the task is a familiar one, group interaction may serve mainly as a vehicle for implementing an already well-learned strategy for proceeding with the task, and no evidence of "working on performance strategy" may be visible in the overt interaction among members. It is true, nonetheless, that members inevitably will encounter interpersonal obstacles that impair their efficiency in implementing even a very well-learned strategy—in other words, a process loss that makes the group less effective than it could be.

Developing or Reformulating Strategic Plans   Few tasks constrain a group from overtly discussing and reformulating its performance strategies (or from developing new strategies from scratch). Yet, there appears to be a pervasive norm in groups *not* to address such matters explicitly, even when group members are aware that it is to their advantage to plan strategies before starting actual work on the task (Shure, Rogers, Larsen, & Tassone, 1962; Weick, 1969, pp. 11–12).

To the extent that norms against strategy planning exist, the chances are lessened that the preexisting strategies members bring to the group will be altered and improved upon, or that new (and possibly more effective) strategies will be generated by group members. This obviously can limit the effectiveness of the group on many types of tasks.

On the other hand, there is evidence that in

some circumstances overt consideration and discussion of task performance strategies can "unfreeze" group members from their traditional and well-learned approaches to task performance, and thereby open the possibility that a new and more effective way of proceeding will be invented. In one study, for example, discussion about strategy tended to occur only when a group member made a suggestion that was deviant from preexisting and shared notions about what would be an "appropriate" strategy for the task at hand (e.g., suggesting a bizarre solution to a routine problem-solving task). Yet, even as group members explained to the deviant why his ideas were faulty, they fell into a discussion of alternative ways of proceeding with the task, some of which subsequently were adopted and led to significant increases in measured group creativity (Hackman & Morris, 1975). Such findings suggest that it may be possible to help groups improve their effectiveness on some tasks by encouraging members to examine and alter existing norms that discourage open discussion of strategies.

Summary Variable 3: Members' Knowledge and Skill

The knowledge and the skills of group members—and the way these are brought to bear on the group task—is the final summary variable to be considered. In this case, the functions of group interaction are as follows: (1) group process is the means by which the contributions of different members (who presumably differ in the amount of task-relevant talent they bring to the group) are *assessed and weighted;* and (2) the patterns of interaction that develop in the group can lead to *changes in the level of talent* held by members and applicable to the task.

Assessing and Weighting Knowledge and Skill of Members For tasks on which knowledge or skills are important in determining performance, it often is possible to predict how well the group will do solely on the basis of the talents of its members (Davis, 1969; Kelley & Thibaut, 1969; Steiner, 1972). The specific predictive model required, of course, depends on the task. For some tasks, the group will operate at the level of its *most* competent member, as in Steiner's "disjunctive" model of group performance (e.g., a track team). For others, performance will be determined by the *least* competent group member, as in Steiner's "conjunctive" model (e.g., a roped-together mountain climbing team). For still others, the group would be expected to perform approximately at the level of its "average" member.

In general, tests of such predictive models have been reasonably successful. Of special interest, however, is the recurrent finding that when actual group productivity is at variance with predictions, it is usually because the model has overpredicted group performance. That is, given the level of members' talent, the group "should" have performed better than it actually did. The implication is that the interaction process of the group, through which the talents of members are assessed, weighted, and brought to bear on the task, must have been inadequate in some way.

For some tasks, such process losses should not be substantial. For example, when the specific knowledge or skill required is obvious, and when obtaining the solution does not involve complex teamwork among members, sophisticated or subtle social processes are not required to identify the necessary talents and to apply them to the task. Instead, group interaction may serve merely as a vehicle for exchanging data, and for informing other members that one "knows the answer." There is little opportunity in such circumstances for process foul-ups (cf. Laughlin, Branch, & Johnson, 1969).

On other tasks, however, the role of group process may be more substantial and the risk of process losses substantially greater. A novel case in point is the prediction of the performance of professional athletic teams from data about the skills of individual team members (Jones, 1974). As would be expected, substantial relationships were found between measures of individual skill and team performance: teams with better athletes did better. However, the *level* of prediction attained was higher for some sports than for others. For example, nearly 90 percent of the variation in baseball team effectiveness was predictable from measures of team member skill, as compared with only about 35 percent for basketball teams. As the author notes, success in basketball is especially dependent upon personal relations and teamwork among players. Thus, process losses might be more likely to impair basketball team effectiveness than would be the case for other team sports.

We have suggested above that when the primary functions of group interaction are to assess, weight, and apply members' talent, process losses are inevitable, and that for some types of tasks the potential losses are greater than for others. In every case, however, considerations of group process determine how *near* a group comes to its potential performance, given the capabilities of its members.

Affecting the Level of Talent Available to the Group Group interaction process can, at least potentially, serve as a means for actually increasing the total amount of members' talent available to the group for work on the task. The issue here is *not* the simple exchange or coordination of existing knowledge and skill, as discussed above; that function of group interaction does not result in a net increase in the total supply of talent available to the group. Instead, the present focus is on how group members can do more than merely share among themselves what they already know—and instead work as a group to gain knowledge or generate skills which previously did not exist within the group.

Virtually no controlled research has been carried out on this latter function of group

interaction. The "training group" approach to the development of interpersonal skills (Argyris, 1962; Bradford, Gibb, & Benne, 1964; Schein & Bennis, 1965) postulates that group members can effectively use one another as resources to increase members' individual competence and thereby increase the level of competence in the group as a whole. But the social processes through which such learning takes place are only beginning to be illuminated (cf. Argyris & Schon, 1974), and additional research on the talent-enhancing functions of group interaction is much needed.

We have examined above the impact of group interaction process on each of three summary variables: (1) the level of effort brought to bear on the task; (2) the task performance strategies implemented by group members in carrying out the task; and (3) the level of knowledge and skill at the disposal of the group for task work. The impact of group interaction on each of these three summary variables is shown in Table 30-1. This table shows that the functions served by interaction process are quite different for each of the three summary variables. The implication is that a researcher who is attempting to understand the process determinants of group performance will have to examine different aspects of the group process, *depending on which of the summary variables are operative in the particular task situation being considered.* By the same token, the approach an interventionist would take in attempting to help group members create more task-appropriate patterns of interaction would vary depending on the variables operative for the task being performed.[1]

As noted in column A of Table 30-1, there are

---

[1]In many complex organizational tasks, all three summary variables will be operative, and a researcher or interventionist would need to examine all of the entries in Table 30-1 to ascertain the process determinants of performance problems, and opportunities for the development of potential process "gains."

Table 30-1   Summary of the Proposed Functions of Group Interaction

Summary variables postulated as important in affecting performance outcomes	Impact of interaction process on the summary variables	
	A _Inevitable process losses_	B _Potential for process gains_
Members' efforts brought to bear on the task	Interaction serves as the less-than-perfect means by which members' efforts are coordinated and applied to the task.	Interaction can serve to enhance the level of effort members choose to expend on task work.
Performance strategies used in carrying out the task	Interaction serves as a less-than-perfect "vehicle" for implementing preexisting strategies brought to the group by members and (often) shared by them.	Interaction can serve as the site for developing or reformulating strategic plans to increase their task-appropriateness.
Members' knowledge and skills used by the group for task work	Interaction serves as a less-than-perfect means for assessing, weighting, and applying members' talents to the task.	Interaction can serve as a means of increasing the total pool of knowledge or skills available to the group (i.e., when the group is the site for generating new knowledge or skills by members).

inevitable process losses associated with each of the three summary variables. A group can never handle the process issues in column A perfectly; the group's performance therefore will depend, in part, on how successful members are in finding ways to minimize these process losses. At the same time (column B) there are potentially important (but often unrecognized) process _gains_ associated with each of the summary variables. That is, at least the possibility exists for group members to find and implement new, task-effective ways of interacting which will make it possible for them to achieve a level of effectiveness which could not have been anticipated from knowledge about the talents and intentions of group members before the start of work on the task. In the section to follow, we explore possibilities for achieving such performance-enhancing process gains.

INTERVENTIONS FOR IMPROVING GROUP EFFECTIVENESS

In this section, we attempt to show how group effectiveness can be improved above the level expected in column A of Table 30-1 by

planned alteration of three aspects of the overall performance situation—three "input variables." In particular, as shown in Figure 30-1: (1) performance strategies can be made more appropriate for each task by the modification of group _norms:_ (2) members' efforts can be increased by the redesign of the group _task;_ and (3) the level and utilization of members' knowledge and skills can be improved by altering the _composition_ of the group. All three factors affect (and are affected by) the interaction process of the group, and all can be adjusted or "set" before the start of task performance activities to minimize the chances of significant process losses—and to increase the likelihood that process gains will materialize.

Task Performance Strategies

The strategies used by members of a group to perform tasks often are well codified as behavioral norms of the group. Group members typically share a set of expectations about proper approaches to each task, and enforce adherence to those expectations. Such norms often make it unnecessary to manage and

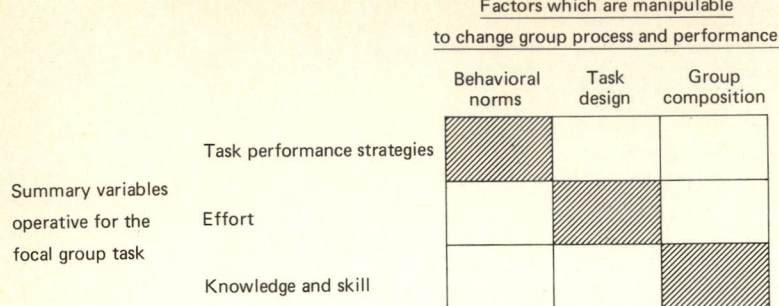

Figure 30-1 The three summary variables and input factors which may be altered to influence them. *Note*: Shaded cells represent sites that are particularly promising for changes aimed at improving group performance effectiveness.

coordinate members' behavior explicitly; everyone knows how things should be done, and everyone does them that way.

Ideally, the presence of such norms should contribute to the effectiveness of the group—simply because little time would have to be spent on moment-by-moment behavior-management activities, leaving more time for actual task work. However, this advantage will accrue only if the norms which guide the selection and use of performance strategies are fully appropriate to the task. If existing norms about strategy are dysfunctional for effectiveness, then performance is likely to suffer unless the norms are changed—despite their time-saving advantages.

As discussed earlier, the problem is that reconsideration of strategic norms in task-oriented groups rarely occurs spontaneously, and may be actively resisted by the group.[2] The challenge, then, is to create conditions that encourage group members to engage in serious explorations of their norms about strategy when there is reason to believe that existing norms are not optimal for the task at hand. Three general approaches for creating such conditions are presented and evaluated below.

Diagnosis-Feedback The Return Potential Model proposed by Jackson (1965) can help group members gain increased understanding of group norms, and can serve as a basis for planning changes in norms. This model addresses the distribution of potential approval (and disapproval) group members feel for various specific behaviors that might be exhibited in a given situation. Its usefulness as a diagnostic device derives, in large part, from its potential for generating quantitative measures of the characteristics of specific group norms (for examples, see Hackman, 1976; Jackson, 1965). These measures can help members increase their understanding of existing group norms, and serve as a basis for deciding whether (and how) they wish to change them.

Diagnostic data about group norms also could be generated using other devices, including observation of behavior in the group by a consultant. The idea is simply to provide systematic and verifiable data about group norms, so that members have a concrete basis for planning how those norms might be altered to make them more appropriate to the demands of the task and the personal needs of the members themselves.

---

[2]The problem may not be as great when the group is dealing with a strange or unfamiliar task. In such cases, few cues will be present in the task materials to engage members' learned views about how they "should" proceed on the task—and they may be forced to discuss strategic options in order to arrive at a shared and coordinated plan for dealing with the task.

Process Consultation   A second general approach to changing group norms about strategy involves the use of an outside consultant to help group members discover and implement new, more task-effective ways of working together. In its most flexible and general form, process consultation involves joint work by the consultant and the group to diagnose the state of the group, and to plan what to do on the basis of that diagnosis (Schein, 1969).

In most applications of process consultation, the consultant spends considerable time with group members, helping them to examine existing norms and to experiment with new ways of behaving. Therefore, broad-gauge process consultation is most effective over the long term—and then only if group members develop their own diagnostic and action skills which reduce their dependency on the consultant and, in effect, allow group members to consult with themselves about the most effective task and interpersonal processes to use in various situations.

An alternative consultative approach, which would appear more useful in the short term, is to educate group members in specific strategic alternatives or techniques for carrying out the task. A number of such techniques have been proposed, such as setting time limits for discussion, temporally separating the generation of ideas from their evaluation, focusing on analysis of the task before beginning to perform it, setting aside time to locate facts and potential obstacles to implementation of the solution, devising specific structures for exchanging ideas and information among group members, and so on (cf. Kepner & Tregoe, 1965; Maier, 1963; Osborn, 1957; Varela, 1971). Some of the techniques proposed are based on research findings; others derive more from intuitive considerations. All are intended to provide procedural strategies which will be immediate aids to group effectiveness.

There are at least two problems with short-term, technique-based approaches to changing preexisting group norms about strategy. First, the value of any given technique depends on the task; yet there is very little information available which would help group members to select those strategic approaches likely to be particularly useful for a given task. Second, some of the techniques involve the use of group relations skills which may not be valued or well-practiced by group members. Moreover, the strategy cannot help the group unless members are both motivated and sufficiently skilled to use it appropriately. At present, little is known about how to introduce such techniques and to train members in their effective utilization.

Probably the most straightforward process consultative technique—for helping members explicitly consider their norms about strategy—is simply to provide the group with a "preliminary task" before they begin work on the primary task. This preliminary task would require members to discuss the task performance strategies they plan to use on the main task—and to consider revising or replacing them if warranted by the discussion. Since in most circumstances, the immediate demands of the primary task drive out any tendencies toward strategy planning, introduction of a preliminary group task could help "hold off" such immediate task demands until strategy planning had been completed. Moreover, the intervention capitalizes on the tendency of group members to follow rather slavishly the demands of tasks they see as legitimate (March & Simon, 1958, p. 185; Shure et al., 1962).

In one recent study, groups (whose main task was assembly of a number of types of electrical components) were given a preliminary task that explicitly required members to discuss their performance strategy before beginning work on the main task (Hackman, Brousseau & Weiss, 1976). Members of experimental groups did follow the requirements of the preliminary task, and discussed their strategic options extensively. Control groups, however, engaged in virtually no spontaneous discussion of strategy, and proceeded immediately to work on the main task in ways that were consistent with their private, a priori notions about how such a task should be done.

Use of a preliminary task does not, of course, guarantee that any new performance strategies that are generated will be more task-effective than members' private, prior hypotheses about how the task should be done. For example, in the study described above, it was found that discussion of strategy increased group effectiveness *when the task required cooperation and coordination among members.* In another task condition, however, where the task did *not* require high interdependence among members, there were no differences in effectiveness between those groups that discussed their performance strategy and those that did not. This finding reemphasizes the importance of the group task in determining what aspects of group process are critical to group effectiveness in a given instance.

Task Design Both the diagnosis-feedback and the process consultation approaches require group members to address directly group norms about performance strategy, and both require some intervention by an outside consultant or researcher. A third general approach to the change of group norms about strategy—task design—deals with norms less directly, and minimizes the role of "outsiders" in the group itself.

Specifically, the group task can be arranged so that it requires, suggests, or provides cues which prompt specific ways of going about performing the task. For example, if a task which requires the assembly of small mechanical devices is physically laid out in a linear fashion, with chairs and equipment for group members placed along the side of a long narrow table, members almost certainly will assume that they should form an assembly line and will proceed to operate as if that is the optimal way of doing the task. But if materials are arranged around a circular table, with a full complement of equipment provided for each member, a strategy of individual assembly probably will be adopted instead, with just as little overt discussion.

At the extreme, of course, a task can be designed so that *no* discretion about strategy is left to the group: members are informed exactly how to proceed to achieve the goal. This is the approach often taken by consultants who attempt to increase the creativity of groups. In the synectics approach, for example, group members are provided with tasks and exercises which specify exactly what strategies group members are to use in working on the task—strategies which are designed explicitly to facilitate the production of original solutions (Prince, 1970). The ultimate success of the group, of course, depends partly on the adequacy of those task-specified strategies.

While, from an "engineering" perspective, task design offers considerable appeal as a device for helping group members utilize more task-effective performance strategies in their work, responsibility for the strategies remains outside the group itself. The task serves simply to get potentially task-effective patterns of behavior underway; whether such behaviors will "stick" and become incorporated into the normative structure of the group depends, in large part, on whether members find the behaviors instrumental for achieving their goals. Diagnosis-feedback and process consultation, on the other hand, probably are less efficient in any given instance, but have the advantage that the group itself "owns" the new procedures it has devised. Moreover, as group members use these techniques, they may learn some group-relations skills or develop some norms that can be usefully applied to other tasks, or in other groups.

Members' Efforts

There is considerable evidence that the effort members expend on a group task, like the performance strategies they use, is powerfully affected by the norms of the group, especially when members value their membership in that group. Much less is known about what determines the *direction* of group norms—that is, whether the norms will encourage high or low effort on the task (Hackman, 1976).

We suggest that whether a group develops a norm of high or low effort depends substantially on the quality of the experiences members have as they work on the task—and that these experiences, in turn, are largely determined by the task itself. For example, if members find the task activities frustrating and unpleasant, they are likely, after some time, to notice the adverse attitudes of others in the group—and perhaps to share these reactions verbally. Gradually, through such interaction, group members may come to an implicit or explicit agreement that the best way to minimize the unpleasantness they experience is to minimize the energy invested in doing the task. If, on the other hand, members find their work on the task exciting, fulfilling, or otherwise rewarding, these experiences also are likely to be shared with one another, and a norm of high effort may be the result.

To the extent that the quality of members' experiences does depend partly on the task itself, then it may be useful to consider task redesign as a strategy for increasing members' efforts, rather than to attempt to address directly norms about effort. To do the latter, in many cases, would be attacking the outcropping of the problem rather than the problem itself.

What task characteristics are likely to lead to high commitment by group members to work hard on the task? Research data suggest that an individual's task motivation often is enhanced when jobs are high on the following five dimensions: (1) skill variety—the degree to which the individual does a number of different things on the job involving use of his or her valued skills; (2) task identity—the degree to which he or she does a whole and visible piece of work; (3) task significance— how much the results of work on the job will affect the psychological or physical well-being of other people; (4) autonomy—the personal initiative and discretion the individual has on the job; and (5) feedback—the degree to which the person learns while working how well he or she is doing (Hackman & Oldham, 1976).

If a group task were designed with these or similar characteristics in mind, one might expect to observe an increase in the motivation of individual group members to work energetically on the task. The result should be a considerable increase in the overall level of effort the group expends on the task (a "process gain"), and over time this increase should be reinforced by the emergent normative structure in the group. Again, as with most of the possibilities for enhancing group effectiveness introduced in this section, research tests remain to be done.

Knowledge and Skill of Members

Consider now tasks for which the utilization of members' knowledge and skills strongly determine group effectiveness. As suggested earlier, the single most powerful point of leverage on group effectiveness for such tasks is simply group composition: a group made up of competent people will do better than a group composed of less competent members (cf. Varela, 1971, pp. 153–157). But if it is assumed that the group originally has been composed to maximize the level of task-relevant talent present, what can be done to increase the utilization and development of that talent in the service of the group task? How, for example, can the group operate to minimize the inevitable process losses which occur when information is combined and members' contributions are evaluated, or to increase the level of knowledge and skills of individual members so that the total pool of talent available to the group also increases?

Achieving such states of affairs in a group is neither a straightforward nor a short-term proposition. Groups usually have difficulty dealing effectively with individual differences in competence: when weighting of individual contributions is done in the group, difficult issues of interpersonal competitiveness, evaluation, and differential status come very quickly to the fore. Dealing with such issues openly is, for most members of most groups, highly threatening and anxiety-arousing. Group members are likely to erect protective shells around themselves in such circumstances, and, as a result, the group as a whole loses access to much of the talent already present within its boundaries. And the chances of members' using one another to learn genuinely innovative patterns of behavior—or to seek out and internalize knowledge that initially is foreign to them—are very slim indeed.

How might a group break out of such a self-defeating pattern of behavior? Possibly the group task could be structured to require explicit and overt treatment of individual differences in knowledge and skill; or perhaps intervention could be made to help members become aware of (and possibly change) existing group norms specifying how such matters are handled in the group. Such interventions can ensure that issues of individual differences in knowledge and skill are brought to the attention of group members—and can prompt explicit discussion of them. But successful resolution of such matters once they have surfaced may be extraordinarily difficult.

What are needed, it seems, are interventions which will help group members learn *how* to deal effectively with issues of individual differences within the group and how to create a climate which supports and facilitates learning and sharing of learning. This suggests the need for a rather long-term program of process consultation (or "team building"), in which members gradually build a climate of interpersonal trust within the group, leading to a reduction in the level of personal threat they experience in the group setting. As such a climate develops, members may become bet-ter able to experiment with new forms of behavior and become increasingly ready to engage in the usually-risky and always-anxiety-arousing activities required to extend one's knowledge and skills in a public setting. Even in the long term, however, there is no guarantee that the group will develop into a site for individual learning and heightened sharing among group members: the process is a fragile one, and fragile things break.

What *is* relatively certain is that if such a long-term team-building program is successful, the members themselves will almost invariably be changed as a consequence—that is, they will perhaps take more risks, experiment more, and be more willing to tolerate stress and anxiety in the interest of increasing and sharing their personal knowledge and skill (cf. Argyris & Schon, 1974). When such a point is reached, if it is reached, the group will have become "recomposed," not by the removal of incompetent members and substitution of more competent ones, but by changes in the attitudes, skills, and behavioral styles of the existing members.

So we come full circle for tasks on which group effectiveness is strongly determined by the level and utilization of members' knowledge and skills. At the first level, we have noted that the most efficient and straightforward means for improving group effectiveness on such task is through group composition: put good people in the group. To move beyond that level, we believe, also requires attention to the composition of the group—but through changes within the group itself, changes in the personal attitudes and interpersonal skills of individual members.

CONCLUSIONS AND IMPLICATIONS
Elusiveness of General Theory

While there have been numerous attempts to integrate findings about group effectiveness and to draw general conclusions about behav-for in groups, so far no general theory of small-group effectiveness has appeared.

We suggest here the possibility that no single theory can ever encompass and deal simultaneously with the complexity of factors which can affect a group's task effectiveness. Instead, it may be necessary to settle for a number of smaller theories, each of which is relevant to a specific aspect or phase of the performance process, or to performance effectiveness under certain specified circumstances. One intent of the present paper has been to help structure the domain within which such smaller theories might be developed. In particular, we have attempted to examine in some depth (1) the role of the group interaction process as a major determinant of group productivity; (2) three summary variables (effort, performance strategies, knowledge and skill) which are proposed as devices for summarizing the most powerful proximal causes of group effectiveness; and (3) some selected "input" variables that we see as having powerful influence on group performance, and thus as being useful points of leverage for changing performance—whether directly, or through the interaction process of the group.

A general framework suggesting how these three classes of variables interact in the task-performance sequence is shown in Figure 30-2. Further research on this input-process-output sequence for different types of tasks may lead to additional understanding that will aid both in predicting and in changing group effectiveness in a large number of performance settings. But a general and unified theory of group effectiveness, we believe, is currently out of reach—and is likely to remain so.

Elusiveness of General Interventions

There is no dearth of small-group intervention techniques available to the practitioner interested in trying to change group behavior and task effectiveness. Yet, just as we have argued that there is not likely to be a general theory of group effectiveness, we also eschew the notion that there can be any single intervention package which will be universally helpful in improving group effectiveness.

Consider, for example, small-group "team building," a popular intervention technique which focuses on the interpersonal relationships and social climate present in the group. Team-building may be of great use in helping group members develop the capability to utilize their knowledge and skills effectively on a task. For this reason, the technique may aid performance effectiveness on tasks for which knowledge and skill are critical. But team-building may be actively dysfunctional (at least in the short term) for tasks where effort is the most important factor, because the energies of group members are siphoned away

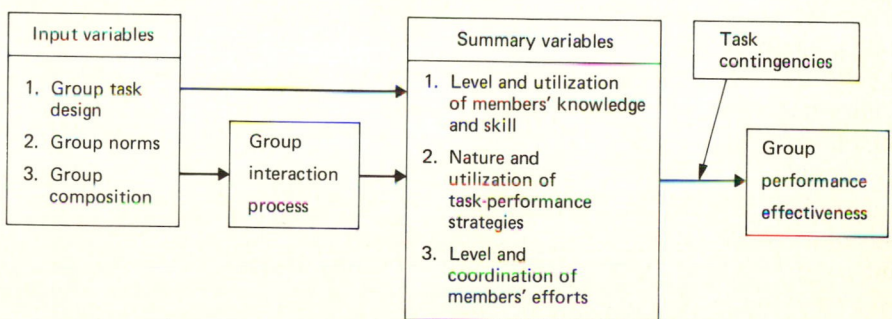

Figure 30-2 Framework showing the relations among certain input variables, group interaction process, and the three summary variables in influencing group performance effectiveness.

from the task itself and applied instead to the exciting and involving interpersonal processes which take place during the team-building process. Similarly, redesign of the group task may aid effectiveness on tasks where effort is an important determinant of productivity, but be much less useful as an intervention if the problem is one of faulty performance strategies.

In general, intervention techniques which have been offered as devices for improving group effectiveness fall into two classes: (1) interpersonal techniques, often utilizing experiential learning devices intended to improve the quality of the relationships among group members; and (2) procedure-oriented techniques, which provide group members (often via the group leader) with specific strategies for going about their work on the task in a more effective manner.

Relatively little research has been done to assess the value of such techniques for improving the task effectiveness of groups. In general, however, research suggests that interpersonal interventions are powerful in changing patterns of behavior in the group—but that task effectiveness is rarely enhanced (and often suffers) as a consequence. Procedure-oriented interventions, on the other hand, often may be helpful in improving effectiveness for the task immediately at hand, but rarely can they be incorporated readily into the ongoing process of the group (cf. Hackman & Morris, 1975).

What seems needed, then, are the following:

1 Development of interventions which enhance effectiveness in the short term, *and* which simultaneously lead to alterations in group processes so that greater overall competence of the group as a performing unit is achieved.

2 Development of a taxonomy of groups, tasks, and situations which specifies the potential utility of various interventions for different types of performance situations. Re-

cent work by Herold (in press) offers some promising leads toward such a taxonomy. In the meantime, however, we believe that interventionists will have to rely on especially careful *diagnoses* of the task, the group, and the situation—and tailor their change-oriented activities to what those diagnoses reveal.

Toward Increased Self-Management by Task Groups

As techniques for modifying situations and intervening in group processes become known and tested, it is tempting for a consultant to a group (whether outsider or group leader) to use this knowledge, perhaps covertly, to move the group toward greater effectiveness. And, indeed, this "engineering" approach has been advocated and used with apparent success in some situations (Varela, 1971, chap. 6).

We believe, however, that, in the long term, it is better if the group members themselves develop the skills and the understanding to manage their *own* development as a productive unit. This will lessen the reliance of the group on the continued expertise of the consultant, and often may increase the commitment of group members to the group and its goals—because they come increasingly to "own," and therefore care about, its processes and its products. Moreover, the problems of a group often are highly idiosyncratic, hinging on rather unique coincidences of people, tasks, and situations. Relying on specific advice and assistance from an outside professional on an ongoing basis would, it appears, be a grossly inefficient way to improve the long-term effectiveness of the group.

There are two major—and quite different—hurdles to be overcome if a group is to gain increased self-control over its own task-performance processes and increased competence in managing its performance activities. The first is the development of a heightened awareness of the determinants of group processes and group performance. The second is the development of the competence (both technical and interpersonal) to respond adaptively to the newly understood problems and opportunities.

Outside assistance would seem to be critical in helping a group overcome both of these hurdles. Members must break out of the reactive stance most people assume in task-performance situations, and take a more active, seeking, and structuring orientation toward their task and interpersonal environment. This is unlikely to occur spontaneously, for reasons discussed at several points throughout this paper. It is, however, likely to become self-perpetuating, once group members become more aware of the determinants of their behavior (assuming that they decide that they do, in fact, wish to take a more active stance toward the task and social environment). With the aid of a competent leader or consultant, the traditional implicit norm of reactivity can be replaced by a new norm of proaction on the part of both individual group members and the group as an interacting unit.

Group members themselves, for example, probably should be as involved as possible in diagnostic activities aimed at determining the demands of the task and the resources the group has at hand to work on the task. By participating in such diagnoses, members should achieve the fullest possible awareness and understanding of the factors which affect their own performance activities and their effectiveness as a group. They should, therefore, become increasingly well-prepared to engage in new activities intended to reduce their process losses—and to chart avenues for realizing previously unrecognized possibilities for process gains.

An especially critical point is reached when group members have become aware of the need for change and have developed the motivation to initiate and carry through specific changes. At this point, they may be in rather desperate need of assistance to learn how, competently, to do what they already want to do—and they may not be aware of many of the problems that they will face in implementing their plans. This is especially important for changes involving the internal process of the group: merely wanting to be "less punitive in dealing with ideas" for example, while often an admirable goal and one that may be task-effective on many tasks, is extraordinarily difficult for most members of most groups to carry off successfully. Similarly, changing the task of the group—something most members of most groups take as an unalterable—requires the use of personal and interpersonal skills which are not well-practiced. Again, members will require assistance in finding ways to carry out their intentions.

The challenge to the consultant is to help the group members to raise their collective consciousness about what "might be" and to learn how to achieve their newly-found aspirations. The challenge to the small-group researcher is to provide, for the consultant and the group members alike, the knowledge and the tools that will help them get there from here.

REFERENCES

Argyris, C. *Interpersonal competence and organizational effectiveness.* Homewood, Ill.: Irwin-Dorsey, 1962.

Argyris, C., & Schon, D. *Theory in practice.* San Francisco: Jossey-Bass, 1974.

Bradford, L. P., Gibb, J., & Benne, K. (Eds.), *T-Group theory and laboratory method.* New York: Wiley, 1964.

Collins, B. E., & Guetzkow, H. *A social psychology of group processes for decision-making.* New York: Wiley, 1964.

Davis, J. H. *Group performance.* Reading, Mass.: Addison-Wesley, 1969.

Hackman, J. R. Group influences on individuals. In M. D. Dunnette (Ed.), *Handbook of industrial and organizational psychology.* Chicago: Rand-McNally, 1976.

Hackman, J. R., & Morris, C. G. Group tasks, group interaction process, and group performance effectiveness: A review and proposed integration. In L. Berkowitz (Ed.), *Advances in experimental social psychology* (Vol. 8). New York: Academic Press, 1975.

Hackman, J. R., & Oldham, G. R. Motivation through the design of work: Test of a theory. *Organizational Behavior and Human Performance,* 1976, **16,** 250–279.

Hackman, J. R., Brousseau, K., & Weiss, J. A. The interaction of task design and group performance strategies in determining group effectiveness. *Organizational Behavior and Human Performance,* 1976, **16,** 350–365.

Herold, D. M. Group effectiveness as a function of task-appropriate interaction processes. In J. L. Livingstone (Ed.), *Managerial accounting: The behavioral foundations.* Columbus, Ohio: Grid Publishers, in press.

Jackson, J. Structural characteristics of norms. In I. D. Steiner & M. Fishbein (Eds.), *Current studies in social psychology.* New York: Holt, 1965.

Janis, I. L. *Victims of groupthink: A psychological study of foreign-policy decisions and fiascos.* New York: Houghton-Mifflin, 1972.

Jones, M. B. Regressing group on individual effectiveness. *Organizational Behavior and Human Performance,* 1974, **11,** 426–451.

Kelley, H. H., & Thibaut, J. W. Group problem solving. In G. Lindzey & E. Aronson (Eds.), *The handbook of social psychology* (2nd ed.). Reading, Mass.: Addison-Wesley, 1969.

Kepner, C. H., & Tregoe, B. B. *The rational manager: A systematic approach to problem solving and decision making.* New York: McGraw-Hill, 1965.

Laughlin, P. R., Branch, L. G., & Johnson, H. H. Individual versus triadic performance on a unidimensional complementary task as a function of initial ability level. *Journal of Personality and Social Psychology,* 1969, **12,** 144–150.

Maier, N. R. F. *Problem solving discussions and conferences: Leadership and skills.* New York: McGraw-Hill, 1963.

March, J. G., & Simon, H. A. *Organizations.* New York: Wiley, 1958.

Osborn, A. F. *Applied imagination* (Rev. ed.). New York: Scribner, 1957.

Prince, G. M. *The practice of creativity.* New York: Harper & Row, 1970.

Schein, E. H. *Process consultation.* Reading, Mass.: Addison-Wesley, 1969.

Schein, E. H., & Bennis, W. *Personal and organizational change through group methods.* New York: Wiley, 1965.

Shure, G. H., Rogers, M. S., Larsen, I. M., & Tassone, J. Group planning and task effectiveness. *Sociometry,* 1962, **25,** 263–282.

Steiner, I. D. *Group process and productivity.* New York: Academic Press, 1972.

Taylor, D. W., & Faust, W. L. Twenty questions: Efficiency in problem solving as a function of size of group. *Journal of Experimental Psychology,* 1952, **44,** 360–368.

Varela, J. A. *Psychological solutions to social problems.* New York: Academic Press, 1971.

Weick, K. E. *The social psychology of organizing.* Reading, Mass.: Addison-Wesley, 1969.

Reading 31

An Intergroup Perspective on Individual Behavior

Ken K. Smith

The history of psychology has been filled with attempts to understand the behavior of people either in terms of their personality, or as an interaction of individual and environmental characteristics (Lewin, 1947). In the latter case, the environment has been conceptualized at many levels, ranging from global influences of the culture at large to specific properties of the groups of which individuals are members. Although a great deal of attention has been given to group influences on individuals' beliefs, values, perceptions, and behaviors (Hackman, 1976), to date the impact on individuals of forces generated by relationships *between* groups has been largely unexplored.

Since there now exists an expanding body of knowledge about intergroup processes (Sherif, 1962; Rice, 1969; Levine & Campbell, 1972; Lorsch & Lawrence, 1972; Smith, 1974; Alderfer, 1977; Alderfer, Brown, Kaplan, & Smith, in press), our understanding of individual behavior can be significantly augmented by including this aspect of the social environment as a determinant of how people behave.

In this paper I explore the proposition that, when intergroup situations exist, *behavior can be viewed primarily as an enactment of the forces those intergroup processes generate.* This is not to claim that individual or group interpretations of the same behaviors have no validity. Rather, it is simply an assertion that if an analysis is made at an intergroup level, a substantial proportion of the variation in individual behavior is explainable in terms of the intergroup dynamics. In particular I propose that intergroup processes: (1) color profound-ly our perceptions of the world, and may play a critical role in determining how we construct our personal sense of reality; (2) help define our individual identities; and (3) contribute significantly to the emergence of behavior patterns that we traditionally label as leadership.

Each of these assertions will be explored and illustrated by examining salient data from three very different social systems: (1) the experiences of a high school principal, and the way his personal sense of reality has been influenced by the various intergroup forces in his school system; (2) the development of the individual identity of a "village lunatic" in an experiential laboratory; and (3) the repeated changes of leadership behaviors in a group of survivors from an aircraft crash.

THE INTERGROUP AS A DETERMINER OF AN INDIVIDUAL'S PERCEPTIONS OF REALITY

It has long been recognized that people in different groups often perceive and understand the same event in radically different ways, particularly when there is an "ingroup" and an "outgroup." In such cases, one group usually will perceive an event in highly favorable terms, while the other sees the same event in an entirely derogatory manner. This phenomenon, referred to as "ethnocentrism" by Levine and Campbell (1972), is so powerful that group members may be unable to develop a view of reality that is independent of the group they belong to. The phenomenon becomes additionally potent when a person is

I wish to gratefully acknowledge the critiques offered by J. L. Suttle, E. J. Woodhouse, and C. P. Alderfer on an earlier version of this paper.

caught in the context of multiple intergroups that involve interlocking sequences of events across time, and when the groups exist in a hierarchy of power relationships. Under these circumstances, the way one constructs his or her sense of reality may be almost completely determined by the interplay of intergroup processes.

Smith (1974) illustrates such a situation in his description of how Lewis Brook, principal of the high school in Ashgrove (New England), constructed his sense of what was taking place within the school system. Brook's perspectives changed dramatically from moment to moment, and these changes often were related directly to changes in his relative position in the power hierarchy of intergroup relationships.

For example, on one occasion Principal Brook was vociferously berating the superintendent, his superior, for something the superintendent had recently "done to" him. Lewis's recounting of the episode was cut short by a teacher who entered his office. Whereupon Lewis, without a moment's pause, responded to the teacher exactly as the superintendent had interacted with him. When confronted with this resounding obviousness, Lewis refused (or was unable) to see the similarity. When the two sets of events were dissected so that Lewis was caught by the brutal certitude of the similarities, he responded, "But it's different! I have reasons for treating the teacher that way." And when it was suggested that perhaps the superintendent had reasons for his treatment of the principal, Lewis, with more than a hint of impatience in his voice, retorted, "But mine were reasons; the superintendent's were merely rationalizations!"

This observation led me to formulate a theory of hierarchical intergroup relations in which the behavior of a person can be examined from the relative positions of upper, middle, and lower in the organizational structures in which he or she is embedded. Lewis Brook, as principal of the Ashgrove high school, had three assistant principals and a staff of one hundred teachers who served the educational needs of some 1,400 children in the ninth to twelfth grades. Relative to these two groups, the teachers and the students, Lewis was in an *upper* position. Superimposed on the school was an administrative and political hierarchy of a superintendent and an elected Board of Education. In relation to these two groups, Lewis was in a *lower* position. Finally, Lewis was in a *middle* position in the constellation of relationships between his subordinates (the teachers and students) and his superiors (the superintendent's office). Brook's life as principal can be examined from each of these three relative positions in the hierarchical structure, as shown in Figure 31-1. In particular, it is possible to see how his perceptions of events were influenced by the position he happened to occupy at the time they took place.

Lewis as a Lower

When in a lower position, Brook regularly demonstrated a high degree of suspicion and excessive personal sensitivity. For example, on the day following each Board of Education meeting, Lewis would sit for long, anxious hours waiting for a call from the superintendent advising him of Board discussions that might be relevant to the life of his school. Usually no such call would come, and Lewis complained regularly and bitterly about how he was so faithfully ignored. But his protestation never triggered anything more than a retort from the superintendent that if anything

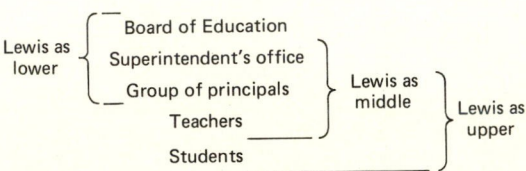

Figure 31-1 Constellation of intergroup relations with Lewis Brook in each of the three positions.

relevant to his high school was discussed, he would be contacted within hours.

From the Board of Education's upper perspective, it was simple to conclude that if Lewis heard nothing it simply meant that the Board had not been debating anything relevant to his school's life. But from Lewis's lower perspective, hearing nothing did *not* mean that nothing was happening. Rather it meant "all hell is about to break loose," an inference that activated his "lower paranoia." Because Lewis assumed there was a conspiracy of silence, he would fantasize with meticulous dedication about all the possible things that could be "done to him," and would search for cues that might validate his worst suspicions. His failure to uncover a "plot" designed to undo him as principal was never interpreted by Lewis to mean that no such plot existed. Instead, he would conclude that his detection devices simply lacked the finesse required to detect what was happening in the "closed" ranks of the uppers.

Ironically, while Lewis was overcome with all this suspicion, reality for the Board of Education was that they were doing "nothing to anybody." In fact, they felt so paralyzed by their own stagnant inactivity that they would have been simultaneously dismayed and pleased to discover that someone, in his wildest imagination, was perceiving them as being in a state other than immobility. Ignorant of this alternative view, Lewis continued to construct a picture of the world about him that hung on trivial contingencies, but which for him was the pillar of his personal reality.

Brook's suspiciousness and oversensitivity when in a lower position can be seen as being a direct consequence of how people who feel powerless respond in intergroup exchanges with more powerful groups. Lower groups often develop strong protective devices and high cohesion to lessen their feelings of vulnerability. And one result of this response is that a lower group comes to define its essence in terms of this very cohesion and unity. In order to feed this sense of unity, members feel the need for the external threat to be continued. This creates a double bind: if the uppers cease to present a threat, that situation may be experienced by lowers as equally threatening, for it lessens the demand for their cohesion. This, in turn, recreates the sense of vulnerability of the lower group, because the *lack* of overt attack is a challenge to the very basis of unity on which group life is predicated. Either way it becomes imperative for members of the lower group to treat the uppers with suspicion. The bind reads as follows: "If they're getting at us, we've got to watch out. If they're not getting at us we've also got to watch out because they'll probably be getting at us in the long run by taking our unity away from us now by lessening the threat we feel." It is this process that ensures a lower group's paranoia and which, in my opinion, stirred Lewis Brook's intense feelings of sensitivity and suspiciousness when relating to his superiors.

Lewis as an Upper

Despite the disdain Lewis felt about his superiors' failure to consult him on matters in which he believed he had a basic right to participate, he reacted toward his own subordinate teachers and students with an equally elitist air. When in his upper position, Lewis always had a myriad of reasons why it was impossible to let the teachers participate fully in decisions that influenced their lives. The teachers felt these reasons were without substance, and they were perpetually distressed by the lack of confidence shown toward them by their principal, who demanded that approval be obtained for even the most trivial and routine of tasks.

When Lewis was in an upper position, he acted out the tendency of superior groups to see the behavior of subordinates in pessimestic terms—the very behaviors that he reacted to so negatively when he was a lower.

As a member of the upper group, Lewis, like other uppers, tended to delegate responsibilities very willingly, but not the authority required to carry through on those responsibilities. This behavior of superiors guarantees that the actions of subordinate groups will not fulfill satisfactorily the expectations implied when the responsibilities are delegated. Although such shortcomings are caused largely by the uppers' withholding of necessary authority, they also are used by the superiors as justification for their original unwillingness to delegate authority. This phenomenon ensures a self-reinforcing and self-repeating set of perceptions, in that it heightens the likelihood that the subordinate groups will be seen as less competent than is desirable.

An insidious dimension of this phenomenon is that it enables upper groups to avoid taking full responsibility for their own behavior. In taking for themselves the role of designing organizational policy—but then delegating the implementation of that policy to the middle group—the uppers are able to build for themselves the perfect defense against failure. They can always conclude that their own policy was good but that the middles simply failed to implement it satisfactorily. Negative feedback can then be viewed merely as an indicator that subordinate groups are not as competent as is necessary. And, at the same time, the superiors can continue to avoid confronting their own expertise (or lack thereof) as uppers. Such a process locks upper groups into a way of viewing the world that ensures they will see the behavior of subordinates in increasingly depreciating terms.

Lewis Brook, as a member of an upper group, was caught by this intergroup dynamic as strongly as he was by the double binds of suspiciousness when he was located in a lower position.

Lewis as a Middle

When Brook was in a middle position, he was always espousing the need for "better communication" within the system. Despite this, he became caught in the trap of wanting to restrict information flow by making sure upper and lower groups communicated with each other only through him and his middle group. This situation is illustrated by the event described below.

Lewis was regularly embarrassed by learning about what was happening in his school for the first time from superiors who had been "leaked" information from below. Since he was an upper within the confines of the school itself, he often was unheeding to things teachers were trying to say to him. Therefore, they regularly felt the need to circumvent him in order to have their concerns attended to by the superintendent or the Board of Education. When teachers made attempts to contact the superintendent directly, Lewis became highly threatened and eventually decreed that no one could have access to the superintendent without first obtaining permission from one of the principals. By this action, Lewis clearly was working to preserve the centrality of his middle group's role as moderator of information flow.

Not to be daunted by this restriction on their liberties, the teachers found informal ways to gain access to the superintendent. The most frequently used device was to apply for study leave, even when not qualified for it. Such an application automatically led to an interview with the superintendent, which Lewis Brook allowed to occur without questioning his teachers. When ritualistically informed by the superintendent that they had not met the prerequisite conditions for study leave, the teachers willingly withdrew their applications and then confided the real reasons why they had sought an audience with him.

Lewis Brook never became aware of this practice, but he always felt distressed by the amount of information about his school of which the superintendent was aware. This distress only reinforced his dedication to make sure that teachers used his office alone as the means of communicating with the upper echelons of the system—an aspiration that he never realized.

To legitimize their own place in the system, middle groups need the uppers and lowers to be operating in a relatively polarized and noncommunicating fashion. Indeed, one of the ways for middle groups to be "confirmed" in the system is for them to become the central communication channel between the two extreme groups. This is possible primarily because both upper and lower groups use the withholding of information as a major strategy for dealing with each other. Upper groups limit information flow by using labels (such as "secret" or "in confidence") that designate who has legitimate access to what. For lowers, ground rules specifying what constitutes loyalty to the group determines what can be said to whom and under what circumstances, with the major concern being to minimize the vulnerability of the group.

If it were not for the rigid polarization of uppers and lowers, and their refusal to allow information to flow freely in the system, the middles might not be needed. But once the middle's role has become established as the communication link between upper and lower groups, the middles become very anxious to keep those polarized groups from talking frankly and openly. The middles become most threatened when the other two groups pass information to each other directly, or through any channel other than those the middles feel they have legitimized for the system. For this reason, the middles invest an inordinate amount of energy in defending the principle that all communication must pass through them. The net result of this dynamic is that middles will be constantly talking about the need to improve system-wide communication—while at the same time playing a vigorous role in restricting direct communication between other groups.

Summary

From the above account it is possible to recognize that intergroup processes cause groups at each of the three levels to become locked into a particular set of binds, and to create unique views of reality that are characteristic of those specific levels of the system. If these intergroup phenomena are conceded, it is predictable that an individual in a lower position will be supersensitive and suspicious of the activities of others. In an upper position, he or she will view the behavior of subordinates in a pessimistic light, and accordingly will delegate responsibility without the necessary authority. When in a middle position, the individual will espouse the need for greater communication, while acting to keep many communications restricted.

All these behaviors were exhibited by Lewis Brook in his role as Ashgrove's high school principal. It is easy to attribute these behaviors to Brook's unique personality. Yet, when viewed in the context of the intergroups operating in Brook's school system, it also becomes possible to understand how powerfully his own behavior and sense of reality were influenced by intergroup phenomena.

THE INTERGROUP AS A DETERMINANT OF INDIVIDUAL IDENTITY

Smith (1976) describes how intergroup interactions in a five-day power laboratory led to the creation of an identity for one individual that other members of the social system came to symbolize as "the village lunatic."

A power laboratory is an experiential, social, and psychological simulation designed for people interested in experiencing and learning about the dynamics of power and powerlessness. The laboratory is structured to create three classes of people: (1) the powerful "elite," who have access to and control over all the basic resources of the society, such as food, housing, money, and so forth; (2) the "ins," who have minimal control over some resources, at the discretion of the elites; and (3) the powerless "outs" who are totally deprived and have no control over any community resources. All conditions of living, such as standards of housing, quality of food, and so on, are differentiated to heighten "class" differences. For example, the outs live in a ghetto-like life style, while the elites live in comparatively leisurely luxury. On arrival at the laboratory all members are "born into" one of these three classes, without individual choice.

In the power laboratory described by Smith, the elite group of seven arrived half a day before the middles, and produced a plan which would enable them to keep their eliteness hidden. They decided to act as if they were regular, nonelite participants, while they actually would be quietly and powerfully pulling the strings of the social system like backstage puppeteers.

The plan ran into trouble, however, within hours of the arrival of the nine middles. The "birth" trauma of the middles was quite extreme: at induction, they had all their belonging (save one change of underwear) taken from them, an event that stirred their anger and their determination to discern "who did this to us." Anthony, one of the middles, had brought with him a tape recorder that he wanted to use for his learning and post-laboratory reflections. He was not allowed to keep the recorder, however, and his resentment about this heightened his sensitivity as to who was powerful and who was powerless in the system. It took him very little time to differentiate the elites from the nonelites— simply by observing the interactions that took place among various participants. In response to his awareness, Anthony tried to initiate a public debate intended to flush out the elite group. He was generally unsuccessful in this, partly because others lacked his acumen in discerning what was taking place, and partly because of the skill of the elite group in keeping their identity hidden.

After half a day all but two members of the elite group had tired of the charade and had made public their real status. This made the middle group angry, and Anthony became even more determined to end the elites' game

of phantomness. But this did not occur. The most influential member of the upper group— Richard, a tall, strong, bearded, black man— did not identify himself as an elite and remained with the middles, continuing to manipulate them to do exactly as the elites ordained.

The successful smoking out of most of the elite group fanned Anthony's fires. He became consumed with his fixation to force all the elites to become visible, Richard included. That was not to be, because Richard was blessed with a resolve equal to Anthony's and the two became bitterly pitted against each other. Anthony's energies were focused entirely on Richard's eviction from the middle group, while Richard, with a simple indifference to these pressures, worked at massaging the middles into accepting obediently their role as servants of the elites.

Whenever Richard attempted to make an initiative, Anthony immediately attempted to frustrate it by accurately, though boringly, accusing him of being an elite spy, and arguing that the middles should do nothing until such time as all the elites had been ousted. Eventually Richard became symbolized as a force for *activity* while Anthony came to be seen as someone reinforcing *stagnation*. Richard skillfully presented himself as the champion of the middles' cause, and successfully led negotiations with the elites for return of some of their personal belongings. This success elevated Richard to the sole leadership role in the bourgeoise and he accordingly dealt with Anthony's accusations by simply dismissing them as part of a personal vendetta against him as the middles' leader.

The middle group did very little in the first day and a half other than debate the spy issue, and this inactivity produced such intense frustration that some reached the point of being willing to do anything, including being led down any path by Richard, simply to escape the paralysis of their inertia. Whether or not he was a spy ceased to matter much.

Anthony recognized that his group had

adopted the spirit of going along with anything that produced activity, yet he could not reconcile himself to the fact that almost everything Richard proposed served to make the middles into the elite's lackeys. Soon Anthony's fight was being stifled by others in his group who would audibly groan their protest over his persistent regurgitation of a theme they all wanted to ignore. To buffer himself against this visible hostility, Anthony began to preface his remarks with a statement designed to lessen his vulnerability. He could have said, "I know I'm the only person who is concerned about this issue," but that's not the way he phrased his protective remarks. Instead he would say, "I know you think this is just my problem, but . . ."

By articulating this "buffer" statement in this way, Anthony provided other middles with the opportunity they had been looking for. By simply agreeing, "Yes, Anthony, that's just *your* problem," they could quickly close him down and avoid the agony of further monotonous reiteration of the spy theme.

The symbolization processes began to develop at a fast pace, and very soon the middle group had made "Anthony's problem" the receptacle for all of their frustrations. (Of course, the middles would have experienced frustration having to do with their need to keep their relationships with both elites and outs functional, independent of Anthony's role. As middles, they found that whenever they acted in the possible interest of the elites, the outs would abuse them for having been co-opted. And whenever they responded to pressures from the outs, the elites would treat them punitively and leave them feeling alienated and alone. The reality was that no matter what they did—even if they did nothing—the middles would end up feeling uncomfortable.)

Since the middles had begun to believe that the cause of their discomfort was "Anthony's problem," they came to view that "problem" in more extreme form as their sense of impotence heightened. Eventually they settled on the belief that "he really must be crazy." To make matters worse, Anthony had been successful enough to convince many of the middles that the spy issue was critical, but this only reverberated back on him: given the way the group's "problem" had become symbolized and projected into Anthony, it made more sense to many members of the middle group to suspect that Anthony was the real spy rather than Richard.

When this possibility was raised in the group, Anthony recognized that his battle was lost. By then he was so much on the periphery of the group that he knew there was little chance of his finding a comfortable place in the middle group. He therefore began to search for an alternative role in the system. The alternatives were, of course, very limited. The doors of the elites clearly were closed to him. That left only the outs—who in fact welcomed him with open arms. For them, the possibility of someone becoming *downwardly* mobile had real strategic value in this particular society, and they quickly grasped at the opportunity Anthony's plight presented. In addition, the outs had developed a strong emotional support system. They sensed Anthony's pain, and willingly reached out to provide him a haven.

Anthony became so overwhelmed by the level of acceptance and warmth accorded him by the outs that he quickly concluded that this was where he wanted to see out his days in the society. Here he ran into a new problem. It had been their common pain, their collective fears and uncertainties, and their desperate need for each other in psychological survival tasks that had forged the group of outs into its particular shape. Nothing in Anthony's middle experience paralleled those forces, and there was no way to revise the "out history" to allow Anthony to be made a full partner in the "real" life of the group. At best, he could become only an adopted son.

Anthony needed acceptance by the outs so badly that he was willing to comply uncritically to any of the group's wishes. And here,

Anthony's "way of being" changed dramatically. The overly perceptive characteristics he displayed in his bourgeois period now became clouded by an obsessional overconforming to the norms of the out group—a response which attempted to compensate for his sense of historical exclusion from the outs' world, and to pay an adequate price for his acceptance by them.

Another event added appreciably to the complexity of everyone's perceptions of Anthony's behavior. At the time of Anthony's migration to the outs, Richard (keen to keep tranquility disjointed) returned to the relative comfort of the elite group. However, still wishing to maximize deception, the elites continued the charade by refusing to acknowledge that Richard had been one of them all along. Instead they described his move as "upward mobility," provided to Richard because of his good leadership behavior and his service to the society.

The impact of the dual departures of Richard and Anthony from the middles left a powerful vacuum. The remaining middles started to experiment with new behaviors. Collectively (though only temporarily) they gained a new sense of vitality. This caused them to lay, even more vehemently than previously, total responsibility for their earlier stagnation at Anthony's feet. They attributed none of it to Richard. For his departure they grieved. For Anthony's, they celebrated.

The remaining history of this laboratory was filled with examples of how tension in the system—the byproduct of unhandled intergroup conflict—became attributed to Anthony's "craziness." No matter what discomforting event occurred, it was symbolized as being Anthony's fault.

Why?

My basic thesis is that once the society had created for Anthony alone a totally unique experience within the society, and once a chance was provided for his behavior to be seen as "crazy," the system gave him an identity that powerfully served the needs of the intergroup exchanges. The "village lunatic" identity provided a receptacle for the craziness of the whole system—the deceit, the multiple and conflicting senses of reality, the myriad of covert, unarticulable processes, and so forth—which enabled the society at large to avoid having to confront its own pathology. In short, the social system had a vested interest in having Anthony become and remain crazy because it served admirably the continuation of the essential intergroup exchanges of the society at large.

And what became of Anthony himself?[1] Initially he was convinced his own perceptions were accurate. But across time, as others failed to see what was so obvious to him, he began to doubt his own sense of reality (even when he actually was perceiving correctly) and to wonder whether he was going mad. This eventually forced him to experience such discomfort that all of his energy became directed toward uncritically finding a place where he could feel support and acceptance. When the society transformed him into the "village lunatic," it created a form of madness aptly described by the poet Roethke, as mere "nobility of soul, at odds with circumstance."

One further question remains. What was it about Anthony as a person that caused him to become the lunatic? In my view, it was virtually accidental. The fact that he came originally with a tape recorder (and with a very high investment in being able to use it for his personal learning) meant that Anthony felt even more deprived than the others at induction time. This additional sense of deprivation heightened his activity to find out who the elites were much earlier than his fellow mid-

---

[1]Anthony left the laboratory in good emotional health. During the critique phase of the experience, the staff of the laboratory spent a great deal of time with Anthony and others exploring how this "village lunatic" phenomenon had occurred.

dles. Because he saw things differently than did the others, he started to become separated from the dominant sense of "reality" in the system. From there, the processes already described took off.

If Anthony had not come to this laboratory, would someone else have been made into a "lunatic" for the society's purposes? I suspect not. The forces which ended up focussing on him might well have been acted out in some other way—perhaps by creating another special identity for one individual, or by generating conditions of war between the groups, or even by the collapse of the society at large. The intergroup dynamics had to find *some* way to be acted out; the particular circumstances surrounding Anthony and his induction into the system were such that he became a convenient and useful vehicle for meeting that need.

The learning of overwhelming importance from this account is that often the personages or identities we take on may have very little to do with our own desires for ourselves, with our particular upbringings, or with our own values. Instead, they may, in fact, be mostly defined for us and forced upon us by external processes similar to those experienced by Anthony in the power laboratory.

THE INTERGROUP AS A DETERMINANT OF BEHAVIORS CHARACTERIZED AS LEADERSHIP

Perhaps one of the most gripping, passionate, and socially educative experiences ever recorded is the story of sixteen Uruguayan football players and their friends who not only survived an aircraft crash in the completely inaccessible heights of the Chilean Andes, but then existed for ten weeks in icy and desolate conditions with only the wrecked fuselage of the aircraft as their shelter and home (Read, 1974).

Of the original forty-three people on board, sixteen were killed in the crash or died in the next few days from injuries. Seventeen days later the surviving twenty-seven were further reduced to a group of nineteen by an avalanche of snow that buried alive almost the whole group, eight of whom could not be dug out before they froze to death. After the avalanche, the group of survivors (reduced later by another three deaths) kept alive for fifty more days before two of their number, under unbelievable conditions, climbed a cliff-faced mountain of ice to a height of 13,500 feet, and eventually stumbled across civilization and help.

The story is a deeply touching account of human relationships under the most extreme survival conditions. In order to stay alive, it was necessary for group members, despite the repugnancy of the idea, to eat the raw flesh of the dead. Much of the early life and struggles of these survivors revolved around the agonies of acknowledging and accepting this imperative. As dreams of rescue faded, and as the struggle together under intense conditions heightened, the earlier revulsions became translated into a very mystical and religious experience—to the extent that several of the boys, when they realized that their own deaths were imminent, asked their comrades to feel free to eat their bodies.

In the discussion that follows, I will explore the social system composed of the survivors, and show how behaviors that traditionally would be described as personal "leadership" can be understood in terms of the relationships between various groups that emerged within that system. Specifically, I will propose that who becomes focal in leadership activities (and what leadership behaviors are seen as appropriate) changes radically from situation to situation—largely as a function of changing intergroup dynamics.

Immediately after the crash, many of the survivors were bleeding and in desperate need of medical care. In this initial phase, during which group life was defined by the visibility of wounded bodies, the key survival task was seen as caring for the bleeding. Accordingly, two of the group, who had been medical students in the earliest phases of their training, were automatically elevated to dominant status. An intergroup structure emerged which delineated all survivors into one of three classes—the wounded, the potential workers, and the doctors. The medical students were given tremendous power, despite the fact that their skills and competence in the setting were minimal, especially given that they had no facilities or medical supplies. Others willingly subjected themselves to directives the students issued around appropriate work or treatment programs. The need for medical help was so intense that the differential status of the survivors enabled limited skill to become symbolized as expert competence, which, in turn, gave the "doctors" inordinate power to influence everyone else's behavior.

Within a day or so, new demands appeared. The acquisition of food and water, and the preservation of hygiene in the fuselage—which constituted the only shelter from sub-zero temperatures, blizzards, and thoroughly treacherous conditions—became critical. These demands required a group structure that was radically different from the one that had developed in the period immediately after the crash. In particular, it became important for someone to play an overall "social maintenance" role to give coherence to the whole system. The captain of the football team, who had been overshadowed in the first day by the medical students, was reelevated to his former position. Beneath him were two groups of approximately equal status: (1) the medical team of two "doctors" and a couple of helpers, and (2) a group that searched battered luggage for tidbits of food, and who made water by melting snow on metal sheets and bottling it in old soda bottles. At a still lower level, was a group of the younger boys who served as a clean-up crew to maintain livable

conditions in the cabin. The football captain himself became the general coordinator, and at noon each day he distributed the carefully rationed food to each person. In this role he clearly brought with him the ethos of his earlier influence as captain on the sports field.

The hierarchies of social influence changed during this period. The medical group now were granted authority related only to their specialist function, and they lost virtually all of their influence over nonmedical domains of the social system. For several days the football captain remained the key figure, mediating potential clashes over the food, and dealing with conflicts between the medical and work teams. Much of his power was predicated on his effusive optimism that they would all be rescued within a few days. He used this hope, which he constantly rekindled, as the major substance for social cohesion. But as time passed, and it became clear that rescue was not imminent, the hopes he had fostered began to sour and the captain's social maintenance skills slowly became devalued.

A new plight confronted the survivors several days after the crash. The food supplies were nearly exhausted. It was clear that if survival were to be sustained, the group maintenance orientation of the captain would no longer suffice. Parrado, who previously had played no significant role, moved to prominence. During the past few days he had been coping with the loss of both his mother and his sister, who had died from crash injuries. In the process, he had developed an unbelievable desire to survive. Parrado became the articulator of two new and key dimensions in the life of the group: (1) the suggestion that the only hope of rescue was for a group of expeditionaries to walk out of the mountains, and (2) the idea that life depended on consumption of the flesh of the dead, which was being preserved by the freezing cold. The force of these suggestions provided new energy for the group, and started the process of delineating new internal social structures within the mountaintop society.

At the same time, the role of the "doctors" was further diminished. With virtually no medical supplies, their "special expertise" had been exhausted. The worst cases had died, and it was now clear to everyone that there was very little more that could be offered in the medical domain. The collapse of the medical team's function added to the power vacuum and increased the uncertainty about social relationships among group members.

Eventually another new social structure did emerge. It was defined primarily by each person's willingness or reluctance to eat human flesh. Those who did so early, and with a reasonable degree of spontaneity, were the ones who maintained the physical energy to persevere—and thereby to provide vitality for the endurance of the social system itself. Those who could not bring themselves to overcome their natural abhorrence to the idea became weak, and eventually degenerated into a new "poorer class." A third group struggled with the tensions of survival on the one hand, and their natural revulsion to the consumption of human flesh on the other. In so doing, members of this group came to formulate a new way of symbolizing the activity. They developed a very mystical and spiritual interpretation of their group experience, reinterpreting the eating of the flesh of the dead as being parallel to a religious communion in which they would consume the body and blood of Christ. This resymbolization of experience facilitated survival by helping everyone respond to the imperative that they eat the flesh of the dead, no matter how strongly the idea initially had repelled them.

During this period, the football captain moved further from his earlier position of prominence. This was, in part, because of his unwillingness to take the lead in eating human flesh. But, in addition, the captain lost credibility because his repeated assurances that rescue was imminent came increasingly to sound hollow.

When the survivors eventually heard on a transistor radio that all rescue operations had been called off, the energy in the system changed dramatically. Despair and outrage hit members like clenched fists, and produced radically different responses in different people. Parrado was ready to leave on an expedition immediately, while others were ready to resign themselves to the inevitability of death. Despair was heightened further a couple of days later when an avalanche of snow caused the death of eight more persons, including the football captain. Reluctantly, it was concluded that an expedition now offered the only hope for survival. And the internal social structure of the system went through yet another readjustment in response to this imperative.

Any social system can become subjected to crisis conditions which produce extreme pressures from the outside, or from within. When this happens, members of the system must respond to these pressures or else risk long-term internal chaos. One common response is for clusters of people to form which eventually evolve into critical groups for the system. Moreover, the pressures that emerge from crisis experiences invariably demand that groups within the system relate to each other more intensely than had previously been the case. Even the composition of these groups will need to change. In the present case, the medical group was dominant initially, with others subservient to them. This structure was altered by the emergence of the football captain as the major mediator between several specialized work groups, and eventually by the emergence of an entirely new social structure defined in terms of members' willingness to consume human flesh.

When these changes are taking place in response to extreme pressures, it often is most unclear what should happen to produce a new form of stability in which both directionality and internal coherence are present. What an individual might do personally to provide leadership is unclear and speculative. Instead, each new set of stresses causes changes in group memberships or behaviors which, in turn, move the system toward some new equilibrium. As this happens, power, authority, critical resources, and ability to influence events become distributed differently than before. Only when the directionality and coherence of the system achieve a reasonable degree of stability is it possible to determine which behaviors actually moved the system in productive directions, or served to keep the various parts of the system integrated. Acts of leadership, then, are merely responses to the forces that emerge from the exchanges among groups within the system, and it would *not* be valid to construe them as reflecting a conscious intent to lead. If, in hindsight, an act appears to have been one of effective leadership, it may have been virtually accidental at the time it happened—and identifiable as leadership only in retrospect. This phenomenon is especially visible in the next phase of the survivors' experiences.

As preparations for the expedition went forward, all energies were dedicated to that task. Medical duties had slipped from any prominence, and the doctors simply took their place in the mainstream of the social structure. Four identifiable groups emerged as planning for the expedition proceeded. They were: (1) a collection of ten individuals who were designated as too weak to undertake any significant walking; (2) three first choices for the expedition, including one of the ex-doctors and Parrado, whose robust constitution and steely resolve to escape had helped buoy the energy of the fainthearted; (3) three cousins who were not fit for the expedition and who previously had not played significant roles in the system—but who had coalesced as a critical subgroup because of their strong support for each other in a common struggle (theirs, a

blood relationship, was the only precrash grouping of friends that had not been fragmented by the ordeal); and (4) a trio of younger fellows who were potential expeditionaries—but who first had to be tested to prove their fitness.

Eventually a group of four was selected as the key expeditionaries. Once chosen, they became virtually a "warrior class" with extra rights and privileges. They were allowed to do anything that could be construed as bettering their physical condition. The whole group coddled them, both physically and psychologically, and everyone made sure that the only conversations within their earshot were optimistic in tone.

Read (1974) reports that the expeditionaries were *not* the leaders of the society. They were basically a class apart, linked to the rest of the system by the group of cousins, whose cohesion was the only force available to balance the unbelievable power that had been given to the expeditionaries. Because the cousins were the only ones able to keep the "warriors" in check (and thereby keep the system in equilibrium) they became the major locus of power within the remainder of the system. They virtually ruled from then on. The cousins controlled food allocation, determined who should do what work, and mediated when the "workers" (those who cut meat, prepared water, attended to hygiene, and so forth) felt that some of the sick were merely "malingering" and therefore should not be fed unless they also worked.

Beneath the cousins, a second echelon of three emerged. These individuals took roles equivalent to noncommissioned officers, receiving orders from above and giving them to those below. One of this trio, the second of the two doctors, became the "detective" in this phase of the society. He took upon himself the task of investigating misdemeanors and norm violations, and he flattered those more senior to him while bullying those more subservient.

It was several weeks before the expeditionaries departed. There were some valid reasons for the delay, but eventually everyone began to suspect that the ex-doctor was stalling and that he was using his expectant expeditionary status as a way of accruing privileges and minimizing work. At that point, his privileges were terminated. When one of the cousins volunteered to go in his place, the ex-doctor stirred himself and prepared for what proved to be a successful expedition: after a grueling ten-day trek, help was located and the remaining survivors were rescued.

One would have imagined that the ordeal was now over, but the system still had to face another extremely difficult event. Within a short time after the rescue, news leaked that the survivors had sustained themselves by consuming the flesh of the dead. This produced a strong reaction, especially among members of the press, who were poised to give world-wide publicity to this remarkable story. Religious figures, parents, and close friends were basically supportive during this period of new threat. But it soon became obvious that, if the survivors were ever to return to normal lives, it would be necessary for them to confront this issue together. So they called a press conference to tell their story.

The group debated at length as to who should explain the eating of human flesh. Several individuals felt they would be too emotional. It was eventually agreed that Delgado, who had been almost completely insignificant on the mountain top, should describe this aspect of their experience. His public presence and his eloquence—which of course had been of no value during the seventy-day ordeal—now came into its own, and he mediated brilliantly between the survivors, and the press, relatives, and other interested parties. His statement was a moving, passionate, religious, and emotional event, and through it he provided a way for everyone to resymbolize

the meaning of the survival experience, thereby quelling criticism and laying to rest concerns over the consumption of the dead.

In this setting, Delgado's behavior, which to date had influenced nothing, was now seen by others as outstanding leadership. But did he lead? Or was it simply that his particular response to the tensions which intersected in his personhood in that situation touched the nerve fibers of the new sets of intergroup interactions, thereby triggering a new directionality and a wholesome coherence for the system?

CONCLUSION

The literature of organizational behavior is filled with concepts that help us understand the behavior of people in terms of their personal characteristics, or as a response to what takes place in the groups of which they are members. The material presented in this paper offers an alternative view: namely, that it is imperative to move beyond explanations that lie within people and within groups—and to include perspectives that derive from more global and systemic forces, including forces that derive from the dynamics of intergroups.

If, for example, the tools of personality theorists alone were applied to Lewis Brook in Ashgrove or to Anthony's identity struggle, we would obtain only a limited understanding of what affected their perceptions and their behaviors. Likewise, if we restricted our explorations of leadership among the aircraft survivors to traditional concepts that imply specific intentionality on the part of individuals (i.e., using notions such as participation, initiation of structure, socioemotional behavior, and so on), much of the essence of the leadership phenomena that developed on the mountain top would have been lost.

But how much relevance do the principles extracted from the materials presented in this paper have for understanding everyday exper iences in everyday organizations? I submit, a great deal—and more than we usually realize or are comfortable acknowledging.

REFERENCES

Alderfer, C. P. Group and intergroup relations. In J. R. Hackman and J. L. Suttle (Eds.), *Improving life at work: Behavioral science approaches to organizational change*. Pacific Palisades, Calif.: Goodyear, 1977.

Alderfer, C. P., Brown, L. D., Kaplan, R. E., & Smith, K. K. *Group relations and organizational diagnosis*. London: Wiley, in press.

Hackman, J. R. Group influences on individuals in organizations. In M. D. Dunnette (Ed.), *Handbook of industrial and organizational psychology*. Chicago: Rand-McNally, 1976.

Levine, R. A., & Campbell, D. T. *Ethnocentrism*. New York: Wiley, 1972.

Lewin, K. Frontiers in group dynamics. *Human Relations*, 1947, **1,** 5–41.

Likert, R. *New patterns of management*. New York: McGraw-Hill, 1964.

Lorsch, J. W., & Lawrence, P. R. *Managing group and intergroup relations*. Homewood, Ill.: Irwin, 1972.

Read, P. P. *Alive*. London: Pan Books, 1974.

Rice, A. K. Individual, group and intergroup processes. *Human Relations*, 1969, **22,** 565–585.

Sherif, M. (Ed.) *Intergroup relations and leadership*. New York: Wiley, 1962.

Smith, K. K. *Behavioral consequences of hierarchical structures*. Unpublished doctoral dissertation, Yale University, 1974.

Smith, K. K. The village lunatic. Unpublished manuscript, University of Melbourne, 1976.

Chapter 9

Leadership Processes

Leadership is a crucial topic for anyone interested in behavior in organizations. We all have been affected by the actions of leaders, and, at one time or another, most of us have assumed leadership positions. Leadership can be thought of as a special case of social influence. Just as groups can influence individual members, so can particular individuals—those we label "leaders" in given situations—influence other individuals. As one goes through the articles in this chapter, it will be especially useful to keep the notion of social influence to the forefront. Unfortunately, however, attempts to unravel the processes by which certain individuals at certain times—leaders in specific situations—exert this influence have proved to be somewhat difficult for behavioral scientists. Part of the problem is definitional: how does one unambiguously distinguish leadership from all other kinds of influence behavior? Also, though, research has produced relatively little in the way of strongly consistent and reliable findings. Progress has been made, but it has been slower than might be expected given the generally accepted importance attached to the concept of leadership. It seems likely, nevertheless, that the next decade may bring about some substantial advances in our understanding of the topic. Some of the bases of knowledge for making these advances are illustrated in the articles in this chapter.

The opening article, by McCall, provides an overview of issues important to understanding leadership. In this reading, McCall faces the issue of why the popular literature on leadership seems so much more exciting than the scientific literature. After reviewing problems in defining "leadership," McCall outlines the major theoretical and empirical developments in the area. As the reader will see, great emphasis is placed on the necessity of focusing on the "demands of the leadership role" and analyzing the kinds of activities engaged in by leaders. From this material, McCall generates some thoughts about the training of leaders and proposes some new ways of looking at leadership processes.

The next set of articles constitutes a symposium on leadership that involves three of the best-known names in the field: Fiedler, Vroom, and Argyris. The symposium is opened by an introduction by Porter, in which he seeks to make certain key comparisons among the ideas of the three theorists. A study of this introduction should help the reader gain a better understanding of those points on which Fiedler, Vroom, and Argyris agree, and those on which they disagree. Fiedler's contribution reviews his well-known theory of leadership, which concentrates on matching the (potential) leader to the situation—or, if necessary, altering the situation to fit the leader. This approach is based on extensive empirical data, and has been quite influential in affecting the research of organizational scientists. It is referred to by Fiedler as a "contingency model," because of its emphasis on diagnosing the situation as a means of forecasting what leadership style will be most appropriate. Vroom also presents a contingency-type of approach, but he (in contrast to Fiedler) places great importance on the idea that individuals can *learn* how to lead effectively. Vroom stresses the decision-making aspect of leadership, and illustrates his approach with an analysis of how the leader should go about ascertaining whether or not to utilize a subordinate's participation in particular situations. The decision-making model Vroom presents is explicitly normative, in that it prescribes a "correct" style of leadership for various specific situational circumstances. It will be seen that Vroom believes strongly that training can help leaders "enlarge their repertoire" of leadership styles. The final article in this symposium, by Argyris, suggests that leaders, or would-be leaders, must be reeducated to a very different approach to leadership than that used by most leaders in typical organizations. This reeducation process, as Argyris makes clear, is lengthy, difficult, and costly, but—to Argyris —worth the effort.

The concluding article in this chapter, by Mintzberg, provides a synthesis of research results on the question of what leaders in organizations actually do. What sort of *activities* do managers actually engage in? Are these different than the activities we assume they carry out? As the title of the article indicates, the author attempts to separate the facts about the manager's job from the folklore that has grown up over the past half century or so. In this analysis, particular attention is paid to the variety of roles played by any person in a managerial position. While these different roles can be separated for purposes of analysis, the author rightfully emphasizes the *integrated* nature of the job. This article is especially useful for putting the flesh of reality on the skeletal outlines provided by scientific theories of leadership.

Reading 32

Leaders and Leadership: Of Substance and Shadow

Morgan W. McCall, Jr.

There are at least two ways to approach the topic of leadership. The first is from the emotional, experiential frame of reference which captures the colorful and dramatic flavor of myth and legend—of the fate of nations and the course of history. The second is an empirical approach based on research about this nebulous topic. If the former is bright orange, the latter is decidedly slate gray.

The bright orange side of leadership emerges when people are asked to name highly effective leaders. The most frequently mentioned—Hitler, Churchill, Kennedy, Roosevelt, Eisenhower, Gandhi—all played a significant part in world history. The characteristics attributed to such effective leaders—charisma, intelligence, persuasiveness, dynamism, energy—also reflect the almost mystical power of central figures in world events.

The essence of the powerful leader's impact has been captured in song, poem, and novel. One example is Tolstoy's description of Napoleon:

> Napoleon was standing a little in front of his marshals, on a little grey horse, wearing the same blue overcoat he had worn throughout the Italian campaign. He was looking intently and silently at the hills, which stood up out of the sea of mist, and the Russian troops moving across them in the distance, and he listened to the sounds of firing in the valley. His face—still thin in those days—did not stir a single muscle; his gleaming eyes were fixed intently on one spot. . . .
>
> When the sun had completely emerged from the fog, and was glittering with dazzling brilliance over the fields and the mist (as though he

had been waiting for that to begin the battle), he took his glove off his handsome white hand, made a signal with it to his marshals, and gave orders for the battle to begin. (From *War and Peace*)

Given the emotional power of leadership, it is no surprise that social scientists have devoted massive amounts of time and resources to studying it. Researchers have looked at leadership in almost every conceivable setting, from army squads to executives; they have examined personality traits, leadership styles, situational contingencies, and a multitude of other topics pertinent to leadership. With leadership studies appearing at a rate of more than 170 a year,[1] it seems reasonable to ask what we know about this elusive topic.

SKIPPING THROUGH A MINEFIELD

At a recent conference on the "frontiers" of leadership research, the concluding speaker made the following comment:

> The heresy I propose is that the concept of leadership itself has outlived its usefulness. Thus I suggest we abandon it in favor of some other more fruitful way of cutting up the theoretical pie. (Miner, 1975, p. 5)

After over forty years of empirical investigation, leadership remains an enigma. In 1959, Warren Bennis suggested reasons for this state of affairs, and seventeen years later his points still seem valid.

[1]Based on a search of *Psychological Abstracts*. The last eight years contain 1,368 references to leadership.

A similar version of this paper was presented at the annual meeting of the British Psychological Society, Occupational Psychology Section, Keefe, Staffordshire, England, January 1976.

First, the term "leadership" has never been clearly defined. Ralph Stogdill, in a recent mammoth review of the leadership research, pointed out that "there are almost as many different definitions of leadership as there are persons who have attempted to define the concept" (1974, p. 7). Perhaps the closest thing to a consensus on a definition for leadership is that it is a social-influence process. Since most interactions involve social influence, such categorizations of leadership have not helped much.

The lack of a generally agreed upon definition of the central concept has led to a proliferation of terms to deal with leadership phenomena. The last ten years have seen the appearance of at least four different "contingency" models, as well as path-goal and open system models, not to mention transactional and vertical dyad approaches, normative and integrative models, and four-factor and behavioral theories.

Second, the "growing mountain" of research data has produced an impressive mass of contradictions. The dimensions of the mountain were suggested by Stogdill's (1974) review of the leadership literature which covered over 3,000 studies. While numerous models, theories, and approaches exist, the accumulated research has not yet produced a unified and generally accepted paradigm for research on the topic, much less a clear understanding of the phenomenon. In fact, Warren Bennis's summary is even more accurate today:

> Of all the hazy and confounding areas in social psychology, leadership theory undoubtedly contends for top nomination. And, ironically, probably more has been written and less known about leadership than about any other topic in the behavioral sciences. (1959)

Naturally enough, much of the early work on leadership attempted to isolate the characteristics of people, distinguishing leaders from nonleaders, or successful from unsuccessful leaders. Almost every conceivable trait and characteristic, from activity to weight, have been examined, but the results have been equivocal. The initial hope that leaders shared common characteristics across situations has not been borne out, and it now appears that personal characteristics are related to leadership outcomes only in the context of specific situations (Gibb, 1969; Campbell, Dunnette, Lawler III, & Weick, 1970). Unfortunately, it is not yet clear which aspects of the situation are most critical.

Another major approach to leadership involves the "style" a leader uses in dealing with subordinates. Many different labels have been generated to describe essentially two styles of leadership (the number of "styles" ranges from two to five): (1) task-oriented and (2) person (consideration)-oriented. While initially intended to reflect the *behavior* of leaders, styles are most commonly measured by one of several paper-and-pencil questionnaires; thus, they represent self or others' reported perceptions rather than actual behavior.

The human-relations school at first contended that leaders should emphasize considerate, participative styles. Consideration of employees' feelings and allowing employees' participation in decision making would result in increased satisfaction which, it was thought, would improve performance. While considerate behavior by leaders did generally lead to increased satisfaction, satisfaction did not necessarily lead to improved performance. Equivocal and sometimes negative results (Stogdill, 1974) indicated that this normative approach was not the answer in all situations.

Other researchers (e.g., Blake & Mouton, 1964) argued that an effective leader must be high on structuring *and* high on consideration. Again, the data did not clearly conform to the normative prescriptions (e.g., Larson, Hunt, & Osborn, 1975). Further refinements aimed at isolating the specific situations in which certain styles are effective (e.g., Vroom & Yetton, 1973) have replaced the earlier, simpler models, but as yet no adequate taxonomy of situational components exists.

Data do exist, however, which indicate that leaders change their behavior in response to situational conditions (Hill & Hughes, 1974) and to subordinates' behaviors (Lowin & Craig, 1968; Farris & Lim, 1969; Greene, 1975). Leaders are not perceived by subordinates as having "one style" (Hill, 1973). Thus, the search for invariant truth—the one-best-way approach—may not hold answers, even when the model includes situational moderators. Leaders may have numerous behaviors to choose from (not two or three) and may face a wide variety of different situations. A number of leadership behaviors may be equally effective in the same situation. As researchers include task structures, power, hierarchical level, subordinate expectations, and other organizational characteristics in their models, predictive power and model complexity increase. But only one thing is clear—no one leadership style is effective in all situations.

Thus early work made an important contribution to understanding leadership. It showed that neither personal characteristics nor styles of leadership behavior could predict leadership effectiveness across situations. More importantly, these findings steered researchers toward identifying the characteristics of situations which might interact with personality or style dimensions to generate positive outcomes.

Most of the current theories have retained the basic ingredients of the earlier models while adding situational contingencies. Although the specific variables included vary, the basic contingency approach is illustrated in Table 32-1.

The relationships studied in contingency frameworks still reflect leadership's research origins in individual and group psychology. The focal unit is the leader and a group of

Table 32-1 The Basic Model for Contingency Approaches to Leadership

Characteristic of leader (e.g., style, personality)	Characteristic of situation (e.g., group task, members' expectations)	Relationship with group outcome (e.g., performance or satisfaction)
A	X	Positive
A	Y	Negative or unrelated
B	X	Negative or unrelated
B	Y	Positive

followers. The outcomes (dependent variables) generally represent an index of the performance or satisfaction of the follower group, and the independent variables are still characteristics or "behaviors" of the leader. The relationships between the leader and group outcomes are contingent on some aspect of the situation.

Fiedler's (1967) contingency theory has been a focus for many current researchers and provides a good example of the contingency approach. Fiedler postulated that the effectiveness of a group depends on the leader's motivational orientation (person versus task) and on the nature of the situation (determined by the structuredness of the task, the position of power of the leader, and the quality of leader-member relations). The elaborate model contains a continuum of situational favorableness (from highly favorable to highly unfavorable) and postulates that task-motivated leaders are effective in both highly favorable and unfavorable situations, while person-motivated leaders are effective in the moderate situations.

The path-goal model (Evans, 1970; House, 1971) provides another example of the contingency approach. Built on an expectancy-theory framework, the path-goal model argues that a leader's style (task or person orientation) is effective when it clarifies linkages between subordinate effort and valued outcomes. Thus, leaders' behavior has contingent effects on group outcomes depending upon the presence or absence of performance-outcome linkages.

In spite of their logical appeal, the contingency models have still yielded contradictory research results. As Korman (1974) has pointed out, the contingency approach "has been a great leap forward in the complexity and sophistication of theoretical formulations and the range of variables which have come under consideration," but he adds, "There has also been a neglect of some basic considerations." Included in such considerations are issues of measurement, the continued focus on personality constructs, a static rather than dynamic view of leadership processes, and a failure to extend situational factors beyond those relevant to the immediate work group.

In the long run, the test of leadership theory is its utility for those individuals who find themselves in leadership roles. The bulk of current research has made some contribution by sensitizing practitioners to the differences among leadership styles and, in general, to the complexity of the leadership process. But researchers are still a long way from an integrated understanding of leadership processes, and equally far from providing organizational leaders with integrated and validated models of leadership.

Relative to the bulk of research on styles, characteristics, and contingencies, a small number of studies have examined what organizational leaders actually do. Many researchers dismiss the results of such studies because, it is argued, leadership and management (or headship) are different things. Unfortunately, the lack of consensus about the meaning of "leadership" makes it difficult to find leaders and follow them around. People who occupy leadership roles in organizations (foremen, managers, executives), however, can be identified and studied. The results of

such efforts have produced some thought-provoking approaches which might clarify some of the confusion in the more traditional leadership literature.

DEMANDS OF THE LEADERSHIP ROLE

No es lo mismo hablar de toros, que estar en el redondel.[2]

Data on the day-to-day activities of those who occupy leadership roles shed some light on (1) the pace of management work, (2) the degree to which the work group itself is a focus of managerial interaction, (3) the kinds of media central to managerial activity, and (4) a global picture of what life is like in the leadership bullring. These, in turn, challenge several assumptions which seemingly underlie leadership theories based on the leader-group paradigm.

The Pace of Managerial Work

Many models of leadership, particularly those advocating participative management or situational determination of an appropriate leadership style, seem to assume that leaders have (1) a relatively small number of events about which style decisions must be made, and (2) enough time to analyze the situation and choose a style.

Two studies of foremen provide an interesting insight into these assumptions. In one study, foremen engaged in an average of 583 activities in a day (Guest, 1955–56); and in another, foremen averaged between 200 and 270 activities per eight-hour day. Other studies of higher-level managers confirm the unrelenting pace of managerial work. One study of a Swedish top executive found that he was undisturbed for twenty-three minutes or

[2]This is an old Spanish proverb which means, "It is not the same to talk of bulls as to be in the bullring."

more only twelve times in thirty-five days (Carlson, 1951). Mintzberg (1973), in a study of five top executives, found that half of their activities lasted nine minutes or less, and only a tenth lasted more than one hour. Mintzberg's observations led him to conclude that a manager's activities are "characterized by brevity, variety, and fragmentation" (1973, p. 31).

The hectic pace of managerial work is exacerbated by the manager's relative lack of control over it. Mintzberg (1975) found, for example, that the managers in his study initiated only 32 percent of their contacts and that 93 percent of the contacts were arranged on an "ad hoc" basis.

The pace of the work has implications for training, research, and practice. Because there are so many activities in a day and because there is so little uninterrupted time, the occupant of a formal leadership role must be, as Mintzberg (1973) calls it, "proficient at superficiality." Training models which advocate "rational" decision strategies (e.g., analyzing each situation to determine the appropriate decision style) make sense, but they are extremely difficult for a manager to implement. Research approaches which ignore the day-to-day process of leading are missing what may be critical dimensions—the crunch of the pace and the breadth of the activities. Finally, managers themselves can be easily overwhelmed. The work is demanding and largely reactive. Activities that require little time and are relatively routine may postpone other activities that are ambiguous and have no routine solution. Thus, larger decisions may be made by default.

Time with the Work Group

The fact that almost all current models of leadership focus on the leader and the immediate work group, suggests that the relationship between leader and led is the most important aspect of the leadership process. Translated into what managers do, one might expect that almost all of a manager's time is spent with members of the group.

Dubin's (1962) review indicates that foremen spend between 34 and 60 percent of their interaction time with subordinates. Mintzberg's (1973) executives spent only 48 percent of their contact time with subordinates, even though the subordinate groups contained most of their respective organizational memberships. This indicates that managers spend between 66 and 40 percent of their time with nonsubordinates—a group including superiors, peers, professional colleagues, members of other departments and units, and outsiders. Dubin concluded in his review:

> It cannot be too strongly emphasized that horizontal relations among peers in management and the nonformal behavior systems through which such interactions are carried out constitute a dimension of organizational behavior long neglected and probably as important as authority relations. (1962, p. 15)

Surprisingly, managers spend relatively little of their interaction time with their superiors (Brewer & Tomlinson, 1963–64); seldom more than one fifth and usually closer to one tenth (according to Mintzberg, 1973).

The mosaic of available data shows that there is considerable variability in the amount of time a manager spends in contact with subordinates. While it is generally true that interactions with subordinates consume the largest single block of a manager's time, it should not be concluded that leader-subordinate relationships are the only—or even the most important—aspect of the leadership process. In one study of sixty managers, group members accounted for an average of only 23.4 percent of the total number of information sources listed by the leader (McCall, 1974).

More research on leadership needs to focus on the leader-system relationship and how the organizational leader fits into the interaction matrix. Sayles (1964) and Mintzberg (1973), among others, have emphasized the major importance and complexity of the managers' information network. Unfortunately, empirical investigation of the impact of nonsubordinates' interactions on leadership effectiveness is sorely lacking.

Many leadership development programs also suffer because of narrow leader-follower paradigms. Since there are few data on the impact and nature of other relationships, it is not surprising that few training programs deal with them. One cannot help wondering, though, if we are creating a generation of managers who believe that their style with their immediate subordinates is the only matter of concern.

Managers and Media

Studies of what managers do consistently find that their work is primarily oral. Dubin and Spray (1964), Mintzberg (1973), Brewer and Tomlinson (1963–64), Burns (1954), and Dubin (1962) all cite evidence emphasizing the high percentage of managerial time spent talking. Much of this talk is directed at exchanging information (Mintzberg, 1973; Horne & Lupton, 1965), and very little of it is spent giving orders or issuing instructions (Horne & Lupton, 1965).

With between 60 and 80 percent of their time spent in oral exchanges, formal leaders cannot spend too much time with written communications (Dubin, 1962). A successful leader, therefore, must have the ability to selectively "hear," retain, and transmit vast quantities of oral information and, perhaps even more difficult, selectively utilize a vast volume of written information provided routinely by the organization.[3] In communicating

with others, the manager would do well to remember that other managers, too, are focusing on the spoken word—things in writing just do not get the time, in general, that is available for an oral communication.

What Leaders Do: An Integration

For formal leaders in organizations, the data indicate that the world consists of many activities (most of them of short duration), frequent interruptions, a large network of contacts extending far beyond the immediate work group, and a preponderance of oral interaction. How do these characteristics fit in with the mythology and empirical work on leadership?

First, notice that these dimensions of leadership represent the day-to-day processes that go on between the leader's "moments of glory." It is easy to latch onto the "Ich bin ein Berliner" and "I have nothing to offer but blood, toil, tears and sweat," thereby ignoring what Kennedy or Churchill did in the daily conduct of their leadership roles. To the extent that we do know what these leaders were like, we owe that knowledge to journalists and not to the empirical leadership literature.[4] Most of the leaders with whom we have direct contact—our bosses, politicians, community figures, and gang leaders—have less grandiose moments of glory, but they too engage in the process of leading. What observational studies have shown us is that the leadership we react to—the inspiration, or lack of it, the autocratic or democratic behavior—is only a part of the larger and more complex set of phenomena comprising the role of leader.

Second, leadership models which emphasize the "style" of a leader vis-à-vis the follower group have limited utility, even when they introduce situational contingencies. They have no explanatory power when it comes to nonsubordinate interactions, and it is difficult

---

[3]Ackoff (1967) has discussed the problems managers face with one type of written information—that provided by managerial information systems. One of his conclusions is that managers have too much, rather than too little, information.

[4]Vaill (in press) made this point by arguing that the *New Yorker* is the best social science journal.

to understand the relationship between some global measure of a leader's style and the literally hundreds of activities that are part of the daily life of a manager. The concentration on leadership style that pervades all of the mainstream leadership research reminds one of what Omar Bradley once said in a different context: ". . . This strategy would involve us in the wrong war, at the wrong place, at the wrong time, and with the wrong enemy."

Third, the results of observational studies suggest a host of different variables and questions that might direct future leadership research and which pose challenges to leadership trainers. The presence of nonauthority relationships and the emphasis on oral communication, coupled with the nonrational way decisions get made (e.g., Cyert & March, 1963; March & Simon, 1958; Katz & Kahn, 1966; Pettigrew, 1973), suggest that a major element of the leadership process is political. While social scientists have advocated the inclusion of political activity in studies of leadership (e.g., Lundberg, in press, has talked about coalitions, lieutenants, and shadows), little empirical work *in leadership* has confronted these issues directly.

Another approach involves looking systematically at the impact of oral communication on leadership processes and outcomes. Skill in oral communication is measured routinely in some assessment center operations (Bray, Campbell, & Grant, 1974), but it has not received adequate attention as a variable in leadership (except in some small group studies where total talk time has been related to the group's nomination of a leader, e.g., Jaffee & Lucas, 1969). Related to the communication dimension are the cognitive processes whereby individuals in leadership roles somehow retain the information transmitted in oral interactions. Unlike the written word, which automatically creates a record for future reference, the spoken word is easily lost.

More intriguing yet is Mintzberg's notion of proficient superficiality. Plagued by interruptions and activities of short duration, how do leaders synthesize, integrate, and understand the larger picture? Direct observation of behavior can produce a catalog of activities, but it cannot shed much light on the actor's mediation of events. How do all those activities fit together for the leader? One interpretation of the huge number of activities in the manager's day is that each activity represents a different situation. Most current leadership theories would imply that the manager should apply the correct style in each situation and thereby achieve the greatest effectiveness. Another way of looking at the problem is to say that leaders face a near-infinite set of situations and engage in a near-infinite set of behaviors. Many different combinations of behaviors may be effective in a given situation, so there may not be any one best way of responding. If so, the search for invariant truth is an academic exercise and any real understanding of leadership will involve a more holistic approach—one that looks beyond superficial behaviors and simplified taxonomies of situations.

TRAINING AND LEADERSHIP

If our understanding of leadership is less than adequate, then we might predict that training based on that knowledge would produce equivocal research results. Campbell reviewed the empirical literature on training and development and concluded, "In sum, we know a few things but not very much" (1971, p. 593). Stogdill also reviewed the leadership training literature and reached a similarly concise conclusion: "It must be concluded that the research on leadership training is generally inadequate in both design and execution. It has failed to address itself to the most crucial problems of leadership. . . ." (1974, p. 199).

Most leadership training based on the behavioral-science approach to leadership repeats the mistakes of leadership research: (1) It tends to focus quite narrowly on the relationship between the leader and the group, and specifically on the issue of leadership style. (2) It fails to take into account the nature of managerial work—many activities, fragmentation, variety, nonhierarchical relationships, etc. (3) When situational considerations are included in training, they tend to be limited to the situation of the immediate work group (e.g., the task of the group or the nature of the immediate problem).

It may be useful for leaders to develop a knowledge of leadership styles and a sensitivity to their contingent application, but applying such learning on the job is a different matter. Instead of teaching content, leadership training courses might better focus on creating situations reflecting the daily demands of the leadership role, and, through the use of extensive feedback, allow the trainees to study their performances and their impact. While the value of simulations for research and training purposes has been articulated for some time (e.g., Weick, 1965), few *organizational* simulations have been designed and utilized.[5]

One result of the hectic pace of managerial work is that managers seldom have time to reflect on their behavior. On-the-job feedback is likely to be fragmented, badly timed, vague, or even entirely lacking. One valuable outcome of a training experience is that it can provide the time for reflection on the process of being a leader. To maximize this potential, the training must generate behaviors approximating those of the organizational role and must provide valid feedback on what the behaviors were and what their impact was. T-groups are high in generating feedback, but they create a situation with few parallels in the organizational setting. Thus, transfer of learning from the training situation to the job is

[5]One review of the literature turned up only two organizational simulations used for leadership assessment (Omstead, et al., 1973).

difficult (Campbell & Dunnette, 1968). Simulations, too, can only be approximations of reality, but we do know enough about the context of managerial work to create reasonable approximations.

TAKING PROCESS SERIOUSLY

In 1970, Campbell et al. depicted the leadership process as a function of the person, the behavior, the outcomes of behavior, environmental influences, and feedback. Advocacy of a "systems" perspective on organizations and the leadership processes within them is not new (e.g., Katz & Kahn, 1966; Weick, 1969; Rosen, 1970; Rubin & Goldman, 1968), and the current abundance of contingency models of leadership is a sign that researchers are moving more in that direction. Still, a number of current trends in leadership research seem to be holding back progress: (1) attempting to categorize a wide range of leadership behaviors into a few simple categories (e.g., structure and consideration), (2) defining the situation as a few simple categories focused on only the immediate situation (e.g., the task of the group) and the interpersonal relations between leader and led, (3) measuring leadership outcomes solely on the basis of group effectiveness, and (4) emphasizing static rather than dynamic components of the organizational context (i.e., assuming that the situation stays the same over time).

While it is relatively easy to be critical of social science, it is more challenging to offer alternative approaches. Fortunately, there are alternatives for looking at leadership.

First, Mintzberg (1973) has shown that the classification of leaders' behaviors can be extended beyond the two basic styles of structure and consideration. Drawing on his observations of managerial work, he generated ten basic roles which he argued are typical of most managerial jobs. Only one, what he calls "leader," focuses exclusively on the leader-subordinate interaction, while the other nine encompass such activities as monitoring and disseminating information, acting as a figurehead, negotiating, handling disturbances, etc. Mintzberg's work is only a beginning, but breaking the set of leadership styles—and moving toward a more representative sampling of the behaviors involved in leadership —heralds a productive advance in research and training.

Second, the introduction of environmental (as opposed to situational) variables into the leadership context has yielded some interesting results. Pfeffer (in press), for example, has argued that leadership doesn't matter as much as we think it does. Reviewing a number of studies which examined the impact of such things as budgets, economic conditions, changes in top executive positions, and role-set expectations, he found that these and similar factors frequently override the effects of leadership on organizational outcomes.

To date, most leadership theories make the implicit assumption that the leader has a great deal of unilateral control: if the leader only used the appropriate style, the group would be more productive; if the leader understood group processes, the group would be more cohesive, creative, and effective. Understanding how nonleader variables influence such outcomes would help both researchers and leaders by providing a more realistic perspective on just what the leader can and cannot hope to achieve.

Third, the measure of a leader's effectiveness is not and cannot be a simple index of group productivity or satisfaction. While group-level variables are important, there are too many factors mitigating the effects of the leader's behavior on work-group outcomes; and there are many leadership roles for which the "work group" cannot be identified precisely (for example, the role of senator) or for which group output is almost totally determined by some factor such as technology (for

example, on the assembly line). At a minimum, both researchers and practitioners must realize that leadership effectiveness involves a number of areas of functioning—including how well the leader deals with nonsubordinate relationships, how structures are designed and modified, development of human resources in the organization, utilization and dissemination of knowledge, creating and coping with change, and actual task performance by the leader. The point is that simplified criteria are misleading, and breaking the rut of current leadership research will require increasing emphasis on the development of realistic performance measures.

Fourth, in most leadership research (and training) the situation is treated as a given. The technology is this, the climate is that, the task is something else. In reality, these and other components of a system are constantly changing. New machinery, new policies, new people are always entering systems (though the rate of change may vary), and the degree to which organizational components are interdependent is itself a variable (Weick, 1974). Leaders, then, do not simply face a number of different situations, but the situations themselves are changing. Part of the leadership process is clearly the leader's attempt to map the organizational dynamics which influence his or her functioning in the leadership role. Another component is how leaders influence the dynamics of their organizational environments by using, modifying, and implementing structure.

SOME CONCLUDING REMARKS

When managers are told that their work is characterized by brevity, variety, fragmentation, a lot of activities, and oral communication, they frequently respond, "You didn't have to tell us that." But these characteristics of managerial work, coupled with the organizational and environmental context within which the work takes place, suggest some new ways of focusing on leadership processes.

First, it is a mistake for leaders or researchers to assume that "the situation" is composed of a small number of fixed parts. The organization, and its environment, are dynamic. An act of Congress, a new invention, or a new corporate president may change all existing cause and effect relationships overnight. Effective leadership behavior must involve flexibility in thinking about the givens of organizational life. Fire-fighting is the bane of many a manager's existence, but the ability of a leader to negotiate successfully through a constant barrage of changes and incongruities is an important component of the leadership process.

Second, it is a mistake to assume that a leadership role, even with its trappings of authority, implies unilateral control by the leader. Organizational rewards and structures, as well as external forces, limit both the leader's and the group's flexibility. Another important component of leadership, then, is how the role occupants create, modify, work around, or ignore the structures imposed on them and their followers. Kerr (1975) has provided numerous examples of how organizations (and the leaders in them) hope for one behavior and get another by inadvertently rewarding the wrong things. DeVries (in press) has shown that relatively simple structures used by a teacher can facilitate classroom learning. These two examples indicate that leaders can succeed not just because of personal charisma or social influence, but because of a sensitivity to, and awareness of, organizational structures and reward systems.

Third, much of human learning is dependent on the receipt of valid and timely feedback on the results of behavior. With all its variety and fragmentation, managerial work provides inadequate feedback—and sometimes none at all. Occupants of leadership roles carry a double burden because they must not only assure themselves of adequate feedback, but also must facilitate feedback to their subordinates (and to other units or individuals working with the unit). Since much of managerial communication is oral, the job of obtaining and transmitting feedback requires substantial effort. No individual in a leadership role can hope to take full responsibility for providing feedback for all who need it. While the personal element cannot be ignored, the leader's use of structural (e.g., designing tasks to provide feedback or *using* an appraisal system to generate valid data) and reward (e.g., basing part of promotion or salary on feedback generation) systems may be a critical component.

Fourth, political activity—in the sense of developing and maintaining a network of contacts throughout the organization and its environment (Mintzberg, 1973)—is a real part of managerial work. Research has not revealed much about how these networks are created and utilized, but most people in leadership roles know how important contacts can be. Many of the contacts are in nonauthority relationships with the leader, and this may be the arena where the critical social and political influence aspects of leadership are played out (Pettigrew, 1973). Certainly, leadership research and theory should begin including this dimension, and practitioners might look at some of their problems in "getting things done" in light of their own interconnectedness with key people in the organization.

The four areas outlined above by no means cover all of the possibilities for expanding thinking about leadership processes. They do reflect some areas which have received insufficient attention in leadership research and training. In sum, the focus on leader-group interactions has yielded some useful information, but much remains to be learned about the leadership processes going on outside of the immediate work setting. By learning more about what leaders actually do, researchers can expose themselves to numerous activities not considered by most traditional approaches to the topic. It is in the day-to-day activities of leaders that the situational-organizational context of leadership is sharply reflected.

Peter Vaill (in press) has defined an art as "the attempt to wrest more coherence and meaning out of more reality than we ordinarily try to deal with." In this context, he has described management as a performing art (1974). The analogy of leaders as artists is potent because effective leaders orchestrate a complex series of processes, events, and systems. Understanding bits and pieces—using a stop-frame on Nureyev—can never capture the whole. Perhaps neither researchers nor practitioners will ever understand the particular magic that makes the legends of leadership. To the extent that constant practice makes the artist more than he or she might have been, expanding our knowledge of the complex processes involved in leadership may, one day, provide part of that magic formula for success.

REFERENCES

Ackoff, R. L. Management misinformation systems. *Management Science*, 1967, **14**, B147–B156.

Bennis, W. G. Leadership theory and administrative behavior: The problem of authority. *Administrative Science Quarterly*, 1959, **4**, 259–301.

Blake, R. R., & Mouton, J. S. *The managerial grid*. Houston: Gulf, 1964.

Bray, D. W., Campbell, R. J., & Grant, D. L. *Formative years in business*. New York: Wiley, 1974.

Brewer, E., & Tomlinson, J. W. C. The manager's working day. *The Journal of Industrial Economics*, 1963–64, **12**, 191–197.

Burns, T. The directions of activity and communication in a departmental executive group. *Human Relations*, 1954, **7**, 73–97.

Campbell, J. P. Personnel training and development. In P. Mussen & M. Rosenzweig. *Annual Review of Psychology* (Vol. 22). Palo Alto: Annual Reviews, Inc., 1971, 565–602.

Campbell, J. P., & Dunnette, M. D. Effectiveness of T-group experiences in managerial training and development. *Psychological Bulletin*, 1968, **70**, 73–104.

Campbell, J. P., Dunnette, M. D., Lawler, E. E., III, & Weick, K. E., Jr. *Managerial behavior, performance, and effectiveness*. New York: McGraw-Hill, 1970.

Carlson, S. *Executive behavior*. Stockholm: Strombergs, 1951.

Cyert, R. M., & March, J. G. *A behavioral theory of the firm*. Englewood Cliffs, N.J.: Prentice-Hall, 1963.

DeVries, D. L. Teams-games-tournament. *Simulation and Games*, in press.

Dubin, R. Business behavior behaviorally viewed. In G. B. Strother (Ed.), *Social science approaches to business behavior*. Homewood, Ill.: Dorsey Press, 1962.

Dubin, R., & Spray, S. L. Executive behavior and interaction. *Industrial Relations*, 1964, **3**(2), 99–108.

Evans, M. The effects of supervisory behavior on the path-goal relationship. *Organizational Behavior and Human Performance*, 1970, **5**, 277–298.

Farris, G. F., & Lim, F., Jr. Effects of performance on leadership, cohesiveness, influence, satisfaction, and subsequent performance. *Journal of Applied Psychology*, 1969, **53**, 490–497.

Fiedler, F. E. *A theory of leadership effectiveness*. New York: McGraw-Hill, 1967.

Gibb, C. A. Leadership. In G. Lindzey & E. Aronson (Eds.), *The handbook of social psychology* (Vol. 4, 2nd ed.). Reading, Mass.: Addison-Wesley, 1969.

Greene, C. N. The reciprocal nature of influence between leader and subordinate. *Journal of Applied Psychology*, 1975, **60**, 187–193.

Guest, R. H. Of time and the foreman. *Personnel*, 1955–1956, **32**, 478–486.

Hill, W. Leadership style: Rigid or flexible. *Organizational Behavior and Human Performance*, 1973, **9**, 35–47.

Hill, W. A., & Hughes, D. Variations in leader behavior as a function of task type. *Organizational Behavior and Human Performance*, 1974, **11**, 83–86.

Horne, J. H., & Lupton, T. The work activities of

"middle" managers—an exploratory study. *The Journal of Management Studies*, 1965, **2**(1), 14–33.

House, R. J. A path goal theory of leader effectiveness. *Administrative Science Quarterly,* 1971, **16,** 321–338.

Jaffee, C. L., & Lucas, R. L. Effects of rates of talking and correctness of decisions and on leader choice in small groups. *Journal of Social Psychology*, 1969, **79,** 247–254.

Katz, D., & Kahn, R. L. *The social psychology of organizations*. New York: Wiley, 1966.

Kerr, S. On the folly of rewarding A, while hoping for B. *Academy of Management Journal*, **18,** 1975, 769–783.

Korman, A. K. Contingency approaches to leadership: An overview. In J. G. Hunt & L. L. Larson (Eds.), *Contingency approaches to leadership*. Carbondale, Ill.: Southern Illinois University Press, 1974.

Larson, L. L., Hunt, J. G., & Osborn, R. N. The great hi-hi leader behavior myth: A lesson from Occam's razor. In A. G. Bedeian et al. (Eds.), *Proceedings of the annual meeting of the Academy of Management*. Academy of Management, 1975.

Lowin, A., & Craig, J. R. The influence of level of performance on managerial style: An experimental object-lesson in the ambiguity of correlational data. *Organizational Behavior and Human Performance*, 1968, **3,** 440–458.

Lundberg, C. The unreported research of Dr. Hypothetical: Six variables in need of recognition. In M. W. McCall, Jr., & M. M. Lombardo (Eds.), *Leadership: Where else can we go?*, in press.

March, J. G., & Simon, H. A. *Organizations*. New York: Wiley, 1958.

McCall, M. W., Jr. The perceived cognitive role requirements of formal leaders. In N. A. Rosen (Chair.), *Some neglected aspects of research on leadership in formal organizations*. Symposium presented at the meeting of the American Psychological Association Convention, New Orleans, August 1974.

Miner, J. B. *The uncertain future of the leadership concept: An overview*. Paper presented at the Southern Illinois Leadership Conference, Carbondale, Ill., 1975.

Mintzberg, H. *The nature of managerial work*. New York: Harper & Row, 1973.

Mintzberg, H. The manager's job: Folklore and fact. *Harvard Business Review*, 1975, **53**(4), 49–61.

Omstead, J. A., et al. *Development of leadership assessment simulations* (HumRRO Tech. Rep. 73-21). Arlington, Va.: Human Resources Research Organization, September 1973.

Pettigrew, A. M. *The politics of organizational decision-making*. London: Tavistock, 1973.

Pfeffer, J. The ambiguity of leadership. In M. W. McCall Jr., & M. M. Lombardo (Eds.), *Leadership: Where else can we go?*, in press.

Rosen, N. A. *Leadership change and work-group dynamics*. London: Staples Press, 1970.

Rubin, I. M., & Goldman, M. An open system model of leadership performance. *Organizational Behavior and Human Performance*, 1968, **3,** 143–156.

Sayles, L. *Managerial behavior: Administration in complex organizations*. New York: McGraw-Hill, 1964.

Stogdill, R. M. *Handbook of leadership*. New York: Free Press, 1974.

Vaill, P. B. *On the general theory of management*. Presented at the Washington, D.C., chapter of the Society for Humanistic Management, November 19, 1974.

Vaill, P. B. Towards a behavioral description of high-performing systems. In M. W. McCall, Jr. & M. M. Lombardo (Eds.), *Leadership: Where else can we go?*, in press.

Vroom, V. H., & Yetton, P. W. *Leadership and decision making*. Pittsburgh: Univ. of Pittsburgh Press, 1973.

Weick, K. E. Laboratory experimentation with organizations. In J. G. March (Ed.), *Handbook of organizations*. Chicago: Rand McNally, 1965, 194–260.

Weick, K. E. *The social psychology of organizing*. Reading, Mass.: Addison-Wesley, 1969.

Weick, K. E. Middle range theories of social systems. *Behavioral Science*, 1974, **19,** 357–367.

Reading 33

A Symposium on Leadership: Introduction

Lyman W. Porter

Leadership—an eternally fascinating subject for both businessmen and academics—receives three contrasting treatments in the articles that follow. Each piece is authored by a distinguished contributor to the literature not only on leadership but on the whole field of organizational behavior. While all three are academic psychologists, the reader will see that there is considerable diversity in the way each writer deals with the subject of leadership. This diversity reflects the contrasting interests and styles of the three, which in turn has led in recent years to their undertaking quite different types of research programs in the leadership area.

Perhaps the most useful way of introducing the three approaches to leadership represented in this symposium is to ask a series of questions that are relevant to all the articles. The answers will highlight the ways in which they agree—and disagree.*

1 Are the Three Authors Addressing the Same Leadership Issues?

Only in the broadest sense could we say that Argyris, Fiedler, and Vroom deal with similar leadership issues. All are concerned with how the quality of leadership can be improved in organizational settings. Beyond that, the authors diverge both in the ways they define

*The comments on the three approaches to leadership covered in the following articles represent the opinions of the author of the introduction. They do not necessarily agree with the way in which Argyris, Fiedler, and Vroom would each characterize his own approach and theory.

leadership and in the ways in which they think an overall improvement in organizational leadership can be accomplished. Nevertheless, as we will see, there is often agreement between Vroom and Fiedler. First, however, we can try to summarize briefly what seem to be the issues that are of most concern to each author:

Argyris focuses on the learning or "re-education" of managers to move from one set of behavior strategies (which he terms Model I) to a different and, he presumes, clearly better (for both the leader and the organization) set of behaviors (termed Model II). Argyris wants to break away from an approach that analyzes existing patterns of "good" and "bad" leadership and instead attempt to help managers learn what is *possible* by way of effective leadership, even though it is currently seldom seen in practice. The emphasis is on how the manager or prospective leader can be aided in developing *skills* that enable him to move from his current modus of operating to a new and "better" way.

Fiedler focuses on the effective diagnosis of the *situation* in which the leader will operate. Thus the emphasis is on understanding the nature of the situation and how it will simultaneously provide assistance to the leader and make demands on him. The implication, as Fiedler makes clear, is that if the situation can be correctly diagnosed, then the *matching* of leader to situation can be improved, which in turn will result in effective leadership. Such matching involves either assigning the leader

The papers by Porter, Fiedler, Vroom, and Argyris (Readings 33, 34, 35, and 36) were originally presented at the 1975 annual meeting of the American Psychological Association, and subsequently were published in *Organizational Dynamics*, Winter 1976, 2–43. They are reprinted by permission of the publisher. Copyright © 1976 by AMACOM, a division of American Management Associations.

to the situation appropriate to his basic personality or altering the situation to fit the leader.

In this approach, if anything has to be changed it is primarily the situation rather than the leader. Leadership training, for Fiedler, becomes something that varies with the individual and that helps him analyze and change the situation rather than himself.

Vroom focuses on the development of a normative or prescriptive decision-making model for leaders, but one that is limited to a single type of leadership decision: the extent to which the leader should encourage subordinates to participate in decision making and hence the degree to which the leader should share his decision-making power. In this sense, Vroom deals with only one aspect of the broader topic of leadership. He assumes that individuals are already in leadership-type positions and that the one type of decision they constantly face is the question of how much subordinate participation is required for an effective decision. His research focuses on both the development of the model and on how leaders can be trained to understand the model and its implications so that they can see how their natural tendencies toward using participation compare with what the model prescribes as the ideal. The leader, in effect, is given a mirror to see how his own decision-making practices stack up against an ideal image.

2   Is Effective Leadership Contingent upon the Nature of the Situation?

Clearly, Fiedler would answer "yes." As we pointed out, he explicitly advocates different types of training for different potential leaders because in his view research shows that no single kind of leadership approach is effective across a wide spectrum of situations. To give the same training to everyone may help some individuals but may actually cause others to become less effective leaders. Vroom would also answer "yes" to this question. His model explicitly takes into account a number of situational variables that must be considered (in proper sequence) by a leader in deciding whether or not to employ participation in a specific decision. Thus in some situations the use of participation would be the "correct" answer (according to the model), while in other situations unilateral action on the part of the leader would be the prescribed solution.

Argyris, by contrast, seems to advocate a set of behavioral strategies for the leader (that is, Model II) that would be good in *all* situations. Because Argyris is talking about a general process of dealing with organizational situations, he would appear to reply "no" to the question—that is, the Model II strategy is valid regardless of the situation.

3   Can Leaders Learn to Behave Differently?

Vroom clearly says "yes," at least as the question concerns the issue of whether leaders should involve subordinates in decision making. If managers or leaders learn to understand his model and have a chance to see how their typical approach compares with the model's prescriptions, then they can (if they are so motivated) learn to make a larger percentage of correct decisions in this area. Argyris's paper also indicates a positive answer, but in his description of his approach to helping managers learn to move from "Model I" to "Model II," he makes it clear that such learning is a very difficult, time-consuming, and anxiety-arousing process. Fiedler, by and large, seems pessimistic on this score. While leaders can learn to improve their diagnosis of organizational situations, Fiedler is not sanguine as to the prospects of leaders' being able to make any fundamental changes in their customary or personally comfortable ways of handling leadership situations.

4   Do Leaders Need Help in Skill Development?

All three authors would agree, in one way or another, that they do. For Argyris, this is the heart of his approach. He feels that good intentions and motivation are not enough; managers need professional assistance—and lots of it—to move to a better model. Vroom, likewise, appears to feel that managers need training and help in understanding and applying his normative decision-making model. Fiedler would agree that they need help, but only of a particular type: namely, achieving better diagnoses of organizational situations.

5 What Are the Criteria for Measuring Effective Leadership?

Fiedler has always been very clear about this, from the perspective of the kinds of leadership issues that interest him. He advocates using so-called "hard" criteria: for example, number of problems solved, number of games won, production records, and the like. His "contingency model" grew out of numerous analyses comparing various combinations of leader personality dispositions and situational characteristics with the performance of the leader's group.

Vroom developed his model of how leaders "ought" to make decisions on the basis of research of many investigators who used various types of criteria for effective decisions. And he is in the process of validating the model by asking managers to compare successful and unsuccessful decisions they made in the past with the method of decision making advocated by the model. In general, Vroom also would appear to advocate the use of "hard" criteria to determine whether actual decisions turned out to be good or poor decisions.

Argyris, as previously discussed, puts much more stress on developing a leadership process that he feels is desirable but that is currently being used only in rare instances. He is not interested in comparing current practices on some existing "hard" (or "soft"—that is, impressionistic) criteria. He assumes that there is an inherently better way to carry out a leadership role, but that we will never arrive at

it by dividing present leaders into better and worse categories on any existing criterion or set of criteria and then finding out what characterizes those leaders who perform better with respect to that criterion or criteria.

6 What Are the Costs in Using Each Approach to Improve Leaders' Effectiveness?

Vroom's approach is relatively low-cost for the purpose intended—that is, for the purpose of training individuals to compare their decision-making style with the normative solutions based on a careful situational analysis.

Fiedler's approach involves relatively low costs in relation to training leaders to make situational diagnoses, but the really critical (and unanswered) question is: What are the costs of training leaders to *implement* or put into effect what they have learned from their diagnosis? Understanding a situation is usually a prerequisite for good performance, but surely does not guarantee it.

As Argyris's article makes clear, his approach involves relatively high costs. He illustrates this concretely by describing how much time (over three years) and effort have been involved in helping just six presidents move partway from Model I to Model II. Of course, it can be argued that future costs can be reduced considerably as the researchers (and those helping managers change their behavioral strategies) gain more experience with the process.

7 What Are the Benefits Obtained from Using Each Approach?

This, of course, is a difficult question. To answer it comprehensively would require considerably more space than is available and would get us into some issues not easily resolved. However, as a first approximation of an answer, several things seem reasonably clear: With Argyris's approach, the costs appear to be high. However, the task that he is undertaking is also extremely challenging.

Thus the potential benefits, if numbers of individuals can actually learn to move from Model I to Model II, also seem significant. At the least, we can say that the six executives mentioned in his article learned (finally) something that was not superficial, something that appeared to be deeply ingrained and changed the way in which they approached the entire fabric of their relationships with others within their organizations.

Fiedler's approach seems potentially applicable to an analysis of all kinds of leadership situations. Thus, if he is on the right track first in identifying the crucial situational variables and second in his judgment about the relative lack of malleability of the adult personality, then he provides an approach that should be useful to some degree regardless of the type of organizational setting.

Vroom's approach deals with a more limited aspect of leadership. However, to the extent that having subordinates participate in decisions is a key aspect of any managerial job, he offers a kind of approach that can add to the leader's repertoire of responses in dealing effectively with such situations.

In conclusion, all three articles address themselves to a topic of continuing importance to both individuals and organizations. The articles give some of the best available thinking on the subject of leadership, and they indicate what kinds of progress have been made in learning more about it and, particularly, how such knowledge can be put into practice. Just as there will never be *the* definitive investigation of leadership, there will never be *the* definitive article on it. The present articles, however, represent progress in research and point the way toward some possibly exciting advances in the future.

Reading 34

The Leadership Game: Matching the Man to the Situation

Fred E. Fiedler

Most people in management would agree that leadership training accomplishes something. Whether it always does what it is intended to do is another question. Most of us know someone whose behavior changed or whose performance improved after he went through a leadership training program. Unfortunately, most of us also know about as many people who have gone through one training program after another and still perform as poorly as ever. Even more intriguing are the many outstanding leaders who have had little or no leadership training at all—Joan of Arc being a stellar example.

Empirical studies of leadership training generally reveal the same disappointing results. On the average, people with much training perform about as well as people with little or no training, and reviews by Stogdill; Campbell, Dunnette, Lawler, and Weick; and others present no evidence that any particular leadership training method consistently improves organizational performance.

Research by my associates and me has revealed the same disappointing results. When we compared a group of Belgian navy recruits and a well-trained and experienced group of petty officers, for example, we found no over-

Reprinted from *Organizational Dynamics*, Winter 1976, 6–16, with permission of the publisher. Copyright © 1976 by AMACOM, a division of American Management Associations.

all differences in leadership performance. In a follow-up study in Canada, basic trainees performed their leadership tasks as well as captains and majors who had graduated from military college. These experimental studies are supported by results from field research. Nealey and I found no relationship between amount of training and performance of post office managers as rated by their immediate superiors. In addition, I found zero correlations between amount of training and performance of police patrol sergeants. Recent studies show similar findings for officers and noncommissioned officers of an American infantry division.

This does not necessarily mean that leadership training need be ineffective. Quite the contrary. Our data suggest that leadership training, under certain conditions, systematically improves the performance of some leaders while it decreases the performance of others. Obviously, we have to understand the conditions under which leadership training is effective if we are to make much progress in this area.

While recognizing the legitimacy of leadership training designed to improve job satisfaction and to enhance personal growth, I want to confine my remarks here to training that aims to improve task performance as it is defined by an organization.

First, let me briefly comment on present training approaches. Then I will propose a preliminary theory of leadership training as well as present some data that support this formulation. Last, I will describe the training program that we have developed on the basis of this theory and that we are currently validating.

CURRENT PRACTICES BASED ON QUESTIONABLE ASSUMPTIONS

Let us first look at present practices and, in particular, their underlying assumptions. One assumption that guides many training programs is the notion that there is one ideal kind of leadership behavior or attitude that is related to good performance under all conditions and that every trainee therefore needs to adopt. For example, several prominent authorities contend that a good leader has to be permissive, participative, or human-relations-oriented.

If we take a close look at the empirical results, however, it is obvious that neither the permissive, considerate leaders nor the autocratic, directive leaders obtain optimum performance under all conditions. Yet any training program that seeks to develop the same kind of leadership behavior or attitude implicitly assumes that there is one best leadership style.

A second major assumption in many programs is that leadership behavior is under voluntary control, that a few weeks of telling a leader how to behave or convincing him that a certain kind of behavior is best will result in the appropriate behavior changes.

This ignores the fact that leadership situations are highly emotion-charged, interpersonal relationships that mean a great deal to the subordinate as well as to his boss. We probably expect more change in interpersonal behavior than a routine training program can hope to deliver. The manner in which we relate to authority figures and subordinates is for most of us a very important interaction that we learn over many years. And it is very difficult indeed to change such significant emotional relationships. It is essential, therefore, that we ask just how much control the typical leader actually has over his own behavior.

Our studies suggest that a leader can voluntarily change his leadership behavior only in situations in which he has a great deal of control. In situations in which a leader is under pressure, in which there is considerable uncertainty and insecurity, leadership behavior seems to depend on the way the individual's personality interacts with his leadership situation. A didactic approach—telling a leader to be more considerate, permissive, or decisive—is about as effective as telling someone that he should be more lovable or less anxious.

A third assumption is that the more powerful and influential leader will be more effective because he will be able to make his group work harder on the organization's tasks. On the basis of this assumption, many training programs try to increase a leader's control and influence in various ways. They give him human-relations training so that he can make himself more acceptable to his subordinates. This supposedly will enable him to motivate his subordinates to work harder. These programs may give a leader technical training so that he can increase his expertise. They teach him the intricacies of an organization so that he can make full use of his legitimate power, knowing where power lies within the organization as well as knowing what rewards and punishments the organization has to offer.

This approach ignores the fact that the leadership situation is an arena in which a leader must satisfy his own needs as well as the needs of his organization. Where a leader's and an organization's needs are incompatible, the leader's needs are apt to take precedence. At the very least, they are likely to interfere with satisfying the needs of the organization.

An equally questionable assumption is at the basis of participative management training, which holds that a leader who shares his decision-making functions with his subordinates will therefore be more effective. As Jon Blades has recently shown, the effectiveness of participative management depends in large part on the intelligence and ability of the group members. The leader who listens to the advice of unintelligent people can hardly expect brilliant answers.

Let me stress again, however, that training in participative management or in any other kind of leadership approach is not necessarily bad practice, nor will it be ineffective for all trainees. Rather, we need to be more discriminating about whom we train and the situation for which we attempt to train a particular leader. Most leadership training programs fail to do this because they give all trainees the same training, despite the fact that practically all of the empirical evidence tells us that the performance of a group depends in part on the kind of task and the situation in which the leader has to operate.

Where do we go from here?

THE CONTINGENCY APPROACH TO LEADERSHIP TRAINING

My position on training, not surprisingly, is based on the contingency model of leadership effectiveness. In essence, this theory holds that the effectiveness of a group or an organization depends on the interaction between the leader's personality and the situation. Specifically, we have to match the leader's motivational structure (that is, the goals to which he gives the highest priority) with the degree to which the situation gives the leader control and influence over the outcomes of his decisions.

We measure the leader's motivation by the *Least Preferred Co-worker Scale* (LPC). This scale asks the individual first to think of everyone with whom he has ever worked, and then to describe the one person with whom he could work *least* well. This can be someone with whom he worked years ago or someone with whom he works at the moment. (See Figure 34-1 for the scale of opposing attributes used to describe the least preferred co-worker.)

An individual who describes his or her least preferred co-worker in very negative and rejecting terms (a low LPC) in effect shows a strong emotional reaction to people with whom he or she cannot work—in effect, *"If I can't work with you, you are no damn good!"*

Think of the person with whom you can work least well. He may be someone you work with now, or someone you knew in the past. He does not have to be the person you like least well, but should be the person with whom you had the most difficulty in getting a job done. Describe this person as he appears to you.

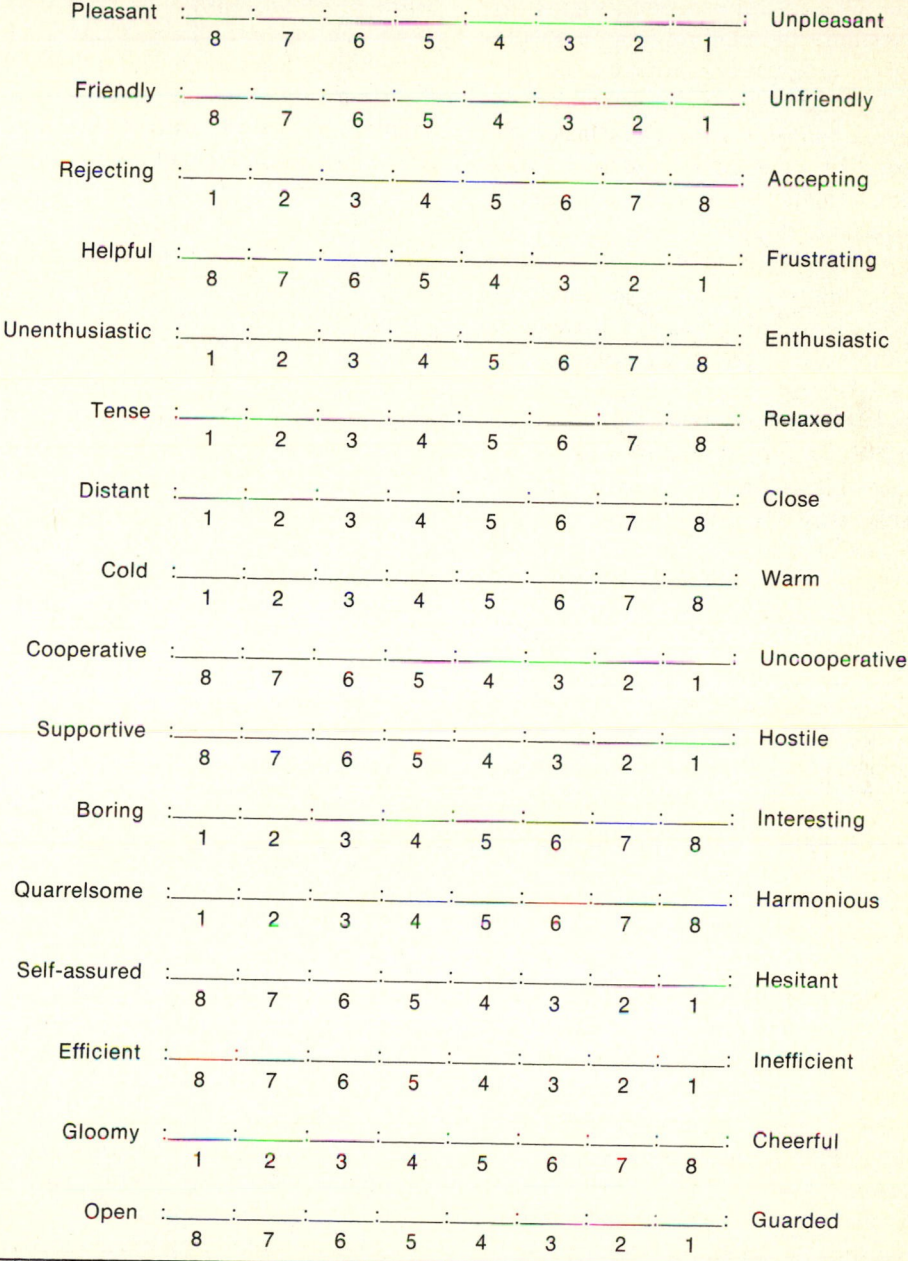

Figure 34-1 Least preferred co-worker scale.

This is the typical pattern of a person who, when forced to make the choice, opts first for getting on with the task and worries about his interpersonal relations later.

Someone who describes even his least preferred co-worker in relatively more positive terms in effect looks at the individual not only as a co-worker but also as a person who might otherwise have some acceptable, if not admirable, traits. The "high LPC" leader sees close interpersonal relations as a requirement for task accomplishment.

Let me, however, strongly emphasize that we are here talking about different priorities of goals. We are not speaking about leader behaviors. The accomplishment of the task might well call for very considerate and pleasant interpersonal behaviors, while the maintenance of close interpersonal relations might be possible only by driving the group to success. In this latter case the relationship-motivated, high LPC leader might be quite single-minded about accomplishing the task. In general we find that uncertain and anxiety-arousing conditions tend to make the low LPC leaders concentrate on the task, while the high LPC leaders concentrate on their relations with their subordinates. The opposite is the case in situations in which the leader is secure and in control.

The other major factor in this theory is defined by the "situational favorableness" that basically indicates the degree to which the leader has control and influence and, therefore, feels that he can determine the outcomes of the group interaction. We generally measure situational favorableness on the basis of three subscales: leader-member relations, task structure, and position power. The leader has more control and influence if (1) his members support him, (2) he knows exactly what to do and how to do it, and (3) the organization gives him the means to reward and punish his subordinates.

The crucial question then is to determine the specific situations under which various types of leaders perform best. The contingency model has consistently shown that the task-motivated (low LPC) leaders tend to perform most effectively in situations in which their control and influence are very high and in situations in which it is relatively low. By contrast, relationship-motivated (high LPC) leaders tend to perform best in situations in which their control and influence is moderate.

Validating the Model

This relationship has now been found in well over 50 different studies; in fact, a carefully controlled experiment by Chemers and Skrzypek showed that the contingency model accounted for 28 percent of the variance in task performance. The model is most easily described by the schematic drawing in Figure 34-2. The vertical axis shows the group's or the organization's performance. The horizontal axis indicates "situational favorableness" —that is, the degree to which the situation provides the leader with control and influence. The solid line shows the performance of high LPC leaders, and the broken line the performance of low LPC leaders. As can be seen, the high LPC, or relationship-motivated, leaders generally perform best in situations in which their relations with subordinates are good but task structure and position power are low. They also perform well when their relations with subordinates are poor but task structure and position power are high (both situations of moderate favorableness as defined in Figure 34-2). Task-motivated leaders perform best when all three factors that define their control and influence are either high or low.

It should be clear from Figure 34-2 that we can improve group performance either by changing the leader's motivational structure —that is, the basic goals he pursues in life— or else by modifying his leadership situation. While it is possible, of course, to change

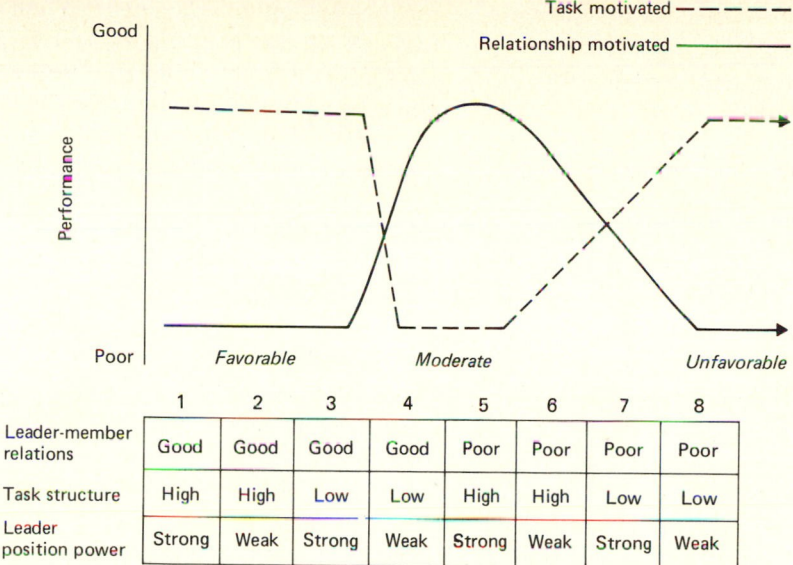

Figure 34-2 Schematic representation of the performance of relationship- and task-motivated leaders in different situational favorableness conditions.

	1	2	3	4	5	6	7	8
Leader-member relations	Good	Good	Good	Good	Poor	Poor	Poor	Poor
Task structure	High	High	Low	Low	High	High	Low	Low
Leader position power	Strong	Weak	Strong	Weak	Strong	Weak	Strong	Weak

personality and the motivational structure that is a part of personality, this is clearly a difficult and uncertain process. It is, however, relatively easy to modify the leadership situation. We can select a person for certain kinds of jobs and not others, we can assign him certain tasks, give him more or less responsibility, or we can give him leadership training in order to increase his power and influence.

As we said before, most leadership training seeks to increase the favorableness of a situation—that is, it increases the leader's control and influence. It follows that leaders who, for example, start off in an unfavorable situation will gradually move into a zone of moderate situational favorableness. Such a change in control and influence would also change leadership performance: The task-motivated leader who performs well in the unfavorable zone will perform less well with training, while the relationship-motivated leader should improve with training as he moves from the unfavorable to the moderately

favorable zone, toward the left of the graph. Training should, therefore, decrease performance of some leaders but increase it for others.

This was recently demonstrated by a laboratory experiment conducted by Chemers, Rice, Sundstrom, and Butler at the University of Utah. These researchers assembled four-man groups composed of ROTC and psychology students, with an ROTC cadet as the leader. Half the leaders were high and half were low LPC persons. Half were assigned at random to receive training, while the others were given an assignment unrelated to the task.

The group task consisted of deciphering a series of cryptograms. Training consisted of teaching leaders such rules as counting all the alphabet letters and then assuming that the most frequent letter would be an *e*. A three-letter word with an *e* at the end would be *the*. The only one-letter words in English are *a* and *I*, and so on. As it happened in that particular study, the groups had very poor leader-member relations, low position power, and an unstructured task if the leaders were untrained—thus an unfavorable situation.

We would therefore expect that the task-motivated leaders would perform better than would relationship-motivated ones. With training, the task would become structured and the situation would become moderately favorable. The relationship-motivated, high LPC leaders should then perform relatively better than would task-motivated, low LPC leaders.

Figure 34-3 shows the results of this study. As expected, the low LPC leaders performed better than did high LPC leaders in the unfavorable situation, while high LPC leaders performed better in the moderately favorable situation. However, as the theory predicts but we would not normally expect, the low LPC leaders with training also performed less well than did the low LPC leaders who had not received training.

Similar findings have been reported in real-life situations. For example, we conducted a study of 32 consumer cooperative companies in which we obtained objective measures of performance on all companies in the federation. When we then divided the general managers into those with high and those with low LPC scores, as well as those with relatively little experience and training and those with relatively high experience and concomitant training, we obtained Figure 34-4. Evaluations from several judges indicated that the experienced and trained general manager had a favorable leadership situation. A relatively inexperienced and untrained manager would have correspondingly less control and influence, hence a situation that would be only moderately favorable.

As Figure 34-4 shows, the task-motivated leaders with experience and training performed better than did relationship-motivated leaders. However, the relationship-motivated general managers with relatively less experience and training performed better than did the more highly experienced and trained general managers who were relationship-motivated. Several other studies give similar results.

The question usually arises as to whether the leader could change his motivational structure or his behavior to suit the situation. I would not want to preclude this possibility, but I also really do not think that this is done very easily. As we said before, leadership is a very ego-involving relationship, and in such relationships it is very difficult to control our behavior. It is certainly much more emotionally charged than, say, the interaction between a salesman and a customer or a lawyer and his client. We are talking about patterns of interaction that are fairly central to our personality. The degree to which a person is affected by his relations with others, or the degree to which he is driven to get a job done, is not very easily changed from one day to the next. I don't really think that you can make someone who is cold and businesslike into a warm, cuddly leader in the course of a few hours or even days. Chris Argyris's account of these difficulties documents this point all too well.

A NEW APPROACH TO TRAINING

Let me now get to the point of this symposium. What kind of training would the contin-

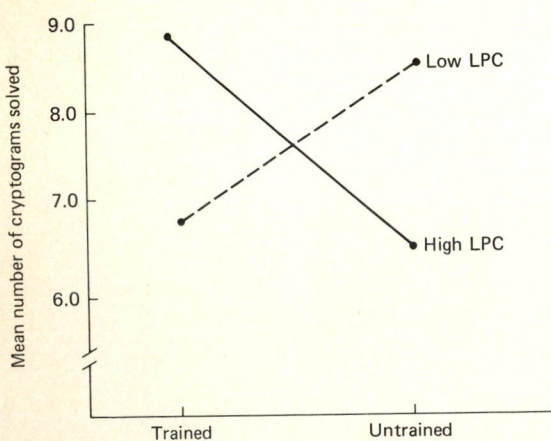

Figure 34-3 Interaction of training and LPC on group productivity.

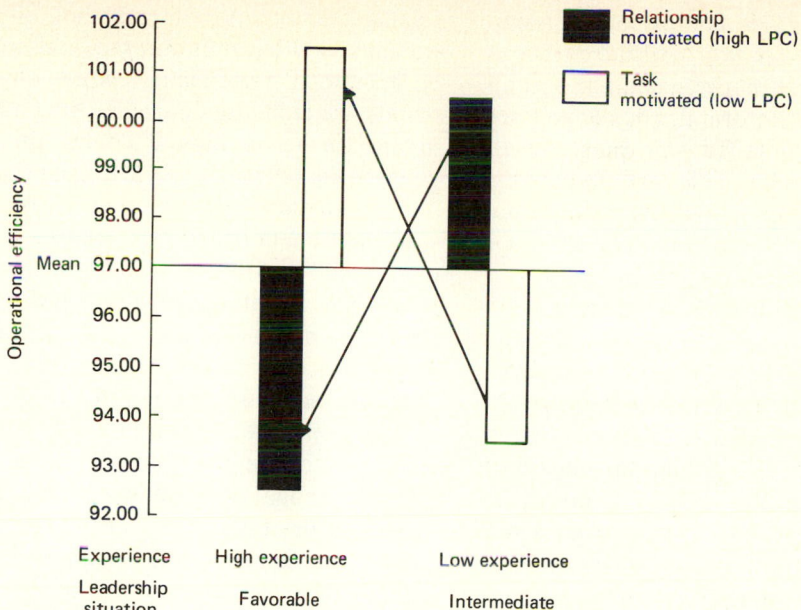

Figure 34-4 The presumed change in performance of relationship- and task-motivated company managers as a function of increased experience.

gency model call for? We have tended to look at people as infinitely malleable, as infinitely capable of changing their behavior and of being changed by just a few hours of training even though the behavior we are trying to change may have been acquired over a whole lifetime. In contrast, we have tended to look at the organization as relatively inflexible and rigid. Most people see themselves as having very little control over their work situation. This is clearly not true. We have to teach people that they have much more control over the relevant aspects of their own leadership jobs than they generally realize. We have to teach them, therefore, that they can change the situation so that it will better match their personality.

The research on the contingency model shows that effective leadership depends on maintaining the right match of personality and of situation. We can certainly teach people how to recognize the particular situations in which they are likely to succeed and those in which they are likely to be less effective. And we can tell them, "If you avoid jobs in which

you are likely to fail, you are bound to be a success."

We now have reason to believe that we can teach people with reasonable accuracy to assess the degree to which their subordinates and their superiors are supportive, the degree to which a task is structured, and the degree to which they have position power.

The next step is to give trainees guidance in seeking or developing leadership situations in which they are most likely to be successful, or to modify their situations to match their personalities. We can also train them in ways to provide their subordinate leaders with conditions that match their motivational patterns.

Successful leaders do this intuitively. They may say about a person that "You have to give him a lot of backing if you want him to be effective." For one person, they may spell out in detail what to do and how to do it; for another, they may just explain what the problem is and then let him run with the ball.

We may not be able to change the warmth and emotional closeness of our relations with others. However, we can frequently modify our accessibility to subordinates, the degree to which we share information, and the extent to which contacts with subordinates are formal and businesslike or informal, social, and relaxed. We can give detailed, step-by-step task instructions or general policies and guidelines. We can use our position power under some conditions and share decision making under others.

Martin Chemers, Linda Mahar, and I have developed a self-administered programmed manual for leadership training called *Leader Match* that attempts to teach managers how to diagnose their leadership situation, how to determine the kind of situation that best matches their personality or motivational pattern, and how to modify the situation so that it does match their leadership style. One validation study has now been successfully completed, using second-level leaders of a volunteer public health organization that operates in Latin America. Another one involves middle managers of a government agency. In these studies the leaders who were trained with *Leader Match* performed significantly better than did leaders in a comparable, randomly selected control group. At the time of this writing, a third validation study also seems to be producing significant results. These early results are highly encouraging, and we hope to obtain further evidence during this coming year.

In summary, my own position is that we must train people differentially—not everyone should be trained to behave in the same way or to adopt the same attitudes. In fact, we will be better served by training our leaders in how to change their leadership situations than in how to change their personality. Leadership effectiveness depends on the proper match of person and situation, and trying to change personality is the hard way of achieving this balance. It is an effort with uncertain success that requires years, not weeks. Our recent studies of contingency model training show that leaders can recognize the situations in which they tend to be most successful, and they can modify their situations so that they perform more effectively. We have reason to believe that this approach holds considerable promise for the future of leadership training.

Reading 35
Can Leaders Learn to Lead?
Victor H. Vroom

Like my fellow authors, I start with certain preconceptions. These preconceptions—some may call them biases—influence the way in which I view issues of leadership, particularly leadership in training. I have tried to depict these preconceptions in Figure 35-1.

The central variable in this figure is the behavior of the leader, which I believe is determined by two classes of variables, attributes of the leader himself and attributes of the situation he encounters. Furthermore, I assume that many of the differences in the behavior of leaders can be explained only by examining their joint effects, including interactions between these two classes of variables.

The left-hand portion of the diagram is the descriptive side of the leader behavior equation. Much of my research has focused on these relationships in an attempt to under-

Reprinted from *Organizational Dynamics*, Winter 1976, 17–28, with permission of the publisher. Copyright © 1976 by AMACOM, a division of American Management Associations.

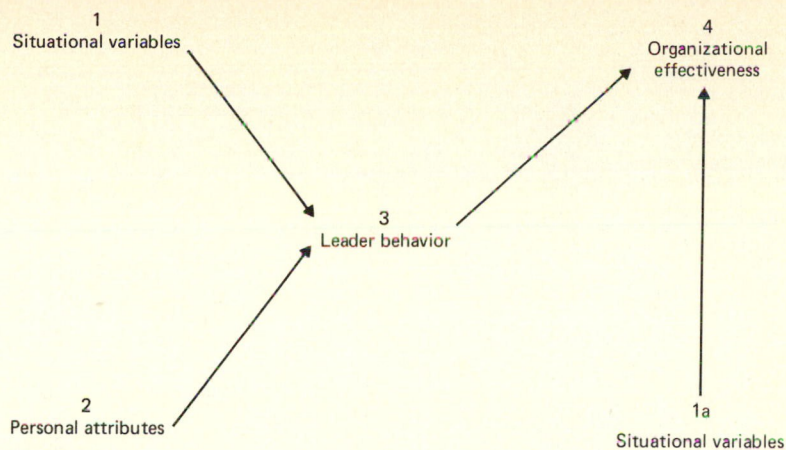

Figure 35-1 Schematic representation of variables used in leadership research.

stand the ways in which managers actually respond to situations that vary in a number of dimensions. If you examine the right-hand side of Figure 35-1, however, you encounter issues that are potentially normative or pre-scriptive in character. They deal with the consequences of leader behavior for the orga-nization and here I share with Fiedler (and probably disagree with Argyris) a conviction that a contingency model is required. I do not see any form of leader behavior as optimal for all situations. The contribution of a leader's actions to the effectiveness of his organization cannot be determined without considering the nature of the situation in which that behavior is displayed.

WORKING WITH THE CONTINGENCY MODEL

I am going to assume that most of you are familiar with the model that Phil Yetton and I developed and have described in detail in our recent book. As a normative model, it deals with the right-hand side of Figure 35-1, but it is a limited model because it deals with only one facet of leadership behavior—the extent to which the leader shares his decision-making power with his subordinates.

Figure 35-2 shows the latest version of our model. For purposes of simplicity, the presen-tation here is restricted to the model for group problems, that is, problems or decisions that affect all or a substantial portion of the manag-er's subordinates. At the top of the figure are problem attributes—that is, situational varia-bles that ought to influence the decision pro-cess used by the leader—specifically, the amount of opportunity that the leader gives his subordinates to participate in the making of a decision. To use the model, one first selects an organization problem to be solved or decision to be made. Starting at the left-hand side of the diagram, one asks oneself the question pertaining to each attribute that is encountered, follows the path developed, and finally determines the problem type (num-bered 1 through 12). This problem type speci-fies one or more decision processes that are deemed appropriate to that problem. These decision processes are called the "feasible set" and represent the methods that remain after a set of seven rules has been applied. The first three of these rules eliminate methods that threaten the quality of the decisions, while the last four rules eliminate methods that are likely to jeopardize acceptance of the decision by subordinates.

A. Does the problem possess a quality requirement?
B. Do I have sufficient information to make a high-quality decision?
C. Is the problem structured?
D. Is acceptance of the decision by subordinates important for effective implementation?
E. If I were to make the decision by myself, am I reasonably certain that it would be accepted by my subordinates?
F. Do subordinates share the organizational goals to be attained in solving this problem?
G. Is conflict among subordinates likely in preferred solutions?

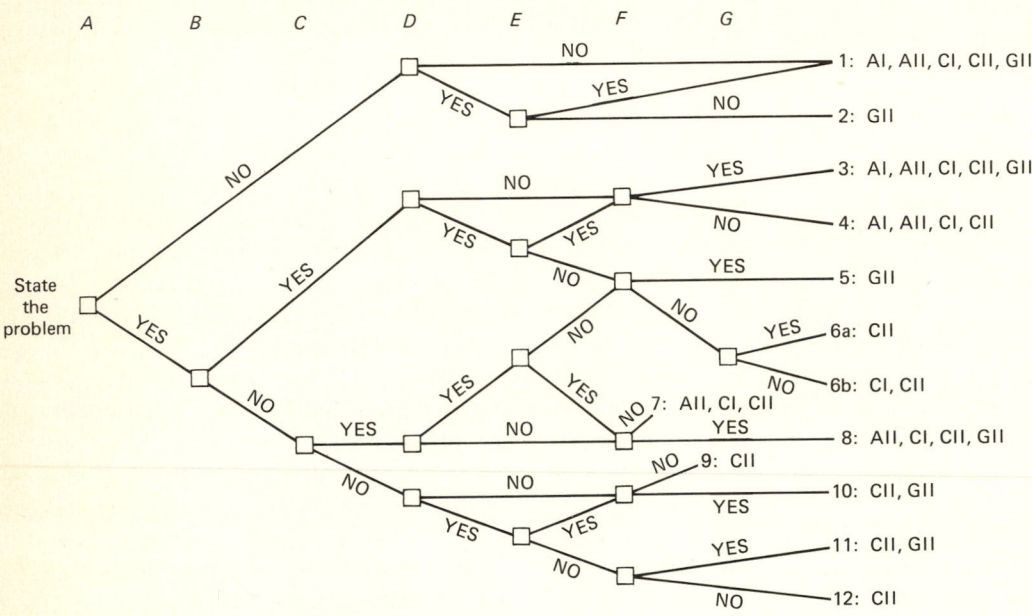

Figure 35-2 Decision process flowchart (feasible set).

For those who are unfamiliar with the Vroom-Yetton model, let me point out that the decision processes are described here in a kind of code. AI and AII are variants of an autocratic process. In AI the manager solves the problem by himself using whatever information is available to him at that time; in AII he obtains any necessary information of a specific nature from his subordinates before making the decision himself. CI and CII are variants of a consultative process. In CI he shares the problem with relevant subordinates individually, getting their ideas and suggestions before making the decision; CII is similar, but the consultation takes place within the context of a group meeting. Finally, GII corresponds with Norman Maier's concept of group decision in which the manager's role is that of chairperson of a group meeting aimed at reaching consensus on the action to be taken.

The part of the model described so far specifies how decisions should *not* be made, not how they should be made. For most problem types, there exist more than one decision process consistent with the rules and therefore contained in the feasible set. We have also been concerned with the consequences of various ways of choosing from these alternatives. There is considerable evidence that the time required to make the decision (defined either as the elapsed time or the number of man-hours needed to make the decision) increases with the intensity of involvement or participation of subordinates.

Thus a time-efficient model (which we term Model A) would select the most autocratic alternative within the feasible set, a choice that would be clearly indicated in crisis or emergency situations and in situations in which one seeks to minimize the number of man-hours that enter into making the decision.

Of course, time is not the only dimension to include in deciding the degree to which the leader should encourage the participation of his subordinates in decision making. In addition to the possibilities that participation may increase decision quality or its acceptance (considerations that are incorporated into the rules referred to previously), there are also grounds for believing that participation contributes to individual and team development and is likely to result in more informed and responsible behavior by subordinates in the future. Hence Model B, which could be thought of as a time-investment or developmental model, dictates the choice of the most participative process within the feasible set. It is important to note that Models A and B are consistent with the same rules (to protect decision quality and acceptance) but represent extremely different ways of operating within these rules. Model A maximizes a short-run value—time; Model B maximizes a long-run value—development.

What is the image of the effective leader portrayed by this normative model? He is neither universally automatic nor universally participative but utilizes either approach in response to the demands of a situation *as he perceives them.* Above all, he is a flexible leader who has thought through his values and who has a repertoire of skills necessary to execute effectively each of the decision processes.

VALIDATING THE MODEL

When Philip Yetton and I wrote our book, we had no evidence validating the model other than the consistency of our rules with existing empirical evidence concerning the consequences of alternative approaches. During the past six months, Art Jago and I have been working to remedy this deficiency. We have asked managers, all of whom were unfamiliar with the model, to select two decisions that they had made—one that proved to be successful and one that proved to be unsuccessful. Each manager wrote up each decision situation as a case and specified the decision process he used in solving the problem. Later these managers were trained in the problem attributes and went back over each of these two cases, coding each in a manner that would permit the researcher to determine the problem type and the feasible set of methods for that problem type.

The data for this study are still coming in. To date, we have written accounts of 46 successful decisions and of 42 unsuccessful ones. (It seems that some managers have difficulty in recalling the decisions they made that did not turn out too well!) Figure 35-3 shows the results available so far. These results clearly support the validity of the model. If the manager's method of dealing with the case corresponded with the model, the probability of the decision's being deemed successful was 65 percent; if the method disagreed with the model, the probability of it's being deemed successful was only 29 percent.

It is important to note, however, that behavior that corresponds with the model is no

	Percent successful	Percent unsuccessful	Total
Method used agrees with feasible set	65	35	100%
Method used disagrees with feasible set	29	71	100%

Figure 35-3 Relationship between model agreement and decision outcome.

guarantee that the decision will ultimately turn out to be successful—nor is behavior outside the feasible set inevitably associated with an unsuccessful decision.

To create a model of decision processes that completely predicts decision outcomes (that is, which generates 100 percent observations in upper left and lower right cells) is an impossibility. Any fantasies that we may have entertained about having created a model of process that would completely determine decision outcomes have been permanently dashed against the rocks of reality! Insofar as organizations are open systems and decisions within them are made under conditions of risk and uncertainty, it will be impossible to generate complete predictability for a model such as ours. To be sure, we may be able to use the data from the study I have described to improve the "batting average" of the model, but the limit of success must be less than perfection.

IMPLICATIONS FOR TRAINING

I would now like to turn to the central issue of this symposium, the use of the model in leadership training. Over the past few years, several thousand managers have received training in the concepts underlying the model. The workshops have ranged from two to over five days in length, and the participants have included admirals, corporation presidents, school superintendents, and senior government officials. I have been personally involved in enough of this training to have learned some important things about what to do and what not to do. And because I believe that there are substantial but understandable misconceptions about how training based on the Vroom and Yetton model works, I would like to describe the things I have learned.

It would have been possible to build a training program around the model that was completely cognitive and mechanistic. Partici-

pants would be sold on the model and then trained in its use through intensive practice—first on standardized cases and later on real problems drawn from their own experiences. Such an approach would represent a new domain for Taylorism and could even be accomplished through Skinnerian programmed learning. I believe that, at best, this behavioral approach would influence what Argyris calls espoused theories and would not have any long-lasting behavioral effects.

Our methods have been much more influenced by Carl Rogers than by B. F. Skinner. We have assumed that behavioral changes require a process of self-discovery and insight by each individual manager.

One method of stimulating this process is to provide the participant with a picture of his own leadership style. This picture includes a comparison of his style with that of others, the situational factors that influence his willingness to share his power with others, and similarities and differences between his own "model" and the normative models.

In advance of the training program, each participant sits down with a set of cases, each of which depicts a leader confronted with an actual organizational problem. We call these cases "problem sets," and the number of cases in different problem sets ranges from 30 to 54. The common feature in each of the eight or nine problem sets that have been developed is that the cases vary along each of the situational dimensions used in the construction of the normative model. The set is designed such that the variation is systematic and that the effects of each situational attribute on a given manager's choice of decision process can be readily determined. This feature permits the assessment of each of the problem attributes in the decision processes used by a given manager.

The manager's task is to select the decision process that comes closest to depicting what he would do in each situation. His responses are recorded on a standardized form and processed by computer along with other participants' responses in the same program.

Rather than talk about the information contained on a printout, I thought that it might be more efficient to let you see what it looks like. The next figure reproduces three of the seven pages of feedback that a manager recently received. Examine the first page of the printout shown in Figure 35-4. Consider A first in that figure. The first row opposite "your frequency" shows the proportion of cases in which the manager indicated he would use each of the five decision processes. The next row (opposite "peer frequency") shows the average use of these processes by the 41 managers constituting his training group. A comparison of these two rows indicates the methods he used more and less frequently than average.

The third row shows the distribution of decision processes that would be used by a manager using Model A, the time-efficient model in the 30 cases. The final row shows a distribution for Model B, the developmental or time-investment model.

To obtain an overall picture of how participative this manager's responses are in relation to other members of his training group and to Models A and B, it is necessary to assign scale values to each of the five decision processes. The actual numbers used for this purpose are based on research on the relative amounts of participation perceived to result from each process. AI is given a value of 0; AII a value of 1; CI a value of 5; CII a value of 8; and GII a value of 10.

With the aid of these scale values a mean score can be computed for the manager, his peers, and both models. These are obtained by multiplying the percentage of times each process is used by its scale value and dividing by 100. These mean scores are shown in B along with the standard deviation (SD), a measure of dispersion around the mean—that is, an indi-

cator of how much behavior is varied over situations.

These mean scores are shown graphically in the figure at the bottom. Each asterisk is the mean score of one of the group members. The symbol X is printed underneath this manager's mean score, the symbol P under the group average, and the symbols A and B show the location on the scale of Models A and B respectively.

D through F in Figure 35-4 show the second page of the printout. As we have previously mentioned, the normative model identifies 12 problem types corresponding to the terminal nodes of the decision tree shown in Figure 35-2. There is at least one case within the set of 30 problems that has been designated by the authors and most managers as representative of each type. The problem types and corresponding problem numbers are shown in the two left-hand columns of D. In the third and fourth columns, the prescriptions of Models A and B are given, and the fifth column shows the feasible set for that problem type. The last column, marked "your behavior," indicates the manager's responses to each of the cases of the indicated problem type. If there is more than one case of that type, the methods used are shown in the same order as the problem numbers at the left-hand side.

E reports the frequency with which the manager's behavior agreed with the feasible set, with Model A, and with Model B. For comparison purposes, the average rates of agreement for members of the manager's training group are also presented.

Each time our manager chose a decision process that was outside the feasible set, he violated at least one of the seven rules underlying the model. F in Figure 35-4 reports the frequencies with which each rule was violated both by this manager and by his peer group. The right-hand column shows the specific cases in which the rule violations occurred. It should be noted that each manager under-

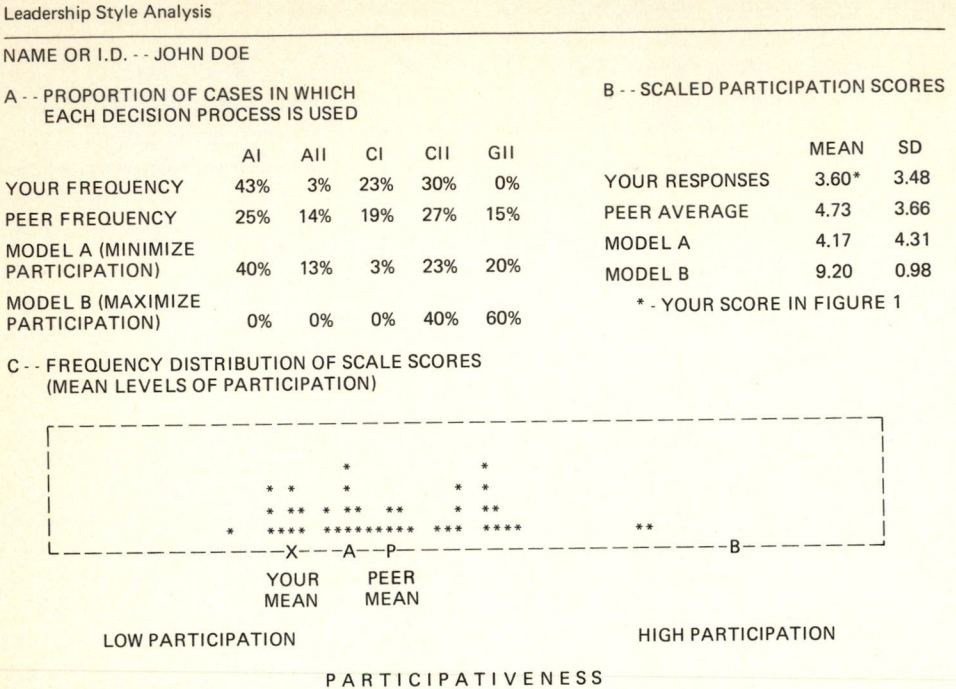

Figure 35-4   Page 1 of printout.

stands the seven rules by the time he receives the feedback, and it is possible for him to reexamine the problems with the appropriate rule in mind.

We have previously noted that the cases included in a problem set are selected in accordance with a multifactorial experimental design. Each of the problem attributes is varied in a manner that will permit the manager to examine its role in his leadership style. Figure 35-4 (page 3 of printout) depicts these results. Consider problem attribute A—the importance of the quality of the final solution. The problem set contains cases that have a high quality requirement and those without a quality requirement (the identifying numbers of these cases are shown at the right-hand side of this table).

The mean scores for the manager's behavior on these two sets of cases are specified at the left-hand side of each row and are designated

by the symbol X. They are also designated by the symbol X on each of the scales, and the slope of the line made by connecting the two letters (X) provides a visual representation of that difference.

If the score opposite "high" is greater (that is, more toward the right-hand side of the scale), it means that the manager encourages more participation from his subordinates on important decisions than on so-called "trivial" ones. However, if the score opposite "high" is lower, it means that the manager is willing to use more participative methods on problems for which the course of action adopted makes little difference and is more autocratic on "important" decisions.

The letter P shown on both scales designates the average effects of this attribute on the manager's peer group, and the letters A and B designate the effects on Models A and B respectively.

D ---- BEHAVIOR BY PROBLEM TYPE

PROBLEM TYPE	PROBLEM NUMBERS	MODEL "A"	MODEL "B"	FEASIBLE SET		YOUR BEHAVIOR		
1	14,15,17,28	AI	GII	AI,AII,CI,CII,GII	AI	AI	AI	AI
2	3,5,	GII	GII	GII		CII	AI	
3	2,22,27,30	AI	GII	AI,AII,CI,CII,GII	AI	AI	AI	CII
4	12,25,26,29	AI	CII	AI,AII,CI,CII	AI	CI	CI	AI
5	7,8,20	GII	GII	GII	CII	CII	CI	
6A	1,10	CII	CII	CII		CI	CI	
6B	11	CI	CII	CI,CII		CII		
7	21,24	AII	CII	AII,CI,CII		CII	AI	
8	19,23	AII	GII	AII,CI,CII,GII		AI	AII	
9	4,16	CII	CII	CII		CII	CI	
10	6,9	CII	CII	CII,GII		AI	CI	
11	13	GII	GII	GII		CII		
12	18	CII	CII	CII		CII		

E ---- FREQUENCY OF AGREEMENT WITH THE NORMATIVE MODEL

	YOUR MEAN	PEER AVERAGE
AGREEMENT WITH FEASIBLE SET	17 (57%)	20.8 (69%)
AGREEMENT MODEL A (MINIMUM PARTICIPATION)	12 (40%)	12.1 (40%)
AGREEMENT WITH MODEL B (MAXIMUM PARTICIPATION)	4 (13%)	6.3 (21%)

F ---- FREQUENCY OF RULE VIOLATIONS

	RULE	RESPONSES IN VIOLATION	YOUR FREQUENCY	PEER AVERAGE	PROBLEM NUMBERS
1	LEADER INFORMATION RULE	AI	3.0 (25%)*	0.7 (6%)	6 19 24
2	GOAL CONGRUENCE RULE	GII	0.0 (0%)	1.3 (10%)	0
3	UNSTRUCTURED PROBLEM RULE	AI,AII,CI	3.0 (50%)	2.8 (47%)	6 9 16
4	ACCEPTANCE RULE	AI,AII	1.0 (10%)	1.3 (13%)	5
5	CONFLICT RULE	AI,AII,CI	3.0 (60%)	1.9 (39%)	1 5 10
6	FAIRNESS RULE	AI,AII,CI,CII	2.0 (100%)	1.3 (63%)	3 5
7	ACCEPTANCE PRIORITY RULE	AI,AII,CI,CII	4.0 (100%)	2.9 (72%)	7 8 13 20

*---PROBABILITY OF RULE VIOLATION (THAT IS, FREQUENCY OF VIOLATION EXPRESSED AS A PERCENTAGE OF RULE APPLICABILITY)

Figure 35-4 (Continued)   Page 2 of printout.

406

G --- MAIN EFFECTS OF PROBLEM ATTRIBUTES

		YOUR MEAN = X	MODEL A MEAN = A
		PEER MEAN = P	MODEL B MEAN = B

PARTICIPATIVENESS ON PROBLEMS WITH ATTRIBUTE

PROBLEM ATTRIBUTES		< LOW PARTICIPATION .... HIGH PARTICIPATION >	PROBLEMS WITH ATTRIBUTE
IMPORTANCE OF THE QUALITY OF THE FINAL SOLUTION (ATTRIBUTE A)	HIGH X=4.17 P=4.97 A=4.38	----------------------------------XA----P-------------------------------B----	(1,2,4,6,7,8,9,10,11,12,13, 16,18,19,20,21,22,23,24,25, 26,27,29,30)
	LOW X=1.33 P=3.75 A=3.33	------------X---------A----P------------------------------B	(3,5,14,15,17,28)
ADEQUACY OF MANAGER'S INFORMATION AND EXPERTISE (ATTRIBUTE B)	HIGH X=3.67 P=4.24 A=2.75	--------------------A------X----P------------------------B---------	(1,2,8,11,12,20,22,25,26, (1,2,8,11,12,20,22,25,26, 27,29,30)
	LOW X=4.67 P=5.71 A=6.00	------------------------------X---P A------------------B---------	(4,6,7,9,10,13,16,18,19, 21,23,24)
DEGREE OF STRUCTURE IN PROBLEM (ATTRIBUTE C)	HIGH X=3.67 P=4.97 A=3.67	----------------------X------------P---------------------B---------	(7,10,19,21,23,24)
	LOW X=5.67 P=6.46 A=8.33	------------------------------X--P----------A---B--------	(4,6,9,13,16,18)
IMPORTANCE OF SUBORDINATE ACCEPTANCE (ATTRIBUTE D)	HIGH X=3.80 P=5.30 A=5.35	-----------------------X----------P---------------------B---------	(1,3,5,6,7,8,10,11,12,13,14, 15,16,18,19,20,22,24,29,30)
	LOW X=3.20 P=3.59 A=1.80	---------------A----------X---P-------------------B---------	(2,4,9,17,21,23,25,26,27,28)
PROBABILITY OF LEADER'S SELLING HIS OWN SOLUTION (ATTRIBUTE E)	HIGH X=1.30 P=3.68 A=1.80	----------X--A----------P-------------------------B---------	(6,12,14,15,16,19,22,24,29,30)
	LOW X=6.30 P=6.91 A=8.90	-----------------------------X----P-------------------A---B-------	(1,3,5,7,8,10,11,13,18,20)
DEGREE TO WHICH SUBORDINATES SHARE GOALS (ATTRIBUTE F)	HIGH X=3.58 P=5.45 A=4.83	-----------------------X----------A---P--------------------B	(2,6,7,8,9,13,19,20,22, 23,27,30)
	LOW X=4.75 P=4.49 A=3.92	------------------------A--P---X-------------------B--------	(1,4,10,11,12,16,18,21,24, 25,26,29)
PROBABILITY OF CONFLICT AMONG SUBORDINATES (ATTRIBUTE G)	HIGH X=3.27 P=3.99 A=4.27	----------------------X----P--A------------------------B-------	(1,2,5,8,9,10,13,15,16,19, 21,22,26,28,29)
	LOW X=3.93 P=5.47 A=4.07	------------------------X------------P------------------------B-------	(3,4,6,7,11,12,14,17,18, 20,23,24,25,27,30)

* * * * * * NOTE: THE THREE ATTRIBUTES WITH THE GREATEST EFFECT ON YOUR RESPONSES ARE A, C, AND E. * * * * * *

Figure 35-4 (Continued)   Page 3 of printout.

A similar logic can be used in interpreting the effects of each of the other attributes in the model. At the bottom of the page, the computer prints out the three attributes that have the greatest effect on the manager's behavior—magnitude of effect referring to the amount of difference the attribute makes in his willingness to share his decision-making power with subordinates.

The results shown in Figure 35-4 pertain to only one manager and to his peer group. Similar data have been obtained from several thousand managers, a sufficient number to provide the basis for some tentative generalizations about leadership patterns. One of our conclusions is that differences among managers in what might be termed a general trait of participativeness or authoritarianism are small in comparison with differences within managers. On the standardized cases in the problem sets, no manager has indicated that he would use the same decision process on all problems or decisions—and most use all methods under some circumstances.

It is clear that no one score computed for a manager and displayed on his printout adequately represents his leadership style. To begin to understand his style, the entire printout must be considered. For example, two managers may appear to be equally participative or autocratic on the surface, but a close look at the third page of the printout (Figure 35-4) may reveal crucial differences. One manager may limit participation by his subordinates to decisions where the quality element is unimportant, such as the time and place of the company picnic, while the other manager may limit participation by his subordinates to those decisions with a demonstrable impact on important organizational goals.

In about two-thirds of the cases we have examined—both those used in the problem sets and those reported to us by managers from their experiences—the manager's behavior was consistent with the feasible set of methods given by the model. Rules that helped ensure the acceptance of or commitment to a decision tend to be violated much more frequently than rules that protect the quality of the decision. Our findings suggest strongly that decisions made by typical managers are more likely to prove ineffective because of deficiencies in acceptance by subordinates rather than deficiencies in decision quality.

Let me now turn to another thing that we have learned in the design of this training—the usefulness of the small, informal group as a vehicle in the change process. The first four or five hours in the training process are spent in creating six- to eight-person teams operating under conditions of openness and trust. Each participant spends more than 50 percent of the training time with his small group before receiving feedback. Group activities include discussing cases in the problem set and trying to reach agreement on their mode of resolution, practicing participative leadership styles within their own groups, analyzing videotapes of group problem-solving activities; then group members give one another feedback on the basis of predictions of one another's leadership styles.

After feedback, group members compare results with one another and with their prior predictions and share with one another what they have learned as well as their plans to change. The use of small, autonomous groups greatly decreases the dependence of participants on the instructor for their learning and increases the number of people who can undergo the training at the same time. I have personally worked with as many as 140 managers at the same time (22 groups), and 40 to 50 is commonplace.

One criticism that has been correctly leveled at the Vroom and Yetton work stems from the fact that the data on which the feedback is based are, at best, reports of intended actions rather than observations of actual behavior. While we have evidence that most managers honestly try to portray what they think they would do in a particular situation rather than what they think they should do, I am persuaded by Argyris's evidence that many people are unaware of discrepancies between their espoused theories and their actions. Small groups can be helpful in pointing our these discrepancies. I have seen managers who were universally predicted by other group members to have a highly autocratic style, who were provided with very specific evidence of the ground for this assumption by other group members, but who later received a printout reflecting a much more participative style. I am less concerned about the relative validity of these discrepant pieces of data than I am about the fact that they are frequently confronted and discussed in the course of the training experience.

In fact, we have begun using a different source of potential inconsistencies, and it is logical to assume that this source will have more information about a manager's behavior than do the other members of his small group. I am referring to the manager's subordinates. In a recent variant of the training program described, they were asked to predict their managers' behavior on each of the cases in the problem set. These predictions were made individually and processed by computer, which generated for each manager a detailed comparison of his perceptions of his leadership style with the mean perception of his subordinates. Not surprisingly, these two sources of information are not always in perfect agreement. Most managers, as seen by their subordinates, are substantially more autocratic (about one point on the 10-point scale) and in substantially less agreement with the

model. Once again, I am less concerned with which is the correct description of the leader's behavior than I am with the fact that discrepancies generate a dialogue between the manager and his subordinates that can be the source of mutual learning.

We are still experimenting with methods of using the Vroom-Yetton model in leadership training and, I believe, still learning from the results of this experimentation. How effective is the training in its present form? Does it produce long-lasting behavioral changes? I must confess that I do not know. Art Jago and I are in the first stages of designing an extensive follow-up study of almost 200 managers in 20 different countries who have been through a four- or five-day version of the training within the past two and one-half years. If we can solve the incredible logistical and methodological problems in a study of this kind, we should have results within a year.

On the basis of the evidence, I am optimistic on two counts: first, as to the leader's potential to vary his style to meet the requirements of a situation; second, as to the leader's ability, through training and development, to enlarge the repertoire of his styles. In short, like Argyris and unlike Fiedler, I believe that managers can learn to become more effective leaders. But like Fiedler (and unlike Argyris), I believe that such effectiveness requires a matching of one's leadership style to the demands of the situation. I also am confident that 50 years from now both contingency models will be found wanting in detail if not in substance. If we are remembered at that time, it will be for the kinds of questions we posed rather than the specific answers we provided.

Reading 36

Leadership, Learning, and Changing the Status Quo

Chris Argyris

Changes in the status quo involve leadership. Yet an examination of the current literature on leadership, including the studies conducted by the other two contributors to this symposium, shows that most studies describe leadership activities as they exist and/or utilize criterion variables embedded in the present state of affairs. We need more research that illuminates how the present state of affairs can be changed and what role leadership can play in this quest.

Implicit in my position is the assumption that there may be something ineffective or dysfunctional in the current state of society. Donald Schon and I suggested that our society presently programs individuals with theories of action that generally are counterproductive to individual growth and organizational effectiveness. Moreover, these same theories are used to design organizations. One consequence is that even if applied effectively, they tend to create organizational stagnation or organizational deterioration. Knowledge is needed to suggest how we may break out of this self-sealing cycle that, as John Gardner has argued, could lead to a societal catastrophe.

Leadership has been defined as effective influence. In order to influence effectively, a leader requires on-line, repetitive learning about his influence. In order to solve ill-structured, complex problems, a leader also requires on-line, repetitive learning about how well substantive issues are being explored. Effective leadership and effective learning are intimately connected.

Studying about learning in terms of potent, real-life problems for which solutions are to be applied and tested in the noncontrived world means that the research methods to be chosen must meet certain criteria. They must not rule out the complexity of real life—or, if they do, they must specify precisely how the knowledge learned in the experimental setting can be used in the noncontrived world. They must involve their subjects easily and deeply so that they maintain their interest over long periods of time. They must not require keeping secret the design of the experiment from their subjects; indeed, they should permit their involvement without losing the power of making generalizations about human learning. They must be capable of eliciting behavior on the part of their subjects in such a way that the subjects cannot hold the design responsible for their actions. Otherwise, they may see no reason to accept personal responsibility for their behavior. The methods must be so powerful that the intended consequences can be brought about even under the most adverse circumstances, recognizing first, that their subjects may initially question their applicability and effectiveness (but not their moral validity); second, that their subjects are not able initially to behave in ways required by the experiment; third, that group behavior initially will be counterproductive; and last, that there will be few societal supports or rewards for learning the new behavior (otherwise we would be educating for the status quo).

I believe that it is possible to create these conditions in adult-learning environments with the requisite attracting, holding, and learning power. Part of this article will describe actual experiments in creating these conditions. But first we need to take a look at the theoretical foundations.

Reprinted from *Organizational Dynamics*, Winter 1976, 29–43, with permission of the publisher. Copyright © 1976 by AMACOM, a division of American Management Associations.

THEORETICAL FOUNDATIONS: THEORIES OF ACTION, ESPOUSED THEORIES, AND THEORIES-IN-USE

We start with three key assumptions:

1 Human action is shaped by the theories of action held by people. Leading and learning are examples of shaped human action.
2 People hold two kinds of theories of action. First is the theory that they are aware of and report; this we call their *espoused* theory. Second is the theory they hold that can be determined by observing their behavior; this we call their *theory-in-use*.
3 Espoused theories vary widely. However, there appears to be very little variance among theories-in-use. To date, 95 percent of the variance may be included under one model—what we call Model I. The reason should become apparent as the research is described.

Picture human beings who have programmed themselves to behave in ways that are consistent with four governing values or variables (Table 36-1). These are to (1) achieve the purpose as the individual has defined it; (2) win, not lose; (3) suppress negative feelings; and (4) emphasize rationality. In any situation, human behavior represents the most satisfactory solution people can find consistent with their governing variables.

I have further hypothesized that human beings have also learned a set of behavioral strategies that complement their governing values or variables. The primary strategies are to control unilaterally the relevant environment and tasks and to protect themselves and others unilaterally. The underlying behavioral strategy is control over others. People vary tremendously in the way they control others, but few people do not behave in ways that control others and their environment.

These behavioral strategies, in turn, have consequences for the individual himself, for other people, and for the environment. Briefly, they tend to produce defensiveness and closedness in people because unilateral control does not tend to produce valid feedback.

Table 36-1 Model I

Governing variables for action	Action strategies for the individual and toward his environment	Consequences on the individual and his environment	Consequences on learning	Effectiveness
Achieve purposes as the individual perceives them	Design and manage environment so that the individual is in control over the factors relevant to him	Individual is seen as defensive	Self-sealing	Decreased effectiveness
Maximize winning and minimize losing		Defensive interpersonal and group relationships	Single-loop learning	
Minimize eliciting negative feelings	Own and control task	Defensive norms	Little public testing of theories	
Be rational and minimize emotionality	Unilaterally protect self	Low freedom or choice, internal commitment, and risk taking		
	Unilaterally protect others from being hurt			

Moreover, unilaterally controlling behavior may be seen by others as signs of an individual's defensiveness.

In addition, I have hypothesized that the consequences above will tend to generate a particular kind and quality of learning that will go on within the individual and between the individual and the environment. There will be little public testing of ideas (especially those that may be important and threatening). Consequently, individuals will neither seek nor receive more than a modicum of feedback that genuinely confronts their actions. They will tend to play it safe; they are not going to violate their governing values and upset others, especially if the others have power. Moreover, whatever learning individuals acquire will tend to fall within the confines of what is acceptable. This is called single-loop learning because, like a thermostat, individuals learn only about those subjects within the confines of their program. They will find out how well they are hitting their goal (maintaining a particular temperature). However, few people will confront the validity of the goal or the values implicit in the situation, just as a thermostat never questions its temperature setting. Such a confrontation would constitute double-loop learning. A teacher in a classroom, for example, may learn (single-loop) to ask students more specific questions in order to control student responses more readily; or the teacher may learn (double-loop) to reduce requirements for control in the classroom.

For most people there is a gap between their espoused theory and their theories-in-use, a gap of which they are unaware. Two reasons underlie this blindness: First, most people's theories-in-use include a proposition that states in effect, "If you see someone whose behavior is incongruent with what he or she espouses, for heaven's sake don't tell him or her because it will upset him or her and you will run the risk of eliciting feelings of rejection and hostility." Second, people pro-

grammed with Model I theories-in-use are so busy controlling others in order to win, to advocate their position, and to do so in a way that cannot be disproved or publicly tested that they create self-sealing processes. The others, for their part, are so busy fighting back (they, too, are trying to win, advocate, and control) that there is little incentive for helping others to learn, especially if it may strengthen their position.

MODEL II AND DOUBLE-LOOP LEARNING

One possible model has been recently suggested that would lead to consequences that are the opposite of Model I, a model identified by Schon and myself as Model II. The governing variables of Model II are valid information, free and informed choice, and internal commitment. On the other hand, the behavior required to satisfy these values is not the opposite of Model I. For example, Model I emphasizes that individuals be as articulate as possible about their purposes, goals, and so forth and simultaneously control others and the environment in order to assure achievement of their goals. Model II does not reject the need to be articulate and precise about one's purposes. However, it does reject the unilateral control that usually accompanies advocacy because the purpose of advocacy typically is to win. Model II couples articulateness and advocacy with an invitation to others to confront one's views and possibly to alter them in order to reach a position that is based on the most valid information possible and to which everyone involved can become internally committed. This means the individual (in Model II) is skilled at inviting double-loop learning (Table 36-2).

Each significant Model II action is evaluated in terms of the degree to which it helps the individuals involved generate valid and useful information (including relevant feelings), solve a problem in such a way that it remains

Table 36-2   Model II

Governing variables for action	Action strategies for the individual and toward his environment	Consequences on the individual and his environment	Consequences on learning	Effectiveness
Valid information	Situations or encounters are designed to enable participants to orginate actions and experience high personal causation	Individual is experienced as minimally defensive	Disprovable process	Increased effectiveness
Free and informed choice		Minimally defensive interpersonal relations and group dynamics	Double-loop learning	
Internal commitment to the choice and constant monitoring of the implementations			Frequent public testing of theories	
	Task is controlled jointly	Learning-oriented norms		
	Protection of self is a joint enterprise and oriented toward growth	High freedom of choice, internal commitment, and risk taking		
	Protection of others is bilateral			

solved, and do so without reducing the present level of problem-solving effectiveness.

The behavioral strategies of Model II involve sharing power with anyone who has competence and who is relevant in deciding or implementing an action. The definition of the task, the control over the environment, is shared with all the relevant participants. Saving one's own or the other person's face is rejected because it is seen as a defensive, nonlearning activity. If face-saving actions are necessary, they are planned jointly with the people involved.

Under these conditions, individuals will not tend to compete to make decisions for others, practice one-upmanship, and outshine others for the purposes of self-gratification. In a Model II world, people seek to find the most competent people to make a decision. They seek to build viable decision-making networks in which the major function of the group is to maximize the contributions of each member so that a synthesis, whenever it develops, is based on the widest possible exploration of views.

Last, under Model II conditions, if new concepts are created, the meaning given to them by the creator and the processes used in developing them are open to scrutiny by all who are expected to use them. Also, the creator feels responsible for presenting evaluations in ways that encourage others to confront them openly and constructively.

If the governing values and behavioral strategies just outlined are used, the degree of defensiveness within individuals, within groups, and among groups will tend to decrease. Free choice will tend to increase as will feelings of internal commitment. The consequences for learning should be an emphasis on double-loop learning that confronts the basic assumptions behind ideas or present views and that publicly tests hypotheses.

The end result should be increased decision-making or policy-making effectiveness, increased effectiveness in the monitoring of decisions and policies, and increased probability that errors and failures will be communicated openly and that participants in an action will learn from the feedback.

CASE OF THE NONPROFIT ADMINISTRATORS

So much for theory. Does it sound like a tall order? Is it clear that the switchover from a Model I to a Model II mode of behavior will take much time, involve much pain and agonized self-doubt, and require much professional assistance for the few with the motivation to run the course? All true—as our experience with a dozen different groups over the past several years has demonstrated. One study, research of managers in the governmental sector, illustrates the hypothesis tested in these dozen different learning environments: Knowing the models and having the opportunity to practice—under supportive conditions—may be a necessary, but is not a sufficient, condition for individuals to discover-invent-produce-generalize about the new Model II behavior.

The majority of the 100 manager-students were people with two to five years' experience as educational administrators, teachers, middle managers, governmental officials, middle- and top-level city and state officials, and a few first- and second-level business managers. All had read *Theory in Practice*, which described Models I and II in detail. The models were discussed in three two-hour class sessions. Toward the end of the sessions, the oral examinations that were held illustrated that the class members had mastered the key concepts in both models. Also, the students reported a strong interest in learning to behave in accordance with Model II.

At the beginning of the fourth session, the students were asked to read the following short case:

One of your subordinates has been performing inadequately for several months now. You've talked to him/her several times, and each time he/she has promised that performance would get better, but you don't see any evidence of this. Since you prefer not to fire him/her, you decide to make one more attempt. He/she walks into your office and asks: "Did you want to see me?"

They were asked to discover-invent-produce a solution. The production had to contain two parts, a short scenario of what the students as the actors in the case would say and do plus their feelings and thoughts about their behavior. They kept the original copy for a week as the basis for class discussion, and they gave the carbon copy to one of the faculty.

During the period between classes, the faculty members analyzed the cases to infer the degree to which they approximated Model I and Model II. All of the scorable cases (about 85) were categorized crudely in terms of the behavioral strategies manifested by the actors. Six behavioral strategies were identified:

1 The respondent attempts to get directly to the point that the subordinate is not producing adequately.

2 The respondent believes the subordinate is wrong but he wishes to start out indirectly and hopefully on a positive note.

3 The respondent couches the issue by asking if he (respondent) is a problem. ("Yes, come in, I want to talk about a problem that I have.")

4 The respondent begins by describing his feelings of discomfort, by attempting to place the subordinate at ease, and then by describing the problem with the subordinate's performance.

5 The respondent asserts that the subordinate has a problem, that the respondent is there to help and not to punish (not to fire).

6 The respondent asserts that both have problems and perhaps both can be of help to each other.

All these behavioral strategies approximated Model I. No matter how direct or indirect, how warm or how cool the interviews began, the respondents tended to approximate Model I theories-in-use. To illustrate how this judgment was arrived at, let us examine a scenario that illustrates the first of the behavioral strategies listed:

Respondent: (*Hope this won't hurt his feelings too much.*) Yes . . . I'm disturbed because I don't see much improvement.

Subordinate: I think my work has improved. I've had more work lately so that may be why you think there are more errors.

Respondent: (*He doesn't really understand that there's a problem. That's a lie about more work. This is aggravating. I ought to just fire him, but actually he's kind of nice and comfortable to have around.*) I don't agree that you've had more work to do. In any case, I simply can't go on seeing this kind of work. What do you think we ought to do?

Analyzing this scenario we find:

1   The respondent began by telling the subordinate he was disturbed because there had not been any improvement in his work (illustrates making judgments without publicly testing them).

2   The respondent's first feelings (the italicized parenthetical inserts) illustrated an attempt to satisfice to Model I governing variables of minimizing the expression of negative feelings.

3   The respondent's reaction to the subordinate's comment was an assessment made of the other subordinate that was stated in such a way that it was not testable. Moreover, no attempt was made to test it publicly.

4   The covert assertion that the subordinate was lying was not tested publicly, partially in order not to arouse hostility.

5   The feelings of aggravation were suppressed (again minimizing the expression of negative feelings).

6   At this point, the respondent asserted that the organization could not be used to fulfill the subordinate's needs; the subordinate must perform. Yet the respondent, by being willing to keep the subordinate when he believed he or she should be fired, was fulfilling his personal needs in a way that may be inimicable to the organization.

7   The first two sentences in the final voiced response showed the respondent's taking unilateral control. The last sentence appeared incongruent with unilateral control. The subordinate probably experienced it as the crucial question—namely, what he or she was going to do.

How typical are these responses? If we examine scenarios that are five to ten times longer than this, the pattern remains the same. That is, if the individuals begin with a Model I theory-in-use, they continue using the same theory-in-use. The changes that may be noted are that the dialogues become even more entrenched in Model I and the inconsistencies become more pronounced and glaring. The self-sealing processes become compounded and the level of holding back and/or deception increases. Moreover, these results continue when people use different modalities to express themselves (for example, going from writing to speaking to tape recording).

Subsequently, the manager-students broke down into small groups and studied the first strategy, chosen because it represented the most frequently used strategy. As consultants to the writer of the case, their task was to design an intervention to help the writer of the case cope with the problem in ways that approximated Model II. They were asked to invent a strategy and to appoint someone to produce the strategy.

After one-half hour of small group discussion, the class reassembled. The faculty member said that he would take the role of the writer. Each group representative described the intervention that they invented and then he/she would produce it through role playing.

The faculty member asked that the class

monitor his behavior to make certain that he was not making it difficult for each group representative. The dialogues were all tape recorded. All of the inventions by the 11 small groups represented a mixture of Model I and Model II theories-in-use.

For example:

1 "He (the superior in the first case) should create an atmosphere where both can be open and share their feelings."

2 "He should create a situation so that each of them can develop the other's behavior rather than simply focus on her behavior."

3 "He should clarify for her the concrete expectations of work performance and the area that prevented him from firing her in spite of her inadequate performance."

4 "He should not control every aspect of the situation, including trying to minimize her expressing her negative feelings."

It appears that the students were learning Model II because they were inventing strategies that approximate Model II conditions. But such learning was at the conceptual level. What happens when the students attempt to transform the inventions (espoused theory) to theory-in-use?

We were able to obtain data to answer this question when the representatives from each group attempted to produce the inventions in the role-playing with the instructor. All the productions were judged by the class, the faculty members, *and the representatives who produced the inventions* (the latter after reflection), as approximating Model I. Moreover, an analysis of the transcript of the class discussion showed that when the productions were analyzed and discussed by the class members, these discussions also adhered to Model I.

Thus we have people who had read *Theory in Practice;* who had discussed it with one of the authors for three two-hour sessions; who met for a half hour to design the beginning of a Model II intervention; who invented Model I

and II interventions, but who produced only Model I interventions. Moreover, it was the members of the class who had identified the inventions and productions as approximating Model I. Also, the class agreed that the faculty member could not be held responsible for the Model I behavior. Finally, an analysis of the members' behavior while they were commenting on the production of each group showed that these responses also approximated Model I.

It is important to keep in mind that no representatives were aware that, when they produced their group's solution, they had produced a Model I intervention. Nor were the students aware that they did the same thing when they tried to help the representatives become aware that they were not producing Model II interventions. Thus the class members could invent Model II solutions but were unaware that they could not produce them.

Looking back on these cases, we note that the students produced solutions that, the class concluded, illustrated Model I theories-in-use. For example: In the first example of an invention for the case on page 413, the respondent invented a solution that was to create an atmosphere of mutual inquiry, yet the respondent (and the class) judged the production to be the opposite. Attributions and evaluations were made about the respondent's behavior that were never tested. The attributions and evaluations were hidden by the use of questions. The camouflage apparently worked only for the producer. Everyone else recognized the covert meanings.

In summary, motivation by itself is not the key to learning. As Don Schon and I explained in *Theory in Practice,* the learning process is a cycle that involves (1) discovering the problem, (2) inventing a solution (conceptual map), (3) producing the invention (performing in terms of actual behavior), and (4) generalizing what has been learned to other settings.

Each step in the cycle involves getting the

participants to become aware of something of which they had habitually been unaware—for example, the discrepancy between their espoused theories and their theories-in-use.

People who wish to learn Model II theories-in-use must re-educate themselves in each phase. They need to learn to discover-invent-produce-generalize about how to discover, how to invent, how to produce, and how to generalize. Fortunately, people are not computers: They do not expect to be locked into their programs. They become increasingly frustrated, angry, and tense as evidence accumulates on their inability to help themselves or others to gain the competence they seek. Such feelings are a necessary part of the learning process. Learning that involves change in the governing variables of a theory-in-use comes about only through dilemmas—through an individual's gradual realization that he is confronted with a progressively intolerable conflict of central elements in his theory-in-use.

It is these reactions that lead people to become defensive—which, in turn, may lead people to use learning cycles that are protective. These cycles themselves may increase the difficulties that created the frustration and anger in the first place. Hence we have self-sealing processes that create cumulative defensiveness in the actors involved. In the hands of competent faculty, however, it is these cumulative, self-sealing, defensive reactions that can provide a breakthrough to learning to learn Model II.

PRESIDENTS APPLY MODEL II

Another group consisting of six entrepreneurs, all presidents of their respective companies, are in the process of moving from Model I toward Model II. They have attended six sessions (ranging from two days to one week) over a period of three years. After the presidents had successfully invented and pro-

duced Model II solutions in the classroom (a painful process similar to that undergone by the 100 administrators), they faced the big challenge—taking their solutions and experimenting with implementing them in their own companies.

Two problems were foremost in their minds. First, and the one to which they alluded throughout their sessions, was concern about the reaction of their subordinates when they began to exhibit their new leadership behavior. Second was discomfort about the prospect of behaving incompetently—as one man put it, "Making asses of ourselves in front of our people."

Turning to the first problem, the presidents had serious doubts that their subordinates would understand or see Model II behavior as relevant or practical. Because they themselves had expressed the same reactions toward Model II early on in their education, this lent credibility to their fears. Another, and probably more powerful source of fear, was the presidents' knowledge that, in their relationships with their vice-presidents, they had made many hidden assumptions, practiced many deceptions, and suppressed many doubts, all in the name of acting constructively toward them. For the presidents now to begin to behave in ways that they had previously rejected could arouse concern if not disbelief and bewilderment on the part of subordinates. And if this did happen, subordinates would probably withhold these feelings. This, in turn, would mean an increase in suppressed tension and/or an increase in overt discomfort on the part of subordinates. All these conditions would make introduction of Model II theories-in-use even more difficult.

To compound the problem, the presidents did not believe that they had mastered the new theory-in-use. Indeed, part of the process of mastering it required that they use it effectively in the "real" world. This greatly concerned the presidents because collectively their view of an effective president was one who was "strong." To be strong included behaving with confidence and approximating perfection. They believed that they could achieve neither criterion if they attempted Model II interventions at this time in their home settings.

The presidents began to experience several new dilemmas. On the one hand, after years of hard work within the seminars, they had begun to discover, invent, and produce new behavior and meanings that they valued. On the other hand, they feared experimenting with the new behavior back at home because of the negative reactions of their subordinates.

They had also learned in the seminars to handle such dilemmas by testing publicly the assumptions embedded in them. For example, their fears about negative reactions on the part of their subordinates required surfacing and testing. If they did not feel fully competent in behaving in accordance with Model II, they had learned to say so publicly. They had also learned to openly assert that what they were going to do was an experiment and that it might not be as successful as they had hoped.

Unfortunately, these cures made the illness worse. If they feared going public with their assumptions, testing these fears publicly would compound their fears; if they felt unsure about their new behavior, candidly saying so would make them appear weak in the eyes of their subordinates. To test this publicly would be embarrassing and bring to the surface their feelings of weakness—feelings that, in their minds, presidents should not express.

"I would not mind going through all this," said one president, "if I knew they wouldn't become confused and disorganized." The faculty member (one of my associates in the seminar) asked this president if he were willing to test that assumption publicly. "There you go again," he responded, "suggesting cures that make the problem worse."

The presidents realized that they were in a double bind. If they chose to experiment, they believed that they could be embarrassed and also harm the functioning of the top group. If they decided to withdraw, however, they would have to admit to themselves that they were controlled by fear and feelings of weakness. To be controlled by such fears obviously would be a sign of weakness, something they all found difficult to accept or admit.

This was a key moment in the group's learning process. Examining the transcript indicates that, although the diagnosis was painful, the choice to move ahead appeared natural and relatively simple. They decided that they had to be masters of their own fate; therefore, if the next step was to experiment, experiment they would.

The learning seminar became the base for the new operation. Each president chose a key issue—such as confrontation of an ineffective executive, development of an effective top-management problem-solving process, or reduction of an operating budget by 20 percent. They discussed it in detail and, with the help of others, invented a range of solutions. Each was produced by the president with the other presidents acting as hard-nosed, disbelieving, confused, concerned subordinates.

After continual practice that helped them to discover, invent, produce, and generalize new interventions, the presidents began to feel confident enough to try their respective experiments in their own organizations. Several had designed experiments involving one or two persons. Several were interested in exploring Model II theories-in-use with their entire top group. Some experimented alone; others invited a faculty member. All tape-recorded their experiments or wrote detailed scenarios that became a rich source of data for further learning. In all cases, the presidents experienced both success and failure. It was most interesting to see how easily they accepted their failures as episodes from which to learn and how willing they were to say so publicly. This, in turn, unfroze their subordinates and opened them up to explore their relationships not only with their superiors but also with each other and their own subordinates.

Not all subordinates liked Model II interventions (rare *or* well done). Some preferred the old ways of behaving and were frank to say so. Reading the transcripts, we saw that the presidents were attacked for behaving in ways that were perceived as weird, impolite, and potentially destructive of group cohesiveness. The fears the presidents had expressed were confirmed. However, the presidents did not become angry or punitive. They encouraged these expressions and, drawing from their seminar experience, used them to explore their impact as well as the foundations of cohesiveness within their groups. Perhaps one reason that the presidents could begin to deal with other people's fears effectively was that they had learned no longer to fear their own fears. Because they had begun to learn how to manage their own fears, they could use their newly acquired skills in helping others express and manage their fears.

Implications from the Six Entrepreneurs

At the most obvious but still meaningful level, there is the fact that the six entrepreneurs have made progress in experimenting with Model II in their own organizations, are making progress at the present time, and hopefully will make further progress in the future. That few people at the top would currently choose Model II as their preferred theory-in-use, that even fewer people are competent to make the changeover from Model I to Model II even with prolonged professional assistance, does not diminish the significance of what the six entrepreneurs have achieved so far. Only a few years ago, I wrote that "our own experience and the published research suggest that there now does not exist a top-management group so competent in meeting the requirements of the new ethic (the values incorporated in Model II) that they do not lose their

competence under stress." I also expressed the belief that some groups and some organizations eventually would achieve that competence—a belief that our experience with the six entrepreneurs is in the process of confirming.

At another level, our experiences with the six entrepreneurs have deepened our knowledge of what is involved in learning to learn. This newly acquired knowledge, in turn, should enable us to help other groups similar to the six entrepreneurs in traveling the same road with a little less travail and pain.

What did we learn about learning? The adult learning processes with which we have experimented have turned out to be primarily cognitive. This does not mean that feelings did not surface. Indeed, the fear of fear and fear of embarrassment, hostility, failure, and so forth were continually experienced. However, the presidents coped with these feelings as components of their theory-in-use. Instead of asking, for example, why they feared failure, the participants learned to ask how they could test their fears and behave in ways that made them obsolete.

Following Model II theories-in-use, for example, the presidents did not choose to explore their personal histories to discover the roots of their fear of fear. A theory-of-action perspective informed them that the way to cope with fear of fear was to create learning conditions with those people with whom they were presently involved—initially the other presidents in the seminar and eventually their own subordinates back home. As you may recall, this strategy created some problems, but it was facing these problems that led to progress. To repeat the sequences of action:

- They asked what, in the present context, operated as causes of their fear.
- After some discussion, they concluded that it was their fear that, if they behaved in an experimental, uncertain manner, their subor-

dinates might become anxious because they wanted and expected strong leaders.

- Having made the conclusion explicit, they realized that it was, in effect, a series of assumptions about their respective subordinates. According to Model II, assumptions should be tested publicly before they become guides to action.

- This produced a double bind. Publicly to test these fears would compound their fears and probably upset their subordinates. To refuse to test publicly their attributions would mean that they withdrew from an action that made rational sense because they were afraid. To suppress rationality because of personal fears was to be weak.

- The presidents opted to experiment and learn. They utilized seminars to design their experiments, make many trial runs in front of each other (each simulating their worst fears), and develop confidence in their ability to respond effectively to expected resistance or confusion.

- Each president performed his experiment in his home setting differently, and each had varying degrees of success. However, each collected directly observable data, the Model II approach to testing concepts, and learned from his failures. Many subordinates reported surprise concerning the degree of openness of their superiors to explore their failures as well as design further experiments. Indeed, this openness to learning appeared to lead subordinates to explore some of the ineffectiveness among their own relationships.

- The competence to learn from failure and the way their subordinates rewarded their openness to learning served to raise the presidents' levels of aspiration for the next experiment and served as evidence that their fears were not based on valid information. As a result, their fears about experimenting in company settings began to diminish.

IMPLICATIONS FOR LEADERSHIP

Leadership theory will have to distinguish between results obtained at the espoused level and those at the theory-in-use level. To date,

the preponderance of data employed in leadership research, including the data used by Professors Vroom and Fiedler, is at the espoused level. Research that remains at the espoused level runs the risk of missing (1) the incongruities between espoused theory and theory-in-use, (2) the blindness to these incongruities, and (3) the unawareness of the awareness that people have about their capacity to discover, invent, produce, and generalize theories of action that challenge the unchallengeable and question the unquestionable. If leadership education is ever to tackle core issues, these factors cannot be ignored.

To the extent that these factors are ignored, leadership education becomes a part of the existing theories-in-use. To the extent that this happens, leadership education will not tend to question the group, organizational, and societal factors that encourage Model I behavior. Leadership education becomes limited to education within the status quo—education that, at best, may transform the world of espoused theories of action and yet have little or no impact on theories-in-use.

Leadership theory and theory about everyday life may overlap much more than has hitherto been assumed. Theories of action shape human behavior under all conditions, and theories-in-use are all minitheories of leadership in that they are theories of influencing others to increase one's own effectiveness. Our research suggests that even those who seek to be followers do so because that is their most effective way of gaining the level of control they seek over their personal lives.

Moreover, Model I theories-in-use are explicit leadership theories that focus on advocacy and unilateral control in order to win. These theories-in-use are consonant with those presently embedded in formal pyramidal structures and management theory. Indeed, this is probably no accident and requires much research.

Strong leaders in a Model I world may well

be effective enough to control the world adequately to achieve organizational goals. Leaders whose strength is based on high advocacy and unilateral control over others also tend to hold attitudes that their subordinates need to be controlled, that they fear confronting people with power, that the competition among themselves is great, and that, if left to themselves, the group would fall apart. These assumptions are self-sealing because they are caused by the leadership style in the first place (or, if subordinates had these predispositions before the leader arrived, this style reconfirms and reinforces their utility).

One result of attributing fears and brittleness to one's subordinates is to make such attributions undiscussable because, as we saw in the example of our six entrepreneurs, such a discussion would be a cure that makes the illness worse. Granted, introducing Model II theories-in-use in organizations is fraught with potential failure and fear; but under Model II conditions, these possibilities must become discussable.

As our experiences with the six entrepreneurs have shown, it is possible over a period of years to change the theories-in-use of a group of company presidents from Model I to Model II, to create conditions in which their espoused theories and their theories-in-use are congruent, and to introduce Model II theories-in-use in the organization despite the fears and possibilities of failure. We can say about our six presidents (who in each case began as the quintessential Model I manager —"the kind of man I would never work for myself," as one self-description put it) that they had made the transition to being the kind of Model II manager who habitually practices double-loop learning. Once we can say that about the man at the top, the organization is on its way.

Many of the problems confronted and resolved under Model II conditions were serious problems that might never have been confronted at all under Model I or, had they been confronted, might have been less effectively resolved. One organization cut nearly 20 percent of its operating budget with the entire top-management group participating in the process. In another case, the need for an executive position that the president believed the vice-presidents wanted was eliminated when, after a more open discussion, the presidents and the vice-presidents developed a new set of operating procedures that made the proposed executive vice-presidency unnecessary. The relationship between a chairman of the board (and owner of the company) with the president (whom the former had appointed personally) began to deteriorate because the latter's performance had not measured up to expectations. The problems were discussed openly and solutions were generated that pleased both men. More importantly, the resolution of the problem did not place the vice-presidents in the dilemma of having to take loyalty oaths toward the owner or the president. An unprofitable venture that the president hesitated to close down (because he had originally decided to create it) was cancelled with the help and advice of the vice-presidents, who had become more open with the president. Last, an organization faced up to the problem of what would happen when and if the president sold out—this being the kind of problem that probably never would surface in a Model I world.

Of course, we have made only a beginning. The presidents have taken the essential first steps in creating a Model II behavioral world with their immediate subordinates. In those instances in which subordinates responded positively, they, in turn, have taken the first painful steps toward creating a Model II behavioral world with their own subordinates. Actually, at this point most of the vice-presidents are where their bosses were three years ago. Relations among the vice-presidents and with the vice-presidents and their subordinates constitute an important inhibiting factor within these organizations.

Much remains to be done. We have said that the formal pyramidal structures that characterize most organizations are embodiments of a Model I theory-in-use. Before we can give an organization a Model II label, its structure, planning mechanisms, and policy-making procedures must all become congruent with Model II theories-in-use. And everyone within the organization, from the highest to the lowest, must understand, accept, and practice Model II as his or her theory-in-use.

All this will take years—and may never take place except in a relative handful of organizations. None of which detracts from the progress so far. Progress worth recognizing, even celebrating. And worth advancing.

Reading 37

The Manager's Job: Folklore and Fact

Henry Mintzberg

If you ask a manager what he does, he will most likely tell you that he plans, organizes, coordinates, and controls. Then watch what he does. Don't be surprised if you can't relate what you see to these four words.

When he is called and told that one of his factories has just burned down, and he advises the caller to see whether temporary arrangements can be made to supply customers through a foreign subsidiary, is he planning, organizing, coordinating, or controlling? How about when he presents a gold watch to a retiring employee? Or when he attends a conference to meet people in the trade? Or on returning from that conference, when he tells one of his employees about an interesting product idea he picked up there?

The fact is that these four words, which have dominated management vocabulary since the French industrialist Henri Fayol first introduced them in 1916, tell us little about what managers actually do. At best, they indicate some vague objectives managers have when they work.

The field of management, so devoted to progress and change, has for more than half a century not seriously addressed *the* basic question: What do managers do? Without a proper answer, how can we teach management? How can we design planning or information systems for managers? How can we improve the practice of management at all?

Our ignorance of the nature of managerial work shows up in various ways in the modern organization—in the boast by the successful manager that he never spent a single day in a management training program; in the turnover of corporate planners who never quite understood what it was the manager wanted; in the computer consoles gathering dust in the back room because the managers never used the fancy on-line MIS some analyst thought they needed. Perhaps most important, our ignorance shows up in the inability of our large public organizations to come to grips with some of their most serious policy problems.

Somehow, in the rush to automate production, to use management science in the functional areas of marketing and finance, and to apply the skills of the behavioral scientist to the problem of worker motivation, the manager—that person in charge of the organization or one of its subunits—has been forgotten.

My intention in this article is simple: to break the reader away from Fayol's words and introduce him to a more supportable, and what I believe to be a more useful, description of managerial work. This description derives from my review and synthesis of the available research on how various managers have spent their time.

In some studies, managers were observed intensively ("shadowed" is the term some of them used); in a number of others, they kept detailed diaries of their activities; in a few studies, their records were analyzed. All kinds of managers were studied—foremen, factory supervisors, staff managers, field sales managers, hospital administrators, presidents of companies and nations, and even street gang leaders. These "managers" worked in the United States, Canada, Sweden, and Great Britain. [A brief review of the major studies that I found most useful in developing this description, including my own study of five American chief executive officers, is informative.]

A synthesis of these findings paints an interesting picture, one as different from Fayol's classical view as a cubist abstract is from a Renaissance painting. In a sense, this picture will be obvious to anyone who has ever spent a day in a manager's office, either in front of the desk or behind it. Yet, at the same time, this picture may turn out to be revolutionary, in that it throws into doubt so much of the folklore that we have accepted about the manager's work.

I first discuss some of this folklore and contrast it with some of the discoveries of systematic research—the hard facts about how managers spend their time. Then I synthesize these research findings in a description

of ten roles that seem to describe the essential content of all managers' jobs. In a concluding section, I discuss a number of implications of this synthesis for those trying to achieve more effective management, both in classrooms and in the business world.

SOME FOLKLORE AND FACTS ABOUT MANAGERIAL WORK

There are four myths about the manager's job that do not bear up under careful scrutiny of the facts.

1

Folklore *The manager is a reflective, systematic planner.* The evidence on this issue is overwhelming, but not a shred of it supports this statement.

Fact *Study after study has shown that managers work at an unrelenting pace, that their activities are characterized by brevity, variety, and discontinuity, and that they are strongly oriented to action and dislike reflective activities.* Consider this evidence:

• Half the activities engaged in by the five chief executives of my study lasted less than nine minutes, and only 10% exceeded one hour.[1] A study of 56 U.S. foremen found that they averaged 583 activities per eight-hour shift, an average of 1 every 48 seconds.[2] The work pace for both chief executives and foremen was unrelenting. The chief executives met a steady stream of callers and mail from the moment they arrived in the morning until they left in the evening. Coffee breaks and lunches were inevitably work related, and ever-present subordinates seemed to usurp any free moment.

---

[1] All the data from my study can be found in Henry Mintzberg, *The Nature of Managerial Work* (New York: Harper & Row, 1973).

[2] Robert H. Guest, "Of Time and the Foreman," *Personnel*, May 1956, p. 478.

• A diary study of 160 British middle and top managers found that they worked for a half hour or more without interruption only about once every two days.[3]

• Of the verbal contacts of the chief executives in my study, 93% were arranged on an ad hoc basis. Only 1% of the executives' time was spent in open-ended observational tours. Only 1 out of 368 verbal contacts was unrelated to a specific issue and could be called general planning. Another researcher finds that "in *not one single case* did a manager report the obtaining of important external information from a general conversation or other undirected personal communication."[4]

• No study has found important patterns in the way managers schedule their time. They seem to jump from issue to issue, continually responding to the needs of the moment.

Is this the planner that the classical view describes? Hardly. How, then, can we explain this behavior? The manager is simply responding to the pressures of his job. I found that my chief executives terminated many of their own activities, often leaving meetings before the end, and interrupted their desk work to call in subordinates. One president not only placed his desk so that he could look down a long hallway but also left his door open when he was alone—an invitation for subordinates to come in and interrupt him.

Clearly, these managers wanted to encourage the flow of current information. But more significantly, they seemed to be conditioned by their own work loads. They appreciated the opportunity cost of their own time, and they were continually aware of their ever-present obligations—mail to be answered, callers to attend to, and so on. It seems that no matter what he is doing, the manager is plagued by

the possibilities of what he might do and what he must do.

When the manager must plan, he seems to do so implicitly in the context of daily actions, not in some abstract process reserved for two weeks in the organization's mountain retreat. The plans of the chief executives I studied seemed to exist only in their heads—as flexible, but often specific, intentions. The traditional literature notwithstanding, the job of managing does not breed reflective planners; the manager is a real-time responder to stimuli, an individual who is conditioned by his job to prefer live to delayed action.

2

Folklore *The effective manager has no regular duties to perform.* Managers are constantly being told to spend more time planning and delegating, and less time seeing customers and engaging in negotiations. These are not, after all, the true tasks of the manager. To use the popular analogy, the good manager, like the good conductor, carefully orchestrates everything in advance, then sits back to enjoy the fruits of his labor, responding occasionally to an unforeseeable exception.

But here again the pleasant abstraction just does not seem to hold up. We had better take a closer look at those activities managers feel compelled to engage in before we arbitrarily define them away.

Fact *In addition to handling exceptions, managerial work involves performing a number of regular duties, including ritual and ceremony, negotiations, and processing of soft information that links the organization with its environment.* Consider some evidence from the research studies:

• A study of the work of the presidents of small companies found that they engaged in routine activities because their companies could not afford staff specialists and were so thin on operating personnel that a single ab-

---

[3]Rosemary Stewart, *Managers and Their Jobs* (London: Macmillan, 1967); see also Sune Carlson, *Executive Behaviour* (Stockholm: Strombergs, 1951), the first of the diary studies.

[4]Francis J. Aguilar, *Scanning the Business Environment* (New York: Macmillan, 1967), p. 102.

sence often required the president to substitute.[5]

• One study of field sales managers and another of chief executives suggest that it is a natural part of both jobs to see important customers, assuming the managers wish to keep those customers.[6]

• Someone, only half in jest, once described the manager as that person who sees visitors so that everyone else can get his work done. In my study, I found that certain ceremonial duties—meeting visiting dignitaries, giving out gold watches, presiding at Christmas dinners—were an intrinsic part of the chief executive's job.

• Studies of managers' information flow suggest that managers play a key role in securing "soft" external information (much of it available only to them because of their status) and in passing it along to their subordinates.

3

Folklore *The senior manager needs aggregated information, which a formal management information system best provides.* Not too long ago, the words *total information system* were everywhere in the management literature. In keeping with the classical view of the manager as that individual perched on the apex of a regulated, hierarchical system, the literature's manager was to receive all his important information from a giant, comprehensive MIS.

But lately, as it has become increasingly evident that these giant MIS systems are not working—that managers are simply not using them—the enthusiasm has waned. A look at how managers actually process information makes the reason quite clear. Managers have

five media at their command—documents, telephone calls, scheduled and unscheduled meetings, and observational tours.

Fact *Managers strongly favor the verbal media—namely, telephone calls and meetings.* The evidence comes from every single study of managerial work. Consider the following:

• In two British studies, managers spent an average of 66% and 80% of their time in verbal (oral) communication.[7] In my study of five American chief executives, the figure was 78%.

• These five chief executives treated mail processing as a burden to be dispensed with. One came in Saturday morning to process 142 pieces of mail in just over three hours, to "get rid of all the stuff." This same manager looked at the first piece of "hard" mail he had received all week, a standard cost report, and put it aside with the comment, "I never look at this."

• These same five chief executives responded immediately to 2 of the 40 routine reports they received during the five weeks of my study and to four items in the 104 periodicals. They skimmed most of these periodicals in seconds, almost ritualistically. In all, these chief executives of good-sized organizations initiated on their own—that is, not in response to something else—a grand total of 25 pieces of mail during the 25 days I observed them.

An analysis of the mail the executives received reveals an interesting picture—only 13% was of specific and immediate use. So now we have another piece in the puzzle: not much of the mail provides live, current information—the action of a competitor, mood of a government legislator, or the rating of last night's television show. Yet this is the information that drove the managers, inter-

[5]Unpublished study by Irving Choran, reported in Mintzberg, *The Nature of Managerial Work.*

[6]Robert T. Davis, *Performance and Development of Field Sales Managers* (Boston: Division of Research, Harvard Business School, 1957); George H. Copeman, *The Role of the Managing Director* (London: Business Publications, 1963).

[7]Stewart, *Managers and Their Jobs*; Tom Burns, "The Directions of Activity and Communication in a Departmental Executive Group," *Human Relations* 7, no. 1 (1954): 73.

rupting their meetings and rescheduling their workdays.

Consider another interesting finding. Managers seem to cherish "soft" information, especially gossip, hearsay, and speculation. Why? The reason is its timeliness; today's gossip may be tomorrow's fact. The manager who is not accessible for the telephone call informing him that his biggest customer was seen golfing with his main competitor may read about a dramatic drop in sales in the next quarterly report. But then it's too late.

To assess the value of historical, aggregated, "hard" MIS information, consider two of the manager's prime uses for his information—to identify problems and opportunities[8] and to build his own mental models of the things around him (e.g., how his organization's budget system works, how his customers buy his product, how changes in the economy affect his organization, and so on). Every bit of evidence suggests that the manager identifies decision situations and builds models not with the aggregated abstractions an MIS provides, but with specific tidbits of data.

Consider the words of Richard Neustadt, who studied the information-collecting habits of Presidents Roosevelt, Truman, and Eisenhower:

> "It is not information of a general sort that helps a President see personal stakes; not summaries, not surveys, not the *bland amalgams*. Rather . . . it is the odds and ends of *tangible detail* that pieced together in his mind illuminate the underside of issues put before him. To help himself he must reach out as widely as he can for every scrap of fact, opinion, gossip, bearing on his interests and relationships as President. He must

[8]H. Edward Wrapp, "Good Managers Don't Make Policy Decisions," HBR September-October 1967, p. 91; Wrapp refers to this as spotting opportunities and relationships in the stream of operating problems and decisions; in his article Wrapp raises a number of excellent points related to this analysis.

become his own director of his own central intelligence."[9]

The manager's emphasis on the verbal media raises two important points:

First, verbal information is stored in the brains of people. Only when people write this information down can it be stored in the files of the organization—whether in metal cabinets or on magnetic tape—and managers apparently do not write down much of what they hear. Thus the strategic data bank of the organization is not in the memory of its computers but in the minds of its managers.

Second, the manager's extensive use of verbal media helps to explain why he is reluctant to delegate tasks. When we note that most of the manager's important information comes in verbal form and is stored in his head, we can well appreciate his reluctance. It is not as if he can hand a dossier over to someone; he must take the time to "dump memory"—to tell that someone all he knows about the subject. But this could take so long that the manager may find it easier to do the task himself. Thus the manager is damned by his own information system to a "dilemma of delegation"—to do too much himself or to delegate to his subordinates with inadequate briefing.

4

Folklore *Management is, or at least is quickly becoming, a science and a profession.* By almost any definitions of *science* and *profession*, this statement is false. Brief observation of any manager will quickly lay to rest the notion that managers practice a science. A science involves the enaction of systematic, analytically determined procedures or programs. If we do not even know what procedures managers use, how can we prescribe them by scientific analysis? And how can we call management a profession if we cannot

[9]Richard E. Neustadt, *Presidential Power* (New York; John Wiley, 1960), pp. 153-154; italics added.

specify what managers are to learn? For after all, a profession involves "knowledge of some department of learning or science" (*Random House Dictionary*).[10]

Fact *The managers' programs—to schedule time, process information, make decisions, and so on—remain locked deep inside their brains.* Thus, to describe these programs, we rely on words like *judgment* and *intuition*, seldom stopping to realize that they are merely labels for our ignorance.

I was struck during my study by the fact that the executives I was observing—all very competent by any standard—are fundamentally indistinguishable from their counterparts of a hundred years ago (or a thousand years ago, for that matter). The information they need differs, but they seek it in the same way—by word of mouth. Their decisions concern modern technology, but the procedures they use to make them are the same as the procedures of the nineteenth-century manager. Even the computer, so important for the specialized work of the organization, has apparently had no influence on the work procedures of general managers. In fact, the manager is in a kind of loop, with increasingly heavy work pressures but no aid forthcoming from management science.

Considering the facts about managerial work, we can see that the manager's job is enormously complicated and difficult. The manager is overburdened with obligations; yet he cannot easily delegate his tasks. As a result, he is driven to overwork and is forced to do many tasks superficially. Brevity, fragmentation, and verbal communication characterize his work. Yet these are the very characteristics of managerial work that have impeded scientific attempts to improve it. As a result,

the management scientist has concentrated his efforts on the specialized functions of the organizations, where he could more easily analyze the procedures and quantify the relevant information.[11]

But the pressures of the manager's job are becoming worse. Where before he needed only to respond to owners and directors, now he finds that subordinates with democratic norms continually reduce his freedom to issue unexplained orders, and a growing number of outside influences (consumer groups, government agencies, and so on) expect his attention. And the manager has had nowhere to turn for help. The first step in providing the manager with some help is to find out what his job really is.

BACK TO A BASIC DESCRIPTION OF MANAGERIAL WORK

Now let us try to put some of the pieces of this puzzle together. Earlier, I defined the manager as that person in charge of an organization or one of its subunits. Besides chief executive officers, this definition would include vice presidents, bishops, foremen, hockey coaches, and prime ministers. Can all of these people have anything in common? Indeed they can. For an important starting point, all are vested with formal authority over an organizational unit. From formal authority comes status, which leads to various interpersonal relations, and from these comes access to information. Information, in turn, enables the manager to make decisions and strategies for his unit.

The manager's job can be described in terms of various "roles," or organized sets of behaviors identified with a position. My de-

---

[10]For a more thorough, though rather different, discussion of this issue, see Kenneth R. Andrews, "Toward Professionalism in Business Management," HBR March-April 1969, p. 49.

[11]C. Jackson Grayson, Jr., in "Management Science and Business Practice," HBR July-August 1973, p. 41, explains in similar terms why, as chairman of the Price Commission, he did not use those very techniques that he himself promoted in his earlier career as a management scientist.

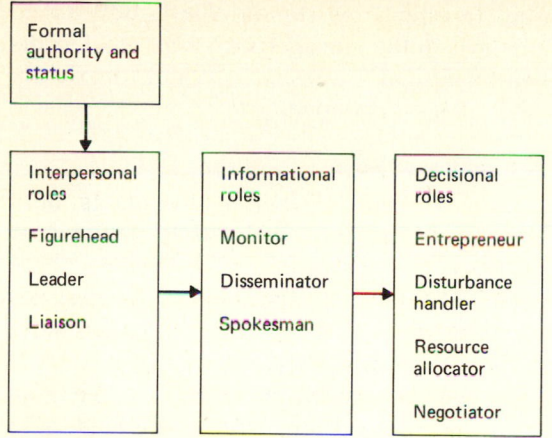

Figure 37-1 The manager's roles.

scription, shown in Figure 37-1, comprises ten roles. As we shall see, formal authority gives rise to the three interpersonal roles, which in turn give rise to the three informational roles; these two sets of roles enable the manager to play the four decisional roles.

Interpersonal Roles

Three of the manager's roles arise directly from his formal authority and involve basic interpersonal relationships.

1 First is the *figurehead* role. By virtue of his position as head of an organizational unit, every manager must perform some duties of a ceremonial nature. The president greets the touring dignitaries, the foreman attends the wedding of a ' lathe operator, and the sales manager takes an important customer to lunch.

The chief executives of my study spent 12% of their contact time on ceremonial duties; 17% of their incoming mail dealt with acknowledgments and requests related to their status. For example, a letter to a company president requested free merchandise for a crippled schoolchild; diplomas were put on the desk of the school superintendent for his signature.

Duties that involve interpersonal roles may sometimes be routine, involving little serious communication and no important decision making. Nevertheless, they are important to the smooth functioning of an organization and cannot be ignored by the manager.

2 Because he is in charge of an organizational unit, the manager is responsible for the work of the people of that unit. His actions in this regard constitute the *leader* role. Some of these actions involve leadership directly—for example, in most organizations the manager is normally responsible for hiring and training his own staff.

In addition, there is the indirect exercise of the leader role. Every manager must motivate and encourage his employees, somehow reconciling their individual needs with the goals of the organization. In virtually every contact the manager has with his employees, subordinates seeking leadership clues probe his actions: "Does he approve?" "How would he like the report to turn out?" "Is he more interested in market share than high profits?"

The influence of the manager is most clearly seen in the leader role. Formal authority vests him with great potential power; leadership determines in large part how much of it he will realize.

3 The literature of management has always recognized the leader role, particularly those aspects of it related to motivation. In comparison, until recently it has hardly mentioned the *liaison* role, in which the manager makes contacts outside his vertical chain of command. This is remarkable in light of the finding of virtually every study of managerial work that managers spend as much time with peers and other people outside their units as they do with their own subordinates—and, surprisingly, very little time with their own superiors.

In Rosemary Stewart's diary study, the 160 British middle and top managers spent 47% of their time with peers, 41% of their time with people outside their unit, and only 12% of their time with their superiors. For Robert H. Guest's study of U.S. foremen, the figures were 44%, 46%, and 10%. The chief executives of my study averaged 44% of their contact time with people outside their organizations, 48% with subordinates, and 7% with directors and trustees.

The contacts the five CEOs made were with an incredibly wide range of people: subordinates; clients, business associates, and suppliers; and peers—managers of similar organizations, government and trade organization officials, fellow directors on outside boards, and independents with no relevant organizational affiliations. The chief executives' time with and mail from these groups is shown in Figure 37-2. Guest's study of foremen shows, likewise, that their contacts were numerous and wide ranging, seldom involving fewer than 25 individuals, and often more than 50.

As we shall see shortly, the manager cultivates such contacts largely to find informa-

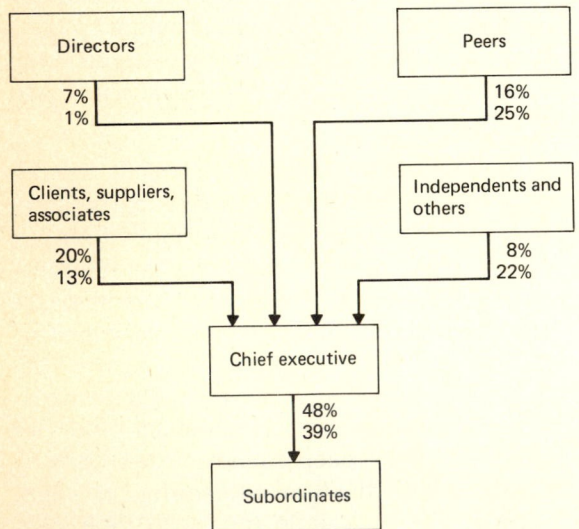

Figure 37-2 The chief executives' contacts. *Note*: The top figure indicates the proportion of total contact time spent with each group and the bottom figure, the proportion of mail from each group.

tion. In effect, the liaison role is devoted to building up the manager's own external information system—informal, private, verbal, but, nevertheless, effective.

Informational Roles

By virtue of his interpersonal contacts, both with his subordinates and with his network of contacts, the manager emerges as the nerve center of his organizational unit. He may not know everything, but he typically knows more than any member of his staff.

Studies have shown this relationship to hold for all managers, from street gang leaders to U.S. presidents. In *The Human Group*, George C. Homans explains how, because they were at the center of the information flow in their own gangs and were also in close touch with other gang leaders, street gang leaders were better informed than any of their followers.[12] And Richard Neustadt describes the following account from his study of Franklin D. Roosevelt:

> "The essence of Roosevelt's technique for information-gathering was competition. 'He would call you in,' one of his aides once told me, 'and he'd ask you to get the story on some complicated business, and you'd come back after a couple of days of hard labor and present the juicy morsel you'd uncovered under a stone somewhere, and *then* you'd find out he knew all about it, along with something else you *didn't* know. Where he got this information from he wouldn't mention, usually, but after he had done this to you once or twice you got damn careful about *your* information.'"[13]

We can see where Roosevelt "got this information" when we consider the relationship between the interpersonal and informational roles. As leader, the manager has formal and

[12]George C. Homans, *The Human Group* (New York: Harcourt, Brace & World, 1950), based on the study by William F. Whyte entitled *Street Corner Society*, rev. ed. (Chicago: University of Chicago Press, 1955).

[13]Neustadt, *Presidential Power*, p, 157.

easy access to every member of his staff. Hence, as noted earlier, he tends to know more about his own unit than anyone else does. In addition, his liaison contacts expose the manager to external information to which his subordinates often lack access. Many of these contacts are with other managers of equal status, who are themselves nerve centers in their own organization. In this way, the manager develops a powerful data base of information.

The processing of information is a key part of the manager's job. In my study, the chief executives spent 40% of their contact time on activities devoted exclusively to the transmission of information; 70% of their incoming mail was purely informational (as opposed to requests for action). The manager does not leave meetings or hang up the telephone in order to get back to work. In large part, communication *is* his work. Three roles describe these informational aspects of managerial work.

1 As *monitor*, the manager perpetually scans his environment for information, interrogates his liaison contacts and his subordinates, and receives unsolicited information, much of it as a result of the network of personal contacts he has developed. Remember that a good part of the information the manager collects in his monitor role arrives in verbal form, often as gossip, hearsay, and speculation. By virtue of his contacts, the manager has a natural advantage in collecting this soft information for his organization.

2 He must share and distribute much of this information. Information he gleans from outside personal contacts may be needed within his organization. In his *disseminator* role, the manager passes some of his privileged information directly to his subordinates, who would otherwise have no access to it. When his subordinates lack easy contact with one another, the manager will sometimes pass information from one to another.

3 In his *spokesman* role, the manager sends some of his information to people outside his unit—a president makes a speech to lobby for an organization cause, or a foreman suggests a product modification to a supplier. In addition, as part of his role as spokesman, every manager must inform and satisfy the influential people who control his organizational unit. For the foreman, this may simply involve keeping the plant manager informed about the flow of work through the shop.

The president of a large corporation, however, may spend a great amount of his time dealing with a host of influences. Directors and shareholders must be advised about financial performance; consumer groups must be assured that the organization is fulfilling its social responsibilities; and government officials must be satisfied that the organization is abiding by the law.

Decisional Roles

Information is not, of course, an end in itself; it is the basic input to decision making. One thing is clear in the study of managerial work: the manager plays the major role in his unit's decision-making system. As its formal authority, only he can commit the unit to important new courses of action; and as its nerve center, only he has full and current information to make the set of decisions that determines the unit's strategy. Four roles describe the manager as decision-maker.

1 As *entrepreneur*, the manager seeks to improve his unit, to adapt it to changing conditions in the environment. In his monitor role, the president is constantly on the lookout for new ideas. When a good one appears, he initiates a development project that he may supervise himself or delegate to an employee (perhaps with the stipulation that he must approve the final proposal).

There are two interesting features about these development projects at the chief executive level.

First, these projects do not involve single decisions or even unified clusters of decisions. Rather, they emerge as a series of small decisions and actions sequenced over time. Apparently, the chief executive prolongs each project so that he can fit it bit by bit into his busy, disjointed schedule and so that he can gradually come to comprehend the issue, if it is a complex one.

Second, the chief executives I studied supervised as many as 50 of these projects at the same time. Some projects entailed new products or processes; others involved public relations campaigns, improvement of the cash position, reorganization of a weak department, resolution of a morale problem in a foreign division, integration of computer operations, various acquisitions at different stages of development, and so on.

The chief executive appears to maintain a kind of inventory of the development projects that he himself supervises—projects that are at various stages of development, some active and some in limbo. Like a juggler, he keeps a number of projects in the air; periodically, one comes down, is given a new burst of energy, and is sent back into orbit. At various intervals, he put new projects on-stream and discards old ones.

2 While the entrepreneur role describes the manager as the voluntary initiator of change, the *disturbance handler* role depicts the manager involuntarily responding to pressures. Here change is beyond the manager's control. He must act because the pressures of the situation are too severe to be ignored: strike looms, a major customer has gone bankrupt, or a supplier reneges on his contract.

It has been fashionable, I noted earlier, to compare the manager to an orchestra conductor, just as Peter F. Drucker wrote in *The Practice of Management:*

> "The manager has the task of creating a true whole that is larger than the sum of its parts, a productive entity that turns out more than the sum of the resources put into it. One analogy is the conductor of a symphony orchestra, through whose effort, vision and leadership individual instrumental parts that are so much noise by themselves become the living whole of music. But the conductor has the composer's score; he is only interpreter. The manager is both composer and conductor."[14]

Now consider the words of Leonard R. Sayles, who has carried out systematic research on the manager's job:

> "[The manager] is like a symphony orchestra conductor, endeavouring to maintain a melodious performance in which the contributions of the various instruments are coordinated and sequenced, patterned and paced, while the orchestra members are having various personal difficulties, stage hands are moving music stands, alternating excessive heat and cold are creating audience and instrument problems, and the sponsor of the concert is insisting on irrational changes in the program."[15]

In effect, every manager must spend a good part of his time responding to high-pressure disturbances. No organization can be so well run, so standardized, that it has considered every contingency in the uncertain environment in advance. Disturbances arise not only because poor managers ignore situations until they reach crisis proportions, but also because good managers cannot possibly anticipate all the consequences of the actions they take.

[14]Peter F. Drucker, *The Practice of Management* (New York: Harper & Row, 1954), pp. 431-342.

[15]Leonard R. Sayles, *Managerial Behavior* (New York: McGraw-Hill, 1964), p. 162.

3 The third decisional role is that of *resource allocator*. To the manager falls the responsibility of deciding who will get what in his organizational unit. Perhaps the most important resource the manager allocates is his own time. Access to the manager constitutes exposure to the unit's nerve center and decision-maker. The manager is also charged with designing his unit's structure, that pattern of formal relationships that determines how work is to be divided and coordinated.

Also, in his role as resource allocator, the manager authorizes the important decisions of his unit before they are implemented. By retaining this power, the manager can ensure that decisions are interrelated; all must pass through a single brain. To fragment this power is to encourage discontinuous decision making and a disjointed strategy.

There are a number of interesting features about the manager's authorizing others' decisions. First, despite the widespread use of capital budgeting procedures—a means of authorizing various capital expenditures at one time—executives in my study made a great many authorization decisions on an ad hoc basis. Apparently, many projects cannot wait or simply do not have the quantifiable costs and benefits that capital budgeting requires.

Second, I found that the chief executives faced incredibly complex choices. They had to consider the impact of each decision on other decisions and on the organization's strategy. They had to ensure that the decision would be acceptable to those who influence the organization, as well as ensure that resources would not be overextended. They had to understand the various costs and benefits as well as the feasibility of the proposal. They also had to consider questions of timing. All this was necessary for the simple approval of someone else's proposal. At the same time, however, delay could lose time, while quick approval could be ill considered and quick rejection

might discourage the subordinate who had spent months developing a pet project.

One common solution to approving projects is to pick the man instead of the proposal. That is, the manager authorizes those projects presented to him by people whose judgment he trusts. But he cannot always use this simple dodge.

4 The final decisional role is that of *negotiator*. Studies of managerial work at all levels indicate that managers spend considerable time in negotiations: the president of the football team is called in to work out a contract with the holdout superstar; the corporation president leads his company's contingent to negotiate a new strike issue; the foreman argues a grievance problem to its conclusion with the shop steward. As Leonard Sayles puts it, negotiations are a "way of life" for the sophisticated manager.

These negotiations are duties of the manager's job; perhaps routine, they are not to be shirked. They are an integral part of his job, for only he has the authority to commit organizational resources in "real time," and only he has the nerve center information that important negotiations require.

The Integrated Job

It should be clear by now that the ten roles I have been describing are not easily separable. In the terminology of the psychologist, they form a gestalt, an integrated whole. No role can be pulled out of the framework and the job be left intact. For example, a manager without liaison contacts lacks external information. As a result, he can neither disseminate the information his employees need nor make decisions that adequately reflect external conditions. (In fact, this is a problem for the new person in a managerial position, since he cannot make effective decisions until he has built up his network of contacts.)

Here lies a clue to the problems of team

management.[16] Two or three people cannot share a single managerial position unless they can act as one entity. This means that they cannot divide up the ten roles unless they can very carefull reintegrate them. The real difficulty lies with the informational roles. Unless there can be full sharing of managerial information—and, as I pointed out earlier, it is primarily verbal—team management breaks down. A single managerial job cannot be arbitrarily split, for example, into internal and external roles, for information from both sources must be brought to bear on the same decisions.

To say that the ten roles form a gestalt is not to say that all managers give equal attention to each role. In fact, I found in my review of the various research studies that

> . . . sales managers seem to spend relatively more of their time in the interpersonal roles, presumably a reflection of the extrovert nature of the marketing activity;

> . . . production managers give relatively more attention to the decisional roles, presumably a reflection of their concern with efficient work flow;

> . . . staff managers spend the most time in the informational roles, since they are experts who manage departments that advise other parts of the organization.

Nevertheless, in all cases the interpersonal, informational, and decisional roles remain inseparable.

TOWARD MORE EFFECTIVE MANAGEMENT

What are the messages for management in this description? I believe, first and foremost, that this description of managerial work should

[16]See Richard C. Hodgson, Daniel J. Levinson, and Abraham Zaleznik, *The Executive Role Constellation* (Boston: Division of Research, Harvard Business School, 1965), for a discussion of the sharing of roles.

prove more important to managers than any prescription they might derive from it. That is to say, *the manager's effectiveness is significantly influenced by his insight into his own work.* His performance depends on how well he understands and responds to the pressures and dilemmas of the job. Thus managers who can be introspective about their work are likely to be effective at their jobs. . . .

Let us take a look at three specific areas of concern. For the most part, the managerial logjams—the dilemma of delegation, the data base centralized in one brain, the problems of working with the management scientist—evolve around the verbal nature of the manager's information. There are great dangers in centralizing the organization's data bank in the minds of its managers. When they leave, they take their memory with them. And when subordinates are out of convenient verbal reach of the manager, they are at an informational disadvantage.

1

The manager is challenged to find systematic ways to share his privileged information. A regular debriefing session with key subordinates, a weekly memory dump on the dictating machine, the maintaining of a diary of important information for limited circulation, or other similar methods may ease the logjam of work considerably. Time spent disseminating this information will be more then regained when decisions must be made. Of course, some will raise the question of confidentiality. But managers would do well to weigh the risks of exposing privileged information against having subordinates who can make effective decisions.

If there is a single theme that runs through this article, it is that the pressures of his job drive the manager to be superficial in his actions—to overload himself with work, encourage interruption, respond quickly to every stimulus, seek the tangible and avoid the abstract, make decisions in small increments, and do everything abruptly.

2

Here again, the manager is challenged to deal consciously with the pressures of superficiality by giving serious attention to the issues that require it, by stepping back from his tangible bits of information in order to see a broad picture, and by making use of analytical inputs. Although effective managers have to be adept at responding quickly to numerous and varying problems, the danger in managerial work is that they will respond to every issue equally (and that means abruptly) and that they will never work the tangible bits and pieces of informational input into a comprehensive picture of their world.

As I noted earlier, the manager uses these bits of information to build models of his world. But the manager can also avail himself of the models of the specialists. Economists describe the functioning of markets, operations researchers simulate financial flow processes, and behavioral scientists explain the needs and goals of people. The best of these models can be searched out and learned.

In dealing with complex issues, the senior manager has much to gain from a close relationship with the management scientists of his own organization. They have something important that he lacks—time to probe complex issues. An effective working relationship hinges on the resolution of what a colleague and I have called "the planning dilemma."[17] Managers have the information and the authority; analysts have the time and the technology. A successful working relationship between the two will be effected when the manager learns to share his information and the analyst learns to adapt to the manager's need. For the analyst, adaptation means worrying less about the

[17]James S. Hekimian and Henry Mintzberg, "The Planning Dilemma," *The Management Review,* May 1968, p. 4.

elegance of the method and more about its speed and flexibility.

It seems to me that analysts can help the top manager especially to schedule his time, feed in analytical information, monitor projects under his supervision, develop models to aid in making choices, design contingency plans for disturbances that can be anticipated, and conduct "quick-and-dirty" analysis for those that cannot. But there can be no cooperation if the analysts are out of the mainstream of the manager's information flow.

3

The manager is challenged to gain control of his own time by turning obligations to his advantage and by turning those things he wishes to do into obligations. The chief executives of my study initiated only 32% of their own contacts (and another 5% by mutual agreement). And yet to a considerable extent they seemed to control their time. There were two key factors that enabled them to do so.

First, the manager has to spend so much time discharging obligations that if he were to view them as just that, he would leave no mark on his organization. The unsuccessful manager blames failure on the obligations; the effective manager turns his obligations to his own advantage. A speech is a chance to lobby for a cause; a meeting is a chance to reorganize a weak department; a visit to an important customer is a chance to extract trade information.

Second, the manager frees some of his time to do those things that he—perhaps no one else—thinks important by turning them into obligations. Free time is made, not found, in the manager's job; it is forced into the schedule. Hoping to leave some time open for contemplation or general planning is tantamount to hoping that the pressures of the job will go away. The manager who wants to innovate initiates a project and obligates others to report back to him; the manager who needs certain environmental information establishes channels that will automatically keep him informed; the manager who has to tour facilities commits himself publicly.

The Educator's Job

Finally, a word about the training of managers. Our management schools have done an admirable job of training the organization's specialists—management scientists, marketing researchers, accountants, and organizational development specialists. But for the most part they have not trained managers.[18]

Management schools will begin the serious training of managers when skill training takes a serious place next to cognitive learning. Cognitive learning is detached and informational, like reading a book or listening to a lecture. No doubt much important cognitive material must be assimilated by the manager-to-be. But cognitive learning no more makes a manager than it does a swimmer. The latter will drown the first time he jumps into the water if his coach never takes him out of the lecture hall, gets him wet, and gives him feedback on his performance.

In other words, we are taught a skill through practice plus feedback. whether in a real or a simulated situation. Our management schools

need to identify the skills managers use, select students who show potential in these skills, put the students into situations where these skills can be practiced, and then give them systematic feedback on their performance.

My description of managerial work suggests a number of important managerial skills—developing peer relationships, carrying out negotiations, motivating subordinates, resolving conflicts, establishing information networks and subsequently disseminating information, making decisions in conditions of extreme ambiguity, and allocating resources. Above all, the manager needs to be introspective about his work so that he may continue to learn on the job.

Many of the manager's skills can, in fact, be practiced, using techniques that range from role playing to videotaping real meetings. And our management schools can enhance the entrepreneurial skills by designing programs that encourage sensible risk taking and innovation.

No job is more vital to our society than that of the manager. It is the manager who determines whether our social institutions serve us well or whether they squander our talents and resources. It is time to strip away the folklore about managerial work, and time to study it realistically so that we can begin the difficult task of making significant improvements in its performance.

[18]See J. Sterling Livingston, "Myth of the Well-Educated Manager," HBR January-February 1971, p. 79.

Part Five

Improving Organizational Effectiveness

Chapter 10

Approaches to Organizational Change

How does one go about changing an organization? Are the behavioral sciences really of use in bringing about change that persists over time and spreads throughout an organization? Or do the forces that most influence what happens in organizations lie beyond the domain of behavioral science—deriving instead from technological developments, from changes in the national economy and the labor market, and from government legislation and regulatory practices?

There certainly is no dearth of behavioral techniques for change. Some techniques take a strongly psychological approach, and aspire to organizational change by improving selection and placement practices, by improving the training organization members receive, or by increasing employees' motivation and commitment. Other approaches have a social psy-chological focus, and attempt to improve the quality of communication that takes place within and between groups in organizations, to reduce dysfunctional conflict, and to improve the quality of managerial leadership processes. Still other change approaches involve structural alterations, including change of the organization structure itself and the redesign of the roles and jobs of organization members.

While there are cases of great success using such behavioral approaches to change, there are at present few documented cases in which long-term changes in organizational life and effectiveness have developed from the planned use of any of these techniques. In this chapter, therefore, articles have been selected that address broad questions and assumptions having to do with behavioral interventions. Rather than exploring in depth particular techniques or strategies for change, these readings attempt to identify what will be required if the behavioral sciences are to become increasingly useful in planning and implementing changes that will yield robust, beneficial, and long-term effects on life in organizations, and on organizational effectiveness.

The first article, by Argyris, deals with *assumptions* that underlie behavioral approaches to change. Argyris offers a theory-based definition of intervention, and then identifies three conditions which he believes must be met for effective change: (1) the generation of *valid information*, (2) the creation of conditions for *free, informed choice* by members of the client system, and (3) the creation of conditions that encourage members of the client system to generate *internal commitment* to the choices they make. These conditions turn out to have a number of important implications for how one proceeds with intervention activities—including implications that differ from practices commonly used by consultants in the behavioral sciences.

Bowers, Franklin, and Pecorella, in the second article, propose that there is no "generally useful" approach to behavioral change. Instead, they argue, the effectiveness of an intervention very much depends on how well the intervention fits with the organizational unit where it is utilized. The authors identify several antecedents to various kinds of "problem behaviors" in organizations, and then offer a number of alternatives for how one might proceed to identify and use interventions that are well-suited to the given problems and to their antecedents. The article

concludes with a number of practical implications for practitioners of organization development.

In the next article, Walton probes for reasons why "successful" innovations in one part of an organization rarely diffuse throughout the organization as a whole. He reviews eight firms in which comprehensive and successful work restructuring activities were carried out, and reports that impressive diffusion of the changes occurred in only one of these eight organizations. After identifying a number of steps in the change process that were common to most of the eight projects, Walton points out several significant problems that were encountered—and rarely overcome—in attempts to diffuse the successes throughout the firms. The nature and extensiveness of these problems are both unsettling and instructive to those who are interested in designing and installing changes that will, over a period of time, lead to broad and profound changes throughout an organization.

One of the problems identified by Walton deals with the kind of involvement organized labor has in the change. This issue is explored in depth by Strauss in the final article. Strauss begins by identifying a number of quandaries faced by unions themselves when innovations affecting the quality of work life are being contemplated in an organization. He then proposes several mechanisms by which union and management can collaborate in carrying out change—mechanisms which are rarely used, but which offer the opportunity for developing broad commitment to a project and, potentially, for designing changes that are of higher quality than is typically the case.

Reading 38
The Primary Tasks of Intervention Activities
Chris Argyris

A DEFINITION OF INTERVENTION

To intervene is to enter into an ongoing system of relationship, to come between or among persons, groups, or objects for the purpose of helping them. There is an important implicit assumption in the definition that should be made explicit: the system exists independently of the intervenor. There are many reasons one might wish to intervene. These reasons may range from helping the clients make their own decisions about the kind of help they need to coercing the clients to do what the intervenor wishes them to do. Examples of the latter are modern black militants who intervene to demand that the city be changed in accordance with their wishes and choices (or white racists who prefer the same); executives who invite interventionists into their system to manipulate subordinates for them; trade union leaders who for years have resisted systematic research in their own bureaucratic functioning at the highest levels because they fear that valid information might lead to entrenched interests—especially at the top—being unfrozen.

The more one conceives of the intervenor in this sense, the more one implies that the client system should have little autonomy from the intervenor; that its boundaries are indistinguishable from those of the intervenor; that its health or effectiveness are best controlled by the intervenor.

In contrast, our view acknowledges interdependencies between the intervenor and the client system but focuses on how to maintain, or increase, the client system's autonomy; how to differentiate even more clearly the boundaries between the client system and the intervenor; and how to conceptualize and define the client system's health independently of the intervenor's. This view values the client system as an ongoing, self-responsible unity that has the obligation to be in control over its own destiny. An intervenor, in this view, assists a system to become more effective in problem solving, decision making, and decision implementation in such a way that the system can continue to be increasingly effective in these activities and have a decreasing need for the intervenor.

Another critical question the intervenor must ask is, who is he helping—management or employees, black militants or Negro moderates, white racists or white moderates? . . . At this point, it is suggested that the intervenor must be concerned with the system as a whole even though his initial contact may be made with only a few people. He therefore focuses on those intervention activities that eventually (not necessarily immediately) will provide *all* the members' opportunities to enhance their competence and effectiveness. If any individual or subsystem wishes help to prevent other individuals or subsystems from having these opportunities, then the intervenor may well have to question seriously his involvement in the project.[1]

[1]There is an important function within the scope of responsibility of the interventionist that will not be discussed systematically [here]. It is the public health function. There are many individuals who do not ask for help because they do not know they need help or that help could be available to them. The societal strategy for developing effective intervention activity must therefore include a function by which potential clients are educated about organizational health and illness as well as the present state of the art in effecting change. . . .

Excerpt from chap. 1 of C. Argyris, *Intervention theory and method: A behavioral science view.* Reading, Mass.: Addison-Wesley, 1970.

BASIC REQUIREMENTS FOR INTERVENTION ACTIVITY

Are there any basic or necessary processes that must be fulfilled regardless of the substantive issues involved, if intervention activity is to be helpful with any level of client (individual, group, or organization)? One condition that seems so basic as to be defined axiomatic is the generation of *valid information*. Without valid information, it would be difficult for the client to learn and for the interventionist to help.

A second condition almost as basic flows from our assumption that intervention activity, no matter what its substantive interests and objectives, should be so designed and executed that the client system maintains its discreteness and autonomy. Thus *free, informed choice* is also a necessary process in effective intervention activity.

Finally, if the client system is assumed to be ongoing (that is, existing over time), the clients require strengthening to maintain their autonomy not only vis-à-vis the interventionist but also vis-à-vis other systems. This means that their commitment to learning and change has to be more than temporary. It has to be so strong that it can be transferred to relationships other than those with the interventionist and can do so (eventually) without the help of the interventionist. The third basic process for any intervention activity is therefore the client's *internal commitment* to the choices made.

In summary, valid information, free choice, and internal commitment are considered integral parts of any intervention activity, no matter what the substantive objectives are (for example, developing a management performance evaluation scheme, reducing intergroup rivalries, increasing the degree of trust among individuals, redesigning budgetary systems, or redesigning work). These three processes are called the primary intervention tasks.

PRIMARY TASKS OF AN INTERVENTIONIST

Why is it necessary to hypothesize that in order for an interventionist to behave effectively and in order that the integrity of the client system be maintained, the interventionist has to focus on three primary tasks, regardless of the substantive problems that the client system may be experiencing?

Valid and Useful Information

First, it has been accepted as axiomatic that valid and useful information is the foundation for effective intervention. Valid information is that which describes the factors, plus their interrelationships, that create the problem for the client system. There are several tests for checking the validity of the information. In increasing degrees of power they are public verifiability, valid prediction, and control over the phenomena. The first is having several independent diagnoses suggest the same picture. Second is generating predictions from the diagnosis that are subsequently confirmed (they occurred under the conditions that were specified). Third is altering the factors systematically and predicting the effects upon the system as a whole. All these tests, if they are to be valid, must be carried out in such a way that the participants cannot, at will, make them come true. This would be a self-fulfilling prophecy and not a confirmation of a prediction. The difficulty with a self-fulfilling prophecy is its indication of more about the degree of power an individual (or subset of individuals) can muster to alter the system than about the nature of the system when the participants are behaving without knowledge of the diagnosis. For example, if an executive learns that the interventionist predicts his subordinates will behave (a) if he behaves (b), he might alter (b) in order not to lead to (a). Such an alteration indicates the executive's power but does not test the validity of the diagnosis that if (a), then (b).

The tests of valid information have important implications for effective intervention activity. First, the interventionist's diagnoses must strive to represent the total client system and not the point of view of any subgroup or individual. Otherwise, the interventionist could not be seen only as being under the control of a particular individual or subgroup, but also his predictions would be based upon inaccurate information and thus might not be confirmed.

This does not mean that an interventionist may not begin with, or may not limit his relationship to a subpart of the total system. It is totally possible, for example, for the interventionist to help management, blacks, trade union leaders, etc. With whatever subgroup he works he simply should not agree to limit his diagnosis to its wishes.

It is conceivable that a client system may be helped even though valid information is not generated. Sometimes changes occur in a positive direction without the interventionist having played any important role. These changes, although helpful in that specific instance, lack the attribute of helping the organization to learn and to gain control over its problem-solving capability.

The importance of information that the clients can use to control their destiny points up the requirement that the information must not only be valid, it must be useful. Valid information that cannot be used by the clients to alter their system is equivalent to valid information about cancer that cannot be used to cure cancer eventually. An interventionist's diagnosis should include variables that are manipulable by the clients and are complete enough so that if they are manipulated effective change will follow.

Free Choice

In order to have free choice, the client has to have a cognitive map of what he wishes to do. The objectives of his action are known at the moment of decision. Free choice implies voluntary as opposed to automatic; proactive rather than reactive. The act of selection is rarely accomplished by maximizing or optimizing. Free and informed choice entails what Simon has called "satisficing," that is, selecting the alternative with the highest probability of succeeding, given some specified cost constraints. Free choice places the locus of decision making in the client system. Free choice makes it possible for the clients to remain responsible for their destiny. Through free choice the clients can maintain the autonomy of their system.

It may be possible that clients prefer to give up their responsibility and their autonomy, especially if they are feeling a sense of failure. They may prefer, as we shall see in several examples, to turn over their free choice to the interventionist. They may insist that he make recommendations and tell them what to do. The interventionist resists these pressures because if he does not, the clients will lose their free choice and he will lose his own free choice also. He will be controlled by the anxieties of the clients.

The requirement of free choice is especially important for those helping activities where the processes of help are as important as the actual help. For example, a medical doctor does not require that a patient with a bullet wound participate in the process by defining the kind of help he needs. However, the same doctor may have to pay much more attention to the processes he uses to help patients when he is attempting to diagnose blood pressure or cure a high cholesterol. If the doctor behaves in ways that upset the patient, the latter's blood pressure may well be distorted. Or, the patient can develop a dependent relationship if the doctor cuts down his cholesterol—increasing habits only under constant pressure from the doctor—and the moment the relationship is broken off, the count goes up.

Effective intervention in the human and

social spheres requires that the processes of help be congruent with the outcome desired. Free choice is important because there are so many unknowns, and the interventionist wants the client to have as much willingness and motivation as possible to work on the problem. With high client motivation and commitment, several different methods for change can succeed.

A choice is free to the extent the members can make their selection for a course of action with minimal internal defensiveness; can define the path (or paths) by which the intended consequence is to be achieved; can relate the choice to their central needs; and can build into their choices a realistic and challenging level of aspiration. Free choice therefore implies that the members are able to explore as many alternatives as they consider significant and select those that are central to their needs.

Why must the choice be related to the central needs and why must the level of aspiration be realistic and challenging? May people not choose freely unrealistic or unchallenging objectives? Yes, they may do so in the short run, but not for long if they still want to have free and informed choice. A freely chosen course of action means that the action must be based on an accurate analysis of the situation and not on the biases or defenses of the decision makers. We know, from the level of aspiration studies, that choices which are too high or too low, which are too difficult or not difficult enough will tend to lead to psychological failure. Psychological failure will lead to increased defensiveness, increased failure, and decreased self-acceptance on the part of the members experiencing the failure. These conditions, in turn, will tend to lead to distorted perceptions by the members making the choices. Moreover, the defensive members may unintentionally create a climate where the members of surrounding and interrelated systems will tend to provide carefully censored information. Choices made under these conditions are neither informed nor free.

Turning to the question of centrality of needs, a similar logic applies. The degree of commitment to the processes of generating valid information, scanning, and choosing may significantly vary according to the centrality of the choice to the needs of the clients. The more central the choice, the more the system will strive to do its best in developing valid information and making free and informed choices. If the research from perceptual psychology is valid, the very perception of the clients is altered by the needs involved. Individuals tend to scan more, ask for more information, and be more careful in their choices when they are making decisions that are central to them. High involvement may produce perceptual distortions, as does low involvement. The interventionist, however, may have a greater probability of helping the clients explore possible distortion when the choice they are making is a critical one.

Internal Commitment

Internal commitment means the course of action or choice that has been internalized by each member so that he experiences a high degree of ownership and has a feeling of responsibility about the choice and its implications. Internal commitment means that the individual has reached the point where he is acting on the choice because it fulfills his own needs and sense of responsibility, as well as those of the system.

The individual who is internally committed is acting primarily under the influence of his own forces and not induced forces. The individual (or any unity) feels a minimal degree of dependence upon others for the action. It implies that he has obtained and processed valid information and that he has made an informed and free choice. Under these conditions there is a high probability that the individual's commitment will remain strong over time (even with reduction of external rewards) or under stress, or when the course of action is challenged by others. It also implies that the individual is continually open to reexamination of his position because he believes in taking action based upon valid information.

IMPLICATION OF THE PRIMARY TASKS FOR INTERVENTION ACTIVITY

1 There is a Congruence between Effective Intervention Activity and Effective Client Systems

The first implication states there is little difference between the activities an ongoing client system requires for effective daily operation and those activities required to intervene effectively. A client system will be effective to the extent that it is able to generate valid information, free and informed choice, and internal commitment.

Effective intervention activity helps the client system learn not only how to solve a particular set of problems but how to operate more competently. Presumably, this greater degree of competence should help to decrease the probability that if the set of problems recur, it will be solved without the help of an outside interventionist.

The concept of competence places constraints upon the interventionist. He may not design change strategies, which even though they may bring about change, can also reduce free choice or internal commitment. Such strategies increase the client's dependence upon the interventionist and reduce the probability that the client system will become self-regulating. [In some cases, for example, organizational development programs have been instituted, or an ineffective manager has been dismissed,] in such a way that the client system became more defensive and apprehensive. Everyone knew about the increase in this tension except the interventionist and the president. The data were kept from them because the clients perceived the interventionist as having sided with the president (some described it as bought out by the president) to design a change program that did not

alter that basic unilateral directive managerial philosophy of the president.

Another way to conceptualize the issue is to note that the processes of management are not separable for the substantive human problems of systems. Indeed, many of the human substantive problems arise because of the process of the management used in many pyramidal organizations. To attempt to alter the human substantive problem—say resistance to change—without altering the processes of management is comparable to making changes without getting at the basic causes. From a client's viewpoint, the only worse strategy is for the interventionist to articulate intervention values, as described, yet behave in a manner that is not congruent and is blind to his incongruence.

2 Change Is Not a Primary Task

A second implication states that change is *not* a primary task of the interventionist. To repeat, the interventionist's primary tasks are to generate valid information, to help the client system make informed and responsible choices, and to develop internal commitment to these choices. One choice that the clients may make is to change aspects of their system. If this choice is made responsibly, the interventionist may help the client to change. However, the point we are making is that change is not a priori considered good and no change considered bad.

This position may seem out of keeping with the emphasis in the literature. Change is described as the challenge of the future, the basic characteristic of the next decade, and the only certainty. These proclamations may be true and they may be, partially at least, self-fulfilling prophecies.

If an interventionist assumes that the client's biggest problems are related to change, he has already made a choice for the client. It may very well be that change is the most important problem or need facing the client. However, it is important that the decision not be prejudged by the interventionist, and, according to this framework, the client should be helped to make the decision. The interventionist can help the client by assisting him in obtaining valid and useful information.

If the majority of interventionists conceptualize problems as involving and requiring change, the potential clients may come to perceive their problems as those of change. The definition of the expert may become the expectation of the nonexpert. But when the executive nonexpert decides (and the interventionist agrees) that he wants to create change in the system, those subordinates responsible for the system may prefer to generate valid information and then see if change is their choice. Such action may be viewed by the top executive (and the interventionist) as resistance to progress, a view which would be incorrect.

Perhaps if the people making interventions, at any level in our society, would focus more consciously and with greater commitment on the primary tasks, we would not experience as much pressure for change. Change may be our biggest societal problem, but it may not be the deepest problem. Indeed if the deepest problems were dealt with effectively, change might not be as important.

Research from task theory shows that the task requirements may have significant effects on the individual's perceptions, attitudes, and performance. If the intervenor assumes that change is his primary task, he may tend to cast the client's problems into ones related to change. In recent years the focus has been so strongly upon change that interventionists have usually been called "change agents." Change agents may be so imbued with the importance of change that they enter the situation without realizing they may have a bias against stability. It is not uncommon to hear change agents speak of the challenge of unfreezing, confronting, or blasting the client system. The pressure for making changes can be made so strong that a change agent may attempt to circumvent the generation of valid

data and development of free choice. For example, in too many organizational development programs the only members who have had a free choice about the program have been the top management. In several inner city projects, the interventionist in the interest of proceeding with change has agreed to black-white confrontation sessions with no previous development of valid data. Indeed, in several cases they have called the meetings so that the blacks could confront their "white oppressors" and have a cathartic experience. None of these sessions provided *all* the clients with free choice or an opportunity to develop internal commitment.

Who is to say that stability and equilibrium are bad or undesirable, or at the least uninteresting and unexciting? Readers familiar with the life sciences, for example, know of the complexity and beauty of the wisdom of the body. Anthropology has provided evidence for the delicate and intricate way by which complex social systems maintain themselves. Social psychology has shown that one of the most difficult tasks in any group is to create a cohesive, well-functioning, goal-achieving group.

Moreover, will clients who should seek help come to interventionists whom they perceive evaluate the desire for stability as wrong or unexciting? How helpful can interventionists be with such clients?

The almost compulsive idealization of change may even lead some scholars and interventionists to evaluate organizational development as being effective to the extent that it can be shown to bring about change. For example, Buchanan and Greiner have presented analyses of successful and less successful organizational development programs.[2] Their primary criteria for success

[2]Paul C. Buchanan, *"Crucial Issues in Organizational Development,"* in Goodwin Watson (ed.), *Change in School Systems*, NTL., Washington, D.C.: 1967, pp. 57–67; Larry E. Greiner, "Organization Change and Development," Doctor's Thesis, Cambridge, Massachusetts, Harvard University Graduate School of Business Administration, 1965.

were the extent to which output behavior (productivity, morale, communication) was reported to have increased and the extent to which changes in behavior could be found to have spread throughout the system. Little or no data were presented in the successful studies related to the degree of free choice and internal commitment experienced by the members of the client system. In two of their successful cases the documentation suggests that there was little opportunity for free choice and internal commitment on the part of all those involved. In one study that they labeled unsuccessful because the program did not spread, it was shown the interventionist had actually helped to stop the program because he helped to generate valid information that the highest level of management was not interested in free choice and internal commitment.

The point is *not* being made that change is unimportant. Change is very important, but its long-range effectiveness may be questioned if it is born of processes that violate the primary tasks. If an interventionist helps a system unfreeze and refreeze at a new level, his task is not complete. The task is complete when the refreezing occurs in such a way that change in the future will be equally possible (or even more possible). Producing a change is therefore not an adequate criterion for judging the effectiveness of an interventionist. A change that leaves a client system more rigid and more apprehensive of future changes may have actually crippled the client system in the long run. For example, a governmental agency such as the State Department has undergone many reorganizations. Each one, although managed by a blue ribbon commission, has tended to make the insiders more wary of change and more defensive about making further changes. The same may be true about the older divisions of large corporations. A large number have undergone so many unilaterally planned and masterminded changes that the insiders no longer feel much responsibility for keeping their system alive and viable—"That

is the top's job," a middle manager said, "We janitors just carry out the orders and sweep up the mess afterwards." This sense of resignation and feeling of nonresponsibility have, in some cases, gone so far as to lead some participants to gain their satisfactions by carefully and creatively fighting changes.

Focusing on the three primary tasks also helps an interventionist prevent himself from falling into the trap of being associated ahead of time with certain types of managerial styles. For example, some interventionists have written that participation is the most effective managerial style; that power equalization is good; and that democratic management is inevitable.

All these statements may or may not be true for the particular client system being served at this time. It may be that from a careful analysis the client system chooses autocracy for certain decisions, makes the power differential between subordinate and superior even greater, and decreases the amount of participation under certain conditions. The information needed to support the validity of these choices will not tend to be generated with the help of an interventionist whose values are already committed to the effectiveness of a particular management style.

3 Primary Tasks Are Used As Criteria for Selecting Client Systems

Defining the primary tasks as generating valid information, free and informed choice, and internal commitment may help to cast light on some difficult value questions regarding the choice of client systems. For example, should one help a system which has, in the eyes of the interventionist, undesirable goals? Would one help the Ku Klux Klan? Most interventionists would say no or at least hesitate for a long time before they would help an organization whose members had been accused of racial hatred and murder. Perhaps this is the organization that needs help more than many others? If members of the KKK have killed, have they killed more than the most optimistic estimates of the impact of the recent edict by Pope Paul on birth control upon children in the poorly developed countries?

If the interventionist keeps the three primary tasks in the forefront, it will be possible for him to help organizations that may be questionable in his eyes without implicating himself (or them) with his values or with change. What would happen if the KKK invited an interventionist to generate valid information about its internal system and to create conditions of informed and free choice for all who became part of its system? Why should it not be helped to accomplish these purposes? Might its successful accomplishment lead to new self-inquiry within the client system? If it does, an important step forward has been taken; if it does not, the intervenor can choose to leave without being charged with bias.

The latter statement leads to another interrelated issue. Should an interventionist be permitted to decide unilaterally which client system he will help and which he will not. Medical doctors and lawyers discovered many years ago that one way to keep their respective professions alive and viable in a society was to offer their aid to anyone who needed it. To be sure, there are medical doctors and lawyers who refuse to take lower class clients, but these refusals are subject to investigation by the local medical or legal professional societies. Such denial of help is not condoned by fellow professionals.

If an interventionist is not to be granted power of unilateral choice of clients, it seems important that he be able to offer initial aid to any system that will not tend to compromise his values. Adherence to the three primary tasks offers such aid without committing the interventionist to remain in the system in order to help it change or to maintain its present equilibrium.

The relationship between the interventionist and client system forms a system in itself. The primary objective of the intervention system

is to introduce into, or build upon, the client system's capacity to generate valid information, free and informed choice, and internal commitment. For two reasons, this objective is a difficult one to achieve in most client systems. As we will see, most client systems tend to be designed and managed in ways that minimize the probabilities of generating valid information (for critical decisions), free choice, and internal commitment. Moreover, in view of the small amount the client system may have of these three activities, the probability is quite high that it was reduced even further and that this fact was one reason an interventionist was invited.

In order to graft onto the client system significantly higher dosages of the capacity to generate valid information, free choice, and internal commitment, the intervention system requires all the assistance it can get. First, the client system must be open to and capable of learning. Client systems at any level of complexity that are closed and not capable of learning are not going to be helped very much by an intervention strategy based on valid information, free and informed choice, and internal commitment. This means that behavioral science intervention theory may be seriously limited in what it can do for client systems that cannot or do not want to be helped. This limitation may be partially overcome by actions described later. However, the limitation is also an important social safeguard. It means that interventionists cannot help anyone unless he wants to be helped. The decision, therefore, is with the client. If it were possible to help someone who does not wish to be helped, it would also be possible to harm someone who does not wish to be harmed.

Second, the intervention system should be linked with the power points in the client system that are the keys to the problem being studied. In pyramidal organizations this usually means the top of the organization. Changes in attitudes, values, and behavior at the top can lead to changes in administrative controls, structure, and organizational policies. All of these combined can produce clear messages to those below of the willingness to change the system.

Linking the interventionist with the top does not mean that the linkage should be limited to the top of the pyramidal structure. Free choice and internal commitment are necessary at all levels. The interventionist may differentiate in terms of the ones who have organizational power, but he may not give differential treatment in line with this power.

There are, unfortunately, many examples of executives who inflicted consultants on their organizations because they felt the system would not change. They gave the consultants full power to explore every issue and make any recommendations they thought necessary. In most cases, the clients participated half-heartedly; resistance, if any, was covert and carefully measured. After the report was issued and the changes announced, the living system was able to incorporate these changes in such a way that the participants proved they were incorrect and misguided. The system competence became worse rather than better.

There are a few cases in which changes have been ordered and unilaterally instituted against the will of the participants and the changes did last. Unfortunately, we do not have systematic data about these cases. Several themes, however, seem to come to the surface from the case material available. First, the top executives were committed to these changes and they relieved any subordinate of his job if he did not accept them. Second, meticulous control procedures were established to catch any major resistance. Third, the top brought in new people whose loyalty to the changes could be high and gave them power positions to apply pressure. Fourth, the old timers learned to fight the changes in a more covert manner and to feed into the

control procedures data that would make effective monitoring difficult. Their resistance went underground and it began to be felt years after the changes were instituted. The costs, in short, were very high. In most cases they were much higher than necessary because the changes developed resistance and organizational tension.

But, for the sake of argument, let us assume that it could be proved that the costs were worth the change achieved and that no other way would have been more successful. If this were so, then the clients do not need the kind of interventionist that this book describes. Indeed, the clients are probably experts in this kind of change. They are experts because it is a natural extension and magnification of the kind of management philosophy with which they are intimately familiar and highly competent to execute. Theory X managers use theory X^2 to bring about change.

Even if executives were not experts in theory X^2 change strategies, we would still recommend that behavioral science interventionists not align themselves with this strategy (except in some few cases) for several reasons. As we shall see, theory X intervention strategy will decrease the probability of getting valid information. Thus the diagnostic and research competence brought to the situation by the interventionist will be blunted. Also, if the interventionist takes sides, he runs the risk of becoming "big brother" who covertly manipulates individuals in the Orwellian 1984 mode. No society has, to date, permitted professionals to flourish freely and under their own self-regulation who, when in action, reduced the freedom and self-regulation of the people living in that society.

There are two conditions under which a unilateral controlling strategy may be utilized by the interventionist. First, it may be used when the problem being discussed is unimportant and therefore does not involve the client's feelings of self-acceptance and competence and where the problem is clearly out of the expected range of competence of the clients. There are, for example, technical issues that an interventionist can answer more competently than the client (how large should a T-group be? how can one define a valid sample of questionnaire? how may tape recordings be content analyzed? etc.). Second, a unilateral directive strategy may be helpful when the client system is in extreme danger and feels helpless, yet deserves to be helped. Under these conditions the interventionist could provide the clients with the information and choices that are needed, recognizing that their commitment will be external. If he takes this strategy, he should be open to the clients about the temporary nature of these controlling and unilateral interventions. He may emphasize that he is willing to behave in these ways in order to prevent the system from dying. One price he may exact for his cooperation is the planning of a growth-oriented program to begin simultaneously or immediately after the immediate danger to organizational life is overcome. In short, as survival seems guaranteed, the interventionist, with the participation of the clients, may plan a program for helping the system reduce its closedness and increase its openness and growth orientation.

As the reader may have surmised by now, the involvement of top management of any system is seen as being critical in effective intervention activity. This does not mean, however, that intervention activities cannot be initiated at other levels. There are conditions under which a beginning at lower levels may be productive. These conditions are discussed later in more detail. At this point we should like to emphasize that if the beginning is at levels other than the upper ones, there should be some respectable probability that if valid information were obtained indicating changes were necessary, top management would be open to consideration of it. If, however, changes are being considered that can be made at lower levels of a client system and do not require the approval of top management to institute and maintain, the involvement of upper management may not be required.

4 Adherence to Primary Tasks Minimizes the Probabilities for Client and Interventionist Manipulation

Selecting a client system with these three criteria in mind tends to create the conditions which will minimize intentional or unintentional client manipulation of the interventionist or vice versa. Neither will be able to control the other because valid information is being produced, free choice encouraged, and internal commitment generated.

The probability of unintentional manipulation by the interventionist is not so infrequent that it may be dismissed. As we shall see, the interventionist may have needs (of power and affiliation) and defenses (about authority and conflict) that may lead him to want to control and coerce the client into specific courses of action. Moreover, the concepts and methods for intervening are so primitive that distortion and manipulation could occur without either party being aware of their existence. The clients are also not above trying to use the interventionist for their own purposes. There are cases on record where top management has invited interventionists into their system in order to find ways to discharge or neutralize other senior executives; school systems have invited interventionists to help frustrated teachers experience some catharsis by interacting with persons who seemed interested in them and their problems; and black militants have used interventionists to create a confrontation with whites where their purpose was to hurt the whites.

One of the most frequent manipulations attempted by clients is to demand that the interventionist shortcut the three primary tasks and get on with change. Industrial organizations seeking help to overcome a crisis see little need for careful diagnosis. Governmental representatives giving money to help correct inner city problems focus on change, not on diagnosis.

This pressure for action without careful attention to the three primary tasks should be resisted by the interventionist. What would have happened if in 1954 interventionists had been brought together in Birmingham to help the citizens generate valid data, develop informed and free choices, and generate internal commitment to these choices? It probably would have taken five years of continuous effort. Would that not have led to quicker, more meaningful, and more effective desegregation? Would that not have helped to begin creating a climate of trust among the several constituents which now rarely exists?

Finally, even if the client and interventionist have the best of motives, it is possible that the client system exists in such a turbulent environment that the interventionist cannot be of significant help. This state of affairs is most quickly diagnosed if valid information is generated and the clients are asked to make their own informed and free choices.

Because the profession of intervening is so primitive, many client systems tend not to ask for help until they are in serious difficulties. Their logic claims that it does not make much sense to invite an interventionist whose professional skills seem to be little ahead of those of the clients. When interventionists are invited into the system under these conditions, the situation may be in such a difficult state that almost any semi-skilled intervention activity will be helpful. Even contradictory advice may be accepted uncritically by the client. For example, if one reads the literature one will find that some interventionists recommend giving and receiving of minimally evaluative feedback as facilitative of growth. An equally large and vocal group of interventionists insist that evaluative feedback can facilitate growth.

One group advises clients to begin only at the top; another admonishes them to begin anywhere in the system that is open to change.

Clients who feel helpless and see their system in deep trouble may permit a good deal of interventionist ineffectiveness because they are either not aware of it or they want some help even if it is not too effective (if for no other reason than to convince themselves or others they are trying to solve their problems). If the interventionist focuses on generating valid information, he helps to bring such conditions to the surface earlier than would otherwise be the case. Moreover, if he focuses on free choice and internal commitment, he will have to make it easier for the clients to confront the interventionist when they see him as not being helpful and they believe that it would not be in their interests to continue his services.

5 Primary Tasks Are Used As a Criterion for Leaving the Client System

One of the difficult choices that an interventionist may have to make is on the time to leave a client system. This decision is especially difficult when the interventionist has worked with the client system for some time. His leaving could be viewed as an act of betrayal by the clients.

The concept of primary tasks may be used in several ways to facilitate responsible decision making in this difficult area. The interventionist may, during the introductory phases when he is being evaluated by the clients, make clear the criteria for remaining within the client system. He may state, for example, that as long as there is an observable thrust toward obtaining valid information, informed and responsible choice, and internal commitment, he is able to remain. If and when pressures mount against such activities, he must ask the clients to discuss his leaving the system.

The interventionist may wish to specify

these criteria more concretely. With regard to the criterion of valid information, if the clients begin to forget their interviews, unilaterally turn down questionnaires because they are difficult to use, unilaterally prevent observations of important meetings, or the like, these actions become cues for the interventionist to consider whether or not he is going to be of help to the clients.

Similarly, if the key power people within the client system begin to ask for private meetings to make decisions about aspects of the program; if they call meetings with subordinates which are loaded against informed and responsible choice (through lack of time or pressure to make decisions); or if they request that data be withheld from subordinates, the interventionist may again wonder if he will be effective within the client system.

Another way of stating the position is that the interventionist remains with the clients as long as the clients seem to be more open than closed to learning.

Two points should be made about open and closed systems. All closedness is not necessarily bad and all openness is not necessarily good. An individual may increase his openness and growth potential if he remains closed to being influenced, to hurting others, or to expressing destructive feelings. An organization may increase its effectiveness if it remains closed to overloads in information. An individual may be so open to learning that he becomes incapable of choice. The same may be true for organizations.

Second, closedness is usually a response to threat. The source and impact of threat may be varied. The system may become closed because it is being threatened by external factors; or a system may have learned that a degree of closedness is necessary for survival. We know that many top management systems reward their executives for survival orientations rather than growth orientations. This type of executive closedness may be called external in order to indicate that it comes primarily from outside the individual. Such closedness is usually not internalized and may be reduced by eliminating the external forces. Closedness that is due to factors stemming from within the individual or system (for example, lack of trust or openness, crisis management) may be called *internal*. Such internalized closedness is rarely overcome by simply eliminating the causal factors. The defenses that have been built up to defend against internal threat may become ends in themselves and so interconnected with healthier portions of the system that an immediate reduction could be temporarily harmful. Internal closedness is more like drug addiction where the elimination of the drug temporarily increases the pain of the system.

Closedness may also be viewed in terms that the threat producing it could be of short or long duration. Moreover, the threat could be related to inner, peripheral, or to central, aspects of the system. Peripheral parts are those that have a low potency for the system, while inner parts tend to have a high potency. The central parts can be peripheral or inner. The key differentiating property is that change in a central part tends to create changes in the surrounding parts, be they inner or peripheral.

An interventionist may begin to move a system from survival to growth orientation by focusing on helping the clients change those central parts that are relatively peripheral but which can provide the clients with some immediate feelings of success. Exactly how this is done is difficult to specify. Research is badly needed.

6 The Primary Tasks Are Related to the Advancement of Basic Knowledge As Well As Practice

Intervention theory is so primitive that there needs to be heavy emphasis upon collecting systematic information and conducting empirical research regarding effective and ineffective interventions. If possible, each case should be viewed as having the potential to contribute to the professional body of knowledge. Medical doctors and lawyers have long recognized their responsibility in this area. It is frequently the highly successful and respected lawyers who take cases for little or no fee, if they believe the case will lead to a reshaping and strengthening of the law.

The requirement of obtaining valid information encourages the interventionist to add to the basic knowledge in his field. The existence of free choice and internal commitment increases the probability that clients will confront the interventionist, and he will confront himself, regarding the validity and usefulness of the information generated. Adherence to the three primary tasks, therefore, allows the interventionist to be better able to make some contributions to his field.

To summarize, an interventionist is someone who enters an ongoing system or set of relationships primarily to achieve three tasks. They are (1) to help generate valid and useful information, (2) to create conditions in which clients can make informed and free choices, and (3) to help clients develop an internal commitment to their choice.

The interventionist and the clients may then develop secondary tasks of change, increasing system stability, etc. An interventionist's decision to select or remain in a particular client system depends upon the client's capacities to fulfill the three primary tasks.

Reading 39

Matching Problems, Precursors, and Interventions in OD: A Systemic Approach

David G. Bowers

Jerome L. Franklin

Patricia A. Pecorella

Many have stated quite accurately that there is no general theory of organizational change and development. Nevertheless, activities abound under the general rubric of "OD." Some such activities have been generally effective and have contributed to the upgraded functioning of some of the systems they set out to help. Others have been well intentioned but generally ineffective. The reasons for the effectiveness or ineffectiveness of the various techniques may lie in the nature of the techniques themselves. That is, some techniques may simply be more effective, useful, and feasible than others, in more situations. If this is the case, the ineffective ones should be modified or discarded. Equally likely, though, is the possibility that the success or failure of any one OD activity is contingent on the "goodness of fit" between the intervention and the organizational unit in which it is utilized. Some techniques may be very effective in units experiencing certain kinds of problems created by certain conditions, while other techniques are most effective in very different circumstances. The validity of OD approaches may well be confounded by differential ability of organizations to choose the best intervention. Thus, the notion of "fit" between settings and interventions offers a fruitful area for exploration.

Reproduced by special permission from *Journal of Applied Behavioral Science*, 1975, **11**, 391–409. This work was supported by the Office of Naval Research, Contract N00014-67-A-0181. The cooperation and help of that agency is hereby gratefully acknowledged.

THE NATURE OF CHANGE

Change is movement, and the very nature of this concept requires that one begin with its antithesis, the steady (or homeostatic) state. Change is, therefore, some form of interruption of a preexisting steady state. Perhaps the clearest descriptions of what is involved in the change process come from the literature of pathology where an interruption of a steady state (a change) is termed a "lesion" (cf. Congdon, 1972). The occurrence of a lesion requires the coincidence of two sets of factors:

Factors of realization usually extrinsic occurrences which bring about the event in time, as for example the occurrence of radiation or trauma, or surgery;

Factors of determination usually intrinsic conditions which are necessary for the event to occur at all, as for example the structure or properties of a cell.

Implicit in these notions is the proposition that both sets of factors are present and must in some way "match"; otherwise change will not occur. A simple medical example may illustrate this perhaps obvious point: an antibiotic drug, as a factor of realization, will produce a variety of different effects, depending upon whether the patient has (a) an infection, (b) a common cold, (c) no illness at all, or (d) an allergy to that drug. In the first instance it will likely help him; in the second and third cases it will have little or no effect, and in the final instance it may send him into anaphylactic shock. Analogizing to the problem of organizational change and development, this implies that the change process is in all likelihood multiplex, with outcomes determined by the interaction of treatment with the condition and its etiology.

From this brief discussion we may derive what would appear to be a fundamental principle of organizational change, which we may arbitrarily label the *Principle of Congruence:*

For constructive organizational change to occur, there must exist an appropriate correspondence of the treatment (action, intervention) with the internal structural and functional conditions of the organization for which change is intended. Since by definition these internal conditions pre-exist, this means that treatments must be selected, designed, and varied to fit the properties of the organization.

Implicit in the notion of factors of determination is yet another proposition. Pathology literature states that change is most likely to occur at what are termed "sites of predilection," which ordinarily consist of points where two or more kinds of tissue meet. Atherosclerotic plaques are more common where an artery branches, for example (Congdon, 1972). The resemblance of this precept to a similar statement made by many writers in the area of organizational change is uncanny. Leavitt (1965) and many others as well talk about "entry points." Lippitt, Watson, and Westley (1958) discuss "leverage points," which may be either some strategically located unit or some functional aspect of the organization from which change may proceed to other areas. Katz and Kahn (1966) similarly seem to see change as originating (a) where the system meets its input source, (b) where system meets supersystem, (c) where echelon meets echelon. Thus, general agreement is rather apparent with what we might term the *Principle of Predisposition:*

There are certain points in organizational space where change will enjoy its greatest likelihood of success; these points are, at least in terms of the change strategy, boundary points, and change starts at that boundary and works inward.

Finally, a third proposition may be extracted by considering simultaneously the ideas of several writers and disciplines. Leavitt has distinguished between primary targets of change (those characteristics immediately impinged upon) and ultimate targets (those characteristics which are sometimes changed indirectly, through change in primary targets). From pathology come the notions of cardinality—that there are main or major processes on which other things depend, and order—that things lead to other things. Lippitt, Watson, and Westley (1958) discuss "linkage," the idea that there must be at least a possible line of change progress from the leverage point to the change objective. The *Principle of Succession* is an implication of all these views:

> *Change is accomplished indirectly, not directly, by a process in which the intervenor changes some things in order to change other things, only ultimately arriving at the true target.*

Several points emerge from all of these various conceptual statements and primitive principles. First, responsible change practice requires that one must be able to say that a particular treatment produces the condition which it is intended to produce. Yet it seems obvious that change design is not a simple matter of treatment selection—a choice of treatments whose impact is uniform whenever used. It is instead one of interaction between the treatment and the existing multidimensional conditions within the organization. Stated more simply, a particular intervention behavior or action is one thing under one set of organizational conditions and a completely different thing under others.[1] The point of all this is that the change agent or designer may delude himself into believing that by using a single intervention or treatment he or she has in some sense "controlled" for extraneous factors by conducting one specific set of activities, when, in fact, precisely the opposite has occurred.

Second, one never changes "it" (the condition which one proposes ultimately to affect);

instead, one changes things (makes inputs of a kind) presumed to lead to "it." Thus, we provide information, conduct skill-building sessions, or alter the situation because we believe that this is likely to change the behavior of the persons involved. In no instance do we—nor can we—"change their behavior" directly. Only the persons involved are capable of that.

The problem of change in organizations, therefore, involves simultaneous consideration, and then appropriate sequencing across many persons, roles, and settings, of three important aspects and their potential interactions: 1) the *problematic behaviors*, 2) the *conditions* which create those behaviors, and 3) the nature of *possible treatments*.

A BEHAVIOR CLASSIFICATION SCHEME

Descriptions of processes and states of organizations are simply shorthand descriptions for perceived constellations of the behavior of many individuals at various points in organizational space and time. The process of formulating these shorthand descriptions involves several steps. First, one must decide which behaviors to measure and how to measure them. Once the behaviors have been measured, individual scores on the measures are averaged across persons. From these average scores, conceptual categories emerge which describe the processes and states of organizational functioning.

Two things are different, then, when one talks about organizational processes and states as opposed to when one talks about the original behavior configurations occurring in an organization. When talking about organizational processes and states: (a) a limited number of behaviors are included, and (b) a higher level of abstraction is present. These shorthand descriptions of organizational processes and states are useful for diagnostic and evaluative purposes. One can assess how an organization is functioning now (with reference to

---

[1] Rubin, Plovnick, and Fry (1974) support this notion in their discussion of health care systems. According to these authors strategies of change must be differentially formulated for client systems according to existing structures, norms, and values.

some ideal or normative score on the measures) and whether major changes are taking place in an organization, by using the measures of the processes and states as benchmarks.

However, a major goal in the OD field is to improve organizational functioning—to make interventions (alternative inputs) that add positively to the ultimate output/input ratio of the organization. Pragmatically speaking, one cannot impinge directly upon a "process." Instead one must work with specific individuals and must be able to help these individuals change the original behaviors that created the ineffective processes. Since there are neither the resources nor the time to attempt to change any or all of the original behaviors in some random order, it becomes paramount to identify some limited number of behaviors which, if changed, will cause changes in other behaviors. One should first change the behaviors that will eventually cause the greatest positive change in the processes and states of the organization and thereby lead to the greatest improvement in outputs. It is important, then, to have an understanding of the causal flow of events in organizational functioning so that change efforts can concentrate on the problem areas which, if changed, are likely to produce the greatest improvement.

We view leadership behaviors as prime causal variables determining the groups' processes and the system's output. According to one formulation (Bowers & Seashore, 1966), leadership is comprised of four categories of behavior: Support, Goal Emphasis, Work Facilitation, and Interaction Facilitation (Team Building). Evidence presented elsewhere (Bowers & Seashore, 1966; Butterfield, 1968; Taylor & Bowers, 1972) suggests that the Four-Factor Theory of leadership is reasonably comprehensive and is related to effectiveness. While the exact nature of the influence of behaviors other than leadership on organizational processes must be explored and stud-

ied, the causal nature of leadership behavior establishes a good starting point for classifying problem behaviors. That is, by changing ineffective leadership behaviors first, one can be relatively confident that positive changes in basic organizational and group processes will occur, and that output variables will also improve.

Precursors to Problem Behaviors

As stated, a critical skill in organizational development is that of obtaining a good diagnosis of the organization, including the problems of its component parts and how they are interrelated. At base, this consists of identifying and then elaborating a definition of "organization." One of the major advances in recent years has been the development of the theories and concepts that treat the organization as a social system (Katz & Kahn, 1966; Miller, 1971). According to this view, the social system consists of complex configurations of the behaviors of its individual members. It is therefore to a consideration of the nature and *causes* of such behaviors that diagnosis necessarily turns. We propose that there are four determinants of behaviors in organizational settings. These include: 1) *information*, 2) *skills*, 3) *values*, and 4) the *situation* in which individuals and groups exist. The first three can be evaluated in terms of individual organizational members. On the other hand, the situation is a more general factor associated with groups and major subunits of organizations. Each factor can be viewed as a precursor to organizational functioning. That is, the presence, absence, and quality of each influence the functioning of the organization. These precursors determine the extent and type of problems that occur in the organization's processes and the variations occurring in organizational outputs.

Information   Individuals base their actions in part upon the information—including perceptions and expectations—they have acquired over time regarding what is effective or appropriate behavior. Insufficient or erroneous information about the technical aspects of the work situation results in misused and damaged equipment as well as accidents and low levels of productive efficiency. Similarly, inadequate information regarding social aspects of work situations results in wasted or injured human resources.

Erroneous models of organizational functioning based on incomplete or mistaken notions about the number and nature of critical variables together with a lack of understanding of the complexities or interactions among them can lead to widespread and severe negative consequences for the organization. A rather typical problem of this type stems from the short-range time frames used by many persons in evaluating the effectiveness of various behaviors. Many problems seem to result from notions regarding motivation based on short-term evaluations without regard for the long-range consequences. Thus, it is common to find managers who strongly believe that high production can be consistently attained through the constant application of threats and pressure, even though evaluations of such behaviors suggest that they become ineffective and quite costly to the organization after relatively short periods of organizational life (Likert & Seashore, 1963).

Skills Individual skills related to behavior in organizational settings also exist in both technical and social (i.e., interpersonal) areas. The ability to operate a piece of machinery or design an accounting system [is an example] of technical skills. Important social skills include those influencing the way organizational members interact and often are referred to as "leadership" and "group process" skills.

The distinction between technical and social skills and the importance of social skills for organizational success seem to be frequently ignored. A common assumption made by many managers is that technical skills are more vital to accomplishing organizational goals while social skills are less important. This assumption leads to the relatively large emphasis on technical training in organizations compared with training in the social aspects of work situations. A related assumption regarding these two skill areas is that, while technical skills require special training, social skills can be generally "picked up" by nearly anyone who has technical competencies.

Perhaps the clearest indication of this assumption is the practice of promoting individuals to managerial positions on the basis of their demonstrated technical abilities. The fact that such appointments frequently are made with little more than cursory training in management concepts—often including only an exposure to the organization's official managerial policies—in part reflects the notions that the social skills required of managers are not terribly important and are adequately acquired through minimal training and by performing in a managerial position.

A contradictory but common assumption is that social skills are essentially untrainable. Accordingly, one is either born with appropriate interpersonal competencies or acquires them very early in life, after which they cannot be altered significantly.

Experiences, observations, and research suggest that the assumptions regarding the relative unimportance of social skills in organizations, the ease in attaining those skills, and assumptions that skills are untrainable are all ill founded. The importance of social skills to organizational performance has been widely observed and is described in various formal theories (Argyris, 1962; Blake & Mouton, 1964; Katz & Kahn, 1966; Likert, 1961, 1967). The importance of such factors has also been demonstrated through analyses of the relationship between social-psychological aspects of organizational functioning and organizational output variables (Taylor & Bowers, 1972). Further, the ability to train such skills has been documented by Bunker (1965) and Bunker and Knowles (1967).

Values Every individual carries a set of values (i.e., estimations of desirability, importance, usefulness, etc.) which influence behavior. These values are related to many areas and are of varied intensities. In general, one might think of the range of intensity beginning with rather superficial opinions which are relatively unimportant to the individual, to beliefs which are more important, and finally to basic values central to the individual's self-concept and behavior. The ties that exist between values at the individual level and ideologies at the organizational level are complex and bidirectional, a point made eloquently by Miller (1971) and by Harrison (1972). Thus, when an individual's values foster behavior incongruent with effective organizational functioning, the consequences for the organization are likely to be detrimental. An extreme example of such a situation would be a manager whose values hold that people are relatively unimportant, expendable resources in organizations, compared to the physical plant and equipment. The behavior of such an individual could prove to be extremely costly to the organization in terms of wasting valuable human resources through turnover, lack of motivation, accidents, and psychologically triggered physical illness.

Situation The behavior of any individual member of an organization depends in part on other individuals and groups and on the physical setting or technological requirements of the job (Davis & Taylor, 1972). As was the case in our consideration of information and skills, we find that the situation can be evaluated in terms of both technical and social aspects.

Examples of how technology and structure influence behavior are easily identified. Machines and standardized procedures (e.g., accounting systems) generally require a limited array of behaviors. Their design dictates which behaviors are to be exhibited and in what order. For example, task design requires that a punch operator follow approximately these steps in order to accomplish the task: 1) obtain a piece of unpunched material; 2) place the material in the machinery; 3) clear one's body from the machine—sometimes with the aid of the machine, which actually pulls parts of the body away from danger; 4) operate a control to punch the material; and 5) remove the material from the machine.

Like technology, the structure of the organization has tremendous influence over individual and group behaviors within an organization. Structure greatly determines the patterns of work-related and purely social relationships found in organizations. Individuals of approximately the same status (i.e., those located at about the same level in the organizational hierarchy) and those whose work dictates that they be in close physical proximity are more likely to interact more often and in more friendly fashion than are those of greatly disparate statuses or those experiencing great physical distance.

The following examples illustrate how the behavior of each organizational member is partially determined by the combined influences of these social-psychological aspects of organizational life. A situation might exist in which a supervisor is greatly constrained in leadership behaviors by the situation. If organizational policies prohibit or strongly discourage the holding of group meetings, this will have a profound and detrimental effect upon the supervisor's ability to facilitate interaction among his subordinates. Consequently, the subordinates will also be restricted in their ability to work together as a team. The result will be less effective functioning, based upon a lack of task-related interactions among members of the group.

Another example of the effects of the social-psychological aspects of the behavior of organizational members can be imagined in terms of the standard of performance established by a supervisor. In a situation in which objectives are inherently unreasonable, unattainable, or unclear, a supervisor is greatly hindered in his ability to maintain high standards of performance. In such a situation that supervisor is often placed in a position of defending the objectives rather than acting as a facilitator to the subordinates in their attempts to attain objectives.

Summary Each of the four precursors influences the effectiveness of the individual's behavior. The most effective individuals are those who have the information and skills necessary to complete the various tasks, values congruent with effective behavior, and situations which support them in their attempts to behave effectively.

Although each precursor is important, the adequate presence and quality of different combinations of these four elements will have different consequences for the organization as well as for the individual. The consequences for organizational effectiveness depend on various factors, including the number of organizational members operating with these inadequacies, and the level in the organizational hierarchy where various deficiencies are encountered. Organizational functioning suffers most when deficiencies 1) involve more rather than few precursors, 2) influence the behaviors of large numbers of organizational members, and 3) occur at high levels in the organizational hierarchy.

A THREE-DIMENSIONAL MODEL OF ORGANIZATIONAL DEVELOPMENT

The various OD techniques can be classified according to the precursor mode on which they impinge most directly and most immediately. Unlike the classification for the precursor modes, *values* has not been included as a category for classifying development techniques since values are not subject to direct

change. Changes in values occur only as a result of impingement on one of the other three areas. For example, some counseling and some forms of laboratory training employed to change values are classified under the *information* category since these techniques primarily impinge on an individual's information.

Figure 39-1 presents a variety of well-known and accepted techniques classified according to the primary impingement mode of each. In addition, the figure illustrates a three-dimensional (3-D) model which should be considered to facilitate effective organizational development.[2] This model contains three basic dimensions:

1 Problematic behaviors—defined herein in terms of four categories of leadership behaviors: Support, Interaction Facilitation, Goal Emphasis, Work Facilitation.
2 Conditions causing these behaviors—described as the precursors: information, skill, situation, values.
3 The nature of possible treatments—the three categories of development techniques termed impingement modes: information, skills, situation.

The model contains 48 cells (3x4x4) each representing different combinations of the three basic dimensions. For example, the cell labeled "A" describes a problem in supportive behaviors resulting from inadequate information and rectifiable through some strategy related to informational input, such as management seminars or team development.

Matching Precursor with Impingement Mode

From the Principle of Congruence we know that problem behaviors, precursors, and impingement modes need to be matched in some systematic way. However, there are at least three possible competing interpretations of

[2]An alternative three-dimensional model has been presented by Schmuck and Miles (1971) for the classification of OD interventions.

Impingement mode	Strategies and techniques
Information	Client-centered counseling Laboratory training Management by objectives Management seminars Managerial grid organizational development Merger laboratory Motivation training Process consultation Scientific management Survey feedback Survey-guided development Team development Third-party consultation
Skill	Behavior therapy Imitative learning Skill training
Situation	Decentralization Differentiation/integration Flow of work Job enrichment Leadership-situation engineering Operations research Scanlon plan Sociotechnical fit Structural change

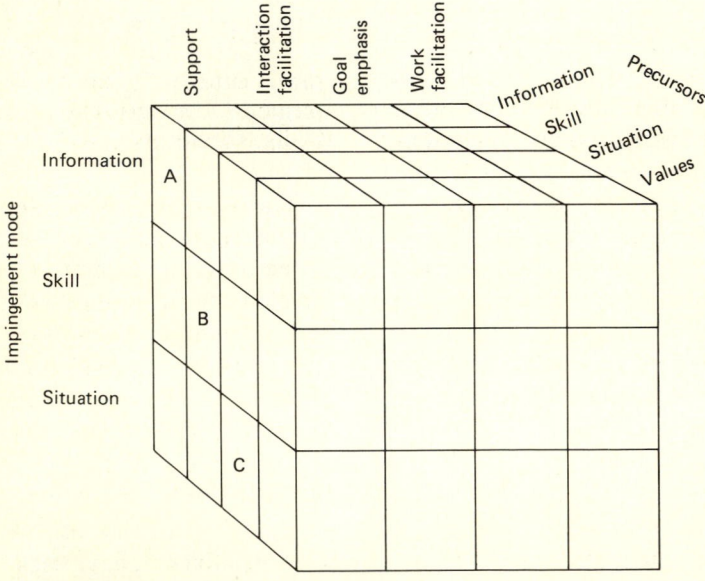

Figure 39-1 Developmental strategies and techniques and the three-dimensional model of organizational development.

the way in which this match should occur. Each interpretation is discussed below.

Interpretation 1 The impingement mode should always be congruent with the precrusor (with the exception of values, which would be changed indirectly by affecting one or more other precursors). For example, if the source of poor work facilitation is diagnosed as lack of information, the treatment should focus on providing information—not skill training or structural modifications. This would suggest that—

When the precursor is:	*The impingement mode should be:*
Information	Information
Skills	Skills
Situation	Situation
Values	(No direct impingement possible)

The match between precursor and impingement mode would not be affected by the specific nature of the problematic behaviors. For example, if members of the client system lack necessary information, the impingement mode should be information, regardless of whether the problem centers around support, interaction facilitation, goal emphasis, or work facilitation. However, the specific *content* of the intervention technique would be determined by the nature of the problematic behaviors. If the problematic behavior is lack of support by supervisors, the information presented, by whatever specific technique, would be information about the meaning, importance, and implications of supervisory support. It would be nonsensical to provide information about supervisory interaction facilitation, goal emphasis, and work facilitation except when this information would clarify the issues relevant to supervisory support. Thus, once the appropriate precursor has been identified, the "Problematic Behavior" dimension

becomes essential for determining the content of a specific technique.

Interpretation 2 The impingement mode should be matched in some other way with the precursor. To use the earlier example, if the cause of poor work facilitation is diagnosed as a lack of information, one might change the situation, with the expectation that the indirect effects would be beneficial (e.g., moving role-related employees into closer physical proximity, thus making information sharing more likely). This would suggest that—

When the precursor is:	*The impingement mode should be:*
Information	Skills or situation
Skills	Information or situation
Situation	Information or skills
Values	Information, skills, or situation

Once again the match between precursor and impingement mode would not be affected by the nature of the problematic behaviors, but the content of the specific intervention would depend upon the nature of the problematic behaviors.

If either of the above interpretations is valid, whole rows in the three-dimensional model would be useful *or* not useful for OD. If interpretation 1 is valid, the rows labeled A, B, and C would be the only useful rows; if interpretation 2 is valid, all rows except A, B, and C would be useful. Quite a different (and more complex) state of affairs would exist if the third interpretation, described below, were the valid one.

Interpretation 3 Precursor, impingement mode, and problematic behaviors must be matched in some specific way. For example, if employees lack the technical skills required to help each other solve work-related problems, then provide skill training; if employees lack the interpersonal skill required to provide emotional support to one another, however, change the situation to one where people who get along well work together. If this interpretation is valid, OD would be a cell-specific (as opposed to a row) problem, with respect to the three-dimensional model in Figure 39-1. There would be at least 48 different states with which we might be faced. The appropriate impingement mode would have to be matched with certain combinations of precursors and problematic behaviors. If this interpretation is valid, *all* of the 48 possible *cells* would have their own "time and season" of usefulness in different OD settings.

While interpretations 1 and 2 are mutually exclusive, interpretation 3 could hold within a framework consistent with either of the other two interpretations. For example, it could be true that a skill deficiency is always best remedied by a skill training input in a specific case of work facilitation, whereas a skill deficiency in goal emphasis normally requires for its correction an information input.

Complications   A critical issue, therefore, is that of determining which interpretation is most valid. Several related issues also arise. For example, more must be known about the nature of particular precursors and problems, since some precursors and problems may be more easily "impinged" upon or be more quickly responsive to impingements than others. For instance, increasing the supportiveness of supervisors may be more difficult and take more time than improving their work facilitation. Or, changing values may take longer than upgrading skills. If these differences are not taken into account, the most appropriate match of impingement modes to problems and precursors cannot be attained.

On the other hand, some interventions may simply be more effective than others (cf. Bowers, 1973). Taking a hypothetical case, a practitioner might apply OD technique "X"—an information-providing intervention—to solve a given problem in one setting, but implements technique "Y"—a skill-building intervention—to solve a very similar problem in a second setting. If the intervention were successful in the first setting and unsuccessful in the second, a definite question of meaning would arise. Are techniques using the information impingement mode more appropriate for solving that *particular* problem than techniques using the skill impingement mode, or is technique "X" generally more effective than technique "Y"?

The number of precursors or problems operating in a setting must also be considered. Thus far, the model has dealt with matching one problem and precursor with one intervention. When a diagnosis indicates the existence of multiple problems or precursors, however, there is a high likelihood that the various problems or precursors operate differently in combination than each operates separately—that is, they probably interact. The presence of such interactions might alter the appropriateness of various impingement modes.

OD Client as Patient: Diagnosis and Treatment

The three-dimensional model proposed is equivalent to a "medical" model, where the problem is described as the demonstrable symptom, the precursor is the underlying cause of the disease, and the impingement mode is the nature of the treatment deemed appropriate. The 3-D model necessitates a differential diagnosis that describes the nature of the disease *and* its causes. The nature of the treatment must be based upon the diagnosis and must be administered at the correct time and in the correct dosage.

There are, of course, dangers inherent in the application of such a model, including the risks that members of the system will reject the diagnosis, and consequently, the treatment. The process of applying such a model is critical in gaining acceptance of the diagnosis and commitment to the corrective intervention. The process requires educative and skill-building aspects to enable the client both to understand the diagnostic and prescriptive procedures and to be actively involved in them.

The essential point is that if OD is to be maximally effective, and if different approaches to OD are to be tested empirically, it must be moved in the direction of more detailed and intensive diagnoses and more exact choices of appropriate interventions.

IMPLICATIONS FOR PRACTITIONERS

The general framework for OD presented here and the principles upon which it is based suggest some important implications for practitioners.

The *Principle of Congruence* teaches that—

Change activities must be matched appropriately with the nature of the problems and their causes and with the nature of the organizational units under consideration.

A systematic diagnosis of organizational conditions and practices, and individual and group behaviors should precede the selection of corrective activities. The completed diagnosis should include a description of problem behaviors and their causes.

Given the particular problem to be solved and its causes, the practitioner should decide whether it would be most effective to eliminate the cause of the problem *directly* or *indirectly*. A direct approach involves choosing corrective activities that have the same primary "target" (i.e., information, lack of skills, inadequate situation). The indirect approach, on the other hand, involves selecting corrective activities with a primary target different from the cause of the problem.[3] An example involving an absence of effective teamwork may help to clarify the difference

between these two approaches. Using the direct approach, an existing structure (i.e., the situation) might be changed to one that utilized work teams, thus encouraging more contact and coordination among subordinates. Using an indirect approach, supervisors might be given information about the benefits of teamwork or given skill training in encouraging teamwork. These interventions might motivate supervisors (if they know they have the support of their superiors) to change their behavior, which would eventually change the organization's structure. Choosing one approach over the other will depend partly upon the relative practicality and acceptability to members of the system of the potential corrective activities called for by each of the two approaches. The choice may also be influenced by beliefs or experiences of the practitioner or system members relevant to how a change in behavior is brought about (i.e., whether to focus on changing knowledge, skills, or situation *first* in order to affect behavior).

The *Principle of Predisposition* suggests that—

Change will occur first and foremost at the following interfaces:
  1 Where the system meets its input sources, culture, or society, e.g., in units where new personnel, younger, better-educated, minority persons are present in atypical numbers; or in boundary units such as sales, purchasing, personnel, research and development.
  2 Where the system meets its supersystem, e.g., in top management groups.
  3 Where major echelons meet, e.g., where first-line supervision meets middle management.
  4 Where functionally different lines merge, e.g., at the interface between production and maintenance functions.

These statements imply that initial change attempts will be more successful in some sections of the "organizational space" than in others. Less obvious, however, is the implication that if problems at the interfaces listed

---

[3] The indirect approach *must* be used when a problem is caused by incongruent values, since no change techniques have a "change in values" as their primary target.

above are not dealt with, change attempts in other areas of the organization are likely to be unsuccessful.

Finally, the *Principle of Succession* is instructive.

> *It is important to consider the sequence in which problems are solved and action steps implemented. Solutions should be designed to solve the problem at hand without creating new ones.*

The practitioner should focus attention first on those problems which may be solved in a reasonable amount of time and which do not require resources (e.g., skills and money) that the organization would be hard pressed to obtain. This statement is based on the notion that it is important to maintain a motivating discrepancy between how an organization functions at a given time and its ideal modus operandi. Choosing a problem huge in scope requiring several months and unobtainable resources to solve would reflect too large a discrepancy, whereas settling for more manageable problems first may lessen the discrepancy enough to motivate and enable people to work on solving problems which previously seemed out of reach.

Secondly, when more than one problem is to be solved, or when a single problem is multifaceted, special attention should be given to implementing action steps in the appropriate order. Some problems, or aspects of a problem, need to be worked on before others can be solved. Some action steps have to be taken before others can be attempted.

Professionalism before Prescribing

As the general change framework, the 3-D model, and practitioner implications suggest, movement toward a more systematic approach to OD requires extensive knowledge and skill. Diagnosis, which includes the analysis and integration of information from individuals, groups, functional areas and hierarchical levels, is a complex process requiring extensive knowledge of organizational functioning both of a general nature and for the specific unit under consideration. In addition, great skill is required for organizing this information in such a way that it is intelligible and useful as a basis for matching and sequencing interventions to coincide with problem causes. Although the requirements of such an approach are considerable, the potential payoffs from moving OD in this direction seem worthy of the effort.

REFERENCES

Argyris, C. *Interpersonal competence and organizational effectiveness.* Homewood, Ill.: Irwin, 1962.

Blake, R. R., & Mouton, J. S. *The managerial grid.* Houston: Gulf Publishing Co., 1964.

Bowers, D. G. OD techniques and their results in 23 organizations: The Michigan ICL study. *Journal of Applied Behavioral Science*, 1973, **9** (1), 21–43.

Bowers, D. G., & Seashore, S. Predicting organizational effectiveness with a four-factor theory of leadership. *Administrative Science Quarterly*, 1966, **11** (2), 238–263.

Bunker, D. R. Individual applications of laboratory training. *Journal of Applied Behavioral Science*, 1965, **1** (2), 131–148.

Bunker, D. R., & Knowles, E. S. Comparison of behavioral changes resulting from human relations training laboratories of different lengths. *Journal of Applied Behavioral Science*, 1967, **3** (4), 505–523.

Butterfield, D. A. An integrative approach to the study of leadership effectiveness in organizations. Unpublished doctoral dissertation. Ann Arbor: University of Michigan, 1968.

Congdon, C. C. *Pathological processes* (Part 1, Notes). Knoxville: University of Tennessee, 1972.

Davis, L. E., & Taylor, J. C. *Design of jobs.* Middlesex, England: Penguin Books, 1972.

Harrison, R. Understanding your organization's character. *Harvard Business Review*, 1972, **50** (3), 119–128.

Katz, D., & Kahn, R. L. *The social psychology of organizations.* New York: Wiley, 1966.

Leavitt, H. J. Applied organizational change in industry. In J. G. March (Ed.), *Handbook of organizations*. Chicago: Rand McNally, 1965.

Likert, R. *New patterns of management*. New York: McGraw-Hill, 1961.

Likert, R. *The human organization*. New York: McGraw-Hill, 1967.

Likert, R., & Seashore, S. E. Making cost control work. *Harvard Business Review*, 1963, **41** (6), 96–108.

Lippitt, R., Watson, J., & Westley, B. *The dynamics of planned change*. New York: Harcourt, Brace and World, 1958.

Miller, J. G. The nature of living systems. *Behavioral Science*, 1971, **16**, 278–301.

Rubin, I., Plovnick, M., & Fry, R. Initiating planned change in health care systems. *Journal of Applied Behavioral Science*, 1974, **10** (1), 107–124.

Schmuck, R. A., & Miles, M. B. (Eds.) *Organization development in schools*. Palo Alto, Cal.: National Press Books, 1971.

Taylor, J. C., & Bowers, D. G. *Survey of organizations*. Ann Arbor, Mich.: Institute for Social Research, 1972.

Reading 40

The Diffusion of New Work Structures: Explaining Why Success Didn't Take

Richard E. Walton

When organizations engage in experimental projects in work restructuring, an underlying assumption is that if the innovation is effective, it will be adapted and used by other units in the organization. Most of us would expect that an organizational pattern that is working better than the one it replaced will be recommended by superiors and emulated by peers. Experience, however, shows this to be not necessarily true: The assumed tendencies are sometimes nullified and offset by competing organizational dynamics.

I have studied a sample of organizations that made early efforts at the comprehensive redesign of work, asking: How much diffusion has occurred, particularly within the same firm? What are the vehicles for diffusion? What barriers are encountered? How does the character of the innovation affect the rate of its diffusion? Answers to questions such as these can help us formulate better diffusion strategies and tactics.

EIGHT EXPERIMENTS

The eight firms included in the study had the following characteristics: All started their research on work redesign in the 1960s; their early experiments involved relatively comprehensive work restructuring; these experiments were all judged initially successful; the firms had a number of physically separate facilities, usually geographically dispersed; the change efforts of all the firms received substantial publicity.

Of the eight firms, two are in the U. S., two in Canada, one in Great Britain, two in Norway, and one in Sweden. The firms in the U.S. are Corning Glass, which initiated a study in its Medfield, Mass., assembly plant in 1965, and the General Foods Corporation, which initiated an experiment in its pet food plant in Topeka, Kansas, in January 1971, although it had begun planning for change in 1968. The Canadian organizations are the Sales and Fabrication Division of Alcan and the Advanced

Devices Center, a division of Northern Electric Company, subsequently renamed Microsystems International, Ltd. In 1964, a group of Alcan managers launched a project in one plant in the works at Kingston, Ontario; over time the innovations developed in the first effort at Kingston were extended to other existing Sales and Fabrication Division plants and eventually to a new cold rolling mill. The Northern Electric unit designed a radically different organization for a new semiconductor facility that was occupied in January 1966.

The European companies form the remainder of the sample. Shell U.K. introduced change in several locations in the mid-1960s, including a new refinery at Teesport, which came on stream in 1968. Several Norwegian projects were carried out in different industries under the Industrial Democracy Project, an action research program sponsored jointly by the Norwegian Federation of Employers and the Trades Union Council of Norway and guided by social scientists associated with the Work Research Institute in Oslo. The two projects included in this study were the fertilizer plants at Norsk Hydro in Porsgrunn and a department in the Hunsfos pulp and paper complex near Kristiansand. They were initiated in the mid-1960s.

A Swedish experiment in Volvo's truck assembly plant in Lundby, begun in 1969, has been followed by similar changes in a neighboring auto assembly plant, the design of a revolutionary car plant at Kalmar that went on stream in 1974, and a commitment to an advanced form of work structuring in a new Volvo plant in the U.S. planned for 1975.

An important similarity existed in the change strategies employed by seven of these eight firms. An early experiment in one unit of the firm was regarded as a pilot project from which the larger organization could learn. The positive results, if any, could demonstrate the value of work restructuring. Lessons gained from the experiment then could be made available to other units. The eighth, Shell U.K., by contrast followed a change strategy in which the demonstration projects were not the point of departure.

The extent of diffusion that has occurred within these eight firms has varied widely. In four companies (Corning, Northern Electric, Hunsfos, and Norsk Hydro) diffusion has been nonexistent or small. In three companies (General Foods, Shell U.K., and Alcan) somewhat more diffusion has occurred; however, the rate either has been slow or it has not been sustained. Only in one company in my sample, namely Volvo, was diffusion truly impressive. Managers involved in all the changes, including those at Volvo, clearly had expected more rapid and extensive change.

GENERAL MODEL

Before exploring the diffusion of "work restructuring," or the lack of diffusion, let us clarify what we mean by the term. The work restructuring approach pursued in the eight cases studied embraces many aspects of work, including the content of the job, compensation schemes, scope of worker responsibility for supervision and decision making, social structure, status hierarchy, and so on. The design of each element is intended to contribute to an internally consistent work culture—one that *appropriately* enlarges workers' scope for self-management, enhances their opportunity for learning new abilities, strengthens their sense of connectedness with co-workers, increases their identification with the product and manufacturing process, and promotes their sense of dignity and self-worth. The word "appropriately" is used in the preceding sentence to signify that the extent to which work structures can realistically depart from today's conventional work organization depends upon many situational factors, especially the type of technology involved, composition of the work force (Is it educated and skilled?), and economic forces (Do they favor the expenditures of time and money involved in a comprehensive attempt at job restructuring?).

Each diffusion effort had its own unique characteristics, but they all also shared many points. A generalized model of the change efforts, containing seven aspects or steps, will highligh both the similarities and the differences. Although I have viewed the early experiments as the first of a number of steps in transforming work throughout the larger corporation, they were not necessarily so conceived at the time they were initiated, either by direct participants or by corporate officials.

Step 1: Initiation of the Pilot Experiment

Although perhaps similarly inspired, pilot experiments took a variety of forms. Some were in new plants—GF's Topeka, Corning's Medfield, Alcan's Center Plant at the Kingston Works, and Northern Electric's plant at Montreal. Others were in established plants—Hunsfos' pulp and paper mill and Volvo's Lundby truck plant. At Norsk Hydro, experiments were initiated simultaneously in an existing and a new fertilizer facility. The Shell U.K. demonstration projects occurred as a later step in the process of restructuring work, but they too embraced both existing and new facilities.

Some experiments involved relatively radical and comprehensive work restructuring at the outset—especially GF's pet food plant, Norsk Hydro's fertilizer plants, Hunsfos' chemical pulp department, and Shell U.K.'s new Teesport refinery. Significantly, each of these four facilities is relatively small, employing fewer than 100 workers, and involves a continuous-processing technology. Also, the way work was restructured in these continuous-processing plants is remarkably similar: Self-managing teams were formed to take responsibility for large segments of the process. Job rotation among team members was encouraged both to improve control of the technology and to provide intrinsically satisfying learning experiences for workers. Support activities, such as maintenance, quality control, and cleaning were incorporated into operating team responsibilities. Because of the diverse abilities required to manage, operate, and maintain these technologies, team members received heavy doses of skills training. Pay was based on the relevant skills and knowledge a worker had acquired rather than on the particular job he was performing. New information and measurement systems were developed to enable teams to keep on top of their enlarged responsibilities.

Northern Electric's Advanced Devices Center, because it focused mostly on professional and managerial personnel, differed from the four continuous-processing facilities. The Advanced Devices Center featured a matrix organization, functional and business teams, elaborate communication schemes, open office layouts, and nontraditional titles and reporting relationships.

Other experiments—in the new plants at Alcan and Corning and the existing facilities at Volvo and Shell U.K.—involved more moderate change. Significantly, two of these, Corning and Volvo, are assembly plants where the nature of the tasks and technology provided relatively little opportunity for upgrading the abilities of the work teams. Thus in these plants emphasis was placed on freeing workers from the tedium of short repetitive work cycles and on steps that would improve communication. Within those constraints, both were bold efforts at work restructuring. The changes that evolved over several years were rotation among and/or enlargement of assembly tasks, the formation of teams, and mechanisms for worker participation or consultation.

An incremental approach to work restructuring in the initial projects in both the Alcan plants and Shell's existing refineries was necessary in part because of constraints related to collective bargaining.

The initial experiment in a majority of cases occurred at the urging of a middle-level line manager, typically a plant manager, or with his active participation. Staff people and outside consultants or researchers also played an active role in designing and implementing most of the initial experiments. In the Norwegian projects, the researchers actually sought out the companies and persuaded them to collaborate in undertaking the projects. Similarly, in the Corning experiment, a corporate consultant began by stimulating interest among supervisors to try their own mini-experiments, which, if successful, could lead to plantwide work restructuring. Interestingly, although the management and worker members of the Norwegian and the Corning experiments subsequently came to "own" the projects, dependency upon outside experts long remained a factor in these cases, each of which resulted in little intracompany diffusion.

Step 2: Pilot Experiment Declared Early Success

The study included only those experiments that were judged successful after a year or two, when participants had had significant experience with the new work structures and when operating results could be assessed.

Spokesmen for these projects claimed that they had produced improved performance, increased worker knowledge and skills, and resulted in a generally more responsible and motivating work culture. In no case were there wholly independent performance audits or measurements that would persuade the most ardent skeptics of work restructuring. While my own field visits led me to conclude that in most cases some discounting of claims seemed to be required, I accept the original judgments of early success.

Results claimed on both the hard and soft sides of the benefits ledger varied: Only about 25 percent of the Northern Electric workers said they experienced a relatively large gain in the quality of their working life; among General Foods workers it was 80 percent. The balance, at least during the initial periods, would fall somewhere between. Six cases reported quality improvement and more efficient production due to decreased scrap, less down-time, or more efficient methods. Also, most companies reported reduced turnover and absentee rates. A case in point: The pet food plant after 18 months reported an overhead rate that was 33 percent lower than the old plant. The absentee rate was 9 percent below the industry norm, and turnover was far below average.

Step 3: Recognition and Resources Provided for Further Work Restructuring

After becoming acquainted with the results of the pilot experiment, top management typically gave its blessing to the approach. In several cases, notably GF, Alcan, and Norsk Hydro, it became company or division policy to diffuse work restructuring throughout the various facilities. In Hunsfos, it became company policy to spread work restructing to other departments in the mill complex. In the case of Volvo, the recognition of work restructuring became very strong. The new president took a special interest in the subject and had made a dramatic commitment to the program in existing plants in the early 1970s. He personally had pressed for and contributed to a revolutionary approach to the designing of a new auto assembly plant in Kalmar that involved a 10 percent higher capital investment to accommodate the desired work structure. This action gave work restructuring a high priority in other plants. Exceptions should be noted in the cases of Corning and Northern Electric, where apparently no strong encouragement of diffusion came from the corporate level other than from organizational development groups.

In Northern Electric, in fact, the reverse was true. A new manager who took over in the third year of the experiment terminated it before it could have reached the diffusion stage. The new organization was regarded as a success at its home base, but corporate management took a different view.

In a few cases, recognition eventually took the form of a management philosophy hammered out by a group of line managers with the assistance of staff consultants more familiar with work restructuring. A General Foods statement, for example, emerged shortly after other corporate measures had been taken to promote diffusion.

Another diffusion measure was the assignment of specific responsibility for promoting work restructuring. For example, in General Foods, the line manager responsible for pet food operations at the divisional level was transferred to the corporate level and made an internal consultant to several dozen plants.

Step 4: More General Interest in Work Restructuring Aroused

In every case, these experiments have been the subject of widely circulated written reports in the news media, oral presentations to other groups, and visits by interested parties to the experimental site. Dissemination activities often helped the project leaders secure top-management recognition and approval, but they had other objectives as well. They were intended to interest and inform managers and union officials of sister units within the same firm and those outside the firm. The visibility and favorable acclaim, of course, were gratifying to the participants, who were proud of the work culture they had created and the performance results they had achieved.

Step 5: Change Agents' Interventions Extend throughout the Corporate System

We have already noted the tendency to designate some individuals or committees to help initiate projects and monitor their development. The change interventions led by the internal consultant at General Foods will help illustrate this aspect of a diffusion effort, although the activities are more elaborate than in other cases, except Shell U.K.

In late 1971, the newly appointed GF internal consultant, Lyman Ketchum, addressed a group of 150 top managers from operations, engineering, quality assurance, and personnel, together with several corporation group vice-presidents. Forms of work restructuring and their rationale were discussed. The chairman of GF and a key vice-president were present and sanctioned the role of the new change agent.

A steering committee comprised of the division operating managers was formed to guide the change activities. As a committee the managers assessed the progress of diffusion, and as individuals they were expected to collaborate with the change agent in his work in their divisions.

Change initiatives occurred at the plant level. Priority was given to new and recent plants over existing plants because more progress could be made with less effort. Further priority was given to larger plants because of their greater importance. Recognizing these priorities, the change agent began working with plant managers who manifested the most interest in change.

The change agent's initial work with plants involved a three-day meeting with the plant manager and his staff, who were encouraged to explore their own values and the connections between values and work structures.

These initial three-day meetings by themselves seldom produced much action. After a month or so had elapsed, the change agent usually scheduled another meeting with a group drawn from the next level below the plant manager's staff.

As a parallel activity, the corporate change agent organized three-day seminars on the techniques of work analysis and design; these were attended largely by staff personnel such as engineers.

Where a commitment to work restructuring developed, the change agent helped form a plant steering committee comprised of key line and staff managers, and union officials where appropriate. Subordinate action committees were formed to explore and recommend specific projects within a limited area of the plant. The change agent himself and other consulting resources were made available to the plant committees to assist them in the actual work restructuring.

Diffusion interventions at Norsk Hydro took a somewhat different form: The first major event was a policy clinic where managers and their union counterparts could discuss the ideas and techniques of achieving employee participation at the shop floor in the planning and introduction of change. These discussions were somewhat inhibited by managers who believed that the area manager was authoritarian and unsympathetic. The area manager discovered the content of these policy discussions and stopped them.

In 1971, a second effort was made with the responsibility for work restructuring initiatives assigned to the Joint Consultation Board. A supervisory training program was also introduced. Some new initiatives worked out; others did not.

By 1972 top management concluded that the diffusion policy still was not working. Middle managers were told to "get cracking," and a training program was devised to better equip them to play their role. In the meantime the area manager had been replaced, in part because he had not helped implement the work restructuring project. This development was offset by the departure of an influential union official who was interested in diffusing the work structures pioneered in the fertilizer plants.

A supplementary vehicle for diffusion was the conversion of the ten-man professional staff of the firm's industrial engineering methods group "from MTM engineers to sociotechnical consultants." The head of this department understood the need for reshaping the role of the department and began in 1971 to reeducate the staff. Over time this development may greatly facilitate diffusion of the work restructuring ideas pioneered in the fertilizer plants.

Step 6: Facilitative Networks Develop

This is a step taken in only a few of the change programs studied. An interunit network of personnel involved in work restructuring is created to exchange ideas, to provide a supportive reference group for its members, and to build a constituency for change in corporate policies and procedures more favorable to work restructuring. In GF, networks of plant managers and their personnel managers are evolving to a point where many of their members can serve others generally as outside consultants.

Step 7: Personnel Movement Occurs

The transfer of experienced personnel from an innovative unit is a way of exporting the knowledge, values, and skills at the heart of work restructuring. The innovative unit then can educate the new managers who transfer into the unit.

A few favorable moves can be cited to illustrate the possibilities. In a strategic move at Norsk Hydro, the person who had been personnel manager in the Porsgrunn area was promoted to corporate headquarters. He was intimately familiar with the fertilizer project and an articulate proponent of the underlying philosophy. He moved to a better position to advise top management on the diffusion of work restructuring. Not surprisingly, the advantage of this move to headquarters was partly offset by the loss felt in the local area.

The manager at Alcan's Kingston Works was promoted to a division-level position after the program was well under way at Kingston. Later, however, he reportedly lost touch with the innovations and became less supportive.

In Shell U.K., the transfer of key personnel

was disruptive of the program under way in the U.K., but some moves seeded other parts of the Shell International organization—for example, the Australian unit—with managers who were committed to finding better ways of organizing work.

THE SHELL U.K. APPROACH

A major variation on the procedure in the other seven firms—that of starting small with a single experiment—is provided by Shell U.K. From the outset, the approach was conceived as companywide, comprehensive in its effect on the work situation, and planned to last from five to ten years.

The first step was not a demonstration project. Work redesign was undertaken only after large amounts of organizational time had been spent in sessions developing and affirming a supportive managerial philosophy.

Attitudes, in short, were changed before structure. Tavistock social scientists worked closely with an internal staff resource group to design the activities in this and subsequent phases, beginning in 1965 with the development of a philosophy to which senior managers could commit themselves.

The second phase was intended to ensure that the operating philosophy was freely accepted by all 6,000 members of the organization from senior managers to hourly workers. To accomplish this dissemination—involving active testing and consensus building—required 18 months, from fall 1965 to spring 1967—and a cascade of conferences.

The implementation phase was launched in March 1966 by a third top-management conference. The first strategic approach to implementation was to set up pilot projects that "could act as centers of organizational learning." These projects, set up in one refinery, did not go well. Moreover, the concentration of attention on a few groups at one site created resentment among many others who had been through the philosophy discussions, and who were emotionally and intellectually primed to implement the philosophy.

Next, the implementation strategy was altered, and responsibility for change was placed on the department-manager level across the company—an approach made possible by the massive dissemination process. To enable department managers to initiate their own change projects, short training courses were provided to teach them techniques of work analysis and principles of work restructuring.

A network of committees representing both management and unions helped to change work rules that otherwise would prevent many types of restructuring, such as flexible manning patterns and paying workers for multiple job skills.

Although pilot projects as centers for organization learning no longer formed the primary foundation for implementation, it was decided to apply the concepts to a new refinery at Teesport, where construction began in 1965 and which came on stream in April 1968.

Evaluation conferences were held in March 1967 on the previous two major sites covered, Stanlow and Shell Haven. Shortly therafter, a number of changes took place that served to arrest the diffusion process and tended to demoralize the innovative systems already introduced.

PROBLEM AREAS IN DIFFUSION

My investigation attempted to find out why diffusion was not more rapid and extensive. The reasons ranged from defects in the design of the original experiment to unanticipated consequences of the success of the initial pilot project.

Regression in the Pilot Project

Because diffusion typically occurs over a significant period of time, the sustained success of early experiments can help build momentum for companywide change; conversely, emergent weaknesses in the pilot projects can erode initial support for change.

A clear correlation between the continued success of initial projects and the rate of diffusion is found in several extreme cases. Volvo's truck plant experiment has continued to be effective and has been followed by relatively high diffusion. The Northern Electric experiment was discontinued, and also produced no significant diffusion within the company. A similar consistency is found in the demoralization of Corning's Medfield experiment, after a period of effectiveness, and the lack of diffusion throughout the firm.

Both Shell U.K. and Alcan experienced moderate effectiveness in their early experiments and have shown moderate amounts of diffusion, although causal connections are not indicated. Shell U.K. achieved its diffusion soon after its change program was undertaken; the initial projects subsequently became somewhat demoralized and no further diffusion has occurred. Alcan has recently diffused the ideas of the earlier experiments into a new mill, although there has been a decline in management and worker involvement in the plants in which the earlier innovations were established.

There is not always a correlation between initial project success and diffusion. The strong success of the Topeka plant in GF is not matched so far by a high amount of diffusion, and in the cases of Norsk Hydro and Hunsfos, there is even less correlation. Continued success of initial change projects appears to be only one of the many influences on diffusion.

What can cause a successful early experiment to deteriorate later on? I have noted several factors: (1) internal inconsistencies in the original design; (2) loss of support from levels of management above the experimental unit; (3) premature turnover of leaders, operators, or consultants directly associated with a project; (4) stress and crises that lead to more authoritarian management, which in turn demoralizes the innovative unit; (5) tension in the innovative unit's relations with other parties—peer units, staff groups, superiors, labor unions; (6) letdown in participants' involvement after initial success with its attendant publicity; (7) lack of diffusion to other parts of the organization, which isolates the original experiment and its leaders.

The seventh factor or principle, succinctly stated, is "diffuse or die"; it suggests that a circular relationship exists whereby lack of diffusion can *eventually* undermine the viability of the initial project, just as weaknesses that develop in the initial project can undermine the diffusion effort. The converse of this circular relationship is not strong; as I have noted above, continued success in the initial project does not necessarily lead to diffusion throughout the larger organization.

Poor Model for Change

Even if the pilot project remains viable over time, it may be an ineffective model for diffusion in the firm because it lacks either visibility or credibility. These deficiencies may reflect the behavior of leaders of the experiment, or they may relate to the way policy is formulated by higher officials. Also, many characteristics inherent in the site of the initial experiment affect its ability to stimulate further change. Consider the many conditions of the GF pet food plant that enhanced the success of that project: The Topeka plant was new, was located in a favorable labor market, required few workers, and was geographically separate from headquarters and other existing facilities of GF. Since it was a new plant with a new work force, no union agreement was required to establish the new work structure. Many of these conditions, of course, did not exist elsewhere in GF, and many managers asked, "Is work restructuring possible in other situations—for example, in a large, established, unionized plant?"

The credibility of the Corning and Northern Electric projects suffered not only for similar reasons but also from an additional site characteristic: The technology involved in the experimental plant was significantly different from that employed in other plants in the system.

In terms of site characteristics, Volvo, Alcan, and Shell U.K. appear to have presented relatively good prospects for further diffusion of a successful experiment. They were initiated in large, established, unionized facilities and involved technologies typical of the larger systems of which they were a part.

The prospects for diffusion of the work restructuring innovations at the Norsk Hydro fertilizer plants would have to be regarded as even more favorable. By 1973 a dozen different plants were adjacent to each other in the Porsgrunn area, each producing a different product—ammonia, nitric acid, urea, formic acid, magnesium, plastics, and so on. They were similar in ways that made the fertilizer work organization generally relevant: They employed continuous-process technologies, and large pieces of capital were manned by relatively small work forces. In addition, Norsk Hydro had operations in a number of other locations, and in fact was the largest industrial undertaking in Norway. Thus, one could project the spread of demonstrably successful ideas throughout the Porsgrunn works and other parts of the firm, and because of the firm's prominence in Norway, to other industrial firms in this small country. Obviously, for an explanation of why much diffusion did not occur, we will have to look elsewhere than to site characteristics.

The way the project leaders present the experiment to others in the firm will influence its visibility and credibility. One basic choice is whether to maintain a low profile or to seek visibility in the corporate environment.

A low profile reduces the career risks associated with failure, and less publicity also minimizes the risk of creating a "showcase" complex with longer-run adverse effects on the work climate. However, in the cases studied, the incentive to publicize the experiments increased substantially once they appeared to be successfully established. Visibility, it was felt, was essential if diffusion were to occur, and the natural pride in the innovation was accompanied by a desire for wider recognition—inside the company and beyond. Some favorable publicity often created an appetite for more. The project leaders sometimes lost control of publicity to other corporate officials and the media.

Except possibly for Corning's Medfield and Northern Electric's Advanced Devices Center, the initial experiments in my sample achieved sufficient visibility throughout their corporate organizations.

Confusion Over What Is to Be Diffused

Even if the initial site is favorable for eventual diffusion and the project leaders manage the publicity effectively, higher management can botch up the process in the way they formulate and communicate the diffusion policy.

If the form of work structure indicated by company policy is stated too conceptually, the policy may be dismissed as abstract and platitudinous or action may be delayed because managers don't know how to translate the concepts.

On the other hand, if the ideas about the desired forms of work structure are stated too operationally, then they may be rejected as inappropriate by managers whose units have different types of work forces, different technologies, or different economic conditions.

Norsk Hydro presents an interesting case in point. Six years after the initiation of the fertilizer experiment and many years after it had become official company policy to diffuse this type of work innovation, managers still complained about the lack of clarity. Was the policy to diffuse "job enrichment," "autonomous groups," "organizational development," "socio-technical systems," or something more general that underlies all of these?

There was general agreement that diffusion would have proceeded more rapidly if it had been clear that the policy was for managers to pursue certain *aims* (such as making better use of the talents of employees and allowing for more day-to-day influence by employees over their work) rather than to employ particular *techniques*.

Inappropriateness of Concepts Employed

The long-run diffusion of work restructuring is affected by another issue: While the concepts should be inspiring, they must also be realistic.

"Autonomous groups" was the key concept employed in the Norwegian experiments to characterize the work restructuring innovations. The term, which many found inspiring, was later dropped because it was not feasible for many groups to become truly autonomous.

"Equal status" was a concept in the design of Shell U.K.'s Teesport work system. The term captured the imagination of the workers as well as the orginators, but overstated what higher management was prepared to do. Differences persisted between blue- and white-collar workers, although all employees were placed on salary. The differences remaining were especially resented because of the expectations aroused by the "equal status" concept.

Deficient Implementation

The initial project may be viable in itself, but the follow-through may be inadequate, in terms of locating accountability for the change and providing "how-to" knowledge.

The first point has already been illustrated. Norsk Hydro unsuccessfully attempted to place the responsibility for diffusion with Joint Consultation Boards and then shifted it to middle management. Shell U.K. started implementation by selecting a few projects with

heavy reliance upon a few staff people but then shifted to a policy in which all department heads become accountable for change in their units. Accountability for work restructuring in Volvo was clearest—it was an essential part of the plant managers' responsibility, period!

As is true with many types of change in organizations, "how to" knowledge must be provided through training, consulting, or both. Resources for this seemed to have been a limiting factor at one time or another in GF, Corning, and Alcan.

Lack of Top Management Commitment

A period of sustained priority for work restructuring is important in achieving diffusion. The continuing interest and commitment of Volvo's president is a prime case in point. By contrast, the shifting priority given work restructuring in several other firms' studies hindered diffusion. An illustrative case is Norsk Hydro, where the work restructuring objective received lower priority during 1970-73 than it did in the period 1967-69.

Priority declined for several reasons. First, when the initial experiment was launched there was a high sense of urgency about improving industrial relations and productivity. But with a general improvement in industrial relations and the competitiveness of the business, the sense of urgency declined.

Second, according to middle-level managers, they have come under increasing pressure to meet demanding volume and cost objectives, making it risky in the short run to start any major projects. One manager said, "I have the freedom to innovate but not the time."

Third, the company has been transformed by rapid expansion and revolutionary change in the raw materials and processes used in much of its business. The changes absorbed the attention of top management and the director-general became more formal and less accessible to members of the organization—at least to those who wanted to lobby for work restructuring.

The Shell U.K. managers perceived a similar set of changes as weakening their work restructuring program. In 1971, Hill reported that after mid-1967 there was a lack of continuing visible commitment at the top. In 1967, the U.K. company was reorganized to include North Sea exploration and production as well as U.K. refining activities, and a new chief executive was appointed. The refineries repeatedly requested assurances that the top management of the enlarged company endorsed and supported the philosophy behind the work restructuring program. When the new management team became absorbed in supply problems created by the 1967 Middle East War and failed to formally endorse an amended statement of philosophy tailored to the company's enlarged role, managers in the refineries became less willing to embark on change.

In many cases, including those just mentioned, inconsistencies in higher-management behavior weakened diffusion efforts. Even before they perceived that the program was down-graded, Shell U.K. managers were concerned that although they were asked to protect and develop their human resources, they were being assessed mainly on their handling of the technical system alone.

In the latter part of the 1960s, Alcan division management reportedly shifted toward a more directive, top-down type of leadership and away from a consultative, problem-oriented management pattern. This directly contradicted and undermined the innovative work structure that had been developed at the Kingston works and had an inhibiting effect on further diffusion of work restructuring in the division.

Union Opposition

Like sustained top-management commitment, union support or acceptance is a necessary condition for any significant diffusion of work restructuring. In some cases, union support has been, on balance, a positive factor. In other cases, perceived opposition by the union has been a reason for not trying to diffuse work restructuring into unionized plants. Mostly, unions have had more complicated effects—on the process of introducing change, the nature of the work structures introduced, and the work climate.

The Scandinavian union movement has been more positive toward work restructuring than trade unions in the U.K. and North America. Clearly, joint union-management sponsorship of the Norwegian experiments served to legitimize the program for workers. However, the actual effects of the union officials on diffusion within Norsk Hydro and Hunsfos were mixed, just as the effects on the management side were mixed.

In Norsk Hydro a particularly key union official had moved from the area and the loss of his support hurt the diffusion effort. In Hunsfos, where the chief shop steward and the company president were strongly committed to the diffusion program, local effort received no backing from the trade union movement. Although the trade union movement as a whole was not averse to the changes pioneered at Hunsfos, the chief shop steward reported criticism from other quarters. He said he took risks with his own constituency every time he "stuck his neck out" (for example, on a change that resulted in a crew reduction). Also, radical sociologists accused him of selling out to management, increasing company efficiency at the expense of workers.

At Volvo, the unions have played an active and positive role in the work restructuring program. Management had initiated the job redesign aspects of the program and the union the consultative aspects. Both parties, moreover, claim joint ownership of the total program.

In the case of the Shell U.K. program, the union deliberately slowed down the rate of diffusion of work restructuring during 1965-68 until productivity bargaining had progressed to the point where they had been able to establish the economic quid pro quo for certain changes.

The union had played its role in the recent demoralization of the Shell U.K. change program. Management negotiated wage increases in 1971 and 1972 that were below the national pattern, and then in 1973 the government constraints prevented the parties from making up the difference. The union has reflected and perhaps amplified worker resentment.

Another factor at Shell is tension around manning. Top management continues to put pressure on refinery managers to reduce the work force. When we recall that guarantees against dismissal and provisions for extra pay were a quid pro quo in the initial change program, we can see how reviving the issue has led to poorer union-management relations and inhibited the further diffusion of work restructuring.

Three projects started in nonunion plants of firms whose other plants were mostly unionized. Unions representing these other plants were expected to oppose or otherwise complicate work restructuring in them. The three firms were General Foods, Corning, and Northern Electric. In the case of GF, where work restructuring effects have actually been undertaken in unionized plants, the collective bargaining relationship complicated change in the early steps but has not prevented it. With Corning and Northern Electric little or no attempt was made to diffuse change to union plants.

To summarize, unions' effect has taken many forms:

First, unions have influenced the basic climate for change. Sometimes the effect was positive, helping to legitimize work restructuring or entering into an informal problem-solving pattern consistent with the work culture sought by the work restructuring experiment. Sometimes the effect of unions was negative, inhibiting management from trying to diffuse change or formalizing and politicizing relations contradictory to the spirit of the work culture being diffused.

Second, unions have complicated the change process by requiring additional consensus-seeking efforts.

Third, unions have affected the preconditions for change or limited the nature of the change itself. Sometimes they have obtained assurances on job security and earnings maintenance and have bargained for workers to obtain a share of the increased productivity that resulted from more flexibility and reduced work crews. Sometimes they have prevented certain changes, e.g., modifications in job content that affect union jurisdictional boudaries or historical patterns.

Bureaucratic Barriers

The importance of this issue belies the simplicity with which it can be stated. Diffusion efforts are frustrated by vested interests and existing organizational routines that limit local autonomy.

Innovative plant managements have often felt harassed by staff groups, who for their part have often become irritated and impatient with many of the plants' demands for self-sufficiency and exemption from uniform company policies. These tensions may be present during the establishment of the initial experiment, and they are escalated when serious diffusion begins. "Experiments," by definition, minimize the scope and duration of the effects of the change involved. However, when the changes are declared enduring or an attempt is made to spread them, the stakes are raised for groups affected.

Bureaucratic barriers can be illustrated from the experience of one company, where managers themselves introduced the term. One problem relates to the level at which decisions are made in the line organization. In 1973, workers were operating informally without supervisors on two of the four shifts, but formalization of this arrangement and extension to a third and fourth shift was not within the authority of the manager of the innovative plant.

Another example involved the method for judging operator qualification for increased pay in the innovative plant. Central personnel insisted that the "theoretical" tests of knowledge appropriate for each job had to be mastered before "practical" knowledge could be compensated. Previously, theoretical knowledge could be learned and compensated *after* a person had shown he could perform the day-to-day operations associated with a particular job and had received an adjustment for that practical mastery. These events not only demoralized the participants of the project, but also discouraged other managers from initiating projects.

The experience of General Foods, Shell U.K., and other firms in which an ambitious diffusion effort has been undertaken are rich with similar illustrations, involving such issues as whether quality assurance procedures at plant level must be uniform throughout the corporation, whether a common job evaluation scheme should be applied to plants with radically different work structures, what should be the respective roles of central engineering and local staff in plant expansion programs, how much local autonomy should exist in creating and filling plant management positions, and whether reporting requirements must be applied uniformly throughout the system.

Threatened Obsolescence

A restructured work situation requires new roles and new skills and makes others obsolete. We have already mentioned the resistance of staff groups who may have to acquire new knowledge, develop new consultative patterns for imparting their expertise, and see some of their functions being performed by nonspecialists.

However, the greatest threat was to first-line supervision. The number of first-line supervisors was often decreased. Sometimes the position was even eliminated. Where the position was retained, the role was changed in the ways that required new attitudes and greater interpersonal and group skills.

Supervisors individually and as a group are weak compared with other groups potentially affected by new work structures. They themselves have not mounted much effective opposition to the diffusion or tried to shape the form of work restructuring, with one exception—Volvo, where within the past year the supervisors' union has taken an active role to protect its members' interests. In at least one case, Hunsfos, concern by workers about the effect of work restructuring on their supervisors created a major snag in the diffusion process. In many other cases, management's uncertainty about how to handle the potential obsolescence of existing foremen has been a factor inhibiting diffusion.

In some cases the resistance of supervisors and other salaried personnel was not due to a direct threat to their existing roles; rather, they felt neglected by comparison with blue-collar workers. They resented the fact that the blue-collar worker's job was enriched and his status and influence upgraded, while their lot had not improved.

Self-limiting Dynamics

In companies that employed the most comprehensive diffusion strategy, there was a tendency for pilot projects to be self-limiting or "self-sealing." The tendency was strongest in instances like Norsk Hydro, Hunsfos, and General Foods, where a single small unit was involved in the original experiment and where serious efforts to introduce work restructuring into other units came only after widespread publicity on the success of the experimental unit.

One dynamic involved a "star-envy" phenomenon, which can be illustrated by Norsk Hydro. The original experiment in the fertilizer plants received an enormous amount of publicity within Norway and outside. The fertilizer plants became the object of innumerable visits by managers, trade union officials, social scientists, and schoolchildren. Top management looked approvingly on the project and made it company policy for others to follow the lead of the fertilizer project. Not surprisingly, the attention given the fertilizer groups engendered resentment and envy among the other persons who were asked to adopt the innovation in their own operations. The resentment was accompanied by resistance to the work restructuring program. The experience of the Topeka plant in General Foods was strikingly similar.

A second dynamic involved a shift in the reward structure. Payoffs for pioneers and those who followed them in the same organization differed in important respects, providing a much less favorable benefit-risk picture for the subsequent users of organizational innovations. Managers who adapted the innovation and succeeded received less credit than the pioneer received, and if they had failed, they probably would have lost more standing in management than the pioneer would have if he had failed. Managers who did not utilize the innovation often figured that while they might be prodded and goaded for not taking any organizational initiatives, ultimately they would be judged on the basis of production and profit performance. In short, they felt that they could afford to resist pressure.

A third dynamic involved the tendency for participants to feel special and to regard their experimental work system as superior. On the one hand, this feeling reinforced their commitment to the group and was a positive factor in helping to establish a new form of social organization. On the other hand, this tended to lead outsiders to conclude that the culture created was unique and to discount the general applicability of the experiment.

A fourth dynamic came into play at a later date. Rivalry sometimes developed among those engaged in work restructuring. They stressed minor differences in their approaches, while ignoring the similarity in underlying values and assumptions. One effect of this form of rivalry among change agents and among innovative units was to weaken their ability to form the collegial networks described as part of the general diffusion model.

A fifth dynamic also came into play at a later stage in those cases where diffusion did not occur fairly rapidly. It was a secondary consequence of two factors related above: the bureaucratic barriers and the special self-image developed by experimental units. The leaders of some innovative units had engaged in so many skirmishes with superiors and staff groups over corporate practices and were so aggressive in asserting the correctness of their positions that they hurt their careers. Observing this, some peers resolved not to get similarly burned.

OTHER INFLUENTIAL FACTORS

After having studied the diffusion process in eight companies and after having analyzed the situational factors that seemed to account for a generally slower-than-expected rate of diffusion, I became interested in assessing how inherently difficult or easy these new structures are to diffuse.

The early classic studies of diffusion traced the adoption of improved agricultural practices. More recent studies have covered other innovations, including farm practices, medical drugs, educational techniques, machinery, management control techniques, and so on. Should we expect diffusion of work restructuring to be relatively slower or faster than diffusion of innovations in these other fields?

Recent reviews of the literature on diffusion consistently concurred on a number of attributes of innovations that influenced their adoption rate. Most are plausible, at least on the surface.

1 *Relative advantage.* This is an obvious attribute that enhances the rate of diffusion.

The cost-benefit analysis implied in this attribute includes not only financial but also perceived social costs and benefits. The problem with work restructuring is that there is a singular lack of agreement among its proponents over the benefits derived. Some stress tangible impacts on such factors as productivity and turnover; others choose to emphasize the psychic dividends paid to workers.

2 *Communicability.* Diffusion will be enhanced if the innovation can be explained easily and if its effects are easily separable from other influences in the environment. Work restructuring innovations rate low on this attribute compared with all other types of innovations cited. Volvo may be an exception. The changes were straighforward and readily grasped. Well-established production norms permitted an easy assessment of any loss of efficiency, and the desired decrease in turnover was quickly measured (although not always persuasively explained). Thus communicability may help explain why Volvo's relatively simple changes on the existing assembly lines were diffused relatively rapidly.

3 *Compatibility.* Diffusion is aided if the innovation is perceived as being congruent with existing norms, values, and structures. Again, work restructuring innovations must be rated low because by definition they call for important structural and normative changes in the existing industrial organizations. (Work restructuring threatens what many managers in the United States continue to regard as their prerogatives.) However, the same innovations would rate higher in compatibility in Scandinavia than in the U.S.

4 *Pervasiveness.* This term refers to the number of aspects of the system affected by the innovation. Less pervasiveness permits more rapid diffusion. By definition, what we refer to as "work restructuring" strives to be comprehensive, embracing division of labor, rewards, supervision, status systems, and power relations. This factor, too, makes diffusing work restructuring inherently difficult.

5 *Reversibility.* Can an innovation be adopted on an experimental basis and reversed without serious consequences? If the status quo ante cannot be readily restored, diffusion will be inhibited. Many managers believe that work restructuring creates expectations that will become a liability if the innovation must be abandoned. My limited observations support that belief. Thus work restructuring may rate moderate to low on the reversibility factor.

6 *Number of gatekeepers.* Numerous approval channels that must be satisfied before an innovation can be adopted will tend to inhibit the rate of diffusion. In work restructuring, top management, departmental or plant managers, staff groups, supervisors, unions, and the workers themselves all have some gatekeeping role to perform. One could hardly imagine gatekeeping conditions less favorable for diffusion of new work structures.

Finally, a major difficulty in diffusing work restructuring is that frequently it's not literally a matter of "adoption." Because work forces, technologies, and economics affect the appropriate work structure, tailored application of the general principles of work restructuring is required rather than adoption of a predetermined model.

CONCLUSION

One important reason for the unimpressive rate of diffusion in the eight companies studied is that, especially in their more comprehensive form, these innovations have many attributes that make their diffusion inherently slow. Even if they offer relative advantages over existing work structures, their character and results are not highly communicable; they are not congruent with existing norms and values; their potential effect in a given work situation is pervasive rather than fractional; they are not readily reversed without incurring social costs; and too many affected parties serve as gatekeepers for the effective implementation of the innovations.

Another set of explanations for the actual diffusion observed in the eight companies relates to the barriers the diffusion efforts encountered and the efficacy of companies' strategies and tactics.

Many key areas are readily identifiable: Does the experiment continue to show good results? Is the experiment sufficiently visible and sufficiently convincing? Is organizational accountability for initiating change clear, and is know-how for implementation available? Is there sustained support for diffusion from powerful groups such as top management and union officials? Careful planning is required to ensure that the answers to these questions are positive.

Two problem areas deal with organizational dilemmas generated by the nature of the innovations. Work restructuring requires an increase in local autonomy, thereby threatening the power of central staff groups and some managers. It also threatens to make some roles obsolete or to eliminate the positions of some staff specialists and first-line supervisors. These problems are not easily resolved and require imaginative solutions—solutions not yet obvious to me.

Last, perhaps the most interesting type of barrier to diffusion is the self-limiting dynamics of pilot projects. Ironically, several of these are unexpected consequences of the success of the project: The greater the attention given pilot units, the more likely are managers of peer units to be "turned off" by the example. The more successful the pioneer, the less favorable are the payoffs and the greater the risks for those who follow. The more esprit de corps and sense of being special that develops in the unit, the less generalizable it appears to others.

Some of the implications of our analysis of these and other self-limiting tendencies are apparent once the dynamics are understood: There is an advantage in (1) introducing a number of projects at the same time in the same firm, (2) avoiding overexposure and glorification of particular change efforts, and (3) having the innovative program identified with top management at the initial project stage.

As the examples of work restructuring in the larger society become more numerous, however, the self-limiting tendencies should pose less of a problem.

In conclusion, I expect relatively little diffusion of potentially significant restructuring in the work place—over the short run. Hopefully the long run may tell a different story.

Increasingly, what many employees expect from their jobs is different from what organizations are prepared to offer them. Work restructuring is the preeminent answer to closing the gap. I would expect the latent dissatisfactions of workers to be activated and pressure for work restructuring to increase as the issues receive more public attention and as more successful examples of comprehensive work restructuring raise the general level of worker expectations. I would also be surprised if future experiments did not profit from the pioneering efforts. Together, these factors should generate an increase in the number of diffusions and a hastening of the pace of diffusion. But how many diffusions and how fast the pace, I can't even begin to guess.

Reading 41

Quality of Work Life and the Union

George Strauss

Much has been written about reforms (such as job enrichment) that management might introduce to improve the quality of work life, and thereby to raise workers' satisfaction and motivation. Before introducing such reforms in unionized organizations, however, management should take into account the interests of the union. Most reforms aimed at improving the quality of work life, for example, require workers' participation; in many cases, such participation is their essence. Such participation is unlikely if the union disapproves. Cooperation by the union is especially critical if changes involve practices previously subject to collective bargaining. Changes in career ladders, for example, may require modifications in seniority systems, while job redesign alters job descriptions—issues that traditionally have been set through negotiation and rendered unalterable by the contract.

Beyond this, the union itself represents an important means of providing a better quality of work life, both as a channel for upward communications and as a vehicle for participation. Neither productivity nor morale is likely to be high in an atmosphere of constant bickering and suspicion, even if strikes are few. Thus, good union-management relations are essential to introducing reforms in the workplace, and are themselves a determinant of job satisfaction.

This reading first discusses the quandaries that issues of job design pose for unions, and then makes some specific suggestions as to how management might effectively enlist the cooperation of unions in dealing with problems in this area.

UNION QUANDARIES

Issues concerning the quality of work life present problems for unions, and many union leaders are uncertain as to how best to deal with these problems (in this, they are no different from members of management). Nevertheless, unions are involved as equal participants in three projects being monitored by the National Quality of Work Center, and a union played an important supporting role in what is so far perhaps the most elaborate (and best reported) company reorganization according to principles of behavioral science, at the Weldon Company (Marrow, Bowers, & Seashore, 1967). Unions have been involved in numerous changes under the auspices of the Scanlon Plan, and without using the concept of quality of work life specifically, unions at the shop level have initiated and supported countless job changes which have had the effect (and frequently the purpose) of increasing teamwork and individual discretion. Finally, Scandinavian unions have been the leaders in seeking reforms in the quality of work life in their countries.

Despite these experiences, issues about the quality of work life still present some serious quandaries for unions. Union leaders are generally suspicious about the movement to improve the quality of work life, and uncertain as to how they should react to it. In part, their uncertainty arises from lack of knowledge and even interest in these areas, since unemployment and inflation generally have higher priority for them than quality of work life. In part, their suspicion has been caused by the way reforms in quality of work life have been

Adapted from chap. 7 (Managerial Practices) of J. R. Hackman and J. L. Suttle (Eds.), *Improving life at work: Behavioral science approaches to organizational change.* Santa Monica, Calif.: Goodyear, 1977.

"packaged," i.e., many union leaders doubt the sincerity of management's sudden interest in workers' welfare and they wonder whether management may have in mind such other objectives as introducing a speedup or weakening the union. Even those who are sympathetic to the goal of improving the quality of work life recognize that implementing these changes may require painful adjustments, on the part of unions as well as management, to traditional values and collective bargaining procedure.

Let me briefly discuss some of the union's concerns, for only with an understanding of these concerns can management develop a realistic plan for dealing with them.

Suspicion of Motives

Much of the writing on quality of work life totally ignores the union. Almost all the early experiments in this area took place in nonunion plants. At least one prominent consultant has publicly argued that job enrichment is an effective way of keeping unions out. And a number of social critics have charged that the labor movement has been so single-mindedly concerned with workers' material needs that it has been insufficiently responsive to their needs for personal growth and development. Management, these critics conclude, has been more up-to-date and, as a consequence, unions have become somewhat outmoded.

Unions naturally react to such charges with anger. They hotly claim that they have contributed more to improving the quality of work life than management ever will. And any fair observer will agree that this response contains a large element of truth. For example, workers in union plants usually earn higher wages than those in nonunion plants. Unions also have fought hard—and generally successfully—for safer working conditions, more humane supervision, and more equitable application of management rules. Above all, they provide the single most significant means whereby workers can meaningfully and effectively partici-

pate in resolving matters of importance to them.

Given this impressive record of protecting workers' interests, unionists feel considerable annoyance with the self-congratulatory tone of some social scientists and management spokesmen who have suddenly discovered, after all these years, that problems do exist in the work place—and then propose to solve them on management's terms and without recognition of the union's role.

Furthermore, many union officers are apprehensive of behavioral scientists and academicians in general. Early consultants were frequently time-and-motion experts, and, as an article in the official AFL-CIO journal put it, "Substituting the sociologist's questionnaire for the stopwatch is likely to be no gain for the workers" (Brooks, 1972, p. 1). The recent interest in quality of work life by those in "radical-chic academic and intellectual circles" (Brooks, 1972, p. 4) is viewed as being somewhat patronizing, especially when this interest is accompanied by suggestions that union officers no longer know what their members want.

In sum, therefore, there is considerable (and perhaps justifiable) suspicion among workers and union leaders concerning the motives of management, as well as suspicion of the motives of the behavioral scientists who are associated with the movement to improve the quality of work life. However, the extent of this suspicion doubtless varies from work site to work site—and depends heavily on the past history of the labor-management relationship in question. Where the relationship has developed amicably and an atmosphere of trust has been created, management's interest in the quality of work life will more probably be accepted in good faith.

The Adversary Relationship

Unions often find it a bit difficult to deal with problems concerning the quality of work life because, as Nat Goldfinger of the AFL-CIO put it, "A union demand is a negotiable demand which, if not satisfied, can be met by a strike. How do you talk about these questions [quality of work life] in terms of a negotiable demand and a possible strike?" (Jenkins, 1974, p. 317). In general, unions have resisted making management decisions, particularly when this requires making invidious choices among members or when it might lead to resentment by union members (as in the case of union participation in the discipline of fellow employees). As an official of one union commented, "We want management to make the decisions so we can be free to start a grievance about it. Otherwise we could be accused of helping make bad decisions. So we have always left decisions up to management."

These comments may exaggerate the problem, however. In the first place, unions frequently participate in making hard decisions which favor one group of members over another. They do this whenever they negotiate a new seniority system or agree to a contract which provides greater benefits for one group (for example, skilled tradesmen) than for others. Such decisions may not always affect the quality of work life, but they do require the union to make a potentially unpopular choice. Further, experienced negotiators are able to live in "mixed motive" situations (to use the terminology of Walton & McKersie, 1965) in which "distributive" bargaining (where one party can gain only at the cost of the other) exists side by side with "integrative" bargaining (where the solution can provide gains for both parties). The quality of work life is an integrative issue par excellence.

Fortunately, unions have a long history of dealing with such integrative problems—from plant picnics to job evaluation—through the establishment of joint union-management committees which function separately from mainstream, distributive bargaining (Sayles & Strauss, 1953). Improvements in the quality of work life may well be more likely, and more effective, through the use of such committees.

Fear That Traditional Economic Objectives Will Be Downgraded

Implicit in *some* of the writings relating to the quality of work life is the assumption that workers' economic needs have already been reasonably well satisfied and that personal "growth" should now be given top priority. Unionists reject this assumption and object strongly to any effort to downgrade the primacy of economic needs. They are in no way prepared to trade off concrete gains, such as wage increases, for anything as nebulous as greater freedom to make work decisions. In general (as the evidence below suggests), unions have been willing to experiment cautiously with changes affecting the quality of work life, but only if these are the side show. They will strongly resist any effort to move economic questions off center stage.

Table 41-1, adapted from a recent survey of union activists in upstate New York (Kochan, Lipsky, & Dyer, 1974), provides some indica-

Table 41-1 Attitudes of Union Officers toward Selected Issues

	Issue "very important"[a]	Issue integrative[b]	Issue appropriate for joint program[c]
Earnings	92%	26%	6%
Fringe benefits	79	48	4
Safety	75	68	41
Job security	68	44	12
Control of work	47	34	54
Adequate resources	46	46	61
Interesting work	41	39	68
Productivity	30	30	51
Work load	22	29	44

[a] Percent rating issue "very important."
[b] Percent reporting that with regard to given issue "my union and company want to accomplish completely the same thing" or "my company and union want to accomplish somewhat the same thing."
[c] Percent feeling that the "best way" to deal with issue is to "set up a joint program with management outside collective bargaining."

tion of unions' attitudes. Several interesting conclusions emerge from this study. As expected, basic economic issues are ranked most important. Yet, substantial numbers of unionists also rate as "very important" such elements in the quality of work life as safety, control of work (described as "having more to say about how the work is done"), adequate resources (described as "improving conditions that interfere with getting the job done"), and interesting work.[1] Both productivity and work load receive reasonably low votes. In sum, the results suggest that improving the quality of work life is a secondary but still important issue for these activists.

The second column in Table 41-1 contains some surprises. With the exception of safety, a majority of the activists do *not* believe that their companies wish to accomplish the same thing as their unions in these areas. Even "adequate resources" was viewed as being a distributive issue. Presumably (we can't be sure) this majority felt that the company was not interested in "improving conditions that got in the way of getting the job done."

The third column suggests considerable union support for joint programs in these areas. (Other data, not reported here, indicate that collective bargaining was not felt to be effective with regard to these issues.)

The study reported above is consistent with the trend of discussion in a two-day "Workers' Assembly" sponsored by the Institute of Industrial Relations, University of California at Berkeley, and attended by about fifty active unionists. The announced subject of this 1974 conference was "The Changing World of Work"; nevertheless, most of the comments in various small groups during the first day emphasized the need for higher wages and job security during a period of combined inflation

and recession. By the end of the day, however, the discussion in most groups seemed to switch to conditions on the job, with the stress at first on such grievances as tyrannical supervision, oppressive management policies, job hazards, and excessive work loads. During the second day, some individuals began distinguishing between various kinds of jobs, especially between those which were closely supervised and those which allowed a man to be his own boss. By the end of this second day, there was general (but not unanimous) agreement that unions should move in the direction of increasing freedom on the job and that perhaps there should be experiments with work groups without foremen.

Thus the conference discussion reinforces the following conclusions of the attitude survey: (1) union leaders are concerned about the quality of work life, although the degree of their concern probably varies from one situation to another, (2) they are somewhat uncertain as to how to handle these issues within a collective bargaining context, but (3) economic issues still are of primary concern. From this I draw one further generalization—if properly approached, unions will support reforms of the quality of work life; on the other hand, like management, they will have to "feel their way" into this terra incognita.

Fear of Speedup

For management, higher productivity is an unquestioned good. Union leaders are less sure about this. While there is general recognition that companies must be profitable if they are to pay decent wages, the term "productivity" is often associated with the speedup and loss of jobs. Note that, of the union sample discussed above, 70 percent viewed productivity as an issue about which the union's interests were likely to diverge from those of management. Thus, union leaders are hardly likely to be enthusiastic about changes in the quality of work life sold in the name of increasing productivity. (Two important

[1]The standard deviations for the quality of work life items are considerably higher than for the economic items—thus suggesting more disagreement among union leaders as to the importance of questions relevant to the quality of work life.

exceptions—these leaders' attitudes may well change if (1) higher productivity is clearly needed to save jobs, or (2) higher productivity will be compensated by higher wages.)

Fortunately, there are numerous other issues, besides productivity, where changes in the quality of work life can be focused.

Traditional Work Rules

Regardless of how they are introduced, programs affecting the quality of work life will have an impact on a number of collectively bargained policies. The thrust of collective bargaining in many industries has been to rigidify and codify managerial practices—e.g., to define job classifications ever more strictly, and to insist that no one work outside his job classification. Job enrichment requires movement in the opposite direction—e.g., the combination of some jobs, the blurring of boundaries between others, and even the blending of workers' and supervisors' functions. Also, new career patterns disturb established promotional ladders, and reforms of reward systems involve the heart of bargaining agreements.

Some unions may adopt the policy of "no backward step" and refuse to make concessions of any kind, even when these concessions might bring about a higher quality of work life. But this attitude is unlikely to be the norm. Once unions' suspicions are allayed, exceptions and changes may be permitted (subject, of course, to carefully negotiated safeguards). After all, difficult problems like those mentioned are constantly being resolved through bargaining; for example, work rules in many plants are the subject of constant renegotiation. Once union leaders discern a clear mandate for an improved quality of work life from their members, problems of job redesign may well be solvable within this work-rule context.

In short, once their initial (and well founded) suspicions have been laid to rest, unions may well cooperate in introducing changes in the quality of work life. Before this happens, however, both parties may have to develop some innovative new mechanisms which will overcome the problems which we have been discussing.

MECHANISMS FOR COOPERATION

As suggested above, issues concerning the quality of work life pose new questions both for unions and for the collective bargaining relationship. How should management approach the union in these matters? The approaches discussed below may be useful in determining the most effective approach.

Separate Committees on the Quality of Work Life

Experience with negotiations regarding such subjects as job evaluation or safety indicates that it might be better to establish separate joint union-management committees (and, in large organizations, separate committees for each major department or area) to deal with issues of the quality of work life than to subject issues in this area to the regular bargaining process. Although many of the same personnel may participate, a separate institutional framework may help divorce the quality of work life from the adversary atmosphere usually surrounding collective bargaining. Nevertheless, it will never be possible or desirable to make decisions in this area without considering their impact on the broader union-management relationship.

Joint Diagnosis of the Problem

It certainly would be a mistake for management to make up its mind in advance as to the kinds of changes it wishes to make in the quality of work life—new compensation systems, for instance, or job redesign—and then to "propose" these to the union (regardless of how tentatively). This smacks too much of traditional bargaining procedure. The union may well react to these proposals by demanding offsetting concessions, and soon the parties are back to bargaining as usual.

Hopefully, proposals for change can be developed jointly by the parties, as a result of mutual agreement about the nature of the problem to be solved. One approach is for the joint committee on quality of work life to begin its task with an assessment of the present quality of work life (though there is a danger that assessment may degenerate into accusations). For the most part, this assessment can be based on the committee members' own experiences. However, outside consultants, *jointly selected*, may be useful in determining workers' attitudes by polling or in suggesting other ways of making the assessment activity more successful.[2]

Once the parties diagnose their problems and agree on their nature, the next step—not always an easy one—is to move to suggested solutions.

Proceeding Experimentally

It may be helpful to consider every step in the procedure as tentative. The fact that a suggestion is made by one party should not bind that party to it. Similarly, every change should be first tried on an experimental basis. Wherever possible, final agreements on changes should be deferred until all parties have agreed on their desirability.

Stressing Areas Other Than Productivity

Given workers' fears that improving the quality of work life may involve speedups and possible losses of jobs, productivity should be deemphasized, particularly at the beginning. Safety, housekeeping, equipment maintenance, and supplies are all issues which in-

---

[2]Standard attitude analyses may not be of much value to such committees, possibly because workers are accustomed to think in qualitative rather than quantitative terms. An attitude survey was taken at the beginning of a quality of work life experiment at the Bolivar plant of Harman International. However, the Bolivar workforce did not show much interest in the results of the survey; only a handful of the workers ever saw or wanted to see the results of the questionnaire.

volve less radical changes in thinking than job redesign or new reward systems. The committee on the quality of work life may wish to defer moving into these areas until its members gain confidence in working together on more traditional types of reforms. (On the other hand, in some situations, it might be a great mistake for the committee to get itself bogged down on trivia. Possibly the important issues should be tackled first. For example, Lawler (1977) suggests that, under some conditions, changes in the quality of work life may *begin* with issues related to pay.)

When the time comes to deal with job redesign, it should be approached from the standpoint of making the job more intrinsically rewarding and satisfying, and not from the standpoint of simply raising productivity. (If the experiment is a success, production will increase in due course.) Similarly, new reward systems should be viewed as a means of increasing workers' incomes and job security.

Economic Guarantees and Payoffs

Workers need to be reassured that programs affecting the quality of work life will not hurt them economically. If feasible, guarantees should be provided against possible layoffs due to these reforms. There should also be recognition that redesigned, enlarged jobs involve greater responsibility. Once workers assume some of management's functions, they legitimately demand some of management's pay as well. Psychological rewards may not be enough; increased earnings may also be required. The Scanlon Plan (Lesieur, 1958) provides one mechanism for rewarding productivity gains achieved through participation.

Maintaining Union Involvement

As experiments in the quality of work life evolve, decision-making authority gets transferred to workers on the shop floor and the functions of the joint committee may be downgraded. Nevertheless, management should continuously acknowledge the role of union leadership in helping to initiate the project. Perhaps the best way to keep the involvement of union leadership high is to bring a continuous stream of new problems to the joint committee for consideration.

Consultants

Outside consultants can be useful, both in suggesting new approaches to problems concerning the quality of work life and in helping the parties work through human-relations problems which may develop at various levels from the shop floor to management. Unfortunately, not every consultant will be equally successful in this regard. Some consultants have developed life styles, value systems, modes of grooming, or specialized language which tend to alienate the average worker. Experience with management groups through Organization Development (OD) efforts does not automatically qualify one to deal with union-management relations. Fortunately, there are some able consultants in this area, and it is reasonable to expect that others will develop—possibly out of the union movement, as did the late Joe Scanlon himself.

The Rushton Project

This project, jointly sponsored by the United Mine Workers and the Rushton Mining Company, illustrates some of the principles described above. The following is taken from a report on the project to the Ford Foundation.

> The first action step at the workplace site is the establishment of a labor management committee, sometimes called a work improvement committee, or a quality of work committee. The project does not begin unless this committee has total project control and a lifetime sanction from the highest levels of the International Union and of the company. . . .
>
> At Rushton . . . it took the participants in the committee a while to fully understand that the quality of work committee was to improve work and work performance at the mine and not to focus on the usual contractual and/or grievance

matters discussed in meetings between the two parties. At first, particularly among the union members, there was hesitance to speak out. This passed quickly. They found themselves beginning to examine all work-related aspects of the mine and how to improve them. The result was the preparation of what they still call "the document" (which described the experiment).

> The document was ratified by a vote of the full membership of the union as an experiment. . . . A joint labor-management committee . . . supervises and monitors the experiment. . . . The original and larger group of management and union officers who drew up the "proposal" still remain. . . . This group (now called the steering committee) deals with broader policy issues while the joint labor-management committee deals with day-to-day operations.[3]

In addition, the project has an outside consultant and an independent evaluator. One final point—in keeping with the experimental nature of the project, participation is purely voluntary and any worker may withdraw from the experimental groups at any time (and some workers have done so).

CONCLUDING REMARKS

Given the tremendous diversity within the union movement and the wide variety of collective bargaining relationships which have developed throughout the country, it is very difficult to generalize with any confidence as to how unions are likely to react to issues concerning quality of work life, except that the nature of the reactions will probably be a function of the previous bargaining history. Where the parties have developed trust and the ability to resolve differences amicably, this trust will probably carry over to quality of work life. Otherwise, however, the discussions regarding quality of work life may well be marked by suspicion and resistance.

For participation to be effective, it must be

---

[3]This information was taken from a document of agreement between the United Mine Workers and the Rushton Mining Company, 1974.

recognized that the union can provide an extremely important vehicle for the expression of workers' views. If management expects to make workers so happy with participation in experiments on the quality of work life that they will cast off their union, mistrust will be inevitable. In fact, the tensions and uncertainties which will almost inevitably arise during the period while reforms in the quality of work life are being introduced may well bring workers closer to their unions. Careful coordination between union and management will be required during this transition period; certainly the human-relations skills on both sides will be sorely tested. But if the parties work together successfully in introducing changes, relations overall are likely to get better. Indeed, good union-management relations with regard to experiments on the quality of work life may reinforce good relations in other matters (including collective bargaining); thus issues about the quality of work life can provide an opportunity to improve labor relations generally.

REFERENCES

Brooks, T. R. Job satisfaction: An elusive goal. *AFL-CIO American Federationist*, October 1972, **79**, 1–8.

Jenkins, D. *Job power*. New York: Penguin, 1974.

Kochan, T. A., Lipsky, D. B., & Dyer, L. Collective bargaining and the quality of work: The views of local union activists. In G. G. Somers (Ed.), *Proceedings of the twenty-seventh annual winter meeting*. San Francisco: Industrial Relations Research Association, December 1974.

Lawler, E. E. Reward systems. In J. R. Hackman & J. L. Suttle (Eds.), *Improving life at work: Behavioral science approaches to organizational change*. Santa Monica, Calif.: Goodyear, 1977.

Lesieur, F. G. *The Scanlon Plan*. Cambridge, Mass.: MIT Press, 1958.

Marrow, A. J., Bowers, D. G., & Seashore, S. R. *Management by participation*. New York: Harper, 1967.

Sayles, L., & Strauss, G. *The local union: Its place in the industrial plant*. New York: Harper, 1953.

Walton, R. D., & McKersie, R. B. *A behavioral theory of labor negotiations*. New York: McGraw-Hill, 1965.